ALDER

Theatre

Who pulls the strings?

THE ULTIMATE CONSPIRACY!

Volume II

About The World Order, bloodlines, Atlantis,
The World Grid, Magnetic Reversals, Global Weather, Magicians,
Cosmic Powers, Secret Lodges, Secret Codes, Phi, Pi, Occult, Scientologists
UFOs, European Union, Extra-terrestrials, Cosmic Computing Intelligence,
Apocalypse, Iraq, Genetic Engineering, DNA, Atoms, Standing Waves,
The Hidden Science, God Genes, The Minoans, The Holy Grail, Druids,
Re-incarnation, September 11, Galactic Confederations, Crop Circles,
Rosicrucians, Mind Control, a Conspiracy against Planet Earth
and a plan that has never ceased to exist.

For book orders including other books written by the Author (referenced)
please address to:
Alpha Education Ltd
P.O. Box 2
Rottingdean
Brighton
BN2 8JW
U.K.

ISBN 0-9529567-2-1
First printing 2001-05-27
Printed & bound by Antony Rowe Ltd, Eastbourne

THE PLATONIC MAXIM IS 'BEFORE YOU CAN CURE A MAN 'S
BODY YOU MUST CURE HIS MIND AND BEFORE THAT HIS SOUL '
–THE QUESTION BECOMES HOW DO YOU CURE A

MANS 'S <u>SOUL</u>?

THIS BOOK IS ABOUT THE BATTLE FOR MAN 'S <u>SPIRIT</u>

This book is available in four volumes and can be ordered from all good bookshops as well as Amazon. It may also be purchased directly from the publisher through the internet *www.alpha-education.co.uk* The contents of the volumes are listed in the frontice pages.

**THIS BOOK IS DEDICATED TO THOSE IN ALLAGES
WHO HAD THE COURAGE TO FACE THE TRUTH
AND SPEAK OUT**

CONTENTS AND ORDERING DETAILS
OF FOUR VOLUMES OF THEATRE EARTH

Volume I   ISBN 0-9529567-1-3

The Hidden Science; In the Beginning was the MRC (Magnetically Reversed) Case; The World Grid; The Keys to the New World Order; UFO's; Domes and Pies in London and New York; Order in the asylum; Dome Theatre; Prehistoric Atomic Wars; Transgenerational Collective Intelligence; Cabalistic origins of the Hidden Science; The Rosicrucians; The One Dollar Note of America; Spiritual Seership Manipulation of the Grid; A Coded Secret Doctrine; Cyclical Cosmology and Atomic Theory; Cabalistic Symbology; Who Killed the Minoans? Acting on Orders no Questions Asked; Hidden Masters; The Holy Land of Scotland; A Matter of Genealogies; Egypt; The Vine Man that Draws Together; The Celts and Druids; The Essenes; The Bible; The Celtic Commonwealth; Esoteric Theology; Gnosticism; The Knights Templar; The World Order of the Rose; Crete as Atlantis? Cretan Zeus and a Theocracy; The All-Seeing Eye; The Vacuum Pattern; Hidden Archaeology; A Stone-Age World Order; Climatic Mysteries; Hydrophobia; Free Energy; anti-Gravity Propulsion; Hitler and Occult Science; Spirals; Spirit and Anti-Worlds; Mind Energy Grid Interface; Thought Imprints or Implants? One-ness; The Universal Mind; Ron Hubbard's Space Opera; Xenu; Incident One; Yatrus.568 pages with 43 Figures.

Volume II   ISBN 0-9529567-2-1

Hill Figures; Gogmagog; The Lost Thirteenth Tribe of Israel; The Secret War Against Beliefs (Re-incarnation); Scientology – A Secret Group? The Great White Lodge and Brotherhood; Britain a Tribal Battlefield; The Hidden Agenda; Existing Policy; Changing the Script and Policy; God Genes; The One Slit World; Bohemian Grove and 'Shape Shifting Reptiles'; Two Jerusalems; Actual Incident One; September 11. 602 pages and 14 Figures with Plates 1-28, which cover volumes I & II.

Volume III ISBN 0-9529567-3-X (NEW)

The Hidden Christian Card; Dan; Y Chromosome; Evolution of the Y Chromosome; DNA Music; DNA Phantom Biowave Computer; Quantum DNA; Virtual Reality; La Place's Demon; Schwarzschild Geometry; Quantum Postulate versus Egg Timer; The Geometric Construction and Administration Point; TheGE Survival Trap; Synchronization of Prophecy to Galactic Clock; The 4-D rhombus Computer; Close Packing of Atoms to create the Rhombus Computer; Trapped in the geometry of the Rose; How Long is a Piece of String? Von Neumann Architecture and the Self-Replicating System; Fibonacci

Bees and Numbers; Games for Atoms – End Day Game Cycle; Kelley's Heroes and Iraq; Root Race Embryology and Metapsychosis; Inside the Mind of the GE and World Order; Borromean Rings; Federation of Faith's or World Order Religion?; The Reshel Grid; The Master Magician's Final Trick at the End of Days; The Möbius Net; Building the Temple of Solomon; Decoding 9/11 and the Judgement Card. 602 pages and 161 Figures.

Volume IV ISBN 0-9529567-4-8 (NEW)

Atomic World War and the Battle for the Mind of Europe; The Noble Lie of Blood and Soil and Neoconservatives; Secrets of the Sphinx and Merovingian Line; A Mad Hatter's Tea Party in Europe and Washington; Muscle-Bound Minoans and European Union; Visions of Hell? Occult background to the Iraq War; The Hidden Energy Recycling Programme; Genesis to Revelations according to Standing Waves; The Cosmic Mind; Euro 2004 – Football and Atoms; Weapons of Maths Destruction; The Mirror Maze of Mind Control; A Personal Note. 696 pages and 71 Figures with 11 Plates (9 in colour).

I very gratefully acknowledge the contribution of all quoted authors cited in reference and in acknowledged diagrams. I am particularly indebted to B. Dunford who wrote *The Holy Land of Scotland* and Comyns Beaumont who wrote *Britain The Key to World History* . I also very gratefully acknowledge the 'saplings 'Ru-Barn who had the courage to stand with the author. I also acknowledge Heraklion MuseumCrete, for iconography and sealings;The Ashmolean Museum for sealings; The Bibliotheque Nationale Paris; The Archives Nationale Paris; The British Library London; Cardiff Castle Wales.

"Actuality means 'What is '...Are you facing in yourself what actually is going on...You don 't take actuality and look at it ".

"Man has been concerned throughout the ages to discover or live in 'Truth '."

(Taken from a series of discussions between Krishnamurti and David Bohm, Professor of Theoretical Physics at London University.In Truth and Actuality by J.Krishnamurti –London Victor Gollancz Ltd.–1986)

TABLE OF CONTENTS

TABLE OF FIGURES AND PLATES

PLATES

INTRODUCTION

In 1986 the author as a Biochemist, set out to resolve the mechanism of cancer outside of the orthodox establishment. No funding or grants were made available to the author for this research, despite the numerous attempts and requests from grant funding bodies and Trusts for a slice of the solid gold 'gravy train' of funding that is available for cancer research: the eventual bill was to cover 15 years of intensive research. Utilising the methods of Dr. Max Gerson M.D. (1881 –1959) the author was soon to recognise that orthodox medical research had dismissed this genius, who initially applied his nutritional therapy to patients with "incurable" Lupus in the 1920's and obtained a 99% success rate in 450 cases. In 1928 he healed his first three "incurable" cancer cases: one advanced, inoperable bile duct cancer and two advanced inoperable stomach cancers. Gerson went on to cure many so-called "incurables" with terminal cancer and Dr. Albert Schweitzer the Nobel Prize humanitarian and physician and one of the 20th Century's most honoured men was treated successfully by Dr. Gerson at the age of 75, for advanced diabetes. After treatment by Dr. Gerson, Dr. Schweitzer returned to Africa and won the Nobel Prize and worked past the age of 90. Dr. Schweitzer was to later write of Dr. Gerson: "I see in Dr. Gerson one of the most eminent geniuses of medical history".

Dr. Gerson in the 1940's appeared before a Senate hearing in America to present the medical histories of some of his cured cancer patients, in attempts to gain a slice of the multi-billion pound 'gravy train' of research funding and grants. The Editorial in the AMA (*American Medical Journal of Nov. 16 1946*) mentioned Dr. Gerson's appearance before the Senate sub committee that year. The hearings also covered "A Bill to authorise and request the President, to undertake to mobilize at some convenient place in the United States, an adequate number of the world's outstanding experts, and co-ordinate and utilize their services in a supreme endeavour to discover means of curing and preventing cancer". Don C. Matcham wrote in *Herald of Health* magazine: "The Committee report of 227 pages, Document No. 89471, gathers dust in the archives of the Government Printing Office". Dr. Gerson was to die a discredited man professionally, despite the brilliance of his work and presumably not fully understanding the role of The Syndicate and goals of a World Order, who had not intention (or policy) of resolving the first part of the Platonic Maxim – the cure of the body.

Whilst the author recognised the importance of Dr. Gerson's work in healing the body, it was evident from the author's own research that there was a mental component working in cancer and that cancer was a psychosomatic condition of *mind and body*. In 1989 the author published a scientific paper on cancer, utilising the Gerson Therapy with counselling, in order to resolve two parts of the Platonic Maxim – mind and body (*R. Henry, S.McLean "A Theory for Cancer based on a Study of Cancer Patients Using The Gerson Cancer Therapy in Conjunction with Psychological Counselling": Complementary Medical Research Spring 1989 Vol. 3 No. 2 –British Library Medical Information Service, Document Supply Centre, Boston Spa, Wetherby, west York's LS23 7BQ United Kingdom*). *The Second Millennium Working Report into Cancer*, by the author, outlining fully the mechanism proposed, subsequently supported the paper. The mechanism lies, after many years of attempting to gain professional support and evaluation in the U.K., collecting dust in the archives of the British Museum Library (*Appendix I and II*).

The author has always retained a scientific and open viewpoint in her quest for truth and thus after reviewing many psychological models and theories, the only model that meshed with the biochemical (body) mechanism of cancer as outlined in *The Second Millennium Working Report into Cancer*, was the mechanism of the mind forwarded as a thesis by Ron Hubbard in *Dianetics – The Modern Science of Mental Health*. Ron Hubbard was the founder of the Church of Scientology and from the moment that the author placed her scientific foot into this field – all hell let loose! It became apparent to the author that not only was there a hidden barrier to the freedom of science in the field of the body, orchestrated by the pharmaceutical industry and what can only be termed the chemical Syndicate (*Appendix I*), but that there was a virtually identical battle and hidden agenda, being played out in the field of the mind between The Syndicate or psychiatry and Scientology. If the field of the body was a battlefield of conflicting orthodox and alternative viewpoints, then the field of the mind was another virtually identical battlefield of conflicting interests. If Dr. Gerson failed in his radical new dietary approach to cancer, to gain financial and professional backing, manpower and research facilities to further his research and clinical testing, then one could only view the battle to gain acceptance for *Dianetics* as the same battle game, of orthodox and alternative viewpoints. The author was willing to accept the story and this background to Scientology promoted by The Church of Scientology, until she herself was to astoundingly become a victim of Scientology. After a horrendous series of events, depicted on the front cover of *The Second Millennium working Report into Cancer*, it very soon became apparent to the author that the barrier to the freedom of science and the resolution of the Platonic Maxim, was not only inclusive of the profits to the pharmaceutical and psychiatric medical Syndicate that would be threatened by a resolution of the Platonic Maxim and healing of mind and body by alternative methods, but a deeper barrier existed in the resolution of the final part of the

Platonic Maxim – the soul.

The cancer research like an errant child, led the author through the mined battle fields of history, religion, politics, psychology, biochemistry, archaeology and anthropology and finally into the forbidden no-man's land of metapolitics - or the politics of the soul. The author on instinctive intuition returned to Greece in 1993, on one level to escape the vicious attacks shown on the front cover of *The Second Millennium Working Report* into cancer, but on another level not quite clear to the author at that time, it was a Cycle of Eternal Return. The result of the research in Greece was the author's first book, *The Battle of The Trees*. The book was produced in a 'T-Shirt' factory in Crete over the period of 1994/5 against appalling odds. A band of spiritually aware people from around the world responded to that book and the author's second book *Alternative 4 – UFO's Mind and Body Control*, with a positive spiritual understanding, despite the lack of editing. There were some however who appeared not to grasp the research at all. I acknowledge that a student only understands as well as his teacher explains it, however as I hope this book will explain, this was no ordinary story or research/book. I hope that in this book, it will be understood that the author was grappling not only with attempts to regain her own memory, but whatever the Grid and Masters might throw to prevent that! The barriers to freedom were *formidable* and at each turn there was no assurance that the author would survive to tell the tale, thus the decision to print regardless of editing or aesthetics of printing. This was always a far more serious battle than the majority realised and in the author's loneliest moments, there was always the thought that if something was published, some may remember that truth – the alternative was to wait until the author discovered the whole truth and the entire track of time, but then this story is not about publishing books, **it is about the battle for man's soul.** This thesis reveals the entire conspiracy from the beginning to the present day and is crucial in understanding the mind and goals of The World Order.

Given optimal circumstances one could produce a product, even research that is perfect, which seems to be the requirement in this age of spin and gloss, however this is not a story about perfection, it is a story about *imperfection* and the highly uncertain and improbable attempt by the author to place an alternative viewpoint on the last 10 000 years, which contradicts most of what mankind has been led to believe in. I thank Dagmar in Canada who wrote after reading the first two books: "Do not ever give up writing, our children are depending on you" – a message that appeared at a particularly low ebb. The author also thanks others that wrote to her and passed on support, which gave the author the impetus for this book, believing that there were still a few out there, who were earnestly searching for the truth. This was far from an easy book to write, it has taxed the author to present it to you the reader, in some form that may indeed warn you of the crisis that humanity now faces, whilst unravelling the great misunderstandings in occult science and the hidden science that have led man into this predicament: Indeed I doubt whether those who are manipulating this science, unknown to humanity understand or know of what I have written here and yet the unknown manipulation of this science stands to destroy humanity. These misunderstandings on the nature of the past and space-time have remained within hidden initiation levels, which drive the World Order and secret groups. If man thought that he would reach the end of the cycle, without any trouble or soul searching, he was only a fool unto himself. This crisis is of an individual nature, there will be no safety in numbers, and it is for each man and woman to search their own soul on what I say here.

This story is really about the hiding away of certain natural laws of science and physics within the secret groups, however I was once told that if you put one scientific equation into a book, your reader numbers are immediately halved! I have tried to keep the science to a minimum, so that anyone without a background in science can understand. It would be helpful if the reader had some background into the World Order, which can be gained from back editions of *On Target* magazine (cited in reference), along with authors such as Mullins (cited) and Professor Noam Chomsky (cited): also *Tragedy and Hope – A History of The World in Our Time* by Professor Carroll Quigley (*GSG and Associates P.O. Box 6448 Rancho Palos Verdes California 90734)* is another source of excellent background material. Whilst the author's first two books provide important background and research material to this book, I hope that this work will clear up misunderstandings that readers may have had. No man or woman however owes man a complete story, for it is eternal spiritual struggle that provides one with the keys to freedom. Further you must accept that there are some things that cannot be said, for there are always forces that would use that information against mankind and it is not my intention to hold secrets, but one must be cognisant that there are some things which must remain unsaid and only you the reader will find those unsaid things, by eternal struggle and searching – It is the route and search for the Philosopher's Stone. I first advertised *The Battle of The Trees* in Athens in March 1995 and on returning to the U.K. the author carried on her research and published *Alternative 4 – UFO's Mind and Body Control*, which provided further insight into the hidden science and the World Order. Although the research seemed very far removed from the cancer research and the final attempt to resolve the third part of the Platonic Maxim – the soul, it was in fact another convoluted turn in the hidden agenda of the World Order and the battle for mans'soul. The first two books provide important insight into the scientific research process and illustrate just how one arrives at the final conclusion. One should not discount that process as it evolves, for it is a testimony to never using the Grid and its memory, but your own. This point is crucial to this thesis and the search for truth. In fact I could have in the production of my books omitted my past life memories or the one that I recount in *Chapter I of The Battle of The Trees* and the statement in this book that I was a witness at the events of Golgotha and the alleged Crucifixion of Jesus; however to do so would be to negate or omit the message of The Holy Grail. The message is one of recognition of the continuous immortality of the soul. This message finds expression in the resolution of the Platonic Maxim: **'before you can cure a man's body, you must first cure his mind and before that his soul'**; and the healing of the soul further finds a mechanism that was outlined in the cancer research.

In 1996 the author felt that she had enough evidence to challenge the World Order, including the vast cover up on the treatment of cancer and approached her local MP Tim Rathbone, then Conservative MP for Lewes, with a Petition to Parliament (*Appendix II*). Despite the support of the Rt. Hon Tim Rathbone MP who agreed to table the Petition in The House of Commons in the U.K., the Petition was predictably scuttled and the author was referred to the procedures of Open Government, where supposedly the various organisations and body's that the author's questions were presented to, were obliged by law to answer. As one eventually comes to realise in World Order politics and policies, those policies and the World Order are not only above the law, but also above the democratic process. In effect the Petition as part of the law and democratic process, was 'lost' down the avenues and cul-de-sacs of labyrinthine and secret government policies and hidden agendas. The Power of the private banking system was such that governments lacked the will and were increasingly unable, to issue their own money at low interest into the economy to finance public expenditure, instead borrowing their own money, from private banks, such that the compounded geometric rise in the national debt and the interest needed to serve that debt, led to the practice of selling off national assets. In the United Kingdom in the 1980's during the regime of Margaret Thatcher as Prime Minister, privatisation of public sector services and academic activity occurred. The freedom of science to search for truth, declined in proportion to subservience of academics to private sector research funding. The big pharmaceutical and emerging 'Life Science' companies were mainly those who paid the grants in research establishments and thus science no longer became impartial, but merely a tool in the hands of the multinational companies associated and interlocked through directorships and consultancies. It became impossible for the individual scientist to engage in true research or in fact any research that threatened private sector profit and monopolistic control (*Appendix I*). Any scientist that approached the truth or questioned current methods, would be excommunicated as a 'heretic' by the 'Inquisitional Church' of a secret hierarchy with tentacles that reach out and control every aspect of politics, religion, commerce and industry, research, publishing and media, banking, insurance, the drug trade, the petroleum industry – a group that is answerable to no one, but its members. With the increasing debt and globalisation of the economy it has been argued that the private sector has been driven in turn to ever expanding growth, as the debt inherited from privatisation continues to "chase its own tail", as part of the overall corporate debt. The greater the commercial operation in the global markets, the greater are the stakes and the greater the concentration of Power at governmental levels.

The Chairman of Biotechnology Investments is the powerful establishment figure of Rothschild director and former Cabinet Secretary Lord Armstrong of Illminster. His deputy is former Cambridge University don, Dr John Bradfield. Another university don, Sir Brian Richards, co-founded British Biotech., linked through its directorships to the Daily Mail (newspaper in the U.K.), Glaxo-Wellcome and Royal Dutch Shell. The Oxford Molecular Group is linked to Pfizer, manufactuerer of Viagra. Sir Brian Richards also sits on the board of Peptide Therapeutics, linked to N.M. Rothschild, Aventis Pasteur and Smith Kline and Beecham Pharmaceuticals. International Biotechnology Trust, in 1997, listed Professor Sir Keith Peters and Sir Mark Richmond amongst eight academic and scientific advisers. This is just the tip of the networking process that occurs worldwide and provides a safe inner sanctum of power, which is impenetrable to questions from alternative and independent viewpoints, particularly when those viewpoints seek to question policy. Virtually, if not all official advisory and regulatory bodies are disproportionately populated by individuals beholden to the multinational conglomnerates, through investments, consultancies or directorships. The same situation prevails in the United States where the term "revolving door" is openly applied to the relationship between the biotechnology Corporation of Monsanto and the Food and Drug Administration (F.D.A.). The F.D.A and Medical bodies such as the American Cancer Society have been instigators (along with the FBI as enforcers), in blocking alternative cancer therapies in America.

Alternative therapist Jimmy Keller was kidnapped by the FBI in 1991 after he fell foul of The National Council Against Health Fraud (NCAHF) and alleged front organisation for the AMA (American Medical Association). The FDA (who are not a law enforcement agency) with the help of police stormed a natural Health Clinic in Washington, where guns were used to terorrise the doctor, staff and patients. Dr Jonathon Wright a renowned doctor along with the community was absolutely and rightly outraged that this incident could occur in the Capital of Americ in 1992. People are not afraid of alternative medicine, so *who* is exactly afraid? Illness is BIG BUSINESS and profits to the multinational companies and the vice-like grip on monopoly can only be maintained, through a hidden agenda or policy *acting through governments*. The Senate Bill 3642 and the NLEA (Nutrition Labelling Education Act) in America which was claimed by Dr Wright as seriously bias against natural health products, mirrors the bully-boy tactics in Britain orchestrated by the Medicines Control Agency (proposal MLX 249) and backed by forthcoming European legislation (*Appendix I*). The reach of the tentacles of an Elite hierarchy into governments and subsequent determination of policy is not as has been suspected, merely driven by power, profit and money. The World Order Elite have continuoulsy throughout millennia existed through and within secret groups, where the actual policies and hidden agendas of national governments originate, thus stripping the electorate of any meaningful control over their own destinies and the environment. It has been the aim of the author to discover what drives the mind of the World Order, where and why this Order evolved and the true nature of their identity, along with their hidden agenda and goal. Secret levels of initiation are revealed in this book, which furthers research and the cracking of various secret codes, which as 'keys' have unlocked many of the inner sanctum mysteries that surround the World Order and the variously associated secret groups. The conclusions are astounding even to the author, who has long since passed the stage of being surprised by the World Order. The author asks whether a case of treason can be brought, on the basis that this is a significant and all encompassing treachery against humanity and in the case of The United Kingdom the conclusions are pivotal to that question.

I trust the Scientologists will not view what I say here as an attack, but rather they will view it as reasonable scientific valid critique and evaluation. In some respects what the author states on the basis of her research, is validation of the secret initiation levels in Scientology, however the author as with Christianity and other religions, offers a varying scientific viewpoint, opinion and belief. The philosopher Alfred North Whitehead stated: "The worst homage we can pay to genius is to accept uncritically formulations of truths which we owe to it". Whilst Alfred North Whitehead was speaking of Einstein, I could equally apply this statement to Ron Hubbard. The question arises in this book, whether or not Hubbard was a genius or whether Scientology is a secret group, with an inevitable higher Order behind it. The same question could be applied to Christianity at the time of its inception, which includes the very secret events of Golgotha covered here. All human knowledge should be preceded by a disclaimer, such as the referral in my own research to "Working Report", signifying that the research is ongoing, however this book is meant as a final personal statement, as I intend to resign my post. Man should accept that he does not know very much at all and knows even less, when he places barriers to truth. The search for truth requires that man does not accept dogma or wrote word of law: an open mind and acceptance that at any one given time – this is the way it appears now, would invite improvements and open discussion. Religion and the World Order invite dogmatism and stuck viewpoints, purely for the purpose of control or power and financial gain. The truth however, is the evolving front of spiritual and scientific research that has every barrier to freedom placed in its path - such is the author's story and the barriers placed to her research, even sadly by those who claim truth or the freedom of humanity as their goal. If there were nothing to hide, then those barriers would not exist, since the truth would pose no threat. The fact that the author's research has taken 15 years (at least!) to evolve, whilst jumping barriers on a daily basis, with a trail of secrecy and lies, emphasises that there are many groups on this Earth, who have great fear of telling the truth. Truth is the ultimate reality and only from that reality will mankind ever achieve understanding, it is for those few who have no fear of reality and wish to understand and confront that reality or ultimate truth, that this book is written It may spoil your day, but far better than to destroy your eternity! I am afraid there was never any safe group ticket out, or assurance of safety or salvation in numbers, this is the story of **the individual** and the ability of that individual to think, reason and on balance decide the fate of his own soul: that is a horrible thing to face, but then the problem here on Earth was always viewed as *a desperate case and the fate uncertain* – "They don't stand a chance unless...". All religions however have warned man to nurture and keep his soul clean from wrong-doing and one can see much truth in that, for it will not be so much the "books" (the account of the individual) that are opened at the end according to the book of *Revelations*, but the anti-matter holographic electro-magnetic imprint or **soul recording**. Man's **conscience** will become his own judge. The World Order misunderstood the **HIDDEN SCIENCE** from the very beginning in their rush to utilise the power, control and wealth to be made from it; and just how that misunderstanding has weaved its way into occultism, occult science, certain New Age therapies, politics, metapolitics, religion, archaeology, history and current biotechnology creating the insanity we are now witnessing on Earth is taken up in this thesis. The Dunces of the World Order might even cause one to roar with laughter, if this was not a very Greek Tragedy for Mankind, as humanity stands on the precipice of disaster. Now that you have opened 'Pandora's box', read on!

HILL FIGURES

Thirty or more hill-figures (*Plate 20*) cut into the turf of Southern England are allegedly a uniquely British phenomenon, however I have found a hill figure in America, which I will come to in the last section of the book. A number of these figures such as the Long Man of Wilmington in Sussex and the Cerne Giant in Dorset show giants, whilst there is a White Horse at Uffington in Oxfordshire. It has proved difficult to date the figures, but is thought that they were constructed in the Bronze Age. Archaeologists have long puzzled over these giants and the appearance of two giants in London Gogmagog and Corineus, whom some thought might be Celtic Deities, but we know Gogmagog in this book, as the grandson of Noah and therefore 13 th tribe.

The White horse is as old as Stonehenge in Wiltshire, the Druidic Apollonian Temple. According to Paul Newman [157] the Revd. Plender Lealth (1885) drew attention to the similarity of the horse to *stylised* steeds on old British coins. These coins showed *sun-wheels*, *half moons* and *dumb-bell* shaped limbs and the dumb-bell was uniquely a feature that I pointed out appeared on Late Minoan Seals, after the Religious Revolution in Crete c. 1400 B.C. The coins show marked similarities to the Uffington horse, particularly in such details as the *rounded eye* with dot in the centre and beaky jaws and small legs.

The Aylesford bucket another archaeological find in Britain, shows horses more birdlike or Serpentine than equine, with the 'S' or snake design prominent and the *arch backs*, all of which are reminiscent of the arch backs of the bull vaulter in the 'Bull-vaulting' fresco, which was a Solar Lunar calendar which incorporated the belief of The Cycle of Eternal Return, a belief I equate with Re-incarnation. The arch back featured in the Bull-Man Seals of the Late Minoan period, after the Religious Revolution, when the whole belief system and Cosmology had been overtaken and stolen by the Semitic invaders. Thus the introduction of the Bull-Minos cult was the basis of the Religious Revolution. The heads of the horses on the Aylesford bucket remind one of the archetypal *Lily* from Knossos and the flowing contours of the horse are very Minoan, particularly I note that the rear of the horse is rather circular and resembles the womb (*Plate 18*).

The ring and dot eye of Uffington horse is also seen in the Silchester horse, which is extremely interesting, since the circle and dot, was considered a top secret sign, by Adam Weishaupt, the founder of the secret group, the Illuminati. The Illuminati by association with Bavaria, the birthplace of the founder Weishaupt, occurs as the front illustration cover of *Vaincre* magazine, with its archetypal portrayal of a Universal Political and Religious Kingdom, based on hermetic philosophy. The eye then, is the hermetic Eye of Intelligence. It is not inconceivable that the Bull-Minos cult was followed by the Equine cult, as both animals had a part to play in the history of The Holy Grail, as totem beasts, with the horse being a totem beast in Celtic religion. There is also a connection to Norse legend, in so far as Odin was the Norse God of prophesies, inspiration and battle and Odin was the focus of a horse cult. The Uffington horse may well symbolise these connections. In *The battle of the Trees*, I mentioned a specifically Irish account of a King, who ate the flesh of a horse in a cauldron as symbolic of re-birth, where the flesh of the totem beast provided the ancestral memory of the tribe. The breaking of bread (and partaking of wine) as manna is a Christian ritual based on this earlier memory. During the ceremony a *wand* was used, being specifically attributed to the Druids and symbolic of the god Hermes as necromancer and magician. Thus there is some connection here between horse, Druids and Celts. Caesar of course suppressed the Druids along with the political aim to enforce a Semitic One World Order Religion on Britain and Europe, identified in the events of the Crucifixion. I proposed that the Druids existed in secret after that at Caerleon-on-Usk in Wales. Optical Stimulated Luminescence (OSL) an archaeological dating technique has dated the Uffington horse to between 1400 - 600 B.C. The earlier date co-inciding with the Religious Revolution in Crete.

In the 1930's, Christopher Hawkes, near Ringwood in Hampshire U.K, found a third-century water jar. On the lid was scratched a horse, reminding one of the Uffington horse, bearing not a rider but a *phallus*. I have commented elsewhere, that the floor of the Freemasons Temple in London has a design, which I concluded was an archetypal symbolisation of the labyrinth or womb, with a penetrating male phallus. The phallus was to turn up in Late Minoan seals after the Religious Revolution, where an egg, was shown penetrated by a phallic member, between the two upright pillars of the shrine of a solar or Twin sacred King. The phallus also represents the wand, the herm around which the snakes are entwined in the caduceus of Hermes and the baetyllic pillar or support between the two upright lintels, which figured in the tomb of Sun Kings and was portrayed at Golgotha in the tomb of Jesus as Sun King. A phallic emblem was found at Wroxeter also exhibiting the four-horse chariot (of Hermes) that appeared in the Inc.1 incident related to Xenu and **mind control.** The Religious Revolution in Crete was the first time I should imagine, that religion or the associated thought patterns and symbols had been imprinted on the bioplasma (spiritual). We know that the Atlanteans whilst clever, had a despotic King over them and it is likely that body control and Yatrus type control was recorded on the morphogenetic bioplasma, simply because the only religion on this Earth was black magic and voodoo, with miss-use of the hidden science (only Black Cabalistic science). Thus thought associated with the higher realms of the spiritual bioplasma had not yet been imprinted I believe. A terrific spiritual battle occurred when spiritual intervention occurred c. 10 000 B.C and that battle became a **battle for the mind**, in Bronze Age Crete.

In *The Battle of The Trees*, I described how the Cabal that invaded Knossos took over the matriarchal symbols and re-positioned them, changing the belief system at the same time and further utilising opium as a suggestive drug. Hermes combined Twin Kings and Goddess into one personage and since Hermes was the master magician, we can assume that the Cabal took certain information that hitherto they did not possess. That information allowed them access to the higher spiritual realms and thus in terms of survival data the spiritual bioplasma would record data from *the majority* i.e. the Druids or thirteenth tribe. One suspects that is why the number 13 arose in connection with the Yatrus incident (body control) and the Religious Revolution images (angels, horn, chariot etc.) appeared in Inc.1 It is thought that the Uffington Horse, may have had a similar addition of a chariot on the back. Perhaps the Romans edited out the truth here! The Westbury horse, on a slope of a *hill* at Bratton Down in Wiltshire, borders on an area enclosed by the Ministry of Defence and may have exceptional ley or magnetic Grid properties. The whiteness of the horse and its oblique symbolisation of the Moon-Goddess in her death aspect, is apparent in all the white chalk hill carvings, once again symbolising that the woman was to play no future role in the religion, after the knowledge was taken. The MMRC had no intention of relinquishing his control over Homo sapiens. The eye once again is prominent in this figure and is curiously represented as a *dome* of white chalk. The One World Order was to adopt the all-seeing eye of the Patriarchal God Hermes, as the sign of intelligence and the hermetic eye, which would become a significant archetypal symbol of the One World Order, to be found on the One-dollar bank note of America.

Richard Gough, the editor of Camden's Britannia, surveyed the Westbury horse in 1772 and Gough's depiction of the horse shows the prominent eye in the centre of the forehead, again with a prominent dot. The eye of Cyclops in myth is intimated together with the Late Minoan icon of man with hand held to the third eye. This undoubtedly relates to the chakra of the crown and the pineal or magnetic body, utilised is psychic prophecy. Further the drug opium was introduced into Minoan Crete at the same period, with the Poppy Goddesses, indicating that opium was used to produce some form of *altered mind state*. Thus there is every indication that the method of Grid channelling was being utilised in the Late Minoan period. In Gogh's depiction, the horse wears a *saddle*, which I previously discussed as a proposed Cosmology. The saddle was to turn up in Salvador Dali's painting *'Persistance du Memoire'* - indicating that he himself had some connection to this knowledge (*The Battle of The Trees*). One notable feature of the Westbury horse is the tail, which has an almost crescent Moon appearance of the dragon (World Grid circling Earth). It also has undertones of the Bull-Minos Cult and the gates of horn, which marked the entry into the abode of the dead. This replaced the earlier Minoan belief that one met with her the Great Goddess, whose gift was Immortality. The overall implication is that the horse was a belief system and Cosmology, taken and adapted by a British based Patriarchal cult, who I identified as the Druids. From an aerial view, the Westbury horse shows one horse superimposed upon another. T.C. Lethbridge in *Gogmagog* (1957) claimed that the: "shadowy figure of the older animal is visible close behind it and appears very much as if it had the beaked head of an Iron Age Monster". The amorphous figures of Palaeolithic times, has a similar shaped nose, resembling a reptilian form. Lethbridge included a sketch of a beast, with sinister tusk-like extensions, jutting from the mouth and once again a blanket or saddle over the body. Further the pointed ears, which are very pronounced of the Uffington and Westbury horses, seem to symbolise the earlier Bull-Minos cult, where the horns are symbolic of the gates of horn. This is certainly absorption of the Late Minoan beliefs, which replaced the truth with archetypal significances. I suspect that the bull's horns became achetypally transferred to the "Beast", of the *Revelations* account in the Bible, where the horns of the bull, became the horns of the Christian Devil. What a nice twist for the 12 tribes to swing on the 13th tribe in this battle! Still playing the game of dynasties I see.

At the village of Southam, near Coventry in the U.K. in the eighteenth Century a Godiva festival took place. The procession was headed by a man wearing a bull's horns and mask (*Plate 20*), who was dubbed 'Old Brazen Face' - intimating radiance and solar power, which reflects the earlier memory of the Bull-Minos cult and once again Knossos in Crete. The iconographic finds of oxen and cart at Knossos remembered in Homer's time as 'oxen of the sun' and indicative of Solar Kingship, may have been superseded by the chariot of Hermes. The fact that there is an older horse or more accurately a tusked animal (bull?) behind the present Westbury horse, indicates Solar Kingship and its derivation of combining Twin Kings of the year, the old dying King giving way to the new Solar King. Following 'Old Brazen Face' in the festival were *two* Godiva's (originally Twin Kings – male!), one dressed in white lace, the other stained entirely in black, after the fashion of the early British tribes during their festivals. Pliny records that they resembled swarthy Ethiopians, which may reflect the appearance of the mysterious "Missionary" woman in Africa, who may have given rise to a tribe there. A Black Madonna appears on the roof of Cardiff Castle Wales, so I am told, but I could not obtain permission to go up to the roof. One suspects though, that two Semitic ancestries are being indicated, one presumably the old Atlanteans a white race and presumably the biblical Adamites, the other some other branch from Noah, which rests on an earlier Babylonian Flood epic and perhaps the tribe of Levi. There was some interest in the 80's, when a book claimed that the Knights Templar had been in Ethiopia looking for the Ark of the Covenant. Coventry was in the area occupied by the

Brigantes a people who worshipped a female deity, later Christianised as St. Brigit, but who was curiously also known as Danu or Anu or black Annis of Leicestershire, thus finding some connection to the Tuatha de Danaan the Greek tribe from the Peloponnese who were regarded as gods by Celtic tribes and allegedly (although questioned in this book) formed the matrilineal line of Jesus.

The Bull-man figure, denotes a Solar deity, and the black and white Godiva's have a much deeper history, although probably were presented at the festival as the winter and summer aspects of the Goddess, representing sterility and abundance in the agricultural festivals. Black was also associated in festivals in Perthshire (Scotland) with the god Baal, who was a Phoenician and Semitic weather -god, sometimes depicted with horns. Scholars have previously queried why such a God was included in British festivals, but it rests on the folk memory of the Minoan Religious Revolution. Whilst it has been previously concluded that Baal may be a corruption of Belinus a Celtic pastoral (flock) God, the Druids may have seen themselves as the Shepherd leading the flock (sheep!), a parallel idea was to turn up in the story of Jesus. The term in Freemasonry Nautonnier, guiding the ship (or Ark) undoubtedly refers back to this earlier idea and the biblical Adamites from whom Noah descended. The Beltane fires and rites of the village of Callander in Western Perthshire (Scotland), required a person who drew the unlucky portion of a black cake, to leap through a fire three times, evidently then, the memory of the old Trinity, with Twin Kings and Goddess, was still retained in festivals. Fire representing the god Hermes and subsequently the Patriarchal God Jehovah. Why was thirteen considered to be unlucky? It must rest on the number of times that the thirteenth tribe nearly came to power, but were thwarted by the tribes of Israel and Levi.

I explained in *The Battle of The Trees*, just how far religion had re-positioned the archetypes, such that many of the biblical archetypes can be found in earlier rites. The Lamb of Christian terminology, was to arise in the story of how Pythagoras went to Crete and was initiated by the Iadian Dactyls, who were in all probability, the secret cabal (Druidic), that conducted the Religious Revolution. Pythagoras was clothed in a lambs skin and drank the milk of the goat that represented Almathea who had fed Zeus. Given that we decided that Jesus was a Druid, it is entirely understandable that this term of the Lamb was applied to him: as the 13 th leader of a group of twelve as was Zeus the Captain of the 12 Olympians. The archetypal symbols were used and changed out of all recognition, to their original intention as taught in the Matriarchal equivalent of the OT level levels in the Bronze Age. The actual meaning was to have no comparable recognition in the manipulated archetypes, which as a point was to arise when Picasso pointed out that his symbolic art *set out to destroy reality*, and oddly enough he drew women as monsters! A theme that was to arise over and over again in biblical patriarchal Jewish texts of the One World Order and

Christianity! - The Serpent being a specific example.

St. George who epitomised philosophical dualism between good and evil, was to ride on a white steed and do battle with the dragon - the Christian Saints became riders of white steeds - white symbolising not only death of the Goddess, but the incorporation of her into their beliefs to be USED. White was the colour of the 13 th tribe, I would maintain and what horror and dramatization of that occurred in the white hoods of the Klu Klux Klan! The Madonna and child based on an earlier belief of Minotaur-child emphasising matrilineal succession, placed on his mother's knee in the classical icon already referred to as the red-figured kylix, had a basket symbolic of the Druids Osier or sacrifice basket, which was to become the Christianised version of sacrificed Sacred Solar King - the Crucifixion on the Taur or 'T' - shaped cross. The entire ritual depended on the sacrifice of a Twin King of the Old year to make way for the Twin King of the New Year, which ensured virility of the tribe. The King of the Old Year disliked having to be sacrificed, so he invented a longer cycle of 19 years in conjunction with the religious calendar. Thus the 9-year cycle was to give rise to a 19-year cycle, after which the monarch or reign could be exchanged. This was eventually changed to give rise to continuous solar monarchy combining Holly and Oak, which is the position today. However as I have commented before, you won't get past the Grid on that one, simply because it is totally incompatible and accumulates karma.

The three Kings as I pointed out in the icon of a stone ring from Naples, was based on an earlier tradition and knowledge, where the middle King of the trio is represented as Hermes, with his petasos (cap). This ring from the 6th Century A.D. clearly remembers that the Christ-child was son of the hermetic God (of Freemasonry and the Druids). The presence of three Kings clearly remembers, that the Herm or Hermes was the central position or pillar and the transcendent third stage beyond death, combining Twin Kings and Goddess. This however was not the original truth, but a repositioning of the truth after the Religious Revolution. The so-called Holly or Holy one was the woman in the Trinity. This has caused the Catholic Church to try and give the position to the mother of Jesus - Mary. I am afraid the truth has so often been swapped about, that the real story has been either forgotten, or it can no longer be confronted. The skull was a symbol that was to turn up in Poussin's painting on the top of a tomb entitled 'Et in Arcadia ego....' Hermes was born in Arcadia in the Peloponnese and the fuller discussion of this painting is given in *The Battle of The Trees*. The Third Reich who were obsessed with the story of the Holy Grail, with Hitler at one point in 1936 being depicted in a poster as a Grail Knight, was to use the symbol of the death's head, in SS regalia. Death's heads figure predominantly in Himmler's Black Order, where SS officer's regalia bore the symbol of death's head rings, which were first presented by Himmler to the SS Old Guard on 24th

December 1933, four months before publication of the Order, which elevated the Totenkopfring to the status of an official SS award. The guerrilla warfare badge is the most symbolically potent of all Nazi decorations and uses an altered Greek symbol of the Caduceus of Asklepios *the healer*! The central Herm or Hermes is the dagger, with the death's head at the base together with the Oak leaf, which the Druids revered as their Tree of Royalty and sacred Solar Kingship; also serpents entwine the Herm or dagger. The Oak club was symbolic of Celestial Hercules, whom the Druids revered in their alphabet, as Duir or Oak and entry of the New King through the door of the New Year. Evidently then Hitler was a New Solar King and did not realise that Solar Kings were puppets to a higher Order or priesthood and usually were sacrificed when they were of no further use. Thus was the Third Reich a bid for power by the thirteenth tribe of Judah, white supremacy and the Aryan Super Race. In which case it is understandable why the Jews never revealed the story of Hitler and perhaps explains why the British betrayed the Arabs when the Jews were given a State of Israel – it was not in the interests of Judah to upset the Jews. Meanwhile the Palestinians became refugees in their own land and even now they travel 4-8 hours to and fro from the West bank to work in Israel –in addition to their job and many men with young families: since they are not allowed to stay overnight. How can this be right?

The archetypal symbolism of the number 7 in the Book of *Revelations*, is encountered in the Beth-Luis-Nion Alphabet, or Tree alphabet, which the Druids used together with a secret signalling keyboard or finger alphabet, which I suspect is where the Masonic handshake appeared from. The seventh tree is Oak, the tree of Zeus, Jupiter and Hercules, the Dagda (the Chief of the elder Irish Gods), Thor and all the other thunder gods including the Semitic God Jehoweh. 'Duir', was the Beth-Luis-Nion word for Oak and we see therefore that The Third Reich was another quest for the One World Order, which would come in the form of European Union after the war, millions sacrificed to pave the way! Virgil mentions the Oak, whose roots run deep underground (magnetic ley line knowledge) and its branches reach high into the air (the Grid) and whose law (*The Covenant*) runs both in Heaven and in the Underworld (death and rebirth of Sacred Kings). Jesus as Holly and Oak and a sacred King, would be re-born, which is the basis of The Second Coming. The Oak oracles that were introduced into Greece by the Achaeans, significantly held the power of prophecy, which was really based on the hidden science and channelled information. The Duir or Oak month takes its name from Jupiter the Oak-God and begins in the Tree alphabet on June 10th and ends on July 7th. Midway comes St. John's Day, June 24th on which a number of UFO researchers met their mysterious death!! (they won't get past the Grid on that one, since the worst crime is to fight The Holy Grail) The Grid and associated phenomena was jealously guarded and seen as the rightful property as it is now of secret groups and the master magicians or old Atlanteans. Presumably their justification is that a Covenant was made with God and in order to keep the Covenant, they must retain charge of the Grid and all phenomena associated with it. St. John was to figure prominently in Cardiff Castle Wales, with no representation of Christ whatsoever. This was explained as Lord Bute holding John as his patron Saint. However it cannot be missed that St. John may well have been the Twin King of Jesus, or he may have brought the Jesus child to Scotland after the murder of the Mary Magdalene in France; thus providing a royal dynastic line, which may be the alleged Davidic line of the Merovingians.

This brings us to another unique hill figure carving on British hills - the Cerne Giant (*Plate 20*). This ancient figure is of a man, displaying large and prominent genitalia particularly emphasising the phallus (wand) and he carries an Oak club: The Oak club being the emblematic sign of a Solar King and the phallus depicting virility of the King and therefore the whole tribe. In a Krater from Ruvo Hermes is about to slay Argos. Argos significantly has nine eyes, revealing that he is a Solar King with the Janiform double head, covered by Petasos, the cap of Hermes. He holds a panther skin and Herculean Oak club. The Oak club was also emblematic of a belief in Twin Kingship, which is depicted here as Hermes, the bisexual incorporation of male and female in the transcendent third stage beyond death, thus absorbing the earlier belief of The Cycle of Eternal Return - Re-incarnation and the role of the woman. The Oak club of the Cerne giant signifies his role as a Solar King, a Herculean figure. He is carved once again into a hillside, with Druidical implications. Further the giant shows the round baby like head (a head incidentally that has been utilised by Hollywood in their secret propaganda games to depict the Alien of UFO's), which is a Celtic feature, and thus we assume he is the King of the New Year. A sight line taken vertically up the 30 foot penis, aligns true East with the summer sun, as it rises above the hills, thus this is another indication, that he is a Solar King, of the New Year. The club is a huge crab tree club, and therefore complements the crab mural at Cardiff Castle, where Hercules cuts the left arm of the crab, with a sword on which a secret is written (*The Battle of The Trees*) and further holds a club in his hand. This represented the second and third cuts of the arm, the second was Knossos and the Religious Revolution, the third was the Magdalene's arm and the events of the Crucifixion and they have missed out on the first cut, which they obviously do not know about.

Dr. Stukeley an important antiquarian in 1764, at a meeting of the society of Antiquarians offered a solution to the Cerne Giant, saying he was the first Hercules, the Phoenician leader of the first colony of Britain. The homeland of these Phoenician wanderers was Ethiopia or Arabia and Dr. Stukeley informed the members: "and from Arabia our first Britons came, and were of the same Patriarchal religion as those Arabian Magi, properly Druids, who came to worship our infant Saviour". Dr. Stukeley tried to combine the ideology of Christianity and Druidism, and promoted worship of the Sacred Serpent. He identified henge monuments as dracontia or snake temples, the snake being the object of veneration in early Egyptian, Babylonian and Hellenic cultures.

John Sydenham in 1842 explained that the Antediluvians, worshipped the snake. The coiled rings of the snake were evidently somewhat symbolic of the Grid and its hyperbolic spiralling. However the snake was in Greek times a symbol of re-birth, since it shed its skin, to be re-born. Thus the snake carried in both symbolic meanings the hidden science and the belief system. The snake as Grid knowledge was in the myth of the Flood glossed for secrecy and the reason given for Jehoweh sending the Flood was idolatry, after the Flood the Antediluvians worshipped both snake and Flood! They deified creatures' half-fish and half-snake, and reptilian water monsters, which must have been in memory of the phylogenetic line. John Sydenham proposed that the Cerne Giant was laid in honour of the victory of sun worshippers over the Serpent cult; and the old name for Cerne Hill was 'hill of the sun-God'.

The biblical *Revelations* account of Satan bonded in chains beneath the Earth, is somewhat paralleled by the Scientology view forwarded by Hubbard, that Xenu was locked up, electronically it would seem in a mountain in Madeira. The idea that Xenu was on the loose again is somewhat paralleled by the *Revelations* account, that Satan is freed at some point. In his *Parallel Lives of Illustrious Greeks and Romans*, the Greek writer Plutarch (AD 54 - 117) refers to Demetrius whom the Emperor had commissioned to explore the Islands around Britain:" More over there was one Island there, wherein Saturn was confined by Briareus in sleep; for that sleep had been devised for his bonds; and that round him were many genii as his companions and attendants". Saturn (Satan) was in Greek Cronus, who was allegedly the protagonist of another British giant Gogmagog. Thus there is some parallel here, between Scientology and Christian texts that are Semitic and British myth an important point that I will return to shortly.

Hitchins in 1772, discovered three letters cut in the turf between the legs of the Cerne giant, which were translated by Mr. Colley March in 1801 as J (Jehoweh), followed by an N-shaped squiggle (the mediaeval Saturn sign), and D which has been interpreted as (Destruxit) or 'God has destroyed Sturn'. However equally it could mean Oak-God (D or Duir in the Tree alphabet) and the Serpent cult who used the Grid. It is thought that the left extended hand of the Cerne giant initially grasped a severed head. The Celts as we know observed the practise of severing the heads of their enemies and keeping them as trophies, which was dramatized en-masse in the French Revolution, which was a Masonic affair that may be further identified here. The word 'Cernel', the old name for Cerne, is composed of Latin Cerno (Isee or ISA –Son of God?) and Hebrew El or Hel (God).

A wishing well named St. Augustines well, which was set up at an Abbey at Cerne near to the giant, is said to mark the advent of Christianity in the village, but it clearly shows the *rosette* emblem, the rose being the emblem of the One World Order and as I have shown previously an emblem of the Rose-Croix, Scottish Rite Freemasonry and the Rosicrucian's. Ron Hubbard on one occasion in his writings wrote a poem concerning a rose, which was most unlike Ron's style! The Cerne giant originally went by the name of Helis (Helios - sun in Greek). Helios was worshipped in Rhodes, where in similar fashion to the Cerne giant, he was naked and highly maculated as a Herculean God. The Knights of St.John occupied Rhodes for many centuries. It was puzzling that so many Greek myths were portrayed in symbolic form at Cardiff Castle, until I deciphered the floor and its association with Scottish Rite Freemasonry and the whole history of Minoan Crete and the Religious Revolution: why a Herculean figure was carved onto a British hillside has puzzled archaeologists also, but is solved here. Hercules was born at Argos, and he was a Sacred Solar King. We know from the Krater from Ruvo previously discussed, that the original King of Argos was a Twin Sacred King. In the krater from Ruvo the Petasos cap of Hermes unites Twin Kings, as it does in coins from Voltera *(fig. 44)*. The club of the giant, which also appears in the volterra coin, is the club of Hercules, once a sacred King whose club was originally a fertility bough. The Krater shows him wearing a panther skin, which is the usual robe of Dionysus, who was a dying god derived also from the archetype of a sacred Sun-King.

The nine eyes on the body of Argus are sun symbols and the fact that the equine carvings contained one eye, gives us the connection to the political system of Iluminati and One World Order. The eye appears in numerous mythic contexts as a symbol of the all-seeing Sun and becomes associated with Hermes and the hermetic Eye of Intelligence. A number of Minoan seals after the Religious revolution show the all-seeing eye, thus implying that the Religious Revolution was another stage in the One World Order plan. The Cerne giant is thought not only to have carried a severed head, but also a lion's skin. The Krater from Ruvo, once again provides the link, with a panther skin, the sign of royalty; in this case it is a lion's skin as the lion was an important royal totem beast in the Semitic Beth-Luis-Nion alphabet, employed by the Druids. Why did Hermes kill the Twin King of Argos? - The answer must surely be that Hermes hoped to combine both Twin Kings in a transcendent third stage beyond death, thus eliminating the woman and her truth. The introduction of a hermetic god enabled a King to avoid his ritual sacrifice, thus giving rise to solar monarchy, which could become a political power, puppeted by a Theocratic priesthood. This is the entire story of Knossos and the installation of King Minos and the Bull- cult, which must be Druid. Orthodox mythographers eventually during the classical period, lost sight of the archetypal Hermes as Thrice Great Hero, who combined male and female and Hermes became a bisexual god.

Fig.44a **Etruscan coin from Volterra. At left, a Janiform head capped by the petasos of Hermes.** *The obverse exhibits a crescent moon and a club and the Etruscan inscription "VELATHRI" (c.350 B.C.)*

Fig.44b. **Coin fromTenedos.**
At left,a Janiform head composed of a male and female face. The obverse displays a double axe between twin pillars.

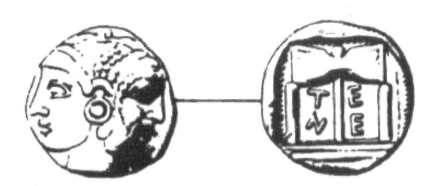

Fig. 44c. **Sketch of seal design from Knossos.**

> *Middle Minoan III (HM. 1597) this seal has a fourth face engraved with two standing birds. (Illustration not available). Labykrinth motifs and serpent with cranes.(Heraklion Museum).Compare with Plate 28 and prehistoric geometric designs.*

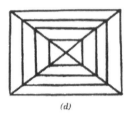

(a)　　　　　(b)　　　　　(c)　　　　　(d)

Fig.44d. **From the labrys (double axe) to the labyrinth. Related motifs from four Cretan seals.**

> *Middle Minoan III – Late Minoan Age. From Knossos and vicinity a. (HM.337) b. (HM.152) c. HM Gallery II, Case 28, No. 1786 d. HM. Callery V, Case 65, no. 2180. Heraklion Museum.*

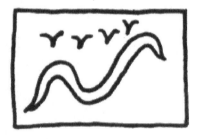

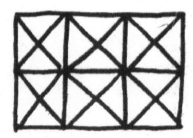

GOGMAGOG

Geoffrey of Monmouth, the twelfth century Benedictine Chronicler, stated that the British were descendents of Brutus, son of Sylvius, grandson of Ascanius, the Son of Aenas i.e. they were descended from Trojan heroes. The story goes, that Brutus was told that Britain was a land where giants once lived and he brought the exiled Trojans after the fall of Troy, to live in Britain. Prince Corineus as leader of another band of exiled Trojans joined Brutus and upon landing at Totnes in Devon, found a dwindling tribe of giants. The leader of the giants was Goemagot, who wielded an Oak tree as his club. Legend has it, that Goemagot and Corineus, engaged in a wrestling match and Goemagot was thrown off the cliff at Lam Goemagot at Totnes. What does all this mean? The story of Jason and the Argonauts has a similar tale, where Amycus Son of Poseidon challenged the Argonauts and Polydeuces who was an Olympian champion boxer accepted. Polydeuces and his Twin Castor were known as the dioscori or "Divine Youths" because Zeus was the father of the former, although not the latter, but both shared the same mother - this is a story of matrilineal succession then. Castor and Polydeuces were Twin princes of Sparta and their mother was Leda, their Twin sisters were Clymnestra and Helen of Troy. Zeus was the reported father of both Polydeuces and Helen. Thus their Twin Kingship has roots in a pre-historic context. Further Amycus customarily had strangers thrown off a cliff into the sea, if they would not box with him. Importantly sacred kings of the pre-historic period sometimes escaped being ritually sacrificed at the end of a year or great year (19 years), by substituting a captive as surrogate victim. There is also evidence in both myth and icon, that the victim or pharmacos was sometimes sacrificed by being hurled into the sea from a height.

Thus the wrestling contest between Goemagot and Corineus looks suspiciously like a ritual contest, in which Twin Kings were engaged. Boxing matches were also employed at festival rituals among the Late Minoans after the Religious Revolution. The rulership of King Minos may have become hereditary monarchy, where the victims or pharmacos as seven maidens and youths were brought from Athens, seven being a propitiatory number to Great Goddess, whom was ousted by the Druids, I concluded at Knossos. Ariadne helped Theseus to overthrow the rule, by giving him the knowledge (golden ball of thread), to get in and out of the maze. Excavations on Thera (Santorini) discovered a Minoan city buried by the eruption of Thera's volcano c. 1520 - 1500 B.C. This has been put forward as the reason for the fall of Knossos causing a tidal wave, however I would claim myth and icon and legend tell a completely different story, apart from the fact that Knossos was covered in Gypsum (which dissolves in running water) and therefore the story of a tidal wave is untenable. A fresco on the walls of a building on Santorini showed two Twin Kings engaged in a boxing match (*The Battle of The Trees*). Further it is curious that the princes wore hair dressed like dread-locks and a resistivity survey by Rodney Castleden on the Cerne giant revealed the possibility of a severed head in the left hand: "a fist grasping a wild mop of dread-locks from which is swinging a severed head". Thus it might be concluded that a Greek line of kings had remained in Greece who retained some links with their Druid counterparts in Britain. Although I put forward a plausible explanation for the stolen genealogies of the Magdalene, there is also the possibility that she may have been from a Greek source and dynasty.

Further the Minoan fresco shows the boxers naked but wearing tight belts, which is paralleled by the Cerne giant who appears to be naked, but to have a line drawn at the belt level. The Minoans wore boxing gloves on the right hand, which were leather thongs wound over the hand, reminding one of the ancient stones, which were bound in thongs. Presumably power from the Grid or some cosmic energy or Divine source (as it was believed) was the idea behind this. The Minoan Princes in the post Religious Revolution era passed their hair through blue headdresses and allowed it to flow from the back, a picture of 'The Prince', is given in *The Battle of The Trees*. Professor Maarinatos pointed out that this identified them as Royal Princes. Homer the Greek also mentions blue hair as an attribute of royalty of Eastern derivation, which appears to have been traditional among the Minoans of Thera. In passing, it should be noted that the Picts of Britain painted themselves blue, indicating this ancient memory.

The phallus of Cerne giant reflects ancient ideas of Kingship. At Domboshawa a 'Bushman' painting of the Palaeolithic period from Southern Rhodesia, shows the death of a King who wears an antelope mask and is restrained as he dies and ejaculates, where his 'seed' serves to form a heap of seed corn, representing fertility of crops and tribe in one sense but dynastic lines in another. There is an old priestess lying beside a cauldron and close by, young priestesses dance beside a stream, surrounded by fruit and heaped baskets, where a priestess accompanied by an erect python pacifies a huge *bison bull*. In Minoan Crete after the Religious Revolution, square sarcophagi depicting scenes of bull sacrifice replaced the bath-shaped sarcophagi with their oval rims representing The Cycle of Eternal Return and Re-incarnation I concluded. The square being symbolic of the Beth-Luis-Nion alphabet of a Semitic groups probably the Druids, or the forerunner of that group, which was the Bull-Man cult.

The Stag cult is older than the Bull-Minos cult and the Stag as the totem beast, was featured in the Spanish caves of Altamira in Spain; and in the cave at Trois Frères in the French Pyrennes, dating back 20 000 B.C. at least. The persistence of festivals in Britain, which retained a masked bull and horned figure, such as

'Old Brazen face' and the Dorset 'Ooser' are clearly a memory of an ancient religion in Britain. Centuries ago, it was the custom in Dorset Britain, for a wild bull-masked man to run through the streets and villages, stopping at houses to demand refreshment (taxes!) This figure was called the 'Ooser' and the implication is that it is derived from the Druids Osier basket, which appeared as the chequer design on the icons of the Late Minoan period, after the Religious Revolution. The appearance of the Osier basket in the icon of Minotaur on the knee of Pasiphae, refers to the ritual sacrifice of the Sacred King. The Druids also sacrificed many people in massive Osier or wicker man baskets, representing a propitiative act in memory of the overthrow of the Great Goddess at Knossos. In Shillingstone in Kent in Britain, the 'Ooser', was known as the 'Christmas Bull' and this reflects the Minos cult and the Minotaur as Divine child, who would herald in the New Year as new babe or Twin King now combined into one king as solar monarchy. This was to be repeated in the birth of Jesus as New Year Solar King, who was destined to be sacrificed after his rule, on the Taur (os) or bull or 'T' shaped cross. In fact when a Sacred King was of no more use to the Theocratic priesthood, they simply got rid of him and elected another one. The Aurignacians also combined the Stag and Minos cults. In a Dordogne cave painting, a bull-man is dancing a playing a musical instrument shaped like a bow (or crescent moon). As the floor of the summer Smoking Room at Cardiff castle in Wales illustrates, the history of Christianity goes back to Greece. The mural at Cardiff Castle showing Almathea feeding the young Zeus, must give the pre-history, in so far as the Minotragos goat-cult in Crete seems to have been intermediate between the cults of Minelaphos and Minotaur. Amalthea, the nurse of Cretan Zeus, was a goat, which is presumably the symbolisation of the Devil with goat's horns, which as a symbol in Freemasonry led to the view they were Satanic, without recognising the earlier source.

Returning to Brutus who arrived in Britain to find Goemagot: Brutus had killed his father allegedly accidentally, whilst hunting and was expelled from Italy for parricide, before coming to Britain. This reflects the history of Evander who was banished from Arcadia for killing his father and religiously implies the suppression of the Triple Goddess by Zeus i.e. patriarchal domination. The implication is that Brutus held his Sacred Kingship by Matrilineal succession and challenged Goemagot, who was evidently a sacred King by Patrilineal succession. I have already alluded to the fact, that Fenuisa farsa was an ancestor of the Irish Milesians, who was also described as a Scythian and a grandson of Magog who himself was the grandson of Noah. Gog and Magog are closely connected names. 'Gogmagog', Gog the son of Gog, was then the giant Goemagot, whom "Brut the Trojan" is said to have defeated at Totnes at the close of the second Millennium. B.C. Where did Gog Mac Gog, as he is sometimes curiously referred to as 'Mac' is Scottish, come from? In *Genesis X,*

33

2 Magog is described as a son of Japhet, who figures in Greek myth as Iapetus the Titan, the father by the Goddess Asia of Atlas, Prometheus and Epimetheus; and as a brother of Gomer, Madai, Javan, Tubal, Meshech and Tiras who are generally agreed to have been the Cimmerians, the Medians, the Ionians, the Tibarenians, the Moschians and the Tyrrhenians. The Moschians and the Tibarenians were tribes of the South-Eastern Black Sea: This region was given by Robert Graves as the region in which the Beth-luis-Nion and Ogham Script originated, which was the alphabet of the Druids. This may supply a solution to the channelled evidence of the Rev. Walker who spoke of "Prince", "lake" and a "net" and implies some form of alteration of matter had occurred here, or misuse of the hidden science, otherwise it would not have been recorded on the morphogenetic bioplasma, which is solely concerned with survival (and changes) in matter. Thus we might assume that Gog Mac Gog did not originally come from Scotland, but the Black Sea area. If Noah's Ark did land at Mt. Arat, then that would make sense.

Thus as we get to the bottom of this secret, we find that Fenuisa farsa was the grandson of Magog and according to Keating's History of Ireland:

> "Fenuisa farsa, a grandson of Magog and King of Scythia, desirous of mastering the Seventy-two languages created at the confusion of Babel, sent seventy-two persons to learn them. He established a University at Magh Seanair near Athens, over which he and Gadel and Caoith presided. These formed the Greek, Latin and Hebrew letters. Gadel, digested the Irish (Goidelic) into five dialects; the Fenian for the soldiers; the poetic and historic for the Senachies and bards respectively; the medical for physicians; the common idiom for the vulgar"

That the tiered alphabet (reflecting Semitic superiority) was invented in Greece was insisted upon, in *The Hearing of the Scholars*. Further Caoith as Coieus was the (British?) Hyperborean grandfather of Delphic Apollo and the Druids laid out their henge in Apollonian style and revered Apollo above all other gods. We also know that Fenuisa farsa as the grandson of Magog was the vine-man, who joins together and as Foeneus father of Atlanta, was the first man to plant a vineyard in Greece, which I assumed was the origin of the Brotherhood or Freemasonry in its earliest conception. This was probably an effort to "join together" members of the lost 13 th tribe of Judah, the biblical Adamites. According to Greek legend, this Foeneus or 'Oeneus' was a son of Aegyptus and came from Arabia (Ethiopia?) or Southern Judaea. This may be why the Druids, chose to act out the Crucifixion in that part, because as the biblical Adamites, they saw a rightful claim to the throne, based on perhaps their origins in the region. The State of Israel was later to be claimed on similar reasons of biblical authority. The Irish bards related that Feniusa farsa was turned out of Egypt, for refusing to persecute the children of Israel. In fact given that Feniusa farsa was a grandson of Magog, who was a grandson of Noah, and thus Semitic this was understandable, although evidently the connection had been lost even in this time. After exile from Egypt Feniusa farsa wandered for forty-two years (alphabetic significance) and then passed northward to the: "Alters of the Phillistines by the **lake** of willows" -Hebron in *southern Judaea* and was later to be found in Greece (for emphasis refer back to Rev. Walker's channelled account). If Feniusa farsa was the grandson of Magog, then is this a story of the origin of Freemasonry ('Vine-man who joins together') in Greece? As I asked in Alternative 4, will Greece be claimed eventually (as Israel was claimed) as the jewel in the crown? Magog was then the grandson of Noah according to Robert Graves in *The White Goddess*, thus Magog the giant who was defeated by Brutus must have been Semitic. Further since Noah in the Ark, was said to have come to rest on Mount Arat, which is in Armenia, then Magog is usually held to stand for Armenia, although Jospehus interprets the word as meaning "the scythians" - which was an inclusive name for *all the Black Sea tribes of the day*. The King of Gog of Meshech and tubal was mentioned in *Ezekiel, XXX VIII, 17*; who is now identified with Mithradates VI of Pontus. This becomes more complicated by the minute, but it seems the history of Foeneus was the *mass emigrations* from Canaan as the Canaanites and Agenor who became King of Argos, who drove the tribe of the Tuatha de Danaan out of Greece and this tribe was to end up in Ireland and one assumes that they propagated a Celtic Royal Dynasty there, which eventually was to produce Jesus through the matrilineal line and grandmother Anna (Danu or Dana). Thus it seems that a Semitic tribe derived from Noah, may have *produced or intermarried with the Tuatha de Danaans* and when the mass Canaanite invasions took place c. 2900B.C. they came to Britain, via Denmark giving that country its name. Further the group who conducted the Religious Revolution in Crete were either Druids from Britain or Agenor, which seems to be connected to the same Semitic line. However given the huge number of connections in iconography between the two locations (Britain and Crete) it seems likely that the Religious Revolution was indeed conducted by the Druids, who were considered as "gods" by the Celts. If the Tuatha de Danaan were the remnant biblical Adamites, who held their own knowledge of the hidden science, then this would account for this. The Tuatha de Danaan were a matriarchal tribe and thus it seems that their source of knowledge came from tutorage of the Early Cretan mysteries probably via the Teacher. Perhaps it was, that they viewed themselves as the rightful divinity on this planet and thus jealously removed the woman from the story, creating a *patriarchal* religion but using matrilinear succession (a compromise to guilt!) using Hermes to combine male and female. Thus it seems that the root was Noah, whose grandson Gogmagog was defeated by Brutus, who was a *matrilineal* Sacred King from Greece (Troy). Magog's grandson Fenuisa Farsa as the 'Vine-man', sought to unite the tribe and once again become a ruling power. Fenuisa farsa and the invention of tiered alphabets at Babel, which was reputedly a tiered or step building (layered secrecy) reflecting the tiered and flounced dresses of the Minoan Snake Goddesses, was an attempt to lock up all the history of the of the biblical Adamites and the hidden science in the uppermost tier whilst releasing glossed religious mysteries to the bards and removing all history and religion from the masses, who would be controlled ("the vulgar").

The giants of Britain were often depicted as the child eating Ogre type and this must derive from pre-historic Greek Kings, who sacrificed a child as his surrogate to avoid ritual slaying at the end of his 9-year reign, which became extended to 19 years. The victim as Interrex was made King for a day, the day of the solstice and then sacrificed. The connection of Sacred Kingship to Goemagot and Corineus (and Brutus) was made when Richard Carew, an Elizabethan historian writing in 1602, reported that the two figures held "clubbes" in their hands. Brutus as the victor, set up New Troy or Trinovantum on the River Thames near London and after the death of Brutus his sons Locrinus, Camber and Albanactus reigned over England, Wales and Scotland respectively. This provides some connection of Alba (white) to the Isle Alba and the Goddess in her death aspect in Scotland, where she was now truly buried and combined with Twin Kings in the personage of Hermes. It is almost too predictable of the puppet Masters to use the symbols once again in their eternal games in the plans for a £20 million rose garden, which will be the first public memorial to the late Princess Diana. The gardens will form the backbone of a redeveloped Royal National Rose Garden, significantly in St Albans Hertfordshire U.K. The oblique connection with Gog and Magog cannot have been missed, since for some obscure reason (although I am sure some excuse will appear) the centrepiece will be a 45ft wide rock from China and a 97ft high golden spire, which will glow in the sunset. Gold as a solar king's colour glowing in the light of the moon (the goddess in her pale death aspect) is implied. The spire will represent "purity and hope, and the rock determination and strength of purpose", which is evidently how the 13th tribe view themselves? The connection to China is obscure, although one of the figures at The Guildhall in the Gog and Magog statues had Mongolian-type eyes, which also occured as a symbol in manipulated UFO incidents, which were described by witnesses as "slant-eyes". "The lady of the Lake" in the Arthur and Round Table stories may also be implied, since a 975ft-long pool at the bottom of the commemorative garden will be backed by bronze friezes by international artists, showing Diana throughout her life. If the artist's impression of the future garden is anything to go by for accuracy, I note a semi-circle pool (crescent moon) at the base of the spire and predictably those twin-pyramidal conifers significantly placed! Presumably the numbers are significant and Bronze appears to refer to the

Bronze Age Minoans? Diana the Goddess in her death aspect then, between twoTwin Kings. Pretty story and commemoration, which no doubt will evolve into myth and fantasy and become another twist in the future story of The Holy Grail, but not the truth of what happened in Bronze Age Greece, where the Holy Grail and its guardian had nothing whatsoever to do with Kings, Monarchy or Goddesses! The Holy Grail was in fact stolen from its true guardian and has been used by the Elite ever since in their eternal games of two Kings, denying the source of The Holy Grail and the messengers that brought it.

Mohamed Al Fayed, father of Dodi who died alongside Diana on August 31, 1997 refused to accept the findings of the French judge who ruled that the Princess was killed because her driver was drunk and speeding. Mr Al Fayed does believe the deaths were an accident and has launched numerous legal challenges wich would help him to prove a conspiracy he believes was perpetrated by M16 also implying that Prince Philip was involved. In America, he asked a federal judge to order the release of 1 056 pages of classified documents held by the U.S. National Security Agency, which he claimed proved the crash was not an accident. Back in France in April 1999, he went to the country's highest court to urge the judge conducting the inquiry into the crash to question British diplomats about the plot to kill the Princess and his son. He asked the criminal division of Paris's Appeal Court to quiz two alleged British security service spies and an American agent about documents said to prove Diana was under surveillance. His application was rejected two weeks later -the story continues.

The Guildhall in London today displays huge carvings of two giants or images entitled "Gog and Magog". This is curious, why not Corineus or Brutus and Goemagot, depicting the original battle? Thus Goemagot now appears as two personages, which tends to confirm his role as Sacred Twin King. Curious when we realise that they replace two earlier images destroyed during the blitz in the Second World War. In the original carvings, one giant of the pair i.e. Gogmagog was shown as barbarous and more formidable than the other and was equipped with bow and arrow and a spiked globe, known as *'Morning Star'*. Corineus the Trojan hero was depicted in Roman dress, with a bird (the epiphany of the goddess in Greece) on his head, and holding a spear. Both figures regally crowned by Laurel. (*Fig.45*).

Fig.45 **Gog and Magog**, *London Guildhall, 1953 (TheTwins?)*

Gog and Magog *destroyed in the Blitz 1940*

Jesus was identified with the holly or holly-oak (holy one and oak royal), which was inappropriate since despite his pacific role, he declared that he had come to bring not peace, but the sword, in his war on woman and the 13 th tribe of Judah, which had incorporated her as Hermes and the truth of the original woman long forgotten now. The tanist was originally his twin's executioner; and it was the oak-king, not the holly-king, who was crucified on a T-shaped cross. Despite my conclusions here, that it was neither Jesus as holly or oak who was crucified on the cross, I refer to Lucian in his *Trial in the Court of Vowels* (about 160 A.D.) where it is explicit:

> Men weep, and bewail their lot, and curse Cadmus with many curses for introducing Tau into the family of letters; they say it was his body that tyrants took for a model, his shape that they imitated, when they set up the erections on which men are crucified. Stauros the vile engine is called, and it derives its vile name from him. Now, with all these crimes upon him, does he not deserve death, nay, many deaths? For my part I know none bad enough but that supplied by his own shape – that shape which he gave to the gibbet named **Stauros** after him by men" (*author's emphasis*).

Stauros (Taur or Tauros = bull; and Star= Mercury the star of Hermes(13th tribe) or Sirius (12 tribes), which appeared in the stone ring from Naples at the birth of Jesus; os = osier basket the sacrificial basket of the Druids) thus this gives some background to the morning star globe of Magog. This implies a secret group named Morning Star, which held the plans for the Crucifixion and Golgotha, further implying the plan was one set up by the 13 th tribe of Judah or the biblical Adamites. The fact that the star is in the form of a spike globe implies tentacles reaching out all over the globe and by further inference a plan of World domination, allied to Christianity. St. Paul effectively commandeered the story and despite Jesus' brother James protesting that it was a specifically Jewish religion marketed it worldwide. The arrows further turn up as a weapon symbol on the One-dollar note of America.

In the Gnostic *Gospel of Thomas*, composed at about the same date, the same theme recurs in a dispute between Jesus and his schoolmaster about the letter T. The schoolmaster strikes Jesus on the head and prophesies the crucifixion. In Jesus' time the *Hebrew* character *Tav*, the last letter of the alphabet, was shaped like the *Greek Tau*. Further the holly rules the eighth month, and eight as the number of increase was assigned to the month of the barley harvest, which extends from July 8th to August 4 th. Eight also refers to the figure-of-8, with all the implications of the hidden science. T is the evergreen oak (with implications of The Cycle of Eternal Return) that rules the waning part of the year. The association of T with Holly or T and the Taur shaped cross, implies when considered with D as oak royal which rules the waxing part of the year, a plan instigated at Golgotha which would remove holly or holy one and initiate a period of royalty or **power**. Placing this in the context of the globe in Gogmagog's hand and its spiked 'tentacles' reaching out from all surfaces of the globe, which as an archetypal symbol turned up in the Marine Vase (with octopus tentacles) in Late Minoan Greece, after the Religious Revolution conducted again by the tribe of Judah; then we might assume that the plan for World domination set in motion at Knossos based on solar monarchy, was to find its zenith in the events of Golgotha and was only to surface again in the events of World War II, which I conclude merely paved the way for the finalisation of that plan in a Federal Europe, coming to fruition in our own times: Predictably with that third battle (Armagghedon or World War III) looming on the horizon.

The interesting point here, is that when the new versions of the statues were made for the Guildhall in 1953, Corineas now has those "Masters", slit Mongolian type eyes, and now the bird (the epiphany of the Goddess) has gone altogether! Gogamagog now has a crown, looking suspiciously like the thousand- petalled lotus (opening of the crown chakra and channelling) on his crown, but both are regally crowned by laurel. Further Gogmagog has *round eyes* and somewhat baby face, which is typical of Celtic art, symbolising the new-year king and babe. Given that this was just after the war and the implication of the hermetic Eye of Intelligence, which as a circle and dot, was the secret sign of the infamous political power pyramidal group of the Illuminati, then putting the clues together what is really being implied here is a new World Order, with triumph presumably for the 13 th tribe and now Israel which had been founded. Thus the plan for a Federal Europe is implied even at this early date after the war. The further implication is that both were sacred Kings, the history of Corineus as Matriarchal King is now erased and the bird of epiphany of the Goddess gone. Further he has become Eastern and somewhat reminiscent of Madame Blavatsky's "Masters", which she claimed were in the Himmalayas.The presence of the thousand-petalled lotus strongly indicates that these so-called Masters have been channelled from the Grid straight off the Akashic Record. Further, Corineus and Goemagot (Twin Kings) now become Gogmagog (Solar King) the supposed grandson of Noah. Presumably now that the Grid had been channelled, perhaps with help from German scientists who went to America after the war, there was no need to retain power through the history of the tribe, since all powerful technology could be developed (from channelled past information and technology) and would render the Adamites great and far reaching power. The Greek nature of Corineus is being changed to now represent a type from the Himalayas and Gogmagog as the fully enlightened one with open crown chakra, which implies that the 13 th tribe had combined power with the Masters (past thought on the Grid!) and removed the woman entirely and forever. Thus whatever conscience they developed through contact with source and the spiritual message that came to Earth c. 10 000 B.C. was forgotten in the quest for power. It was a crossroads in the rehabilitation of the MMRC case and he took the road to a Theocracy and elitist Communism governed by formidable technology, thus repeating his karmic past. The question of whether he now sought to placate his conscience by giving back to man the apples of immortality in the form of Scientology but for the elite few only, thus retaining his grip on power and wealth, can only be guessed at.

Archaeologists have always been at a loss to explain why biblical figures should appear in Britain, however there is many a folk tale that tells of the ferocity and sacrifice of the giants Gog and Magog. Further in *Ezekiel*, there is the prediction that the **Jews would destroy Gog and Magog**. If Hitler tried to implement Atlantean (Aryan) supremacy, he may have sought to kill the Jews, to avoid the prophesy of *Ezekiel*. Thus it seems that The One World Order plan involved two groups who were both Semitic and both desiring to create a One World Order. Presumably, the 13 th tribe of Judah elitist, aristocratic and obsessed with dynastic bloodlines, versus the twelve tribes who could not compete on the subject of dynasties and therefore sought elitist Communism. In actual fact, the former and the latter groups *both* supported Communism for the masses and were both elitist, thus it really did not matter, whether you voted right or left, the outcome was the same: this would account for historians who note that at some high level, there is some form of cohesion between right and left politics (and I would add religion). Both groups had significant religious and political aims, with religious and political leaders taking one side or the other, as was evidenced by the Illuminatus pope, who presumably was 13 th tribe with the Socialists in Britain on the side of 12 tribes and Conservatives in their anti-European stance as 13 th tribe or at least some remnant of those ideologies? You could probably say that it really does not matter what political party it is, they are still subservient to the One World Order or Federal Europe Masters, who hold all the arrows as evidenced on the One-dollar note of America. In fact you could probably define the whole of religion and politics in terms of the battle of 12 and 13 and their ramifications along with the hidden science: indeed the Eye in the sky, the morphogenetic and spiritual bioplasmas appear to have kept a complete record of Arch controllers from Xenu or Yatrus and Hermes upwards, which they follow! – Hey ho! Welcome to the insane asylum that is Earth.

London's Gogmagog had been modelled faithfully on the *Ezekiel* account, including the weapons: "And I will smite the bow out of the right hand, and I will cause thy arrows to fall out of thy right hand". This evidently shows that the 12 tribes were in control of Britain after the war (at least in 1953) and obviously has some connection to those secret Masters in the Himalayas. Presumably then, Hitler's 13 th tribe (as Aryans) bid for power and the annihilation of the Jews, was to save the thirteenth tribe (as Aryans), before indeed they were wiped out by the Jews – hence the Holocaust? No doubt the SS saw themselves along with Hitler as the saviours or sun kings of Europe, in a bid against a Federal Europe? Which was very well developed as a plan even then. This would certainly account for much of the evidence I gave in *Alternative 4* concerning Hitler's obsession with the Holy Grail, cosmology, root races and esoteric matters including the SS Nazi symbolism and his referral to the woman in the story, at the time of his arrest and trial for treason, prior to his rise to power. It is not in my opinion co-incidental, that Britain has been run down to the level of a Third World country since World War II and Scotland has become a separately governed and parliamentary controlled sector of Britain, whilst retaining politicians (of which there are a number in Tony Blair's government) in The House of Commons in London, which is the UK parliament. However no English MP sits in Scotland. This must depend on Scotland as the true Holy Land and home to the 'cuckoo' – the biblical Adamites.One might theorise that it is the intention of Israel and the One World Order to break Britain and I strongly suspect, that Britain has been designated as "the Great City" in the Apocalyptic account of *Revelations*: where it suffers a large earthquake and is destroyed. Notably Rothschild who was heavily tied up in the One World Order, was the first person to coin the term "City" for London, thus plans might have been on the table for quite some time. *The Bible* indeed predicts the destruction of the 13 th tribe in the *Ezekiel* account, whether that irrationally extends on the basis of dramatization, to the people of England is unsure, although the symbolism of "7 (white?) Mountains" in *Revelations* could be applied to the Seven Sisters white cliffs along the south coast of England. Equally as I mentioned before, it could refer to the seven 'mountains' or Pythagorean triangles obtained from geometry applied to the tops of the mountains that surround Knossos and the psychro cave, where Zeus was allegedly born in Crete. The Greeks presumably believe that Communism and the One World Order will save them from the MMRC case, as they hook up with the 12 tribes and the 13 th? Having myself observed a light brought from Israel to Patmos (where St. John a member of the 13 th tribe wrote *Revelations*) for the first time in 1994. The Greeks should reminisce on the pith of Britain that has been spat out, when the juice has gone and the fruit is no longer of any USE. For those who gave their life-blood in this country in the Battle for Britain and stood against Hitler, when most of Europe was subjugated and having given a home to the Jews and taken an active part in the birth of the State of Israel, even honouring a Holocaust memorial day, it must be considered somewhat of an *Arch* betrayal even by Semitic group standards, if this is indeed the case. Certainly the British people are mystified why *their culture* is fought and "Britishness" has become a dirty word. Where every *culture* is respected and represented in the "multicultural society", but the Briton is accused of racism if he expresses his own *culture*: whilst any portrayal of Nationalism still enjoyed by all other nations (despite the MMRC plan for globalisation) is subject to the propaganda line of a (pro-Jewish) press that it is an expression of colonialism and British Empire (which was a 13 th tribe affair). "Britishness" to the Jews and Federal Communistic Europe, is seen as 13 th tribe nationalism and probably at the top of the power pyramid, you will find a merging of the 12 tribes and the

13 th, who as the global elite "movers and shakers" over nations and money markets, that profit Jew and Judah or 12 th and 13 th tribes, the mass of Britain's are dispensable. Now the leaders of the 13 th tribe have moved on and out of Britain, the British are suffering from an identity crisis, without knowing who they are. They certainly like the rest of the world have no inkling of this story.

As Britain receives bad press for the crisis in BSE and now foot and mouth disease, it is just a little too predictable that Britain should be paraded as the pariah of Europe aided by a pro-Jewish press. Since the latter disease came into the country *from abroad*, whilst Britain was still importing meat from countries known to have the disease, then it either shows a governmental level of incompetence or?! American media joined the bandwagon of European press; hot on the tail of pro-Jewish Hollywood and the film the *Patriot* and somewhere along this line I can smell the rat of the MMRC case. If you suppress a nation enough, as with an individual they simply fall down the emotional scale and tune into the Grid and self-survival behaviour. The very noticeable suppression in this country by high taxes, high living costs and expensive housing not to mention the weather! Coupled with governmental policies that are running down transport, police, education and healthcare, together with self sufficiency from farming which may have seen the final coup de grace in the latest crisis, with increasing costs from high levels of *welfare dependent* alleged political asylum seekers (*irrespective of race*), can only represent a mind boggling level of governing incompetence or treason?! Politicians are entrusted with the will of the people and quite clearly the people in Britain do not want a Federal Europe or a European army, they have paid their taxes and expect things to be kept in running order and good shape. When a politician does not **govern by the will of the people** and betrays that trust, he will destroy the nation. I suggest that politicians look up their job description and they might find, that they are a (British) politician owing their allegiance to the British people and not "the vine man who draws together". Further the British may yet find their identity, if they ask for the real **truth** of their history including the 'cuckoo' in the nest. The dictionary defines betrayal as: 1. Betrayal of one's sovereign or country, esp. By attempting to overthrow the government. 2. Any treachery or betrayal. The British people have been betrayed, along with the French, Germans, Greeks and many other nations.

Some accurate memory of the history of the giants existed in the reign of Henry V, since when he was passing over London Bridge on the way to his coronation; the City of London's first recorded giant greeted him. Two years later, after the triumph of Agincourt (1415), he was greeted by *male and female giants* at the Southwark gate entry to London Bridge; the *male* held the City *Keys*, as if porter of Hermes of London. The role of the woman is more difficult to find, which has probably not changed in Apollo's Britain! At other Royal functions after this date, the giants were either specific personages e.g. Hercules and Sampson or appear as Corineus, Brittanus and Gogmagog *Alb*ionus. The Great Fire of London in 1666 destroyed the original giants and a new pair was made, which were again destroyed in the blitz during the Second World War[158] It appears then, that originally the giant inhabitants of Britain and Goemagot or Gogmagog, were patriarchal descendents of Noah. They assumed matriarchalism after contact with Greece and the idea of political power as Twin Kingship was superimposed onto a BELIEF system (Re-incarnation or The Cycle of Eternal Return) and this belief and a whole cosmology were taken from the Early Minoans. The history of this was retained within the secret groups, principally with the Druids one would assume, the biblical Adamites and it appears in archetypal symbolism on the floor of the Summer Smoking Room at Cardiff Castle, which represents Scottish Rite Freemasonry at Rose-Croix degree level and Rosicrucianism.

THE LOST THIRTEENTH TRIBE

A. Yarker[159] stated: "The symbolic tracing of the Rosicrucian's was a *square* Temple approached by *seven steps*...here also we find the *two pillars* of *Hermes*, the *five* pointed *star*, *Sun* and *Moon*, *compasses*, square and *triangle*". Obviously here is solar Kingship (sun); Goddess (Moon); seven (Matriarchal number - 5 dactyls who tutored Zeus and two Twin Kings = 7); Hermes (Twin Kings/woman, fused in transcendent third stage to remove the woman); and the square Temple (four pillars of equal height of the Beth-Luis -Nion alphabet used by the Druids); star (Staurus or Morning Star a descendent group of the Rosicrucian's and an ascendant group of the Druids involved with the Crucifixion as a front group for the Druids and 13 th tribe). Thus in this statement alone, we can connect the Rosicrucian's with many events on the world stage and particularly the case of stolen apples from Crete in the form of a belief system and cosmology involving science.

Rosicrucianism was not the beginning, but a link in the long chain connecting Freemasonry, with far earlier groups and cults starting with the Stag cult in Palaeolithic times. Ultimately though the top echelon of Freemasonry is Jewish and the 'Vine-man', who joins together or Fenuisa Farsa the great grandson of Noah, or the grandson of Magog. The twelve tribes of Israel and the thirteenth lost tribe, which must be the Druids or originally one assumes the tribe of Magog grandson of Noah: with further connections to the Tuatha de Danaan from the Black Sea region. The Jewish writer Bernard Lazane, noted there were Jews around the cradle of Freemasonry and the Masonic coat-of-arms used by the Grand Lodge of *England*, was a Jewish design. Lucien Wolf[160] stated: "an attempt to display heraldically the various forms of the cherubim pictured to us in the second vision of *Ezekiel* - an ox, a man, a Lion, and an eagle belongs to the highest and most mystical domain of Hebrew symbolism". The Druidic Beth-Luis-Nion Alphabet which Graves believes originated in the Black sea region and thus holds implications of a connection to the Tuatha de Danaan and the Semitic tribes that wandered into Greece, was governed in the four stations of the year (and the four pillars of equal height in the square), by four beasts. The year of Bull, Lion, Serpent, and Eagle is Babylonian: a calendar beast having the body and horns of a bull, forelegs and mane of lion, head and scales of the serpent, hind legs of the eagle. *Ezekiel* glossed over, or someone has edited out, the serpent and replaced it with man, since it either represented the hidden science or had some relationship with the woman. Further the number of vowels was increased in the alphabet, to make 7 and the proportion of all the letters in the alphabet to the vowels is 22 to 7, which is the mathematical formula of π and the relation of the circumference of the circle to the diameter: again with implications of the UVG120 sphere or Grid. It is also "pie" as in: 'to put a secret in a pie and place a pastry crust on top', which although a term for bardic glossing and secrecy referred to by Robert Graves the poet, it has also been referred to in this manner by secret groups at the time of the French Revolution. The number of aggregate strokes for the Ogham script in the entire alphabet was 72, and since the Ogham script was utilised by the Druids, then the fact that Jesus' Resurrection was reported as covering a period of 3 days or 72 hours, connected him to the Druids and this secret wisdom. Further the use of 72 implies control of the entire alphabet and by inference its religious mysteries, which must include the two cycles or pulses of matter (360 degrees) and anti-matter (360 degrees). Thus one assumes, that this was intimated in the transparent nature of Jesus' alleged body after the Crucifixion, where he passed through matter in much the same way as was reported of the crew in the alleged Philadelphia Experiment. The implication being that He had become anti-matter (anti-Christ?) and *that* was heaven and not Earth.

Further the seal on the diplomas of craft Masonry show the woman and man combined, which must be Hermes and reminds us strongly of the millennium icon as a symbol of 'Britain's' millennium (or should I say the 'cuckoo's' millennium). When Jesus spoke of the joining of male and female in the previously quoted Alexandrian text, he referred presumably to the triumph of Jewish Freemasonry and Hermes, which would through Fenuisa Farsa and the 'Vine-man' who 'joins together', create a Semitic One World Religion – Christianity for the masses and perhaps another religion for the elite. When the ritual and constitutions of Masonry were drawn up in 1717, although certain fragments of the ancient Egyptian and Pythagorean doctrines were retained, the *Judaic* version of the secret tradition was the one elected by the founders of Grand Lodge on which to build up their system. However as I noted in *The Battle of The Trees*, there have always been two groups who have fought for world supremacy, both groups Semitic, but one group in the past, holding significant knowledge of the Greek background, which inherently carried the matriarchal knowledge. Neither can the possibility be dismissed, as I have pointed out, that both groups 12 and 13 act in *unison at the top*: otherwise it would be inexplicable why Israel should have sent a light from there to Patmos in Greece in 1994, the alleged place where St. John wrote *Revelations*. St. John I concluded was a Druid or 13 th tribe. Although I had not quite clarified this matter in *The Battle of The Trees* I did propose that the highest aspirations of Israel in the political arm of Zionism, were retained within a secret group at the top, where one might pose the conclusion, that the secret and alternative version of St. John's *Revelation* and the *Secret Doctrine*, is being followed by that group. The B'nai B'rith the secret International Zionist and Masonic order that tried to round up all Comyns Beaumont's books, which give Scotland as the true Holy Land, must have some connection to this group, if not part of that group itself. One could place virtually all World Revolutions and Wars at the doorstep of these two groups as RELIGIOUS WARS: where both groups have fought their ridiculous battles over this Planet in their equally ridiculous goal of a One World Order, both politically and religiously. Man should always have choices be that political or religious. That goal is nothing more than the pre-Flood Atlantean quest for monopolistic and despotic control, which was retained in this cycle by the Adamites through Noah.

The Prieuré de Sion, a secret group, who were around the cradle of European Union, held the number 13 to be significant. Obviously this not only held significance through the Beth-Luis-Nion alphabet, with its 13 consonants, but implied Jesus and his twelve disciples making a company of thirteen and the Druidic or thirteenth tribe. From decoding of certain connections of this group including the *Vaincre* illustration in *The Battle of The Trees*, I concluded that when the impetus for European Union was set up, through the secret groups, that there had been some form of agreement between the top echelons of the groups and specifically the two groups which I have termed 13 and 12 (the thirteenth tribe and the twelve tribes of Israel) as to the religion that would form the One World Order. Evidently both groups believed Marxist communism as Illuminism would provide the political pyramid of control, which is noted on the left hand side of the One Dollar note from America – far left Socialist politics, which is the political world revolution. I concluded further, that there had been some kind of disagreement between these groups in the 1980's and the form of the religion displayed on the right hand side of the One Dollar note, would not take the path originally intended, but was to centre on Christianity or Orthodox religion for the masses, whilst concentrating on the more immediate goal of political and monetary union, which undoubtedly forms a power Communistic pyramid run by the far right rich Elite. This disagreement one concludes, must have led to the group 13 making alternative plans that were set in motion in the 1980's a date that co-incidentally that was contemporary with Ron Hubbard's death (left the body) although Hubbard is alleged to have lost control of the Church in the 1970's.

Thirteen must have become an unlucky number, considering the number of times the group has tried to achieve power. But what of this thirteenth tribe - where is there any mention of it? Josephus (*Antiquities V. 5, 5*) writes of the *three* wonders of the sanctuary (Mother Goddess and Twin Kings making an ancient Trinity) namely the table of shew bread, and the alter of incense:

> "Now, the seven lamps signified the seven planets, for so many there were springing out of the candlestick; the twelve loaves that were upon the table signified the *circle* of the zodiac and the year; and the alter of incense by its *thirteen* kinds of sweet smelling spices with which the sea replenished it; signified that God is the Lord of all things in both the uninhabitable and the habitable parts of the earth, and that they are

all to be dedicated to His use." (*Author's emphasis*)

These thirteen (rather than four) spices must belong to an early secret tradition not mentioned in the Law, coeval with the instructions in *Numbers XX iX, 13,* for the sacrificed of thirteen bullocks on the first day of the Feast of Tabernacles. The Beth-Luis-Nion alphabet with its significant number of 72, a number associated with the Resurrection, signifies Mosaic Law, a Law that was employed by the Druids. The total number of bullocks sacrificed from the inauguration of the critical seventh month to the end of the seven days of the Feast, was the sacred number of 72 again. Josephus hints that the number thirteen refers to Rahab, the prophetic goddess of the *Sea* ('As I flow away, so must I return' - Re-incarnation) Guardian of Sheol ('the uninhabitable parts of the World - the abode of the dead). Thus the thirteenth number is matriarchal and signifies a belief concerning the after-life. I would maintain that the thirteenth tribe held a belief in Re-incarnation, which was held by the Druids. This belief came from Early Minoan Crete (and prior) and was taken, along with the knowledge of a whole cosmology. Thus the thirteenth tribe I would conclude is matriarchal as opposed to the Twelve Tribes of Israel, which are patriarchal. The Jews or the group 12, were promised: "no more sea", at the end of times, since evidently as in the *Ezekiel* text, they believe that they will kill Magog and overcome the thirteenth tribe and the sea was traditionally connected to the Goddess or the woman in the story. The original intent of "sea" was to teach the concept of The Cycle of Eternal Return and Re-incarnation: "As I flow away, so must I return". However that was lost very early on to mankind, sequestered into secret groups and specifically into the 13th tribe - Druids and the highest levels eventually of particular branches of Freemasonry.

What appears to have been a jewel-sequence corresponding with Ezekiel's tree-sequence was arranged in *three* rows on the golden breast-plate worn by the High Priest, called in Greek the logion, or 'little word-giver' (*Exodus XXVIII, 15*). Significantly it was made by the Egyptian craftsmen and the King of Tyre wore a similiar one in honour of Hercules Melkarth (*Ezekiel, XXVIII, 13*) The jewels (crystals?) gave oracular responses (receiver properties extracting information from the world Grid or UVG 120 crystal sphere?), by lighting up in the dark of the sanctuary (free energy from the vacuum?); and were probably hollow cut with a revolving drum behind them in which was a small strip of phosphorous. When the drum was revolved the message was spelt out in the Ouija style as the strip of phosphorous came to rest behind different letters in turn. This is effectively then, channelled information from the Grid. I am sorry to say that many prophecies are information of PAST EVENTS, which only occur cyclically when used to predict *future* events - a most important point.

The account of the breastplate in *Exodus* mentions twelve precious stones, inscribed with the names of the Twelve Tribes of Israel, set in a *gold* plaque *eight* inches *square.* I have emphasised the significances, which you should be able to recognise by now. The Israelites in Exodus were led by Moses, himself evidently a fostered (or adopted) child of 13 th tribe origin, which was a method of gaining leadership among the twelve tribes and in Moses case he was taken in by an Egyptian dynasty. He is connected to the basket (Druid osier basket) and the reed (royalty) and thus I assume he was Druidic *and* royal. The basket of course was the Osier, the sacrificial basket of the Druids, the Celtic custom being to offer sacrifices in an Osier. This is curiously hinted at, since there is a thirteenth stone, which is given such importance elsewhere in the Bible, for example in *Isaiah, LIV, 12*; that it is presumed to have been part of the original series. This is the Kad Kod, mistranslated in the authorised version as 'agate', probably the red carbuncle, and we may assign it to the tribe of Gad, which disappeared early on in Israelite history. Whether Gad became God and combined *G*ogmagog and *Ad*am all of which reveal Father - Dad, with the corresponding idea that the Adamites were gods, which the Celts believed of the Tuatha de Danaan, until finally through constant channelling identified themselves as God, reflects the condemnation of man implied in religious texts. Further Dad implies *D*anaan and *Ad*am, with Anna in the matrilineal dynastic line allegedly of Jesus providing the Greek dynastic line from the Tuatha de Danaan: this probably finds a solution to the *Isaiah* text: "The Father is the Mother" a quote that apparently cost a Pope his life. All the jewels are mistranslated in the authorised version! And a slightly different set appears in *Revelation, XXI, 19*; where only twelve stones are given and "twelve pearls" are referred to, once again reflecting the *Ezekiel* prophesies that the twelve tribes would eradicate the thirteenth tribe. Whether such a religious dramatization will descend on the heads of the British, sacrificed to the cause of a 'script' – *Revelations* and The "New Jerusalem", can only be concluded on the past and the dogged way this 'script' has been followed as the One World Order plan. Ah yes, and all "vile" and "dirty" things come out of her and let me prophesy what the pro-Jewish if not controlled press will print "ah yes, did '*she*' not give us BSE and foot and mouth and football hooligans!" And the people will wonder in awe that his all come to pass as prophesied. Meanwhile today as farmers grapple in Britain with the foot and mouth disease, that came **from abroad**, and struggle to cope with one of the biggest agricultural crisis in this country, as the livelihood of tourism and agriculture is threatened together with hauliers, what is the British government doing in Parliament? According to Quentin Letts *Yesterday in Parliament* (*Daily Mail March 16, 2001*) as the Agricultural Minister rose to speak on the crisis in the House of Commons: "The only Cabinet minister who could be bothered to attend his 90-minute Commons statement on the epidemic yesterday was Ann Taylor, who as Chief Whip was doing little more than her basic duty". In his usual witty style Letts stated of the lack of interest in country jobs: "Come off it, though! It was lunchtime. Mr.

Brown's (Agricultural Minister) statement started at 1.18 pm, an hour when Blairites are sitting down to their endive and crostini starter at some Conran restaurant". Treason to the British people?! The question remains *why* do they show no apparent concern? Where the only concern is the short- term politics of re-election.

The **twelve** jewels in the Revelations account, form the foundations of the "NEW JERUSALEM" - which is the ONE WORLD ORDER PLAN WITH ITS POLITICAL AND RELIGIOUS SYSTEM: which may co-incide with a plan for a World Order, laid out as a map on the Floor of the Summer Smoking Room at Cardiff Castle, which mentions "Australia, Asia, Europe and Jerusalem". The pyramid or hive of world Marxism or Illuminism, clothed as Socialism and Christianity, is the One World Order of the twelve tribes of Israel. The difficulty here is in deciding whether the 13 th tribe has some other World Order in mind, or whether the two have now combined. Given the history of these two groups and the conflict, one might suppose there has been some form of agreement, which retains political Illuminism, but allows two religious groups. I will come to the proposal of an alternative religious group shortly. The twelve tribes of Israel in the *Revelations* account achieve victory and become "the chosen ones" or the "144 000" that are saved, from the catastrophe. *The Covenant* maintained presumably, before the next Magnetic Reversal or the next boundary event that physicist Harold Aspden spoke of: whereupon the "New Jerusalem", will be destroyed, the world's stage and Theatre cleared for the next cyclic production. However something can be learnt from the past 'script' and the Antediluvian era, in that a nuclear war seems to have been precipitated *before* a cataclysm and may well have caused the actual event itself, through the misuse of the hidden science. Personally I believe there is still time left, but the urgency with which I have always worked, is soul intuition, coupled with observation of world events and the completion of the plan for a One World Order, bringing man precipitously close to the misuse of the hidden science. Further since the MMRC case cannot finish a cycle of action, then I am afraid that the pattern will wipe the board clean long before "paradise" or the "New Jerusalem". I tried to bring the game to a rational halt, to assess the ethics and misuse of the hidden science, through my Petition to the British Government demanding TRUTH. However there is a whole hidden battle going on here and I personally do not hold out much hope of the entire audience lifting themselves from their seats! In support of the few hecklers who have blown raspberries at the leading players!

You may remember that the Yatrus incident and the control of bodies with "distortion of data" whereby "data of his own was added". L. Kin agreed that it was difficult to date the incident, since there were only one or two 'frames' in hundreds of feet of 'film roll'. This is certainly interesting, in so far as one might propose, that such meddling with what I propose as the morphogenetic bioplasma or master blueprint, the data for the survival of the phylogenetic line of the species, may have occurred in the past and then terminated for some reason. We might further propose, that such an incident was just prior to a Magnetic Reversal, which terminated it. Such meddling today is seen in the field of genetic engineering and cloning of species, which as I have pointed out is bound to confuse the master pattern, where the conclusion would be, that a certain phylogenetic line has failed to survive and is now mixed e.g. with pig or porcine DNA. Would such a conclusion indicate to the master blueprint, that recombination of DNA had occurred, thus precipitating a corresponding change in the master DNA or phylogenetic pattern on the hermetic principle: 'As above, so below' and vice versa? Thus would the master pattern now implement a fusing of tri-partite biofield information or "jelly mould" of pig and human? Thus giving rise to species that are deformed? In 1999 the Australian biotech firm Stem cell Sciences in Australia, produced an embryo that was part human and part pig and recently research has produced human-pig mutants for use as spare body parts in medicine! Human DNA and a small proportion of porcine or pig DNA was implanted in a hollowed-out pig's egg in secret cloning experiments. This mirrored the production of Dolly the sheep at the Roslyn (Rose-line) Institute in Scotland. According to the report in an Australian newspaper, the pig-human embryo was grown to the 32-cell stage and American scientists have conducted similar work, injecting human DNA into unfertilised cows eggs. Surely they will be trying Bulls next, in the hope of a Minotaur hybrid! Some dramatization! In Britain Dr Richard Nicholson, editor of the *Bulletin of Medical Ethics* said that the Australian research devalued life and was an: "odious activity" and: "They seem to be treating human DNA as a commercial substance to be played around with in the laboratory". Quite! Everything has a price in the world of the MMRC case. Finally Dr Nicholson stated: 'its just scientists saying, "we can do what we like".' Reflecting Alister Crowley's cry and that of the One World Order, Atlanteans, Adamites, 13 th tribe, 12 tribes and the MMRC case of old Yatrus (lets see how far we can take it) or: "Do what thou wilt, is the whole of the Law": The age of satanic will, unreason and misuse of science, with man playing God.

The breastplate was still in existence in the time of Josephus, although it no longer lighted up and significantly contained all the stones *except the thirteenth stone of Kad Kod*. Robert Graves in *The White Goddess*, states that the: "order given in the Bible ...has been purposefully confused for reasons of security". Graves the master poet and undoubtedly with a past life in this area as bard? re-arranges the order with the: "yellow cairngorm, lessem, belonging to the glaring hot D and T months". Significantly D is Duir or Oak (royal) and T is Tinne or holly (Holy one) in the Tree alphabet: the Twin Kings, which Jesus as a Solar (hot) King hoped to combine in one personage. The blood-red carbuncle of the *thirteenth stone is Kad Kod* and assigned to S (Saille or Willow in the Tree alphabet), which is the month of the "razzia" or RAIDING PARTY. Obviously there is some religious mystery tied up in this and the Bible is full of stories about one brother tricking and gaining power over another, which is the glossed matriarchal and patriarchal battle or matrilineal and matrilineal succession: Cain and Abel, Set and Osiris etc. Also the willow was the Druid osier basket and a willow allegedly stood outside the psychro cave, where Zeus was born and I concluded also the Religious Revolution, conducted by a secret Druid cabal at the cave. According to my own witness account, a raiding party took the genealogies of the Magdalene in France and the Jesus child was taken presumably to Scotland, to propagate a royal dynastic line – the Merovingians; who allegedly descended from Morovee and perhaps that Jesus child. The Religious Revolution in Crete, where the belief system and cosmology was taken, presumably by the Druids (13 th tribe) or their earlier incarnation as the Bull-Minos cult. Evidently the thirteenth tribe and the missing thirteenth stone are synonymous.

Why should the thirteenth stone or missing thirteenth tribe, be associated with S or Saille for Willow in the Tree alphabet? The answer becomes clear if we remember that the Willow or fifth tree is the Osier (Ooser the Bull-Minos figure in the British Folk Festival) associated with the Druids. The basket that Moses was placed into, the chequer pattern that turned up in Minoan iconography and a tree sacred to Hectate, Circe (Cerne?) Hera and Persephone, all Death aspects of the Triple Moon Goddess. Culpepper in his *Complete Herbal* states: "The Moon owns it" female or matrilineal then. The Druidical human sacrifices were offered at the full of the Moon in wicker baskets. According to Pliny, a Willow tree grew outside the cave where Zeus was born, thus connecting the Druids (as Bull Minos cult) not only to the Religious Revolution in Crete at Knossos, but to the One World Order plan and I would conclude European Union, named after Europae, who was a Phoenician Princess taken to Crete for marriage to a solar King.

Commenting on a series of coins from Cretan Gortyna (where the first laws of Europe are laid out post Religious Revolution c. 1400 B.C.) A.B. Cook in his *Zeus*, suggests that Europae, who is shown seated in a Willow tree, osier-basket in hand, and made love to by an eagle, is not only Eur-ope, 'She of the broad face', i.e. the Full Moon, but **Eu**-rope! "She of the flowering Willow withies" - alias Helice and sister of Amalthea. Thus in its conception European Union looks very much like a thirteenth tribe conception, that was eventually shared by the 12 tribes in order to bring about their *own* Order. The *Vaincre* magazine illustration, produced by a man who was around the cradle of European Union, definitely shows the Greek symbolism of Knossos, together with the hermetic knight riding down the road, towards the 'Etats Unis' or the United States of the West, or EU. The road has 'Bavaria' (political Illuminism) on one side and on the other side the word 'Brittany' occurs, linking it to the Merovingians and hence ultimately to the thirteenth tribe or Judah. Thus, one might conclude that the original concept of Europe was a Marxist political hive coupled with a pagan religion run by a royal dynasty derived from a child as the product of a relationship between Magdalene and Jesus or a royal bloodline. This however, was obviously thrown out in the 80's when a rift between the two groups occurred and whilst the political goal has been retained, there is a question over which religion will become universal – Christianity or perhaps some other religion? The only contender that I can see is Scientology. The connection of the Willow to water, typically and archetypally associated with the Goddess, is why the Jews or twelve tribes of Israel are promised "no more sea" at the end of things, which also represents the Covenant with God, that there would be no cataclysm, if man behaved himself (no abuse of the hidden science). Further the prophesy of Ezekiel's vision was that the 12 tribes would destroy the thirteenth tribe. The fact that the willow grew outside the cave of Zeus, co-inciding with the Religious Revolution, signifies power and the birth of the plan for EU or Europae (Eu-rope) was initiated in the Late Minoan period c. 1 400 B.C The mention of 'rope' is interesting, since I decided that the ball of string (which can be considered a rope) was Ariadne's gift to Theseus in order to find his way in and out of the labyrinth, to kill the dreaded Minotaur. The Minotaur was a hereditary solar king, who committed human sacrifice in myth and thus was matrilineal or should I say pre-hermetic, but utilising a system of patriarchal control as solar kingship. Water and the Willow are further connected to the 'Underground Stream', the spring or well of life, the significance of which was that often wells were built near religious places in Britain and represents healing and hidden knowledge. It might be proposed then, that the original concept of EU and perhaps the one that Lord Bute (Cardiff Castle) supported was a healing of Europe based on a political power pyramid headed by a priestly aristocratic dynastic hierarchy, or 13 th tribe. This however requires some form of religion and must find some practical observation of the contender for that religion today. Which religion is it then? World War II it seems was planned to pave the way for the healing process! of European Union. Millions sacrificed to a cause of 12 and 13.

The Goddess' bird of epiphany was the dove in later times, but originally the goddess' prime bird, was the wryneck or snakebird, or cuckoo's mate! Which hisses like a snake. The fact that the skull appears in Poussin's painting covered previously in *The Battle of The Trees*; connects the Holy Grail with Twin Kings (as shepherds) and was to appear on Third Reich iconography, together with the labyrinth motif as Trieskelion or Swastika of Minoan symbolisation. Thus increasingly we come to view World War II as a Religious War between the twelve tribes and the thirteenth tribe for dominance, with the Third Reich carrying the symbols and variant (Aryan) ideology of the 13 th tribe. However if both the 12 tribes and the 13 th tribe desired the goal of European Union, then how can one not conclude that there was at a very high level, a master plan which was accented to by *both* groups. Whilst that ascent obviously covered the political goal, the question is whether there was also a religious goal.

The Philosopher's stone: "the stone that fell from the heavens", had a Semitic significance of *stone* attached to it, but in terms of Holy Grail symbols it was the colour of lapis lazuli or sapphire blue. Jeanne D'Arc carried a banner of a white/silver bird on a blue background which not only depicted healing, but Magdalene and the Goddess' in their epiphany as bird and the entire cosmology and belief in re-incarnation. Thus it represented a religious goal. She also carried the small "hammer", which was the Minoan Axe indicating The Cycle of Eternal Return with implications of 13 th tribe. The blue however was a colour of the tribe of Levi, perhaps having taken that or borrowed it, as was their want, from the Early Minoan symbols for death. The battle of Orleans it appears was a religious war of the 13 th tribe versus the 12 tribes (the inquisition) who at that time were dominant in England and Europe: burning heretics and witches at the hermetic stake in, the symbolisation of fire as Hermes or 13 th tribe. H (Uath) or whitethorn was the sixth tree in the Tree Alphabet and depicted the philosopher's stone, the first month of summer as sapphire, since it typifies the blue sky. Blue was the colour of the precious stone associated with the tribe of Levi. The Late Minoans in the Religious Revolution transition era employed blue to depict death, but also re-birth or Re-incarnation. Sappur is translated as "saphire" in the authorised version of the Bible, and *Ezekiel* mentions it, as the colour of the throne of God. H was the Greek goddess Maia, whose son was Hermes and marriage was considered hateful to the goddess, simply because her truth had been merged with Semitic groups with Hermes the bisexual god of joined male and female was the result - thus Hermes was Maia's son. Generally mother and son or father and son relationships in Greek myth portray religious mysteries or changes in religious beliefs. Thus blue signified Maia in Greece and since she was the mother of Hermes, then we can assume, that this was a period BEFORE the Religious Revolution when the symbols were taken over. Blue sky became not Re-incarnation but the sky God and Heaven (total death). The 'Spiritual Marriage' of Jesus and Magdalene, deciphered from the Nag Haamidi scrolls and recounted in *The Battle of the Trees*, was believed by Magdalene to signify the first Minoan and ancient truth which incorporated Re-incarnation as a world healing indeed after the Crucifixion she went to the Greek colony of Marseilles in France where she was healing using past life regression; but the Patriarchal group- the Druids or 13 th tribe, who had instigated the plan of Golgotha fully intended to betray her and the hopes of the Millennium, by substituting Hermes, the bisexual god, who incorporated male and female in a transcendent third stage beyond death, thus removing the woman and her apples of immortality entirely. Jesus himself referred to this in the Alexandrian text, with the joining of male and female until they "become one" – Hermes.

It was always realised that a terrible spiritual injustice had occurred and the Greeks propitiated Maia at marriages and the Romans did not marry in Maia's month of May, considering it very unlucky. Interestingly Plutarch remarked that this was the month in which puppets called argeioi (white men) were thrown into the river as an offering to Saturn. In Welsh mythology, the Hawthorn or Uath, H in the Tree alphabet, appears as the malevolent chief of the giants: Yspaddadem, Penkawr, the father of Olwen ('She of the White Track'), another name for the White Goddess. Further Joseph of Arimathea's staff had thorns (Hawthorn) attached to it in legend. Jesus wore thorns as a crown (Hawthorn) placed on his head significantly by the Jews (the twelve tribes) under the Roman administration, which supported them. This undoubtedly showed Jesus to be matriarchal a Sacred King of the Druids and Celts, who was crucified on the Taur-shaped cross, symbolic of the Bull-Minos cult and identifying him as the Twin King ruling through matrilinear succession through his grandmother (Anna), who was no doubt descended from the Tuatha de Danaan from Greece and the biblical Adamites.

The confusion whereby Jesus was at first accepted by the Jews and then crucified by them becomes clear if my claim that he was fostered by the Druids (or adopted by the Essenes?) into a Jewish family were accepted, then clearly his background would not have been known. Although evidently the stone ring from Naples in the 6th Century A.D. still retains a memory of His hermetic background and the Druids. However Mary Magdalene also had significant genealogies and it was probably the find of either these genealogies, or associated information, that became the mystery of Rennes-le- Chateau, which I recounted in *The Battle of The Trees*. Briefly Rennes-le-Chateau is a tiny village on the French side of the Pyrenees. In early times, it was known to the Phoenicians and the Romans as Reddae, which may hold significance, since the 13 th tribe were sometimes known as 'red men' and in the Late Minoan period in Crete, Princes were coloured in red. The holly bush (or Holy one) bears red berries and is represented by Tinne in the Druid Tree Alphabet. In 1885, the new priest was a man called Berenger Sauniere and something of a rebel, thus being sent to Rennes-le-Chateau was something of a punishment. In 1888, he started repairs on the church and workmen lifted the top of the high altar, and discovered that one of the *two pillars* on which it rested was hollow (signifies hermetic symbolism) and that hidden inside were *three* wooden tubes containing rolls of parchment (signifies old Trinity of Twin Kings and Goddess) The parchment seemed to be in some kind of code. Sauniere tried to decode it, and then showed them to the bishop of Carcasonnne, who sent him to Paris to consult experts at St Sulpice. By the time Sauniere returned to Rennes-le-Chateau he was a rich man, No-one knew where his wealth came from. He also had the church elaborately and strangely decorated in what I concluded in *The Battle of The Trees*, was Scottish Rite Freemasonry symbolisation and which must be 13 th tribe.

The only clue to what was found, is that whilst he was in Paris, he brought reproductions of two pictures - *St Antony the Hermit* by Teniers and Poussin's *Les Bergeres d'Arcadie* ('The Shepherdesses of Arcadia') which I reproduced in *The Battle of The Trees*. Undoubtedly the priest had uncovered something significant concerning the story of The Holy Grail and perhaps knowledge of the Magdalene, who had died in France after the Crucifixion. I did decode certain icons connected with the mystery in my first book. It has further been suggested that he discovered some instructions on the whereabouts of the legendary Cathar treasure, a heretical sect associated with the region, whose last adherents were burned alive in 1243, after being besieged at Montseguar. It is said that three men escaped carrying the 'treasure of the Cathars' to a safe place. However, others believe this treasure was the holy book. Henry Lincoln and Baigent in *The Holy Blood and The Holy Grail* discovered a tomb close to the village of Rennes-le-Chateau, which reflects the painting of Poussin, with its tomb and dark and foreboding sky, which I claimed was symbolic of the Crucifixion. Lincolon claimed that the village was once called Aereda (Aeries/ ram totem beast after the Bull-Minos cult: and dad/father/Adam?) and was an important centre of the knights Templar, the order dedicated to guarding the Temple of *Jerusalem*. Thus one assumes that the Templars held the truth of the events of the crucifixion and may even have known of the plan for a One World Order through guarding the temple at Jerusalem, which would account for that 'peculiar marriage' with Scottish Masons or 13 th tribe, who presumably instigated the plan. The Templars were connected with an even more ancient Order -The Priory of Sion, also connected with the Temple of Jerusalem. There was strong evidence that this secret society had continued down the ages, and that the Rosicrucian's, launched in the seventeenth century, were the Priory of Sion under another name. In short Sauniere had discovered some secrets of the order of Rosicrucians, which I further identified as Scottish Rite Freemasonry and Druids. I strongly suspect that what Sauniere found also contained documentary proof of the Crucifixion. When Sauniere died, he made a confession that deeply shocked the priest who heard it. In 1910 his Bishop suspended Sauniere from his duties as a preist, but he continued to say Mass in a chapel he built himself. I conclude that Sauniere on the basis of what he found, which must have been substantial documentary proof then pledged his allegiance to the ancient Holy Trinity and Goddess.

Returning to the lost tribe, Kad Kod, the red carbuncle and the lost thirteenth jewel, Graves maintains that: with the help of the names given to the tribes by their mothers in *Genesis XXIX* and *XXX*, and of the prophetic blessings or curses bestowed on the m by Jacob in *Genesis XLVIII* and *XLIX*, a letter can be assigned from the Beth-Luis-Nion alphabet to each tribe.

B	Dec.24	Red Sard	Reuben
L	Jan.21	Yellow Chrysolite	Issachar
N	Feb.18	Sea-green Beryl	Zebulon
F	March 18	Fire-Garnet	Judah
S	April 15	Blood-red Carbuncle	Gad
H	May 13	Lapis Lazuli	Levi
D	June 10	White Carnelian	Asher
T	July 8	Yellow Cairngorm	Simeon
C	Aug.5	Banded Red Agate	Ephraim
M	Sept. 2	Amethyst	Manasseh
G	Sept. 30	Yellow Serpentine	Dan
Ng	Oct. 28	Clear Green Jasper	Dinah
R	Nov. 25	Dark Green Malachite	Naphtali

(*The White Goddess* - R.Graves)

Little Benjamin their ruler belongs to New Years Day, the day of the Divine child. The serpentine month of G was assigned to Dan, 'like a Serpent'; which was replaced by Ng - the tribe of Dinah; for Dinah, the female Twin of Dan, was another tribe that disappeared early. Mary Magdalene could even have been the female Twin of Jesus, or from the tribe of Dinah, which was matriarchal. The Ng tree was the Ngetal, or reed and was a symbol of royalty in the Eastern Mediterranean and Moses significantly was found among the reeds and was I concluded Druidic. He was a Solar King and the Druids held Mosaic Law. A royal reed was placed into the hand of Jesus when he was attired in Scarlet. The willow was of great importance in the worship of Jehovah at Jerusalem, and the Great Day of the *Feast of Tabernacles*, a fire and water ceremony, that was called the *Day of the Willows*. In Tanaitic tradition, dating from before the destruction of the Temple (and from the combination of water and fire indicates hermetic philosophy was practised and thus 13 th tribe) it was prescribed that the red-twigged willow with lanceolate leaves, i.e. the *purple osier* (Druid and 13 th tribe) should be the sort used in the festival thus utilising thyrsus of palm, quince (apple - immortality) and willow; if none were obtainable, then the round-leaved willow, i.e. the sallow or palm might be used. Thus Jesus' association with the palm presumably symbolised 13 th tribe connections and mauve would indicate that through the purple osier made of willow. The Ailm or A in the Beth-Luis-Nion alphabet is a female tree and ailm, in Old Irish, also stood for the palm, a tree not native to Ireland. The phoenix bird was born and reborn in a palm, which implies re-incarnation and may account for that phoenix allegedly erected in His Royal Highness Prince Charles garden. The Prince as a believer in re-incarnation appears to hold different beliefs from his parents then and must place him in a very difficult position as future monarch. The poetic connection of the phoenix and palm with birth is that the sea is the Universal Mother and that the palm thrives close to the sea. Apollo was born under a palm tree and Apollo was venerated in Britain above all other gods, whilst the Jews (12 tribes) were promised: "no more sea" as a reward for keeping The Covenant with Jehovah, which presumably centred on not miss-using the hidden science. If Princess Diana tried to play the Holy one or holly and set up a rival court to oak royal, then even by the events of her death, it should be remembered: "For I am a jealous God" as Jehovah warned and Jehovah would have no truck with goddess's. Further the thought of a rival court and Egyptian dynasty must have sent ruffles around the 13 th tribe and the 12 tribes blamed it all on the woman and dispatched her as Eve in *Genesis*: whilst the 13 th tribe preferred to immortalise the goddess in her death aspect and despatched her as co-joined to the Twins in the personage of bi-sexual Hermes. Which of these tribes had more motive (if not both at the top), can only become another turn in the convolutions of so-called conspiracy theories, which generally prove to be unsolved assassinations committed by 12 and 13. Witness the mysterious deaths of UFO researchers on June 24 St. John's day – 13 th tribe, but one must not forget the light brought to Patmos from Israel and thus there must be a unified group of 12 and 13 at the top.

It is odd in the above sequence that DAN comes under G (Gort or Ivy) in the Tree Alphabet and Judah under F (Alder). In the original *Battle of The Trees* (from which my title was taken) the alder *fought on the front line*, which holds no other significance in my pen name. However we know that the Celts were battle veterans and quite formidable opponents. It is odd that the 13 th tribe of Judah should be distinguished from DAN or Ivy. The Tuatha de Danaan, who were probably derived from a Semitic tribe from the Black Sea region are associated with Ivy and I proposed that Fenuisa farsa "the vine man" and "he who joins together", was the grandson of Magog who was the grandson of Noah. Thus here there is some corroboration, that the Tuatha de Danaan were in fact biblical Adamites derived from Noah and the post Flood race. This would infer that they were perceived as "gods" by the Celts, because they held some form of the hidden science, which had been retained and saved in the Ark presumably from the pre-Flood era or prior to a Magnetic Reversal and the Atlantean stock. The fact that the jewel is yellow serpentine indicates the sun and the serpent indicates the hidden science. Thus as I concluded earlier in this book, it looks as though the white stock was the Celts and the Tuatha de Danaan were Semitic stock. This may account for that curious "Missionary woman", half black and half white indicating intermarriage between two types vine and ivy. Vine and ivy come next to each other at the turn of the year, in the Beth-Luis-Nion alphabet and are jointly dedicated to resurrection. Thus we might assume that the Druids or Judah held the belief in resurrection of divine or sacred solar kings, which Jesus became.

Vine and Ivy are the only two trees that grow spirally and this has implications for the Grid, but also infers development spiritually, with furthr implications of Jacob's ladder reaching into the heavens. The vine also symbolises resurrection because its strength is preserved in the wine. The rivalry mentioned in mediaeval English carols between holly and ivy represented a domestic war of the sexes and must represent a religious mystery also. The holly replaced the holly-oak in the Beth-luis-Nion alphabet. The holly oak was also known as the scarlet oak. Presumably the royal scarlet dye that was extracted from it, was responsible for the red Prince at Knossos and the Druids probably utilised it. The dye signified royalty and as oak (royal) and holly (holy one) were combined, this probably fitted the political form of power via sacred sun kings. Since the scarlet-oak is the evergreen twin of the ordinary oak, this also probably suited the concept of the Cycle of Eternal Return (evergreen) and Twin Kingship. However twin kingship was replaced by holly oak and hereditary monarchy, combining royalty with divinity and Jesus wore kerm-scarlet when attired as King of the Jews (*Mathew XXVII, 28*).

One might speculate that the lost thirteenth tribe and jewel in the series above, was perhaps the Tuatha de Danaan from Greece (Dan), or Judah who were matriarchal and exiled from Greece c. 2900 B.C. by hordes of Semitic invaders who broke into Thessaly. The fact that the palm is associated with Jerusalem and the plan for the religion of a New World Order incorporates a: "New Jerusalem" and implies that the hermitic religion will be returned, to rebuild the Temple. The building of the Temple is a significant part of Freemasonry. Further, I concluded the Tuatha de Danaan were probably a tribe of Adamites that wandered from the Black Sea region, where the palm grew. The Tuatha de DANaan were known as "gods" by the Celts and when in 1522 Emperor Charles V visited London, two giants greeted him at the drawbridge gate - Hercules and Samson. Why these names and not Gogmagog and Corineus? The name 'Samson' means 'of the sun' and 'DAN' was his tribe. Samson, like Hercules, killed a lion with his bare hands and one of the tiled murals at Cardiff Castle in Wales, shows Hercules in one of his twelve labours, killing a lion with his bare hands. Since I concluded that this was Scottish Rite Freemasonry - Druidic, then one assumes that the lost tribe of DAN is being implied. This tribe of DAN must have been considered special in some way either through descendency, or by way of knowledge of the hidden science and since they gave rise to a royal dynasty in Scotland as Anna the alleged grandmother of Jesus, one can assume they had both dynastic and scientific power. Certainly they must have had contact with the Early Minoans and the religious mysteries they held, which were given openly. Sampson was chained symbolically between two pillars

(Hermes) and his problem of how to get off the wheel of life (karmic re-incarnation?) was symbolised in the hermetic third herm or pillar and Sampson solved it, by pulling the Temple down, signifying the power of the hermetic God. Thus in 1522 in London there was an open display of Twin or Sacred Kingship - in the form of giants Sampson and Hercules - London being matriarchal or at least hermetic at that point.

Judah must have held Cabbalistic knowledge of the hidden science, which had been handed down through the Patriarchs even from the Flood. The advent of superior knowledge and the new concept of re-incarnation with the connection to goddess, seriously challenged superiority of Judah and the cabalists of the 12 tribes and the battle between the male and female ensued. However the message that arrived c. 10 000 B.C. had nothing whatsoever to do with tribes of Israel, the patriarchs, Cabalistic knowledge, Kings, solar Monarchy, Twin Kings or secret groups. It was merely a message (Re-incarnation) and knowledge of the Grid and the trap here on Earth and how to exit from it. The Holy Grail as two inherent parts, one a belief system (Re-incarnation) was only one half of the Grail. The other was material power 'Rex Mundi', of the Cathars and relates to the power that was inherent in the hidden science and Grid knowledge. To exit however, one would have to know one's past lives, in order to rectify all wrongs, otherwise there was no possibility of passing the first stage of the life review and the second stage of spiritual review. This depended more on the laws of physics than of moral issues, although conscience is vital. Undoubtedly through Cabalistic magic, the old Priesthood knew of magical methods of channelling and utilised such magic in weather phenomena, but they had never lost control over that knowledge and religion really if one could call it that, centred on the Black Cabala, magic and cannibalism. This position altered c. 10 000 B.C. The battle was on, when the knowledge was taken and withdrawn into the secret groups, principally it would seem into the thirteenth tribe initially - the tribe of DAN and Judah, the biblical Adamites or the Ivy and vine of the "vine man", which was conceivably the true origins of the Brotherhood. Danu or Anna was to become it is alleged from heraldic documents, the grandmother of Jesus.

It seems at some point that white Celtic women presumably from the tribe of DAN may have provided Queens for the various Solar Kings and some of the Egyptian mummified remains definitely show women with fair hair, although the male Kings had typically Semitic traits. It appears that the Druids or the Bull-Minos cult stole information from the Early Minoans, which pertained to the spiritual message and knowledge from c. 10 000 B.C. It may have been realised at that point, that the thirteenth tribe no longer needed the other twelve tribes and could form a One World Order under their own superior knowledge. Curiously after the Religious Revolution, iconography involving bees and the goddess occurred. There is a sealing from Knossos that I reproduced in *The*

Battle of The Trees, which showed the Goddess on a beehive or a mountainous honeycomb, with two lions either side. This parallels finds mentioned previously of early Palaeolithic times, including a coral and a honeycomb like structure. She curiously holds out a wand or stick. To her left is the bullhorn motif, which shows evidence of the presence of a Bull-Minos cult, which I now equate with the Druids. The stick or wand would provide further evidence, as would the mountain, both of which were utilised by the Druids. This then in itself, is some evidence that the knowledge that enabled the Druids to channel or miss-use the Grid, came from the woman. However, this knowledge was being used in Palaeolithic times to create the equivalent of the OT levels, **to free man from the trap**. The raiding party having taken that knowledge then went on to miss-use it, as they had always mis-used the hidden science even in their cabalistic rituals prior to 10 000 B.C. The MMRC however always selects the wrong target for blame and never ceases to whinge about what was done to him (self) whilst ignoring what he has done to others. Thus the trap and man remained and woman was blamed for the misuse of the hidden science! Presumably also she was blamed for the violation of The Covenant, where the Jews had made an arrangement or agreement with God over their *own* salvation "the chosen ones". Perhaps they feel that they gave man religion and thus deserved to be saved, but I am afraid that is not the case; man would still be conducting human sacrifice and black magic unless he had received help. The Holy Grail however was not meant as the elixir of life for the elite or sacred kings, but *everyone*.

The lions represented in the Late Minoan seals indicate Twin Kings. The Goddess wears the curious tiered flounce skirt, which reminds one of the layered or secret levels of knowledge, which as a design turns up in the step pyramid, representing the equivalent of Masonic knowledge, the hidden science and the plan for a World Order. The step design is also a feature of Lenin's tomb in Red Square Moscow. Now if we put all the clues together, then we might conclude that the twelve tribes were more prolific, dominant and held all secrets of the Black Cabalistic science and thus controlled man and tracts of land via Kingship, whilst perhaps the thirteenth tribe provided white Celtic Queens as a nominal token of power. However this position of dominance by the 12 tribes evidently altered, once the 13 th tribe came into possession of the secret and more evolved hidden science, stolen from the woman along with the Holy message (Re-incarnation) and a whole cosmology. The thirteenth tribe then sought a hierarchal control over this knowledge and sought the 'Rex Mundi' or power and treasure that was synonymous with the jewelled cup of the Grail in myth: and thus tagged on Twin Kings to the belief of Re-incarnation, transferring re-birth to Sacred and solar kings under the bisexual god Hermes. Politics and religion (Re-incarnation) became inseparable from that time. These Kings became dispensable by terminating their reign at the end of the 9 year period, which was extended to 19 years in order to change a monarchy and install indefinitely a continuous Monarchy. The true battle of holly (holy one) and oak (royal) is the incompatibility of the two on grounds of historical truth and the Holy Grail Message, which was not the gift of the man or monarchy. Why should it matter especially whose gift it was? That point would only be answered in the bid for exit at the spiritual level. (the spiritual review in the Death Experience as one soul passes through the spiritual bioplasma)Where one confronts one's involvement as action and thought in the totality of one's past in terms of spiritual survival along all levels from self to man to a spiritual hierarchy (God in Christianity). At that point will come the truth of the gift and what an embarrassment if you were involved with stealing it from source! Despatched no doubt for a cycle of return with a slam of a book on the head, lesson not learnt! Thus it only matters on a *personal level* and whether you value your exit from the trap. Whilst this is a humorous explanation, once again it has more to do with physics of energy and a deadly serious trap.

The idea of bees (and ants), fascinated men like Adam Weishupt who discussed this point with his initiate Philo. Weishaupt as founder of the Illuminati was part of the One World Order political power pyramid plan. The beehive was to turn up on iconography in an omphalos (matriarchal womb symbol), from Delphi in Greece and also on a similar structure from Coventry England (the scroll-work on the latter reminiscent of the scroll-like forms of horses on the Aylesbury bucket). Bees figured on the ancient Phaistos disc from Crete and a gold pendant from Mallia in Crete post Religious Revolution era, showed two bees clasping a globe of honeycomb. The beehive concurrently appeared in the ancient Greek alphabet! (*The Battle of The Trees*), which also included the mathematical correlation between the circle and its diameter or π It seems likely then, that the ancient alphabets in Greece hold religious mysteries and the symbol for π also came to represent the two upright pillars, with lintel across which signified the tomb of a sacred king, which was symbolised at Golgotha and where the central herm or lintel represented Hermes the master magician. Placing these clues together, one might conclude that a considerable secret was taken from the woman at the time of the Religious Revolution and immortalised in the alphabets by the pie or π with its secret inside and a lid on top! The association with bees, not only as with the coral of Palaeolithic finds, represented a social colony, but a system of control politically: but one also suspects through the Grid or morphic resonance from that one controlling signal from Queen bee at the top, man as a controlled slave-species, which has been the goal of all World Orders instigated by the MMRC case. It would be interesting to analyse the humming sound of the bee for cycles per second and note the effect on the human biofield, but I will leave that to a scientist with some inclination.

The secret that I decoded on Hercules sword at Cardiff Castle contained an apple and in another mural at the Castle, Hercules kills the lion with his bare hands. There is a further mural with a woman wearing a crown sitting above a lion. Thus here we have some indication of the background and history of Crete and the implication of the idea for a One World Order. Aristaeus was the Pelasgian Hercules and father of Actaeon, the stag-cult King, and son of Cheiron the centaur. Thus the Bull-Minos cult was another ascendancy of man-beast virility groups. Aristaeus like Hercules killed a lion with his bare hands on Mount Pelion and from the wound the first swarm of bees emerged. In the Cuchulain version of the same story, Blodeuwedd is named Blathuat and extracts from her husband King Curoi, the secret of his soul that is hidden in an apple in the stomach of a salmon, which appears once every seven years in spring on the side of a mountain (which sounds highly Druidical). This apple can be cut only with his sword (very Arthurian). Her lover Cuchulain waits for seven years and obtains the apple. Blathuat then prepares a bath and ties her husband's long hair to the bedpost (as with Sampson in the biblical form of the same story), she takes his sword and gives it to her lover, who cuts the apple in two. The husband betrayed, loses his strength and cries out "No secret to a woman, no jewel to slaves!" Thus the hidden science and the hidden history, is really the secret of the soul and the woman always carried the Holy Grail openly and the man in secret (in his soul). Thus the emasculation of the man via his hair or crown chakra, which resonates with the Grid, is really a story of the biblical Adamites, Judah and the 12 tribes who have built their power on such secrets.

The Adam and Eve story in Genesis implies that Eve *gave* Adam the apple whereby man acquired knowledge "of the tree of life", immortality and the secrets of the soul that were always associated with the apple. The association of tree with Adam refers to the religious mysteries of the Tree Alphabet but more succinctly to the Grid pattern. It is no co-incidence that Newton, who was a member of the Rosicrucian's used the story of the apple to supposedly formulate his gravity laws. The trillions of bioplasma vortices which occur at Grid cross points, not only store information as I have explained, but also represent channels of exit and *anti-gravity* anomalies, if only man could pass through the life and spiritual review without his conscience bringing him back to clear all his karma. As the Bible states: "you won't get out of that place, until you have paid the last coin of least value". The presence of the Serpent also implies the hidden science and immortality. In actual fact woman gave man knowledge to free him from the trap and since this knowledge was evidently taken by the thirteenth tribe, then obviously the twelve tribes would have reported the woman badly in the story, particularly as the twelve tribes and their Cabalistic magicians were jealous of the new knowledge and power, since hitherto they had represented a political power throughout the Middle East. The lost secret of the 13 th tribe is implied on the mural at Cardiff Castle, by association with Greek myth and provides the reason why the husband shouts: "No secret to a woman."

Presumably at some point, the woman must have disseminated their secrets, reflecting the myth that the woman carries the Grail openly and presumably also provides the reason why Freemasonry is an all boys club, whilst immortalising the woman in her death aspect or as conjoined in Hermes. A secret is as good as money in the bank and yet, it won't buy you a ticket out, only a sourjourn presumably somewhere in space until, mankind has received his implants or imprints for 36 days, whilst the Earth is submerged with all species under water and fantastic black storms blow. How can they ever get out with that on their conscience? – the answer of course is they can't, the laws of physics can't allow it, even if man's Law can. It has a great deal to do with the mechanics of thought and the unified field, rather than exterior judgement. Anyone who ultimately tried to stop the Holy Grail message and knowledge is in BIG trouble! Unless he reverses that and unfortunately he is going to have to find **all** the personnel in the basic or **first** hologram in what will probably be a chain and carry out amends in order to erase the hologram chain.

Gogmagog through his connection to hills, oak-tree and mistletoe was a Druid. Mistletoe is actually a parasite! The word 'Druid' has been translated as 'knowledge of the oak'. Maximus of Tyre observed that the Celts venerated the tree as a *symbol of Zeus*, who mythically was born (with the One World Order plan) in the Psychro cave on Crete, from where the Religious Revolution was conducted I concluded. The Herne Oak in Windsor Forest was connected in folklore to the Stag-cult, which I assume was the earliest descendent group of the Druids. This is also indicated by the iconography of the Floor of Cardiff Castle. The Oak was the lightening tree, as it was frequently struck by lightening, which gave rise to the belief that it was a magnetic centre, which obviously had implications from point of view of the hidden science and the secrets that were tied up in the alphabetic mysteries, including 'Lightening man' who apparently even in the Palaeolithic age was utilising his pointed Luis or quick beam finger of the Druid signalling alphabet, with its decoding of secrets. The Gogmagog Hills just south of Cambridge in England have held varying names and Richard Coates (1978) drew attention to the parallel of the word ' hodmedod' or 'hodmandod', meaning snail. The shell of the snail displays the hyperbolic spiral as concentric rings and sea shells displaying this feature were enclosed in burials in Early Minoan times, where the dead were buried in the foetal position, awaiting re-birth (Re-incarnation). This once again points to the Early Minoans as the source of knowledge acquired by the Druids. The concentric ring pattern is also displayed at Wandlebury Camp an archaeological site close to the Gogmagog Hills. The Hills then, may exhibit some Grid vortex property and signify the spiralling of 'filaments' that I posed in the morphogenetic bioplasma.

T. Lethbridge the archaeologist, set out to recover the lost giant of the

Gogmagog Hills and to his amazement using a sounding bar to test depths below the turf, he found a giantess with a horse. Lethbridge also discovered a second male giant warrior carrying a shield, which shows a distinctive circular shape with seven (five male dactlyls and Twin Kings from the Religious Revolution in Crete) circles patterned on it. Lethbridge was confused that the giantess, was a composite pattern of whorls and loops, which is completely synonymous I would conclude, with the labyrinthine pattern or maze, the emblematic symbol of the abode of the dead. In this case her head is composed of a circular maze also, which may indicate the crown chakra and its connection to the morphogenetic bioplasma with its phylogenetic and event history. Lethbridge claimed to have uncovered a sun god to the left of the Goddess and labelled the Goddess "Magog" ('Mother -God').

The hillside mural (*Fig. 46*) is interesting, in so far as the eyes of the Goddess or giantess, are a spiral design, one connecting the other and which in the Early Knossos frescoes, portrayed symbolically the thought, when traced with a finger in and out of the spiral "Into a life, and out of it, Into a life, and out of it etc" - i.e. Re-incarnation. However the appearance of icons in the Late Minoan period, showing a hand raised to the third eye, associated with the pineal gland at the base of the brain, with its potential function of a magnetic centre associated with the opening of the crown chakra, means that the spiral connecting the eyes or 'goggle' appearance probably symbolises this connection. This perhaps gives us another way to interpret UFO witness accounts of men with goggle eyes, or "frog-like"! Symbols from the past impinging via the 'Onion-Ring model' I produced to explain the way in which the natural UFO phenomenon works. The fact that the 'goggle' men appear in the UFO phenomenon, means that they had some impingement **on matter**: you will remember that the bioplasma is only interested in the survival of matter and thus records data/event that had some impingement. If channelling had occurred through the opening of the crown chakra, then obviously this would have been recorded. The hologram then contains a whole event and sequence that is not apparent; it is coded if you like in pictorial or holographic form, in much the same way as hieroglyphics can record complex thoughts. This is really the point of an archetypal symbol, it conveys in one simple picture a complex thought(s) and events, which is why the secret groups are so obsessed with symbols, which can like devil's horns convey a great deal more to the initiated, than the "cattle" or slaves.

Paul Devereux former editor of the *Ley Hunter*, reported in *Edition 84*, that his new and expensive camera fell apart at the precise moment when infrared pictures of the Gogmagog figures were to be taken! I know the feeling well! As I have had 15 years of vanishing documents, computers *who* (as almost humans) swallowed up whole sections of books and refused point blank to tell me where they had put them and refused to print them! Typists who caved in, printing companies that caved in, where I was often told: "I am sorry we just don't know where it went to, it just vanished! Or: "this job should have been simple, but it's the worst job we have ever had" (tell me about it!) One poor chap had his entire company search for missing originals and told me mysteriously they had checked a pile of papers no less than 6 times, but eventually after 2 hours they found them in the pile. He kept repeating: "I just don't know how it happened, I checked that pile 6 times page by page". His hair was virtually standing on end! I eventually realised that unless I did everything myself, not being subject to the Grid 'scripts', I would never get the research out there! It proves if anything the power of the Grid, when you try to introduce a *new pattern or thought* which is contrary to the mind control thoughts and patterns from the past that dominate it - some trap! some barriers to freedom! I felt rather like a hunt jockey jumping fences for 15 years (at least!) through a mined field - followed by the dramatizing hunt and mad dogs naturally (front cover of *The Second Millennium Working Report into Cancer*). As I reported earlier as I finished this book, the entire power cable in the road blew up! And I carried on by hand as the computer ground to a halt, whilst a crew of workman, who found it most odd, when I shook my fist at the sky, dug up the road! The Grid almost in apparancy has grown a sentience of its own, in its *own* bid for survival.

Fig. 46 **Complete chart of the Wandlebury figures.** *The solid lines represent Excavated areas and the sunded areas are indicated by broken lines. Note: 'goggle eyes', chariot, horse or octopus or bird, dolphin? To The right is a Celtic warrior with round shield and sword as plotted by T. Lethbridge from soundings and test cuts.*

The work of Lethbridge was undoubtedly interesting and should have been covered. Professor Gly Daniel reviewed Lethbridge's book *Magog* in *Antiquity*, describing it as an: "unfortunate book" commenting that Lethbridge was: "not finding any genuine antiquities but probably confusing geological features". Despite some of Lethbridge's assumptions, there was no doubt that there was a basis in pre-history for his findings, which have so tallied with the whole scene, that one cannot but help think, that Lethbridge may have experienced the all too familiar attempts by the research establishment to ridicule any new idea refusing to publish, on the grounds that it is "**new**" (don't you just love Grid *past* dramatization and mind control!) and if you do manage to get it published as I did with the cancer research in a scientific journal, a politician tells you they can't spend the time to look at an answer to cancer, because it is not published! Grid thinking is very moronic and the array of excuses (all irrational) that you get as to why you can't change the pattern or the 'script' would be laughable, if they were not a part of this Greek tragedy. The eyes Lethbridge describes and the labyrinthine nature of the goddess's body, undoubtedly give the whole mural an air of authenticity, particularly as Lethbridge evidently did not know about the story I give here. It is unfortunate indeed, that research has so many barriers placed before it, particularly if it approaches the hidden science.

The Long Man of Wilmington is another unique hill figure, which holds according to Paul Newman (cited): "a pair of staves or wands" in his outstretched hands. The man is obviously central to the two upright pillars (staves or wands) and thus represents the herm (lintel or baetyllic pillar) and therefore one might conclude, Hermes the incorporated male and female god. The mention of wands together with Hermes also suggests Druids. The fact that all the hill figures are composed with a layer of white chalk, is in honour of the goddess in her death aspect, now fused with Hermes in one sense, but in another the knowledge of Crete now in the possession of the master magician and necromancer – Hermes. In Late Minoan iconography the central member between two upright pillars has various motifs including egg, a tree, a baetylic pillar (the Herm), an omphalos, a double axe, a labyrinthine design, but all represent without contradiction the womb of the Mother-Goddess, as well as the union of the male and female principles. The labyrinthine womb came to represent a place of re-birth for solar kings, removing the entire belief in Early Minoan Crete, of Re-incarnation and a Cycle of Eternal Return.

Robert Graves in *The White Goddess* points out in the *Song of Amerigin* an ancient Celtic poem that he decoded:

"God speaks and says:	**Author's interpretation**
I am a wind of the sea	{Magnetic Reversal and Flood?}
I am a wave of the sea	{Contact with Early Minoan beliefs
I am a sound of the sea	'As I go so shall I return'-the tides}
I am an ox of seven fights	{Bull- Minos cult}
Or I am a stag of seven tines,	{Stag cult}
I am a Griffon on a cliff,	{Royalty Twin King seen in frescoes at
or I am am a hawk on a cliff	Knossos}

I am a tear of the sun	
I am fir among flowers	{Silver Fir is A or Ailm in Tree Alphabet
I am a boar,	Female tree sacred to moon –Ist tree}
I am a salmon in a pool,	{wisdom = salmon}
I am a lake on a plain,	{origin near Black Sea region –Thothmes III
	Great White Lodge Lake Moeris?}

I am a hill of poetry,	{Druid}
I am a battle-waging spear,	{World Order –Celtic
I am a god who forms fire for a head }	Commonwealth hidden science}
or I am a god who forms smoke from}	{Fire god – Hermes and channelling
	via sacred fire for a head.}
	Crown chakra?}

1. Who makes clear the ruggedness of the mountains?
   or *who but myself knows the assemblies of the dolmen -house on the Mountain of Slieve Mis?*
2 Who but myself knows where the sun shall set?
3. Who foretells the ages of the moon?
4. Who brings the cattle from the House of Tethra and segregates them?
5. On whom do the cattle of Telthra smile?
   or For whom but me will the fish of the laughing ocean be making welcome?
6. *Who shapes the weapons from hill to hill?*

Invoke, People of the sea, invoke the poet, that he may compose a spell for you.

For I, the Druid, who set out letters in Ogham,
I, who part combatants,
I will approach the wrath of the Sidhe to seek a cunning poet that *we may concoct invocations*
I am a wind of the sea".

This poem appears to carry the secret group history of the Druids (13 th tribe) together with their thoughts. As Robert Graves pointed out: "English poetic education should, really, begin not with the *Canterbury Tales*, not with the *Odyssey*, not even with *Genesis*, but with the *Song of Amerigin*, an ancient Celtic calendar-alphabet, found in several purposely garbled Irish and Welsh variants, which briefly summarizes the prime poetic myth." In other decodings Graves refers to the lines: "I am the queen: of every hive" and "I am the tomb: of every hope". The former thought was to be conceived at Knossos, in the plan for a One World Order with religious aspirations as well as political. One cannot deny that political aspirations had been in existence since early Palaeolithic times, as evidenced by the coral (colony) archaeological find, however there was no religious aim, until after the appearance of the Holy Grail. The communistic hive was a method of despotic control by kings dating back to the Atlanteans and presumably Xenu and Yatrus. The latter line from the poem quoting "tomb" was a conception born at the tomb of Golgotha as the World Order religion of Christianity and re-birth (the Second Coming of a sacred solar king – Jesus ostensibly a Druid). This was merely the concept of a World Religion taken from the Early Minoans but changed to suit the 13 th tribe. The line above: " who shapes the weapons from hill to hill", evidently holds secrets of Ley lines, the hidden science and connection to the Grid. Further "invocations" implies a ritual of morphic resonance, either for the purpose of channelling or producing phenomena associated with the Grid and explains perhaps why the chariot (Of Hermes?) should occur in Inc. I of Hubbard's Space Opera, since it was probably the first time for billions of years, that the MMRC case had access to the spiritual bioplasma. However his new- found knowledge gained from the woman, was coupled with channelling and thus, since that would alter survival of spirit, it was bound to be recorded on the spiritual bioplasma as holographics of that change or event. This was of course, the Religious Revolution in Crete I conclude c. 1400 B.C. To drive this point home fully, you will remember that I explained **emotion**, as the principle form or mechanism of morphic resonance. Before the Holy Grail arrived, man was in the emotional state of *fear*, which is verging on resonance of matter. The post Flood races were in fear not only of the event of a Magnetic Reversal which they knew as: "the sea bursting its bounds", but they were also ruled by despotic rulers, who kept fear firmly in place. Thus at that level where voodoo, black magic and cannibalism were the rule of the day, coupled with fornication on the level of gratified animal behaviour, love and higher emotions were not part of man's thinking process. The longevity of the body in pre-Flood times and the era of giants had passed and man now had lost the idea of re-incarnation. Thus the appearance of the Grail was to disperse fear and allow man an ascent on the emotional scale and therefore ascent to the spiritual bioplasma. The fact that chariot (Hermes?) and the sound of a horn (horn of plenty, Bull-Minos, horn of plenty?) also appear in Inc.I, *appearing* to signify the start; means that Inc. I need not necessarily represent the *actual start* (the birth of the spirit) but may indeed signify a time c. 1 400 B.C., when man channelled information from a higher level and consequently in changing the energy pattern within the spiritual bioplasma, caused the hologram to become imprinted.

Wilmington man carries two spears a symbol that occurs also in the poem, which is Druidic. Further the spears are each 70.3 metres and 71.8 metres long and although not exactly 72, given the period of time over which this hill figure has been in existence and allowing for cleaning of the white chalk, then the spears may well have been intended to be 72 metres long, which would hold significance in the Beth-Luis-Nion Alphabet, which was known to the Druids and was signified in the three day (72 hours) resurrection period of Christ. The significant number of 72 is also reflected the anti-matter matter cycles and was inferred as anti-matter, in the description of Jesus, after his alleged crucifixion. The poem also speaks of "dolmen-house". The Beth-Luis-Nion alphabet was arranged in a thirteen-month calendar form, significantly paralleling my conclusion that the tribe of DAN was synonymous with the Druids, the 13th missing tribe of Israel. This alphabet was often arranged as a dolmen (*fig. 47*). A dolmen is a burial chamber, a 'womb of the Earth', consisting of a capstone or lintel across two upright pillars, in which a dead hero is buried in the crouched position, like a foetus in the womb, awaiting re-birth. This was a form of matriarchal burial in Greece, where the belief was openly displayed by the foetal position of the dead person in the early bath-shaped sarcophagus. Further the tomb of Golgotha as I have already pointed out, was representative of this dolmen-type burial chamber. We have seen from iconography as late as 6th Century A.D. that these archetypes were remembered by the people. Thus the symbolic tomb of Jesus would in terms of the archetypes, immediately have been recognised in terms of the belief system portrayed. If Jesus were laid in a tomb, with two upright pillars with lintel across, it would have signified the tomb of a Sacred King compare also the Lion's Gate at Mycenae (*Plate 7*) where entry is via this structure signifying a city of a Sun King. If He were laid on a horizontal pillar or baetylic pillar as He was, that would have signified the Herm or the god Hermes and 13 th tribe. If he had been positioned in the foetal position that would have signified re-birth or Re-incarnation. If Jesus had been in the tomb and had left it, *with* the Mary Magdalene, who was the first to arrive after the Crucifixion, then she would have been identified with the Goddess and *re-birth* as *her* gift, would have displayed the *Early* Minoan belief system. If Jesus had been in the tomb, the belief system would have been re-established, the mystery revealed to the people and a whole cosmology and the trap of the Grid taught. However it was not to be and the plan of Golgotha became the ultimate conspiracy. The belief became Immortality for Son of God, the promise of a Second Coming and the Grid ("you and me forever") stayed firmly in the hands of the 13th tribe, to be wielded as a power base, whilst plans for a One

World Order, with Christianity as the Universal religion forged ahead. It suited both the twelve tribes and the 13th tribe - woman betrayed again and removed from the story. Further, one has to consider whether the Second Coming is not a variant of the Cycle of Eternal Return, where the cabal that overran Knossos (13 th tribe) used the newly acquired information, to concept this idea of a Sacred King who would return (in the next cycle) after man had got his dose of the 'cinema reel' and 36 days of "implants": naturally, whilst the MMRC misses his, via some safe haven. Can't you just see the next cycle, when the 'script' now has the MMRC returning in his space ship, as "gods" and dramatizing his past 'script', believing himself to be the Second Coming and since he has big overts on woman, then the next cycle will be rough for women as he pulls in the justification: "It's all *her* fault!"

Fig 47 **Beth-Luis-Nion Alphabet arranged as a Dolmen.**
Compare with Lion' Gate at Mycenae (Plate 7)
And figure 19 (Alphabet as a square ruled over the year by four totem
beasts. The entry (gate) to the New Year was through the vowels
AOUEI – the tomb At Golgotha was the entry to the new Aeon.

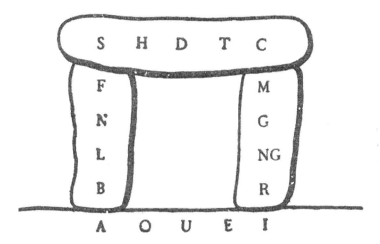

The beginning of the poem *The Song of Amerigin* above appears to mirror the end of the poem, implying that it was recognised through the new knowledge obtained in Crete, that events and catastrophes were cyclical and particularly the Flood. This was a fine power base for the 13 th tribe, who could now set about channelling the events of the Grid and then presenting them as prophesies for the future, which they impressed on the minds of the people and others not in the know, which gave them "god-like" power of prediction. Hitler's obsession in the timing of his campaigns and his association with an unidentified woman at Berchtasgaden, may rest on this point. The twelve tribes had made a Covenant with God which was their answer to not provoking the sea: "to burst its bounds", which the Druids feared most. What a release from such fear, when they came to realise from their new found knowledge, that they could USE this knowledge to empower themselves. They disliked the idea of sharing such knowledge with the people, since for millions of years, they had as the Atlanteans before them, exercised despotic control: where black magic and fear or darkness ruled. Then there came light on dark and the Holy Grail Message, along with certain knowledge.

Wilmington man is the Herm or Hermes a combination of the spears (Twin Kingship implied) and the Goddess. The "Sidhe" are now popularly regarded as fairies, but in early Irish poetry, they appear as real people, a highly cultured and dwindling nation of warriors and poets who occupied stockaded forts including the matriarchal barrow - New Grange in Ireland, which in *The Battle of the Trees* I concluded had connections to the Tuatha de Danaan. From the point of view of the Aryan super race programme the Sidhe are interesting, since they all had blue eyes, pale faces and long curly yellow hair. They were ruled over by **two** *virgin-born* Kings (with connotations of Twin Kings and the alleged birth of Jesus - although I suggested fostering or adoption). The Sidhe were sexually promiscuous 'without any blame or shame'. The Picts were allegedly some descendents of them - known as the tattooed men. The 'blue-eyes' were not actually blue, but had two interlocking blue tattooed rings around them giving the 'goggle' (or frog?) appearance, which held religious significance. In The *Song of Amerigin* there is mention of a mountain "Slieve Mis", a mountain in Kerry Ireland, which may have been the equivalent of the Masonic Lodge and one of the early ones in Britain, before the "Mother" Lodge at Kilwinning was founded in 1286 A.D. in Scotland. Finally the reference of "Hill" and "weapons" in the same line of the poem, suggest the use of the magnetic centres and UVG120 Grid anomalies for the purpose of covert warfare.

The poem *The Song of Amerigin* Graves admits was *'pied'*, meaning to make a pie and put secrets inside, which as a unique verb *'to pie'*, introduced by Robert Graves is very descriptive of history on this Planet. Graves when placing the lines in 13th month calendar form as a method of decoding found: "I am a hill of poetry" occurred in the Vine month, which connects with Fenuisa Farsa - the 'vine-man', or 'he who joins together' - which I thought was the earliest form of Freemasonry for the 13th tribe. "I am a threatening noise of the sea" - reminds us once again of the fear of the Druids for the sea and a past cataclysm, which originally was the reason The Covenant was undertaken, to dispel fear. The thirteenth tribe once they had taken the knowledge from Crete, believed that there was no need for the Covenant, kept by the twelve tribes and presumably saw themselves as "gods", who could avoid a cataclysm. Who however can exit if they have no concept of truth? The reference to the "sea" is placed in the reed or royal month of Ng, which was associated with the lost 13th tribe, through Jesus and Moses. Graves places: "I am a battle-waging spear", significantly enough in the holly or **Tinne** month, which is 'Holy One'. This would certainly explain that odd statement for the pacific Jesus: "I have come to bring a sword not peace". The sword of Arthur, the sword of Hercules displayed with its secret at Cardiff Castle and what about *that* battle of Scientology?! - Another Holy War! 'T' (for) Tinne or holly in the Tree alphabet, must hold significance on 'Taur', in the Greek alphabet and Sacred Kings were crucified on the Taur-shaped cross. The idea of war as the sacrifice of bodies to a holy crusade was born and replaced the need to sacrifice bodies in wicker osier baskets, in order to propitiate the goddess who had been duped and her gift stolen. It also eventually replaced the need for cannibalism and the imbibing of the spirit of another (very degraded being) since now the high emotion of battle and the cause, with millions dead on battle fields, would feed the insatiable appetite of the MMRC case, for controlling bodies and minds. "Do what thou wilt is the whole of the Law!" The end justifies the means and the mountains of human suffering of both body and sprit, would all be worthwhile in the end. This however is a complete dramatization of 13 th tribe mentality, history and the past. "Was it really worth it my friend?" The battle of 12 versus 13 has given rise to the majority of World Wars and Revolutions on this planet, which were in the main ostensibly - HOLY WARS, but in reality are complete dramatizations where Grid rules. The horror of war and what man is capable of inflicting on another spiritual being, is worse than any animal pack survival mechanism, simply because it is not wholly the morphogenetic survival mechanism that comes into play, but the control thoughts of the MMRC case – nasty fellow is "666". The Holocaust and the reign of terror in France at the time of the French Revolution (which saw men's skin sewn into lampshades and fat boiled down) were both dramatizations of an occult power, which would be dramatized again in the case of the Jewish holocaust.

In the poem arranged in thirteen month calendar form, Graves places the Hercules "stag" (or "wild bull") at the beginning of the year as B for BETH in the Beth-Luis-Nion alphabet i.e. Birch in the Tree alphabet. Birch was considered FEMALE and Self-propagating which implies a dynastic line. The "Griffon" is a griffon-vulture and was found either side of the King's throne at Knossos after the Religious Revolution. The vulture in myth as the eagle removed Thalia and the myth was previously shown in the red-figured vase from Nola (*The Battle of The Trees*) Zeus as vulture stealing away the woman (or more accurately her knowledge) and significantly in the icon, there is a ball of string, which in Greek myth Ariadne gave to Theseus, to find his way in and out of the maze or labyrinth (womb and cnothic underworld of the dead) in order to kill the Minotaur. Thalia in the icon, significantly wistfully looks at the thread. The thread however is the UVG120 sphere and a whole cosmology, which was to be found in the curious stones wrapped with leather thongs that were recovered from Crete. The appearance of the chequer pattern or basket weave signifies the Osier Willow baskets of the Druids - and thus perhaps we glimpse the group who stole the source.

In the Song of Moses (*Deuteronomy XXXII, 22*) Jehovah is identified with the heraldic griffon, which is a lion with griffon-vultures wings and claws and represents the sun god as King of the earth and air: and as the equivalent of eagle, was employed on the American One Dollar note and in Third Reich symbols. The "salmon" in the poem, is associated with the nut month of C or COLL. The connection of nuts to salmon is 'wisdom'. The referral to Ng as the month when the terrible: "roar of the breakers and the snarling noise of pebbles on the Atlantic seaboard fill the heart with terror", is a reference to the Druid's fear of a cataclysmic event. The positioning of the reed or Ng (Ngetal tree), to this cataclysm is significant in so far as it is the TWELTH tree. The implication is that a ruling body of twelve (disciples, knights of Arthur, twelve tribes of Israel or Galactic Federation? etc) is connected to the event of a Magnetic Reversal and Flood, with the inference that such a group would have power to overcome that. Power over the sea, was seen as a sign of Divinity and Moses naturally, parted the waves of the sea in *Exodus* to allow the Israelites to pass. In Irish legend Cuchulain and Fionn as sun gods fight the waves with sword and spear, implying the magician Hermes and by inference the Grid. The thirteenth member as Zeus Captain of the twelve Olympian gods, Jesus as head of the disciples, Merlin as magician of Arthur and his knights of the *round* table, signified a matriarchal belief, with her gift now locked up in the tomb or secret, magic circle of the thirteenth member a representative of the tribe of Judah and the Adamites.

A corresponding text given by Graves in *The Romance of Taliesin*, appears once again to give a further history of the Druids: "I have been a blue salmon" implies the Picts of Britain, who showed the 'goggle' eyes, tattooed their bodies blue, a colour of death in Late Minoan Crete, presumably with implications of a sky god (Heaven for the masses and an old man with a white beard and judgement in the after life) and the Grid (to the initiates, total power, wealth and man as God himself). How a little knowledge went to their heads! In this poem, which Graves deciphered, there are a number of references to *survival* and *water* corresponding once again, to Tree alphabet months. Thus, the L month or LUIS or Quickbeam becomes: "I have been a boat on the sea"; and NION or Ash becomes: "I fled vehemently...on the foam of the water". This implies the Druids are giving Noah as their origins and indeed Gogmagog was the grandson of Noah. Further the Ash was sacred to Poseidon the Greek god of the sea and in British folklore it is the tree of re-birth and also as the third month is associated with FLOODS. The association of L or Luis is interesting, because this finger is the pointed index finger of the Druid finger-signalling alphabet, which I covered in *The Battle of The Trees*. This finger appears significantly in a painting by Poussin and refers to the requirement to answer difficult questions, which must refer to the crucifixion. Hitler pointed prominently with it during his speeches and Greek oratators utilised it. In the above poem it is associated with the phrase: "I have been a boat on the sea". Thus this must refer to the Ark, Noah and some secret that requires answering (presumably the question of how they survived the Flood where all other life was extinguished). Continuing with the decoding Graves gives: "on a boundless sea I was set adrift" as the R month and: "I have been a boat on the sea" as the L month. R is RUIS or Elder, the THIRTEENTH tree. The Elder was said to be the Crucifixion tree and has a long association with death. I commented in *The Battle of The Trees* and earlier here, that the reason why certain codices of the Nag Hamaadi scrolls have been withheld, is that e.g. the day or month that Noah's Ark came to rest and which wood the Ark was made from, are all part of the eternal 'pies' - 'pied' politics and religion! Obviously no one wanted anyone to get to the bottom of this particular story. Who pulls the strings indeed!

With regard to Wilmington man and his proposed hermetic-god nature, the appearance of long barrows from the Bronze Age surrounding the hillside figure confirm his role in the afterlife as incorporating male and female as the transcendent third stage beyond death. Curiously there is a memory which Paul Newman (cited) discussed of the so-called giants feet pointing one to the left and the other to the right, which further indicates the petasos of Hermes and the mirror image face or Janus, representing Twin Kings in one sense and perhaps gravitational spin and centripetal spin and the cycles of anti-matter and matter in another sense, since Hermes was the master magician. This mirror-image motif often appeared in Late Minoan iconography to show Twin-Kingship and was later employed in the Janus head pointing in different directions as in the coin from Volterra (*Fig.43*). I was somewhat intrigued to find a number of these archetypally significant motifs employed in the early stages of the New Labour's rise to power in Britain after which Tony Blair became Prime Minister. Tony Blair was depicted on advertising posters as Hermes with Janus head pointing both ways and of course that emblem of the Rose for their party not to mention *that* dome and *that* Eye in London or indeed the bisexual-type millennium icon for Britain! Some dramatization! Or some game by the boys! And Rupert Murdoch a media mogul who owns *The Times* newspaper and the masses daily *The Sun* appeared with devils horns and pointed index finger, to be followed by a biography in *The Express* entitled: "*Fear reigns at the Court of the Sun-King*". Some dramatization or some game! For those in the know of who is in group12 and who is in group 13 - guessing the name of the god was some game in ancient times, a game it appears that is still being played, simply because the page of the 'script' and plan is being religiously turned and followed. Arrogance and "Do what thou wilt is the whole of the Law".

To clinch the connection to the Minoans, a resistivity survey of Wilmington Man in 1969 showed that there might have been a plume emerging and curving upwards from the top of his head. The plume significantly appeared on Late Minoan frescoes and in The *Battle of The Trees*, I produced the fresco of *The Prince*, which showed this plume as the attribute of Sacred Kingship. Above the figure of Wilmington Man, lies the largest burial mound in Sussex - Windover Long Barrow, which almost certainly identifies the figure with the cnothic underworld of the dead and presumably Hermes. The burial mound is long and thin with its "implicitly rounded tip" resembling the phallus. This would also in its phallic symbolisation of the importance of the male, reflect Minoan seals, where between two upright pillars in one seal there was an egg, which was pierced by phallic member or Druid wand. Just as the fertility bough, the Oak club of the Druids and Hercules sword symbolised fertility and power in the male, as with the laurel of Apollo, an attribute of Sacred Kings depicting virility. The laurel was seen on the heads of the giants Gogmagog at the Guildhall London. The phallic member is not only a symbol of union after death as male and female (Hermes), but also represented the male as the potential source of life. Greek Leda was courted by Zeus in the form of a swan and gave birth to the Dioscuri, the Twins Castor and Polydeuces who emerged from a swan's egg. In Britain it is a long-standing tradition, that swans are protected by *royal* warrant. Corineus one of the giants at the Guildhall in London, in earlier models, wore a crown with a bird in it, which was the epiphany of the goddess and may have been a swan. Finally Wilmington Man has no genitalia unlike the Cerne giant, which might indicate he is of a later date and possibly Bronze Age, since the absence I would conclude is indicative of Hermes - the bisexual god. A god that still rules in Britain!

That Wilmington Man was formed earlier and may have been added to is noted by Paul Newman, who stated that: "An embanked freeway running South eats up the hill and tapering near the summit has been arduously hammered out with antler pricks nearly 3 500 years ago". Thus the earlier Stag cult, which was a forerunner of the Druids I conclude, were probably responsible. Mr. Heron Allen (1939) took up a suggestion first advanced by A.D. Passmore (1937), comparing Long Man to a coin showing the emperor Ventranio holding in each arm the standards of his authority. The staves are comparable to the 'labrum', the small hammer corresponding to the double axe of Late Minoan Crete, which Jeanne D'Arc carried. The Banner of Christ t features on numerous coins after adoption by Constantine in A.D. 312. To quote Newman:

> "The original standard, the Vexilium, consisted of a long gilded spear from which hung (banner wise), a square of purple silk or cloth. Later this square was attached to the spear like a modern flag and bore the

Christogram, the sacred monogram Christo P/X, and under Emperor Jouian (A.D. 363-4), when Christianity was established as the State religion, this became the general standard of the army".

Further, if the spears of Long Man, did contain a labrum to impress "the faith" on native Britons as Newman suggests, then it is as well to remember the meaning and source of the labarum (Late Minoan Crete, Druid, Twin Kings and stolen apples) The X of P/X is derived from Late Minoan iconography and the symbol of the double axe; which was a symbol of the Minoan Great goddess, who was mistress of the Labyrinth or "Lady of the Labyrinth", as a Linear B tablet from Knossos calls her. The Labrys was a sacrificial axe, with two crescent-shaped blades. This is a well kept secret with the layered esoteric meanings of the crab at Cardiff Castle (re-produced in *The Battle of The Trees*), where the crab holds a petal (aesthetic beauty and love) in one sense, but an axe blade at the same time, which Hercules returns with a cut to the left claw. Left was **knowledge for all** a concept that became degraded in the pyramidal power of socialistic and communistic politics, which proved no better than the right of facism, which as a point was illustrated by the fall of the Third Reich, to be re-placed by the hive of a communistic Federal Europe, run by the elitist groups who incepted it. The labrys was a sacrificial axe, with two crescent-shaped blades. Solar Kings were symbolically to die, to be re-born, the blade cut both ways, (reflecting the Janus head of Hermes) slaying the Calendar beast the Solar-bull and the Solar lion in turn, but each are re-born in a Cycle of Eternal Return. This was a complete downgrade of any Early Minoan truth and was obviously the Druid idea of sacrifice to their eternal cause. The tribes of Israel both 12 tribes and 13th tribe brought the idea of sacrifice to a Cause into the world, through Holy Wars and the sacrifice of millions in the goal of a World Order. The labrynth was not only a symbol of death and life after death, but of rebirth for sacred kings (only!) -"chosen ones". Why would the labrys be chosen as a symbol for Christianity, unless Christ had been a Druid employing what was essentially to become hermetic Freemasonry, derived from Minoan Crete after the Religious Revolution, where the Bull-Minos cult was installed, which was a fore-runner of the Druids.

P for Peith was not an original letter in the Beth-Luis Nion alphabet, it is a Brythonic substitute for the original letter Ng. However P is the reed, royalty and Jesus (by carrying the Reed) was depicting his royalty. This has been explained away as the royal Davidic line, but it goes much further underground like the royal druidic oak tree roots. The banner that employed P/X really symbolised the Great goddess and royalty as Solar King (Twin King combined) i.e. a Sacred King - the story of the Mary Magdalene and Jesus. In *The Battle of The Trees*, I gave the derivation of the double axe from the labyrinth design as the X shape. The labyrinth archetype is presented as a maze, often symbolised by a circle or concentric circles, which was a feature of the Cerne giant and the Goddess in the hill mural. The spider's web with its UVG120 sphere undertones must be the real foundation for the Cosmic Circle pattern, or concentric ring design such was employed on the Floor of the Smoking Room at Cardiff Castle. The step pyramid has the same connotation of *tiered knowledge*, with the hierarchal and apical power group at the top of the pyramid, corresponding to the centre or *inner* enclosing ring of the labyrinth or maze: which in the case of Cardiff Castle, shows a map for a Universal Political and Religious Kingdom or One World Order, which is reflected in the One dollar note of America and European Union, concepted by the inner enclosing ring or Brotherhood. Homer describing the shield of Achilles in the *Iliad*, says that it pictured youths and maidens engaged in a complicated spiralling dance on a: "dancing floor like that which Daidalos once fashioned in spacious Knossos for Ariadne of the lovely hair": These maze-like dances were mentioned by Aenid and Lucian who mentions a dance called "the Labyrinth". These maze dances have turned up in Europe, Wales, and even in north eastern Russia and in folklore it is sometimes referred to as the: "Troy Dance". Cretan folk dancing still retains this form of dance pattern, although when I asked one troupe about the pattern they could not say why it was that particular pattern, the memory lost.

Corineus the giant represented at the Guildhall in London came from Troy and was I decided matriarchal and in my first book, I produced a figure of an Etruscan Oinchoe from Tragliatella (7th Century B.C.) which showed Twin Kings as horsemen together with a foetus emerging from a labyrinth labelled "Troy". One Twin holds a spear as the tanist and the King of the New Year (babe) who will slay the dying King of the old year; and significantly the giant Corineus held a spear, which further connects Gogmagog and Corineus as Twin Sacred Kings and the defeat of Gogmagog by Corineus. This was a mythic tale about a change of dynasty and matriarchalism triumphing over patriarchalism. It is certainly odd that whilst Corineus *defeated* Gogmagog, later giants of obvious significance greet Monarchy and yet are called Gogmagog and in a final twist of the tale, since Corineus was matriarchal then Gogmagog must originally have been patriarchal i.e. derived from Noah. The answer one suspects is that the Druids descended from Noah, stole significant knowledge from Crete after defeat by Corineus and re-asserted their power under the flag of Hermes, having combined male and female and then sought to cover the tracks, by at least removing the goddess's bird of epiphany from the head of Corineus and supplying two new giants now confusingly combined as one personage, such that Goemagot one of the original giants, becomes Gogmagog, with no tell tale symbols of the past. A typical Patriarchal trick one comes to know very well on the track of time (dusting the tracks).

The biblical account of the Crucifixion of Jesus records that a spear by a Roman soldier pierced His side. Evidently the plan was very well worked out, right down to the last symbol! This has symbolic significance emphasising He was a Sacred King of the *old* year, his tanist is Roman (aided by the 12 tribes of Israel) and Caesar sought to wipe out the Druids and the Celtic Commonwealth was crushed, by mass slaughter or ethnic cleansing of the Celts, which came back to haunt the Jews in the Holocaust. St. Paul then set about marketing the new religion of Christianity to the gentiles, much to the dismay of Jesus' brother James, who claimed it was specifically for Jews and required circumcision! The Christian martyrs only convinced the public, that this was the coming religion – sacrificed to the cause. The twelve tribes under Roman protection had ostensibly won then. However the ultimate conspiracy had that double cross or the double agent at the back of it, as I previously described. There was a persistent legend that Joseph of Arimathea may have travelled to Solway Firth in Scotland after the Crucifixion and Barry Dunsford in his book *The Holy Land of Scotland* pointed out: "could Glasten (now Glasserton) in Galloway, have been the real Glaston associated with Joseph of Arimathea rather than GLASTEN (Glastonbury), in Somerset...In support of this the Scots historian, Archibald B. Scott, comments as follows: " 'Glais-ton' of Whithorn, now Glasserton, was represented by 'Glasten'. The first attempt made by the mediaeval Romanists to divert these names away from Candidia Casa, was to identify 'Ros-nat' or 'Ros-naut' with 'Ros' at Menevia II, and to change it into 'Ros-nant'". Recent archaeological discoveries in Galloway Southern Scotland, in the region of Candida Casa, Whithorn, suggest that there may have been early Celto-Christian activities dating back to the first century A.D." Perhaps the Romans sought to change 'Ros-nat' or 'Ros-naut', from detection as Rose, Rose-line, Rose-Croix and the connection to Freemasonry, Judah and the biblical Adamites; including 'nat' with its connection to nut as in wisdom, and nautonier as in the chief mariner guiding the boat (Ark) or the Brotherhood, dating from Noah. "Nautonier" is a term used in Freemasonry.

One cannot dismiss the connection of 'Withorn' to White-thorn or hawthorn, in the Tree alphabet, which not only I propose was the crown allegedly placed on the head of Jesus (or Simeon), but formed in legend some part of Joseph of Arimathea's staff. One might suppose that he brought the crown back to Scotland after the Crucifixion. Certainly the crown in conjunction with the spear, indicated a matriarchal religion and the hawthorn in the tree alphabet, was sacred to the Goddess and as H or UATH, was considered as her Tree. Thus overall one would conclude that a plan of the 13th tribe was a complex one even by today's standards and centred a Universal Political and Religious Kingdom or World Order, bringing Christianity to the Gentiles, whilst exhalting the Jews and giving man hope, whilst slowly removing his freedom from him. Whereas James the brother of Jesus specifically reminded St. Paul that Jesus intended His religion for Jews and the question of circumcision arose.

The enigmatic phrase in Guercino's painting (c. 1618) *Et in Arcadia Ego* which was the first known painting to use this phrase, almost certainly refers to the birth of the god Hermes mythically in Arcadia. Arcadia is in the Peloponnese Greece. I assumed in *The Battle of The Trees* that the two male shepherd figures looking at a white skull on top of a square (Semitic) tomb, carrying the phrase was a symbolic portrayal of the old Trinity of two males (Twin Kings) and the Goddess, which was combined in the figure of Hermes the transcendent third stage beyond death - the god that Jesus referred to in the Alexandrian text. The later painting by Poussin (c.1640 -42), entitled *Les bergers d'Arcadia*, uses the druidical significance of the finger signalling key-board of the Beth-Luis-Nion alphabet and the Tree significance of LUIS or quickbeam in the use of the forefinger, to intimate the secret of why the Goddess was buried in the square (Semitic) tomb. Twin Kings with staves are present once again intimating Druids, and a third member, which must be Hermes as the woman looks wistfully on. The Twin Kings are therefore tanists (staves) and the New Year babe of Hermes, who has killed the old ruler of the year and therefore it signifies the removal of the woman and therefore the truth of the story.

It is not generally known that Jeanne d'Arc was similarly betrayed. She carried the labrys in battle, but never killed anyone (the poor girl also had to have a cup of wine to face the courage of it all). The labrys was the banner of Christianity with the Greek matriarchal background. Her banner also carried the white dove as the epiphany of the Goddess against a sky blue background. She therefore in a similar fashion to the Magdalene was the misfortunate dupe of Hermes and the thirteenth tribe. She was USED in a Holy War by France against the English to drive them from France.*La Fontaine de Fortune* painted in 1457 by her betrayer and mentor King Rene d'Anjou has an inscription that says the **sorcerer** Virgil brought the spring (water) forth. Rene's contemporaries would have associated Virgil with Arcadia and therefore Hermes. Despite Hollywood's portrayal of Jeanne a truer picture of her appearance may be seen in this picture. This is the first surfacing of Arcadia's underground stream Alpheus, in modern Western culture. The painting implies that the underground stream associated with its wisdom was the work of Hermes and thus the 13th tribe, which is a very large lie, since it belonged to the Early Minoans from whom the cosmology and belief system was taken. The painting also shows a white horse, which connects Jeanne to the 13th tribe through the Celtic line (horse) and to the Goddess in her death aspect (white). One assumes that this period, which was the Catholic inquisition to come, was an attempt to rid France of the twelve tribes of Israel and presumably their support by the English.

Paul Newman (ref. cited) describes an Anglo-Saxon belt buckle excavated from a cemetery at Finglesham in Kent Britain, by Sonai Chadwick Hawkes (*Plate*

19). The nude man holding *two spears* in *left* and *right* hands, with an *oval* buckle at the waist and exhibiting a demure *penis* below, wears a *horned helmet*, which is said to be: "tipped by a pair of curving beaks". This may be the Minos-cult bull's horns or the gates of horn and the abode of the dead. Helmets also turned up at Knossos with swords after the Religious Revolution c.1 400 B.C. The helmet worn on the head also implies the cap of Hermes and petasos and further may imply opening of the crown chakra and its use in channelling for purposes of gaining past technology for war. The oval egg-shaped buckle also symbolises Hermes in the central position between two upright pillars (the spears). Both feet point to the right (of the man) or left (facing the motif), which is a parallel position to the Long Man of Wilmington hill figure. Christopher Hawkes, archaeologist husband of the excavator, pointed out the similarity of this find and Long Man, to the God Odin, god of inspiration, magic and battle, which he thought was the infusion of Swedish culture into Britain. However, obviously this culture goes back to Minoan Greece, the Celts who were warriors and the 13 th tribe. The two spears not only imply Druids and their Holy War, but also are emblematic of Twin Kings, with the egg motif central, as is the case in a number of Late Minoan seals. The belt buckle of the figure is oval with a line across it, which in Greece is the sign of Theta θ in the Greek alphabet. The line is both symbolic of the wand or the central herm (Hermes) and the joining of the Mother Goddess and Twin Kings represented either side of the line.

The alphabets always carried the religious mysteries and a change in religion always brought about a change in the alphabet. The oval with line is emblematic of male and female principles with the central figure as wand (magician Druid or Hermes) and as such is a sign of the old Trinity (Twin Kings and Goddess) that is also retained in the Greek letter ψ (Psi) connected to the sea and more famously found in the hand of the sea god Poseidon. Ron Hubbard highly significantly in my opinion, was to use the sign and Greek letter of Theta θ to denote 'Theta' which was used as 'Thetan' a spirit or who you are. As I will come to shortly, it is also significant that I personally perceive in Scientology a mixed bag of matriarchal and patriarchal knowledge with that unmistakable hand of Judah and the Illuminati style (wealth and power and tiered secrecy culminating in an apex) that is so characteristic: and what remarkably resembles those female stolen apples of immortality and knowledge, which was her gift to humanity, now locked up in the tomb it would appear with another red-headed 'Messiah' Ron! Significantly then Hermes as transcendent third and his connection to the Bull-Minos cult and Druids were still remembered in Anglo-Saxon times in Britain. Three-way knot buckles of the Celts depicted the ancient Trinity also. The Goddess tied interminably to the Twin Kingship created by the Semitic group who invaded Knossos and signified in the knot, which explained the ability of Odin to "bind, the maiden who holds a cup or chalice". The cup or chalice signified the Holy Grail message - Re-incarnation, as her gift to humanity along with a whole cosmology and with it, the chance to exit the trap. Thus the Druids and Celts, and the events of the crucifixion really centred on the god Hermes and the ancient mysteries of Crete. Mercury as we saw in the stone ring from Naples signified Hermes. As Caesar was to remark: "Among the Gods they worship Mercury, there are numerous images of him, they declare him inventor of all arts, the **guide for any road and journey** and they deem him to have **the greater influence for money-making and traffic**". (*Author's* emphasis)

In hermetical alchemical lore, which had very ancient sources, Hermes as "Mercurius" was a prime symbol in the search for the Philosopher's Stone, because it was thought to combine "sol" and "luna" or Sun and Moon and male and female respectively. "The stone that fell from the heavens", with stone a Semitic addition, implying The Word (of God). Newton's apple reflected this fall from the heavens in the form of an apple (of immortality – the Message) under the gravitational field of the vortices of the grid and the spin motion. Surely the Message and the word did come from a higher source, but it was never intended to have the attached significances that have been adhered over many thousands of years of battle between 12 and 13. The Holy Grail cup came to signify wealth and jewels, but it was an emblem of power derived from *knowledge* of the hidden science. The cup however contained "the elixir of life", which I associate with the Holy Message Re-incarnation and provided evidence for that in *The Battle of The Trees*. Hermes as "Trisheros" is a title, which appears on two tablets from Pylos in Greece (*Fr 1204*), where he is the recipient of an offering of oil, and on the second tablet (*Tn 316*) he is the recipient of a votive offering of a gold cup. Once again this reflects the two halves of the Grail, the contents (message and knowledge which is matriarchal) and the container (the hiding of that message and knowledge for profit and power). The gold cup has become part of the history and archetypal memory of the Holy Grail, but essentially we see *Gold* (money and power) as a Solar King colour (Silver was the Goddess's colour). Thus money and power overtook the purpose of the message and knowledge that came to Earth c. 10 000 B.C which was to remind man he was his immortal soul and the requirement of re-incarnation where there is karma to be dealt with: further unless all wrongs (in all past lives on Earth) were redressed, then man would not be able to leave. The Grid and the cosmology also had to be understood, for even if man passed the first post, there was still two more to pass. The Early Minoans gave it away for free, but I am afraid it did not place them in a position of material power and today I know that purposes are necessarily tied in the material world to the problem of money. Even the cost of researching cancer without a grant for 15 years is relatively, if not totally bankrupting! Tablet Tn 316 is interesting since it lists sacrifices of men and women, which was part of druidical practise and Solar Kings who wished to avoid ritual sacrifice at the end of their reign. Sacrifices were offered to appease the Goddess in some peculiar idea that this somehow would balance out two wrongs -Twin Kings (which do not make a right). At Knossos after the Religious Revolution, we find Poseidon called Ennosigaion, or "Earth shaker" and Hermes Areia as Enyalios or **"Battle God"**. The Celts and even Hitler (*Alternative 4*) used the woman as the *justification* of a Holy War - and Jesus it would seem.

Caesar remarked of the Long Man "The heathens brought him victims to slay" and according to Paul Newman:" it was claimed by the Reud Chancellor Parish that a cock stood to his right, a bird sacred to Mercury in his manifestation of Asclepios, god of healing. The early British revered the cock, the goose and the hare; a relief from York in Britain depicts Mercury holding a caduceus or snake *wand*, in his left hand and *purse* in his right! On which side he is flanked by a cock" (*author's emphasis*). *The thirteenth tribe in relation to healing and money!* Jesus the god of healing was of course betrayed after three crows of the cock, inferring I suppose that the ancient Trinity behind his teachings had been discovered i.e. Hermes as transcendent third of goddess and Twin Kingship: or he was as I concluded betrayed by the Thirteenth tribe of Judah and indeed Judas Iscariot The cat was out of the bag, but why did Jesus predict it all as part of the plan? I will leave you to work out the obvious conclusion. Thus the picture of evidence presented here, shows quite clearly that the ancient Trinity and its connection to the Bull-Minos cult and the Druids and the background to the crucifixion was known even to the early Christians in Britain. Great power and wealth was to be had, by retaining the religious mysteries and utilising the inherent power of the message and hidden science. This knowledge known as The Holy Grail and the Underground Stream, was searched for by many and hence the phrase 'In search of the Philosopher's Stone'. When you find it, you simply find the way out or exit. Magdalene was right to prophesy of this hidden story and the cut on her left arm from the sword of Hermes that: **"There will be no peace on this Earth, until the cut is healed"**.

They could not wipe out all the truth though, the story is still present in myth, icon legend and folklore: for example, Paul Newman records a fragment first published in the *Countryman*, which features the giant Wandil, a little-known English monster, quite feasibly related to the giant of the Gogmagog Hills, Cambridgeshire. T. Ryder was given the following account, by an old man living in Stroud in Britain, thus illustrating that a folklore memory had survived:" The giant Wandil *stole the spring*, so winter grew longer and harder till it seemed the world must die. At last the gods caught Wandil and made him give up into the sky and he became the constellation of Gemini, with his eyes, Castor and Pollux glare down, as on the night of our encounter, there will be a keen frost, and there was". Gemini the Twin e.g. Pollux and Castor represents Twin Kingship and the spring represented re-birth (Re-incarnation). Further, Pollux and Castor as Twin

Kings were, shown in ancient art in the company of Helen as Helle or Persophone a Goddess of death and **Resurrection**. As I pointed out the effects of the Crucifixion, were that Re-incarnation was lost as a belief, replaced by resurrection or re-birth of Solar and Sacred Kings ('Son of God'). The fact that the hill carvings were executed in white chalk emphasised the Goddess in her death aspect, as Twin Kings or two opposing groups on Earth 12 and 13 with the knowledge and belief now in their hands had replaced her.

Stepped crosses *(Plate 20)* on ancient coins reflect the step pyramid of the Illuminati system. The cross itself is Greek, as is the architectural design of Alfriston Church in Sussex, which formed the starting point of *The Battle of The Trees*. The Greek cross was not generally used in western Christianity, for obvious reasons, with its implication of Hermes, the old Trinity and the God of Resurrection and 'Taur', the 'T' shaped cross the sign of the Minos- cult and druidical sacrifice of sacred kings. In one coin, the origin of the Trieskelion, the swastika and fire drill is shown, again indicative of Hermes as he is credited with the invention of fire. The Whiteleaf Cross and Bledlow Cross, carved into the Chiltern Hills in Britain, are both constructed on the sign of the Greek cross. Further the Whiteleaf Cross has significantly a pyramidal base.

THE SECRET WAR AGAINST BELIEFS (RE-INCARNATION)

In my first book I concluded that the One World Order contained both political and religious goals for a "Universal Kingdom". I also concluded from the decipherment of the codes for the names of the two groups in the past at the time of 'The Cutting of the Elm (arm) Ceremony' at Gisors in the 12th Century (CAPUT and ORMUS); that those two groups had entirely different aims based on a patriarchal and matriarchal religion. Their disparate philosophies were often pronounced and yet similar and both groups were willing to sacrifice individuals for their cause. There was a cold, hard thread that I followed through time and the battlefields of Earth and undoubtedly Christianity, as a world religion has been the goal of one group, including the Vatican.

The fact that Pope John XXIII (Angelo Roncalli) was initiated into a secret Illuminatus society[161] and took part in a secret ceremony where a woman, egg and wand were involved, indicates that a secret Freemasonry group which is clarified here as the 13 th tribe and Judah, still held aspirations of power over the Vatican, presumably holding the document revealing the true events of the Crucifixion as the sword of Damocles over their heads. No Catholic would have recognised these symbols or the sun-face depicted on John's glove, as a symbol of a Sun-King. Further the Illuminati founded by Adam Weishaupt, were notorious for being involved heavily in the World Revolution scene, with communistic goals, which are more fully discussed in my first book. The high level of co-operation between East and West at the top, even during the so-called Cold War, was a common goal of World Communism. At the time the Pope underwent this ceremony, the Vatican was to become heavily embroiled in the notorious P2 Freemasonry affair involving corruption of many senior figures with connections to Freemasonry in Italy.

I have already referred to the One Dollar bank note with its power political pyramid on the left, which might have some bearing on the position of the feet of the giants in the hillside carvings. The pyramid is marked MDLCLXXVI or 1776, the year of the American Revolution and The Declaration of American Independence drawn up by Thomas Jefferson, who was mysteriously handed The Great Seal of The United States, by a men in black, which is strongly indicative of the ancient Holy Trinity (Twin Kingship and Mother Goddess) paralleling the Trinity of Hermes. This is also indicative of the thirteenth tribe, or Druids. 1776, was also the year that infamous Adam Weishaupt founded the secret group, the Illuminati, with its Communistic One World Order goal. Indeed on the One Dollar note is the inscription "Annuit Coeptis, Novus Ordo Sectorum" (New Order of the Ages).The motto was borrowed by the colonists from the works of the Roman Philosopher Virgil, and on an occult level, from the Freemasons and Roman Catholics and as previously covered has connections to Hermes and his birth in Arcadia. Further the Latin motto "Epuribus unum" which also appears on the note, is translated as 'One out of many' and identifies the pyramidal and Illuminatus political and religious secretive structure of Freemasonry. On the right hand side of the note is quite clearly illustrated all the archetypal symbols relating to Twin Kingship and mother Goddess i.e. hermetic. I can only conclude that at the top the goals of the twelve and thirteenth tribe are the same. The New World Order aimed at removing National boundaries and frontiers in a political goal, but the boundaries of religion would be eradicated by implementing some other form of religion, which would become Universal.

The New World Order was further displayed in its two- pronged goal of political and religious aims on the front cover of the magazine *Vaincre* (*Fig.48*), which was produced by a man who was in the secret groups around the cradle of European Union. Here again, there are the archetypes of Christianity dating back to the Religious Revolution in Crete, with Hermes as knight riding down a road to a: "United States of the West" or European Union, between the names of 'Bavaria' (Illuminism) and 'Brittany' (Merrovingians and a dynastic line produced from a union of the Mary Magdalene and Jesus). But I have already suggested that the Jesus child was taken back to Scotland after the murder of Mary Magdalene and thus I assume that the religious goal was with the thirteenth tribe and the political goal was Illuminism, which is Communism. However it seems reasonable to assume, that the 12 tribes held the political goal and the thirteenth tribe was to hold the religious goal. The World carved up on the chess- board between King and Queen, reflecting the Egyptian mummies where the queen was Celtic and the King Egyptian/Semitic? The end of the road in the *Vaincre* illustration is marked by a blazing sun, emblematic of Solar Kingship (and the Pope's glove) Hermes god of fire: and whilst the beginning of the road is marked 1937 (the origins of World War II), the end of the road is marked with the date of 1946, the date at which European Union started to become a reality.

Fig.48 **Illustration from the first issue of** 'Vaincre' - *21 st September 1942.The road towards the United States of the West (European Union) 1937 to 1946 between Bavaria and Brittany (Bibliotheque Nationale Paris).*

It might appear then, that the twelve tribes and the thirteenth tribe had joined in their goal for a Universal Religious and Political Kingdom i.e. Communism and Christianity for the masses and some other religion for the elite coupled with the political ideology: "Do what thou wilt is the whole of the law". I noted in *The Battle of The Trees*, that there appeared to be another 'Cutting of the Elm (arm) Ceremony' within the secret groups in the 1980's, which may have rested upon a difference of agreement between the religious goals; the thirteenth tribe could have decided that they would pursue their own universal religion, which must have its foundations in hermetic thought. At any rate in this period the two sides appeared to separate on the basis of priority of goals, with the political and monetary unification of Europe seen as being of critical importance: the stranglehold of control sought in the control of money by bankers working for Satan. As a lesson in Revolution and how things are manipulated every child should study carefully the true facts of the French Revolution. When Louis XVI was in debt he borrowed from the bankers, but if he had borrowed on the land, he would not have been the puppet of the bankers. As agriculture in Britain today collapses, whilst curiously the Socialist government have hardly moved on the crisis, preferring to concentrate on re-election, Britain will no longer in the future be self-sufficient and will become the puppet of a higher power. I believe it is no co-incidence that British farming is collapsing: they are trying to break Britain and subdue her to her master and as I pointed out may have earmarked London as the "Great City" of the *Revelations* account.

Pope Angelo Roncalli was followed by the untimely and mysterious death of Pope John Paul I (Albino Luciani), who had quoted the *Isaiah* text: "The Father is the Mother" shortly after his election, immediately revealing either he supported the hermetic God or he stood to reveal matters! The fact that he was embalmed within 24 hours of death and no post mortem carried out, has led many to suggest that he was murdered. Following the death of Albino Luciani, Pope John Paul II (Karol Wojtyla) the current Pope was elected to the Papacy and received something like a hero's welcome because he was a Pole, from behind the 'Iron Curtain', where religion, especially Christianity was suppressed. It was generally believed that such credentials, would determine the politics of Karol Wojtyla - Communism. Pierre Bourgreignon, writing in *Didasco*, a French publication that appeared in Brussels, April 1979, said: "No one capable of coherent thought will easily believe that a Cardinal from behind the Iron Curtain can be anything but a Communist plant." The Abbe de Nantes leader of the catholic Counter-Reformation of the Twentieth Century was more forthright: "We have a Communist Pope." Piers Compton (cited) wrote: "Someone had noted that during the conclave in the Sistine Chapel, at which he was elected, the solemnity of the occasion, and the fact of being overlooked by Michelangelo's gigantic frescoes of the Last Judgment, did not prevent Wojtyala reading from a book that he had thought fit to take in for instruction - or for a little light relief from the gravity of choosing the Vicar of Christ? It was a book of Marxist principles."

Curiously the new Pope praised Paul VI for having revealed: "the true countenance of the Church": somewhat bad form then, not to reveal that "true countenance" to the millions of Catholics. Piers Compton noted that after Vatican Two the church's position was to secure: "the acceptance of fulfilment of Vatican Two in accordance with its authentic content. In doing this we are guided by faith...We believe that Christ, through the Holy Spirit, was with the Council Fathers, that the Church contains, within its magisterium, what the spirit says to the Church, saying it at the same time in harmony with tradition and according to the demands posed by *the signs of the times" (author's emphasis)*. One must at least applaud the Archbishop of Canterbury (Head of the Church of England) in Britain for stating of the resurrection: "We cannot be sure". Compton went on to comment that: "It was essential to renew the Church, in structure and function, to bring it into line with the needs of the contemporary world; and from that admission it needed but a step for Wojtyla to emphasise the revolutionary principles of 1789, with the glorification of man, liberated man, as a being who is sufficient unto himself. Man was the only idol deserving the reverence of those on earth, his stature being confirmed by and classified as the Rights of Man." In fact as the One World Order with its Communistic doctrines pressed ahead for completion, there was only one acceptable Pope for the Vatican, and that would have been a Communist Pope. As Compton noted: "The Pope then proceeded to pass from verbal to more active approval of the political system from which he had emerged." World communism is the political goal of the One World Order.

Speaking of the Church in Poland, Wojtyla said that: "its relationship with *Communism* could be one of the elements in the ethical and *international order in Europe* and the modern world" (my emphasis) .The Soviet Minister, Gromyko spent audiences with the Pope and he was the 'star' speaker at a Latin American Congress in Panama City, where the theme was not religious, since the organisers were the Communist dictator, General Torrigos, and the Marxist Sergio Mendez Arceo, of Cuernavaca: curiously Islam with its denial of Christ's divinity and of the redemption was commented on by the Pope in an audience with Moslems where upon he told them that their Koran and the Bible "are in step". More recently Christians in Britain were puzzled by the Archbishop of Canterbury's statement (*Mail on Sunday Aug. 1 1999*) when he raised doubts over the Resurrection of Jesus Christ. In his Millennium message to millions of Christians, Dr George Cary stated: "We cannot know". The same edition in a feature article asked: "If the Church questions Heaven, Hell and even the Resurrection, what does it believe in?" Clearly both the Catholic Church and Church of England adjust "according to the signs of the times", but truth is not adjustable to the times, it is as true today as it was 10 000 B.C. One of the Pope's letters, dated 15 September 1981, on the subject of private property and capitalism, shows a marked contradiction of and a departure from the Church's teaching. For in the letter he says: "Christian tradition has never upheld the right of private property as absolute and untouchable. On the contrary, it has always understood the right as *common to all to use* the goods of the whole creation." This is a particularly Communistic ideal and was the very basis of my trouble with Scientology. We might conclude then that the Papacy is not elected without political considerations and after at least one Masonic Pope and one doubtful one, who clearly both referred to hidden symbology retained by the highest echelons of Freemasonry, we assume that the current Pope Karol Wojtyla was chosen for his Communistic sympathies which aligned with the One World Order politics of Communism for the masses, run by the rich far right and dominated by 12 and 13.

World Revolution and Communism did not begin in Russia in 1917, with the Russian Revolution; it began at least in France in 1789, with the French Revolution and the goal of a Federal Europe and One World Order. That goal as I have claimed in my research, was conceived as far back as the Tower of Babel in the post Flood or Magnetic Reversal era. After significant knowledge was taken from the Early Minoans, the lost 13th tribe I concluded conceived of their 'own' One World Order based on a matriarchal religion, and certainly just as elitist as the other side. It has long been realised and covered more fully in the case of the French Revolution, in my first book, that behind all secret societies there existed and continues to exist, a hidden centre of direction. At the top of Freemasonry there is a hidden group, as one previous member who had reached the 30th degree noted in Martin Short's Book *Inside the Brotherhood*, when asked to enter by a 'side door', into a group that was *not listed* in the degrees. Further it has long been recognised that such unofficial groups may form what is known as 'the secret Government of the World'. Whether that group is the Bildebergers or the Rose-Croix, 33rd degree of Freemasonry and above or whether these levels are synonymous, has been the deliberate confusion placed to prevent the goals of such groups being identified. The B'nai B'nrith is a secret group who work for the political Zionists and Israel and is International, operating in the majority of countries including the United Kingdom. This secret group, which pulls strings everywhere, is unelected and undemocratic and yet wields great power. Eustace Mullins in her book *The World Order - Our Secret Rulers*[162] and the books of the respected Noam Chomsky[163] refer in detail to this secret Government. It was this secret Government that brought about the French, Russian and British Revolutions and the American Revolution had the same swirling background, each was one step nearer a goal of a One World Order. Each was planned with that goal in mind, with a *predicted and manipulated* outcome. The French were such dupes in the Revolution parroting every word from the paid agents of the Masons, whilst believing that they were fighting for the *Rights of Man*. Maria Antoinette with her wit, was often to be found quoting their book at them (the Commune), whilst fighting for the rights of her family not to be murdered; further employing the chief of police in order to find out who was the driving force behind the Revolution. However she was too naive and too late and after her death the Commune turned on the citizens of France in an occult blood bath, known as the reign of terror, that surpassed the Holocaust, for its breathtaking ferocity and vileness. Cannibalism and its dramatization must find its outlet, as the occult cry of "Do what thou wilt, is the whole of the Law" found its expression in the *Rights of Man*.

A number of commentators have noted that the hidden power was not French or British, since everywhere the activities of World Revolution, was directed at France and England, seldom against Germany and *never against the Jews*. In the past that power has been described as Pan-German power, Jewish power or Illuminism. These headings are undoubtedly too simple to cover the complexities of International Finance or the cross-fertilisation of groups e.g. Pope Angelo Roncalli was initiated into a secret Illuminatus group, who held significant symbology on the Greek background to Christianity, thus connecting with the Rose-Croix degree and Rosicrucianism and Scottish rite Freemasonry. The powerful Bilderberg group described as the 'World Shadow Government' has never publicly acknowledged its goals or secret agenda and yet has contained members who are some of the most publicly and politically active people on the world's stage, including democratically elected politicians! (David Rockefeller, Peter Carrington, Karl Otto Pohl Wilfred Martins, Henry Kissinger etc were noted as attendees in the past) [164] Only but the very naive or uninformed would believe that their Government is the real ruling power. As Disraeli a past Jewish British Prime Minister noted: "You would be very surprised to know that the World is governed by very different personages than you would imagine".

On Target [165] noted that this International group of immense power retains the philosophy of destruction of the existing Order and where the: "real target of this Revolution had always been Great Britain, the greatest imperial power of the times and her Empire". However we must decide whether this was not anything but the battle of 12 versus 13 being played out on the world's stage. Many historians have noted a preponderant Jewish presence behind the chain of secret societies of the Revolutionary period; which On Target, points out: "effectively dominates much political action and the present day mass communications media and entertainment industry. These are simple, quantifiable facts without prejudice. It is of great concern because considerable pressure is being brought by organised Jewry such as the Board of Deputies of British Jews in order to suppress exposure and discussion of these truths on the basis of race "hate" and Holocaust "denial". It is also worth noting that a Jew, the rabbi Don Marmur, identified the connection between Secular Zionism and atheistic Marxism". The same edition of On Target went on to comment on the: "close links between the Communists and organised Jewry".

In October 1999, British Home Secretary, The Rt. Hon Jack Straw, uncovered a Government proposal for a "Holocaust Commemoration Day". On Target devoted a whole issue to this topic saying: "the proposal has enormous potential consequences for both Gentiles and Jews, not only nationally, but world-wide and for all of whom there are widely ranging and differing perspectives and convictions. Ultimately as the noose tightens around our traditional freedoms, it is essential seriously to ask 'Exactly who governs the United Kingdom?'" Anyone who has followed past issues of On Target including the history of the Power of Zionism and organised Jewry[166] will be aware that the foundation of a State of Israel was as "absurd" as quoted from Nesta Webster in her book Secret Societies as the proposal in 1999, for: "the commemoration by an entire Nation of the Holocaust on the basis of crimes committed by another country against others on foreign territory. The proposed commemoration purports to be in the name of all atrocities against mankind, but the alternative suggested dates corresponding to the liberation of Auschwitz relate to the Jewish Holocaust".

However as I have noted in this book, Hitler, World War II and the Holocaust were a complex battle and plan of the secret societies, where 12 and 13 played out or should I say dramatized on the world's stage the goal of a One World Order. It seems to me a commemoration of the pie! Should we by the same reasoning declare a commemoration day for the atrocities of the French Revolution, carried out in the name of the people by the Freemasons? During which the "reign of terror" and the occult forces behind the Revolution saw the leaders turn upon its own citizens and although never published, children, women and priests were slaughtered; dead bodies boiled in their thousands load to extract fat and sold, lampshades made from skin of the dead etc. That one is kept very quiet indeed. Should we have a commemoration day for the real truth behind World War II and the occult influences and secret groups who surrounded the puppet Hitler? Should we Commemorate the day on November 2nd 1917, when Mr. (later Lord) Balfour penned his signature to the Balfour declaration, in a letter to Lord Rothschild stating: "His majesty's Government view with favour the establishment in Palestine of a National home for the Jewish people, and will use their best endeavours to facilitate the achievement of this object, it being clearly understood that *nothing shall be done which may prejudice the civil and religious rights* of existing non-Jewish communities in Palestine" (my emphasis). Should we commemorate the Palestinians and the loss of their land and homes? Or the tragedy of both Palestinian and Jew with the death of loved ones in the incessant wars that have resulted from the Balfour agreement, with its treachery to the Arabs that appears to rest on an agreement between 12 and 13?

Should we commemorate the British Revolution and remember that letter from Oliver Cromwell to Ebeneezer Pratt, on 16th June 1647:

> "In return for financial support (for the Revolution) will advocate admission of Jews to England. This however impossible while (King) Charles living. Charles cannot be executed without trial, adequate grounds for which do not at present exist. Therefore advise that Charles be assassinated..."

Or the reply from E. Pratt on 12th July 1647:

> "Will grant financial aid as soon as Charles is removed and Jews admitted. Assassination too dangerous. Charles shall be given opportunity to escape, his capture will make trial and execution possible."

The same formula was applied to Maria Antoinette as she tried to escape with her family, in order to bring about an international peace keeping force in France, which idea was to become the United Nations. How did Nostradamus predict the exact spot where Maria Antoinette would be captured? *Planned* and prophesied. What about a commemoration day for the Russian Revolution as we remember a Report from the Netherlands Minister at Petrograd on the 6th September 1918 forwarded to Mr. Balfour in the British Government:

> "I consider that the immediate suppression of Bolshevism is the greatest issue before the world, not even excluding the war which is still raging, and unless as stated above Bolshevism is nipped in the bud immediately, it is bound to spread in one form or another over Europe and the whole world, as it is organised and worked by the Jews who have no Nationality and whose object is to destroy for their own ends, the existing order of things."

Further Lord Kilmarnuck wrote to Lord Curzon from Petrograd on February 3rd 1919:

> "The Bolsheviks comprise chiefly Jews and Germans". Mr. Alston to Lord Curzon, forwarding a Report from the Consul at Ekaterinburg on 6th Feb. 1919 stated: "From examination of several labour and peasant witnesses, I have evidence to the effect that a very smallest percentage of this district are pro-Bolshevik, the majority of labourers sympathetic with summoning a Constituent Assembly, witnesses further stated that Bolshevik leaders *did not represent Russian Working classes*, most of them being Jews" (my emphasis)

> The Rev. B.S. Lombard wrote to Lord Curzon on March 23rd 1919:
> "I have been for ten years in Russia and have been in Petrograd through the whole of the Revolution (I) had ample opportunity of studying Bolshevik methods. It originated in German Propaganda and was being carried out by International Jews. The Germans initiated disturbances in order to reduce Russia to chaos".

The world as a big chess game with "the chosen ones" or God's people as the master puppeteers, despite that embarrassing comment by God in *Isa.I, 1-17*; and *Ezek XX 13*. The idea of a Jewish Conspiracy has been vehemently denied, but the problem of the formation of the State of Israel was very simple to Gandhi, who could not be described as anti-Semitic, since both arguments of biblical authority and persecution of the Jews in Europe were far removed from India. In the late 30's Gandhi accurately diagnosed the problems in Palestine as between Jews as *settlers* and Arabs as *natives* and stated unequivocally that Palestine belonged to the Arab natives and that their rights took precedence over any other claims he stated:

> "The cry for the national home for the Jews does not have much appeal to me. The sanctions for it are sought in the Bible and the tenacity with which the Jews have hankered after a return to Palestine. Why should they not, like other people's of the Earth, make their country their home

93

where they are born and where they earn their livelihood? Palestine belongs to the Arabs in the sense that England belongs to the English and France to the French. It is wrong and inhuman to impose the Jews on the Arabs. What is going on in Palestine today cannot be justified by a moral code of conduct".

It is perhaps the case, that the Adamites having first originated in the Middle East, in the region of the Black Sea, then migrating to Greece where I proposed that they were the Tuatha de Danaan and on to Britain, only adhered as a group through the Brotherhood and had long hankered after a nationality of their own. The 12 tribes of Israel however, were scattered all over and the State of Israel would provide all Jews with both State and nationality. If this is correct, then it would be considerably difficult for the British to deny the Jews a State of Israel, since British politics was obviously pro-Jewish having had a 'cuckoo' in the nest for a long time. The Arabs had to be sacrificed and would become refugees in their own land. As Gandhi asked, why could they not call their country of birth, their home? The answer must lie in the fact, that they hankered after their 'spiritual' birth as *the Brotherhood*, which was in the Middle East in the area of the Black Sea and such claim was supported on the apparent authority of The Bible but in reality must have rested with secret Masonic history.

Theodor Herzl, the founder of political Zionism stated in 1897, following the French Revolution that: "It may take five years or fifty years, but the Jewish State is a fact now"; and on November 29th 1947, the United Nations general Assembly passed Resolution 181 (ii) which called for the partition of Palestine and the creation of a Jewish State. Following that Israel popped up in all the world's trouble spots and developed her "peripheral foreign policy", which centred on her own Security among the developing and emerging Arab States, which was responsible for many wars in the area. *On Target* in the above issue, has noted the growth of Political Zionism in Britain where: "Rarely do British politicians, public figures or journalists now care or dare to stand openly against this Power"; and where: "The pivotal question in many cases, however, has been the distinction between an exclusive commitment to the United Kingdom, as opposed to dual loyalty and double standards exercised with primacy for the Zionist "State" of Israel, and *automatic* and *unequivocal* bias in favour of Jewish interests regardless of the circumstances." This bias of course rests on the 'cuckoo' or 13 th tribe that has existed in Britain in the past and obviously still has an overriding control and influence today on politics. The Labour government has pledged to legislate against Holocaust denial and has sought the help of the Jewish Community in Britain's moral crusade. But how far has this "unequivocal" and "automatic" support of Jewish interests spread beyond the field of politics into the field of religion?

In Britain we have noticed a suppression of the freedom of speech and the right to peaceful protest, expressing different viewpoints. Several students at Sussex University in Britain this year were threatened with expulsion, when they protested against Cherie Blair's (wife of Tony Blair Prime Minister) visit to their University: despite the fact that the new Rights of Man, state in the form of *Human Rights* legislation, that every man/ woman has the right to express an opinion, or viewpoint and find an avenue for expression of that viewpoint and such legislation being supported by Cherie Blair. In the late 60's and 70's student protests were an impetus for social reform and change and it is a sign of the deterioration of liberty and freedom in the West, that students are no longer granted the right of peaceful protest or indeed a variant viewpoint from the One World Order: not being "On Message" has become the millennium inquisition. No hope for me, since I have never been "On Message" from the Grid! As the door of freedom rapidly closes, we noted that during a visit of China's President Jiang Zemin to Britain in October 1999, that once again the right to peaceful protest and freedom of speech was denied to those who sought to question the role of China in Tibet. Newspapers reported the absence of Prince Charles from the State banquet in honour of the President's visit, which is unheard of in terms of etiquette and one could only view this, as a personal protest by the Prince evidently on the subject of Re-incarnation? Those who sought to wave Tibetan flags peacefully in The Mall in central London, as the President's car passed, were not allowed that protest and had their flags wrestled from them! What newspapers failed to report in the case of Prince Charles, was the connection to his belief in past lives (Re-incarnation). *The Telegraph* newspaper (*Oct 22 1999*) reported that Prince Charles had met privately with the Dalai Lama at least twice in the preceding five months at Highgrove his home. Astoundingly *The Telegraph* pointed out that the meetings with the Dalai Lama were: "**in defiance of Government Policy** " (my emphasis!) This is truly amazing and gives some background to Prince Charles and his desire on becoming King to become 'Defender of Faiths' as opposed to the current position of 'Defender of the Faith' i.e. Church of England and Christianity. The Declaration of Human Rights certainly at least in theory (if not in practise as I was to discover many times in my own journey), allows everyone the *right to their own belief*, the use of the word "policy" undoubtedly underlines a secret and covert war here on beliefs, which is allied one must assume to the One World Order and *Communistic* programme which is connected to political *Zionism.*

Rupert Murdoch the media mogul who I have previously mentioned, owns a good slice of British media, and supports the One World Order politics of Communism despite being far right rich in his personal life (which is the hypocrisy of the elite). Murdoch owns a joint venture Chinese language television station *Phoenix*, which is produced in Hong Kong, (which was handed over to the Communists from the British), and aimed at the mainland's new middle classes. Coverage of Jiang Zemin's visit to Britain omitted any reference to protestors in London, including the arrest of a man who was peacefully protesting in The Mall, holding a Tibetan flag. Neither was there any mention of the debate in Britain over police heavy handedness. The removal of the demonstrator was an infringement of certain basic rights that have been **laid down in legislation!** which have taken many hundreds of years to build up in this country and dating back to Magna Carta; rights that certainly do not exist in China as the students who were murdered in Tianamen Square, demonstrating for Democracy were to sadly illustrate. This control of the press has become the most insidious aspect of the control exerted by the elite, where people are simply not given the facts.

Rupert Murdoch has built up a formidable link inside China with the Communist Security and propaganda machine and whilst Chinese Internet surfers must log on through 'Big Brother' and the State-controlled gateways, which block hundreds of sensitive sites, including Amnesty International and Tibetan sites, how much longer will the West be free of such political and religious suppression, under the Communistic European Federal Super State and One World Order programme and how much longer will it be before a Universal Religion becomes compulsory? It is the time and perhaps the *one last exit* through the closing door of freedom, to place the view of Re-incarnation and expose the lies behind world religion and politics that have suppressed the truth. It may not be true for you, but then that is **your choice** and religion and politics *are* a matter of personal choice and MUST remain so. No secret and hidden agenda should seek to pull strings on man. Our spiritual journeys and development are different; we pass through those stages at our own pace and through our own Karmic path, which should not be *dictated* by anyone overtly and NEVER covertly. Our purpose here on Earth is spiritual and therefore it is not surprising that a hidden and covert battle for man's soul has raged for thousands of years. What I say in this book, is open and spoken in freedom of speech, you may disagree with it, but we should all embrace that freedom as part of spiritual awareness and development. If you cannot allow freedom of speech today, tomorrow you will find that freedom has disappeared, for it is only by wedging one's foot in the door of freedom, that it remains open.

How long will it be, before it becomes a crime to produce this knowledge and the background to the events of Golgotha or claim any form of beingness as an accumulation of all past life identities. World Marxism and Animal Farm has decreed that all men must be equal in *beingness* and no man can therefore rise to any greater *spiritual* height. As early as 1970 Zbigniew Brzesiski later National Security Advisor to President Jimmy Carter, predicted a: "more controlled and directed society", would gradually appear linked to technology and ominously stated that this society would be dominated by an elite group.

Could the Military revolution and its marriage with the Court of Justice happen in Europe? The final Report on biotechnology Research requirements for Aeronautical Systems through the year 2000 in the U.S. indicates in certain terms that future capability and policy is directed toward mind control and interrogation application. The neural-chipped society has much deeper and sinister implications. *On Target* covered this issue and I covered the issue with application to the UFO phenomenon in my second book. Prophetically and intuitively *On Target* stated: "In the Elite's misguided judgement, the ideal form of control will be via a micro-chipped population connected to a global computer. Transactions will be carried out via a microchip inserted under the skin..". [167] The horrible reality however, is that man has for millions of years has been controlled via the mega-computer in the sky (www-com/grid along with his controllers who follow faithfully their own thought forms or programmes from the past - what a computerised Theatre!

According to statistics, 360 000 tasks are carried out in cyberspace EVERY SECOND, in the U.K. alone! That includes e-mails, accessing and browsing websites and downloading material from the Internet. With more and more people logging on to the Worldwide Web, the volume of traffic world wide, will vastly increase Linx, the London Internet exchange, which carries more than 90% of the UK's Internet data flow revealed recently that Internet traffic rose to six gigabits per second –equivalent to 360 000 e-mails passing through its network every second. The level is more than three times that of nine months ago and is increasing. Traffic has roughly doubled every day through the 1990's. However, e-mails have also been blamed for rising stress levels in offices, where one survey claimed that office workers dealt with an average of 39 e-mails each day, on top of 150 faxes, voicemails, post and courier items, phone calls and message slips. The world is spinning faster and faster. My question here, is whether the disruption of the human biofield under duress or stress, communicates that decrease in survival to the morphogenetic bioplasma, that watchful eye in the sky that monitors event and survival data for the phylogenetic line of the species? I have covered at length, that it does indeed record changes in the human biofield in relation to environment and matter. The electro-magnetic nature of computers must also challenge the Grid, since the Grid itself is composed of electro-magnetic fields of force. I would not like to suggest, that if enough computers and stress combine in a message back to the Grid, that computer = stress (disruptive biofield) = non-survival = programme for survival faulty = mega computer = non- survival. What would the eye or mega computer 'think' to that! Perhaps like man as god on Earth or the MMRC case, it will wipe out the entire species rather than accept from the minions below that *it* has a programming fault! For years I struggled along on an antique typewriter and sent letters by post, rather than compromise my knowledge, but it is swings and roundabouts where time is a factor, before we reach the final scene and the curtain comes down. It is impossible to say whether the knowledge that was obtained this time in the cycle, allowed computers to uniquely appear, as man raises his evolutionary and spiritual awareness of connectiveness and the web, but it may be so. Did Nostradamus predict 1999 as the year of the spider? – with its web woven in concentric fields interconnected into a pattern, with its victim trapped as a fly on the 'filaments'. Whether information technology will speed up a Magnetic Reversal is another question that there can be no answer to, but I think it is highly probable. How can a master pattern, cope with that much information per second, multiplied worldwide? Thus one must think of reducing stress levels, as well as the whole computerized system? Man can never go back though and I doubt now whether anything but a Magnetic Reversal would change the system. The advent of electronics may have caused the last cycle to terminate, since as I previously covered electrical artefacts have been uncovered by archaeologists.

The Daily Telegraph (*Oct 22 1999*) reported that Rupert Murdoch's station *Phoenix* was back on the propaganda trail, this time with the spears out for a mystic healing sect - the Falun Gong, who were banned in China. Western governments were quick to condemn the Falun Gong ban as a breach of China's Constitutional rights to freedom of religion but that has never stopped the One World Order. Indeed the bookshop in Athens that was advertised in the *Athens News* (*March 1994*) as the stockist of the author's first book was co-incidentally or not blown up! A Star of David was carved into the author's front door in Crete and the author's car badly damaged. Further what was a useless rhetoric scrap of paper with Briton's signature - *The Declaration of Human Rights* worth, if the government possesses "a policy"; which cost the author £10 000 to fight for the right of freedom of belief in a court in London in 1989 and where the author was warned by a barrister: "remember that from now on Big Brother is watching you": and what about the lack of order in another Court hearing in 1991 when a judge joined in! (failing to keep order in the court) after a barrister ridiculed the author on the subject of beliefs a case of –"do what thou wilt is the whole of the law"?

Phoenix took a different view on Human Rights as Murdoch's company produced yet another video under the Communist Masters, depicting the evils of Falun Gong. In a move remarkable even by News Corporation standards, the video was a co-production with China's *police force*! - the public Security Bureau: government "policy" then. What exactly does the Falung-Gong believe in? – Shooting student's protesting for Democracy? (as their Government did) - No, you have guessed it - RE-INCARNATION! Do you think that the author was exaggerating, when she predicted there will come a time, when beliefs which do not fit with the Universal Religion, will enter the person into police files as a "dissident" and that person as I can testify to in my own case, some of which is depicted on the front cover of *The Second Millennium Working Report on Cancer*, will be harassed bugged and hounded, their children assaulted and run from school to school, refused permission to buy a house etc., through the gamut of mindless dramatizing UVG120 sphere controlled zombies, brainwashed by propagandist literature of the likes of news moguls, working with the Communistic One World Order Elite: And did *The Bible* not predict in *Revelations*, that only those: "with the mark of the Beast", would be able to: "buy and sell in those days"? Neither can it be dismissed, that Rupert Murdoch co-incidentally or not, was depicted as the devil in a newspaper and allegedly found it amusing enough to have it framed. Presumably either he has a generous sense of humour, or he was aware of the symbolisation of 13 th tribe and the Bull-Minos cult. But hang on; did the author not explain the 13th tribe were matriarchal and believed in Re-incarnation? Oh yes that is just for solar kings and as the *Express* Newspaper pointed out: "Fear reigns at the court of the sun king". Fear was indeed the predominant emotion on Earth, before the spiritual message arrived.

This brings the author to that notorious document, *The Protocols of the Learned elders of Zion,* a document more fully discussed in her first book. *The Protocols* were hotly debated at the time when they appeared in Russia in 1905, and condemned by Jewish authorities as a vile "forgery". As *On Target* (cited) pointed out: "forgery or not, the uncomfortable and undeniable truth, is that each of the twenty four individual Protocols have come to pass in the United Kingdom, at the hands of certain powerful elements of the Anglo-Jewish Community". Whilst I agree with *On Target*, that the Protocols are not, together with their virtual fulfilment evidence of any: "collective Jewish Conspiracy for ultimate Power", I suspect that the people of Israel may be as horrified as anyone else by past world events and this story. However I cannot conclude other than what I have provided evidence for here and that is the elitist groups of 12 and 13 have caused the majority if not all world wars and revolutions on this planet and there is a very definite conspiracy. In terms of Murdoch's obvious stance against freedom of belief, is it co-incidental, that the profile of Rupert Murdoch in three successive editions of the American tabloid newspaper *The spotlight* (*1989*) revealed three individuals each of Jewish origin, behind Murdoch's rise to power.[168] On *Target* produced an impressive list of media and publications owned or connected to influential Jews, commenting that: "the fact remains that in the space of the Twentieth Century organised Jewry has achieved a position of pre-eminence in the organs of power of Anglo-Saxon-Celtic society".

Religion shapes the mind and viewpoint; it is a powerful force for good (freedom and truth) or bad (suppression, control and lies). Truth is essential in religion, since as St. John most profoundly stated: "The truth shall set you free". I observe, that rituals carried out in religion also help to fixate viewpoint and in some respects parallel the rituals of magic, in so far as everything must be carried out precisely, in order of sequence, for it to work. The obsession with ritual then, overtakes any meaning and has the unfortunate result of *becoming* the religion. Going to Church does not make a good Christian! but I expect a good Christian goes to Church. What is taught in a religion is vitally important to the viewpoint of the member of that religion and the majority of religions warn about 'looking over there!' or alternative viewpoints. The problem with fixed viewpoints, as any philosopher will tell you, is an inability to OBSERVE, SEE, or TO KNOW. A parent knows the truth on this very well, you say to a child now don't do that because this will happen, but he goes right off and does it and *that*, indeed does happen and now he KNOWS. One never truly knows, until one can experience for one's self and WISDOM is really a matter of how much you really KNOW inside and within you, from accumulated EXPERIENCE. Fixed viewpoints limit experience, wisdom and virtually set you up as a victim of Grid control - after all the Grid is the Master Computer and just as I have explained in the case of Cancer, if you can't solve a problem using your *rational mind* through communication and Spiritual soul memory experience, then the computer which is based on survival of the species, will 'solve' it for you, on the computation of SURVIVAL OF MATTER AND SELF/GROUP *only:*

Hitler who fought for self, Third Reich and nation (group) devastated the whole of Europe and beyond to Russia, simply because he was operating in the field of mind and body control appealing to the Grid to 'solve' it. World War II was just one big dramatization! Hitler's use of the ancient archetypes of Minoan swastika (womb), the death heads, oak leaves etc.; together with the use of the cosmic keyboard in his speeches aimed at morphic resonance of the biofield, triggering primitive survival mechanisms which all appealed to Grid survival. The clever use of the archetypes appealed to the spiritual bioplasma memories that are for the main deeply embedded in man's subconscious, as we have seen in Hubbard's Space Opera and the explanation that I gave of Inc. I. He conducted his rallies at night, which increases hypnotic value, coupled with nationalistic marches and a prominent display of the colour red, which is a high-energy colour. A whole nation went into survival mode, as he appealed to their patriotic past and the injustices of the Versailles Treaty, again aimed at the emotion of survival. Very clever as the' Messiah' method! As one of Hitler's secret group mentors commented: "Follow Hitler, but it was I who played the tune". The problem with these 'Messiah's' is that come to believe they are the saviour, that only they can do it, they stick themselves on the 'cross', set themselves up as "the one" next step-jump from glee, is straight into the asylum where they believe they are God. Hitler honestly believed as a Sun King that the ice would melt before him in his Russian campaign. The Aryan became the religion of Nazi Germany. A religion says stick with me kid its safe with us, we have millions of members so we can't all be wrong can we! "You and I forever", you and I against the world, against all other faiths, - BATTLE STATIONS! Oh dear, that has alerted the moron Grid – did it just hear something about survival? Primitive Reactive mind dramatizations switch on! ('Fright (run) or Fight'?) O.K. Fight! Kill! Cheat! Betray! lie! Go on Homo sapiens *animal*

you will 'solve' it. In actual fact he clocks up just that bit more karma in his primitive or reactive mind that prevents him from getting out of the trap. To top it all, *Revelations*, encourages man to look forward to getting stuck like a fly to fly paper on the "strings", or 'filaments' of the disrupted morphogentic bioplasma during the Magnetic Reversal or space boundary event: "Paradise" for the MMRC perhaps, waiting for things to recover so that he can get on with the 'script' DAY 1 –Plant the vine.

It is believed that the Jewish religion is based solely on The Old Testament, which depicts the Jews as a favoured race by God - a view that Christians believe has been superseded, for which reason the book of *Revelations* in the Bible that depicts the triumph of the twelve tribes of Israel, has been somewhat politically ignored at public level. Notice that no one in the hierarchy ever refers to *that* 'script' or Jesus, much to the puzzlement of Christians. *The Talmud* is an important part of Jewish beliefs and Michael Rodkinson in the Preface to the translation of the *Talmud* (*vol. 1 p.x*) states: "The modern Jew is the product of the Talmud". The Talmud places the Bible as secondary in importance and a Talmudic treatise *Soferim* states:" The Bible is like water, the Mischna is like wine and the Gemara like spiced wine". The Talmud is a meticulous ritual or code applying to the Jew alone. Drach [169] points out: "The Talmud expressly forbids one to save a non-Jew from death...restore lost goods, etc., to him, to have pity on him." The Jews are far from unanimous in support of the Talmud and many have refused to adhere to this teaching to their credit, however Israel and its Rabbis are entrenched in the Orthodoxy of their religion, even it would seem in the dreadful manner they treat women by enforcement of the Daily Prayer. However, it is in the Cabala, that the Judaic dream of world-domination recurs with the greatest persistence. The *Zohar* in fact predicts: "When Israel triumphs over the people of the world... and *dominates them*" (my emphasis) at: "The Feast of Tabernacles". The advent of the messianic era apparently entails another Feast, where naturally "a *female* Leviathan is boiled and pickled"! (My emphasis) Civilized! All her fault I suppose again, which is a justification for having committed a wrong against the woman by stealing the Holy Grail, the overt should really be run on this! The objection against woman is just a complete dramatization! I have already referred to the unbending orthodoxy of requiring women to state the form of their daily prayer: "Blessed be Thou, o Lord our God King of the Universe, that Thou has not made me a woman!" Drach explains that according to the *Talmud* a service can take place in a synagogue only if ten persons (the old Pythagorean sexist pyramid of male numbers thousands of years old) are present, which ensures God's presence. Even if there were nine men and one woman, then the service cannot start! If this is the One World Order thinking, then is it any wonder that women are generally paid less, suffer sexist remarks in their jobs, face sexist courts and have barely a token presence on any top echelon committee of 'movers and shakers' in the One World Order programme. Freemasonry is a sexist organisation that never lets women in to the power levels.

It is difficult to respect a religion and its leaders when they suppress documents (The Dead Sea Scrolls), that are not their property but belong to man's heritage. It is difficult to respect a religion that covertly seeks to suppress other beliefs through political channels and media and even seeks to suppress any moral criticism. *On Target* in the above issue gave the case of a former United States Secretary of State for Defence under President Harry S. Truman, James Forrestal, whose death was claimed as suicide. Forrestal's career was effectively ended, after he had urged that the Palestine problem be taken out of the political agenda, after which orchestrated public attacks began against him. In the case of the Arab Israeli wars of 1967 and 1973 *On Target* stated: "the full weight of organised Jewry was brought to bear, for example, by direct contact with newspaper editors, and through the influence of individuals in the B.B.C. to suppress the Palestinian case or impartial coverage and to ensure preference towards Israel."Nesta Webster[170] pointed out that: "Rabbinical Judaism is the declared and implacable enemy of Christianity. Hatred of Christianity and of the person of Christ is not a matter of remote history, nor can it be regarded as the result of persecution; it forms an integral part of rabbinical tradition." Evidently whilst this must rest on the hidden background of Jesus and his association with the 13th tribe, then both sides in the story know the truth, but neither will confirm that truth. Further Webster asked why the Jews: "perpetually hark back to what was done to them in the past": the answer must lie in the fact, that it prevents questioning of the present and future. Political Zionism is justified thought, in so far as the conscious mind has sought to explain away its own aberration, thus avoiding admitting wrongness, which it seeks to avoid at all costs, that it has failed as a conscious mind: The ultimate humility of having to apologise at least to the goddess and woman and concede that a wrong was committed. Political Zionism seeks to suppress any contradicting viewpoint, simply because at some high level these things are known. As the lie deepens, the mechanism becomes psychotic 'I must be right or I die'. Would a religion survive if it admitted wrongness? And if the conclusion is to go along with a lie, simply so that self or group can survive, then you have just given into the survival mechanism of the Grid. As Hucklebury Finn noted: "You can't pray a lie". The group or religion is bound to fail in its purpose or goal of setting man free even as John remarked and even as it is engraved outside the offices of the CIA: "And the truth shall set you free".

To employ a justifier such as the Jews or Brotherhood employ for the Goyim (non Jews) or the "cattle", means that a person must believe his act was harmful and since he cannot accept that he has harmed, he must require that his act was unmotivated, thus the Jews always portray themselves as victims (everything done to them and nothing to others). We see in the psychological case, the diminishing spiral, where he punishes and restimulates himself, always complaining about what others have done to him, but *never what he did to others*. Once when I was teaching my children the meanings of the various icons at the Knossos Museum, the tail end of a group of tourists being given the official tour, asked if they could tag on to my little group telling me I should run the equivalent of the 'X-files' (The Truth is out there) tour! Man has a great capacity for truth and *making his own choices* and we should grant man the possibility of his noble character, without treating him as "cattle" to be squeezed for money and then spat out when of no further use, a trait that is becoming all too familiar, in many areas of life as man cheats and betrays his fellow man. Nowhere is this more poignant than in the field of education; we owe it to the next generation, to teach them the truth. The appalling liturgy of lies and omissions in curricular education together with the under use of iconographic education in museums is a grand betrayal to the next generation, who will inherit this generation's folly and laziness as we inherited theirs (past life). The wheel of life and the eye turns in a Cycle of Eternal betrayal.

SCIENTOLOGY A SECRET GROUP?

The official biography of Ron Hubbard, the founder of Scientology (1954), has always portrayed Ron Hubbard as a genius, who not only developed an entirely new science of the mind - *Dianetics - The Modern Science of Mental Health* (1950) but at various times Ron's accolades have included explorer, researcher, science fiction writer, philosopher, movie director, script writer, horticulturist, economist, historian, metaphysician, nuclear physicist and so on. *The Current Scene (Vol. I 1983 -1986)* lists the various honours Ron received, including *keys* (?) to various cities! Undoubtedly Ron had a truly amazing life, but left one of the muddiest trails in history, apart from Jesus. I cannot search for truth and then fall short of that goal, by leaving one stone unturned. As a Scientist, Biochemist and Physiologist, with many years research experience, I understand only too well, what long arduous perseverance and painstaking effort and thought, it takes to deduce *any* new thought in science, from basic principles and *original* research. When I came across *Dianetics* a complete science of the mind, I was very sceptical that Ron could have developed this science, without recourse to references and of course apart from one or two extremely vague references, there was only the claim that his genius had been source. Thus it is interesting to look at the biography of Ron, which started in Montana America, where his wealthy grandfather owned a cattle ranch. Ron according to the official line was like the young Jesus, a precocious child, engaging in philosophical discussions with a member of the Indian Black Feet tribe when he was only six years old. Ron allegedly learnt the secrets of the tribe and in 1923 met another illusive influential figure in his life Commander Joseph 'Snake' Thompson of the United States Navy, who taught him Freudian analysis, whereupon he took up a search for life force, culminating in the science of *Dianetics*. He went to China (*the East*) and there allegedly learnt more of the Spiritual side of life, particularly from an elderly magician named Mayo, with ancestral links to conjurers who served in the court of Kublai Khan. Thus goes the official story of Ron Hubbard. The background of magic was to feature a number of times in Ron's life, although the Church politely ignores this.

In fact his father was a naval officer and was posted in various exotic locations around the world and Ron was on occasions taken along, thus despite Ron's claims of travelling alone as a teenager in the East, he was accompanied by his parents, who were very conscientious about Ron's education. In fact Ron was to fail a number of courses, and despite the PR claim that he was a civil engineer, he dropped out of George Washington University in 1930 and his despairing parents went to great lengths to get him to settle down and study for his grades, but Ron always had other things in mind. The creation of Ron the 'Messiah' has somewhat curious parallels to the life of Jesus including the precocious childhood, interest in philosophical ideas, lost years and the emergence of the ministry. The lost years as I have covered with Jesus, are in the case of Ron just as muddy. Prophetically in his early Journal Ron as a teenager wrote: "I will tell you the secret of this strange life I had, Ssch! I was born on Friday the *thirteenth*" (my emphasis). In fact he was born on 13th March 1911, which was in fact a Monday.

Russell Miller's biography of Ron *The Bare Faced Messiah - The True Story of L. Ron Hubbard*, was a book Scientologists tried to ban. Evidently because the story of Ron's life hardly matched that of the official line of the Church of Scientology (COS) and further Miller's book whilst being fully referenced and researched, utilised numerous interviews with Scientologists who had known Hubbard - no doubt an embarrassment to the Church. The book was first published in Britain in 1987, which might account for the cull of Miscavige, where long standing members of the Church who questioned Church policy at this time were declared suppressive and thrown out. This would co-incidentally or not, parallel secret group policy of 'no questions asked'. In a curious parallel to Jesus the myth of 'Messiah' was being re-born on dusting the tracks of the *man*. Miller's book highlights the enormous gap between reality and myth and as an exercise in comparison of Ron's life to that of Jesus, illustrates the predictable attempt and failure to combine holly (holy one) and oak (royal) into one personage: Ron's character was definitely oak. 'The Battle of The Trees' re-enacted once again on the world's stage and the birth of a new 'Messiah', which as a phenomenon was inherent with the 13th tribe. The reference to "thirteen" may not have been entirely co-incidental, since children often display very openly their past life memories in odd phrases, particular talents or interests and fascination with objects, indeed as I have already pointed out, even researchers reclaim their memories through their 'great work', as the philosophers call it. The Dahli Lama of Tibet is chosen on such principles and the child genius has often been a Professor in a past life. There are very curious parallels to thirteenth tribe ideology in Ron's life even down to his red Celtic hair. Even more curious, is the fact that when Ron's son Quentin by Mary Sue, allegedly committed suicide, Mary Rezzonico a Scientologist, turned up with an authorization signed by L. Ron Hubbard and Mary Sue Hubbard, for the release of Quentin's remains and personal effects. Rezzonico said she had personally obtained the signatures over the weekend at: "an unspecified location in Ireland". [171] Apart from this one occurrence, there was no other mention of Ireland in Hubbard's biography, although he spent a great deal of time in New York where there are many Irish Americans.

Scientology PR would claim that Ron from the age of 14 to 18 or 1925 –1929, travelled extensively in between his studies at George Washington University, where he was majoring in Civil Engineering; finding time to act as a director with the Caribbean Motion Picture Expedition in 1931. The underwater films made on the expedition providing the Hydrographic Office and the University of Michigan with invaluable data for their research. In addition he established himself in the literary world, supporting himself at the age of 21, conducting the West Indies Minerals Survey and making the first complete mineral survey of Puerto Rico. This indeed would be impressive for such a young man and whilst there is no doubt that Ron went on expeditions of sorts, the grand titles were an embellishment of assumed importance. This of course would be neither here nor there if Hubbard (the man) had not hung on in later life to a young man's boast. Miller recounts a different story and how Ron, having dropped out of University at George Washington, went to see his parents in Guam in the Philippines, where his father was stationed in the Navy. It was to be his mother, who tutored him for the entrance examination to the Naval Academy, whilst Ron was experiencing the East. This of course is quite a different scenario from travelling alone in the East at the age of 14. Far from showing an interest in Eastern culture Ron shows a certain bias when he notes in his journal: " The Chinese have neither the foresight or endurance to overrun any white country in any way except by intermarriage. One American Marine could stand off a great many yellow men without much effort" Surprisingly there are several more such references in Miller's book, which show this early attitude. As for the Temple of Heaven, probably the supreme achievement of traditional Chinese architecture Ron comments in his Journal: "Very gaudy and more or less crudely done". Only The Great Wall of China was to stir his future ability as a Science fiction writer: "The only work of man's hand visible from Mars". Even from an early age, Ron had ideas on how to make money from history when he added: "if China turned it into a rolly coaster it would make millions of dollars every year". In fact how to make money pre-occupied most of Ron's life until 1954 when he founded The Church of Scientology (COS).

Personally I would be reluctant to trust any biography of Hubbard, if it were not for the inclusion of witness accounts from Scientologists themselves, as is the case with Miller's book. David Mayo, a senior case Scientology supervisor in the COS H.Q. at Clearwater in Florida, was to be summoned to Hubbard in 1978, when Hubbard pursued by the FBI had gone into hiding and was very ill. Mayo would recall to Miller: "He was obviously very ill, lying on his back almost in a coma". Mayo was to audit (Scientology procedures) Ron and bring him back to health, but was deeply disturbed by what he learned during his daily auditing sessions with the old man. "He revealed things about himself and his past which absolutely contradicted what we had been told about him. He wasn't taking any risk because I was a loyal and trusted subject and had a duty to keep such things confidential". Full marks to Mayo for not betraying another's soul, but clearly for such a loyal and trusted "subject" (a curious word) to divulge even that to Miller, meant there was something about Ron's background that was fairly significant and absolutely contradictory. I know Scientologists and they regularly audit rape, murder and the full gamut of man's irrational mind in past lives and nothing like that would concern them enough to comment on it, as The Bible states: "Let no man say he hath not sinned". Neither would Mayo be turned by the occasional yarn that was Hubbard's style – no, this was something much more fundamental. Mayo was to continue: "It wasn't just what I discovered about his past, I didn't care where he was born or what he had done in the war, it didn't mean a thing to me.... what worried me was when I saw things he did and heard statements he made, that showed his intentions were different from what they appeared to be.... when I was with him messengers often arrived with suitcases full of money, wads of hundred-dollar bills. Yet he had always said and written that he had never received a penny from Scientology...I didn't mind the idea of him having money or being rich. I thought he had done tremendous wonders and should be well paid for it. But why did he have to lie about it? I slowly began to realise that he wasn't acting in the public good or for the benefit of mankind. It might have started out like that, but it was no longer so. One day we were talking about the price of gold, or something like that, and he said to me, emphatically, that he was obsessed by an insatiable lust for power and money. I'll never forget it. Those were his exact words, 'an insatiable lust for power and money'". [172]

Ron loved adventure and excitement and there is no doubt he was enterprising as a young man in organising a vacation trip for fellow students describing it as the 'Caribbean Motion Picture Expedition". Why not leave it at that? It was pretty impressive for a young man, but no - in the PR line of genius, building up to those discoveries of a new science, great claims had to be made and yet no traceable benefits from the expedition were recorded. Increasingly as I viewed Hubbard's life and his "expeditions", I was reminded of the early explorers who circumnavigated the globe using Grid knowledge and constructed the ancient maps. Was he in his early life, dramatizing a past life? Re-stimulated by his father's profession as Naval Officer with various postings around the world: which created wanderlust in Ron, which would only be satisfied when he had created the Sea Org (Scientology speak for Organisation) Ron was to give a number of his past lives, although to my knowledge he did not mention any life that would connect him with the 13th tribe apart from one alleged life as Cecil Rhodes and the alleged admission that he had been a member of a Council back on the time track, which may be significant and which I will come to. Hubbard first believed that Australia would achieve the state of Clear (Clear is a Scientology term referring to a state of having no abberative engrams which are comparable in my terminology to holograms), however trouble with the Government of Australia, meant that Hubbard sought a safe environment for Scientology and he turned to Rhodesia, believing that he could also solve the Rhodesia crisis, particularly as he had been Cecil Rhodes in a previous life. The CIA on 7th April 1966 received a request from an agent in Rhodesia asking for information on Hubbard. Hubbard's plan to acquire a hotel on *Lake Kariba* was obviously aimed at the well-heeled (white) market of prospective Scientologists. Hubbard gave an interview in the *Rhodesia Sunday Mail* saying he was re-cooperating from illness, but intended to invest in business in the country, at the same time distancing himself from Scientology, stating: "I am still an officer of the corporation that administers the movement, but it is very largely autonomous now". [173] The CIA have that curious inscription from John outside their headquarters and John I have concluded was thirteenth tribe, so is this a period in Ron's life, when the CIA picked up the potential of Dianetics, along with the thirteenth tribe?

In May of 1966 Hubbard produced (uninvited) a: "tentative Constitution" for Rhodesia which he felt would satisfy the demands of the blacks, while at the same time maintaining white supremacy. It embodied the principle of one man one vote for a lower house, while real power was vested in an upper house elected by qualified citizens with a good standard of English, knowledge of the Constitution and financial standing verified by a bank. Hubbard was convinced the black population would welcome his ideas even though the qualifications to sit in the upper house, would exclude most blacks. The interesting thing to me about this episode is the tiered structure proposed. Hubbard went to some lengths to get his foot in the door of Rhodesia although privately he thought Ian Smith was: "a nasty piece of work". [174] Further Miller in his book gives an interesting insight into Hubbard's character, which was curiously, a parallel ideology in the past of the 13th tribe. Mc Master a Scientologist teaching a clearing course in Johannesburg, revealed this side of Ron when he explained:" similarly, he publicly espoused sympathy for the plight of the black majorities in both Rhodesia and South Africa, while privately admitting contempt for them. Blacks were "so stupid" he told John Mc Master: "they did not give a reading on the E-Meter". [175] Although no racial policy exists in Scientology today and is open to all, money certainly has defining power over treatment, one could hardly imagine John Travolta or Tom Cruise, getting 'roughed up' as a sacrificial victim as was my experience. To be absolutely fair to Hubbard, I distinctly remember a bulletin reminding Scientologists to take great care with the "little people" I believe was the term he used. Ken Urquhart then LRH (Lieutenant Ron Hubbard) Communicator world wide for the COS strongly maintained that Hubbard sought to help the Blacks and that was the reason he was kicked out of Rhodesia - what is the truth?

It is curious that Hubbard allegedly stated his past identity as Cecil Rhodes. John Riskin in 1870 was to be given the chair of Fine Arts at Oxford University and chose to accept, by giving a speech on the Empire and England's downtrodden masses as a moral issue. Ruskin told the undergraduates that they were the possessors of a magnificent tradition, of education, beauty, rule of law, freedom decency and self-discipline, but that this tradition could not be saved, and did not deserve to be saved, unless it could be extended to the *lower classes* in England and to the non-English masses throughout the world. If this precious tradition were not extended to these two great majorities, the minority of upper class Englishmen would ultimately be submerged by these majorities and the tradition lost. To prevent this, the tradition must be extended to the masses and to the Empire. Cecil Rhodes (1853 - 1902) kept the speech with him for thirty years copied out in longhand. Lafayette Ron Hubbard was to Re-incarnate on 10th March 1911 to battle it would seem throughout his life, with the two separate parts of the Holy Grail, torn between oak royal and holly the holy one. On numerous occasions oak royal shocked and upset his followers whilst his apparent genius and research together with the Tech. (Scientology speak for technology and forms the works of Hubbard) would instil great loyalty in them (following the holly or the holy one). Mayo obviously could not accept there was an oak royal, or money and power in the equation, a story that I remember at least once in the past trail of the 13th tribe: Hubbard the man and Hubbard the 'Messiah'. Just as the Nag Hamaadi Scrolls are suppressed, since they show a different account of the life of Jesus, then so are any attempts to reveal the true biography of Hubbard.

Rhodes of course went on to exploit the diamond and gold mines of South Africa, rose to be Prime Minister of Cape Colony (1890 - 1896), contributed money to political parties, controlled parliamentary seats in both England and south Africa and with the financial support of *Lord Rothschild* and Alfred Beit, he monopolized the diamond mines as De Beers Consolidated mines and earned a fortune from Consolidated Gold Fields. Interestingly with regards to a One World Order, Rhodes desired to federate the English-speaking peoples and to bring all the habitable portions of the World under their control. For this purpose or goal, Rhodes left part of his fortune to fund the Rhodes Scholarships at Oxford in order to spread the English ruling class tradition throughout the English -speaking world, as Ruskin had wanted. Further Rhodes formed a secret society in 1891, with a number of prominent people from Oxford and Cambridge, including Arnold Toynbee and Alfred (Lord) Milner, Lord Balfour (who was to become so prominent in the formation of the State of Israel) and Lord Rothschild, all men have been quoted by Mullins (cited) as prominent fomenters of the World Order. Can we assume that contrary to the beliefs of Scientology, that Hubbard's alleged immediate past life had no hold on his goals in his present life and any Federal World Order goal was dropped with his body as Rhodes? As Hubbard himself was to point out, the troubles you have in the current life, are more dependent on previous lives.

Ron by the early thirties was writing pulp fiction and was to marry Polly, his first wife by whom he had two children. However Ron was to leave Polly with his family in Montana, whilst forging a career as a writer in New York. Frank Gruber introduced Ron to the American Fiction Guild and was to remember Ron as a great yarn spinner. "One evening Gruber sat through a long account of Ron's experiences in the Marine Corps, his exploration of the upper Amazon and his years as a white hunter in Africa. At the end of it he was asked with obvious sarcasm by Gruber: "Ron, you're eighty-four years old aren't you?" To which Ron snapped, "What the hell are you talking about?" Gruber waived a notebook in which he had been jotting figures: "Well", he said, "You were in the Marines seven years, you were a civil engineer for six years, you spent four years in Brazil, three in Africa, you barnstormed with your own flying circus for six years...I've just added up all the years you did this and it comes to eighty-four". Ron was furious that his escapades should be openly doubted: "He blew his tack", said Gruber. [176]

Ron's oak character was not the patient studious one that would be required to formulate a new science from basic principles; it is not the way science works or is researched and it is complete fallacy as any scientist who has undertaken original research will tell you. It has taken me 15 years to formulate a mechanism for cancer and I have included many references in that research upon which the quantum leap was made. If you cannot quote references and the hard grinding work of others, it is merely an admission that your ego governs your work and you have so little power to create, that you must deny the power of others and importantly the *source* of the Grail. In fact Ron's school and University life is marked by his inability to conscientiously apply himself to his studies, such as taking up gliding when he was at George Washington University. He did obtain his glider's license, but at the expense of his grades and in fact he never completed the course at University. To Scientology 'spin doctors' and perhaps even to Ron himself he was a walking legend in his own time. His career in Hollywood was to be hyped as with everything else. In fact he did have some success with one script *The Secret of Treasure Island,* aimed at the Saturday morning matinees, which was brought by Colombia, but there appears to be no other major credit, which no doubt John Travolta hopes to rectify with the forthcoming *Battlefield Earth.* Since Hubbard often used whole time track (Akashic Record?) in his books, then one should be careful when one applies that to film and public audiences. *Battlefield Earth* was the story of how Jonnie Good boy Tyler, one of the few surviving human beings still on earth, turned the tables on the huge, shambling, hairy aliens who had taken control of the planet. In fact in myth, legend and in the *Secret Doctrine* (and in the higher echelons of Scientology?) there is a recurring belief that Super masters will try to descend and take control of Earth. This is definitely a belief in the occult, which is not magic as such but the Secret Doctrine of pre-history and particularly Blavatsky referred to it.

At the time *Battlefield Earth* appeared in the early 80's, Hubbard having evaded the FBI for years in safe hiding places wrote to David Mayo in April 1982, saying he did not expect to live long and was assigning responsibility for safe-guarding the "purity" of the technology to his friend Mayo. In fact David Miscavige who in 1982 according to Miller was a "ruthless" and ambitious nineteen-year old who had learned management technique at the Commodore's knee (Ron), as a camerman in the Cine Org (Org is Scientology speak for Organisation); was with Ron in the last years and was one of the few people who knew where he was hiding. Broeker was another senior Scientologist with Ron in those final years when Miscavige: "Apparently at the behest of the absent Commodore directed a massive corporate re-organisation of the Church of Scientology, ostensibly designed to further shield Hubbard from legal liabilities and to ensure that the income flowing to him from the Church, then running at about 1 million dollars per week, could never be traced". [177] David Mayo according to Miller believed that Miscavige and his cohorts interpreted Ron's request that Mayo take responsibility for the "purity" of the technology as a threat to their position and began making plans to remove him. In fact great upset was caused in this period, when many long term serving senior Scientologists were purged from Scientology during the re-structuring and none had redress to Hubbard. As one *Phoenix* (the breakaway group from the COS) member told me, this was completely incomprehensible in so far as these people were only trying to help humanity and inexplicably were declared "suppressive", which in Scientology speak is a declared enemy of the COS. The question of "purity" of the technology was also a point raised by *Phoenix*. I believe the point centres on material written by Hubbard and any material that may have been *added* with the apparency that Hubbard had written it. This reminds me of the character of the so-called Yatrus and the addition of data of his own!

The problem seems very clear to me, having past life experience of the path of the Holy Grail: there were always two ways the Grail could go, when it was a mixed bag of matriarchal and patriarchal knowledge. The Grail is in two parts (although it was never intended that way) there is the elixir or the *contents* – the message of Re-incarnation and the knowledge; and there is the *vessel* or cup with its potential for secrecy power and wealth. Scientology is in my own perception a mix of elixir and cup and as such could go left or right, according to the emphasis placed on either part and as such is indicative of the god Hermes, with his face of two sides – the Janus head. Hermes of course was the god who had the most ability to make money, speaking first this way and then that, which was a point made by the founder of the Illuminati Adam Weishaupt. I perceive that many Scientologists feel that they cannot betray Scientology, with its matriarchal message (Re-incarnation and its knowledge or the tech) but have real conscientious objections to the gold cup (patriarchalism). Unfortunately as with Hermes, the goddess has now been locked up in the tomb with yet another combination of Twin Kings holly or holy one and oak royal, as a sun king! Hermes of course always worked with the Illuminati power pyramid with its layered secrecy, control and extremely hard thinking, where wealth and power are the goal and did not Miller quote Hubbard's auditor as saying that was Ron's goal? There lies the Greek tragedy of the Religious Revolution in Crete once again. The Illuminati being communist never sought freedom for the spirit and thus how could an organisation that has *any* Illuminati influence, ever succeed in freeing the spirit? It is a system of control only. The question becomes as to whether Scientology was taken over by the Illuminati? It's anybody's guess which way the Church went after Hubbard's death and more of a guess whether Hubbard was set up for the eventual take-over, or sold the Church downstream for those wads of money that came in suitcases? However we must accept the official Church line, that Ron was a genius and his sole goal was to help humanity with no connections whatsoever to this story. Deary me, now where have I seen this story on the track of time! One thing is certain, it was scandalous to exclude previous members of the Church, who had only shown the necessary qualities of helping humanity - there would be **no questions of conscience asked** by those who had been at the very origins of Scientology and had known Hubbard *the man*. Illiminati thinking co-incidentally goes through the same thought processes, with its power pyramidal control apex, it will tolerate no questions asked, as my Petition in 1997 illustrated. Miscavige was also to oust Mary Sue, Hubbard's third wife or second (whichever story you believe), after her conviction for Federal crimes.

This was a very messy period in the history of the COS, when Mary Sue took the 'can', for an illegal and covert action of The Guardian's Office (GO). The GO was Scientology's intelligence bureau and as the various United States Government agencies aligned themselves against Scientology the GO had agents infiltrate various Government offices, removing documents on Scientology. The covert operation was eventually discovered and in January 1983 the Supreme Court convicted Mary Sue, who then at fifty-one years old, was sent to prison for four years, whilst Hubbard claimed (unbelievably to some), that he knew nothing about it. Mary Sue loyal to Ron never spoke out. Mary Sue's resignation as controller of the Church after this outcome, under pressure from Miscavige, resulted in the Church issuing a press release piously justifying the "shake-up" as a reaction to the indictments resulting from the covert operation by the GO entitled "Snow White"; and further admitting that the GO "went adrift" by engaging in a battle with the Federal Government. However I believe the statement was issued in 1981 before the indictment, which possibly indicates that the shake-up looked for a justification, which they found in operation "Snow White". It might be pertinently asked *who* advised Mary Sue to go down this route of all out war on the American Government, if not Hubbard? I ask such a question, since agents for the World Order, often infiltrate groups and make ill-advised suggestions to manipulate events for their own means.

With the ousting of those who had known Ron Hubbard the man, those who had strongly believed that the new Science of *Dianetics* and the Tech. would change the world into a more ethical and humanitarian place, were to be gravely disturbed at the phenomenal prices that were to be charged in order to receive help by Scientology auditing including the cost of books and tapes, effectively placing an ascent of the OT ladder to the highest levels (OT 8 in 1991) and Scientology Tech. beyond the reach of the ordinary man. Further there would be no-one around to question the hierarchy a point that I verified, when I personally wrote to Miscavige before I left for Greece in 1993, reporting the horrors and unethical nature of my experience, to which I received no reply and certainly no explanation as to why at least three policies written by the founder had been violated. The "purity" of the Tech. that Mayo had been asked to protect, evidently no longer mattered. The oddest thing, was that what I clearly perceived and reported as wrong and unethical, was to receive the cold comment from one OT8 involved: "There was no read on it" (no charge on the E-Meter indicating upset). Further I could not get once ounce of sense out of it and had the feeling I was talking to *a machine*, with quotes from Hubbard spouted back at me. Even those Scientologists who could recognise the wrong, eventually succumbed to the procedures for getting rid of people who ask questions, even though *those* procedures did not adhere to those Hubbard had lain down. Now if you ever wanted to cave in a soul completely that was an excellent way of doing it! I very nearly dropped the entire postulate! Now where had this particular cave in occurred before? – I fled to Greece with my research not long afterwards, after a string of disconnected or perhaps connected events, which threatened survival and would unravel the story. As I commented, sometimes your perceived worst enemy is your best teacher. Yatrus Xenu and the One World Order have provided very good teachers.

Irrelevant things like authorised qualifications never deterred Ron. On 27th February 1961 when Hubbard was trying to set up Scientology in London, Richard de Mille son of the film director who was a close associate of Hubbard's and a Scientologist, received an urgent telegram from Hubbard in London:

> "PLEASE INFORM DR. HOUGH PHD VERY ACCEPTABLE. PRIVATELY TO YOU. FOR GOSH SAKES EXPEDIATE. WORK HERE UTTERLY DEPENDENT ON IT. CABLE REPLY. RON".

The doctorate that Hubbard required from Dr. Joseph Hough, who was a chiropractor and naturopath, was of a dubious nature, since the good Dr. conferred 'degrees' from his dubious 'University' of Sequoia in a house in downtown Los Angeles, on whomever he thought merited them. In this way Hubbard acquired the letters DD (Doctor of Divinity) after his name followed by D.Scn. (Doctor of science). In March 1961 Hubbard was to append further qualifications in material written for the Saint Hill Special Briefing Course (SHSBC) - C.E (certificate of Education?) Ph.D., and nuclear physicist! The same qualifications appeared on Ron's correspondence with the FBI in 1955. In fact since Ron did not pass his exams and had been occupied with pulp fiction writing in New York, many of his acquaintances found it very odd, that in 1938 he should have claimed to have written a philosophy which he had produced in the manuscript *Excalibur* (very Arthurian and thirteenth tribe) Described as: "a sensational volume which was a summation of life based on his (Hubbard's) analysis of mankind". Much would be heard of this great work in later years, indeed it became the cornerstone of the mythology built around his life. The thesis was said to have been derived, from Ron's discovery that the primary law of life was to SURVIVE. The part played by his journeys and explorations would form the background to explain how exactly Hubbard came up with the work - the myth of the 'Messiah' had to be maintained at all costs and David Mayo who would remember Ron the man, would for that reason be ousted from the COS. Once you have seen this exact scenario before on the world's stage, you begin to smell the proverbial pie.

The manuscript *Excalibur* was never seen or printed and Art Burks remembered Hubbard called him one day and said: " I want to see you right away, I have written *the* book". Burks was to recall that Ron had told him he had written it without sleeping, eating or anything else and had literally worked himself into a frazzle. "He was so sure he had something away out and beyond" anything else that he had written, that he had sent telegrams to several book publishers telling them he had written *the* book. He told Burks that it was going to revolutionize everything, the world, people's attitudes to one another:" he thought it would have a greater impact than The Bible".[178] Burk recalled the manuscript as being seventy thousand words long and began with a fable about a King who gathered all his wise men together and commanded them to bring him all the wisdom of the world in five hundred books. He then told them to go away and condense the information into one hundred books. When they had done this, he wanted the wisdom reduced into one book and finally the word. That word was "Survive".

Given that the OT Levels previously discussed up to Level III, look suspiciously to me, at least in the Inc.2 "implant", like a Magnetic Reversal or space boundary event and whole track *event* data for *Earth*, I personally was interested how Ron knew *what* to audit on the OT levels. Did Ron channel information from the morphogentic bioplasma or the Akashic Record? Thus giving him some idea of *what* to audit, or was this original research, whereby the accumulation of data from regressive (past life) data of Scientologists, was formulated into the OT levels? A case of which came first, the chicken or the egg? In science this would be considered the double blind trial. I am not questioning whether Scientologists have come up with the data, since if this was a Magnetic Reversal, then it would be recorded in the memory banks, however it is the interpretation of data, that is in question i.e. is Inc. 2 an "implant" or is it the downloading of the entire Akashic Record after a Magnetic Reversal or space boundary event? In 1972 when Hubbard was moving from one safe house to he next, pursued by Government agencies, Preston and Dincali two senior Scientologists who were staying with Ron recalled that after dinner, Hubbard had a single tot of brandy and sometimes talked into the night: "He'd jump around from subject to subject", recalled Dincali: "One minute he'd be talking about how an angel had given him this sector of the Universe to look after and the next minute he'd be talking about the camera he wanted me to buy him the next day. I used to watch him talking, sometimes his eyes would roll up into his head for a couple of minutes and he'd be kinda gone". Ron was sixty two by this time, and perhaps with his extra-ordinary life on the run, one might be forgiven for thinking that this was tiredness of the old man; but Dincali recalled that when he was writing Scientology Bulletins: "He wrote tremendously fast by hand. It was *like automatic writing* you get in the occult. He'd have a glazed look, as if he was kinda gone, his eyes would roll up and the corners of his mouth would turn down and he'd start this frenzied writing. I've never seen anyone write so fast" (*Author's emphasis*).[179]

The channeller or Seer, when channelling information, has to write very fast in order to keep pace with the information (Holograms) that is channelled from the Grid, with the brain (or mind as a biofield) acting as dipole radio-receiver. Hubbard had a fatty lump on the top of his head, which he always claimed was shrapnel, but on X-ray showed no metal, which may or may not be significant. Further the eye-roll is also a feature of the Seer phenomenon. We might ask at this point, whether Hubbard was channelling information from the Grid and Akashic Record, or whether he co-incidentally took on the character of Seer whilst writing?! Miller's book quite clearly shows that Ron became increasingly irrational during his time at sea with the Sea Org and his outbursts became more bizarre in later years especially during the cine Org. Period in his later years, a time co-incidentally when Miscavige had joined the cine Org. One might easily put this down to the enormous pressure and stress that he was under and certainly this might be so, however some of the Bulletins that Hubbard allegedly wrote on the destruction by any means of anyone who dared to question Scientology making them "fair game", reminded me very strongly of that notorious document *The Protocols of the learned elders of Zion:* that were brutally cold and very symptomatic of that disease - the World Order plan and sacrifice to a cause. *The Protocols* were an alleged plan by the Jews to create a World Order and whilst they have been hotly disputed as to source, many researchers see today the culmination of such a plan:

> "We will make merciless use of executions with regard to all who may take up arms against the establishment of our power" (*Protocols -page 50*)

> "We must take no account of the numerous victims who will have to be sacrificed in order to obtain future prosperity" (*Protocols p.51*).

> "Our laws will be short, clear and concise, requiring no interpretation, so that everybody will be able to know them inside out. The main feature in them will be obedience required towards authority and this respect for authority will be carried to a very high pitch" (*Protocols p. 56*)

> "The end justifies the means. In making our plans we must pay attention not so much to what is good and moral, as to what is necessary and profitable" (*Protocols p. 40*).

And given my own experience in Scientology:

> "He who wants to rule must have recourse to cunning and **hypocrisy** (Protocols p 3). We must not stop short before deceit and **treachery**: If these are to serve the achievement of our cause.   (*Protocols p6*). (*Author's emphasis*)

The most noticeable thing about the *Protocols* in my view is that they represent Grid survivalist thinking, which is *only* concerned with **survival** of individual or **self** and at the highest level the **group**. Now as I have explained the morphogenetic bioplasma is a primitive mind that records all *events* in the environment, which concern *matter* and therefore the phylogenetic line of the species. Thought and behaviour is very much along the Darwinian principle of 'survival of the fittest'. Ethics, morals and conscience together with compassion do not occur within this bioplasma, after all an animal when faced with survival, does not sit and ponder whether the action it takes is morally right or wrong, or whether it should have compassion for the sick it leaves behind, it simply follows innate behaviour and thought which is dictated by the Grid survival mechanisms. Battle stations! Under threat!   Did I hear that word *survival*? (Rational analytical thinking mind clicks off and primitive reactive or irrational mind switches on): Fright or Flight (run)? No I will fight! The animal has the chance to run or fight and the more power the animal has, then it will fight. Man can choose either, in which case he subjects himself to Grid survival mechanisms and animal survivalist behaviour. Or, he can retain his rational mind and choose to fight within the boundaries of ethics, logic, morals and importantly utilise **communication** as his 'weapon' fulfilling the old adage: 'sticks and stones will hurt my bones, but words will never hurt me'. Words only elicit a physical response, as we all know, when they are true! One cannot deny that the reason *Dianetics* has been fought, is that it is true! (I cannot speak for the rest of Scientology or the OT levels, as I do not have personal experience). *Dianetics* is I believe the answer to man's mind and it is a must have book.

Hubbard had a large fatty tumour or lymphoma on top of his head, which he said had slivers of shrapnel in it. Scientologist close to Hubbard had it X-rayed and had the film enlarged fifty times to find the shrapnel, but there was nothing there, Shrapnel places the origin of the lymphoma at about the time of Ron's naval experience and a time in 1938 when Ron was to come up with the illusive *Excalibur* manuscript .Did this lymphoma have anything to do with Ron's apparent ability to act as Seer? The events in Hubbard's life leading up to *Excalibur* which was in existence in 1938, warrant further examination, since what is not understood, is that the games played on the Theatre stage are big games and only when you have played enough of these games, with enough knives plunged in your back do you understand how One World Orders creep up by many a winding path, under many a mask – witness Christianity. The betrayal and treason to the message and hope for humanity, goes deep within one's soul and it grips one's soul with pain that often takes thousands of years to overcome, such were the events of Golgotha for those who were there to witness it. However the tendency to put up with a half truth or lie, has grave eventual consequences as we saw in the events of Golgotha: for if Jesus had been at the tomb, in the crouching or foetal position and not laid on a Baetylic pillar (herm indicating Hermes) and missing when Magdalene arrived, then the last two thousand years would have seen a very different result. Just two seemingly insignificant details, allowed the One World Order to take root.

When the author first met Scientology she had one overriding feeling, she had seen it all before (on the track of time), it was just a matter of when and where? When the knife came in the author's back as it was bound to do, it was she perceived a   recognition at a spiritual or higher level of the author's goal of **truth**. The author did manage to recover her memory *independently* at great emotional cost, upset and time - but she did remember in the end *without recourse* to the Grid or Akashic Record. To carry the Grail as it was intended, defines the edge of human experience both on an emotional and physical level. It is significant to to the author, that it was Phoenix (the old matriarchal group?) who provided the last jigsaw piece in the puzzle and goal for truth. Let me assure you, that there is no greater pain to my soul or edge to human experience, than to write these words, including the background to Jesus, which to the author is like telling a young child, who dares in his soul to reach for Heaven, that you have no idea of the spiritual forces at work on this planet, which seek to crush man's exit from the trap of Earth. Scientology wa aptly described by one Scientologist who had known Hubbard, when she said: "you are like a cow, you give a good bucket of milk and then you knock it over". Scientology had everything that you could have (at this stage of spiritual evolution) hoped for, in bringing about its *stated* goals of helping humanity, it contained the technology to resolve (the state of clear) the abberative mind of man and past lives recognition (contained in the book *Dianetics*): technology (OT levels 1-3) it would appear that can to some extent access the trap of a Magnetic Reversal and which Scientology refers to as an "implant" (Inc. 1 and Inc. 2): it contains technology that would revolutionise education and communication and has undoubtedly the power to *overcome* any World Order. Equally as the Tech could be used in two ways with that inevitable hermetic flaw, it has the power to *become* a One World Order and prevent man's release from the trap. As Roncali the Scientologist who was with Ron in the Sea Org would recall: "I truly believed he had come to save the planet". Something similar was believed at Golgotha and Nazi Germany thought the same of Hitler. Male Messiah's always seek to join holly the holy one (matriarchal gift) and oak royal (power secrecy and wealth) in that transcendent and hermetic magical third, which is the god of the World Order. Constantly before me, I see that unlucky thirteenth tribe, who fought the World Order of the twelve tribes and consistently failed because an 'out reality' or lie was used, when they utilised the hidden science and never ran a straight line on truth or source; compounding the injustice by locking up the woman with Hermes. When will they ever realise, that **Male Messiah** is not the answer, whilst continuing to defy the Mary Magdalene's words: *"There will be no peace on this earth until the cut healed"*. *The truth revealed.*

Many believe that the manuscript *Excalibur* never existed and it was certainly never published. Burkes a literary associate of Hubbard at the time, could not reconcile his knowledge of Hubbard as a pulp fiction writer, with no apparent philosophical background, with the philosophical manuscript of *Excalibur:* "one envisions the philosopher as quiet grey-beard, timid in all things but thought. It is, withal, rather upsetting to the general concept to think of L. Ron Hubbard as the author of *Excalibur*". Ron unquestionably believed in *Excalibur* because he wrote a long emotional letter to Polly, his first wife in which he expressed his hope that the manuscript would merit him a place in history: "When I wrote it " (*Excalibur)* he was to write: "I gave myself an education which outranks that of anyone else. I don't know but it might seem that it takes terrific brainwork to get the thing assembled and usable in the head. I do know that I could form a *political platform*, for instance, which would encompass the support of the unemployed, the industrialist and the clerk and day labourer all at one and the same time". (*My emphasis*) This was perhaps the first time that the cup or the other half of the Grail emerged as the inevitable use of the elixir in the power pyramid of politics, wealth and power.

Years later when fellow Scientologist Jack Horner and Jim Pinkham were at Hubbard's house in Phoenix, there was a knock at the door and Ron spoke to a man outside for five minutes, returning with a big grin on his face he said the man wanted to give him five thousand dollars, for a copy of *Excalibur*. Then he laughed out loud and said "One of these days I'll have to get around to writing it". He then admitted that there was no such book, despite earlier referrals. Hubbard himself recognised that writing pulp fiction prior to and during 1938 did not give him the credibility he sought:" Writing action pulp doesn't have much agreement with what I want to do because it retards my progress, by demanding incessant attention and further actually weakens my name". Money was a constant problem to Ron and writing to Polly on one occasion he said: "I've got to do something about it and at the same time strengthen the old financial position". Towards the end of the letter he wrote about strange forces, he felt stirring within him which made him feel aloof and invincible and the struggle he had faced to answer the question "Who am I?" These letters were written from New York and it is possible that he had met someone at the Explorers Club, who had introduced him to the concept of Immortality or regressive past life therapy or perhaps some magical circle, although there is no proof of that, at that point in Ron's life. What is evident is the sudden appearance of the ideology that motivates all secret group higher initiates and that is their arrogant belief in their comparable power to that of God: "God was feeling sardonic the day He created the Universe, so it's rather up to at least one man every few centuries to pop up and come just as close to making Him swallow his laughter as possible".

Some years ago when I was promoting my research in London at a stall at the *Fortean Times* conference, I met a young man who mentioned to me that he had attended Michael Hall School, in Forest Row (Rudolph Steiner) with which I was familiar and that his grandfather was a Freemason and had known Ron Hubbard. A Welsh person referred me to a book (no reference) which mentioned that Ron had frequently visited a Traegeda House (?) in Wales. Unfortunately as I was very busy and I did not manage to obtain the young man's name for further details. Further, I always thought it was odd, that Hubbard should have chosen the title of *Excalibur* for his thesis, since it was the sword that only Arthur the thirteenth member of the group of twelve, could pull from its resting place and use. The court of King Arthur whilst believed to be mythical, certainly has ties to the thirteenth tribe in so far as after Caesar purged the Druids, they were believed to have carried on in secret at Caerleon-on-Usk in Wales: and surrounding this place in Monmouthshire U.K. are a number of place and site names that have historical connections to some aspect of the thirteenth tribe: 'Whit (e) church', 'Great Oak', **Magor**', 'King Arthur's Cave' and Cardiff Castle which undoubtedly has Rosicrucian and by descendency Druid knowledge displayed on the floor design. Further Hubbard in his OT material allegedly claimed to have been a member in the long distant past (not this lifetime) of a group of twelve. Certainly the Rosicrucian's have vibratory resonant knowledge which included the very earliest works by Pythagoras who was initiated by the Idian Dactyls in Crete where a whole belief system (Re-incarnation) and Cosmology was withdrawn from the Early Minoans and hidden within secret groups as religious mysteries including the *cosmic keyboard*, which co-incidentally or not, appears in variant form in Hubbard's *Chart of Human Evaluation*. Such knowledge I have no doubt was increased over the millennia and may have well produced a group with tremendous psychological knowledge, which curiously enough came up in a natural UFO incident; "There is a group on this Earth with powerful psychology". This may indicate and probably does, since the UFO incident (natural) is a hologram from the past, that there was in existence a group with such knowledge. Hubbard's *Chart of Human Evaluation* in his book *The Science of Survival* is undoubtedly a highly workable and astonishing chart, but was it all Hubbard's knowledge?

At any rate Hubbard hoped for recognition from *Excalibur* stating: "Sooner or later *Excalibur* will be published and I may have a chance to get some name recognition out of it, so as to pave the way to articles and comments which are my ideas of writing heaven". Hubbard also may have sought to establish his yarns for the purpose he gave in a letter to Polly: "I turned the thing up so it's up to me to survive in a big way. Foolishly perhaps, but determined none the less. I have high hopes of smashing my name into history so violently that it will take a legendary form even if all the books are destroyed. That goal is the real goal as far as I am concerned". Not only do we see something of a Celtic warrior here, but also the Tech or elixir is not evidently so important as the man and legend – the cup. The sadness of it is, if Ron had not been so intent on money and fame, he might have passed *Dianetics* for study to a University or had it subjected to Clinical trials in the treatment of the sick. Unfortunately by the time I tried to get a clinical trial underway in the field of cancer, Ron had indeed smashed his name so well into history that no one wanted to go near the proposed trial with a bargepole! And curiously enough not even Scientology. The Holy Grail was always meant to be applied to healing and yet the COS showed not the faintest interest in my research, reducing me to doubt once again on their goals, which appeared to refer to group alone. The first doubt arose, when I was quite literally thrown out of the COS, to fight The Declaration of Human Rights (the right to one's own belief) in a court of law in Holborn London in 1989. The reason being that the COS did not want any adverse publicity (fear)! Hypocritically COS International from June 21 to July7th, ran an advertising campaign in *USA Today* to hit back at a *Time* magazine article, which had attacked the COS; where the campaign propounded the rights of man including *religious freedom*. Even more hypocritically when against all odds, I did win that case with Compton and Carr Solicitors in London, the case itself being a landmark in religious freedom and the right to one's own belief; the COS did not recognise that win, or indeed advertise the result in their group publications, which supposedly monitors religious freedom, even though I understand that *other religions* (Jehovah's witnesses) have used the judgement. Further after another horrendous experience with the COS I came to realise that "The aims of Scientology" so profusely outlined in words in *USA Today* hardly matched with my own experience or the actions of the COS. When I tried to share the research on cancer with the COS, there was not the slightest interest in the Scientific publication, despite the fact that it had been one of Ron's stated goals to have *Dianetics* applied to the field of health and tested in a scientific manner. I was beginning to realise slowly, that the COS had its *own agenda* and that agenda was clearly demonstrated at their rallies, when Scientologists were awarded on how much *money* they brought into the COS. Clearly cancer and religious freedom for *other* religions was not part of the agenda. As one senior Scientologist told me with respect to cancer: "Help the more able first". I certainly made my views very clear right to the top of the COS International with silence from Miscavige. I stated in *The Battle of The Trees*, that when words do not tally with actions, then there is a LIE that is hidden. That lie is a **hidden agenda**. One has only to look at the total disregard for farming in Britain with the mocked air of consolation, without action and the empty seats in the House of Commons during the foot and mouth crisis, to realise that there is a hidden agenda there.

Was it revelation or initiation? That "turned the thing (*Excalibur*) up". This is not the first time that such a question has been asked on the track of time. Is it not co-incidental that in 1940 Hubbard wrote the book *Fear.* "No-one who read *Fear in unknown* during their impressionable years would ever forget it", claimed Brian Aldiss, science fiction writer and historian. The stream of consciousness narrative, akin to psychoanalysis charts the disintegration of an academic who writes an article debunking the existence of spirits and demons and is punished by being dragged into a nightmare of black magic and hallucinations" *Fear* was very different from Hubbard's swashbuckling adventure stories of his earlier years and thus we might conclude that the years just prior to 1938 and the appearance of *Excalibur*, were very important in the life of Ron. Who is to say whether he knew of the forthcoming World Order plan of European Union, when he wrote *Typewriter in the sky* and *Final Blackout*, both considered to be classics. The latter book created controversy and accusations that it was Communist or Fascist propaganda depending on your viewpoint: that curious mix of left and right which is the two pronged plan of control by the World Order; with left politics (communism) run by the elitist far right which mirrored the ideology of groups 12 and 13 respectively. The story was set in Europe laid waste by generations of war and populated only by marauding bands of renegade soldiers - leading a brigade of "unkillables", the hero, identified as the "Lieutenant" fights his way to England, where he establishes a benign military dictatorship until he is overthrown by his former Commanding Officers, with the backing of the United States. Another short story in December of 1940 *The Case of the Friendly Corpse* held curious significance when we discover that the hero disposed of one character in the story - Harold Shea, with a *magic wand,* which turned into a *Serpent* - very Druidic! - Very thirteenth tribe!

When I was researching in Greece (1993 - 1995) not only did I notice the light brought from Israel to Patmos in 1994, but the large number of Holocaust stories that were televised on Greek television. Some curious incident occurred involving some association with black magic or occult was splashed all over news programmes; where people were being interviewed in hysterical mode, which struck me immediately as some form of black propaganda with a hidden agenda pre-determined outcome or goal. Sure enough the announcement came, that all *Dianetics* organisations in Greece were to be closed, effectively removing the COS from Greece. The accusations of "black magic" and "occult", flew thick and fast in predictable fashion, with its subliminal message: 'don't look over there its too dangerous'. Meanwhile a large communist gathering in mainland Greece occurred. If you put together the clues, with the fact that Greece removed their monarchy and king Constantine, together with light brought from Israel to Patmos, then quite clearly here we see the hidden agenda, as the 12 tribes with the Greek Orthodox Church and the World Order maintaining their control over Greece. This implies that the COS is perhaps thought to have some political significance or hidden agenda, if not the message itself of Re-incarnation – perhaps 13 th tribe? In fact the propaganda line against the church for some time has been the accusation of "black magic" and "cult". The fact that the Black Cabala and resonant ritual, was utilised by patriarchs of the twelve tribes of Israel in a number of so-called religious mysteries has evidently been overlooked: along with the majority of prophecies in The Bible, which I conclude were either dramatizations or Grid channelling. What about Moses? Who was not unabashed to utilise such knowledge and the hidden science on Mount Sinai: or Joshua? When he collapsed the walls of Jericho: or indeed Jesus and the feeding of the five thousand? A case of 'pot calling the kettle black' - as the old English saying goes, in the war of 12 versus 13?

Whether this battle of 12 and 13 is behind the terrorist group the *17 November,* who have targeted American and British subjects in Greece for 20 years, through successive governments is hard to say, but possible. This group have never been identified or their crimes prosecuted, which has led some senior figures in Greece, to maintain that this is government "policy". The last victim was a British diplomat in late 2 000. This is the problem when a country and its people become the victims in this war of 12 and 13 and presumably accounts for the wrangle over the Elgin Marbles retained in Britain, but originating from the Parthenon in Athens. Greek icons and artefacts remain in museums all over the world and are not being fought over for their return to Greece, but for some hitherto inexplicable reason the Marbles have become symbolic in this battle: presumably intimating something of the culture of Greece was taken from the Minoans? Ah well you see, as the twins fight over who should claim the *cup* of the Holy Grail, the *message* or elixir is forgotten, with its warning of karma in relation to exit, reflecting the biblical phrase: "You will not get out of that place, until you have paid up the last coin of least value". The word "policy" noticeably occurs in connection with the Grail, the hidden science, re-incarnation and in fact any facet of the battle of 12 and 13.

The COS claimed in a statement made in December 1969 that: "Hubbard broke up black magic in America ...because he was well known as a writer and philosopher and had friends among physicists, he was sent in to handle the situation". That's an odd statement, which does not make sense. Ostensibly then Hubbard had been "sent" by nuclear physicists? To terminate the practise of black magic being practised in a house in Pasadena. This is a forked –tongue statement and the official line of the COS, because Hubbard did not know any nuclear physicists at the time he came into contact with the secret group in Pasadena the O.T.O (Ordo Templis Orientis) apart from the leader of the Agape Lodge, John Whiteside (Jack) Parsons. Hubbard's life history given in Miller's book shows no sign of contact with nuclear physicists, after all he was writing pulp fiction in New York, which is an unlikely field to draw you into contact with nuclear physicists. If Hubbard was: "sent in to handle the situation", then *who* sent him in? The COS statement continues: "He went to live at the house and investigated the black magic rites and the general situation and found them very bad. Hubbard's mission was successful far beyond anyone's expectations. The house was torn down. Hubbard rescued a girl they were using. The black magic group was dispersed and never recovered". In fact according to Miller's book Hubbard ran off with Betty (Jack Parsons girlfriend) and there was some kind of "confidence trick" according to the letters of Aleister Crowley, who wrote to Parsons. Although Hubbard later denied having married Betty and thus committing bigamy, as Polly was still his wife at the time. Thus there appears to be some inconsistency with the official line put out by the COS and accounts by Aleister Crowley together with the biography of Hubbard by Miller.

Lou Goldstone (Jewish) who was allegedly a science fiction illustrator curiously was the man to introduce Ron to the secret group of the O.T.O in 1945.The group was headed by Jack Parsons who was a rocket scientist and chemist working at the California Institute of Technology. Parson's was evidently one of America's foremost explosive experts and worked on developing jet engines and experimental rocket fuels. It is certainly odd, that I can remember Hubbard referring to rocket scientists as those who used *Dianetics* first. It is not inconceivable, that Parson's in the period after the war was working on Nazi research, which had been brought to America in 'Operation Paperclip' when Nazi scientists, who I claimed had been researching Grid past technology arrived with such knowledge in the U.S. Jack Parsons was to join the O.T.O in 1939 and set up his own lodge in Los Angeles and quickly rose to prominence in the group, which was founded by the infamous English black magician Aleister Crowley. Crowley through notoriety had earnt himself the title of "the beast" ("666") and utilised drugs and sexual practises in his magical rites. In fact Crowley used Cabalistic science to channel information from the Grid, although goodness knows where he actually thought this information was coming from, probably from Masters or Etheric Spirits who he invoked through magical vibratory or morphic resonance. Scientifically speaking, he was pulling down holograms from the Grid and he sought information, as all occultists do. Effectively this was the quest for Akashic Record information or event data from what I term the morphogenetic bioplasma. Obviously in the book here, you have a greater awareness of the exact process, from the point of view of vacuum energies and morphogenetic bioplasma or Akashic Record. However this was not known to Crowley and evidently not to Hubbard or Pa\arsons.

If Hubbard met the O.T.O in 1945, then this is a later date than 1938 associated with the manuscript *Excalibur.* In a letter to Dr. Joseph Winter in 1949, Hubbard claimed that he had worked on *Dianetics* for eleven years, which co-incides with the date of 1938 and *Excalibur.* Thus increasingly we come to associate Excalibur with the origins of *Dianetics,* which *precedes* Hubbard's association with the OTO. Some years after Hubbard left the O.T.O he was to enter into correspondence with the FBI, a report in the FBI files records a meeting with Hubbard where he was trying to 'zip up' Miles Hollister as a Communist. Miles Hollister had gone off with Betty and it was proving to be a somewhat messy affair, with Ron paranoid that he was the victim of some form of plot against him. According to the report: "Hubbard stated that he strongly feels that *Dianetics* can be used to combat Communism: However, he declined to elaborate on how this might be done. He stated that the Soviets apparently realised the value of *Dianetics* because as early as 1938 an official of Antorg, while at the *Explorers Club in New York*, contacted him to suggest that he go to Russia and develop Dianetics there" (*my emphasis*). The Explorers Club looks increasingly like a possible contact venue and *Excalibur* and *Dianetics* both seem to stem back to December 12 1939, when Ron Hubbard was formally proposed for membership to the Explorers Club. Compared to his output in previous years Ron did not produce much in 1939, only seven novels and two short stories, which was nothing for Ron.

In 1939 Hubbard wrote to the Secretary of the War Department to offer his services in the event that America was dragged into the war in Europe. In his letter he claimed that he had spent five years studying psychology and human behaviour, purely for his own benefits. His "pioneering" notes on emotional reactions, he added, would be published in the coming year. Thus one assumes he is referring to what would become the official COS line, that Ron studied psychology with Commander 'Snake' Thompson, looking into Freudian analysis. Thus which is it to be psychoanalytical research and revelation or initiation? Which still does not answer the question of *who* exactly sent Ron into the O.T.O? The question also becomes, did Ron study resonant vibratory or Cabalistic ritual there in the *Secret Rituals of the OTO*, which would provide a method for channelling? Another question becomes whether he stole knowledge from the O.T.O, which would allow him to channel information from the Grid, thus giving him some idea of *what* to audit for his OT levels (I -III)? I have tried to get hold of the *Secret Rituals of the OTO*, but I am afraid that all copies appear to have disappeared.

The logo used on Scientology materials is a four-step pyramid and the managerial structure is along the lines of the Illuminatus power pyramid, with a few or one controlling brain at the top. Further another logo shows two interlaced triangles with an S-shaped letter ostensibly representing Scientology connecting the two. The Scientology sign for Theta (life force) is an oval with a line across θ having significance to the Greek letter theta, but also reminds one of the Finglesham belt (*Plate 19*), with its hermetic Masonic (magical) connotations, although this may in fact be mere co-incidence. We might assume that the COS was correct in stating that Hubbard's goal was to break up the O.T.O and black magic, if it were not for the correspondence between Alisteir Crowley and Jack Parsons which shows a somewhat more complex story. [180] Jack Parsons the head of the Agape Lodge of the OTO wrote to Aleister Crowley in July 1945:

> "About three months ago I met Ron Hubbard...he is a writer and explorer...a gentleman; he has red hair, green eyes, is honest and intelligent, and we have become great friends.... Although Ron has no formal training in Magick, he has an *extraordinary amount of experience and understanding* in the field. From some of his experiences I deduced that he is in *direct touch with some higher intelligence*, possibly his Guardian Angel. He describes his Angel as a beautiful winged *woman* with *red hair* whom he calls the empress...He is the most Thelemic person I have ever met and is in complete accord with our own principles. He is also *interested in establishing the New Aeon*" (*my emphasis).*

Hubbard then, in 1945 was no mere novice since he has an "understanding in the field". Further Parsons addressed Crowley as: "Most beloved father" and signed himself "Thy son, John". I have already referred to the fact that Crowley and his lodge in Switzerland displayed the signs of the Rose-Croix and I assume, that *The Secret Rituals of the OTO* are methods of **the Rosicrucian's**, who had in descendency, links to the Druids and therefore the thirteenth tribe – Judah - descended from the "Vine man" or "he who joins together" and Noah. There is no doubt that the secret rituals sought and acquired some of the top Akashic Record secrets on Earth events. How to attract an elemental which could be turned into one's familiar spirit, was set out in the top secret O.T.O. treatise entitled, *De Nuptiis Secretis Deorum cum Hominibus* ('Concerning the Secret Marriages of the Gods with Men') For this class of magic (VIII degree), one needs no assistant for it is sexual magic of the solitary kind; but Parsons chose nevertheless to perform the rite in the presence of Ron Hubbard. Crowley was wearing a black hooded robe, and Hubbard a white one (very 12 and 13 tribe!). Thundering away in the background was one of Prokofief's piano concertos or Rachmaninof's symphonic poem, *Island of the Dead*. This may have provided the exact morphic resonance on the cosmic keyboard, for pulling down the holograms that were required with the biofield of the mind acting as a dipole radio receiver. Whether or not pre-history of Atlantis was being sought is not known.

What interested me was that in a letter to Crowley Parsons referred to this ritual: "For the last three days I have performed an operation of *birth*, using the *air tablet, the cup*, and a *female* figure, properly invoked by *the wand*, then sealed up in the *altar*. Last night I performed an operation of *symbolic birth and delivery*". I have emphasised the significant symbols. You may remember that Inc. 1 of Hubbard's OT levels included symbols such as the horn, angels and chariot, that I thought could easily be the symbols of the Religious Revolution in Crete c. 1 400 B.C. I questioned whether Inc. 1 was not the *actual* beginning, which I would state as the anti-matter matter explosion as the birth of a spirit; but the beginning of recordings on the spiritual bioplasma. Thus this spiritual event on the Akashic Record as recorded by the spiritual bioplasma, represents a time, when new knowledge and emotions, allowed that information to be recorded on the spiritual bioplasma which is a higher plane of energy than the morphogenetic bioplasma, concerned only with recordings of events of matter. The Religious Revolution being the time when the 13 th tribe came into possession by theft, of new knowledge meant to free mankind from the trap. To access those holographs then the channeller has to be in a *high state of emotion*. Hubbard? and Parsons evidently used solitary sexual magic and highly emotional music to raise biofield resonance, to the point where it would by morphic resonance vibrate with that higher plane, thus allowing the Seer or channeller access to INFORMATION OF EVENT. Further, if one utilised parts of the hologram in this case "birth and delivery", then by the physics of holograms the entire hologram would be pulled down: In other words, if a hologram contains 'bites' or components of information as A, B, C, D, E etc. Then if you re-created A and B you would by the laws of interconnection, pull down the entire hologram and *event*. The fact that the "birth and delivery" elements of the hologram were used, would restimulate holograms of Knossos and the Religious Revolution simply because you have the connection of archetypal symbols of birth to the labyrinth and the take-over by Hermes: thus this may account for the chariot (of Hermes) and the horn (gates of horn and Bull-Minos cult) and cherubim (Tree of Life Jewish Cabala) which Hubbard stated were part of the Inc. 1 "implant": However it may have *appeared* to be the start, but it was in fact only the *start of a battle* to take over The Holy Grail Message. The fact that Hubbard associated Inc. 1 with Xenu and mind control, may be explained by my point of view and the fact that drugs (the Poppy Goddesses) were used to make the Minoans suggestible to religious symbols and initiates appeared to be channelling via the third eye (crown chakra) as was evidenced by icons showing men with their hand raised to the third eye. The problem is, you would have had to be in a lot of places to get the real truth on *actual* event, rather than channelling it from the Akashic Record, where you merely tap into the Masters side of the story! There was of course another story from the other viewpoint. It is interesting that Parsons used solitary sex, since Hermes was an effort to get rid of the woman in the story, after the Grail had been taken.

The Air Tablet or Elemental Tablet of Enoch (the Enochian Keys), is one of the four Watch Towers of the Universe, the others being tablets of Fire, Earth and water. In other words Parsons was working the magical system of John Dee and his scryer, Edward Kelley, which Crowley had successfully worked during 1909 in the North African desert with his chela, Victor Neuburg. The 'wand' was the penis as the talisman that was placed in the altar, symbol for the womb. Jack Parsons had what sounds like a Hermetic alter in his Lodge, which consisted of the horizontal baetyllic pillar or lintel across, flanked by two upright pillars and as such is comparable to the tomb of the Twin Kings combined in the hermetic and transcendent third stage beyond death. This would almost certainly define hermetic magic was being employed. It is quite clear from correspondence that Ron undertook O.T.O rituals. The COS would no doubt claim that Ron's experience and understanding came from Ron's contact with the Chinese magician and the chief of the Blackfeet. The holographic method of pulling down the entire hologram might be illustrated when Parson's known as Frater 210 wrote exultingly to Crowley: "I have my elemental! She turned up one night after the conclusion of the Operation, and has been with me since, although she goes back to New York next week. She has red hair and slant green eyes as specified. If she returns she will be dedicated as I am dedicated!" Her name was Marjorie Cameron.

You may remember that I said that the experience, knowledge and soul memory of the Seer, or even the UFO witness will determine how the holograms are interpreted. One never receives one assumes a full story from channelling and as the case of the Rev. Walker showed, one can put two and two together and make six. The UFO witness who was a farmer spoke of "cookies" and the pilot will speak of "instruments". Thus one may get brief holograms from thousands of miles of 'film reel' but the manner in which those holograms are strung together in a story line of event, may not necessarily represent the truth of the event itself, as I have tried to illustrate over Inc.1 of Hubbard's Space Opera, which appears to me to look like the Religious Revolution in Crete. Who is to say whether Marjore Cameron, was not a part of the Religious Revolution, perhaps a Snake Goddess, since obviously the 13 th tribe or some Egyptian 12 tribe group, who took over Knossos and the Holy Grail, must have supplied these Goddesses. However, with his Scarlet Woman (Marjorie Cameron) and in the presence of Hubbard, Parsons began to perform the IX level of magic to produce another higher being. Parsons wrote to Crowley:

> "I am under the command of extreme secrecy. I had the most important – devastating experience of my life between February 2 nd and March 4 th. I believe it was the result of the IX degree working with the girl who answered my elemental summons. I have been in direct touch with One who is most Holy and Beautiful as mentioned in *The Book of the Law*, I cannot write the name at present. First instructions were received direct through Ron, the seer. I have followed them to the letter. There was a desire for incarnation. I do not yet know the vehicle, but it will come to me, bringing a secret sign. I am to act as instructor guardian guide for nine months; then it will be loosed on the world. That is all I can say now....".

Crowley was not pleased and he replied: "I thought I had a most morbid imagination, as good as any man's but it seems I have not. I cannot form the slightest idea what you can possibly mean...." And to Frater Saturnus (Karl Gemer) Grand Master of the O.T.O in New York, Crowley wrote, "Apparently Parsons or Hubbard or somebody is producing a Moonchild. I get fairly frantic when I contemplate the idiocy of these louts." As Symonds (cited) wrote: "But the 'lout' Hubbard was quietly acquiring through the writings of Crowley, those magical secrets which helped him a few years later to found his celebrated Church of Scientology". This was my question, did Hubbard use channelled data in order to know *what* to audit on the OT levels? Parsons was to quarrel with Hubbard and he ran off with Parson's girlfriend Betty in Parson's yacht and some time later Parson's died in an alleged accidental explosion. In a letter published in *The Sunday Times, 28 December 1969* "Dr Hubbard" claimed that he had "rescued a girl they were using. The black magic group was dispersed and destroyed and has never recovered".

Thus the muddy trail requires us to question whether Fratus Saturnus in New York, was in fact the Grand Master of some parent secret group of the O.T.O perhaps a branch of the Rosicrucian's or the Illuminati? The claim by the COS tht Hubbard knew nuclear physicists, may infer the Rosicrucian's, since I have maintained that it was this group that was always interested in the hidden science and may well have researched it, utilising top scientists: further, was Lou Goldstein an agent working for that group or Illuminatus? Was Hubbard set up, in other words via the Explorers Club? The masters are very clever, they know a man's goal and his character and can assess a man's current life and predict his past lives. Hubbard may have represented the exact personality that was required to set up a group and may have already attained the experience in magic that Parson's was to comment on, through a secret group. Alternatively Hubbard may have co-incidentally and independently through Lou Goldstein come across the O.T.O and then ran off with the secret rituals, realising their potential. The third alternative is to accept the COS official line, in which case the question of who, "sent" Ron into the O.T.O to break it up, still remains unanswered. We must look back to the Explorers Club and the manuscript *Excalibur*. Many a secret group has been founded on the Master of the Lodge coming across co-incidentally significant information. Indeed the Golden Dawn group with its interconnection to the O.T.O. was formed on such a basis and was outlined previously and in *Alternative 4* thus it is difficult to decide exactly the origin of Excalibur and Dianetics, whether it was indeed Hubbard's genius or whether it was in fact research from some branch of the Rosicrucian's.

There is no doubt from correspondence with Crowley, that Jack Parsons used Ron as a Seer. A Seer acts to write down and channel information from the Akashic Record and we have already discussed the testimony of one Scientologist who described the way in which Ron wrote his Bulletins (Tech of Scientology). In fact Parsons was determined to try and create what Crowley had prophesied in his *Book of the Law,* some forty years earlier a 'Moonchild' - a magical child, "mightier than all the Kings of Earth", which some believed had arrived in the personage of Hitler and some thought would arrive in the personage of the Buddha of compassion, depending on your viewpoint. Records of the magical working kept in the *Book of Babylon* show that the group was heavily imbued with **Apocalyptic Psychology**, presumably on the basis of channelled information and some past apocalyptic event. This may certainly provide corroborative evidence for my conclusion, that the Inc. 2 incident is the event record of the morphogenetic bioplasma recording a time of a Magnetic Reversal or space boundary event. Some of the rituals worked by Ron and Parsons produced wind phenomena and of course the storm was a feature of the Inc. 2 incident, which Hubbard thought was an "implant". The wind phenomenon may however have just been a part of the hologram which when restimulated would reproduce in current time significant components of the entire hologram. If that hologram was a Magnetic Reversal with terrific storms in the original event, then one might expect a milder form or wind to occur in present time. A Scientologist was to remark on record to Miller, that Ron could "shift clouds around". Parsons was to write in his Journal: "The wind storm is very interesting, but that is not what I asked for". Unknowingly of course I perceive he had asked for it, by trying to pull down the Inc. 2 event. However they had no idea of the physics involved or Magnetic Reversals. I might add here, that if cloning, genetic engineering, nuclear tests and anti-matter matter experiments are allowed to continue, with the HAARP and GWEN programmes, then these are really just dramatizations of a past event or holograms. Thus by allowing them in present time, you merely by introducing past components of the entire hologram, precipitate the entire hologram or event to be pulled down with its consequences – species extinction and another cycle. Day 1 – plant the vine. Indeed the worldwide weather deterioration might be a sign of this mechanism, which is prophesied in Revelations according presumably to a cycle of events in the past. Thus earthquakes etc on an increased scale, might with other environmental factors such as global warming, may not merely depend on a hole in the ozone layer, but a total re-stimulation of events leading to a Magnetic Reversal, which Dr. Becker who was twice nominated for a Nobel Prize, states has already started.

I assume that the rituals followed hermetic invocations, although I have been unable for many years to locate the book *The Secret Rituals of the O.T.O.* Which would define more clearly what type of system was being used. I suspect that copies of this book have been purposefully traced and removed from general circulation. However from the scientific explanations in this book, I consider that morphic resonance may have been used to retrieve information from the Grid. The Phantom Leaf Effect, which I have previously described, illustrates the persistence of an energy field even though the material subject or leaf has gone. I suspect that when a person (dies) leaves the body that some imprint is left and this imprint may be absorbed into the general morphogenetic bioplasma. Thoughts also persist in the spiritual bioplasma and one suspects that ritual resonance (morphic resonance) is set up to exactly resonate according to the cosmic keyboard with the past energy 'shell' or thought processes of a *bygone entity*, which is just recorded *experience*. All ritual magic seeks INFORMATION ON THE PAST, since by definition, the morphogenetic and spiritual bioplasmas record event and thus the event must have occurred for it to be recorded. I suspect that this was the warning that Marthe Kuntzel gave to Hitler not: "to take the easy route". The hardest route I can assure you, is to follow the story for thousands of years recording YOUR **OWN** DATA AND EXPERIENCE and then try and remember that, through the natural process of regaining memory; in this manner you know what is true and what is not, because you know the limits of YOUR **OWN** JUDGEMENT AND OBSERVATIONS. I once told a colleague about the witness account of Golgotha and the subsequent events in Marseilles France. "I believe that", she said and being an aware and spiritual person, told me that she had twice lost her crucifix in France in that very region. The Spirit is aware of a great deal more, than the conscious mind is willing to confront. To channel information and then represent that as a higher source, is to fall prey to the trap that the majority of thought contained in the bioplasma is that of hermetical magicians or initiates who tried to use the Grid for control purposes; and therefore such change whether in the form of bodies and matter (morphogentic bioplasma) or Cabalistic and hermetic magical ritual (spiritual bioplasma) will contain a very lop-sided view. I once asked a Greek, whether they thought Jesus was crucified and in typical Greek fashion they replied: "I don't know, I wasn't there!" That in a nutshell is the whole moral of OBSERVATION and viewpoint. Quite simply if you were there you would KNOW and if you were not there, you might be tempted to channel and find out. The master no doubt will give you (his) viewpoint.

There are many indications, which I discussed both here and in *Alternative 4*, that Hitler was the puppet of an occult group of Masters who may well have been members of the thirteenth tribe or a joint 12 and 13 effort; precipitating a World War for the end of creating a Federal Europe on the Pollyanna smiles and promises of peace, in the form of Internationalism: thus completing yet another of the goals of *The Protocols of Zion*. There is the curious and recurring question of whether The Third Reich or Hitler were channelling information from the Grid, in order to plan Hitler's campaigns. Nostradamus had given some insight in his visions of presumably a past event or similar scenario in past history, when he predicted World War II. There was a stifling atmosphere at Berchtasgaden, with a feeling of insanity at worst or unreality at best that most people were glad to get away from after visiting. The alleged warning of Marthe Kuntzel, who was an associate of Crowley's and therefore had knowledge if not experience of the *Secret Rituals of the O.T.O.* stated: "My Fuhrer, don't touch Black magic! As yet both white and black are open to you. But once you've embarked on black magic it will dominate your destiny. It will hold you captive. Don't choose the quick and easy successes. There lies before you the power of a realm over pure spirits. Do not allow yourself to be led away from your true path by earthbound spirits, which will rob you of your creative power". [181]

Whilst the person who gave these words of advice was assumed to be Marthe Kuntzel, she denied it, and the person has never been identified. It is claimed that Hitler became Marthe Kuntzel's esoteric pupil and magical child ('Moonchild'), however it was only Crowley who supported this extra-ordinary story, after he read this report in *Hitler Speaks* by Rauschning. The Fuherer frequently either quoted or paraphrased Crowley's *Book of the Law*. However there was a mysterious woman at Berchtasgaden, whom I managed to track down in an old book by Pauline Kohler, *I was Hitler's Maid* (1940). The early date of the book, suggests that in the years prior to 1940 Hitler was being influenced no only by a magical secret Order, but perhaps the woman who lived at Berchtasgaden was a hermetical magician or seer, certainly Hitler it has been claimed was in contact with the Teutonic Gods of old. "The Quick and easy successes" may then have referred to channelled information. Pauline Kohler was to write of the mysterious woman who was not Eva Braun, or: "another woman friend...Fraulein X...All I can say is that she was the best influence Hitler has ever known..." The woman called Fraulein Kirstner (probably a pseudonym) was:

> "Another woman who has played and, for all I know, still does play, a tremendous part in Hitler's life. She is forty, plain, comfortably stout, and with no pretensions to any kind of dazzling charm. To me she will always be the greatest mystery in the Fuhrer's life. She was at Berchtasgaden when I arrived. She was there when I left. She has nothing to do with the running of the establishment. She usually takes her meals in the two rooms in which she lives. But she is a permanency at Berchatasgaden. She does what she likes, goes where she likes, says what she likes – unquestioned. I know she often spends several hours alone with Hitler. And that is about all I do know. But when the history of Hitler's years of power is fully told I am as certain as I am certain of anything that the world will learn more of Fraulein Kirstner. She is the mystery woman of Germany. I am convinced that her influence over Germany's destiny has been enormous. Do not ask me why. I can only say that we all thought that, and I am sure our belief will one day be justified".

When I read the accounts of Scientologists in the Sea Org in Miller's book, it beggared my belief, together with the accounts of those who were around at the time when Hubbard founded the Cine Org. where many people noted there were two sides to Ron's character, the worst side emerging during those periods. The problem with channelling is that as the mystery warning foretold in the case of Hitler: "it will hold you captive". There is no doubt that I could see in Miller's witness accounts of Hubbard, similarities to the worst side of Hitler, who ranted and raved on occasions and Pauline Kohler remarked in her book that:

> "An Austrian psychologist who happened to be a good Nazi and yet a good doctor visited Berchtasgaden. He could not help studying the Fuhrer as a patient. I know what his verdict was, for he told a Munich

doctor who afterwards attended me. These were his words. "The Fuhrer is a great   man, but that is not to say that he is sane. I admire his work for Germany, but I still have my beliefs as a doctor. If I were speaking of him as a patient I should say he was an egomaniac with a split personality. One side of him is brutal. The other is weak and sentimental. When this side predominates he needs the company of women. They flatter his ego, reassure him about his virility,   a n d bolster up his pride. That, I am certain, is the only reason the Fuhrer has affairs with women - not because he is really in love with them, but because he is so madly in love with himself".

Oddly enough Hubbard was to make the same diagnosis of Hitler, "genius but insane". Hubbard produced one of the most beneficial works ever written – *Dianetics – The Modern Science of Mental Health*. It is brilliant stuff and has great power to help humanity, but Hubbard did not understand the science involved to the extent of understanding how the Grid works and what part that has played in the history of mankind. He went for "the easy wins" I believe. I do not condemn Hubbard for it, simply because in this jigsaw piece, the information has been invaluable to the viewpoint I present here. I will not spend time condemning people who have the guts to get up and do something, even if that something is not perfect, when there are so many armchair critics. Scientology never worried me from the point of view of the knowledge or the technology, since I have a very strong viewpoint and can see the wood from the trees, however like all religions it is bound to become dogma and suffer from fixed viewpoints and there is probably not a religion on this planet that does not have the inevitable Hermes of mixed viewpoints i.e. matriarchal and patriarchal. The only thing that ever concerned me was whether the COS had a hidden agenda and the concern of Mayo Hubbard's auditor of Hubbard's goals. If his goal was money and power, it automatically means that there is a possibility the COS may have been sold out by Hubbard either in his lifetime or on his death. The third thing that concerns me now that I have continued in my research is whether Scientology is a secret group with the implication that there is an invisible higher Order.

Scientology (being distinct from *Dianetics*) took on the quality of an entire organisational structure that in its pyramidal form was reminiscent of the Illuminati power pyramid, capable of becoming a major religious and political force, since the technology contained virtually a self-sufficient system of organisation and ideology. I have already referred to the connection of Crowley to Carl Gemer the head of the O.T.O in New York and the Illuminati as we have seen, in the case of the Illuminatus Pope, had headquarters in New York. It would be impossible to say whether the two groups were linked at a very high level. Scientology as I have also noted, in its apparent dual and almost hermetic foundation of a matriarchal and patriarchal base, could have gone one of two ways, since it had the power to fight a One World Order, or become one. There is no doubt that the Scientologists who joined in the 60's and 70's did so against a backdrop of the student revolts, where astoundingly the courageous students in France, virtually re-enacted the French Revolution, this time without Masonic interference and demanding a People's Revolution. As millions of French workers supported the students, De Gaulle was shaken. Ban the bomb marches in London, were all to add to the feeling that the people could take charge of their own destiny and wrestle it, from the forces that had always controlled them - The One World Order. There was a hope that man could rise from the ashes and carve a better world with justice, quality of life both material and spiritual and education for all. Scientology presented an ideology of freedom that mirrored the spirit of the times and many people thought no doubt as I once did, that at last here was the cavalry, the badly needed troops, who would fight fearlessly on the front battle lines for a better world, for truth, peace and justice.

Many believed and wanted to believe, that Hubbard was the coming man, who would lead them out of the cesspit that the One World Order had created. I will cover the battle of Scientology shortly, but I am prepared to give Hubbard the benefit of the doubt. Perhaps Hubbard did try to do something, but his personality and the oak royal overtook the holly and holy one, as the disillusioned Mayo was to find out, when he realised that Hubbard's obsession was money and power, with motives that did not mirror his publicly stated goals. There is the possibility that Hubbard stole the 'apples' from the O.T.O and the ensuing battle against Scientology was an attempt to recover them. And some battle it was! Who can say whether such a battle was designed to create a loyal and dedicated following ("you and I against the world kid!") or whether that battle was a battle of 12 versus 13? However one knows that if the World Order had wanted to eliminate Hubbard it could and would have done so. Perhaps Hubbard did manage to stave of both groups by giving the subject of Scientology Church status thus giving it rights and taking to the high seas with his loyal and dedicated crew who formed the Sea Org, in a stroke of pure genius, since the ship was out of jurisdiction of all countries and the FBI. If Hubbard survived, there is the undeniable doubt that Hubbard may have had connections with Freemasonry and may have been 13 th tribe, trying to instigate a world religion in opposition to Christianity and the 12 tribes. The question then becomes, if it was an attempt to fight the World Order, then why did Scientology not seek to inform the public of this, utilising their vast wealth? I am afraid, that there are many unanswered questions here and things that simply do not tie up. It might be argued as is the case believed by Phoenix, that the Church was taken over after Hubbard's death and that may be the case, since Hubbard's auditor Mayo reported to Miller that Hubbard had requested that he take charge of the technology and keep it "pure". There was certainly no need for the culling that occurred under Miscavige, unless there was an agenda there. There is no doubt that the early Scientologists, many of whom were ousted in Miscavige's shake-up of the COS, would have taken Scientology onto the front battle-lines of Freedom for Man, despite Ron's serious limitations. I believe it was a crossroads for Scientology – the elixir or the cup, matriarchal or patriarchal, freedom or power and wealth; there was always that choice of roads, after the Religious Revolution in Crete. *The Grail legends* that I covered in *The Battle of The Trees* held the memorable line: "WHOM DO YOU SERVE?" If you serve the elixir and the message with the knowledge, then it is a duty that will take you to the black abyss and the edge of human experience.

Urquhart a Scot and Scientologist who had been studying Music at Trinity College in London, before being introduced to Scientology, remarked on the changes in Scientology when "ethics" came in 1965. "Conditions", were an essential part of the new "ethics technology", "devised by Hubbard in the mid sixties, effectively as a form of social control. It was his first, tentative step towards the creation of a society within Scientology, which would ultimately resemble the totalitarian state envisaged by George Orwell, in his novel 1984.Anyone thought to be disloyal, or slacking, or breaking the rules of Scientology, was reported to an ethics officer and assigned a 'condition', according to the gravity of the offence...The worst that could happen was to be declared an SP (suppressive person), who became 'fair game', to be pursued, sued and harassed at every opportunity". Cyril Vosper who worked on staff at Saint Hill, the HQ in East Grinstead U.K. remembered: "What happened with the development of ethics was that zeal expanded at the expense of tolerance and sanity". There again lies the Greek tragedy, in so far as one perceives that unmistakable Illuminatus hand co-incidental or not. Once again too I am reminded of the *Protocols of Zion*:

> "Our programme will induce a third part of the populace to watch the remainder from a pure sense of duty and from the principle of voluntary government service. Then it will not be considered dishonourable to be a spy; on the contrary, it will be regarded as praiseworthy" (*Protocols p.65*)

> "We will make merciless use of executions with regard to all who may take up arms against the establishment of our power" (*Protocols p.50*)

> "We must take no account of the numerous victims who will have to be sacrificed in order to obtain future prosperity" (*Protocols p. 51*)

> "Soon we will start organizing great monopolies - reservoirs of colossal wealth" (*p.22*)

I am also reminded of another Protocol: "Most people who enter secret societies are adventurers, who want somehow to make their way in life, and who are not seriously minded. With such people it will be easy for us to pursue our object, and we will make them set our machinery in motion" (*p.52*). Doreen Smith a 'messenger' for Hubbard, the elite core of mainly females (apart from Miscavige), who hung on Ron's every word, once asked Ron why he chose girls as messengers, to which he replied, that Hitler was a madman, but never-the-less a genius in his own right and the nazi youth was one of the smartest ideas he ever had. With the young people you had a blank slate and you could write anything you wanted on it and it would be your writing. China incorporated much the same idea in its mass indoctrination of the young. In fact whilst I was in Scientology I was told that you did not need to read anything but Scientology, since it was all right there - a somewhat blinkered view I thought, as I continued with my own viewpoints regardless. The same parrot talk came out of Theosophists as well, as they spouted great tracks of incomprehensible Steiner philosophy that jarred on my scientific mind. What exactly is it in these groups that leads to uniformity, hive, mechanistic control, which is a complete about turn on stated goals of freedom? The Janus head which points two ways again, the elixir of freedom and the cup of power and control. In fact even the bulletins of Hubbard were contradictory, one moment he would talk about individuality and the next, was the group survival and I suspect that which way a group goes, is dependent on who runs the pyramidal apex and their goals and spiritual experience.

Hubbard's story to 'Forrie' Ackerman on the manner in which he "turned the thing up" - *Excalibur* may be true, or it may have come after some contact with a group, via the Explorers Club, who is to say since there are so many discrepancies in the life of Ron. Ackerman claimed that Ron had told him of an incident when he had experienced what appears to be a NDE (Near Death Experience):

> "Basically what he told me was that after he died he rose in spirit form and looked back on the body he had formerly inhabited; over yonder he saw a fantastic gate, elaborately carved like something you'd see in Baghdad or ancient China. As he wafted towards it, the gate opened and just beyond he could see a kind of intellectual smorgasbord on which was outlined everything that had   ever puzzled the mind of man: All the questions that had concerned philosophers through the ages - when did the world begin? was there a God? whither goest we? were there answered. all this information came flooding into him and while he was absorbing it, there was a sort of flustering in the air and he felt something like an umbilical cord, pulling him back. He was

saying "No, No, not yet!" but he realized he had re-entered his body. He opened his eyes and found a nurse standing over him looking very concerned, just as a surgeon walked into the room, Ron said, "I was dead, wasn't I?" The surgeon shot a venomous look at the nurse as if to say, "What have you been telling this guy?" But Ron said, "No, No, I know I was dead".

According to Ackerman, after this Ron said he jumped off the operating table, got two reams of paper and a gallon of scalding black coffee and for the next 48 hours, at a blinding rate, he wrote a work called *Excalibur,* or *The Dark Sword.*[182] The date for *Excalibur* was 1938, which as we have seen co-incided with the date that Hubbard claimed he had worked on *Dianetics* in its origins. The manuscript must have contained psychology since Ackaman said: ". When he left the Navy he shopped it around publishers in New York, but was constantly turned down. He was told it was too radical, too much of a quantum leap; If it had been a variation of Freud or Jung or Adler, a bit of an improvement here and there, it would have been acceptable, but it was just too far ahead of everything else..." Oddly when Ackerman acting as agent, did find Ron a proposed publisher who was interested in reading the work, Ron strangely backed off, telling Ackerman it was in a bank vault and it was going to stay there. Later Ron was to joke with Scientologists saying he would have to write *Excalibur* one day, thus denying its existence.

If the account Ron gave to Ackerman is true, then it sounds like a NDE (Near Death Experience), which doctors have recently confirmed is clinical death, where the heart stops beating. I went through such an experience and whilst I returned quickly and never experienced any access to knowledge, Ron may have either accessed his own past knowledge, or the Grid had downloaded information into his memory banks. I belong to IANDS (International Association for Near Death Experiences) and have not come across anyone who had a similar experience to Ron. Thus I am afraid there are a lot of discrepancies here on the subject of *Excalibur*, together with how Ron obtained his: "experience and understanding" of magic, before entering the O.T.O and the origins of *Dianetics*, let alone *who*? exactly sent him into Aleister Crowley's group. What is certain is that Ron could have laid himself open to secret groups, simply because of his obsession with money and power. Sam Meruin who edited the *Thrilling* group of magazines, noted in 1946 that Ron: "was anxious to hit big money - he used to say he thought the best way to do it would be to start a cult". In 1947 Hubbard wrote *The End is not Yet* about a young nuclear Physicist's attempts to prevent the world being taken over by constructing a new philosophical system. Was this Ron? or Ron as part of a secret group that hoped to fight the one world Order? Was this reason for the numerous discrepancies and the need for secrecy? Ron may have had a desire to save the world, but he certainly hoped to gain riches and accolades from his efforts. Sam Moskowitz the writer recalled Hubbard in 1949, stating:"writing for a penny a word is ridiculous. If a man really wanted to make a million dollars, the best way to dot it, would be to start his own religion". Later Richard de Mille a Scientologist and close associate of Hubbard's would remark:" what I didn't understand about him at the time, was lack of personal attachment. He thought people were there to be used, to serve the user, and didn't have any importance in their own right". A thought that would describe my experience and at base has been and still is the mind of The World Order.

If there was no Masonic thirteenth tribe background to Hubbard, then why build a castle for the HQ of Scientology at East Grinstead in Britain? A particularly hermetic knight, thirteenth tribe, middle Ages architectural symbol, which appears in the *Grail Romances* covered in *The Battle of The Trees:* Hubbard as Grail knight, bringing forth the underground stream and hidden science of the Holy Grail, fighting off those who would seek to bury it? Or Hubbard *using* the Grail message, whilst finding greater glory in the Grail cup, the Rex Mundi of power and riches that was always one half of the Holy Grail and which man has never failed to use. De Mille later would reminisce: "when I first saw him (Ron) at the meeting at the Shrine Auditorium I was very impressed. I thought he was great man, who had made a great discovery and whatever his shortcomings they must be discounted, because he had the answer". It is odd that De Mille should have said: "People present new ideas and there are always a certain number of people who believe them. Lenin was the Hubbard of 1917. Hubbard was the Madame Blavatsky of 1950", odd because secret groups and the One World Order backed both Lenin and Blavatsky. In 1960 Hubbard issued an HCO (Hubbard Communications Office) Bulletin covering the newly formed 'Department of Government Affairs', made necessary Hubbard explained because of the amount of time senior Scientology executives were having to devote to governmental affairs, as governments around the world, disintegrated under threat of atomic war and communism. The goal of the department was "to bring government and hostile philosophies or societies into a state of complete compliance with the goals of Scientology". Well I must reflect here on the question – What are those goals? And further reflect on the question of the Grail Legends 'Who do you serve?' (Elixir or cup?)

Miller's book does not cover the serious attacks that the COS underwent throughout a period of 25 years. Miller would like to place Ron's "paranoid behaviour" down to a personality disorder, and there is no doubt that during his time as Commander of the Sea Org and his time as head of the Cine Org that his personality bordered, from Miller's witness accounts, on the oppressive side to say the least. Even a saint can crack under immense pressure however and as I was not there at the time, I can't comment further. Omar V. Garrison an award-winning journalist who was completely independent of the COS wrote in *Playing Dirty -The Secret* War *Against Beliefs* that:

> "After analysing hundreds of governmental documents relating to the Scientology case. Rodney Austin, an expert on Constitutional and Administrative law affirmed unequivocally that the U.S. Justice Department had 'initiated an all agency effort to malign, oppress, criminally prosecute and ultimately end the practise of Scientology'".

Hubbard had produced a 'double whammy', in so far as *Re-incarnation* was allied to a *science of the mind - Dianetics*, such a combination was bound to incite attacks from The Syndicate in the loss of revenue on psychotropic drugs: and as I have pointed out in the case of Tibet, there has been a secret ongoing "policy" and war against Re-incarnation as a belief system for the masses, since at least 1950 if not c. 1 400 B.C. Further that "policy" was referred to obliquely in the media, at the time of the Tibetan incident in London (2 000). The World Order has continually suppressed the belief in Re-incarnation and the battle for the mind has also been ongoing since the Religious Revolution in Crete, which was also evident in the events of Golgotha. Garrison confirmed Austin's conclusion after examining the role of such vested interests as the AMA (American Medical Association), World Federation of Mental Health, Better Business Bureau and other organisations connected to The Syndicate by a thousand and one strings. Rodney Austin went on to say:

> "Given the history of government misconduct so far documented, it may be inferred that the crucial evidence relevant to the Church's allegations of bad faith, selectivity, illegal searches and seizures, entrapment, and provocation has yet to be revealed".

The battle that the COS withstood is indeed astounding. The machinations against the COS did not get into top speed until in 1958, eight years after the publication of *Dianetics*, when the U.S. Department of Justice took over its co-ordination. Late that year, Assistant U.S. Attorney Edward Troxell met in his office with Capt. Ernest Jefferson of the D.C. Police Department's Narcotics and Vice Squad, together with representatives from the Postal Department, the FDA (Federal Drug Administration) U.S. Army Intelligence and others. The attendees at the preliminary coven drafted a master plan for the illegal monitoring, entrapment and ultimate destruction of the COS. The involvement of the Army alone in such a scheme was in violation of the Posse comitatus Act (18 U.S.C. 91385). Undoubtedly the social reform activities of the COS and particularly its vociferous stand against the Therapeutic State of no cure (for the mind and psychosomatic illness), which threatened psychotropic drug profits to The Syndicate sent ripples through the offices of the Pharmaceutical giants apart from the Psychiatric Association, with whom Scientology had been engaged in a running battle with for many years. I have personally experienced the forces that have come into play from The Syndicate in the field of cancer and since the World Order plan is *a battle for man's mind*, the Scientologists would have taken the full force of the Syndicate's ruthless oppression of any organisation or individual who threatens their monopoly over the mind and body.

One cannot dismiss that a belief in Re-incarnation would also bring suppression in the secret war against beliefs. Glenn Hoddle the England football manager expressed a belief in Karma (Re-incarnation) in 1999 and was ousted from his job by the vociferous re-action of the British press, despite that insignificant piece of paper, entitled *The Declaration of Human Rights* and the right to one's own belief, even though Great Britain is a signatory of the Declaration which is now incorporated into law. Significantly the Murdoch press played a pivotal role in the 'witch-hunt' utilising the down market newspaper *The Sun* read by the majority of football fans I would suspect, to shout "Go!" and go Hoddle did. Evidently what passes in China under Communist rule supported by Murdoch, also applies to Great Britain and neither can one say that the Government does not hold a "policy" on this, given the Tibetan demonstration mentioned before. The Metropolitan Police in the U.K. admitted on May 3rd 2000, that officers broke the law during demonstrations against visiting Chinese president Jiang Zemin. Scotland Yard agreed that some officers went too far in their policing of human rights protesters in The Mall in October 1999. Whilst an internal review rejected accusations that the police were heavy-handed during the President's five-day state visit, it took a High Court action by the *Free Tibet Campaign*, to achieve justice. In a very carefully worded additional declaration, the Metropolitan force also said: "It would be unlawful to position police vans in front of protestors if the reason for doing so was to suppress free speech". The fact that the visit was televised and would be shown in China, I suppose had nothing to do with it. This reflected the police's insistence that vans parked out-side Buckingham Palace and the Chinese Embassy were not to 'mask' demonstrators but to prevent public disorder. They must think we are all blind on diktat! The *Free Tibet Campaign* rejected suggestions that only individual officers were at fault and there was no *direction from above*. As Campaign solicitor Julie Holden stated: "It seems surprising that every single officer managed to get it wrong. Someone must have told them what to do". Certainly no doubt Murdoch's television network back in Hong Kong would have found viewers believing that the visit was supported by the British, as a sea of red Chinese flags was permitted, whilst Tibetan flags and banners were wrestled from demonstrators: and Murdoch attended meetings with the President and Tony Blair - quite why is any body's guess since he is Australian! Whilst the Government was accused of putting trade links with China before human rights, this cannot account for the attacks on the group in China - The Felung Gong, who hold a belief in Re-incarnation.

Within Whitehall, it was accepted that the Foreign Office exerted discreet pressure on the police and former Metropolitan Police Federation chairman Mike Bennett said that he believed instructions to block anti-Chinese demonstrations did come from the Government, which confirms the report in *The Daily Telegraph* that referred to "Government policy". Tory foreign affairs spokesman Francis Maude said: "The blame for the handling of the Chinese state visit lies firmly with the Government". There is no reason to doubt that Scientology may have over the years fought a religious battle on the subject of beliefs and whilst the Dalai Lama of Tibet has sought peaceful solutions to the invasion of Tibet by the Chinese in 1950, Hubbard who produced *Dianetics* in the same year, was to take on the whole of the American Government in a battle of some proportions. Indeed if beliefs and threat to the Syndicate were the entire truth here, one would have been completely overjoyed to see at least one group on this Earth with the courage and guts to stand up to the World Order. The ferocity of attacks on Scientology outran any rational cause or purpose and it was my opinion that some deeper battle was being waged, which was not visible – a hidden agenda. I do not say that the official line of the COS and its claim of an all out war with psychiatry is not correct, but this may not be the entire truth or the entire case and battle of Scientology. However it is fairly obvious in the hostile press that Scientology has received, that a pro-Jewish press has incited public opinion as Henry Clay noted:

> "The arts of power and its minions are the same in all countries and in all ages. It marks its victim, denounces it, and excites the public odium and the public hatred to conceal its abuses and encroachments".

The Citizens Commission for Human Rights (CCHR), for the COS continued its attacks on primitive and brutal psychiatric practises of lobotomy, electro-convulsive therapy and abuses by Psychiatry, such as the horror of Pain-Drug-Hypnosis experimentation under the veil of secret intelligence research in Canada. This research had culminated in the MK-Ultra programme of Mind Control in America, which Cathy O'Brien allegedly fell victim to. The attacks on Scientology ostensibly increased in proportion to the pressure that CCHR brought to bear. There is no doubt, that Scientology was instrumental in uncovering and drawing public awareness to psychiatric abuses and violations of Human Rights in the 70's and 80's and where CCHR's continued attacks on dangerous psychotropic drugs particularly Prozac, was to initiate a ferocious attack by *Time* Magazine in the *April 29 1991* edition. The CCHR subsequently took a full-page advertisement in *USA Today (June 15 1991)* entitled *'Who Controls what gets Printed in Time Magazine'*. The article demonstrated the Syndicate web behind the attack and *Time* subservient to its Syndicate big business advertisers had placed the dagger.

Eli Lilly the pharmaceutical giant and maker of Prozac (and earlier heroin and LSD) had become embroiled in litigation with the COS after they exposed the dangers of Prozac, however not before the company lost 5 billion dollars in stock value. Eli Lilly was just one of the clients of WPP Conglomerate headed at the time by Martin Sorrell. WPP also owned J. Walter Thompson Advertising Company, which as a subsidiary placed advertising to Eli Lilly. Another subsidiary of the WPP conglomerate was Hill and Knowlton, who were forced under pressure from Martin Sorrel and the WPP Conglomerate to drop the Scientology account. WPP controlled some 18 billion in advertising annually for many big drug companies such as Eli Lilly, Ciba Geigy, Lederle Labs, Merk Sharp and Dohme, Sandoz Pharmaceuticals, Burroughs Wellcome Co., Smith Kline Beecham, GD Searle and Co., apart from media accounts with Time Warner Inc., Time Life Books and others. WPP could not afford to ignore the demands of the Drug Syndicate in order to retain their monopoly over 'healing'. The One World Order has become a monopoly over the Platonic Maxim: "Before you can heal a man's **body**, you must cure his **mind** and before that his **soul**". Advertising in placing the dagger in Scientology was once again to sell its soul, for pot of gold -advertising accounts. A similar position occurs in cancer, which I have noted in *Appendix 1*.

I have previously referred to the centralised attacks on Scientology that parallel *The Free Tibet Campaign,* in so far as there was a centralised direction allegedly from government, from which the suppression came. In the case of Scientology the attacks appeared to emanate from Washington D.C. I have already indicated that the American One Dollar bill shows both a religious aim on the right hand side of the reverse of the note, with the political aim on the left. The political aim is clearly Illuminatus or power pyramidal World Order and Masonic, whilst the right hand side with the religious aim demonstrated through its archetypal symbology refers to the Rosicrucian's. The Rosicrucian's I maintain hold a long descendency, which is the history of the 13 tribe. Further I have already outlined the connection between Druids, Rosicrucians and the World Order of the Rose. Hubbard, who would have presented the most unlikely poet, once produced a poem about a rose oddly enough as a Bulletin! There is a precedent for Hubbard's *Chart of Human Evaluation* in the Pythagorean tonic scale which I produced in *Alternative 4*, albeit in rudimentary form; also an expanded form may occur in the Cosmic Keyboard and specific charts which give the various resonant vibrations for various bacteria and viruses. The latter charts undoubtedly could be used to beam resonant wavelengths of a virus or bacterium at an individual or population in secret warfare. Why then would Washington D.C. exert an all out attack on Scientology? Did Hubbard take significant material from the O.T.O. that was connected to the Rosicrucian's in the personage of Aleister Crowley who appears to have been a Rose-Croix Mason? Would this account for a terrific battle to end the practise of

Scientology, which far outweighed any sense of rationality? I think you can probably resolve these mysteries if one assumes that a battle has waged between 12 and 13 and the curious thing today, is that despite the battle to close Scientology, the COS prospers and grows in America! And whilst the voice of dissent is still marginally there, to all intense and purposes Scientology has on the face of it won the battle. The same position appears to be the case in the U.K and the Britain is the one country in Europe that has held back from full integration into the European legislature and economy, whilst retaining a "special relationship" with America. The question becomes - why have the attacks scaled down on the Church? Was it always envisioned at a very high level, that Scientology was to become the Universal Religion? Or was it that whilst Hubbard was alive the COS could not be taken over, but after his death the Corporate shake up, was really in effect a take-over? Or is it more what presumably would be the COS line that a policy of litigation has frightened off any attacks? The latter is unlikely since the World Order has colossal wealth and if they wanted to get rid of Scientology they would have done so. All these questions can and must be answered by the COS hierarchy to find the truth here. Neither can one easily dismiss that Jack Parsons, the one person that could throw further light on the matter, died conveniently in a mysterious explosion in 1952, apparently by dropping a bottle of nitro glycerine on the floor, despite the fact that he was an enormously experienced rocket scientist, which has led to speculation that he was murdered. I have already drawn the connection between Crowley, Nazi sympathies and Rosicrucian's and thus if a plan of a Universal Religion emitted from this group, dating back to the Druids and the goal of a Theocracy, then Hubbard's association with the O.T.O cannot easily be dismissed in the terms that the COS provided, limply explaining that Hubbard sought to break up black magic in America.

COS International hit back against *Time* Magazine in *USA Today* (*29th May 1991*), taking out a full page advertisement as part of a prolonged campaign to destroy *Time* magazine, according to policy surrounding those who attack Scientology as "fair game", in response to *Time* magazine's article (*May 6th 1991 - 'Scientology -The Cult of Greed'*). Predictably the *Time* article hit at *Dianetics*, which was I agree totally uncalled for, since this is a very workable science of the mind. The attack was evidently a Syndicate propaganda job, but curiously Scientology chose to hit out against *Time* magazine's support for Hitler in 1936 when the magazine had hailed Hitler as the "Messiah" of the Germans - curious because Ron himself became associated with the O.T.O with its Nazi sympathies at around the same time. Ron was also to refer to Hitler as a "genius but insane". Scientology's campaign ran in *USA Today* on *May 3o th* hitting out at *Time* support for Mussolini; *May 31st* hitting out at *Time* support of LSD; *June 1* hitting out against Prozac;
June 4th hitting out at *Time* magazine's inability to tell the truth; *June 5th* once

again attacking Eli Lilly and Prozac; *June 6th* attacking Eli Lilly and its connection to Heroin and LSD; *June 7th* attacking Eli Lilly and the sale of dangerous drugs; *June 8th* attacking Eli Lilly and the production of the drug Dolophine based on a formula associated with Zyklon B gas used in the concentration camps of Adolf Hitler; *June11th* attacking *Time* for propaganda and lies with an inability to state the truth; *June 12th* attacked Eli Lilly for pleading guilty to 10 charges of concealing evidence from the F.D.A; *June 13th* Eli Lilly once again attacked for dangerous medicines; *June 14th* attacked Eli Lilly and the FDA complicity in the promotion of Prozac. Formidable stuff! The interesting point to me however, was the attack on Nazi Germany and *Time* magazine's support of Hitler in 1936, since Hitler was evidently tutored by some branch of the 13 th tribe. As you can see the old game of guessing a group's god (12 or 13) was not an easy matter. Does this mean, if Scientology was controlled by a group, it was initially the 13 th tribe, but was then taken over by the 12 tribes?

Hubbard whilst on the run from the American Government's all out attack, was depicted as paranoid when he spoke of the enemy forces ranged against Scientology and elaborated on the "International Conspiracy", which he not only levelled at the Communists (World Order), but also curiously he named the "*Tenyaka Memorial*" as a mysterious agency whom Hubbard claimed co-ordinated the attacks on Scientology. In a letter dated 2nd November 1969 and headed *'Covert Operations'* he claimed that he and Mary Sue his wife, were under attack from "members of the World Federation of Mental Health" who were working "for British and US Intelligence agencies". Interestingly Hubbard claimed: "These bastards who are in charge of security in these Western Countries, ought to be simply electric shocked to death. I'm not kidding. Because these same guys ... have meetings with the Russians every year". This co-operation of East and West in the One World Order plan, even at the time of the so-called Cold War, was something I discussed in *Alternative 4*. At some high level of the secret societies there was always co-operation between East and West, which depended on the World Order Communistic plan. However, if the communistic 12 tribes worked in unison with the 13 th tribe at the top, whilst maintaining pretence of separation in the lower levels, this would supply an explanation. Later, Ron decided that the Tenyaka Memorial was run by a *Nazi underground movement*, intent on world domination (*The Guardian 12th Feb. 1980*). Hubbard was to go on to accuse his alleged second wife, Betty (Sara Northrup) who was Jack Parson's girlfriend and a member of the O.T.O. as a Nazi spy, despite that the COS must have referred to Betty, when they declared in 1969 that Hubbard had rescued a girl from the black magic group. If the O.T.O had Nazi sympathies through its founder Aleister Crowley who was not only evidently a Rosicrucian but also a member of the Rose-Croix, then clearly Hubbard did not support them. If the Nazi movement was related to the thirteenth tribe ideology or indeed represented the old goal of a thirteenth tribe – a Theocracy, where the Black Order would become the initiated priesthood, where did this leave Hubbard? One gets the feeling that Hubbard may have been set up by the thirteenth tribe and the 12 tribes in that highest and most secret level, that plays a dualistic game in the lower levels. Perhaps Hubbard believed he was working for the goals of a Rosicrucian Order, who were merely interested in healing the world and furthering the hidden science.

Hubbard did co-incidentally or not, utilise symbols that had some hermetic background and such background is a feature of the 13 th tribe. Thus what was Hubbard really doing in the O.T.O? Was Hubbard really a Communist KGB agent, as Nibs his son by his first wife Polly was to claim in the *June 1983* issue of *Penthouse* magazine? Nibs had already fallen out with Hubbard, unable to support his wife and Hubbard's grandchildren, on the lowly wages of Scientology and was to break away from his father and the Church. Nibs may have served an ulterior motive of revenge or bitterness at his father in his subsequent interviews, but it is not easy to dismiss his claims, particularly since his mother Polly seemed a decent if not long suffering wife. Hubbard did send a letter to the FBI earlier in his career, claiming after he had written *Dianetics*, that the Russians had claimed an interest in his work. Thus Hubbard could have worked for the Russians, or he could have used the FBI to gain contact with the equivalent group in the west. Further there was the curious statement made by the COS that Ron had been "sent into" the O.T.O to break it up, with the question who exactly sent him not answered. Nibs in an interview with the *Santa Rosa News Herald* in *July 1982* claimed that his mother Polly had: "told me about him trying out all kinds of various incantations, drugs and hypnosis". The mention of "incantations" definitely implies channelling and since there is no reason for Nibs to have put this together, it seems that the statement has a ring of truth about it and as I suspect Hubbard did channel information deduced from the account of the Scientologist who compared his Bulletins to automatic writing. Further, Parson's the head of Agape Lodge (O.T.O) had confirmed in a letter to Crowley that Ron had acted as a seer, thus utilising channelling. Parsons had also noted that Ron already had a great deal of understanding about magic, when he first entered the lodge. How he came by such knowledge is not known, but could have come from the Russians as Nibs claimed, or equally could have come from a thirteenth tribe hermetic group, the Rosicrucian's who held the hidden science. The young man I met at the book conference who stated his grandfather was a Freemason and knew Hubbard seems to indicate that Hubbard may have had contact with a group in the U.K The alternatives run thick and fast, Hubbard may have been duped into believing that he was setting up a world religion to help humanity, whilst in reality the cohesion of the two groups of 12 and 13 were actually working in unison to create a World Order religion. Hubbard went straight to **Ireland**, when his son Quentin committed suicide. Did

Hubbard go back to *source*, to find out if Quentin had been murdered? The inference would be that Hubbard's source was in Ireland and 13 th tribe; co-incidently where Bill Clinton ex President of the United States has treturned to, after unprecedented intervention in the Irish problems during his presidency – perhaps reflecting his "special relationship" with Britain.

Why in fact did Hubbard set up his HQ at East Grinstead, a stronghold of the Theosophists and Rudolf Steiner's group? (although, from the author's experience evidently no link is recognised between the two). I have already covered Steiner's connection to the World Order and the Rosicrucians and again Steiner's occult science has some smattering of the hidden science, particularly his recognition of the Akashic Record. Further the young man whose grandfather was a Freemason and who knew Hubbard attended the Steiner school in Forest Row a short distance from the COS castle at East Grinstead. From my own horrid experience of Steiner's group it had that dualistic dichotomy that is so recognisable of World Order Theocracy i.e. communistic method of thinking, run by far right elitism thinking incorporating Grid animal mechanistic behaviour. I have previously discussed that Steiner developed occult science, which holds a belief in Re-incarnation and Steiner himself was to describe the product of occult training, which I feel should be re-stated here:

> "This is the change which the occult student observes coming over himself - there is no longer a connection between a thought and a feeling or a feeling and a volition, except when he creates the connection himself. No impulse drives him from thought to action if he does not voluntarily harbour it. He can now stand completely without feeling before an object, which before his training, would have filled him with glowing love or violent hatred; he can likewise remain actionless before a thought which heretofore would have spurred him to action as if by itself..."

Whilst I have seen somewhat similar training in Scientology under TR's (Scientology 'speak' for *Communication Training Routines*) the object is to train a person not to react in any circumstances without his own volition or will. Thus one might perceive when faced with anger, that it would be a very good thing, not to react and thus escalate the problem. Once again, the knowledge can be used in one of two ways, it can leave you impassive to a situation that requires one to feel one's conscience and react to the needs of another: or it can be used to avoid primitive reactive mind mechanisms, which cause one to react irrationally. Communism always created this impassive response to human suffering, which allows cruelty and the cruelty to animals is very marked, it is a form of dissociation and is patriarchal or Masters thought. An animal feels no conscience as it attacks and devours another as the predator that seeks survival for self: it feels no conscience at leaving the sick or attacking the weakest member of the group. However even in my own experience (of both Scientology and Theosophy) such training was used to impassively stand and watch the horror of a situation created by unethical actions, without so much as a blink of the arrogant eyelid or apparently any conscience on caving in another's soul. In both cases, there was *no recognition* of the upset caused, or the question of *right and wrong* and in both cases there was that Grid survival mechanism of self and group before all else. This is my own personal experience and thus I can state it with some certainty and knowingness.

Weishaupt the founder of the Illuminati and Communistic Organisational Power Pyramid said: "I cannot use men as I find them; I must form them". The problem with all philosophies, which derive from occult sources (hidden), is that they have Semitic (patriarchal) origins and the philosophy bears the unmistakable imprint– Communistic (the method of control of the masses) or elitist (those who control). Further it has stolen the elixir and cup of the Grail (matriarchal) with just enough truth to render it spiritual; thus the philosophy and how it is *weighted* will determine the outcome. Often the both are combined, which gives that schizoid result that was noted in Hitler's personality, simply because one cannot be elitist (oak) and holly or holy one: one suspects that communism removed religion for that purpose. In terms of historical groups, it can only be compared to the Jewish Communistic Essenes and the elitist 13 the tribe Druids with their goal of a Theocracy with themselves as the elitist priesthood, who in all probability formed the parent group and masters of the Essenes in the higher degrees. The Essenes were communistic in the lower degrees, denouncing all their wealth and in effect supporting the elitist 'cuckoo' at the top. If the top echelon has this schizoid nature of holly and oak, so prevalent in the hermetic god which sought unsuccessfully to combine the two in Crete 1 400 B.C in a World Order religion, then any religion which contains this duality or Janus head that can go two ways, will retain that schizoid nature in its writings, action and thought. Communism since it concentrates on survival of self and group is an automatic 'key in' or restimulator to the Grid, which promotes thinking and behaviour that is majority survival for the phylogenetic group (body line). Kill or be killed, cheat and steal to increase one's own survival at the cost to another etc. And the full gamut of what passes for civilization on Earth. The elitist justification for such action at the top is an arrogant superiority of correctness, with the denial that in the history of evolution, it is the individual and not the group who has created change. I will come back to this point later but here it is sufficient to point out that within all groups there is a choice of which way the philosophy can go, but such choice is only evident, where there is not a hidden agenda built into the philosophy in the form of rules and regulations that act as methods of social control. Any group that has been set up by the World Order will always exhibit the dualistic character and if it is a world religion such as

Christianity became, then written into the scriptures will be very definite social control mechanisms, such as 'follow this data to the letter', 'don't ever interpret it', 'don't look elsewhere', 'this is the only truth you will ever need' 'disconnect from anyone who has a different viewpoint' etc. Zealots who seek to impress that control on others, means that diversity and change, including viewpoint of the individual, the very propelling factors for evolution and in this case evolution of the spirit, are sacrificed to the majority group view where the result will be stagnation. The Grid however is not interested in the individual but only the *majority* survival. Thus any communistic group will fight new thought, the individual and any change, simply because they are subject to Grid survival mechanisms and thought. The bourgeoisie "that bag of fear filled with prejudice" as Victor Hugo called them, the middle classes will also fight any change, simply because they have a vested interest in a stagnant pattern, which pays the bills and funds their lifestyle. It was always the man at the bottom that never resisted change, since he had the least to loose. Indeed the animal attack of the pack can be quite ferocious as the cover of The Second Millennium Working Report into Cancer shows! We should embrace change and the new thought and ideas together with discussion, simply because it challenges the Grid and the World Order.

Hubbard was to note with regard to *Dianetics* that it could be used either way to free or control. There is always that crossroads for occult knowledge and which path is taken, which depends on the nature of the person or group at the top of the Power Pyramidal apex. Thus Hubbard could have been working for the Communistic One World Order, as he stated to the FBI, he had been approached by the Russians; equally Hubbard could have been thirteenth tribe, in the form of the Rosicrucian's or Rose-Croix Mason. Equally I suppose there is that third alternative, that Hubbard was a genius, thought it all up by himself and outran both groups, the entire American government, the FBI, the Nazi's, the pharmaceutical Syndicate and the psychiatrists as no doubt the COS will claim. To avoid having the Scientologists initiate "fair game" (Grid attack) policy then I must say here, that of course I believe their version! A Power Pyramid as an organisational structure with one or a few people at the top, which means that it can be very easily taken over in any future corporate shuffle. Hubbard in using this form of management for the Church, was either very naive, or his intention was not a democracy, where people vote on leadership. Further one should *at least* have three people at the top of an organisation for decision-making and **always** employ procedures where leadership can be challenged in the event of wrongdoing or in a vote of a no-confidence situation.

I had always considered that there was a group in France who were thirteenth tribe; historically speaking in *The Battle of The Trees*, I pin-pointed the Prieuré de Sion, not only as a group who held a religious goal, but as a group whose

Grand Master has been historically associated with the illustration in *Vaincre* magazine: which as I have shown depicted a Federal Europe incorporating both political and religious goals. Those religious goals were symbolised by the hermetic (magical) knight who through the open display of occult symbols, drew on ancestral links to Greece and the Bull-Minos Cult, which I have concluded was non other than the Druids and later the Scottish/Scottish Rite Freemasonry and Rose-Croix. However, I did conclude in my first book, that a rift appeared to have occurred in the 1980's, when the religious goal may have been thrown out and the political goal of a Federal Europe had been given priority. It is difficult to decide what form such a religion would have taken, but it is not inconceivable that after Hubbard died in the mid 80's, that the religious goal was pursued in the form of Scientology, which looks increasingly to have perhaps utilised hermetic knowledge to channel past event information from the Grid. Certainly then, Scientology under Hubbard may or may not, have started out as independent from both groups, but there is a possibility that it was as many in Phoenix, the breakaway group from Scientology claim, taken over by some agency in the 80's and which was perhaps a particular branch of the thirteenth tribe? The all out effort of the American government along with heavy suppression from Australia, appears to indicate a battle between 12 and 13 for control. It may even be that the double agent caper of Golgotha was re-enacted and Hubbard may have worked for both sides and when the communists and the 12 tribes found that they had been the subject of a double agent caper initiated an all out attack. Equally the top echelon could have played the lower groups of 12 and 13 in a dualistic battle, to see who was the fittest to survive. As I have stated never underestimate the workings of the MMRC mind or the Masters who have played this dualistic battle time and time again. Hermes in his duality suits this philosophy, with a face that has two sides. Unfortunately there is of course a third person or party in the 'marriage', which profits from the destruction and chaos. However Hubbard or the COS may have eventually shown their true 13 th tribe colours, which would certainly explain why Scientology was excluded from Greece in the period (1993-1994), when I was there. If Greece appears to have aligned itself with the 12 tribes of Israel and World Order Communism, then the only three possibilities for excluding Scientology were a) Hubbard was an independent third group and a threat to both thirteenth and twelve Tribes. b) Hubbard was working for the thirteenth tribe. c) There are two factions within the 13 th tribe or more succinctly within the Rosicrucian's with different goals that I will come to shortly. The fourth possibility of the psychiatry lobby or pharmaceutical lobby actively working on the Greek government will probably be the COS line. Whatever the case, the fact that a light was brought from Israel to Patmos where John allegedly wrote *Revelations* is probably highly significant and the culmination of the plan or 'script' – The New Jerusalem of the World Order is coming to fruition like a pie in the oven.

Federal Europe with its Communistic political programme also incorporates a religious goal, which is encompassed in twelve tribe Christianity: if Greece is dominated by these goals, then what of France?

The *Spotlight* (*Oct. 4. 1999*) reported that: "Seven Scientology officials accused of frequently obtaining money from converts and the illegal practise of medicine are on trial in *Marseilles*" (my emphasis) - my how these overts keep swinging back as karma on one! The Mary Magdalene was murdered just north of Marseilles for the "illegal practise of medicine", teaching past lives and biofield energies, until the thirteenth tribe having taken the genealogies, took the remaining truth and manuscripts. According to the prosecutor (and a 12 versus 13 game?) Scientology is "a monster that devours" its followers money and lives and the main defendant is a "parasite", which is the usual terminology employed: "The defendants, five of whom were women, are accused of "embezzlement, the illegal practice of medicine and violence with premeditation between 1987 and 1990. They are said to have charged for services like "Dianetics", described as a "mental science" aimed a "suppressing illness and undesirable sensations". Deary me, should they not have mentioned some of the side-effects I listed in a *Scientific Appraisal of Electro-Convulsive Therapy* [183] where some of the side-effects of this 'legal' medicine are Grand Mal fits, loss of memory, suicide and death, but there are no side effects from *Dianetics*. However Psychiatry just gets along with this *legal* practise of 'treating' the mind, together with a wide range of psychotropic drugs, worth billions to the Pharmaceutical giants as humanity sinks deeper into One World Order depression! Illness is big business! A somewhat similar tale to Cancer in *Appendix I*. Alternatively I never heard of *Dianetics* harming anyone, on the contrary since it releases one from past memories of Grid action it can only be beneficial. The all too familiar attack from the Syndicate, similar to The Gerson Therapy for Cancer and indeed a number of alternative cancer therapies which have been fought - but there you are secret policies and legislation never cease to pull that Ace card of hysteria on the public as the quote by Henry Clay pointed out. The stories are never simple, always a complex web and we have to decide whether the real game here, is a jealous God and: "Thou shall have no other medicine but mine" (to misquote) or is this a 12 versus 13 attack, playing the orthodox medicine monopoly card?

The unexplained destruction of court documents relating to the case came to light in mid-September and thus the case or plot thickens. The Marseilles trial has been linked to a lawsuit brought 10 years ago by a doctor, Robert Polquer, who said he had paid the equivalent of about twenty thousand dollars for Scientology "services". Basically the only problem with Scientology has always been the immense fees charged, fees one assumes are necessary to an organization that has the power to become either untouchable from political agendas of both groups 12 and 13, *or* a World Order Religion? On Sept. 8th

Minister Elisabeth Guigou ordered an inquiry into the destruction of more than *three tons* of court documents, some of the evidence collected for the Scientology case. Who then had the power to destroy this volume of court documents? Even the Scientologists would not dare to repeat the old GO "snow white" caper which saw Sue Hubbard sent to prison, even a Scientology agent could not walk out of an office with three tons hidden on his person - no, this has all the hallmarks of some support from a very high level or group. Further this was the second time that legal documents relating to scientology in France had disappeared. In 1998, other documents concerning the COS disappeared from the Paris Palais de Justice. That case Gigou said was different, apparently then; "It was not destruction but a *disappearance*, and that was even more disturbing. Then there was *no question of error*" (*author's emphasis*). Thus who exactly had the power to steal court documents? I have already mentioned the mystery surrounding Princess Diana's death in France and the possibility of involvement of groups 12 and 13, is there reason to suppose that such a battle is not occurring over Scientology? According to published reports, the prosecutor said the trial would still go ahead as planned, but pointed out that it would be up to the three-judge court to decide on the importance of the missing papers, once the court convened.

The *Spotlight* newspaper (*Feb.214th 1999*) produced an article that covered the financial power of Scientology, which is too much for even the IRS (Inland Revenue Service) in America to fight, together with a list of alleged "front companies" for Scientology. Scientology produced a booklet at one time that fully denounced the IRS, which is normal Scientology policy of attack as "fair game" anyone that crosses swords with them. That is their policy, however what I find almost hypocritical is that the booklet portrayed itself as in the interests of public, when as with the advertising campaigns taken out against *Time* magazine, this was really a Scientology battle. Fickle in the extreme, if now that the IRS has come to some arrangement with Scientology, Joe public can get along with his own battles. Further in the above article by *Spotlight* one of the alleged 'Front Companies' for Scientology is given as 'The Federation for Religious Freedom', however my feet did not touch the ground when I was thrown out to fight The Declaration of Human Rights and the right to one's own belief in a court of Law in London in 1989. *The East Grinstead Observer* (Thursday 5th April 1984) reported 'Protest March at Sect HQ', where forty-five members of the Scientology splinter group had demonstrated outside Saint Hill U.K. Headquarters in protest at the process of disconnection after the cull by Miscavige and the cost of Scientology courses. This was part of the corporate shake up at the time of Hubbard's death. Whilst the Church denied courses were too expensive for the majority of public Mr. Ballard a spokesperson for the dissident group told the Observer that: "The Church of Scientology currently charges over £150 per hour for lower level counselling and someone embarking on the complete programme of counselling is facing an expenditure in the region of £75 000!" – the costs would be higher now. Further Mr. Ballard asked: "Why does the Church maintain a monopoly in the use of Scientology? And what happens to the sums of money paid into the Church by devotees?" Well, you really can't monopolise the Akashich Record can you? Although Scientists under private research companies are trying to patent the Genetic Code which according to my research, is as good as patenting the morphogenetic bioplasma or Akashic Record on the hermetic principle of: 'As above so below' and vice versa. If you control the pattern below, then you control the pattern above and vice versa. This is really just dramatization of control in the past and what Hubbard would call the Yatrus incident and the "deletion and addition of data".

The Grail was delivered as a **Philosophy** in early Minoan Crete and applied to healing, with the lack of intention of coupling the Holy Grail to any political system: although after the Religious Revolution the Grail was irretrievably linked to a political system of control. That incident appears to be coded in the spiritual bioplasma and recorded as the Xenu or Inc. 1 "implant" in Hubbard's OT levels: an incident that clearly represented a case of *mind control*. That is curious but explained, if one realises that the hiding of truth and knowledge at that period, would be a method of mind control. The hidden group or 13 th tribe who stole that data could now 'marry' it to a political method of control, i.e. communism controlled by a hermetic, elitist secret priesthood. This undoubtedly would become the standard format of religion in Christianity. The irony is, that religion itself would become a major source of spiritual control, reflecting the holographics of the incident recorded it would appear on the spiritual bioplasma ('As above, so below'). Cloning and biotechnology would re-appear in present time, as a dramatization of morphogenetic control reflecting Inc. 2 and Yatrus who: "added his own data". Whilst Xenu with his symbolic alleged "implants" of "horn", "chariot" and "cherubim" clearly indicated the control of the spirit, reflecting the sequestering of the Grail message and knowledge of the trap.

Crowley was evidently a Rosicrucian at Rose-Croix level and that group held significant knowledge on vibratory resonance scales, which may have been subsequently developed to form a Psychology. Jung the Psychoanalyst was pre-occupied with Cretan Seals and archetypal symbolism retained in the "collective conscious" of man and as I covered in *Alternative 4*, there was one UFO incident that pointed to one group on Earth who had a formidable psychology. I can only think that Scientology is at least one group that would qualify in this field. Crowley was directly linked with Grand Lodge Masonry through a man who was one of England's leading Masonic scholars - John Yarker. Yarker admitted Crowley as a 33rd degree (Rose-Croix) Freemason. According to my own thesis here and evidence from Cardiff Castle, this version of the Rose- Croix, or ancient and accepted Rite, would have contained the history of the matriarchal belief in Re-incarnation and the hidden science of vibratory resonance. Indeed Crowley claimed to be a Re-incarnation of Eliphas Levi, a member of the secret groups around the cradle of European Union or a "United States of the West" during the French Revolution. Eliphas Levi spoke of the emergence of a "Universal Religious and Political Kingdom" - a plan that is clearly laid out on the floor of the Summer Smoking Room at Cardiff Castle Wales. Hubbard may have had links to the Freemasons on the basis that the young man I met at the bookstall in London, told me his grandfather was a Mason and knew Hubbard, although there is no direct proof of this.

Yarker ran his group from Manchester, much to the fury of English groups and the orthodox Rose-Croix, which expelled him in 1870. However, United Grand Lodge never expelled Yarker from Craft Freemasonry. He was still giving lectures to its premier research lodge, *Quator Coronati*, forty- two years later. Yarker also inducted Crowley into the 95th and 90th degrees of his combined Memphis -Misraim Order, which may well be Mosaic Law and the secrets of Cabalistic rites since Moses was an initiate of the Rite of Memphis, which pertained specifically to the matriarchal mysteries of Greece. Whether or not Hubbard hoodwinked Parsons, in order to gain access to the rites is not known, however one member of the O.T.O group who lived at Parson's house stated that Ron's typewriter would tap well into the night. Perhaps he was writing pulp fiction in his spare time or working on? The Order of Memphis-Misraim according to Martin Short (cited) was in the 1980's carried on by Desmond Bourke, who is 97th degree Grand Hierophant of Sovereign Imperium of the mysteries. Mr. Bourke told Short, that he held his authority through John Yarker, who had himself, acquired it from the Order's leaders in **France.** As I have stated I suspected that a powerful thirteenth tribe group existed in France, perhaps the Prieuré de Sion or its ascendant Order? And thus it was interesting to find that Bourke was a **Druid,** heading the **Universal Druidic Order**. One assumes then, that the Order is International and present in many countries. One cannot deny the possibility that Crowley as a Rosicrucian with Nazi sympathies was really a Druid and there is the curious mention of Ron wearing a white hooded cloak during one rite at Parson's O.T.O lodge, whilst Parson's wore a black one, reminding us of the 'marriage' of the two groups i.e. 12 and 13 in the form of Egyptian Queens and Kings, with the Queen 'bee' provided by the 13 th tribe of Celts. The curious 'Missionary Woman' in the Palaeolithic cave painting with half black (bottom half) and half white (top half) has curious symbolism.

On *page 172* of *The Battle of The Trees* I decoded a mystery of *The Grail Legends* and clearly the "**Root**" of the Grail is seen as T in the Tree alphabet or holly (Tinne) and the yellow Cairngorm or **the tribe of Judah**, which was Druid in ascendancy; with significance on Ng or reed as *royal one*. The "**branch**" however contains R as Elder and N as Ash and Q as apple, with Y as mistletoe.

The Ash holds significance, in so far as a Druidical wand with a spiral decoration was part of a recent Anglesey find dating from the early first century A.D. The Ash is also connected with floods and water and the sea. In British folklore the Ash is also the tree of *birth* and occurs with the apple in the "branch", thus emphasising *immortality*. The elder or R for Ruis in the Tree alphabet, is the Crucifixion tree, with the white flowers connecting it to the Goddess. Thus in this we see two halves to the Grail, with a kingly royal and elitist half of Judah, Druid and 13 th tribe as *root* or source, coupled or 'Married' to the *branch*, matriarchal knowledge from Knossos and the Early Minoans with the message and the woman. Not correct as I have shown, but the question is: Was Hubbard a Druid then? The new redheaded 'Messiah', so beloved of the thirteenth tribe in their World Order Universal Religion plans? Or was Hubbard as his son Nibs claimed a KGB agent (working for the 12 tribes?): Or did Hubbard merely work for himself independently, although such independence is hardly indicated, when the COS maintained that Hubbard had been "sent" into the O.T.O. I suspect Druidic magical rites were hard to come by, especially since the Druids never wrote their magical rites down, or their esoteric teachings and perhaps Parsons suffered retribution for his indiscretion, from the parent O.T.O in his death, which many believed was not an accident. Thus we have four alternatives Hubbard the entrepreneur who stole the apples, Hubbard the KGB agent working for the 12 tribes and sent into the O.T.O to gain hold of their magical rites: Hubbard the Druid the new messianic hope of the 13 th tribe and given the connection to Jesus- the Second Coming? Or Hubbard the genius who thought it all up on his own? Quite frankly 12 and 13 buried immortality and the hope of the millennium 2 000 years ago, so I do not see much hope this time.

Bourke as head of the Ancient and Archaeological Order of the Druids Hermeticists and the Order of the Holy Wisdom in 1966 authorized the foundation of another Druidic group, known as the Golden Section Order. Bourke is also an eminent Freemason. Further in September 1986, *Masonic Square* reported that Worshipful Bro. Desmond Bourke was President of the *Arcadian* Masonic Study Circle, which would be holding a series of lectures in Freemason's Hall, London. Bourke told Martin Short, that he was no longer President, but a member. Rituals might include Memphis - Misraim, but they have never been published and the Order's immediate forebear was the France-based Rite of Memphis that gave its lodges names such as Osiris and Helipolis in Great Queen Street London. It has long been noted that the Masons have an obsession with ancient Egypt and Greece, with the Cabbala, Mithras, the Essenes and the Druids, for reasons I propose here. Curiously Short ascribes this to: "the obsession of an adopted child desperately seeking its true parents and identity". Desperately seeking its Mother? If they had managed to get the crab story right, at Cardiff Castle, they might have known a bit more! Or if they had managed to get themselves on the equivalent O.T. levels down there in

Palaeolithic times and learnt a bit more about elixir than the cup, they might have avoided all their karma that has accumulated, all of which must be rectified before trying to exit. Alternatively they can play a few more Acts on Theatre Earth, before the light (the sun) and their god goes out, which as an ageing star it will of course.

The oval-shaped egg not only describes the biofield of man, but also in architecture is obtained by the intersection of two equal circles, which pass through each other's centres. The oval shape is also symbolised as two triangles, with a line across. Many religious mysteries are locked up in the early Greek alphabets and one suspects the Greek letter Theta, holds something of this mystery as indeed might be the case with the Scientology logo, although Hubbard merely assigns Greek origin to it. This sign turned up in the Finglesham belt buckle (*Plate 19*), with its Hermetic (magical) and Druidic connotations and the combination of male and female principles in the transcendent third stage beyond death. The combination of Sol (Sun)- male; and Luna -female, which might be described as two interlocking circles with the line across as the Baetyllic Herm.:The combination of holly and oak - the holy one and the oak royal (oh dear not again!). I'm afraid boys, the cycle will repeat and repeat and repeat, until you tell the truth on it, which includes Crete! The oval shape symbolised woman, for obvious reasons. In medieval heraldry it became an acute diamond shape and J.S.M. Ward says that in Freemasonry: "the lozenge is easily represented by square and compass", into which the nose of the initiate is thrust and the masculine tools of Freemasonry are the level and gavel. The level has the shape of the 'T' or Taur shaped cross and this sign, which is synonymous with the Bull-Minos cult, which designated the original Sun-kings and I would propose is synonymous with the Druids and later Rosicrucian's. The symbol came to represent the Cross of Christianity upon which the Sun-king was sacrificed - very Thirteenth Tribe! The gavel is like a hammer, the labrys, the double axe, which is an archetypal symbol of the Great Goddess. These archetypal symbols occurred on the front cover illustration of *Vaincre* magazine in connection with the plan for a Federal Europe - A thirteenth tribe plan of Universal Political and Religious Kingdom, which can only be Illuminatus in its political aspect. There can be no assurance however that this is not a joint plan between 12 and 13. Thus was Scientology with its rigid form of social control seen as the perfect partner? With its power pyramid that is very Illuminatus in structural organisation, with one or two controlling brains at the top. Or is it the case as the breakaway group of Phoenix have maintained, that Scientology was taken over *after* Hubbard's death.

Ward explained that alongside the square and compass in the Masonic Lodge: "lies the gavel or Tau, and so the cross and the vesica piscis (oval) are brought together in conjunction with the third great light in Masonry (the Bible), at the very moment the candidate takes the Oath".[184] This is significant, since obviously as the 13 th tribe are descended from Noah, and then the Freemason must accept biblical history. If Freemasonry were really a cover for Jewish tribal aims, then the Bible would make sense, after all the thirteenth tribe are the biblical Adamites. Was Freemasonry originally the brainchild of Foensia Farsa 'The Vine man that draws together' - the grandson of Magog and the great grandson of Noah? And when Adam and Eve were in the Garden of Eden they ate of the Tree of Life, which esoterically relates to Cabalistic knowledge and thus according to *Genesis 3,7*: "And the eyes of them both were opened, and they knew that they were naked; and they sewed fig leaves together, and made themselves **aprons**". (My emphasis) The significance of aprons in Freemasonry ritual, is I would assume a reference to Cabalistic knowledge handed down from the Adamites.The Tree of Life and Cabalistic knowledge entered Crete after the religious Revolution and in *Alternative 4*, I produced an icon of The Tree of Life, with the dove as epiphany of the Mother Goddess, illustrating how the original knowledge was fused with Cabalistic ritual, which incorporated channelling. Cauldrons and opium were part of the Religious Revolution, which I equate with the Bull-Minos Cult, Druids, and Rosicrucian's in ascendancy. The question becomes whether Hubbard acted independently or whether he was furthering the aims of the biblical Adamites? Alternatively did Hubbard let all hell loose, when he took information from the O.T.O - swiping the apples of immortality and setting up his own organisation? There are certainly a number of alternatives here: however Hubbard I believe would not have survived unless he had been a member of either group 12 or 13. Again however, Hubbard did take the extraordinary step of forming the Sea Org. thus placing his floating Scientology ship out of the jurisdiction of any country and its subsequent laws. If Hubbard did act independently, then one could view such an enterprise as one of the most courageous acts (and definitely a caper the matriarchal team never thought of!) - however there is no way of telling the truth, except Hubbard is unlikely to have been source, which is evident based on archaeological and mythical sources from Crete and the long trail of the hidden science, apart from the universality of the Akashic Record, which cannot be owned: although the World Order have sought to monopolise it, by maintaining secrecy for thousands of years. Whilst a substantial case has been produced here for Crete as the source, in fact the source goes back to 10 000 B.C and Palaeolithic times, although the evidence for that is obviously only present in vague form from the few remaining finds, which I have sought to provide as evidence in this book.

The O.T.O was a neo-Masonic Order said to be of German origin and it is the Germans who have so rigorously sought with the French a unified Europe. Crowley who became head of the O.T.O created a progression of magical rituals offering: "a rational basis for *Universal Brotherhood* and for a *Universal Religion*" (my emphasis). Crowley's religion of Thelema was even paraphrased by Hitler, but we know that he was a Rose-Croix Mason and Rosicrucian and it was in fact in these groups, that the hidden science was held. Thus we cannot dismiss Hubbard's association with the O.T.O lightly. The fact that Crowley and Parsons used the air tablet or Elemental tablet of Enoch, as one of the four watchtowers of the Universe; and cup symbolic of The Holy Grail, which was properly invoked by the wand, intimated that the system of magic being used was that of John Dee and his scryer Edward Kelley. The fact that Hubbard wrote a story line around the wand as serpent used to kill off one of his characters, might indicate some connection to the rituals of Parsons, where there are very definite references to Hubbard's participation. Scrying is a means of practising clairvoyance or divination by gazing into a *crystal ball*. It is a method of acquiring information about things remote in space and time, i.e. the past. Scryers can be considered psychically gifted, in so far as they have the ability to see figures and scenes in a crystal ball, but this is really just a method of channelling. John Dee created the magical incantation or ritual, which presumably sets up a morphic resonance between the crystal ball and the UVG 120 Crystal sphere or Akashic Record. Kelley and Dee used scrying in combination with a complex system of numbered and lettered charts to receive they alleged, dictation from the angels. An angel would it is alleged appear: "in the ball and with a wand would point in sequence to numbers and letters on a chart. Dee called the language of these communications 'Enochian' and curiously it had a consistent syntax and grammar. However I have already outlined new science advances and the ability of the physical crystal to act as receiver and transmitter, retaining a morphic resonance attachment to the Grid, allowing holographics to be pulled down, together with thought forms, which is another aspect of channelling. One may be forgiven for believing that Esoteric Masters or angels live in the etheric domain, when one receives such precise answers to questions.

The UFO natural phenomenon exhibits parallel phenomena as I described in *The Onion-Ring Model*, whereby holographics of past and often mythopoeic thought and symbols impinge upon the witness's mind or brain, acting as dipole radio-receiver. However, there is what one might call in science a variable - the EXPERIENCE OF THE WITNESS. I explained this variable in *Alternative 4* and previously in this book, whereby the Air Force pilot, or the farmer as witness of the phenomenon, explained the symbolisation according to their own experience, however the universality or common experience of the UFO witness, was explained as some form of *initiatory or religious experience*. This I explained in terms of the Akashic Record or morphogenetic holograms containing both event (matter and environment) and in the case of the spiritual bioplasma (spirit and event): thus when such holograms impinge they give some picture of a *past* event and may well be perceived as a religious experience. I further proposed that Hubbard's Inc.1 and

Inc. 2 may be some impingement of these holographs. The field of parapsychology in relation to natural scientific laws is so poorly researched for obvious reasons, that I have had to take my own conclusions from basic or first principles and OBSERVATION, i.e. witness accounts in proposing 'The Onion Ring' model for the way in which the phenomenon works. The postulation of bioplasma vortices and holographic electro-magnetic imprinting are the conclusions I have drawn.

Hubbard may have used the O.T.O rituals to cover whole track material contained on the Akashic Record, to discover *what* to audit on the OT levels, perhaps in his lack of true scientific method, training and discipline, he failed to recognise as have all the esoteric groups, that there is a complex interaction between the *past holographics* and one's own *personal past experience*. The variable to use a scientific term is that the interpretation of data or holograms of past events would thoroughly depend on the person or channeller who is receiving the data. Thus in the analogy I drew in the past of giving several people key words in a story, they may provide different stories, which show essentially similar elements. Hubbard, who was a science fiction writer, sees a chariot, cherubim and horn in Inc.1 as mind control by Xenu the arch controller who is locked up in a mountain presently. As a scientist with the rsearch I produce here, I would write a different story, which would encompass the totality of my knowingness and soul memory of the past. The more places you have been, the more battles you fought and stuck with the holy Grail on the front line, the more you would know and I mean really KNOW. I went through the hard process of soul memory and never used any Grid knowledge. I trust my own judgement and experience and not another. My story based on such experience, would together with my scientific background immediately recognise the X (of Xenu) as the female gene of the chromosome, which determines sex.

The genes in almost all organisms are found in large units called chromosomes, which are usually included in the cell nucleus. The central axis of the chromosome appears to consist of a single, very long DNA molecule comprising hundreds of genes. The chromosomes of almost all species occur in pairs. The DNA as I have explained occurs in a double stranded helix form and carries within the individual units or genes all the necessary information, to control the functioning of the body. The DNA is coded in the form of biochemical bases (Adenine, Guanine, Cytosine Thiamine and Uracil or A, G, C, T and U). The combination of bases e.g. ACG or GAC in a triplet sequence, gives rise to all the necessary codes for proteins, which govern the functioning of the cell and body. Thus the DNA is really an information system. This system I have proposed is derived on the hermetic principle: 'as above so below'. Thus I proposed a master DNA pattern or code within space, which is responsible for the pattern of DNA below in the cells of all species. The appearance of the spectacular DNA crop

158

circle patterns a few years ago, may be natural and some indication of that pattern above, or manipulated either by some secret research imprinting, or mindless agents for the World Order completing these patterns to confuse the issue. The cosmic DNA if you like, is really just a pattern that must find some organisational structure, within the morphogenetic bioplasma and spiritual bioplasma, perhaps themselves wound in electro-magnetic 'filaments' as a double helix also. In human beings, the females usually have 23 pairs of chromosomes, one pair called the X chromosomes; males have 22 similar pairs and two other chromosomes (XY). Consequently female gametes usually contain 23 chromosomes one of which is an X chromosome, but half of the male gametes contain 23 chromosomes corresponding in the group to the female gametes (including an X), and the other half 22 plus the short Y chromosome. Thus the XX   is female and the XY is male.

Thus when I look at Hubbard's so-called Inc.1 I see Xenu as a female X chromosome i.e. female. This is associated in Hubbard's account with mind control and a chariot. Thus the significances in my account might become: female, chromosomes, horn, cherubim and chariot. My research and viewpoint would then provide a different story of the spiritual battle that occurred between male and female in Crete 1 400 B.C. when Hermes (chariot) and the Bull-Minos (horn) cult took over the Holy Grail from the woman. It was the birth of mind control because thereafter Hermes was utilised in a political and religious system of control. That religion itself became a method of social control and mind control is implied. Further the fact that the X occurs in association with the DNA implies control as a matter of function. In similar fashion I associate Y or Yatrus with the male chromosome, cosmic and body DNA and DNA as a method of control. Unlike X or Xenu, the Y or Yatrus is involved with bodies and appears as Hubbard's so-called Inc.2 which I thought was the holographics or memory of a Magnetic Reversal, which Hubbard terms the "implant". The fact that Inc.2 occurs before Inc.1 according to Hubbard, would make sense, since the Magnetic Reversal did occur before the Spiritual message arrived as the Holy Grail c. 10 000 B.C and the Religious Revolution occurred
c. 1 400 B.C. Thus my own account although not channelled, shows similar basic features or holograms, which Scientologists must have accessed through regression into the past? I do not know how it is done, since I have no experience other than a few months in Scientology. The major difference here is that through glimpses of soul memory and acting on intuition derived from that, I conducted my hard grinding research. That research is thus part of my own personal experience combined with personal soul memory. Thus Hubbard came up with a variant and different version to my own, but the basic holographs are there. This is a positive conclusion, since if two researchers come up with a similar conclusion, by two entirely different routes it implies that there are physical laws involved. The fact that the *Revelations* account in the Bible still

assumes that Satan is active, locked up in the "bottomless pit" bound by "chains", parallels Hubbard's description of Xenu, apparently according to L. Kin locked up in a mountain on Madeira "electronically tagged". There is a possibility that the Revelations account has been edited, with the removal of the word mountain, since by association it implies Druid rites and electro-magnetic forces, which are of course inherent in Hubbard's account of how Xenu is retained. Again this may be too simple an explanation and may in more complex form of knowledge of events, refer to the complex background of the use of pits by the Druids to alter electro-magnetic energies, which through morphic resonance connected such alterations to the Grid for purposes of channelling or altering the Grid in some fashion, which must be considered as control. Further the mountains of course are particularly Druid. Overall then there is the other version that X or the female is locked up in the tomb of the Druids, which would parallel the paintings of Poussin and Guercino, which I discussed in *The Battle of The Trees*. In my own experience, Satan, Xenu or Yatru is not some all-powerful mystical master that will descend to Earth but complex pre-history and history relating to spiritual and physical battles, imprinted on the bioplasmas. One thing is certain, after the Grail was stolen, the battle was on for man's mind and his soul.

THE GREAT WHITE LODGE AND BROTHERHOOD

Aleister Crowley worked for years on the magical methods and development of the secret rituals of the O.T.O, which are so rare, they are almost impossible to find, which is evidence to me that there is some secret (or pie) here. In 1913 Crowley worked the Paris Working of magical methods for the O.T.O, with another magical adept (Frater), using the abbreviation of O.S.V which stands for Olf Sonuf Vaoresagi, which means 'I reign over ye', from the first call in the Enochian or angelic language of Dr. John Dee and Sir Edward Kelley. "Ol Sonuf Vaoresagi goho iad balata lansch calz": 'I reign over ye', saith the God of Justice, 'in power exalted above the firmaments of wrath'. This is a reminder of the Flood or 'Firmament', and those masters who reigned supreme prior to the Flood. There is no doubt, that Crowley was channelling from the Akashic Record, and obtained thoughts from the morphogenetic bioplasma and no doubt sought thoughts from the higher level of the spiritual bioplasma; thoughts and events that one must assign to the "Masters", prior to the Flood or the old Atlanteans and in the post Flood era as the Adamites and subsequently the thirteen tribes of Israel, inclusive of Judah and Levi. I would hate to suggest, the spiritual battle that has been fought in Scientology, with all of its high energy and access to past events, together with all the new data that has impinged, has now imprinted on the so-called Akashic Record and in the event of a Magnetic Reversal, will become part of man's future "implants" and WHO is going to take responsibility for it! Or more succinctly who is going to help put the **truth** up there, for those who do not make it out of this cycle? I have to be realistic and I am unsure how many will or can make it out this time. The next cycle will be horrendous, which is why personally I have made every effort to pay up all karma and exit. Total reality never was a ball of fun!

The fact that Cardiff Castle exhibited nine concentric rings based on *the triplet* or *Law of Three* evident in my decoding (*The Battle of The Trees*) signified the hermetic patriarchal God Jehoweh on one level, but on another level, given the map at the centre of the floor design designated I proposed, a Universal Kingdom, both politically and religiously; it also pointed to an authoritive *Hierarchy*. Mystically this may well allude to the celestial hierarchy, which The Great White Brotherhood refer to as The Great White Lodge. This is a group of spiritual or allegorical beings arranged into *nine orders of three triads each*. The nine orders constitute a kind of celestial ladder, with the implication of Jacob's ladder and a patriarchal hierarchy with ascending knowledge. This is in *direct contrast* to the 'matriarchal ladder' and the route or exit out of the trap, which *does not* depend on any earthly hierarchy, only a spiritual hierarchy that sent a message to teach the 'children'. The most spiritually advanced or highest triad of the *patriarchal* hierarchy being the one allegedly most approximate to the *cosmic mind*. The referral in the inscription at the Castle to the "Ages" of man would appear to indicate the stages that must be passed in order to achieve the goal of a Universal Political and Religious Kingdom. The stages that the political goal took, were covered in *The Battle of The Trees*, principally the French and Russian Revolutions and presumably World war II, paving the way for A "Federal United States of the West" or European Union, so clearly shown in the illustration of *Vaincre* magazine. But what "Ages" did the religious goal pass through?

One might consider the various initiations of secret group members like Aleister Crowley, were attempts to widen progressive research into rituals, which would access the spiritual and phylogenetic event history of the Grid. An initiation is a ceremony or method by which a person is introduced to a particular level of knowledge. The ancient mystery initiations were intended to dramatically reveal a secret gnosis or wisdom to the candidate. Equally, Crowley was very talented as a magician and certainly arrived at his own material independently. However it may have been the case that Crowley himself, was used to further the cause of the Universal Religion, believing himself in his religion of Thelema, which Hitler paraphrased. Crowley was working on magical systems that would challenge or at least parallel the power of the kabala or Quabbalah and presumably the 12 tribes? The word is from the ancient Hebrew and literally translated means "Doctrines received by ancient traditions". Such traditions feature heavily in the Old Testament where various prophesies including *Ezekiel* had accessed the Akashic Record. There was in the early days great competition between 12 and 13 and the priesthoods for absolute control. The written teachings of the Kabala go back perhaps no later than the eleventh Century. There is evidence however, that the oral teachings were in existence at a far earlier date and traditionally, they are said to date back to the time of the secret wisdom related by Moses.

By a system of numbers and letters of the Hebrew alphabet, the kabala discloses the esoteric mysteries. Its philosophy in other worlds concerns ontology, the nature of being; cosmology, the origin of the Universe, and theology, the nature of God, and further anthropology, and man's relationship to God and the world. Crowley however also sought information from the ether or vacuum, believing that he was talking to higher Masters, or spirits and developed a progression of magical rituals offering a supposedly rational basis for universal brotherhood and for a *Universal Religion*.Crowley was financially supported by Karl Johannes Germer (Frater Saturnus) a rich man and head of the O.T.O in New York, who with Heinrich Traenker of Weida in Thuringia Germany (Frater Recnartus) received Crowley's *The Book of the Law* for publication. Traenker became head of the O.T.O in Germany in 1924 and was horrified by *The Book of the Law*, initially condemning it. Traenker who had certain clairvoyant ability, at one time saw Crowley as *Head of a group of Masters* but after another vision, he curiously pronounced that he had misjudged Crowley and Traenker was to later describe Crowley's book as a: "glorious manifestation" and said he could condense its meaning into one word - civilization. The book was anti-Christian and Herr Grav another member of the *German branch* of the O.T.O made an interesting comment on this, given that Hitler would soon follow and make the Third Reich and the Aryan Super Race the basis of 'religion' in Germany:

> "I thus to my horror got a glimpse of the *future reconstruction*, as *planned* by the ... of a *primitive World Order* which suggests the *blackest days of Atlantis*. If these ideas had been clearly in my knowledge at the time, Sir Crowley may rest assured that I would not have put myself so certainly before the *chariot* of the... and been invited the 'boot' for services rendered in good faith...These Germans have had this 'boot' too often without unfortunately learning wisdom thereby...".
> [185]   (*author's emphasis*)

One assumes that here, the future world War II or a Federal Europe is being referred to, which evidently was on the chess board and planned as far back as 1924: just after the First World War, which surely must have provided the impetus for the second World War, in the form of the Versailles Treaty, which formed the common cohesive bitterness of the Germans, which Hitler was to utilise and mould the German people to the cry of injustice and war. I have stated previously that World War II, finally paved the way for European Union, which as an idea could only be sold to the peoples of a devastated Europe, on the 'marketing ploy' of peace in Europe - Europeans brought it, hook line and sinker. The referral to the chariot must signify Hermes and the formation of a Hermetic World Order, thus defining perhaps Hitler as a thirteenth tribe puppet. Aleister Crowley was pro-German and very much aware of the plans for a Universal political and Religious Kingdom. Ford the motor car manufacturer, who was to exert a great influence over Hitler and who was anti-Semitic, claimed that he had been approached by *three Jews* (three men in black, as a sign of the Druids and thirteenth tribe?) who convinced him that the Jews had a great plan to dominate the world. This may have been the plan of *The Protocols of Zion*, which outlined such an alleged conspiracy. Crowley himself was suspected of being a German agent and thus in this long and secret trail of the plan for a Federalist Europe, we also see a culminating religious plan placed stealthily on the 'back burner', whilst Crowley unawares, was probably another dupe of a higher Order. Thus I cannot easily, once again dismiss Hubbard's connection with the O.T.O and Crowley or the fact that Hubbard may have been duped or persuaded on financial lines, as clever as he was we have yet to discover where his wads of money came from. Hitler was to claim that everyone had betrayed him at the end, which probably reflected the fact and mind of the MMRC case, that having fulfilled his purpose, he was now no longer of USE.

The fact that clairvoyantly Crowley had been seen as a Master within a secret Council reflects not only his prior life as Eliphas Levi a member of the secret groups and an incarnation at the time of the French Revolution, but also Crowley's acknowledged life as a Master of a secret Council. Levi pronounced you might remember that: a Universal Kingdom (political and religious) would be had by those with the "keys to the East": the Enochian magical keys (rites) to the Grid and past events? Or advanced mind and body control technology as exists in alleged defence technology in America, able to alter the emotional and behavioural states of man and his biofield? Or both. Certainly the UFO manipulated experiences indicate that such technology has been already tested on unsuspecting individuals. Crowley also developed his own technique for arousing Kundalini power (shakti) at the base of the spine, generally associated with sexual activity, which he promoted through sexual magic. This arousal united the crown chakra with the *"cosmic consciousness"* - which I can interpret only as connection to Grid holographics with the inevitability of following the 'script' – Day 1. Plant the vine.

Is it not co-incidental that Hubbard would go on to develop what he hoped would become a Universal Religion? Is it curious also that Hubbard should claim how he attended a Council of Masters (millions of years ago) that would be a familiar story of Crowley, which in his case occurred: "shortly before the time of Mohammed". Whilst Hubbard's Council appeared to occur in cosmic surroundings, Crowley described the location of his Council as: "one of the wildest solitudes of Europe" Scotland in the U.K. would have aptly fulfilled that description and since Crowley was a Rosicrucian and Rose-Croix Mason, then the significance would become that the first Lodge of Freemasonry - Ancient and Accepted Scottish Rite, which holds I propose the mysteries from Crete and a Universal Religious goal, was held in Scotland where a lodge was later set up at Kilnwilling in 1286. Although Kilnwilling was set up much later than the era of Mohamed, there may have always been a religious centre in Scotland, which Barry Dunford associates with the Church of Fortingall at the time of the events of Golgotha. The Druids with their peculiar and unique proposal of a Messiah, in ascendancy of Scottish Rite Freemasonry and the highest Orders of The Rose Croix, may have always sought a furtherance of the religious goal, through a series of "Ages" and Messiah's. Was Hubbard another 'Messiah' or the 'Second Coming' of a plan that sought a Universal Religion? That plan irretrievably mixed with the political arm of the Illuminati?

Crowley said of his secret meeting with the Masters: "The critical questions to be decided at that time - the beginning of the Dark Ages - was the policy to be adopted in order to help humanity". This sounds very Rosicrucian, very White Lodge, very Masters and Council. Crowley wrote in his Journal: "A small minority including myself, was for positive action: definite movements were to be made; in particular *the mysteries were to be revealed*. The Majority, especially the Asiatic Masters, refused even to discuss the proposal. They contemptuously abstained from voting, as if to say, 'Let the youngsters learn their lesson'. My party therefore carried the day, and various Masters were appointed to undertake different adventures". [186] This would form a similar story to Hubbard, whereby Masters for good or bad, were charged with controlling at worst or guiding at best humanity. Crowley's task was to bring oriental wisdom to Europe, and to restore paganism in a purer form. Crowley as I have covered was undoubtedly Rosicrucian and the inn near to the Abbey of Thelema in Switzerland was called the Gasthof Rose and bore the banner of the Rose Croix. The Abbey in an obituary honoured Franz von Liebenfels the important Nazi occultist. Further Crowley always carried a small rose ornament with him. Madame Blavatsky was to repeat a similar tale of "Masters" and claimed she was a student of the master Kut-Hu-Mi (K-H-M). It is said that K-H-M is Deputy Grand Master of the Great **White Lodge of the Great White Brotherhood**, who was at one time known as Thutmose III of Egypt. This is a pie is it not! However, the Zend-Avesta once referred to him as **the Illuminator** and he was known in Egypt as the Kroomata (Kai-Ra-au-Meta), or **Cromat** and if you reverse the initials of the title of the order of **AMORC** or: **The Ancient and Mystical Order Rosae Crucis**, you obtain CROMA (T).

Today the One World Order of the Rose must still retain a religious goal, which may or may not be Scientology and the further release of the mysteries. I have pointed out that the data in Scientology, not only carries resonant vibratory research, such as *The Chart of Human Evaluation*, which bears a striking parallel to the tonal scale of Pythagoras (and the Cosmic Keyboard), who was honoured within Druid ritual Law and knowledge, but Hubbard gives no concrete references for his sources other than his own genius. The Rosicrucian's carry significant research that has been continued throughout the centuries which includes atomic and nuclear data, which was not generally available, but one suspects became available to some extent through scientists like Newton and Boyle, who were members of this society. I suspect that some important nuclear physicists in history have been members and this might account for the official line that Hubbard knew nuclear physicists. When the COS in 1969 issued a statement to cover the reason for Hubbard's association with the O.T.O in 1945, there was a vague mention of Hubbard's association with physicists and the fact that he had been "sent". In fact there is nothing in Miller's biography of Hubbard to suggest that he would ever have moved in the circle of atomic physicists, even though on occasions Hubbard would refer to himself in such qualified terms, despite historical record shows that his qualifications were not standard University certified and he never graduated. Thus the mention of his association with nuclear physicists is somewhat without explanation, unless we realise that Crowley and therefore Parson's group of the O.T.O was a particular branch of the Rosicrucian's.

Crowley owned a property at San Jose California and since Crowley was always on the verge of bankruptcy, how he came by the property is worthy of consideration. Crowley arrived at the ownership of the estate through the activity of one R. Swinborne Clymer, the head of an American Rosicrucian society called the *Brotherhood of the Rossy Cross*. Clymer was the author of an enormous book, written in an attempt to discredit a certain H. Spencer Lewis, the Imperator of **a rival Rosicrucian Order** called the *Ancient Mystical Order Rosae Crucis* (*AMORC* for short). The basis of Clymer's attack on Lewis: "the boastful, pilfering Imperator with black magic connections", was that Lewis had received a charter for his order, which Clymer described as a *commercial enterprise*, from the O.T.O. The two volumes that Clymer wrote, *The Rosicrucian Fraternity in America: Authentic and Spurious Organisations*, was an attack on Crowley and Lewis, but the curious thing is that Lewis did not receive his charter from Crowley's O.T.O. but from Theodor Reuss, the head of the O.T.O in America. Crowley's only connection with Lewis was to write to ask him to surrender his estates at San Jose, the headquarters of AMORC, to him. Lewis' reply to Crowley is not recorded.

If Clymer and Lewis were at loggerheads within the O.T.O that curiously included the objection of commercialisation of the mysteries, then this denotes two dissenting factions or even groups within the Rosicrucian's. Presumably Clymer disliked the *commercialisation* of the secrets of the mystical order and its connection to Crowley and black magic (channelling). The question here is whether Hubbard sought to break up Crowley's group as the COS maintain on the grounds of black magic and commercialism; or whether commercial profit would fair better, if Crowley was eliminated from the equation, together with Parson's group, thus one must look to Theodor Reuss in America and presumably his Masters (Ancient and Accepted Scottish Rite Freemasonry - Druids - Great White Brotherhood?) to discover exactly who "sent" Hubbard into Crowley's O.T.O in America to break it up. It may be, that Hubbard intended to release the secrets and was part of Clymer's group, thus breaking up Crowley's group, which resulted in the 25-year battle Hubbard had with just about every American government agency. Further it might be supposed that AMORC or Spencer's group who intended to commercialise the secrets, took over Scientology after Hubbard's death. Thus there may be an underlying policy within Scientology over prices and that would also account for the fact that whilst Scientology initially was fought, is now accepted in America and Britain. The battle is no longer simple, with the groups 12 and 13; the thirteenth group has appeared to spit up into dissenting factions that centre on the price of the elixir! What a sad and ridiculous end to a very great gift sent to all humanity. I suspect that "Ghusts of laughter the Moon Goddess stir" if she could see the Twins (12 and 13) fighting over her apples! Surely she would welcome the idea of taking the gift back from both and returning from whence she came leaving man to his Magnetic Reversals and 'script'?

One wonders in all this, whether Crowley who was actually a very adept magician or more succinctly was good at gaining information from the Grid, had served his purpose and true to form for both 12 and 13 was **used** and dispensed with. This usurer aspect has defined secret group self and group survival mentality, throughout their entire history. Solar kingship was used as a form of political control, until of no further use, after which Europe's monarchies including the French and Russian monarchs, were murdered to pave the way for a Federal Europe. These long- term goals by secret groups show no conscience in sacrificing one or millions to their cause. Whether or not Hubbard took the secret rituals from the O.T.O., using them to access whole time track or Akashic Record, which gave him the backbone of *what* to audit for the O.T. levels, may find some proof in the statement by Nibs his son, who stated that his mother Polly had told him that Hubbard had used various "incantations". Further we know from Parson's letters to Crowley, that Hubbard acted as a seer. This is not to say that the O.T. levels do not cover personal memories of the time track and what I consider to be, at least in Inc.2 a Magnetic Reversal; however I would have to know the exact methadology and manner of the O.T. procedures including any data that was read *prior* to regression into the incident, if I was going to comment further, since I personally have no experience of the O.T. levels other than the garnered information from L. Kin's book. However all of this is merely splitting hairs, since the source, the data and the method, or the group should not deter from the conclusion; and that conclusion is, that it would be better to leave or exit, prior to a Magnetic Reversal. Quite frankly as a practical person, I don't really care where information comes from, providing that I can garner a thread of truth out of it and if that thread is a warning, then why quibble about who's gift it was, who had it and when and how the truth affects religion today. Goodness me, you can be your bottom dramatization though, that the argument will still be raging, when suddenly rippling waves and flickering of rainbow colours appear in the sky like an LSD experience (so I am informed) signalling the curtain coming down on yet another production on planet Earth, just before the seas envelope the entire argument and man gets his 36 days of downloading of 'script', so he's nice and suggestible for the next production – Day 1 plant the vine, send in the "slaves".

There is a persistent legend that Jesus went to Tibet for his initiation. The Master K-H-M who is said to have passed through a number of Re-incarnations was more recently in an incarnation to be found on the Earth plane, living at a secret monastery and temple near Kichingargha. Thus there appears to be in the background not only to Crowley, but also Jesus some vague presence of a higher Order, which might be the Great White Lodge, which even by its name is a reminder of the thirteenth tribe. The Great White Lodge (GWL) exists apparently on a COSMIC plane, where alleged Masters carry on work and also await incarnation to carry work on the physical plain on Earth. Presumably there must be some channelling or morphic resonant method of contact and one would question exactly *who* or *what* is being contacted? Since I have covered adequately before, the storage of *thought* in the spiritual bioplasma. However this belief in superior Masters who guide humanity, has persisted through the eons. I mentioned in *Alternative 4,* disturbing methods being used by some healers, including those with connections to NASA (National Aeronautical Space Agency) and the Goddard Space Centre (perhaps aptly named), whom I believe may have some connections to Rosicrucian groups or knowledge particularly biofield energies and chakra function and manipulation. NASA may be quite aware of a forthcoming catastrophe on Earth, which becomes the driving force behind the space programme and the quest to Mars, which appeared to be already well underway in the 1970's. The book *Alternative 3* indeed claimed that a base on Mars had been established and a British MP at the time, said: "something is going on". The idea persists in my conclusions of two competitive groups ostensibly separate, but in reality played off against each other only to act in unison at the top as a secret hierarchy, for instance the alleged Cold War of East and West, when there was no such thing, with only co-operation at a high level. The point of such competitive poles or research would be to push scientists into greater heights of achievement by giving them (rather like their own laboratory rats), a game to play and a maze to run (usury). The race by scientists in America and Russian to put men into space, became the new and sexy game of the decade, with no questions asked, as to whether the money would be better spent, in giving Third World countries money for education and food as we watched some of the worst famines and atrocities. The backdrop of the Vietnam War only fuelled the notion of Communist threat. However it has been revealed that even during the alleged cold war, scientists in Russia and America were sharing information, a point that Hubbard himself made. I think you the reader will pretty much be gaining the idea of how these Masters work! The disturbing methods of healers were to recommend that the person who comes (presumably in a poor state of physical and or mental health) for healing, should learn to listen to their "spiritual guides", who being more wise and thus able to direct the person, can give guidance. Massive alarm bells went off in my head, since one should *never* recommend to anyone, let alone the sick, that they should listen to anyone other than their **own mind** and being. The New Age health movement, I believe is being systematically penetrated by World Order Communist control methodology, as a counter progressive measure.

Under the direction of The Great White Lodge (GWL) which you will understand is an "invisible" and therefore a cosmic group, a group of high initiates or The Great White Brotherhood (GWB) are prepared in each incarnation, for higher work in their next incarnation. The GWL is on *a cosmic level* or more succinctly must contain the spiritual bioplasma memories, Aleister Crowley evidently was directed to believe in his purpose along these lines, assigned as magi in a branch of the GWB. This group does not exist on a cosmic level i.e. thought from the bioplasma, it is an *earthly* Brotherhood or real, of which the Rosicrucian Order is the highest. Thus the GWB is the school or Fraternity of the GWL, which has an alleged invisible Brotherhood of Masters. Thus those that work on the physical plane are very much visible, but even so, there is a higher and INVISIBLE DIRECTIVE. This directive then becomes very important in definition and explanation. If the directive was merely thought from *past Masters* retained on the Grid or spiritual bioplasma, channelled by magi as members of the GWB on earth, then since Masters tend to Re-incarnate time and time again into familiar groups with familiar goals, one might consider the possibility that the world is being run on past thought and goals of Masters, who may or may not be the MMRC case with a goal of total control. These masters on incarnation, would simply join the GWB and continue to channel their past thoughts! Deary me, this is a fine 'script' in an ongoing Orwellian plan and may account for the reason that such a plan with its goal of a World Order, has been ongoing for such a long time. Alternatively the idea of cosmic masters may be simply be to hide not an invisible Brotherhood, but the very secret hand that moves, the ULTIMATE GROUP who are in fact quite visible if only one could identify them.

One might reasonably ask *how* instructions from a Master either on the "Cosmic plane", such as in the GWL or on an earthly plane as the GWB, come down to the student or high initiate on the physical plane? Secret groups would claim "Cosmic Illumination" or "Cosmic Consciousness" but do they really mean channelling? Interestingly enough, the initiate becomes aware of passing through a *series of events,* which constitute Initiation. These often occur *during the night* or while he is in *periods of rest* and meditation in the *mountains or caves* and away from worldly affairs. This is the method by which Crowley's servant was to convince Crowley of his own contribution or development. This consciousness can take the form of some *recognition of knowledge*. Whilst one can have illumination under such circumstances, which can give insights, there is the possibility that I discussed in *Alternative 4,* of the use of advanced technology to alter the human biofield, with its storage and memory banks - i.e. unnatural manipulation of the human bio field, with the brain or mind acting as dipole radio-receiver. There are indications that so-called psychotics who hear voices in their head and then commit a serious crime, may have been used in public assassination attempts and certainly today's technology being developed under the cloak of defence, has a capability of being covertly applied by those who hold the strings to this technology. The right to bear arms in the American Constitution is continually questioned over the increasing number of people who commit mass killings, but once again this may merely represent manipulation of public opinion. An armed populace of course, would pose a threat to complete control by 'Big Brother'. There was every indication in *Alternative 4*, that many alleged UFO events were being manipulated and may have provided test cases, for so-called "Cosmic Illumination"!

Initiation is not some kind of prophetic impression, but knowledge and so-called "Cosmic Consciousness" of events now occurring and decreed to occur in the near future. This is not intuition, but prophetic insight, in the sense that cyclical action in the form of construction and destruction (the Flood) has been imprinted on the Akashic Record. One must ask, whether the decreed events are merely a mindless tuning into the Grid or whether thoughts are indeed implanted from so-called "cosmic illumination" which is in fact a rather more visible group of Masters in the ultimate enclave. What part the prophet plays in this is called to question, by the accuracy of prediction of events. The Apocalyptic *Revelation* of St. John is one example where people compare the prophesied events with current world events and nod sagely and say: "ah yes, it is as it was prophesied" and "The Kingdom of Heaven is at hand". The inevitable event wrapped up in Churchanity prevents one looking at such prophesies with a closer scientific eye, particularly when they have 'Religious text', stamped all over them. In *The Battle of The Trees*, I proposed that the Apocalyptic *Revelation* was THE PLAN of The New World Order in its religious aims - i.e. the aim of the 12 Tribes including the 13 th tribe? for I doubt at the top whether they do not work in unison. Such a plan on the alleged cosmic level on the hermetic principle of 'as above, so below' must be shadowed at every move on the physical plane on Earth. Very clever these Masters! And there is a questionable parallel of events, which may well be manipulated to provide the authenticity required to prove some divine and Cosmic Plan at work.

Consider the prophecies of Nostradamus (1555), did he receive "Cosmic Illumination" or downloaded information from some 'Big Brother's plan? Or did he for one moment perceive events from the past as a natural clairvoyant, believing that they represented some future event? One quatrain of the prophesy speaks of two married persons who would come by the forest of Reines by a circuitous route to Varennes - then there would be tempests, blood and beheading (trancher, 'to slice'). Varennes appears only once in French history, when Louis XVI and Maria Antoinnette were arrested there, in the flight from Paris during the Revolution. In the light of the physics I produce here, there is the very remote possibility that in some distant past the event happened and Nostradamus picked up the signal from the Grid or Akashic Record and then produced that as a prophesied future event. However the Grid does not offer such specific holograms, there are only one or two frames in hundreds of feet of 'film reel'. Thus a prophesied event that is so specific, indicates to me that the "invisible" cosmic masters or more succinctly some high order within the Brotherhood may have illuminated Nostradamus either consciously (as their agent) or subconsciously in sleep. The appeal of this sort of prophecy allows a sort of inevitability to surround future events, coupled with a veil of mysticism, which gives it that authenticity which prevents any questions asked, just as the book of *Revelations* offers such prophesy and is not questioned, at least in scientific terms.

It was the Count de Fersen the Swiss army officer who organised the (failed) escape of Marie Antoinette and her family and thus either he was incompetent, or an agent for the World Order, or perhaps an agent of the Duke d'Orleans and Layfayette, the latter being heavily involved in the American Revolution, which virtually bankrupted France against the advice of Maria Antoinette not to use French money to finance it. Maria Antoinette was subsequently with royalty blaimed for the bankruptcy of France, despite her attempts to find out who was behind the French Revolution and her suspicions of the involvement of Freemasonry, whom she warned her brother Joseph (The Hapsburgs) in Austria about, before the Hapsburgs became the victims of the conspiracy. The Duke d'Orleans was often to be found in England and whilst British Freemasonry denied any involvement in the French Revolution, which was eventually laid at the door of German Masonry, one cannot escape the conclusion, that a very secret Order in England may have been involved. Further Cagliostro a magi and Jew and two other Jewish jewellers in the affair of the necklace, did more according to Napoleon, to bring about the downfall of Maria Antoinette, than anyone else. Cagliostro also had links to England. This was a specific plan that Maria Antoinette fell helplessly into, as she tried to escape with her family, in order to set up what was her original idea of The United Nations (U.N.) peacekeeping force. It was her idea by escaping with her family, to gain international support for a tribunal into the events that were occurring in France and a peacekeeping army that would maintain order in the interim. Thus again we see, that a prophecy gave some sort of inevitability to a Revolution that was planned from start to finish by the Masons. It is worth quoting here the opinion of the Grand Master of German Freemasonry over the events of the French Revolution:

> "A great sect arose which, taking for its motto the good and the happiness of man, worked in the darkness of the conspiracy to make the happiness of humanity a prey for itself. This sect is known to everyone: it brothers are known no less than its name, It is they who have undermined the foundations of the Order to the point of complete overthrow; it is by them that all humanity has been

poisoned and led astray for several generations. The ferment that reigns amongst the peoples is their work. They founded the plans of their insatiable ambition on the political pride of nations. Their founders arranged to introduce this pride into the heads of the peoples. They began by causing odium on religion...They invented the rights of man which it is impossible to discover even in the book of Nature, and they urged the people to wrest from their princes the recognition of these supposed rights. The plan they had formed for breaking all social ties and of destroying all order was revealed in all their speeches and acts. They deluged the world with multitude of publications; they deluded the most perspicacious men by falsely alleging different intentions...This is what has been done and is still being done. But we notice that princes and people are unaware how and by what means this is being accomplished. That is why we say to them in all frankness: The misuse of our Order, the misunderstanding of our secret, has produced all the political and moral troubles with which the world is filled to day. You who have been initiated, you must join yourselves with us in raising your voices, so as to teach peoples and princes that the sectarians, the apostates of our Order, have alone been and will be the authors of present and future revolutions...Indomitable pride, thirst of power, such were the only motives of this sect: their masters had nothing less in view than the thrones of the earth, and the government of the nations was to be directed by their nocturnal clubs... we must make for princes and people a complete sacrifice; so as to cut out to the roots... the abuse and error, we must from this moment dissolve the whole Order.

Thus in the opinion of the Grand Master of German Freemasonry, a secret sect working within Freemasonry had brought about the French Revolution and would be the cause of all future revolutions. Whether the Revolution had done its work in destroying the French monarchy and now threatened the security of Germany, or whether the Duke was genuinely disillusioned is hard to decide. Three years after the Duke of Brunswick issued his Manifesto to the lodges; the books of Barruel, Robinson and others appeared laying bare the whole conspiracy. Further in the opinion of Chevalier de Malet, the sect that engineered the French Revolution was absolutely international:

> "The authors of the Revolutions are not more French than German, Italian, English, etc. They form a *particular nation* which took birth and has grown in the darkness, in the midst of all civilized nations, with the object of *subjecting them to its domination*" (*Author's emphasis*)

Whether the Jews or more specifically the tribes of Israel (12 and 13) are implied is not known, but a particular nation that took birth in the darkness, implies not only the nocturnal secret groups that Brunswick referred to, but also how could a nation not have a country but retain the implication that it is international unless the goal of that "nation" was not retained within secret groups or the Brotherhood? The only group that might fit such a description as part of Freemasonry, is the hierarchal and most secret group that binds the 12 tribes and 13 th tribe or biblical Adamites according to the 'script' of *Revelations*, which requires that "**all** the tribes of Israel" (*Author's emphasis*) are honoured at the end in the *Feast of Tabernacles*. According to Hubbard's *Third Party Law* which states that for two groups or individuals to argue or fall out, there must be a *third and hidden party present*, then it is this most secret and hierarchal level that will eventually not only cause a third world war on Earth, but have caused the majority of conflict on this planet. I have covered the French Revolution more fully in *The Battle of The Trees*.

The manner in which Hubbard claimed that he had been illuminated on *Excalibur*, i.e. during what was probably a Near Death Experience during an operation, is only interesting if *Excalibur* formed the illumination and basis of the knowledge of *Dianetics*: as Hubbard was to claim every answer man wanted was laid out like some "smorgasbord" before him. If Hubbard had been illuminated by Cosmic Masters as some part of the plan to release the mysteries to mankind, then Hubbard would not have been aware of it, and generally may have believed it was his own illumination. Alternatively he may have had some form of unmanipulated illumination. However time and time again, we come back to the question of who "sent" Hubbard into the secret O.T.O group and whether or not the two warring factions of the O.T.O or more specifically the Rosicrucian's on the subject of "commercialisation" and release of the mysteries, were thrown together in order to see which group would win. As I stated before, never underestimate the mind of the MMRC case, for this is his game – the Roman arena of Earth, where he throws together two groups and on the Darwinist principle of the 'survival of the fittest', waits to see who wins. Let us not forget, that it was Reuss the head of the O.T.O in America who gave Crowley and Lewis their Order and whether Hubbard unsuspectingly had the opposing Order, created for the purpose of this game is a theory, which can't be proved. However the only way that holograms become imprinted on the Grid, is through a force versus a counter force.

In the case of the morphogenetic bioplasma then the interaction of the species with the environment forms the force and counter force, thus event data and species adaptation is recorded. However as we have seen in the case of the spiritual bioplasma, there has to be a force and counter force on a spiritual level, for the data to be imprinted. The only reason that the events of the Religious Revolution in Crete were imprinted was because the woman fought the man on a spiritual level. The fact that he won is presumably why the archetypal symbols of chariot (Hermes?) and horn (Bull-Minos cult?) occur. The force and counter force or postulate versus counter postulate (thought with high intention) would cause a confusion of energy and that is in fact the hologram. A hologram is made every time two opposing forces meet The fact that Scientology may have been set up for a battle might be for the very purpose of imprinting the battle on the holographic record. The obvious advantage is that after any event that wiped out all the books, then the Masters would simply be able to tap into the bioplasmas or Akashic Record or event and thought data through the Cabalistic method that they carry through each Magnetic Reversal as the Secret Doctrine, just as Noah must have carried it and pick up where they left off. One suspects, that the use of Hermes with the face of two sides has been used to ferment conflict between the two groups 12 and 13 or any number of combinations of those two groups. The world as the great big laboratory and evolutionary test tube of the Masters, who apparently understand evolution in animals, but not in spiritual beings. "Accelerated evolution" as they call it, as the justification of manipulating man on such a large scale, is really built on Darwinist control and the 'survival of the fittest' or he who wins. No doubt in the mind of the MMRC case he believes he is doing man a favour.

The leaders of the O.T.O were well known Grand Masters of Masonry, such as Franz-Hartman, Keinrich Klein and Karl Kellner. They decided to found the O.T.O after Viennese Karl Kellner had returned from an extensive tour in the East, where he had been initiated by the Arab fakir, Soliman ben Aifha, and the Indian yogis, Bhima Sen Pratap and Sri Mahatma Agamya Guru Paramahamsa where the mysteries, yoga and the philosophy of the left-hand path which he called 'sexual magic' had been expounded. In *Alternative 4, I* referred to Hitler's use of the left-handed Swastika, which occultists regard as the equivalent of the reversed crucifix - black magic. Black magic has been used as a term from ancient times to indicate mysterious practices or secret magical or resonant methods and those methods today are not understood, although in the strictest sense they work according to scientific laws of morphic resonance and utilise I would conclude the 'Onion-Ring Model' of the bioplasma vortex, which I covered in *Alternative 4.*Here again then we see the time old manner of setting up secret groups, with a claim that initiation came from the East and Masters. Black magic really formed the basis of ritualistic practise that enabled information to be channelled from the Grid. Presumably the rituals in black magic differ from white magic and the idea of black and white arises. White magic one suspects must be Grid data, where perhaps events, rather than past thought are sought? Black magic perhaps is access to past Masters and their thoughts in the pursuit of knowledge. Event data could however be used to avoid catastrophe's and who is to say whether or not NASA at some top level did not have recourse to event data of the past which has been the impetus for the space programme? The idea that Masters exist in the Ether in reality or allegorically, can only rest on a misunderstanding of the way that thought is imprinted on the bioplasma. Is Xenu or Satan still active? Or is this some past thought form imprinted on the bioplasma? Indeed does the addition of data in the etheric layer, as was the case of Yatrus, really refer to addition or change in the gene pool of the DNA, with its master pattern in the vacuum energy? Did Satan or Xenu really as controlling spiritual beings become trapped on Earth and now exist not in some Ether or vacuum pattern, but rather run Governments and the World Order on Earth? Take a realistic look around, and you might observe the obvious! Black magic or Satan is meant to convey the idea that one mind can call into play certain forces of nature to work injury upon another from a distance. It is assumed that the cosmic space existing between two minds or persons can be a utilized by one of them to transmit evil and destructive thoughts to the other. Further the advance of covert technology presumably can alter the biofield pattern. I believe I have mentioned how this one was tried on me, but provided you know your own mind and thoughts, then one can immediately recognise any foreign thought or emotion. Further people who have witnessed such attacks, have reported physical events in the environment, which precipitate the emotion of fear, which softens one up for the psychic attack so to speak, by causing a resonance of the tri-partite energy field, which would immediately connect to the Grid on a computation of survival.

It was I believe the alleged 'Woodpecker signal', a low frequency signal apparently aimed at the American Embassy in Moscow, which allegedly caused some staff to become very ill and develop cancer. Martin Short in his book *Inside The Brotherhood* (cited) quoted the case of Stephen Knight who wrote *The Brotherhood* an expose of Freemasonry shortly after which he developed a brain tumour and quickly died. In my cancer research I have noted the scientists, who have either lost their academic positions or have mysteriously died or have been imprisoned for trying to reveal some aspect of the hidden science. A number of UFO researchers have also mysteriously met their deaths, on St. John's day June 24 th. One must pity those who created for themselves one more knot or confusion, that will require them to return to Earth and as I stated any battle to suppress the Holy Grail is such a big overt, that one would have to do some major action of good, to reverse the harm and confusion created, in order to satisfy one's own conscience in the life review that forms the first post on the road to exit. One has to be able to nullify the hologram of force that one created, otherwise thought sticks on it, simply from the confusion it creates in the soul memory or holograms of others. Man in self- mode, is made to confront what he did to others. God could not have thought out a better court of justice in the sky, where the pattern concerns the survival of the entire species and thus self, is not a concept within the majority master pattern. The World Order elite or the individual may work on the principle of self whilst on Earth thus posing a force to numerous victims and creating many holograms of confusion for their victims, however I am afraid that once you meet the holographic record, that record has recorded the majority confusion and experience. A man's soul is made to look at his actions and the effect on others in the life review since the holograms are interconnective, thought will stick on a confusion of energy. Thus to get past the trap or at least the first post, you have to be able to mirror image the confusion to make it disappear. This has more to do with physics than morality, however it is ironic justice. This necessarily means that in the so-called 'life review' of the death experience, there is a confrontation with truth or reality. If you can't confront your role in the confusion then I am afraid it is a wrap on the dunce's head, sent back to learn the lesson. To quote a memorable line from a poem by Graves in *The White Goddess*:

> "You who, capped with lunar gold
> Like an old and savage dunce"

The O.T.O founded in 1902, constituted an inner circle of adepts, who had new and exciting knowledge from whatever source. The Ancient and Accepted Scottish Rite was linked to this group and I proposed in *The Battle of The Trees*, that this group held both political and religious goals for a Universal Kingdom, which appears to be laid out on the floor of Cardiff Castle U.K. Eliphas Levi an alleged past incarnation of Aleister Crowley, referred to this Universal Kingdom as being had by "those with the keys to the East". At one level I assumed in *Alternative 4*, that this referred to the hidden science and technology capable of controlling the mind and body of man through the biofield, but here I would suggest another interpretation, which might refer to the Enochian magical rites and secrets, which would allow access to the Akashic Record. Presumably though there are two groups here, one with black magic and access to Masters or in reality their own past thoughts and those who accessed events of the past to attempt to steer mankind free from future catastrophes; or at least the "chosen ones", who might for example exist on a safe base on Mars in the event of such catastrophe? until the Earth has completely recovered from the magnetic cycle. NASA has for many years researched how man can survive for long periods in different gravity conditions from Earth and principally under gravity conditions present on Mars. It is hard to find a rational goal of such research or a justification for the enormous amounts of taxpayers' money involved, if it were not envisaged that Mars for some reason would become a space station. Further, since Mars is not exactly a preferred habitat even in the event of over population of Earth, with its red soil and barren landscape with inferno quality light, apart from the adverse effects of Mars gravity on the physiology of the human body, then one must assume that there is a hidden agenda here. Undoubtedly the goal of setting up space stations was principally to monitor how long man could survive in space, with experiments to extract oxygen and water from biological waste products. Why NASA or the international space effort should be so interested in maintaining man in space for long periods, when there is no real goal in terms of expenditure over practical information garnered is unfathomable unless of course, it is viewed as absolutely necessary to maintain men in space for long periods. The reason for that can only be guessed at in terms of what I say in this book.

The O.T.O or Order of the Oriental Templars refers historically to the Knights Templar, who was to unite in Scotland and form the Ancient and Accepted Rite of Scottish Freemasonry. The Templars presumably held a secret on the Crucifixion openly spitting on the cross referring to Jesus as: "The thief on the cross": they were also matriarchal or at least hermetic and thus one must consider that some version of the events of the Crucifixion that I give in my own witness account was known to the Templars. The Templars also supposedly held sexual practises, which brought about their suppression at the beginning of the 14th Century. The New Templars in the form of the O.T.O derived their knowledge from the East, although they were of German and Austrian origin. Further the accusations against The Templars may have been no more than those made against witches during later times and an attempt to suppress knowledge, particularly one assumes certain resonant rituals that Crowley developed later. The sexual rites and homosexuality claims against the Templars however presumably rests on hermetic and Cabalistic practise of magical rites, which Crowley undertook in the Paris Working. One wonders whether such practise, had specific resonant value and presentation of a part of the hologram that would invite according to holographic science, the entire hologram to be pulled down, via the ritualistic practice and chant or invocation.

The Templars idol was Baphomet, derived from two Greek words - the baptism of Metis (wisdom) or the absorption into wisdom. It is the equivalent to the word wisdom itself. The Templars dictum was glorify Baphomet, he is the true god, renounce Christianity and 'do what thou wilt'; which became

Crowley's basis for his religion of Thelema and 'do what thou wilt is the whole of the law': which Hitler paraphrased. The Oriflame, the central directive of these new German Templars - the O.T.O announced the new directive of their secret society with the words:

O, disciple!
Who seeks it, will suffer;
Who finds it, conceal it;
Who uses it, let no one know.
He who is a true philosopher
Shall remain unknown.   (*Author's emphasis*)

The old idea of secrecy and hidden Masters in relation to the hidden science, philosophy and knowledge is once again evident. Having advised secrecy Oriflame then announced: "our Order possesses *the key* which opens up all Masonic and hermetic secrets, namely the teaching of sexual magic, and this teaching explains without exception all the secrets of Nature, all the symbolism of Freemasonry and all systems of religion". As I have been at pains to point out in all my books, the root of all religion dates back to Crete, and the Message, however the patriarchs as I have also pointed out, evidently knew black magic ritual and had used it from time immemorial to control humanity. One suspects that hermetic magic specifically sought to access information from the Grid dating back to the Religious Revolution in Crete. Indeed one could say that all religion evolved not from that point, as secret groups believe with the birth of the bisexual god Hermes, but from the time of spiritual intervention c. 10 000 B.C., however control of the Grail and mind control started with the Religious Revolution. The elite who were always in control from the beginning held a populace in fear and thus it was easy for them to control man as a body through the Grid, since fear is a level where only the primitive or reactive mind functions and is thus controlled by Grid survival mechanisms relating more to animals and the phylogenetic line. These ideas of ancient high civilizations such as Atlantis are mere efforts of the elite, to maintain the myth that the patriarchs were civilized. The Old Testament rather dispels that idea as I have shown. The rulers as black cabalists, were despotic and ruled by the edge of fear, that thinking is still prevalent in the World Order today, who are merely re-incarnated MMRC cases. This mind might be considered as the 'mind' of the Grid, where the sole goal is survival.

The analytical mind or rational mind, the one that solves problems, only 'clicks on' at higher emotions above fear, anger, or grief and thus man never really utilised this mind. He was a mind controlled being, surviving along animal lines according to Grid survival mechanisms of self and at its highest group. The spiritual message or the Holy Grail, that arrived on Earth, meant for all mankind, was to raise man from these lower emotions and help to raise his conscious awareness to the point, that he could question and solve problems. Agriculture and farming allowed man to stay in one place, such that he could turn his mind to creative pursuits, rather than live on the edge of survival in a nomadic wandering habit. That message was taken over by those who sought to suppress such a healing for humanity where the Platonic Maxim was changed to a method of control i.e. "To control, one must first control the body and before that the mind and before that the soul". The Platonic Maxim for healing was the reverse: "Before you can cure a man's body, you must first cure his mind, and before that his soul". The healer must first cure the soul and that cure rests on truth. Thus if Hubbard set out in his O.T. levels to cure the incidents of confusion created by Xenu and Yatrus in the soul holographs of man, then such cure can only occur, when the real truth of such incidents are known. Secrecy and tiered elitism, was only a deterrent to such cure or healing of soul and mind. Control and secrecy is a horrible thing, it merely is a statement that the being, does not perceive in his or her own spiritual being enough survival or ability to create an effect, without recourse to tying the leg of his or her opponents in the unfair race of Atlanta with the apples of immortality. It says that 'Unless I disable others in some way, I cannot survive and I will no longer have power'. I do not put much of my attention on survival for this reason. A man may torture you, deprive you of all your wealth, ridicule you, imprison you, attempt to take your own story, or even kill you (your body), but he can never ever take away your soul experience or your beingness. The MMRC who in Palaeolithic times cannibalised his victims in an attempt to imbibe their spirit has not changed, together with the process of degraded thought, but he will never ever defeat what is right, true and just. Neither can he take a message that came from a true spiritual hierarchy, since even they do not own this message or the physical laws of physics which govern the knowledge, it is a truth of man's existence in the matter universe: in much the same way that private biotechnology companies cannot own mans genetic code or secret groups cannot own the Grid and sell man back that truth for profit and purposes of control or power.

In 1912 Theodor Reuss head of the O.T.O paid a visit to Crowley upon the death of Karl Kellner, who had died in mysterious circumstances in 1905. Reuss was also a spy for the German Secret Service and a member of the Socialist League. The visit was in order for Reuss to accuse Crowley of publishing the innermost secret of the O.T.O., the ninth degree secret. Crowley denied it, saying he had no idea what their secret was. Reuss pointed to the book *Liber CCCXXXIII: The Book of Lies.* He opened the book at the page that begins: "Let the Adept be armed with his *Magic Rood* and provided with his Mystic *Rose*". Obviously from the research conclusions I make in this book, the "Magic Rood" is not only the phallus, the hermetic god, the

Druid's wand, the biblical Adamites, the thirteenth tribe and the "Mystic Rose" the vagina, the womb, re-birth, Re-incarnation, the Rose-Croix, Scottish Rite Freemasonry, the political arm of Illuminism and the World Order programme of a Universal Kingdom with religious and political aims: but the union of the two held great historical archetypal significance and import as root and branch and the question 'WHOM DO YOU SERVE?' (THE GOLD CUP OR THE ELIXIR?) This symbology almost certainly is part of the symbology that emerged in the Cretan Seals, after the Religious Revolution in Crete, which I proposed was directed by the Bull-Minos Cult who in ascendancy appear later I proposed as the Druids and later the Rosicrucian's and. thirteenth tribe presumably. Such a period in Crete was to 'marry' female and male in a transcendent and bisexual third stage beyond death – Hermes, thus removing the woman in the story and the truth. Crowley's Paris Working is the record of a series of invocations of Mercury or Hermes and presumably the homosexual act that Crowley employed, was to aid the invocation, or in more scientific terms, aided the morphic resonance of the hologram of the bisexual god, thus enabling information to be pulled down from the Akashic Record.

Reuss begged Crowley never to reveal the secret of the O.T.O and Crowley impressed by the eloquence and seriousness of Reuss, never did. One suspects that such an appeal was based on a future Universal Religious Kingdom and the revealing of the mysteries. Such an appeal would have struck a cord with Crowley, since Crowley had no regard for Orthodox religion and called himself "The Beast", although this has been greatly misinterpreted. Thus Reuss may have based his appeal on a long- term goal sought by the thirteenth tribe, of a Universal Religion to reveal the mysteries. Very admirable and I have considered the exact problem myself, since one knows, that there are opposing forces within the elite who are very good at whipping up fear and mind control techniques through the media and publishing that connect man to the Grid, thus reducing intelligent discussion to attack by the animal pack. Very clever these masters! One has only to mention mind control, sexual rites, and black magic as was the case in Greece and public opinion is whipped up to the emotion of threat to survival and ping! 'What was that about survival?', Grid clicks in with reactive mind! There is no wish to harm a good cause, but my decision to write this section rests on Hubbard's confession to his auditor Mayo, that his motives were "power and wealth" and Hubbard's claim that he did not take a penny from the Church, when Scientologists in Miller's book claimed suitcases of cash were brought to Hubbard. In the pursuit of truth (ultimate reality) one cannot ignore a lie (out reality) and the only way to raise the level of reality is by communicating to raise understanding.

As I noted in *The Battle of The Trees*, when I deciphered the names CAPUT and ORMUS identifying two secret groups with entirely different aims, one group wanting to release the mysteries to man and the other group preferring to keep them hidden. The curious 'Cutting of the Elm' ceremony which saw two groups separate on those principles at Gisors in the 13 th century, was to be displayed in symbolic form at Cardiff Castle, in the cut of the claw of the crab, which reflected the cut of the Magdalene's arm after the events of Golgotha. The Mary Magdalene sought the elixir but was thwarted and double-crossed by those who sought the cup. Crowley as part of his alleged Council of Members in a past life at the time of Mohammed, was all for releasing the mysteries and thus would have found a comparable goal if Reuss had revealed a thirteenth tribe plan for such. The twelve tribes would of course base their goal on the continued belief in The Covenant and presumably the magical and Cabalistic rites that the patriarchs had adhered to? Thus the secret revealed to Crowley may have been the goal of the Rosicrucian's and parent O.T.O., to reveal the mysteries. However, my decision to write this book rests on the conclusion that there is no freedom for man, if the mysteries are released without the truth and are commercialised to the extent that they are only available to an elite few and where there is doubt over the goals at the apex of management. Since truth is the ultimate reality, then no understanding can occur without a very high level of reality or truth, which is ultimate reality. Did not St. John state: "And the truth shall set you free". It is simple to my way of thinking, in so far as anyone or any group, who seeks to hide truth, has a **hidden agenda** and is *not* in the business of setting man free. If we really must follow the 'script' then let us have our Armageddon of **WORDS** now, before there really is an almighty bust up (atomic war) and that **third battle (Third World War)** recorded on the holographs of the past, where 12 and 13 or two opposing groups fought it out on the world's stage and precipitated a Magnetic Reversal?

In *Britain - The Key to World History,* the author Comyns Beaumont stated: "The famous Egyptian Book of the Dead, influenced completely by the epic of the Flood and composed in the name of Thoth (Hermes), in its ritual caused the soul of the dead, to undergo a fanciful, final, gloomy pilgrimage to the sacred West, indeed, I contend to the legendary Amenta, identified as the tiny island off Staffa, near Iona, in the Hebrides, whence the wandering spirits were supposed to be judged by Osiris, and were rewarded or consumed according to their lives on Earth.Staffa lay in the very vortex of the greatest destruction at the time of the Flood. Water being but one element concerned - and later became the Underworld of the Celts, as it was of the Hellenes". You may remember that the work of Comyns Beaumont including a book that revealed Scotland as the true Holy Land, were weeded out from libraries in America by the Zionist (the political arm of Judaism) Masonic

Order of the B'nai B'rith. The boat (to the Isle of the dead, or after life), also appeared in the finds of the psychro cave and the alleged birth-place of Zeus in Crete; where I claimed a secret Cabal the Dactyls (Druid and thirteenth tribe?) had conducted a Religious Revolution and removed the equivalent O.T. levels or open mysteries from the Early Minoans and their Teacher. Such knowledge not only involved the belief in Re-incarnation, which was the Holy Grail Message, but it also involved a whole cosmology. The birth of Zeus in myth corresponds then, to the time of the concept of the cup, or power and wealth, to be made from the elixir. The appearance of boat icons in the cave of Zeus is therefore significant, connecting the Religious Revolution once again as with other evidence in this book, with the Bull-Minos Cult, Druids and ultimately Rosicrucian's - the Mystical Rose Croix of the World Order. Pythagoras, who was initiated in Crete, is said to have been the pupil of the British Arch Druid -Abaris and as I recounted in *Alternative 4* possessed research on a resonant scale of emotion, behaviour and music; which may be the source of *the Chart of Human Evaluation* of Ron Hubbard, which compares emotion and behaviour with tonal resonance and life force. If Hubbard did think it all up by himself, then there was certainly already in existence the basis of this chart.

Earlier in this book, I referred to wars this century, which may have really been Grid battles e.g. Afghanistan, which sought to control a particular geometry of the Grid. It is not inconceivable that certain parts of the Grid contain information relating to history of that area. I mentioned that it was certainly co-incidental that 'Dolly' the cloned sheep was produced at the Roslyn Institute in Scotland and the Rose Line running through central Scotland, may be a very strong magnetic Ley line with morphic resonance to the Grid. Grid content over the covered area may affect events below on the hermetic principle 'as above so below'. Scotland may have even been part of the ancient Atlantis, which was never submerged at the time of the Flood, and still retained its physical connection to the Grid, Alternatively when the Nazis went to Thule in Greenland, ostensibly to research their Aryan ancestors, they may have perceived this place as a Grid location, in much the same way as an inorganic crystal holds a connection to the Etheric crystal or UVG 120 sphere. The Scots geologist, Hugh Millar claimed that the rock stratum on the "Black Isle", near Inverness, is among the oldest recorded on the planet. The infamous Loch Ness monster with its prehistoric dinosaur-type description may be a holographic recording of the past, where a holographic impinges on witnesses, in the same way that UFO witness accounts occur i.e. via the 'Onion-Ring Model' described in *Alternative 4*. In early history Scotia (Scotland) U.K., was known as Alban or Albion - the White Isle, which may hold interconnective inference to the O.T.O. and the Great White Brotherhood of the Rosicrucian's, the tribe of the Tuatha de

Danaan or (Dan) and the Druids or thirteenth tribe. Alban therefore may have an earlier derivation – '*Alb*' (white) and '*an*' (Dan?) which not only represented the Goddess in her death aspect, but also represented a white tribe and the Tuatha de Danaan. In the Romance of Taliesin, Gwion's enemy Caridwen, or Cerridwen, was a white Sow-goddess. Her name is composed of the words cerdd and wen. Wen means 'white', and cerdd in Irish and Welsh means 'gain' and also 'the inspired arts, especially poetry'. The 'muse' for the thirteenth tribe was taken from the woman at the time of the Religious Revolution in Crete. White became her colour only in so far as the thirteenth tribe locked her up in the tomb with Hermes. Knossos in Crete was a burial place covered in white gypsum, as was the Celtic New Grange barrow in Ireland. White was also to find its appearance as the colour of the white chalk hill figures in the U.K., which I associate with Hermes and the Druids. Albion or Alba was only initially applied to Scotland, but afterwards in what must have been Druidical influence, was to become the name of the whole of Britain. Little Gwion had every reason to fear her; it was a great mistake on his part to conceal himself in a heap of grain on her own threshing floor. To quote that memorable line from Graves:

> Ghusts of Laughter the Moon stir
> That her Bassarids now bed
> With the unnoble usurer
> While an ignorant pale priest
> Rides the beast with a man's head
> To her long - omitted feast.   (*The White Goddess*)

The White Hill, or Tower Hill, at London preserves Albina's memory, the Keep built by the Bishop Gundulf is still called the White Tower. Alphito, the Barley-goddess gave her name to Britain. Albina or the White Goddess was the eldest of the *Dan*aids - the fifty Danaids appear in early British history. The Latin albus, alphiton was 'pearl - barley' and Alphito seems to have been the Danaan Barley-goddess of Argos. The kings of Argos were solar kings and obviously consumed the goddess and the Holy Grail into their political goals of money and power. The word 'Argos' means 'shimmering white' and gave rise to priestly white vestments! The goddess well and truly locked in with a patriarchal priesthood. Io the white cow was in myth the goddess and nurse to the infant Dionysus, who was guarded by Argus Panoptes ('all-eyes'), the hundred-eyed monster, probably represented as a white dog, with the bardic gloss of 'hide the secret'. Io was also worshiped as a white mare and appears as such in Celtic myth. Graffiti on the head of the piscine on the South Chapel of the Templar-Church at Gallway, shows a winged pyramid and solar emblem of a fish and snake (*The Battle of the Trees*). Thus the Templars were obviously well aware of this story and eventually combined forces with the thirteenth tribe, if they were not actually thirteenth tribe in origin, they contributed knowledge presumably from the Temple in Jerusalem. The connection however of Barley to pearl (of barley) may have some connection to the pearls worn by the alleged 'Missionary type' woman found in the Palaeolithic caves and thus she must be the goddess; already at that early date, locked up with the 13 th tribe in the tomb and the Holy Grail message stolen along with the cosmology and knowledge.

The Gallic Druids lopped the mistletoe from the oak tree with a golden sickle, comparable to a crescent moon. I have already discussed the 'root' as royal and Judah and the 'branch' as the Grail message with the apples of immortality. This ritual must provide some significance for 'the cutting of the elm' (arm or branch?) ceremony where the cup of the Grail (money and power) was obviously with royalty to overtake the branch in importance. The elixir presumably seen as a parasite on the oak royal tree! Here we have the mind of the MMRC at work, with the Grail message and knowledge and immortality only a branch to power and money. The woman became hated, since she tried to make the Grail message and the knowledge the 'root' and further reveal the mysteries to the "profane" as secret groups referred to humanity. Barry Dunford in *The Holy Land of Scotland* (cited) was to ask: "Is there another dimension, not generally recognised, connected to the continuity of purpose of a partially underground secret Christ Tradition which is designed to help and guide the human race along a trajectory of spiritual evolution?" I have already pointed out the mechanics of the third and ultimate hierarchy or party and its concept of "accelerated evolution", by causing competition and conflict between two opposing parties or groups, if one can call that guiding humanity. Certainly the Druids as Adamites and thirteenth tribe, held Theocratic Priesthood as the most desirable form of Government, presumably with a solar kingship and religion in tandem. The religion that they held was clearly very different from orthodox religion and incorporated some form of heresy, which appeared in the Templars as anti-Christian, with a denouncement of the figure of Jesus. Clearly also there is a body of secret history surrounding the life and goals of Jesus that has not been revealed. Further there is also a persistent legend of Jesus and his initiation by Eastern Masters, the same story that has been given by the O.T.O, who I assume are the Druids in some form, who sought a One World Order. It may have suited the plan of the time to evolve a Christian religion, until such time that it could be replaced by another hermetic goal and order – the World Order of the Rose and the Rosicrucian's. That I am afraid is probably the reason why there has always been the injustice of a Third World divide. The Alexandrian text which quotes Jesus and his referral to the joining of male and female principles, can only be interpreted as the hermetic God and triumph of the Adamites - with Jesus working with the thirteenth tribe; although it is clearly evident that Mary Magdalene who believed that the mysteries were to be released, was double crossed in a double agent caper: the twelve tribes and the Roman administration managing to find out the real role of Jesus and putting the attempt down. The Dead Sea Scrolls indicate quite a different story, in so far as Jesus stated he had: "fooled them" and: "they nailed their man to the cross".

In a Tibetan manuscript Jesus is allegedly referred to as Issa, [187] thus making the connection to Tibetan Masters. Jesus is also reported as saying: "He that sent me is true". Once again we come across that curious word "sent", which was to appear in the history of Ron Hubbard. According to Sthya Sai Baba, whom many believe to be the Avatar (Divine Incarnation) of this Age and a male (naturally), with all the implications once again of another Divine Master Jesus also said: "He who sent me will come again", implying that the messianic quest would come for a second time, presumably as another stage in the great plan for a World Order. When the Bible spoke of John the Baptist it was said: "He is Elijah come again", with all its implications of either Re-incarnation or another case of "sent" and another cog in the great plan. A series of Divine Masters or initiates, sent by perhaps the Great White Brotherhood and the invisible Masters of the Great White Lodge. Of course Re-incarnation was not for the masses, the Masters allowed the "cattle" to believe in total death and the masses wept tears of loss and grief over their loved ones, which has contributed to the decline of man's sanity - and just as you think it can't possibly get any worse, just as European Union was introduced after World War II as a political system of peace in Europe: lo and behold along comes new and amazing knowledge that the pulp fiction writer Ron Hubbard co-incidentally or not just happens to come up with. Wow! What a fortuitous co-incidence. The 'Messiah' arrives just in the nick of time, like the cavalry in the action adventure story and the audience gasp! - What a man! What a hero! What action! – My! what a way to enlist recruits into the Christian (sorry time track slip) Scientology army! The well researched and produced 'script scene' of 'THE CAUSE ' (enter stage right or left of the Janus head (unimportant) the Celtic hero chased by villains with 'new' and amazing script lines). "Freedom" and "survival" of Man! The audience gasp Wow! There is hope, we can go on, we can survive and we can be free – "American Express? – That will do nicely!" Of course I do accept the COS line that Hubbard was a genius and came up with it all himself!

The thirteenth tribe certainly knew how to run a religious game! And if it wasn't for the physics of force versus force, emotion versus counter-emotion and the battle of the woman against man, then the winner (the cabal that invaded Knossos presumably 13 th tribe Adamites) would not have had the winning score of the male and Hermes, recorded on the spiritual bioplasma as Inc.1? (the beginning according to Hubbard's O.T. levels). You might have trouble getting a Scientologist to go back earlier than that since this is I believe in Scientology speak would be a "rock slammer" (List One R/Ser)? (as opposed to "rock slam"). It is very difficult now to get recruits on white steeds as they charge into battle, with 'hang on a minute - what is the goal and game plan here?' The recruits shout 'who cares about game plan or goals, Scientology is the best game on the planet!' - maybe it is, then maybe it isn't, it all depends on *who* "sent" Hubbard into the O.T.O., and what the goals are, just as it depended on *who* sent Jesus: and whether or not Hubbard was independent or allied to a group such as

The Great White Brotherhood and Lodge of the Rosicrucian's or whether Hubbard was independent and the COS taken over on his death. If Hubbard cocked the victory sign at BOTH groups (12 and 13) and decided to release the mysteries independently he would be a hero: but realistically given his attachments and his lack of higher level scientific background, together with my own experience of the group, the monetary elitism and the hypocrisy over stated goals and my own experience - then I would have to say that Scientology looks increasingly like at least one other scenario I have witnessed on the track of time. The idea of Ron the superman, or Jesus as 'Son of God' really gives rise to the concept of supermen, Masters and man as a god, which degenerates in such thinking of man as God –you can kiss ethics goodbye at that point.

Ron Laing records that Sathya Sai Baba told him directly that: "He" was the one to whom Jesus was referring to when he stated that "He who sent me will come again". Ron Laing further states that he asked Sai Baba, if "He" was what Western Christians call the Cosmic Christ, to which he received a reply in the affirmative.[187] The "*triple incarnation*" of the personage of Sathya Sai Baba as a) Shirdi Sai Baba (1835 -1918) b) Sthya Sai Baba (1926-2021) c) Prema Sai Baba (2029 -?) i.e. past incarnation, present and future is thought to be explained in *Anacalypsis (VolI)* by Godfrey Higgins, originally published in 1836, quoting from Higgins: "The Sun was always Triplified in his power, and as the **triangle** is another form of the great mystery, they were fond of erecting triple gates in the East, as in the Triple portal or Tripolin of the Rajas of India". *The law of Three* was particularly peculiar to Druids and appears frequently, as the tri-partite embryonic biofield; the head, thorax and abdomen: the triangle of three in Scientology (ARC), as the three wise men at the birth of Jesus and of course we have already discussed the tie between India's caste system and the Druids very early on in this book. The law of three however initially referred to an idea of the matriarchal Teacher, which showed as a man died, he was re-born through her (meaning her gift to humanity based on historical truth). This became mixed up with woman as Great Goddess and thus the idea now became as one died, one was re-born through Her the Great Goddess. The persistent desire for power, wealth and control through kingship allied to a secret priesthood or Theocracy, meant the transition was now to become: as one waning Twin King died, so he was united with Her the Great Goddess, to be reborn as the new waxing Twin King of the Year (New Year babe of Dec. 25 as it was to become). This gave the impression of *divine* kingship and the idea that only Kings possessed immortality; which became confused further into solar kingship and hereditary monarchy with its divine solar philosopher kings. A King did not have to die at the end of his rule of 9 years or even at the end of the Great 19 year cycle, but could retain his power through hereditary monarchy: however to change the ruling power the waning king would be killed after 19 years. Further the theocratic priesthood sought to remove the woman entirely from the story, by fusing the woman to the Twin Kings in the bisexual god of Hermes; thus removing the woman's persistent objection to the gold cup of power and wealth as the 'root' whilst the elixir and the power to release man from the trap had been removed to insignificant 'branch'. The question 'Whom do you serve?' in the Grail Romances is based upon this issue.

Godfrey Higgins, the 19th Century antiquary stated: "A great number of Celtic, Sanscrit and Latin words which are evidently identical prove most superabundantly that the Hebrew is Welsh, and the Welsh is both Sanscrit and Latin; therefore, that the Hebrew is Sanscrit. I believe there were many Sanskrit languages; it was an appellative term, and applied equally to the Gael or Celtic in India, and in Scotland. The Scots Gael or Celtic was the Gael or Singala, of Beni-Gael, of Point-de-Galle, or Oru Gallu of the Syrian or Hebrew or Pushto. This very ancient and first-written syllabic language was, I cannot doubt, the Sanskrit or holy writ, and thus it is found in Scotland" [189] Further Brigadier Wilson pointed out in *Coincidences? Pointers to our Heritage* that: "There is a significant basic similarity between the old indigenous tongues of these Isles (Britain) and ancient Hebrew (not Yiddish which is totally different) e.g. between Welsh and Hebrew, between Gaelic and Hebrew and between Erse and Hebrew, Cornish is similar as also is Breton. How did these old Celtic tongues of these Islands evolve? And why is there this basic similarity to Hebrew?" The fact that the thirteenth tribe as Adomites have existed here as part of their homeland of the old Atlantis, means that the question of the Brigadier is answered. British archaeologists have yet to account for the lack of human remains in certain geological strata, which sounds like a mass cull and clean up the evidence! Is it that the racial stock of that period in Britain may identify the source of the Admits and perhaps that they were not a white race? Genetics became a dirty word after the Aryan Super Race programme and eugenics, however it is still a valuable tool in the discovery of historical truth. The German O.T.O who historically held Nazi sympathies must have aligned themselves with the goals of the thirteenth tribe, if not being members of the tribe itself. Crowley wrote the Gnostic Mass, for the O.T.O., which is a nineteenth degree secret that ran:

> "And I believe in the Serpent and the Lion, Mystery of Mystery, in his name Baphomet, And I believe in one Gnostic Catholic Church of Light, Love and Liberty, the world of whose law is.... (Thelema in Greek)"

It is odd that Crowley should have supported the Gnostic Catholic Church, unless of course here he referred to the old Trinity of woman as Goddess and

Twin Kings. Crowley was invoking Hermes in the Paris Working, where he employed homosexual magic, the basis of which I have already explained in terms of morphic resonance. In a preamble, Crowley announces the programme in his biography *Confessions*:

> "...The *9th year* of the *new aeon* of *Horus* which began in 1904, i.e. 1913). Frater O.S.V. accomplished the task laid on him by the **Great White Brotherhood** by issuing No. 10 of The Equinox..." (*Author's emphasis*).

Crowley thus admits in this quote who: "sent" him, the Great White Brotherhood and by extrapolation The Great White Lodge of "invisible" Masters. I previously commented that Hitler had been in possession of the drug anhalonium lewinii, which in 1920's and 1930's was unusual. Crowley himself used it and in his treatise *Magick in Theory and Practice*, gives more insight into the use of this drug together with cocaine! Which reveals that this drug was used in certain ceremonial rites to aid materialisation of the so-called spirit from which information was requested. Hitler as we know developed a tremble on one side of his body and he often look glazed during his speeches, thus it might be explained here! The drug involved invoking of "gods" and the conjuring up of "demons" (get a grip reader! – probably past thought of the MMRC case in history). In fact the drug anhalonium lewinii is quoted by Crowley as "the drug proper to Hermes". Thus it looks as though Crowley was attempting to access what later Hubbard may have co-incidentally discovered and referred to as Inc.1 (Hermes as Chariot, Horn as Bull-Minos cult, and cherubim as Angel?). Thus here there is some unproven but tenuous link, between Crowley's magical rites, and Hitler, who actually referred at one point to "Her" revealing Twin Kings and Mother Goddess and by implication the hermetic god (*Alternative 4*). The old Trinity (as a first downgrade of the truth) would become the new religion, whatever developing variant form that would take, as decreed by the Masters: just as Crowley referred to his variant religion as Thelema and Hitler was to make the Aryan race the new religion.

The interesting thing is that in one of Crowley's invocations, he evidently refers to this hermetic information as the formulation of "the Universe", or the beginning. However I strongly dispute this, preferring the anti-matter matter explosion and the evolving diablo pattern. Hubbard also thought that Inc. 1 was an "implant" at the beginning and thus a bad thing, which would be correct, since obviously the manufacture of the god Hermes overlaid a former truth. The birth of the World Order plan is indicated when in the invocation Crowley states:

At the Ending of the Light,
At the Limits of the Night,
Stood Mercury before the
unborn ones of Time.   {Mercury represented
                                                          Hermes}

Then was formulated the Universe; {Implies Hermes was the beginning}
Then came forth the Gods thereof,   {Implies religion evolved from here}
The aeons of the Bornless Beyond.
Then was the Voice vibrated;   {Implies channelling Hermes Master}
Then was the Name declared.
At the threshold of Entrance   {New Year, or threshold of Beth-Luis-Nion
                                                     alphabet and threshold of tomb
                                                     of sacred king, also threshold
                                                     to new eon of hermetic magic?}

Between the Universe and the Infinite,
In the sign of the Enterer
Stood Mercury, as before him   {Implies that Hermetic magic opened
                                                     Up whole time track event by
                                                     Channelling}

The aeons were proclaimed
In symbols did he record them: {Implies the recording of event data
In breath did he vibrate them;   pa symbols e.g. chariot,
For between the Light and the
Darkness did he stand.
And horn and cherubim i.e. access

Well Crowley now admits his Masters and the secret order who "sent" him as the Great White Brotherhood: however since we know, that Crowley was a Rose-Croix Mason and Rosicrucian and also an O.T.O member, then this has implications of the Great White Lodge and those "invisible" masters. In the above ritual we note, that Hermes and the "new college of magic" in all probability allowed whole track event data to be channelled, presumably also the thought forms and the technology of ancestors, such as the Atlanteans, with their celestial space cars. I believe that it was this form of magic that Hitler utilised and was warned against as black magic. However the science I produce here shows that there is probably very little difference between black and white magic, in so far as it is a manifestation of the laws of morphic resonance and the whole of hologram science. The worst feature however, is that these channellers including Hitler it would seem, do not recognise that thought retained within the holographics is past thought, which is recorded in archetypal symbols and then requires the interpretation of the channeller. The reason why Crowley was an adept at translating the holographs into event data must to a certain degree have depended on his admitted involvement in past lives with the secret groups and therefore he was familiar with the symbols. Further Crowley may have had previous lives as a Cabalist, as one rarely changes direction; once this path has been taken as Hitler was warned. The main point however, is this misconception that the Universe began with a horn, chariot and cherubim or what Hubbard refers to as Inc.1 when in fact, it is I would emphasise from my own viewpoint, the start of the Religious Revolution and a system of control. The year of Horus which began in 1913 is interesting, in so far as I have claimed that World War I resulting with the Versailles Treaty, which carved up Europe forbidding Germany to manufacture weapons and annexing some of her previous land, was to create the impetus for World War II. In short there was probably and Eye of Horus (comparable to the Illimunatus or Hermetic Eye of intelligence) plan at work, which runs its miserable course through two World Wars, up to European Union and a Federal Super state, as a final stage of the World Order plan, which must include a universal political (Communist/Illuminati) kingdom allied to a religious kingdom. Further, the star Mercury depicts Hermes and the alchemist's metal of Mercury. Mercury is like quicksilver it separates and then as if by magic coalesces into one and this would have suited the mind and goal of the MMRC case, illustrating the phrase on the One Dollar note of America 'Out of many come one', with the Illuminatus power political and religious pyramid. This star appeared over Jesus and the three kings, in the early Christian stone ring from Naples, where evidently it was still remembered at that early time: as a Rosicrucian explained Hermes saw the birth of the divine child: which implies a thirteenth tribe plan, but also it was a plan based on a "new college of magic".

The fact that Crowley believed he was invoking spirits or Masters, was given in the Licence to Depart or dismissal of the evoked forces: "And now I say unto thee, depart in peace unto thine habitations and abodes...and be thou ready to come, whensoever thou art invoked and called!" In fact the sex act was used to invoke Hermes and Crowley often used whatever came to hand (male or female), however one suspects that Freemasonry being an all boys club, may have invited the former, if the rite of Hermes was re-enacted. I suspect that the push towards 'coming out of the closet' is really a Masonic impetus. Crowley was quite an adept at obtaining information and one assumes that Parson's who was the Grand Master of the Lodge Agape in Pasadena to which Ron Hubbard belonged (or was "sent into" according to official COS lines) had access to such rites. In one working or invocation Crowley appears to have a conversation with the god or spirit, who also appears to render information. The convincing interplay of interpretation, holographics of the past and experience of the seer or magician in the past and present is complex, but very convincing of the illusionary presence of an actual spirit. However this is not the case, it is merely this complex interplay of information memory holographic banks and the mind which sorts through its own holographic banks at lightening speed forming associative ideas and story to match the holographics:

The first question that O.S.V. asked was, 'Are we working right?'
'No', was the disconcerting answer.
'What's wrong?' said O.S.V.
'The time and to a lesser extent, the place'.
'What is the right time?' asked O.S.V.
'Three hours before dawn.'
'Does this apply to Mercury alone or to all the gods?'
'To Mercury alone.'

Thus Neuburg who helped Crowley in this invocation and acted as the seer was in a trance, but in response to Crowley's questions (O.S.V.) the reply from Neuberg was thought to be the god or higher spirit speaking through him, in this case Hermes. According to holographic science, if you present one factor in a hologram it will encourage the whole hologram to be 'pulled down'. Thus the more factors, such as resonant emotion, personnel, sound, objects, clothing etc that are utilised, then the greater the likelihood that the entire hologram will be precipitated with its information. However the reason that the magicians so often misinterpreted the data, is that only perhaps one frame, in several hundred feet of 'film roll' would emerge, requiring personal experience and *interpretation* of the data, by the seer or magician. In Aleister Crowley's case his own interpretation of data, would depend on his past lives and in one he described himself as part of a Council, which was attempting to control humanity for good or bad (comparable to the Nautonnier of Freemasonry) as the thirteenth member in a Council of twelve. In one UFO witness account, which I related in *Alternative 4*, there was what seemed a banal question of: 'what time is it?' Interestingly enough the witness claimed the question came from some mechanical being, which is often associated with the UFO experience. Time as we can see from Crowley's magical record, is part of the Black Cabalistic ritual and certainly these rituals are mechanistic, simply because thought and data is being pulled down from the past from that great big computer in the sky, the Akashic Record: a mechanical record if you like. Thus the UFO witness may have picked up a couple of frames in several hundred feet of 'film roll', relating to the Arch controller. The question is whether this was a deep philosophical question, or whether the Cabalistic magical ritual had imprinted on the bioplasma, simply by the magician setting up a morphic resonance that inter-faced present time, with the past. This is the problem with channelling isn't it, if you start to re-stimulate these past holograms and set up a morphic resonance, then you do actually start to 'pull them down' and further **new** holograms will be imprinted. I believe in this way that the time track on these events gets muddled. For instance to take Hubbard's Xenu character a mind controller, there may have been a number of these controllers on the track of time and since they continually use Black Cabalistic methods, then they re-stimulate these past control holograms, but also add data simply through the Cabalistic ritual which relies on morphic resonance. Thus you might get several holograms on the same subject i.e. arch controller, but when the hologram is picked up in present time, the mind confuses the exact date and time sequence simply because data has been added to the original hologram which is now a composite. What is certain though, is that new information was stolen in Crete and subsequently used wrongly in Cabalistic practise and therefore the imprinted archetypal symbols of the Cabal who overran Knossos were imprinted on a higher grade of energy. Why were they imprinted on a higher grade of energy or the spiritual bioplasma? – because a very fierce spiritual battle was fought in Crete. At a subconscious level these archetypal symbols still have the power to control: for which reason I thought that the use 9consciously or unconsciously) of such symbols by Hollywood was unethical. Further, either UFO witnesses are naturally picking up single frames in hundreds of feet of 'film roll' of these holographic events, which Hubbard terms Inc. 1 and Inc. 2 and which I refer to as Religious Revolution and Magnetic Reversal respectively, or the World Order is experimenting on unsuspecting civilians as the FBI did with LSD.

It appears to me, that if Hubbard did go into the O.T.O and therefore Crowley's Order with the intention of breaking up black magic, it may have been to stop, the magical practices of channelling past thought processes through this "new college of magic" or the Hermetic school of magic, which does in fact rely on the past thoughts of the Cabal or Masters that overran Knossos. This cabal are those beings who through re-incarnation have always controlled man through many cycles, including Atlantis or the pre-Flood era. Such beings I term the MMRC case and it was my theory in my previous books, that they originally 'fell' to earth, by trying to manipulate mankind through the etheric morphogenetic bioplasma, which effectively through the genetic line or DNA on the physical level within the body, controls the human being: the puppet Masters who pulled the strings from above and then fell to join the puppets, only to be effectively now pulled by their invisible strings of the past. Effectively the MMRC case tried to add and subtract data from the master blueprint in the sky, which as a master genetic code would obviously affect the phylogenetic line of the species. It appears however, that at some point in pre-history the MMRC case became trapped in the holographics by coming to Earth and in effect became subject to their own past thoughts now retained within the Grid holographics. The dramatization of this incident is seen today not only in an obsession with secret "invisible" Masters or "Guardians", which appears to be the case with Crowley's chiefs i.e. the Great White Brotherhood, controlled by "invisible" Masters OR "Guardians" within the Great White Lodge; but also in the belief, that some day these beings will land again on Earth. In fact as I have proposed, every time a Magnetic Reversal occurs they do like Noah, manage to miss that event, perhaps by space ships of their own and merely return to create a new cycle. I suspect that the appearance of mechanical beings and space ships, in the natural UFO experience is a past holographic memory of this. The farmer who witnessed such an event recounted in *Alternative 4*, spoke of being given "cookies"; once again the personal interpretation of the witness depends on their own past experience and knowledge. The "cookie" may be substituted as 'manna from heaven' or totem beast and the whole memory of a tribe, which is incorporated within the totem beast. One might say that beings in the past descended from space (after a Magnetic Reversal) and then sought to imprint the memory of the tribe on the peoples of Earth: such a tribe being the biblical Adamites or their descendents from way back on the time track of man, which may in fact even go back to some Xenu character. The farmer may not have the relevant holographs in his own memory banks, which allows him to match the holograph with lightening speed, thus 'manna' or totem beast indicating tribal memory in his own memory banks is translated as that the mother bakes for the child. He has experienced some form of these past incidents involving the Religious Revolution, but cannot interpret them, since either he has no background education, or experience. If the farmer had been a witness of the Religious Revolution, then he would have interpreted them entirely differently. Crowley could gain information since it was suspected that in one of his past lives, he had been a Cretan snake goddess, which might have accounted for his obsession with drugs, since opium was used not only be the Cabal who overran Knossos, but drugs have always been used to control man and used in Cabalistic practice. The fact that the young today are overwhelmed with drugs is a reflection of the Cabal who currently runs the world as in the past.

In fact the MMRC case first landed millions or even billions of years ago and would only land again after each Magnetic Reversal or indeed may have initially suffered Magnetic Reversals, before he realised he could avoid them, whilst leaving humanity to mentally and spiritually deteriorate through the experience of such cycles: also spirits became continually trapped by the beauty of Earth and thus the continuing soul population continued to rise. The Arch controllers or MMRC case has lived among humanity unnoticed, apart from the visible and obsess ional desire for a World Order, with themselves always in charge of humanity. They merely dramatize the controlling incident of manipulation of the morphogenetic bioplasma, which is also dramatized as the field of biotechnology and cloning, which in the past was a goal of a slave species. Whilst I have spent much time in this book trying to identify the cabal who took the Holy Grail during the Religious Revolution at Knossos c. 1 400 B.C, that effort centres on the ability to discover who that group is in present time further defining the exact group and goal of the Arch controllers today. There appears to me, to be two groups of Rosicrucians both of Semitic origins, but one with a Greek history and one with an Egyptian history, the former representing 13 th tribe and the latter either the 12 tribes of Israel *or* some remnant group of the 13 th tribe that has aligned itself with the 12 tribes of Israel. Increasingly to me, it occurs that it was the Egyptian group or the Jewish priests that overran Knossos and certainly Egypt did have trading links with the Early Minoans. However, I have noticed that there are many Minoan symbols that turn up in Scotland and equally the Druids with their Greek background of the Tuatha de Danaan could have conducted the Religious Revolution. Thus we are left to decide between 12 or 13 as the origins of the Religious Revolution and the start of mind and religious control that would come to fruition in a plan for a World Order, with its religious and political goals. Who did it, is further complicated by the cunning with which the MMRC case has sought to cover his tracks, by intermixing the two groups with the enormous number of front groups in history.

As I have covered, the events of Golgotha were a ' play out' between these two groups of 12 and 13 and where the last remaining truth held by the Magdalene was stolen, along with her genealogies. Those genealogies however were absolutely critical in deciphering this story, as was the ability to regain my own witness account memory. The genealogies related to a Greek background and thus if I extrapolate that conclusion, then I have to place the Egyptian Jewish priests as the chief culprit. The thirteenth tribe may have tried to regain power and thus organise the events of Golgotha, however the game by that time, had already deteriorated into double agent capers, spying and manipulation of the Grail, thus one group became no better than the other and both groups by now had extensive knowledge of the Religious Revolution and the quest by both groups for a World Order with its political and religious goals. The thirteenth tribe evidently tried to combat Divine kingship and the dynastic rule of despotic kings, by introducing the concept of Messiah, but it was not the truth and was bound to fail, it was a wrong turn and reflected the Semitic background of both groups, in so far as neither group could actually give the gift as intended, without putting a control factor on it. That control factor always required the Illuminatus power pyramid with its one or two controlling brains or a Theocratic priesthood at the top, handing out or not, the Grail according to the elitism and assumed superiority that was inherent within the tribes of Israel. Throughout history there has been the question within both groups, whether or not to release the mysteries and the old question of 'whom do you serve?' cup or elixir or wealth and power, as opposed to release of the elixir hidden within that gold cup. However both groups held the cup more important and even if it were the case, that Scientology wanted to release the mysteries then either Hubbard or his successors succumbed to the cup. Even so there was a control factor on both lines and neither did the message of the Grail and its knowledge belong to either of them.

It is not even certain whether the thirteenth tribe, Druids, Rosicrucian's, Bull-Minos cult, or biblical Adamites as one and the same, were always as one tribe. When the Tuatha de Dannan entered Greece presumably from the region of the Black Sea and Lake Moeris where the Beth-Luis Nion alphabet originated as did Thothmess III the Grand Master or leader one assumes of the original 13 th tribe; it may have been that some remnant of the tribe wandered to Egypt, whilst the Tuatha de Danaan went to Ireland and eventually to Scotland in Great Britain. Since the Tuatha de Danaan were considered gods, there is every reason to believe, if this were the case, that those remnants of the tribe that may have wandered to Egypt also had Black Cabalistic powers that would render them powerful, which as I have shown in the early history of the patriarchs including Joseph appears to be the case. There is thus some indication that there may have been two factions to the Rosicrucian's and although not always known under that name appear to evolve from a common stock that utilised the Black Cabala and then diversified i.e. Egyptian and Greek which in the latter developed Celtic or Scottish links, which depended on the migrations undertaken approx. 2 000 B.C. The Tuatha de Danaan as biblical Adamites originally from the Black Sea region going to Scotland and Ireland from Greece, perhaps whilst another faction from the Black Sea region travelled to Egypt and became reconciled with the 12 tribes of Israel. I will rejoin this line of enquiry again shortly.

The Esoteric record for Crowley's third Working, begins by giving Brother L.T.'s description of Hermes: "the god was essentially phallic, but in his hand is a book called Book II, which has 106 pages. On the last page is a luminous *four-pointed* star, which (the Magicians decide) is to be identified with the eye of Shiva, the symbolic eye in shiva's forehead. It is closed; if however, Shiva should choose to open it, its light would destroy the universe." The sub-title of the book was BIA, 'force'. Presumably to unlock the past Akashic Record on the secrets of atomic science would indeed cause destruction and a third battle before a Magnetic Reversal, or perhaps as the physicists press on with their anti-matter and matter experiments, they just cannot stop themselves in their quest to open Pandora's box and destroy the universe. Hermes of course was phallic, since he was the product of the Religious Revolution by the Bull-Minos cult, who were phallic in the fertility sense where the seed of the king in Palaeolithic times was considered the source of the tribe; and the icons of the Late Minoan period at the time when the Bull-Minos cult took over Knossos, show men with pronounced penis: along with the Late Minoan seals, which show egg with piercing phallic member, or magician's and Druidical wand. We might here interject a new interpretation, that the egg or potential for the world was not only seen in the male (as penis and fertility) but as wand (of magician) and presumably the new magical rites developed ("a new college of magic"), which could access whole time track data and more importantly events and technology of that past. The whole point expressed here in this book, evidently entirely forgotten or missed by the "dunce", is that Cabalistic ritual channelling of *past thought precipitates in present time, the events of the past.* As sure as night follows day, there will be a Third World War on this planet, if man does not question and disband the World Order. Further in the above account, Hermes is associated with force, simply because the woman and male engaged in a spiritual battle for the Holy Grail of some proportion, which the woman sought to save for humanity, however Hermes won and got to record his successes on the spiritual bioplasma. Thus my previous assertion, that the character of Xenu and that of Yatrus are merely the interpretation of that battle of male versus female in the X and Y-chromosomes, really depends on the experience and knowingness of the person who interprets such data.

This would certainly account for the icons found at Knossos, where a man held his hand to the third eye, which I thought was channelling and the opening of the third eye or crown chakra. Also drugs were evidently used and we can thank the World Order for opium and the 'Poppy Goddesses' at Knossos. I believe I have mentioned elsewhere, that I believe LSD connects the mind biofield of the individual user, to the Apocalyptic event of a Magnetic Reversal or space boundary event: and the FBI were utilising this drug in the 1960's and fobbed it off care of the World Order on humanity, presumably because it tunes man, into the 'script' or Grid of past holographics and as such is a form of mind control, for which reason it should with other hallucinatory drugs be banned: those people who sell or deal in these drugs must think carefully about the future of their souls, for the karma on such things is horrific and the amount one must do to rectify that karma is enormous. The mind expansion that users of LSD sought, merely tuned them into Grid holographics. Mind control as was utilised at Knossos and thus Hubbard's Inc. 1 which I explained in terms of mind control, most certainly is imprinted up there along with the symbols that Crowley spoke of. The phallic god of Hermes also was reflected in icons with large penis and presumably the egg with piercing wand or phallus, which as a symbol is displayed in the Freemason's Temple floor in London and aptly named, but perfectly misinterpreted 'Great Queen' Street. The fact that women are not often used in magical practice was commented on by Crowley as it: "is more dangerous to the career of the magician". Presumably the 33 rd magical degree of Freemasonry as a boy's club which together with all the degrees is organised as such for this reason. Crowley does not explain why, but women most certainly would as mothers presumably interpret the material differently and feel some abhorrent concern over the concept of the use of the cup to decide who is to gain access to the elixir. Neither would a woman relish the idea of homosexual practise and the "new college of magic", which sought information from the time of the Religious Revolution with its secrets of the Teacher, cosmology and knowledge dependent on invoking Hermes, the god installed at this time. In practical and scientific terms, the cabalistic rites depended on creating morphic resonance through ritual practice, which involved homosexuality, thus accessing the entire hologram and therefore information. A mother cannot choose between her children and who is the better, she loves them all equally. Just as she would love those terrible Twin Kings equally and tell them they are both wrong, and both right, but overall, so terribly wrong!

I stated that I thought the woman may have been used to intermarry with more deformed types to create a race. The deformed types perhaps remnants of the Magnetic Reversal. In one of Crowley's workings, he was specifically told to gain four men who were deformed and four women from the corners of the Earth. Crowley was led to believe that in this invocation he would receive the wisdom of the serpent:

> "I now see the eightfold star of Mercury suddenly blazing out; it is composed of four fleurs-de-lys with rays like anthers, bulrushes in shape, between them. The central core has the cipher of the grand master, but not the one you know. Upon the cross are the Dove, the hawk, the Serpent and the Lion. Also, one other symbol, yet more secret. Now behold fiery swords of light. All this is upon a cosmic scale. All the distances are astronomical. When I say 'Sword', I have a definite consciousness of a weapon many millions of miles in length....".

Indeed the Grid, together with the vacuum energies is currently being used as the 'sword', under the alleged strategic defence initiative known as the Star Wars programme (HAARP – The High Active Auroral Research Programme) with its mind control capability and further discussed in *Alternative 4*. This allusion to the sword is not uncommon in myth and legend. The idea of the sword as a weapon surfaced in the Indian epics, which told of a third battle. Crowley was to discuss his work, as perhaps Einstein had discussed: "something similar, that men before have had to face". Crowley's discussion centred on the rites unloosing a huge force, and he expressed the fear that, in time, it would become dangerous, 'International complications' and so forth. Indeed his fears were to materialise as the Nazi scientists went to America after the war and took the magical rites with them, presumably now further researched as Rosicrucian knowledge. Whether Crowley foresaw the knowledge of the past, as creating portent for the future in his referral to dangerous "International complications", is unsure but quite possible.

The abberative holograms of the past sacrificial rites were to be again dramatized as the Supreme Rite, which brought about a climax in the death of the victim. How many poor souls or children in the past have been lost to this abhorrent secret rite can only be guessed at, together with how far these secret societies have in the past created man's dramatization in present time of such dramatized rites as paedophilia – there can be no more worse sin, that to betray the innocence of a child: Those who commit this act, must indeed save many children, before their conscience would release them from the first post of the trap, in the 'Life Review' of the death experience. Crowley as if intimating the Druidic and Celtic custom of cannibalism, stated that the victim: "preferably a girl" should not be eaten. Thus if one looks at Crowley's connections to Germany and the Communists, then one perceives indeed a black magic and patriarchal group, presumably descended from the 12 tribes? and the use of the black Cabala. Thus it may be the case that Hubbard as a member of a scientific branch of the Rosicrucian's? did go in to break up this group of Crowley's, for it was noted by Parson's to Crowley, that Hubbard had some magical knowledge and it is still not clear where he obtained that knowledge, if not from another branch of the O.T.O and the Rosicrucians.

The science of holograms is really a science that depends on the laws of physics, where a complete picture of an event is recorded even with the environmental conditions such as wind or weather; as I have explained many parameters are recorded: including personnel, thought, sound, emotion etc. The environment represents a recording of the history of matter and thus is relevant to the bioplasma or Akashic Record. Crowley's Paris Working was a series of magical rites in varying degrees and during the Tenth Working Crowley tried to invoke Jupiter in his Egyptian form of Ammon-Ra, once again this god has some connection to Knossos, since icons show figures with hands raised to the god Ammon-Ra. I have already referred to the quality of art, which declined after the Religious Revolution along with the introduction of stilted icons with an almost mechanical quality that was vastly different from the life force that had flowed through Knossos, prior to the Religious Revolution. The Paris Working was entirely a homosexual rite and the crystal ball was used in the method of scrying. In the Fifth Working, Crowley gave the colours connected to the gods. The god Priapus was the Greek and Roman god of *procreation (fertility)* and interestingly protector of gardens and vineyards ('the vine man' or 'he who draws together' – the biblical Adamites). The worship of this god, whose visible emblem was the phallus, was widespread, and in parts of Italy extended throughout the Christian era to modern times. The colours of Priapus were yellow and purple. With regard to the colours we must remember that the world (circle) was black (magic) and Hermes and the phallic god (Priapus in Crowley's account) superimposed that black, with the triangle of three and mauve. However a purer colour was silver, since it was her colour and carried the apple of immortality and the elixir; it was only later that silver became associated with quicksilver or Mercury as Hermes. The red colour of 'The Prince' that appeared on the frescoes of Knossos after the Religious Revolution, signified Pan, the god of lust and passion and the blood red carbuncle of royalty. This together with the Poppy Goddesses and seals showing orgiastic rites signifies that sexual hysteria and invocations were being utilised, which is presumably why Crowley had to use sexual intercourse to invoke Hermes the god of the cabal at Knossos. The psychro cave, the alleged birthplace of Zeus associated with power and wealth, also contained cauldrons in archaeological finds indicating Cabalistic ritual, which is presumably responsible for the imprinting of archetypes described by Hubbard as Inc.1. The phallic god was also symbolised by the bull, which is the basis of the Bull-Minos cult who overran Knossos: further the figure-of-eight, which as a symbol was to occur frequently in Scotland and Crete, was the symbol of Hermes and I concluded anti-matter and matter cycle, including the electron shell orbital path. This effectively was the knowledge that was stolen and hidden and which the black magician sought. Such knowledge then eventually by ascendancy of secret groups came into the hands of the Rosicrucian's that probably form a line from the Druids in one group and from the Egyptian priest Thothmess in the other group.

It is interesting that the auditory imprint of the holographic appeared to be heard by Crowley during his invocation of Jupiter, during the Tenth Working. Crowley and his assistant Neuberg clearly and distinctly heard the sound of astral bells. This is odd, since Madame Blavatsky worked for a higher Order of her so-called "Masters", but in all probability some branch of the Rosicrucians if not the Great White Brotherhood: she was also a seeress who channelled information by automatic writing and was the chief instigator of racialist doctrine that has plagued the secret groups. The sound of 'astral bells' was frequently heard in her presence, as though she herself was part of the hologram and her mere presence could re-stimulate or pull down the auditory part of the hologram of past memory. This would imply, that she was in fact a channeller for black magic. Interestingly also, other sounds can be heard according to witnesses of practices in Yoga, where the serpent of Kundalini is stirred, such as the drone of the bee, the whine of the flute and the clash of cymbals. Once again such things as the horn or cymbals are merely the auditory input, at the time the hologram was imprinted such as might be employed in Cabalistic ritual in the past. Kundalini is associated with energy at the base of the spine, generally accorded with sexual energy. The manner of behaviour today of teenagers, when they reach puberty and the Kundalini energy of the sexual hormones is awakened, implies that such behaviour is attributable to a connection through the biofield to Grid holographics: inclusive of behaviour, thought and other parameters. One might consider that the teenager connects with the whole of the holographic memory of sexual behaviour and thought as part of the memory of the survival mechanisms of the phylogenetic line. Unfortunately this appears to be an activity in the past associated with the MMRC case that frequently utilised sexual practices in magical ritual and thus imprinted this on the Grid holographics. The MMRC case as we have seen is totally obsessed with himself at the lower end of survival and with the group at the upper end. Adolescents quite literally can be little 'monsters'! For this reason I believe and since this kind of hologram is very re-stimulative, it can certainly drag anyone in the vicinity (the parent!) down to that level, via re-stimulation. I have already discussed teenagers and gangs or groups as part of an animal pack survival activity in the absence of a family 'pack' model. Families pushed to the edges of survival, where a single parent now acts as the substitute for the 'pack' model cannot form the strong anchor point needed, which is part of the phylogenetic memory of the species. The extended family in times before the World Order policies broke down that unit, used to represent the animal 'pack' and there is no doubt, that children in extended families are better protected, simply because that unit provides a majority viewpoint and model. A single parent cannot represent that model no matter how hard they try and despite the growing tendency for broken 'pack' or family units, it is a counter evolutionary survival action. Undoubtedly as children become more estranged from the family or 'pack', you will find that children and teenagers will fall prey to the Grid survival animal pack mechanism. The most interesting observation however is the sound of the bee, which has obsessed as ideas of beehives and ant heaps, World Order thinking including Adam Weishaupt, the arch controller of the Illuminati. The beehive or honeycomb mountain was of course found in Crete, Britain and in the Palaeolithic caves of France, where earliest Palaeolithic finds included the coral, a social colony. These forms of colony fascinated the World Order as dramatizations of the past where rule was despotic and communistic run by the elitist Theocratic priesthood –the hive with Queen bee (Hermes).

Crowley noticeably in his magical rituals often became irritable and quarrelled with his associates afterwards and this would be re-stimulation of holograms, within the magical rite, which remind one of events and experience or memory on the track of time in the past. Despite this, drugs, alcohol and women, Crowley seemed remarkably robust to such things. The Tenth Working or invocation of Jupiter (associated with wealth) was received in the angelic language of John Dee and Edward Kelley, to the effect that the gods wished to regain their dominion on earth. The fact that Crowley had contacted not the gods, but past thought of the Masters or MMRC case, was evident when the gods called for: "sacrifice of cruelty". Crowley had a bad night afterwards and perceived the purpose of the kind of operation that they had performed that night was that of "freeing of the elemental spirit of an animal soul". You may remember, that I explained that a memory or hologram in your own memory banks, could be re-stimulated by meeting in the environment once again an element or part of the hologram of a past event e.g. a dog in present time might re-stimulate a past memory of a dog bite and you might feel a slight pain momentarily in the old scar region. This is the process of *re-stimulation*. Thus, during the Cabalistic rite that was utilised it merely restimulated a hologram held in the morphogenetic bioplasma, which I have explained as the one, which carries event data of the environment in the past, together with the irrational or reactive mind of the species, with its survival mechanisms. This is the primitive mind and a mind that was in the past a despotic mind of cruelty and fear, that contains many holographics of the mind of the Arch controllers. Crowley was right in his perception, since by invoking the hologram of the past, stored either in the morphogenetic bioplasma or latterly after the Religious Revolution in the spiritual bioplasma, he merely brought that forward or re-activated it through the process of restimulation. The conclusion might be, that ostensibly you have loosed some demon or animal form, but in reality, you have merely re-stimulated the *memory of an event*, with personnel and environmental factors. People who use the Ouija board might feel a bad presence and they have re-stimulated the thoughts of past masters, the primitive animal mind. The problem becomes, whether such re-stimulation, then leaves that hologram 'active' and thus able to influence man in present time. Thus it was perceived by Hubbard that Xenu was active again, but is this merely the action of more and more people accessing this particular hologram and the events I would propose in Crete, at the time of the Religious Revolution thus re-stimulating it? The problem is you can't flatten that etheric hologram, to use the Scientology term of erasing the hologram or "engram" (a picture of loss, pain or unconsciousness in the past) from the reactive or irrational mind, since the hologram of Xenu must be seen exactly for what it is (truth) before it will erase. My aim with this book would be to try and erase the hologram by as many people as possible reading this book and understanding how that trap of the spider's web has been woven. Mind and Spirit control stops here!

I have noticed a rise in UFO witness accounts, which report some Greek connection. Equally atomic weaponry must be highly re-stimulative to past holograms, if the past event did contain an atomic war as was suspected in the Indian Epics. Thus do we merely re-create the past event in present time, by ignorance of what is happening in such invocations or memories of the past pulled down by channelling or by the seer using the crystal? The rise in atomic detonations since 1945 must have re-stimulated the etheric hologram of the past with its nuclear explosion and a third battle, which I am afraid, is not good, since that would have operative control on Grid connected or brain-dead types in present time. Further there were a number of natural UFO events, that warned of atomic detonations and a number of witnesses reported being shown pictures of nuclear or atomic detonations. Thus, one has to ask, whether some flux of energy through the ether vacuum energy caused holographs from the past to impinge on the mind biofield of the witness, through the 'Onion Ring' mechanism I proposed in *Alternative 4*. Such witnesses reported a loss of space-time reality and this would be entirely correct, since the memory of the atomic explosion is carried within the holographics of the morphogenetic bioplasma, which carries event data for *matter* and also the primitive or reactive mind holograms. When one accesses such data, the rational or conscious mind switches off, as it does in any shock or accident, which then leaves the reactive or primitive mind only to make sense of the event. The only way to stop the re-stimulation is to erase the event entirely from the bioplasma or confront it with absolute mirror symmetry of truth, thus this book hopes to erase the control master hologram of both the Religious Revolution in Crete and the Magnetic Reversal, which Hubbard termed Inc.1 and Inc. 2. respectively. It might indeed appear as if monsters are awaiting somewhere, to invade Earth as the old myths state, but of course there must also be holograms of such events in the past. More accurately it is the entire hologram of the past event that waits. However if you pull that down, no doubt the MMRC case would start again with his sacrifice and black magical rites, channelling once again information from the Grid. It is certainly interesting in this respect, that Crowley's associate after the invocation of Jupiter, went about the next day 'overshadowed by Jupiter' (having re-stimulated the hologram) and the world appeared to him as a 'vision of the future', a phrase which is best explained by the next sentence: "His eyes are dilated; he cannot read; his manner is as one stupefied or entranced, which implies that was momentarily stuck in the hologram of the past. Crowley utilised great "banquets" of food, in between rituals, which rectified the after effects.

Crowley tells of one of his lives as a Temple prostitute, who conducted sex in religious ceremonies, and he managed to worm out of a priest on one such occasion, the "Secret of the Temple" which was "The Midnight sun". This sounds very much like the lights that burnt continually without apparent means, that Dr. Falk the Jew had in London and who was thought to be a very high initiate in Freemasonry. The lights were also utilised in sealed Egyptian chambers. Crowley explains the secret as: "Globes of fire used to gather on the font, and from the other altar, and begin to revolve in the shrine. They would coalesce and then become one, which stood single and unmoving all the night, only fading with dawn". This is comparable to physics research today into vacuum energies, where balls of glowing light were produced, from tapping the zero point energy! Such balls of light have been reported in UFO witness reports, however in each case they have occurred close to a sensitive research facility. Thus we must consider that the gods of old, had very modern technology or rites even, for tapping the zero point energy. Crowley also accessed one of his other past lives and interestingly enough he had been a priestess in Crete. One might assume given the perceptiveness of his channelling or seer crystal gazing, that his interpretation of data would very much depend on his past life there. Undoubtedly then Crowley had past lives that were a part of the 13 th tribe holographs. Evidently Crowley had a long history of sexual practices and control, allied to the Masters. After the Nineteenth working, Crowley once again came down with flu like symptoms and took opium as the cure for Jupiter, which in effect meant, that he 'keyed out' the hologram, probably re-stimulating holographics of Hermes in the process! The Poppy Goddesses in Crete were evidently used in invocations, it seems that the use of sex in the rituals as with the rituals to invoke Hermes, worked quicker results than the long-winded rituals of theurgy that he had been taught by the Golden Dawn. The orgiastic sexual rites that the Cabal who invaded Knossos used would be a part of the hologram along with drugs. It is my opinion that Crowley simply by using parts of the hologram to re-stimulate the entire hologram was promoting morphic resonance. Once again the laws of a science will cover this. I have been at pains to point out, that I have not channelled any information in this book it has been a hard slog of research and personal soul memory. One simply could not trust data from the Grid, as a higher truth, even though obviously from the scientific point of view and my own research it is interesting. The woman, who advised Hitler not to use black Magic or invocations, was very wise to do so, as she warned once you do use it, you will be captured by it. Personally I also believe that it channels energy from the vacuum ether and there is always a certain amount of euphoria or glee around people who do this, with the resultant arousal of Kundalini and the sexual emotive force, which will badly connect one to Grid survival and sexual mechanisms and event past data along with Grid primitive thoughts. Sexual activity with Grid controlled beings has an animal-like quality, however true union in the physical and spiritual sense has a quality that could never be defined but only experienced as a higher plane of knowingness.

In 1905 Rudolf Steiner joined the O.T.O., and also became General Secretary of the Theosophical Society and later founded his own Anthroposophical Society. Reuss invited Steiner into the Inner Order of the O.T.O., but by 1914, the German Freemasons had become at odds with the O.T.O and looked upon Reuss as a traitor. Whether or not the Germans then set up their own Order, which was to initiate Hitler's association is not known, but discussed briefly in *Alternative 4*. Whilst Crowley utilised sexual coupling in his left-handed path, this was not mere sexual deviation, but a necessary part of obtaining the right experimental resonant emotional frequency to pull down specific information from the Grid. However it appears to me, that Crowley was not only pulling down holograms of specific event data, but also the thoughts of those who conducted the Religious Revolution i.e. from research here the Bull-Minos cult or

13 th tribe and biblical Adamites. In Crowley's form of the Christian Mass, the man and woman partake of the 'Feast of the Five Elements', (Pauchatattva) in a frame of mind not earthly but mystical. The five elements are the four of Western occult tradition, Fire, Air, water and Earth, represented respectively as Wine, Flesh, Fish and Cereals and the fifth element by Spirit or Ether. Crowley's partner in magic was Frater O.S.V. who undertook the Paris Working with him in a homosexual union. Crowley felt obliged to undertake this kind of union and sexual magic as Head of the O.T.O., in the U.K. However during the Paris Working his journal records an interesting connection to the Great White Brotherhood, which was an earthly hierarchy of Masters, who claimed initiation from a non visible cosmic hierarchy, which I assumed was the past thoughts of the Masters, indeed probably going back a long way to Atlantean times and before: all of which remain as a record presumably within the morphogenetic bioplasma and not the spirtual, since the first event in the spiritual records, appears to be the Inc. 1 of Hubbard or the Religious Revolution in my own research conclusions, although I cannot be sure that there are not more controlling holographics on the spiritual bioplasma.

Evidently then, not only was the O.T.O directed by the Great White Brotherhood, which was Rosicrucian, but Frater Crowley hoped presumably to be admitted into the Great White Lodge, after completing his task and the "Magnum Opus". Further the symbol utilised in Crowley's Juournal for the Paris Working was a cricle with a dot at the centre, which was the exact symbol that Adam Weishaupt the founder of Illuminism utilised for his group The Illuminati (*The Battle of The Trees*). Thus increasingly the Universal Religion of the Rosicrucians looks like a part of the Political aim of The Universal Kingdom and The Illuminati. This would appear to be the goal symbolised on the One Dollar note from America. Oddly enough Hubbard used the Illuminatus power pyramid structure in the Scientology Organisation, with one or two controlling figures or brains at the top, which in Hubbard's time was himself. Although Miscavige is now the *visible* head of the COS, I have questioned whether the COS is in fact a secret society, which by definition has unknown goals and superiors at its unseen or *invisible* apex, only the COS can answer such questions and in the interim we must accept that Hubbard was a genius, thought it all up himself and never had any secret group connections.

The term Illuminati refers to the students of occult mysticism - the enlightened ones, with implications to the "chosen ones" in the Bible, when referring to the Jews. It refers to those who have received Illumination or light in the sense of cosmic consciousness and realization of omnipresence, which I assume is the acceptance of past or hidden Masters in the Great White Lodge? Further one has to ask whether such Illumination is natural through knowledge and philosophy with a corresponding opening of the charkas, or some kind of downloading from the Masters, by technological means as in the case of the neural chip. Channelling or seer activity using crystal ball or automatic writing could be considered an illumination, since there is access to past events and thoughts from past Masters. The term Illuminati was historically applied to the Rosicrucian's and Martinists and The Rosicrucian's were often known as "Brothers of the Illuminati" and have also been known as Illumines. The fact that the place name 'Bavaria' occurred in the *Vaincre* magazine illustration, with its proposal for a Universal Religious ('Brittany') and Political ('Bavaria') Kingdom is further paralleled by the dual political and religious aims, seen on the reverse side of the One Dollar note from America. Bavaria was of course the birthplace of Adam Weishaupt, the founder of the Illuminati.The note however shows Rosicrucian symbols and archetypal symbols connected to Knossos and the Order of the Rose, which is paralleled in the Vaincre magazine illustration with its goal of a Federal European Super State. Thus there is a strong indication here, that the Religious aim of The One World Order is a Rosicrucian or White Brotherhood aim and by inference, run by the Great Lodge of "invisible " Masters or "Guardians" who may in fact be visible if only one could locate them as "the constant Sanhedrin of Europe". There is also the possibility, that the "invisible" group of Masters within the Great White Lodge, is merely the thought of past Masters being channelled from the Grid, in which case www-com/grid, is really running politics and religion as that great big mega computer in the sky! Evidently Hubbard's Inc. 1 and Inc. 2 sought to challenge that control, but I do not believe that he had sufficiently understood what is happening in terms of the science involved. This might imply that the Illuminati and Rosicrucian's are operating in both Europe and America as one group, with one Universal Kingdom goal, but according to the Rosicrucian's, there are two groups of Illuminati, with Weishaupt's group bearing no connection to an earlier group of Illuminati. Does this imply that once again that there are two groups on the world's stage each utilising a political system of Illuminism, which really is Communism; but with entirely different religious goals, one group wishing to release the mysteries and the other group trying to hide them? Would this account for the all-out American Government agency effort against Scientology? A battle that enlisted so many Government agencies, that it is hard to see that battle solely in terms of the battle of Psychiatry or The Syndicate against the Church, or even the allegations of bad faith to some of its members; although undoubtedly as in my own case those horrors do exist. There seems to

206

be some hidden reason, as to why the COS has caused such a ferocious battle that has not been disclosed by *either side.*

Hermes who was the god installed as the usurper of knowledge in Crete, commonly the god of thieves and vagabonds. The fact that Thutmose III of Egypt, was given by the Rosicrucian's as the original Grand Master of the Great White Lode, may account for the Step pyramid in Egypt, with its levels of Freemasonry and initiation, which I previously discussed. Crowley invoked Thoth the Egyptian form of Hermes in his Paris Working, which was comprised of 24 workings, but on each occasion Crowley opened the Temple with the Ritual 671 - 'The Building of The Pyramid', which in Masonic ritual may have become the building of the Temple. Presumably accounting for 'Jerusalem' at the centre of the concentric ring design at Cardiff Castle, which indicated a religious goal of a World Order, perhaps as the "New Jerusalem". We might equate the two i.e. building of pyramid and Temple as the completion of a goal for a World Order, with religious and political pre-determined goals. Crowley in his account of the working for once gives some insight of the results: "and upon the stroke of midnight did the first **words** and **acts** of the Accendat strike upon the **Akasa**" (my emphasis). I assume then, not only did Crowley channel thought ("words"), but also events ("acts") from the Akashic Record ("Akasa") or the morphogenetic and spiritual bioplasmas in my own terminology. Rudolf Steiner was to incorporate the Akasha into his work, but never for one moment, giving the secret away. "Accendat" means 'let it be lighted up' and Akasa is Sanskrit word for ether, which we now know as having a patterned energy and further in the bioplasma geometry, which is part of the Grid, contains *information.* Crowley stated that there were many astonishing results, ranging from spiritual illumination to physical phenomena including windstorms, which Parson's working with Hubbard was to comment on, in one of his letters to Crowley. Crowley further claimed, that he had "conversed" with the "mighty well of antiquity" and "**guardians of esoteric tradition**". "One by one they passed before his impassioned gaze; Pythagoras, Plotinus, Auicenna, Paracelsus, Fludd, Willian Blake...He heard them all". (*My emphasis*)

I assume that Crowley in his "esoteric tradition" is really referring to the Secret Doctrine, which was apparently passed down through Moses to St. John and both St. John and Pythagoras were Druids and thus I assume that this is the Doctrine of the biblical Adamites or 13 th tribe? This Doctrine must involve Cabalistic practice and perhaps after 1 400 B.C knowledge of the events at Knossos. At least two of these names, connect with the thirteenth tribe of biblical Adamites. Pythagoras we know to have been initiated by the Dactyls in Crete and Abaris the Arch Druid in Britain and thus I assume Pythagoras was a Druid also. In *The Battle of The Trees (p.143)*, I listed the past Grand Masters of the Prieuré de Sion. That French group I concluded held a religious goal and were matriarchal, with the possibility explored in this book that they were 13 th tribe biblical Adamites. I noted that there still appears to be a group in France today that are 13 th tribe who may or may not be responsible for the lost Scientology court documents. The troubles of the COS in France appear to somewhat parallel those of Greece, in so far as the 12 tribes or one group of Rosicrucian's appear to be in control. Since Germany and France are pushing for a fully integrated Europe and are bent on having a European army independent of NATO, I consider that Federal Europe is the 12-tribe branch of the Rosicrucian's allied to communistic Illuminism. However I noted that COS documents, all three tons of them disappeared prior to a recent trial of Scientologists and proffered the suggestion that such a fete could have only been accomplished with help at a high level. Thus there may be a group in France, the reformed secret group of the Prieuré de Sion perhaps, that is also a branch of the Rosicrucian's, but a specific group that parallels the group symbolised on the One Dollar note of America. Is it any wonder! That America is really concerned about the forthcoming European army, since there appear to be two opposing groups here. To plug this home, then one must remember that a third (nuclear?) battle occurs in the 'script' and has been reported in myth and legend including the Indian epics, just before the 'curtain' comes down in the final 'act. As I have repeatedly tried to warn humanity and especially Europeans and Americans, which I had hope to raise in my Petition questions in the *Appendix II*, that **there will be a THIRD WORLD WAR**, if those questions are not answered and a referendum held on Europe based on the entirety of facts: that war will in all likelihood involve America and Europe.

There are already mounting signs of tension between America and Europe, which until recently took the form of trade disputes with the increasing muscle power of Europe, which has challenged the giant over its hitherto unquestioned and unparallel power. Increasingly though we see the way things are headed and a future picture that I foresaw in 1995, after completing *The Battle of The Trees*. Unfortunately my own attempts to bring this to the notice of the public have been thwarted by the control over publishing and media. America's ambassador to Nato has already warned that the Euro army could destroy the translantic alliance. Alexander Vershbow said that unless many problems were resolved it could "divide" the 50-year-old military pact, "diminish" Europe's capacity to manage crises and 'weaken' U.S commitment to protecting Europe. Predictably plans for the new rapid reaction force to have a separate planning base could cause Europe and America's military priorities to "drift apart". Vershbow warned the EU against seeing the creation of the Euro army purely as a vague political exercise in building a united Europe. The most obvious thing here, is that the EU army follows the same predictable statement line as those of the past, which assured Europeans that European Union, was not going to develop into a European Federal super state with its own army. Its disgraceful that the arrogant Masters, have by stealth and stages unleashed a plan onto the world's stage, that was in evidence, at least from the times of Jesus and as I have illustrated in this book prior to that from the time of the post Flood era. Betrayal and stealth is most certainly the method of the World Order, speaking this way and then that, which as a point is illustrated by the treaty agreed at the Nice summit in December 2 000 which had guaranteed that the Euro army would be "embedded in Nato". Whilst Tony Blair with his Janus head that looks both ways, assured the Americans that Nato would be the primary way to keep the peace in Europe, we find that a general from non-Nato Finland, Gustav Haglund, will head the military committee co-ordinating the new army: with Nato's Supreme Allied Commander in Europe, U.S. General Joseph Ralston, having no automatic right to attend meetings of this crucial committee. The question is whether Tony Blair lied to President Bush?

George W. Bush instigating an international row, after he pulled the U.S out of a landmark treaty on global warming has not eased the tension. The Kyoto treaty of 1997 was not the President claimed, in the best economic interests of the United States. Pacific island nations warned that if nothing is done to stem the melting of the Polar caps, rising seas could soon wipe their islands off the map. The erratic weather that has engulfed large parts of the world and particularly in Britain, where large scale flooding caused unprecedented chaos, caused many nations to condemn America, with veiled threats of trade sanctions if the U.S fails to cut dangerous emissions. The Kyoto agreement commits the world's developed countries to cut emissions of carbon dioxide and other gases by five to seven per cent over the next decade. Environmentalists fear that if the U.S drops out, it simply will not work. Although America has just four per cent of the global population, it produces 25 per cent of the world's so-called greenhouse gases. Most of the pollution comes from its coal and gas-powered energy industry. Economic considerations are certainly not the major concern of President Bush in pulling out of the treaty, since as Europe and other nations press ahead with new anti-pollution technology, it would leave America behind in the technology revolution, which would not be in America's future economic interests and thus the treaty may be a 'trade card' over the issue of a European Army or American scientists may be aware of what I say in this book. President Bush's refusal to reduce human-generated carbon dioxide emissions may rest on the fact that carbon dioxide produced by fossil fuel burning amounts to just 3.5 pc of the total. Earth temperature is much more closely related to solar activity and water vapour from a heated earth is considerably better at trapping heat than carbon dioxide. The Kyoto agreement intended to cool the Earth by a minuscule 20 th of a degree Celsius is an exercise in futility, but helps to assuage the ignorant, on the real science of Magnetic Reversals and the reasons why Earth has gone through periods of heat and intense cold in the Ice Ages. However from the point of view of this book and the method of the World Order hierarchical method, then wherever you have the possibility of dissent between two individuals, groups or nations, the third party of the World Order, will seeks to **create conflict**. Contrary to popular belief, it takes three to make an argument or even break up a marriage. There has probably never been a people's revolution on this planet, apart from the student revolts in the 1960 –1970 period across the world and particularly in France. The World Order has created at least two revolutions and with increasing certainty two World Wars and stands create that final war or battle, which would undoubtedly be atomic, that has according to the 'script' occurred at least once before. Once the control of money in the form of the euro is in place, the stranglehold of Europe will be complete.

If you know the 'script', then Armageddon I am afraid is right there in the final 'act'. No doubt, just before man gets swept up like a fly onto the web of chaotic Grid 'filaments' during a Magnetic Reversal, to receive his next programmed memory and 'lines' of the next 'script' which will be a repeat of the last 'production', he will nod sagely and say: "Ah yes, it has come to pass as it was all prophesied". However the Black Cabala will dominate the next cycle and if you want to stay for cannibalism, torture, despotic kings, control, giants and the Blackest days of Atlantis with the whole gamut of the MMRC case, then ignore this warning. There will of course be few alterations to the 'script' based on this cycle, the inevitable Hermes will appear and no doubt the entire gamut of dramatizations as man descends into an abusive controlling sexual cycle, if he has not already sown the seeds of that in this cycle. You will never challenge the MMRC case and what he considers as his sector of the universe, simply because he never questions whether his actions are sane or not, the only answer is to exit and leave him to it. What kind of arrogance or disregard for international concern over erratic weather conditions, would lead to a President of America refusing to share that concern? One cannot believe that it is only the foolhardy approach of the Ostrich head in the sand, no, there has to be some deeper issue and perhaps the knowledge of American Scientists, that a phenomenon other that global warming is the centre of the trouble – a Magnetic Reversal. You will never rationalise the MMRC case, it has gone too far and whilst man could locate and identify this case, I have to state realistically that man will probably view this book as complete science fiction, rather than the ultimate truth. However I am not out to convince anyone, a man will make his own decisions, however he had better be right on it, for that decision will determine his entire future for all eternity. When a Magnetic reversal occurs and the "sea bursts its bounds", little point then of trying to gain answers to questions that one never got around to asking.

The other name that Crowley mentioned as a guardian of the esoteric tradition was that of Fludd, who was Grand Master, of the Prieuré de Sion (1595 – 1637) and Paracelsus, whom Prince Charles was to quote (*Appendix*). Paracelsus researched the biofield energies and the cosmic keyboard in relation to health. Numerous Grand Masters including Robert Boyle (1654-1691) and Isaac Newton (1691 –1727) belonged to this group and therefore had the opportunity not only to view the secret doctrine that Crowley spoke of, but also to further research and develop that hidden science. Leonardo de Vinci was a member (1510 –1519) also. Fludd was the first cabalistic Grand Master, who had an interest in the speculative side of Judaism, or the Cabala and he was conversant with the Tetragrammaton, which appeared in the upper degrees of Freemasonry, with the triangle or Law of Three forming a part of Fludd's cabalistic system. It is in the higher degrees or Rose-Croix level, that all these men belonged, a degree that is purely **Jewish**.

In the address to the candidate for the initiation into the Rose-Croix degree at the lodge of the 'Contrat Social' it stated:

> "This degree, which includes an order of Perfect Masons, was brought to light by Brother R. Who took it from the Kabbalistic treasure of the Doctor and Rabbi Neamuth, Chief of the synagogue of Leyden in Holland, who had preserved its precious secrets and its costume, both of which we shall see in the same order in which he placed them in his mysterious Talmud". (*B.O.Trees p.163*)

The question is whether, Brother R. Referred to Robert Fludd? or Christian Rosencreutz? However as I cover in *The Battle of The Trees (p.163)* Robert Fludd, was deeply steeped in esoteric knowledge and composed the Necromantic Magic described as:

Goetic, which consists in: "diabolical commerce with unclean spirits, in rites of criminal curiosity, in illicit songs and invocations, and in the evocation of the souls of the dead"
Maleficent which is the adjuration of the devils by the virtue of Divine Names
Theurgic, purported to be governed by good angels and the Divine will, but its wonders are most frequently performed by evil spirits, who assume the names of God and of the angels
The last species of magic is the Thaumaturgic, begetting illusory phenomena and by this art the Magi produced their phantoms and other marvels.

Thus it was in the Rose-Croix, or magical 33 rd degree of Freemasonry and above - Abracadabra, that magic existed and the magical wand of the Druid was the sign perhaps of a Rose-Croix Mason. The word Abracadabra could imply

Abaris the Chief or Arch Druid. The step pyramids no doubt signified the levels of Freemasonry. These magical rites in scientific terms must produce specific resonance, for accessing the Grid holographics and past thought form and action including event. The highest degree of the Rose-Croix was at one time, the Initiated Brothers of Asia, the Masters of the Wise, and the Royal Priests, or the True Brothers of the Rose-Croix. The real origins of the Asiatic Brethren are not known, but a Christian connotation is given, since they were also called 'The Knights and Brethren of St. John the Evangelist'. This is interesting, because not only did St. John, write the book of *Revelations*, with its prophetic apocalypse, but in my witness account of the events of Golgotha, I stated that he may have taken the remaining manuscripts from the Mary Magdalene in France after her murder, together with the Jesus child back to Scotland and the royal Celtic family derived from the Tuatha de Danaan and Anna, the alleged grandmother of Jesus. This line was derived of course from the biblical Adamites, the thirteenth tribe. Thus we find this trail of the Secret Doctrine, held by the "guardians" and passed down through a secret group, throughout the ages: such doctrine being added to and researched. This group was evidently Semitic, but obviously the knowledge now has come to include some elements from both tribes i.e. 12 and 13 including the Cabala and Tulmud according to Fludd.

We must consider, that in fact the Great White Lodge of "invisible" Masters who are said to exist on the "cosmic plane", who control the Great White Brotherhood and presumably also the Rosicrucian's, are no more than this earthly secret and high order, who are in fact visible and who as "guardians" or Masters plan the world according to their Secret Doctrine of past thought and action! The directors of the 'script' who rely on their lackeys the producers, in the subservient world of toady's to ensure that the 'script' is adhered to. I cover the history of these secret Masters and groups in *The Battle of The Trees*, but note here that whilst the real origin of the Asiatic Brethren are not known, apart from their connection to St. John, we do know that the Templars had access to the writings of John through Theoclet, who was sixtieth in succession from John the Evangelist presumably as Master and "guardian" of the Secret Doctrine. There was also the question of where the alternative version of the Gospel of John (which differs from the vulgate) disappeared to, if not retained by the biblical Adamites and the thirteenth tribe; which must represent, an alternative version of the 'script' in *Revelations*, which is written for victory of the 12 tribes against the thirteenth tribe: the world as one big chess game between 12 (king) and 13 (Queen). Dr. Luchet explained that the mysterious order or Rose-Croix in its higher degrees, was entirely Judaic and the "superior direction is called the small and **constant Sanhedrin of Europe**". This group must carry the goal of the Universal Kingdom, or Federalist Europe with its political and religious goals and whilst the political goal is evidently communism, there has to be an alternative religious goal other than Christianity. The names employed in the highest degree of the Rose-Croix are all Hebrew names such as Urim and Thummim. The Elders of Zion, who have been given as one possible and likely source of *The Protocols of Zion*, an alleged plan for world domination by the Jews and Sandhedrin, were admittedly Masons of the 33 rd degree. Thus whilst the Rose-Croix degree is not the highest level, the nature of the Order, was unswerving obedience to unknown superiors, thus bringing up those "invisible" Guardians or Masters, who may be not so much the "invisible" as the visible White Lodge, if one could only ascertain their true identity. The unvarying rule in secret societies is that the true Masters never reveal themselves. No questions asked it would seem and indeed from my own experience, no questions answered. The Third Reich with its earliest philosophical connections to anti-Semitic and Aristocratic Thule society, who increasingly look like some branch of the 13 th tribe, spearheaded the Illuminist doctrine of the cult of obedience and once Europe was devastated by World War II, it was rather too late to challenge the policy of no questions asked. Rudolph Hess as I previously mentioned, was curiously to claim that there had been a misunderstanding between Germany and Britain and one perceives he was probably referring to a thirteenth tribe misunderstanding, when he took the step of piloting a plane to Britain to speak to the Duke of Hamilton in Scotland. His infamous journey no doubt has never in the annals of orthodox pies, been fully explained.

Dr. Oliver concludes that the Rose-Croix degree was certainly Judaic and stated:
> "It was known much sooner, although not probably as a degree in Masonry, for it existed as a **Cabalistic science** from the earliest times in Egypt, Greece and Rome, as well as amongst the Jews and Moors in times more recent, and in our country the names of Roger Bacon, Fludd, Ashmole and many others are found in its list of adepts. (*B.O.Trees P.164*) (*Author's emphasis*).

This statement is interesting since it is admitted that the magical degree or secret doctrine existed in its earliest form in Egypt and Greece, which might support my conclusion that there are two Rosicrucian groups one with Egyptian ancestry and Jewish priests and the other with Greek ancestry and Semitic priests or Druids: both however perhaps originating with the 13 th tribe and separated due to the migrations, or alternatively two completely separate tribes and priesthoods. However both tribes and priesthoods whatever their origin, sought a World Order, with their own particular Theocracy at the head of it. Why should the magical degree have existed in early times in Greece and Egypt however? I assume that the Egyptian Thothmess III the Grand Master of the Great White Lodge, explains the Egyptian branch, but the Greek branch must either refer to the Tuatha de Danaan expelled by patriarchal invaders from the Peloponnese in

Greece at the beginning of the second millennium B.C who went to Ireland via Denmark giving that country its name; or the cabal that took over Knossos during the Religious Revolution c. 1 400 B.C.

Robert Fludd as a past Grand Master of the Prieuré de Sion and I assumed a Rosicrucian and Rose-Croix Mason, identified cabalistic magic in his first three classifications 1. "*Natural Magic* - that most occult and secret department of **physics** by which the mystical properties of natural substances are extracted" and 2. *Mathematical Magic*, which enables adepts the art to: "construct marvellous machines by means of their geometrical knowledge" whilst 3. *Venefic Magic:* "is familiar with potions, philtres, and with various preparations of poisons". Natural Magic or physics including resonant energy and morphic resonance of the human biofield and Grid holographics has evidently been researched to a high level and forms the majority of what is now the hidden science. That science has evidently formed part if not all of the Secret Doctrine or esoteric tradition as Crowley referred to it and incorporated Cabalistic magical ritual. Such research may have involved illicit testing of electronically induced archetypal symbols on unsuspecting UFO witnesses. It is not known, just how far the Rosicrucian's influenced modern day science or physics, by filtering ideas down to research level and how far various scientists who were secretly Rosicrucian's helped to develop the hidden science; but certainly many famous scientists in the past have been members of the Rosicrucian's: and I have previously questioned the Goddard Space Centre and NASA. It was impossible for me as a scientist, to take Hubbard seriously when without anything but dubious and obscure references, he de facto came up with *Dianetics* and his COS data, without questioning whether he had been attached to a particular branch of a secret society, presumably Rosicrucian. *Dianetics* works, just as atomic physics works; it is part and parcel of the natural energy laws. However, I have explained and researched things here in a very different way, even though the conclusions corroborate each other to a certain extent. If science is white magic, then that has been my method. *Dianetics* as a science of the mind is white magic, based on natural laws of physics and predictable phenomena, which is the basis of the method in formulating a new science.

Whilst I have experience of the subject of *Dianetics* and can speak from the point of view of a scientist from my own experience and therefore feel quite assured in verifying the workability of the science of *Dianetics* in its resolution of the mind, I do not as I have stated, have experience other than what I have obtained from L. Kin's book (cited) on the methodology of the OT levels of the COS. If Hubbard did channel the data, then it would of course depend on the experience of the channeller or seer. I have by a completely different method of scientific observation, come up with a different interpretation of Hubbard's Inc.

214

l "implant" which Hubbard views as the beginning and which I view as the Religious Revolution in Crete which was only the beginning of a system of religious and political control, which is presumably coming to fruition in our own times as another World Order. We do know, that at least one Scientology witness, did refer to Hubbard's way of writing Bulletins which was co-incidentally or not, was very similar to automatic writing, which is a form of channelling: and this coupled with his son Nibs statement that Polly, Hubbard's first wife, described him chanting, must place my question 'Is the COS a secret group', into valid comment. Further we know that Hubbard acted as a seer for Parson's the leader of the Agape Lodge in California and branch of the O.T.O and we know, that Parson's considered Ron Hubbard to be experienced in magic, thus the question is how he came by that knowledge, if not in some scientific branch of the O.T.O or Rosicrucian's?

The fact is, that Scientology at least in its lower courses contains very valuable data (I have no knowledge of higher levels and thus cannot comment) which like the classification of Fludd can no longer be regarded as magical arts, since such knowledge has past into the realms of science. However I have questioned the management of Scientology and how Hubbard knew *what* to audit for the OT levels and further where exactly did the whole track data given in *A History of Man*, come from? The COS will argue that it came from auditing sessions, whereby individuals are regressed back on the time track, which will cover the phylogenetic line of the body. This would absolutely accord with my own theory here, that the primitive or reactive mind is really the Universal Mind that carries event and phylogenetic data for the *body*. However I would propose that in the primitive biofield that surrounds the body, the entire events and experience of the body are recorded and as such connect with the morphogenetic bioplasma, with the entire event and phylogenetic data for a body or a species on the track of time. A body for the species Homo sapiens may on the track of past time have been a fish as the recapitulation of the embryonic development of man seems to suggest: with the embryo passing through a fish-like stage with gills and tail and rather looking at one point like a tadpole. I have proposed here a scientific explanation of how such things work and whilst I do not deny, that it was the intention of the Grail to extend knowledge to mankind of this sort, that would allow him to realise the way in which the past is retained in holographic form, there is that question over the right of some groups to retain such knowledge for profit or commercialisation, or whether it should be allied to any political cause of a World Order.

It is the Goetic classification of Fludd and: "commerce or evocation of the souls of the dead", which I believe to be the 'germ', that invariably infiltrates any secret group philosophy which is based on channelled information. This is really just past thought from the Masters and to some extent represents current thought, in so far as those masters re-incarnated and still follow, their past thoughts! There is certainly a question here, of whether the past "invisible" Masters or Great White Lodge, are these channelled thoughts where it is believed that "invisible" Masters or "Guardians" exist in the etheric directing humanity along a supposed spiritual course, or whether in fact there is merely a *visible* group of such men on earth, who constantly hide their purpose of destruction, by utilising such beliefs. There is no doubt in my mind, that a Federal Europe is a recipe for destruction, not only of national identities and boundaries but in the greater 'script' it is a recipe for a Third World War. The MMRC case is not content to rule a country, he must rule absolutely and globally and absolute power corrupts absolutely. I have tried in my own mind to determine whether the World Order follow these "invisible" Masters or merely manipulate the situation and I have to conclude from the wealth of evidence in this book, that it is generally believed that there are Guardians or Masters in the etheric and who simply are in some form 'locked up' waiting to descend to Earth, which for the Egyptian based group and the Great White Lodge and Brotherhood with their first Grand Master of Thothmess III, or the Revelations account of Satan waiting to be released, must be considered a good outcome. However there is no doubt that some groups also believe in these Masters waiting to descend, but consider that a bad thing. Either way hand out the dunce's hat, since the science of holographics is a very different explanation. A little harsh however, as obviously in the event of a Magnetic Reversal, those who escaped the event, have to return, which presumably is responsible for UFO witness accounts of little mechanical men, in space ships, who appear to have a great deal of mechanical trouble with their space ships (Alternative 4). However the Indian epics and other legends, describe how the Atlanteans or some pre-Flood people used the magnetic lines of force at sunrise for their space flights all over the globe, which evidently may have caused a lot of mechanical trouble! What seems clear however, is that these UFO witness reports identify some aspect of pre-history very well and thus my identification of a Jewish manipulatory UFO cover up group, fits with the life's work of that group to destroy all evidence that would ever allow man to discover what really went on, on this planet. Horror of horrors, we might find that the story of the civilized Atlanteans or some pre-Flood group were not the PR picture that has been painted of them, but more despotic rulers where cruelty and sacrifice together with cannibalism and Black Magic through Cabalistic ritual was the order of the day.

Crowley mentions Theophrastus Bombastus von Hohenheim, commonly known as Paracelsus, the son of a German doctor, born about 1493. He is said to have acquired knowledge of some secret doctrine that he acquired during his travels in the East, which is the familiar story of all initiates that wish to cloak their true origins within the secret societies. This Secret Doctrine was elaborated into a system for the healing of diseases. Although his ideas were thus doubtless drawn from some of the same sources as those from which the Jewish Cabala descended, Paracelsus does not appear to have been a Cabalist, but a scientist of no mean order, and as an apparently isolated thinker, he was thought to have no secret group connections, which Crowley evidently persuades us is wrong, by stating that Paracelsus was in fact a: "guardian of the esoteric tradition" and placed in the same category as Fludd, must have been at one time a Grand Master of the secret descendent group of Rosicrucians. The O.T.O and by implication the Great White Lodge (invisible masters) and Great white Brotherhood (visible hierarchy) must also have been directed by this Secret Doctrine. However this doctrine was not the group of so-called "Christian Cabalists", those who may have been directed by the 12 tribes and drew their inspiration from the Cabala of the Jews and perhaps black magic as the Black Cabala with the Talmud. Certainly as I maintain, the Patriarchs utilised the hidden science, but evidently mixed this with black magic and directive thought from past Masters retained on the Grid, presenting that as a higher source e.g. in Ezekiel's vision. The group, to which Paracelsus belonged, was different and more scientifically inclined, along the lines of physics or white magic.

Eliphas Levi, who was evidently 13 th tribe and Jewish held the secret of ever burning lamps and I previously mentioned, that although it was never admitted may have been the top echelon of the 13 th tribe in London at the time. This secret of the burning lamps, together with ball lightening, was obviously some method of tapping vacuum energy and thus I assume that Paracelsus belonged to this group. However, Eliphas Levi related how the Rabbi Jechiel, a cabalistic Jew protected by St. Louis, possessed the secret of ever-burning lamps, which was later claimed by the Rosicrucian's. Thus even from the past accounts of the pre-Flood Atlanteans, it might be concluded that the Black Cabala has held scientific secrets of vacuum energies, which conferred great power on the Jews from time immemorial. Such secrets obviously passed into both groups of 12 and 13, but it was the goal that differed presumably on the course that the knowledge would take. Further, at the time of the Religious Revolution new knowledge came into the hands of one of those groups, presumably the thirteenth tribe or at least a branch of the descendent Rosicrucian's. Such knowledge allowed man access to his past and this produced two conflicting goals and ideologies on Earth. In one group, the secrets were to be released at the inevitable Jewish price and in another group, the secrets were to be hidden and used by only the elite for creating power and wealth, thus repeating past history and pre-history, which is almost certainly the story of the Atlanteans. The Holy Grail came, to disperse and destroy the group who perpetually held man trapped, utilising black magic: thus it was not until the time of the Religious

Revolution in Crete, that new data on the Grid arrived as part of the Grail message, which was sent to free man. The appearance of the thonged stones in Crete, the armillary device and the ellipsoid shape of the sarcophagi together with the message: 'As I go, so shall I return', was astounding new knowledge, which threatened those who had long held power and control those men could not grant man his freedom or loose that control. Even the one group who were in favour of releasing the secrets, could not give back to man the gift, but commercialised it to a "chosen few", who could afford to pay.

The history of the Rosicrucian's has been purposefully clouded. It was thought that the group emerged from the Cabalistic movement and the teachings of Paracelsus. However even from Crowley's statement, the movement goes back much further. The first attempt to cloud the origins of this group was given in a series of pamphlets, which appeared at the beginning of the seventeenth century. The first of these, entitled the *Fama Fraternitatis* or *Discovery of the Fraternity of the most Laudable Order of the Rosy Cross*, was published at Cassel in 1614 and the *Confessio Fraternitatis* early in the following year. These pamphlets contained what became known as the "Grand Legend". The story of how Christian Rosenkreutz a German, became the founder of the Rosicrucian's, is in itself untrue in my opinion and the only interesting point in the story, is the referral linking Rosenkreutz to a European secret society, whereas it was also claimed that Rosenkreutz had been initiated in the east: "there might be a *society in Europe* which might have gold, silver and precious stones sufficient for them to bestow on kings for their necessary uses and lawful purposes." Whether this was the "constant Sanhedrin of Europe" the secret high Order that perhaps Crowley hoped to enter as the Great White Brotherhood and Lodge and therefore 13 th tribe is uncertain. Once again however, the old and tired story of how Rosenkreutz developed his knowledge in the East was given as his source, in much the same way as Hubbard was to start his journey in the East and Jesus was claimed to have been initiated in Tibet. As the Grand Legend goes, there was an agreement drawn up on the founding of the Rossy Cross and one of the statutes was that no Rosicrucian: "**should profess any other thing than to cure the sick and that gratis**". It might be concluded that the row between Clymer and Lewis who headed two Rosicrucian Orders centred on this point and perhaps provides some background to Scientology? On the supposed death of Rosenkreutz, it was alleged his burial place was discovered and certain documents also and the Brethren who discovered them, then knew that after a time there would be: "a general reformation both of divine and human things". Which sounds like the plan followed for aeons of a political and religious World Order. What is quite revealing is a section of the Fama (of the Rossy Cross) that states:

"Our philosophy is not a new invention, but as **Adam** *after his fall* hath received it and as **Moses** and **Solomon** used it...wherein **Plato**, **Aristotle**, **Pythagoras** and others did hit the mark and wherein **Enoch**, **Abraham**, **Moses**, **Solomon**, did excel, but especially wherewith that wonderful Book the Bible agreeth. *(Author's emphasis)*

Thus here presumably is the history of sorts, of the Rossy Cross or Rosicrucianism. Firstly **they admit that the woman gave the hidden science as new knowledge to Adam**! Thus confirming the history of the Religious Revolution at Knossos (1 400 B.C.) which in the Bible is made to co-incide with Genesis and the story of Adam and Eve, which was not the first time the knowledge had been taken, but that period was significant since it was already symbolised in certain archetypal forms, which the Cabal took over and re-positioned against the male, with the invention of Hermes, thus removing the woman from the story entirely. The Fama also gives some history of the patriarchs who were evidently Rosicrucian's or Rossy Cross members utilising the Secret Doctrine or the hidden science and we know that the Druids ascended from the biblical Adamites, used Mosaic Law and Moses himself, utilised the hidden science in the parting of the waves for the Israelites in *Exodus* and in the case of the Commandments on Mt. Sinai. The Enochian keys, which presumably in esoteric language reveal the rites for accessing certain holograms of the Akashic Record, presumably the period of the Religious Revolution are referred to, along with Pythagoras who developed the initial cosmic keyboard, that the Druids utilised. Moses was a high initiate of the Cabala inducted into at least the Rite of Memphis as apparently were Abraham and Solomon and the "Bible agreeth"; since the miracles and prophecies are really an account of the misuse and manipulation of the hidden science by an elite priesthood, co-joined with the Black Cabala to access the whole event record or the Akashic Record, which *Ezekiel* apparently mastered.

According to this manifesto then, it would appear to confirm that the Rossy Cross and the Rosicrucian's are none other than the biblical Adamites and the 13 th tribe. Importantly whatever knowledge or elixir of the Holy Grail that was obtained at Knossos, which presumably was knowledge of the Grid as evidenced in the thong-wrapped stones from Crete, was then mixed with Black Cabala ritual and presumably the whole area of knowledge was to be researched and extended under various Grand Masters that were to follow, in either subsidiary groups such as the Prieuré de Sion, or branch Orders of the Rosicrucians. Crowley presumably as a Rosicrucian and pro-German sympathiser was intent on a German World Order, which probably accounts for the inscription at the abbey in Switzerland linking a senior Nazi to Crowley's group. It might be perceived that this branch of Rosicrucian's was 13 th tribe and incorporated a plan that hoped to avoid a Jewish or 12 tribe World Order. This would certainly explain Hitler's attempts to exterminate the Jews, in his so-called 'Final Solution'. This would also account for the fact that Hollywood has never revealed this section of history, for it was not in the interests of the World Order to reveal the true background of a Federalist Europe. The question which seems relevant to the word **treason** is whether such a World Order will utilise the 'script' of *Revelations*, to claim victory for the 12 tribes of Israel, by revealing Britain as the thirteenth tribe, where London will be sacrificed along with the British in a holocaust incorporating the large earthquake predicted as the fate of the thirteenth tribe in the *Revelations* account. We are assured by the current Pope, that the Book of Revelations is "symbolic", which presumably means that the symbols or the war of 12 and 13 is no longer relevant, which is not confirmed by even a casual glance at world politics today and the events in France and Greece, apart from the transatlantic rift between Europe and America. The fatality exists in the appearance of normality of the Earth, with the apparent sanity of those who are pushing towards a World Order. The misconception lies in the belief that two countries start wars or two leaders, when in actuality it is always a third party that unknown and unseen directs events and hostilities. This third party has always existed in a hierarchal Order that seeks absolute power and wealth, that Order by psychiatric definition are psychotic and insane, they have through constant re-stimulation of the holograms of the past through resonant ritual and Black Cabalistic methods, become entrapped by them. Once you set up a hologram in your own memory banks, if you have changed matter in any way then that hologram is recorded in the morphogenetic bioplasma and will continue to retain an energy connection to all those elements present in the hologram including personnel. The Cabal that conducted the Religious Revolution are still very much a part of the holograms that appear to be retained in the spiritual bioplasma and which Hubbard referred to as Inc.1. That cabal also retain memories of the event in their own spiritual memory banks. If in present time they re-stimulate their personal memory banks they will simply re-activate the hologram in the ether vacuum, which contains a holographic recording, which then directs them. In this manner, the World Order, continue to re-enact the past merely by the control exerted through past holograms and the events contained in them, a process referred to as dramatization. The Great White Brotherhood and those "invisible" masters of the Great White Lodge of course ruled Crowley, but Crowley through his magical practice this lifetime was merely re-peating the holograms of his own past, which he continually re-stimulated and he admitted that he was in all probability a snake goddess in the post Religious Revolution era at Knossos. It seems that the Rosicrucian's or their ultimate Masters used Crowley to develop magical rituals to access the Grid, perhaps to re-work the rituals relating to the garnering of information from the Religious Revolution era, which would later be researched by the Third Reich and after World War II, would go to America with the Nazi scientists. We know that Nazi scientists were researching disc-type spacecraft and methods of vertical take-off, utilising Grid energies.

However whilst it is denied that the Rosicrucian's ever existed, that is not the impression one obtains from the Manifesto or indeed the archaeological finds I outlined from Crete where the rose was in evidence in archaeological finds. Also another pamphlet entitled the *Universal Reformation of the World* again indicated a plan for a World Order both religious and political. According to one Rosicrucian tradition the word "Rose" does not derive from the flower depicted on the Rosicrucian cross, but from the Latin word ros, signifying "dew", which was supposed to be the most powerful solvent of gold, whilst crux, the cross, was the chemical hieroglyphic for "light". If the original intent of the Rosicrucian's, was to dissolve the power of Solar kingship (gold), then it presumably fell foul to man's own innate greed and avarice, since I cannot see any evidence in the world today of any order secret or otherwise, that is not infested with power and greed. The simpler explanation that has been given for the Rossy Cross is that it derived from the Red Cross of the Templars. I refer to the work of the chemist Peter Plitchta (cited) who drew a perfect Templar Cross in his energy diagrams of the atom and electron shells. You may remember that I thought Peter Plitchta might have had access perhaps as a scientist to this information perhaps within a secret society in a past life. The Golden Dawn, which I discussed in *Alternative 4*, was probably another offshoot secret group of the Rosicrucian's or in my conclusion the 13 th tribe.

One suspects, that after contact with the Teacher in Crete, that 13 th tribe began to recognise that there was a science involved and a cosmology and the effort to widen that science and understand the magical treatises of the Cabala in the light of that knowledge became an effort, that would sustain them not in a goal of a more enlightened humanity, bit in a goal of control. Eckert states that the ritual, symbols and names of the Rose-Croix were borrowed from the Templars, and that the Order was divided into seven degrees, according to the seven days of creation, at the same time signifying that their "principal aim was that of the mysterious, the investigation of Being and of the forces of nature" which signifies the hidden science. However the Knights Templar joined with the Scottish order of Rosicrucian's, which presumably means that there was some agreement here. The Rosicrucian Kenneth Mackenzie, in his *Masonic Cyclopaedia*, appears to suggest the same possibility of Templar origin. However I feel it is far more likely that the Druids and biblical Adamites or 13 th tribe, were behind the Rosicrucian's. Mackenzic (a Scottish name) refers to the Rosicrucian's enigmatically as an **invisible fraternity** that has existed from very ancient times, as early as the days of the Crusades, and: "bound by solemn obligations of impenetrable secrecy". This invisible fraternity is the same story given, for the Great White Lodge, which I thought was 13 th tribe even though it is described as a "cosmic" fraternity of "invisible" Masters or Guardians and therefore not earthly. The Rosicrucian's it is alleged are bound together in work for humanity and to "glorify good". I would think that Hubbard may indeed have belonged to this group, however Russell Miller's autobiography of Hubbard and the statements of Scientologists that knew Hubbard haunt me. Further it appears that the oath of the Rossy Cross was to heal without profit. The fact that the witnesses that spoke to Miller were Scientologists, implied a great deal, because I know from experience, when you have given your soul to the cause of good, it is hard to confront reality on what you *observe* (actuality). If anyone feels betrayed at this point, think of Golgotha and the horror of betrayal that some endured on that plan. The Scientologist who felt betrayed when he actually saw suitcases full of money arriving for Hubbard despite Hubbard's claim, that he never took a penny off the Church, must be placed in position, with the account of Mayo Hubbard's auditor, who whilst retaining the secrets of Hubbard's soul, was to express the point that he felt betrayed by Hubbard's confession that his true goal was reflected in his desire for power and wealth. Hubbard may have told the truth when he said he had not received a penny from the Church, but in looking for an alternative source for the money, I am reminded of that "constant Sanhedrin in Europe", with jewels and wealth. Neither can I dismiss Hubbard's one attempt at poetry, which happened to concern a rose. It might be, that Hubbard started out with the science i.e. *Dianetics* and as brilliant as it was, realised that there was no money in it, other than an academic career. He could have put that science into a University or utilised the help of all those who wanted to get the subject seriously looked at by doctors and scientists. Perhaps it is that the crossroads for Hubbard came at that point and whether or not he sold it out, as the Church of Scientology to a branch of the Rosicrucian's is pure speculation. Perhaps Hubbard did start independently and afterwards became attached to a branch of Rosicrucian's and thirteenth tribe, that wanted to heal humanity or perhaps that group after Hubbard's death were taken over by another branch of the Rosicrucian's who were only willing to sell the mysteries at a commercialised profit: or finally the COS line, that Hubbard was a genius and thought it all up himself, with no profit. Which is it to be?

The invisible fraternity that was behind the Rosicrucian's, has never been revealed, but I hope I might have at least made one suggestion here, which is the biblical Adamites, 13 th tribe, Druids, Bull-Minos cult, Stag cult and all the symbology retained on the floor of Cardiff Castle Wales, where Scottish rite Freemasonry appears as some branch or if not the order of the time. Mackenzie notes: "the Rosicrucian's of the sixteenth century finally disappeared and re-entered this invisible fraternity" – from which they had presumably emerged. Mirabeau stated, that the Templars after the suppression of the Order continued in a secret form to the present day. However as I have covered they joined forces with the Scottish branch of Freemasonry, in The Royal Order of Scotland and the first Lodge was set up at Kilnwilling and was termed the "Mother Lodge". Evidently then as I have covered they carried matriarchal knowledge or the elixir, but inevitably that gold cup of wealth and power. The degree of the Rosy Cross according to a legend preserved by the Royal Order of Scotland was instituted by that Order in conjunction with the Templars in 1314, with the Lodge of Kilnwilling. Thus Hubbard's white cloak in the hermetic ritual with Crowley and the poem of the rose may indicate much deeper connections of Hubbard. Rosenkreutz was then a disguise I believe to hide the true origins of the Rose-Croix or Rosy Cross, which had I presume its roots in the oak and holly or oak royal and holy one, the Druids and biblical Adamites.Their so-called 'gift' to humanity however did not arise with that group, even though they did have substantial knowledge of the Cabala and rituals which undoubtedly could produce the miracles and prophesies of the Bible – the historical truth was that it was 'her' gift and even that gift was not hers and did not originate on Earth, although she was entrusted with it. No man or woman owns truth. The original intent of the Holy Grail in its message and science of the trap was intended for everyone, but was soon to be overtaken by that inevitable quest for the cup and that penchant of the Semite, in a belief of his own superiority and "chosen one" status, believed that he could grudgingly give man the elixir, provided he could control it and make a profit from the cup: presumably he has forgotten or does not know the crab story, or the story of source and how the Grail came to be on Earth and believes his own genius thought it all up for himself.

The Rose-Croix, Mirabeau stated were: "a mystical, Cabalistic, theological and magical sect". There you have it, the Holy Grail, mixed up with the Cabala and inevitably those magical rites, which channel information from the Grid, including those "invisible" Masters and their thoughts that probably are in fact visible as "guardians" of the Secret Doctrine. Inevitably then, any hope that the Holy Grail would be used by all humanity, was to be overlaid with those inevitable traits of superiority, power, wealth, control, hierarchy and secret group mentality of tiered secrecy and management. It might be assumed that The Knights Templar held the secret of the Crucifixion and also perhaps the Religious Revolution in Crete. They committed sodomy and were accused of such at their trials, thus this would indicate bisexual Hermes and the sort of Cabalistic rites that Crowley undertook to invoke Hermes. It might seem plausible, that the Knights Templar were drawn into the Royal Order of Scottish Freemasonry, to keep such maters hidden and to avoid having another source for such knowledge, although there is another important alternative here. That alternative, is that the Scottish Order gained significant knowledge from the Templars as far as the Religious Revolution was concerned, which was 'married' to the history of the Druids and the truth of events at Golgotha. This indeed could have been the period, when an alternative Rose-Croix or Rosicrucian Order was set up, with the goal of revealing the mysteries. The Templars may have come by the knowledge of the Religious Revolution in Crete, through guarding the Temple at Jerusalem. Mr. Waite in referring to the alleged connection between the Templars and the Brethren of the Rosy Cross observed:

> "The Templars were not alchemist, they had no scientific pretension, and their secret, so far as it can be ascertained, was a religious secret of an anti-Christian kind. The Rosicrucian's, on the other hand, were pre-eminently a learned society and they were also a Christian sect".

What is clear however, is that from the list of Grand Masters of the Prieuré de Sion and I assume the Rosicrucian's and Great White Brotherhood, there was some scientific background of the hidden science, which was added to over many thousands of years and by a number of famous scientists and also Cabalists. Mr. Waite observed that the publication of the *Fama* and the *Confession Fraternitatis* would not add new lustre to the Rosicrucian reputations:

> We are accustomed to regard the adepts of the Rosy Cross as beings of sublime elevation and preternatural physical powers, masters of Nature, monarchs of the intellectual world. But here in their own acknowledged manifestos they avow themselves a mere theosophical offshoot of the Lutheran heresy, acknowledging the spiritual supremacy of a temporal prince, and calling the Pope anti-Christ...We find them intemperate in their language, rabid in n their religious prejudices and instead of towering giant-like above the intellectual average of their age, we see them buffeted by the same passions and identified with all opinions of the men by whom they were environed. The voice which addresses us behind the mystical mask of the Rose-Croix does not come from an intellectual throne....".

Julius Sperber, in his *Echo of the divinely illuminated fraternity of the Admirable Order of the R.C. (1615)* indicated the place assigned to Christ by the Rosicrucian's. In De quincey's words on comment of the publication:

> "Having maintained the probability of the Rosicrucian pretensions on the ground that such *magnalia Dei* had from the creation downwards been confided to the keeping of a few individuals –agreeably to which

he affirms that **Adam was the first Rosicrucian of the Old Testament** and **Simeon the last** – he goes on to ask whether the Gospel put an end to the secret tradition? By no means, he answers: **Christ established a new "college of magic"** among His disciples, and the **greater mysteries were revealed to St. John and St. Paul".**

Here we have some important facts, firstly as I suspected, Adam was the first Rosicrucian and therefore Rosicrucian is synonymous with the term Druid and biblical Adamite and indeed as I have shown synonymous with the Bull-Minos phallic cult who conducted the Religious Revolution and whose god became Hermes by the attempt to eradicate the woman in the story, combining her with the twin Kings in a transcendent third stage. Further then, the whole history of the 13 th tribe through the Tuatha de Danaan and the alleged matriarchal grandmother of Jesus as Anna is inferred. The cat is out of the proverbial bag, I am afraid boys, since there is a marked difference between the Old Testament and New Testament, that difference centres on the cruelty, murder and sacrifice that were very much a part of the thinking of the Patriarchs: compared to the New Testament, which has very definite Buddhist influences which came from the Magdalene and her descendent line. I have already discussed that the New Testament in the life of Jesus shows marked Buddhist influences, which have been explained away by that Eastern connection again (yawn!) and in the case of Jesus it was Tibetan Masters, that initiated him. However I have produced quite a different story in this book, where I claim that he was fostered (Druid) or adopted (Essene) into a Jewish family in Palestine and his tutorage was initially with the Essenes who were Jewish and communistic. His Tibetan influences came from contact with the Mary Magdalene who was a Princess in her own right from a *Greek root* and where the knowledge of the event of the Religious Revolution at Knossos was known. Jesus in the Alexandrian text, undoubtedly followed hermetic philosophy and Hermes was 13 th tribe philosophy, with the Messiah as a uniquely 13 th tribe or Druid phenomenon; and thus one might assume that the referral in the above text to a new: "college of magic" being established with Jesus, referred to magical rites centred on the invocation of Hermes. There is no doubt, that this is sexual magic and Crowley's rites utilised both homosexual and bisexual alternatives. The Mary Magdalene and Jesus had a relationship and if the Magdalene descended from a Greek root and was in matrilineal possession of the history of the events of the Grail in Crete, then this may indeed account for the fact that some Secret Doctrine passed to St. John, for I claim from my own witness account, that she was with St John in France, just north of Marseilles, when the documents were taken and she was murdered by a raiding party: however Jesus in Jerusalem took her genealogies. It is perhaps these genealogies and some aspect of the truth that the Templars found. Indeed since the events of Golgotha were it appears planned from Scotland by the

Druids, it seems logical that after St. John returned to Scotland following the Magdalene's death, that he would take the Secret Doctrine that belonged to her, with him. He may also have taken the Jesus child who was used to propagate the Merovingian dynasty a supposed kingly line from David and a union of the Magdalene and Jesus. It would also seem natural for the Templars to join with the Royal Order of Scotland, since both had significant knowledge of the same events. Thus I assume that the truth at one time in terms of documentary evidence was held in Scotland at the Kilnwilling Lodge. The forthcoming documentary to be televised on British television on the unfortunate day of April 1st, entitled 'Son of God' and showing Jesus with a Jewish face produced by computer trickery and a study of ancient Jewish skulls, is perhaps more than an April fools joke, since the BBC has become another form of mass brainwashing in Britain, which people pay for the privilege of. The fool's joke I suppose for those in the know, is that Jesus was a Druid and Celt and the Holy Land is Scotland and the fool's finger or psychic finger in the Druid alphabetical finger signalling keyboard, was the requirement to answer difficult questions (in this case on the racial origin of Jesus).

The Nag Hamaadi scrolls show that the disciples especially Peter, were upset at how much Jesus loved the Magdalene and were very jealous of her and the fact that Jesus would "Kiss her on the mouth often". The Mary Magdalene however I stated was from a Greek background and a Princess in her own right and also held the Greek background to the religious Revolution in Crete and hoped to reveal the mysteries to the people, however as I have covered the hope of the Millennium was dashed, when Jesus failed to adhere to the plan. Naturally the greater mysteries were revealed to St. John in the above text, simply because he apparently took the last parchments of truth from the Magdalene. Further, I have already covered the fact that Jesus' brother James had quite a row with St. Paul over the efforts of Paul to bring Christianity to Gentiles. James specifically told Paul that Jesus' teachings were only for the Jews, but Paul evidently was aware of the greater mysteries and the World Order plan, since evidently he was a part of that plan to bring Christianity to Europe and did indeed have considerable trouble convincing the "stupid Galations" or the political Celtic Commonwealth. Further St. John was apparently the preferred saint for Lord Bute who had the floor of the Summer Smoking Room laid at Cardiff Castle, which I concluded was Rosicrucian knowledge and therefore 13 th tribe. It would appear then, that whilst there was a 13 th tribe plan evident at Golgotha, Jesus "fooled them" as Nag Hamaadi documents state and the 12 tribes of Israel high jacked the plan in alliance with the Roman administration, who presumably had no wish to see a Celtic Commonwealth with a religious and political basis forming a power threat to Rome. The Romans indeed invaded Britain and the Druids were said to have been destroyed, although it was rumoured that a few hundred "learned men" existed at Caerleon-on-Usk in Wales perhaps as surviving remnants, which presumably accounts for a Rosicrucian Order there, that may well have initiated Lord Bute in the 19 th Century.

The idea of Christ as an initiate runs through all the secret societies and rests on actual documents held with the secret societies. The fact that the Bible and the Christian version of *Revelations* condemns the 13 th tribe and prophesies that the 12 tribes will triumph, must reflect the *Revelations* condemnation of "frogs". The Rosicrucians were accused of having Satan as their god, which might just have inferred anti-matter and the anti-Christ as heaven as opposed to this Universe which is matter, thus reflecting a different viewpoint on heaven and hell with this Earth as hell and matter. The reverse crucifix presumably had the same meaning and Hitler purposefully utilised the left- handed swastika: which perhaps explains why Rupert Murdock owner of the masses daily newspaper *The Sun,* was so amused by being depicted as the Devil by the Mirror newspaper (2 000). The Rosicrucians or Rose-Cross, were accused of compacts with the Devil, sacrifices of children, of cherishing toads, making poisonous powders and dancing with fiends, however as I have been at pains to point out there is more than one Rosicrucian group and one of those employs the Black Cabala, whilst the other may well have physicists and scientists among its members researching the hidden science. It would seem the *Revelations* account might have been purposefully edited to remove 'toad' and replace it with from, to remove all connections to the Rosicrucian's and therefore the Biblical Adamite. The toad, although not a frog may concern certain hallucinogenic substances that some toads contain in their skin, which may have been used in Cabalistic rites, in much the same way as opium was used at Knossos and Crowley used Allohonium Lewinni in his black Cabalistic rites to conj our up information from Hermes. Thus it would seem that the Rosicrucuians or Rosy Cross had that face of two sides, the Janus head of Hermes that could point both ways, left or right, black or white magic, freedom or control, and cup or elixir and that may simply come from the two groups of Rosicrucian's who may have evolved from two factions of the 13 th tribe, with one Egyptian and one Greek in its descedency. This may also account for the mixed bag of philosophy contained in the secret groups, with its ability to be used one of two ways and the inherent mix of cup and grail. Perhaps that really explains my own experiences of Scientology and Anthroposophy, where actions do not quite tally with words or stated goals, since somewhere in the philosophy of secret groups the knowledge can be used in one of two ways and undoubtedly could be controlled in one of two ways by the two Rosicrucian groups.

The Hermetic god can look both ways, since it incorporates both male and female qualities and knowledge. Man is hooked on the matriarchal knowledge the science, shout of freedom, peace and hope for humanity – buying it hook line and sinker and then comes the power pyramid, the Illuninatus Janus head of the male with its quest for secrecy, power and wealth and the use of Cabalistic science that dates back to the patriarchs and the blackest days of Atlantis. The male and the female destined to battle for all eternity, which as a thought is portrayed at Cardiff castle, where the cat runs up the tree on one plaster relief, chased by the dog. The schizoid nature of the initiate and group, who speaks of helping humanity and freedom for mankind, leaves one with the feeling of a knife in the back, when one sees the actuality of business, big cash, or hypocritical actions. Political parties invariably carry the Janus head. Hermes is portrayed astrologically as the Twins of Gemini, with that inevitable split personality. However man inherently has this personality in his rational and irrational mind, which has more to do with the physics of energy, the Grid and the master pattern, than any esoteric mumbo jumbo. The irrational mind is really just the morphogenetic bioplasma that connects to the embryonic tri-partite biofield of man and carries survival data on the morphogenetic line of the species, with event data. The attempt to persuade man that he has a Universal Mind, merely attempts to connect him to Grid thinking and the whole gamut of behaviour that defines animals and animal pack mentality, which as a philosophy has been badly misapplied to Communism where big brother or the KGB and now Rupert Murdoch in conjunction with the Chinese special police, decide who is to read what, or access certain information in this *Animal Farm* scenario, which is no more than a complete dramatization of the past events also contained on the Grid, where the Arch controllers were no more than dominant males in an animal pack, who ruled by fear as *The Express* newspaper headline of the autobiographical article on Rupert Murdoch pointed out 'Fear reigns at the court of the Sun King'. I believe China leaves girl babies to die, commits untold crimes in its population laws allowing two children only and leaves cats to suffer ignoble and painful deaths packed up in crates waiting to enter the food chain of the Chinese: and this is what happens, when you push a nation down to self and group survival level, it tunes into the Grid and dissociates from human and animal suffering at the level of the Darwinian principle of 'survival of the fittest'. That impassioned stare in response to situations that require one to feel from one's heart and act, can be no better than the statement: "Help the more able first".

There is no doubt too, that the Rosicrucians were experts at poisons and why it should be rumoured that Miscavige head of the COS keeps his water covered is anybody's guess, but if Hubbard did break up Crowley's group and the O.T.O. then since Crowley was a Rose-Croix mason and Rosicrucian with Nazi sympathies, we can perhaps imagine that a branch of the Roicrucians who utilise the Black Cabala, were perhaps none too pleased. A group perhaps that perhaps as a branch of the Rosy Cross, used the scientific knowledge of the Rosy Cross normally applied to healing to a precisely opposite and deadly purpose. This would explain the row between Clymer and Lewis and two different Rosicrucian groups with the claim by Clymer that Lewis' group had wanted to *commercialise* the mysteries. Lewis' group was one that was allied to Crowley and thus perhaps Hubbard did go in to break that up, but the question still remains as to where Hubbard's money came from if not from the "constant Sanhedrin of Europe"? and the observation now, that Scientology is very much a commercial enterprise. However both groups of Rosicrucians despite the commercial objections of Clymer, held the Cabala of the Jews as their source and as I have described the Rose-Croix is a Jewish degree as are all those above that. No doubt the difference between the two groups was the distinction of black and white magic and whose power was the greater i.e. Black Cabala or science? Huysmans however scoffs at this distinction and says the use of the term "white magic" was a ruse of the Rose-Croix. It was this warning or difference of white and black magic that was given to Hitler. Whether white magic today which is more accurately described in terms of Physics, chemistry and Biochemistry, is being conducted by creating resonant frequencies to open the various chakras, with their specific resonant frequencies which is a part of top secret science, rests upon the acceptance that the hidden science, is indeed a science, with phenomena covered by the laws of physics and chemistry. One thing is certain, the aims, doctrines and the identity of the Rosicrucians has been kept a long and guarded secret until now and the profound secret that they were rumoured to hold, must refer to the Universal Kingdom with its political and religious goals, seen on the reverse side of the One Dollar note of America and the floor of the summer Smoking Room at Cardiff Castle: the "Reformation" that was spoken of in the 16 th century. The Continental Brethren of the Rose-Croix form a shadowy group of "Invisibles", that may or may not be, the Great White Lodge but the Rosy Crucians did build castles as did the Templars and the COS co-incidentally or not, in East Grinstead built a castle for their headquarters in the UK next to that other branch of Rosy crucians – Anthroposophy founded by Rudolf Steiner. In history there is a reference to the "Invisible Mountain of the Brethren", which may be the source of the idea of an invisible fraternity or Brotherhood. However we know that the Druids, held their ceremonies on mountaintops and in caves, presumably because the ley line energy found some connection with the Grid at these points, which facilitated channelling. The Assassins a notorious group in history, also utilised mountains. Further the scriptural reference to "House of Wisdom", cannot be un-connected to the Lodge of Freemasonry or the Temple in Jerusalem: and the "New Jerusalem" I would think refers to the "reformation", that is coming and the new religion. That the Rosicrucian's or at least the political arm of the World Order, the Illuminati, were behind two Revolutions i.e. French and Russian and possibly behind World Wars I and II, shows how closely the religious and political aims of the two groups have worked in tandem towards the "New Jerusalem".

Crowley was to receive his particular form of *Excalibur* sanction in China, which co-incidentally or not was one of the sources that Hubbard gave, whilst he was travelling there. He received this form of secret communication from the secret Masters or Chiefs, which could have been natural or manipulated and possibly the "invisible" Order of The Great White Lodge, through the Great White Brotherhood: or given the mention of precious jewels, the "constant Sanhedrin of Europe" which appears to be a group that is a likely source of those so-called "invisible" masters or "guardians" of the Secret Doctrine. Crowley recorded the event in his Journal:

> "One morning I had sat down and..... Salama (a servant) came and sat down by my side, I looked at him in amazement. It was an astounding breach of etiquette. I have often wondered if he did it deliberately, as if to say, 'I am not your headman: I am a messenger of the gods,' He began, however, in a very shamefaced, sheepish way, obviously embarrassed. 'Sahib,' he said, 'last night I had a tamasha.' I reproached him laughingly. Tamasha means an entertainment of any kind, and, in the East, frequently implies a certain amount of liveliness, possibly an indulgence in forbidden liquor and flirtation; but he merely meant a dream.' I was on the shore of a small lake ' he proceeded.' It was a wild country and the lake was surrounded by tall reeds, some of them growing in the water. The full moon was high in the sky, but there were clouds and mist. You were standing in front of me, Sahib; quite motionless, lost in thought as you always are, but you seemed to be waiting for someone. Now there was a rustling in the reeds, and out of them came a boat rowed by two beautiful women with long fair hair, and in the front of the boat stood another woman, taller and fairer even than her sisters. The boat came slowly across to you; and then I saw that the woman held in her hands a great sword, long and straight, with a straight cross-hilt that was heavy with rubies, emeralds and sapphires. She put this sword into your hands and you took it, but nothing was said. They went away as they had come, into the fringe of the reeds across the lake. And that was all I saw.' I remained unable to reply. At this time I was the last man in the world to take anything of the sort seriously. What struck me dumb was hearing an old Shikari tell the story of *Excalibur* in language so near to that of Mallory as to make no odds. Could one of his Sahibs have told him the tale long ago, so that it popped up again in this strange fashion? I had no doubt whatever of the man's sincerity and truthfulness, and he had no motive for inventing

anything of the sort. I cannot believe it a coincidence; I really wondered whether the most reasonable hypothesis is not that Aiwass, (Crowley's Guardian Angel), wanting to remind me that I was chosen to do the Great Work, picked out, on the one hand, Salama as the most unlikely prophet imaginable; on the other, the tale was one which I could not possibly dismiss as trivial." [190]

These sort of synchronicities, arise often when the Masters want to set in operation a further phase of their plan. Woodcott and Mathers, who set up the secret group of The Golden Dawn, just happened to find a secret document in a bookshop with an address on it: also people just happen to meet the acquaintance of the contactee. These synchronicities are undoubtedly manipulation in some form for the purposes of the Masters. It is certainly odd, that Hubbard should entitle his own particular illumination *Excalibur*. This account contains numerous archetypal symbols: triplicity of *female*, sword, reed (royal) in the Tree Alphabet; all associated with the Druids. Further, Thutmose III of Egypt the Master K-H-M and Deputy Grand Master of the Great White Lodge of the Great White Brotherhood at one time resided at Lake Moeris (Morias). This account has a certain similarity to the channelled information of the Reverend Vale Owen's book, *Life Beyond the Veil*, which was allegedly impressed upon his mind by souls who had left their physical bodies and were residing in what appeared to be parts of the astral region, although equally I thought that these may have been past thoughts and events retained on the bioplasma and as single frame holographs required personal interpretation by the channeller. Certainly it is probably this type of channelled information, that gives rise to the concept of cosmic or "invisible" Masters or "guardians"; neither can one dismiss the fact that the true and real life Masters as perhaps that "constant Sanhedrin of Europe" which may or may not be synonymous with The Great White Lodge, manipulate such beliefs in order to remain anonymous and yet weave their plan through men like Crowley or Hitler. The Reverend wrote down these impressed or transmitted thoughts through automatic writing and co-incidentally or not this is the manner and description of the way in which Hubbard wrote his Bulletins in his later years and whether connected or not this is also the way in which the Seer or psychic channeller works. Only the COS perhaps can answer my question of how Hubbard knew *what* to audit on the OT levels, which looks remarkably like data of **past events** from the morphogenetic and spiritual bioplasmas. Neither do I say that it is necessarily wrong in the case of the COS, after all it is some aspect of physics, but my only reservation is who exactly is the upper level of the COS and what is their aim? The natural UFO phenomenon does appear to be a natural insight into past events retained in holographic form on the bioplasmas, however I did question in *Alternative 4*, whether a secret group (Jewish) were manipulating the holographic record for their own purposes, where in fact some UFO incidents were perhaps unnatural or manipulated and therefore in breach of the Human Rights Act. The Arch controllers never for one minute, thought about the right of man to control his own mind and body.

If the Druids or that "constant Sanhedrin of Europe" were synonymous in their highest ascendant and secret "invisible" Master level which also describes the Great White Lodge, then Crowley's "Great Work" or Opum Magnus, may have been to re-work ancient Druidical Hermetic rites, which may have been lost in time and particularly those concerned with Hermes and the events of the Religious Revolution, which I thought may provide the background for explanation of Hubbard's Inc. 1 event. Whilst Hubbard certainly does not himself link that event to the Religious Revolution in Crete, there are archetypal symbols within the event that have parallel archetypal symbolism to that event c. 1 400 B.C. Hermes as chariot, horn as gates of horn of the Bull-Minos cult and the inevitable Cabalistic cherubim portrayed perhaps as the Cabalistic Tree of Life from the Knossos site of the period, with the epiphany of the goddess as bird or dove in the branches. Crowley was a very adept magician and his rites may have allowed greater access to information from the Grid, hitherto not accessible due to incorrect or poorly developed magical resonant rituals. Crowley himself may have been recognised by the Masters as a past (life) Druidical magi, which evidently the sword of Arthur (Excalibur) verified at least in Crowley's mind. I have already explained that the Dalai Lama is chosen on the basis of recognition in this life, of things from the past. Crowley admitted that at the time of Mohamed he was a member of a Council and was all for the release of the mysteries which evidently was his Magnum Opus or Great Work: Hubbard was to go on to state that at one time (no date) but in some cosmic period that he was a member of a Council and of course in my own view, Scientology has released the mysteries to a certain extent although my own research here, provides an alternative viewpoint. The Buddha of compassion was expected in 1950 and it is certainly another great co-incidence that Hubbard, was to release *Dianetics* at this time as a science that would enlighten man on the workings of his own mind and would show the path of healing of mind and body. Co-incidentally too or not it was in the 1950's that plans for European Union were forging ahead with the notion that healing of Europe and peace could be realised through such and organisation of nation states. After the great destruction of two World Wars, would come that clever pre-determined outcome which identifies the hand of the Masters or "Guardians", as the political and religious plan was followed with the predictability of a bus timetable.

Crowley's invocations in one ritual using Eve as a Seeress, involved him asking questions from the Akashic Record:

Q: What is the work of this weekend?
A: Geburah.   (Explained as strength or fortitude)

Q: Geburah applied to what?
A: The **egg**. The egg is resting on the
points of **mountaintops,**   (egg with piercing member Very sharp.
                               Water around, **lotus** flowers on it.
                                    Minoan seals –wand/penis)

Q: Egg is symbol of some **new knowledge**, isn't it?   Psychro cave/Cabal)
A: Gimel, lamed.   (The letters G and L
                                     in Hebrew; add up
                                     to **33** and mean
                                     'spring fountain'

What does that mean?   33 rd degree = Rose-Croix degree of
A: I don't know.   Freemasonry and Rosicrucians)

Q: How are we to **break open the egg?**   **(Gain her secret)**
A: In plain language it means
Thou art to go this Way.   {Janus head of Hermes
                                  male and female}

Q:(That isn't plain language.) How are we to get this **new knowledge?**
A: (Don't ask questions too fast.) Sow the wild oats; go into the ...into the
Mother to be born again.

Q: What about the Mass of
the Holy Ghost?   (Crowley's Gnostic Mass,
                              the text of Which, is printed in
                            his *Magick in Theory and Practice).*

I have outlined in bold the significances (with my own notes in brackets), which again relate to Druidical symbolisation and the Religious Revolution in Crete, by the reference to Mother and re-birth the elixir of the Grail is indicated and the message. The "new knowledge" sought referred to some aspect of knowledge lost within the secret group hierarchy, regarding time track event data and which perhaps Ron Hubbard had access to in the O.T.O group? The egg of course was the Hermetic third or male potential symbolised by the male phallic piercing member or Druid wand as both penis and Excalibur sword: the egg, wand and the figure of Hermes substituted for the woman and labyrinth in Cretan seals of the Late Minoan period. The womb as labyrinth and egg with phallic piercing member is also displayed in the Temple of Freemason's Hall in Great Queen Street in London. The reference to mountaintops again signifies Druid rites, which were conducted on such and the cabal that overran Knossos did so from the psychro cave in the mountains surrounding Knossos and where in myth Zeus the symbol of power was born as Captain thirteen of the twelve Olympian gods. Further, the new knowledge sought evidently was to be found in the 33 rd degree of Freemasonry at Rose-Croix level, which was the defining conclusion of the floor of the Summer Smoking Room at Cardiff Castle, which I thought was Scottish Rite Freemasonry at 33 rd degree level, which is also the magical Hermetic level. The idea that Hermes brought forth the Spring (of new knowledge), which was symbolised in the paintings of Guercino and Poussin, that I reproduced in *The Battle of The Trees*, was incorrect, since the Bull-Minos phallic cult replaced the woman with Hermes and the egg as Easter egg, or potential for the world, was evidently going to come from the magical rites (and access to the Akashic record) wand (penis) of the male! Such potential to heal the world was then given to the Messiah, which was a uniquely Druid phenomenon. The Rosicrucian statement that Christ instigated a "new college of magic", merely refers to the attempt to place the hope of the world into the magical rites that would access whole track event data or man's spiritual record and event data here on Earth. The great mistake was to consider the Religious Revolution as the beginning, when in fact it was only a beginning of a political and religious system of control. The actual beginning goes back a great deal further and I have given an anti-matter, matter explosion and the evolving Diablo geometric as the beginning, which may align to the modern 'string' theory of the physics of space. On a practical level this "new college of magic" must refer to the adepts or initiates within the Rosicrucian's or 13 th tribe, who sought a world religion allied to the political aim. The "New Jerusalem" of the Rosicrucians was no more than the New Atlantis at least in that branch of the Rosicrucian's who utilised the Black Cabala and took directions from the thoughts of past Masters, who were none other than the old Atlanteans or Arch controllers who no doubt had existed on Earth for millions if not billions of years. Curiously enough Crowley set up the Society for the *Propagation of Religious Truth*, his publishing House being situated at Boleskine, Foyers in Inverness in Scotland!

One of the earliest and most eminent precursors of Freemasonry is said to have been Francis Bacon. Bacon is recognized to have been a Rosicrucian, and the secret philosophical doctrine he professed, was closely akin to Freemasonry is clearly apparent in his *New Atlantis*. The reference to the " Wise Men of the Society of Solomon's House" cannot be a mere coincidence. The choice of Atlantis – the legendary island supposed to have been submerged by the Atlantic

Ocean in the remote past would suggest that Bacon had some knowledge of a secret tradition descending from the earliest patriarchs of the human race, whom, like the writer Le Plongeon, he imagined to have inhabited the Western hemisphere. It perhaps would be natural for the biblical Adamites, presumably as the Tuatha de Danaan of Greece, who had migrated from the Black Sea region, where their alphabet the Beth-Luis Nion appears to originate; to find a home in Scotland, where the rocks are suggested by geologists to be some of the oldest in the world. I have already in previous sections of this book, discussed how the crystalline structure of matter when it cools, still retains a morphic resonant connection to the UVG120 sphere or Earth crystal and thus channelling in such places as caves, would undoubtedly aim to utilise this fact in the type of information sought. The Druids perhaps used caves for this reason and St. John was said to have written *Revelations* from the cave on Patmos in Greece and the Religious Revolution was conducted from the psychro cave on Crete, which bore archaeological evidence of cabalistic rites and practise. Icons of chariot (bull drawing a cart) and the cauldrons were found amongst other significant archetypes.

Bacon relates that certain of the Jews, who, whilst accepting the Cabala, rejected its anti-Christian tendencies, preserved the tradition of Atlantis, in its pure form. Thus: "in this island of Bensalem" there are Jews "of a far differing disposition from the Jews in other parts. For whereas they hate the name of Christ, and have a *secret inbred rancour against the people amongst whom they live*; these contrariwise give unto our Saviour many high attributes" (my emphasis). This must surely cover the point that whilst the events of Golgotha were a 13 th tribe plan, Jesus as admitted in the Nag Hamaadi scrolls, "fooled them". But at the same time they believe: "that Moses by a secret Cabala ordained the laws of Bensalem which they now use, and that when the Messiah should come and sit on His throne at Jerusalem, the King of Bensalem should sit at His feet, whereas other kings should keep at a great distance". This passage is of particular interest in showing that Bacon recognized the divergence between the ancient secret tradition descending from Moses and the perverted Jewish Cabala of the Rabbis, and that he was perfectly aware of the tendency even among the best of Jews to turn the former to the advantage of the *Messianic dream*. The Messianic dream and the promise of a Second Coming, in the form of a Celtic male with a muddy background history, together with new and astounding knowledge that bounces onto the world scene, fought by the old religion whereby its leader is crucified, is really such a science of manipulation, that it evidently became a subject in its own right within the Rosicrucian's, who refer in one text to "Messian*ology*"! ('ology' – study of). However, as I have pointed out the 'cuckoo' in the nest of the British Isles may have always sought to elect those Isles for the ultimate sacrifice of bringing about the prophesy of *Revelations* and the destruction of

"The Great City", which Rothschild I believe first used as a term for London: as Bacon admits the 'cuckoo' never held any allegiance to the peoples of these Isles and his imaginary Atlantis is a gloss for the British Isles and the 13 th tribe of biblical Adamites who held Mosaic Law. Freemasonry tried to disown Bacon, simply because his *New Atlantis* contained unmistakable allusions to Freemasonry and in its final transformation like the chameleon of many colours, it was to finally reveal its inner goal and self in the *New Atlantis*; which was a Theocratic priesthood, who may have had extra-ordinary intelligence through manipulation of matter via the Cabala but by ancient accounts or legend they were despots. The New Jerusalem was in fact the New Atlantis, the world run once again by despotic and enlightened Masters.

Rosicrucianism was not the beginning, but a link in the long chain connecting Freemasonry with Adam (the first Rosicrucian), the biblical Adamites, Noah, Tuatha de Danaan, Druid, Bull-Minos cult and stag cult, presumably dating back to 'Lightening Man'. Yarker in *The Arcane Schools* was to write: The symbolic tracing of the Rosicrucian's was a square Temple approached by seven steps...here also we find the two pillars of Hermes, the five-pointed star, sun and moon, compasses, square and triangle". Yarker further observes that: "even Wren was more or less a student of hermeticism, and if we had a full list of Freemasons and Rosicrucian's we would probably be surprised at the numbers who belonged to both systems." Sir Christopher Wren the architect built *St. Paul's* cathedral (significant!) in London with *that* dome! Which co-incidentally has dramatized itself up river (Thames) in *that* dome, along with *that* hermetic London Eye? Professor Buhle emphatically states that: "Freemasonry is neither more nor less than Rosicrucian's as modified by those who transplanted it into England". Presumably the vine or: Day 1 - plant the vine is implied. Whilst many researchers have denied the connection between Freemasonry and the Rosicrucian's, that may be so, but the point is that Rosicrucianism is highly likely to be a very elite form or "root" and whilst retaining a certain form that corresponds to Freemasonry, the Rosicrucian's it would appear have always retained the Messianic dream and the goal of themselves at the head of a world religion. Further they do possess impressive knowledge and the hidden science it would seem, which sets them apart from the Cabalistic aims inclusive of *The Covenant* of perhaps the 12 tribes. One cannot deny that over the extensive period of time through double agents and spies in each group (12 and 13), that the 12 tribes did not borrow from the Rosicrucian's a part of their system and symbols, which they adapted for their own purpose. However, it cannot be denied also, that both groups are Jewish, with presumably a combined interest and goal inherent in The Feast of Tabernacles where the tribes of Israel triumph. Whilst it may be convenient for the highest Order to allow conflicting groups of 12 and 13 to continue, perhaps as witnessed in the battle of the COS, there is

236

every possibility that the pre-determined outcome has already been written by the highest Order or Masters along the concept of 'accelerated evolution' and the Darwinian principle of 'survival of the fittest': the war of the two groups like the stage of the Roman arena, will have a winner in the battle and as we have seen the winner will get to imprint their triumph on the Akashic Record. Who is to say whether a few million years from now, after another Magnetic Reversal or space boundary event, that channelling the Akashic Record, will not throw up single frames in hundreds of feet of 'film roll', the technology of the E-Meter, people holding 'cans', a castle etc? Or in other words the COS story and the story of Christianity will be imprinted which is already evidenced by the frames of a man carrying a cross in the events of Inc. 2 which I thought was the entire Akashic Record downloaded into the memory banks of the spirit of man, at a time of a Magnetic Reversal. My books unless they make a significant impact on matter, with high emotion that creates morphic resonance, will not appear at all – this small and single frame in the 'film roll' with its truth of the side that did not win, the thought processes that I have expressed here, will not appear at all: just as the story in Crete at the time of the Religious Revolution, only imprinted the archetypes of the winning side as Hermes who wrote the woman out of the story. As Ghandi was to eloquently phrase it: "Even if you are in a minority of one, the truth is still the truth". The World Order as Arch Controllers of matter, minds and bodies of man, has always managed to imprint its thoughts firmly on the Akashic Record or morphogenetic and spiritual bioplasmas thus in eons to come, when my books have long gone, there will only be the memory within the individual's memory banks, thus if I were to proffer any advice, it might be, to grasp this story entirely, for if one did not make it out past the third post of exit and had to return for another Magnetic Reversal, this information may be of infinite value. Although I do not know whether the crucial third post in the chain would wait, they have waited already beyond a time one could reasonably hope for or imagine. One cannot expect another to wait in the harshest of circumstances, whilst one sits idly in front of the telly.

The Jewish writer Bernard Lazare has declared that: "there were Jews around the cradle of Freemasonry. In fact the coat-of-arms still used by Grand Lodge of England is undoubtedly of Jewish design. Mr. Lucien Wolf stated that the coat: " is entirely composed of Jewish symbols," and is "an attempt to display heraldically the various forms of the *Cherubim* pictured to us in the second vision of Ezekiel – an Ox, a Man, a Lion, and an Eagle – and thus belongs to the highest and most mystical domain of Hebrew symbolism". In other words, this vision, known to the Jews as the "Mercaba", belongs to the Cabala, where a particular interpretation is placed on each figure so as to provide an esoteric meaning not perceptible to the uninitiated. The Masonic coat-of-arms is thus entirely Cabalistic; as is also the seal on the diplomas of Craft Masonry, where another Cabalistic figure, that of a man and woman combined, is reproduced. The Bull, Lion, Eagle and Serpent, were the calendar beasts and four pillars of equal height in the Beth-Luis-Nion alphabet. The Bull or Ox was found in the psychro cave, from where I maintain a secret Cabal, the Idian dactyls or Druidic priests of the 13 th tribe, conducted the Religious Revolution. The Bull or Ox in the icons pulls a cart, which must be synonymous with the chariot of Hermes. We know that *Ezekiel* tried to distort his vision by changing the symbols whereby Man replaced Woman, who was represented by wisdom and the Serpent. During the re-positioning era at Knossos, the archetypal symbols were manipulated in a transition stage, to represent both male *and* female who would come to represent Hermes. However, eventually Hermes and the combining of male and female in a transcendent third stage beyond death as the bisexual god of **thieves** removed the woman in the story altogether! The ideas of Rhea and the philosophy of 'As I go, so shall I return', which was meant for all humanity, was re-positioned as the Second Coming for Solar Kings and Messiahs'.

Although I could find no reference to Thutmose III, the Deputy Grand Master of the Great White Lodge in history, I assume that the name is Thothmess III who was a priest of the temple of Amon (Adam?) He secured his succession by marrying either Hatshepsut or her daughter and superseded Thothmes I, at a festival during which, the oracle of Amon proclaimed him as the Pharaoh. This sounds like the old oracle trick, where a Theocratic priesthood pulled strings on the election of a new monarch. It seems that he and Hatshepsut, jockeyed for power and at one time *she relegated him to the background.* She must have been a remarkable woman to grasp power and evidently at this time there must have still been a memory of power shared by woman and man, perhaps co-inciding with the fair-haired Celtic (?) Queens provided for union with the Semitic kings presumably chosen for 12 th tribe connections? thus signifying joint power of 12 and 13, which I have suggested may still be the case today. Hatshepsut completed the great mortuary temple at Der-el-Bahari, with its significant *three* terraces and to overcome any objections by the priests of a woman being named "son of the Sun", Hatsheput in mythical scenes was depicted in the company of her male "double" (Twin) and on State occasions wore a false beard! This was perhaps a female attempt to reconcile both sides as Hermes, in order either to gain power or to try and bring the religion closer to its original source? However she would have done much better if that were the case, to take it back to true source, which did not involve Goddess and Twin Kings (the old Trinity) or Hermes, but *only* the knowledge, cosmology, belief and the way out of the trap. There is of course no power in that.

To celebrate her jubilee, Hatshepsut erected *two* magnificent obelisks, nearly 100 feet high in front of the Karnak temple in which Thothmess III was a priest, presumably signifying Thothmess III as the central Herm and herself as archetypal goddess between the two pillars of Hermes signifying the ancient Trinity. Hatsheput it seems was more concerned with religious affairs, than political ones and soon a revolt spread through Syria, where tribal chiefs scorned to owe their allegiance to a woman, especially as she would not enforce her will by the sword. Mysteriously no record exists of how Hatshepsut died and her mummy was never discovered; further her chosen successor her daughter was no longer referred to in any document, and her name was ruthlessly erased from her monuments. Thus we can assume that there was a religious battle that occurred here. Thothmess III, immediately came to the throne, and subdued the Syrian rebellion thus revealing the source of the uprising no doubt as third party and managed! Thothmess III from his mummy, we know to have been a little man with coarse features and despite his age when he died and a jaw that was not tied up before embalming, he still retains significant Semitic features. If Thothmes III is the same personage as the Grand Master of the Great White Lodge, then the mysterious disappearance of all records of Hatsheput becomes significant. Thothmes III was also referred to as Manakhpirria (Men-kheper-ra), which may literally translate as 'men-keeper-sun god'; and may be abbreviated in similar fashion to M-K or K (h)-M, in a circle of cycle of Eternal Return displayed in the word itself by joining it in a circle. The personage of K-H-M was given as the Deputy Grand Master of the Great White Lodge the "invisible" group of guardians or Masters who at one time lived at lake Moeris. This lake was to significantly occur in the channelling of the Rev. Walker and was to occur in the so-called illumination of Aleister Crowley, where his servant related the dream that corresponded to Mallory's tale of *Excalibur* and King Arthur and the Round Table: where Arthur was the 13 th member of a group of 12, just as Jesus was the 13 th member of the group of 12 and Zeus was Captain thirteen of the twelve Olympian gods. Jesus was to significantly state that: "I have come to bring a sword not peace", indicating his own particular Excalibur sanction and in my own witness account conclude he was a double agent for the 12 tribes and Simeon as the last Rosicrucian was nailed to the cross explaining that statement by Jesus in the Nag Hamaadi scrolls: "It was their man they nailed to the cross" and "I fooled them". Further Hubbard was to significantly refer to a manuscript he had written, which laid out all knowledge "like a smorgasbord" as *Excalibur*.

Thothmes was significantly dreaded long after his death, and may have originated the Semitic title "Pharaoh", which was never used by native Kings of Egypt. Under Thothmes III Egypt became a great *Empire* and the foremost power in the world, which indicated that the power and wealth attachment to the Holy Grail may have been used in secret and thus responsible for the eradication of Hatsheput who was concerned with religious affairs, allowing the old plan of a World Order to materialise once again on the world's stage.

The priests of Amon composed a great hymn in honour of Thothmes III, for his many victories and the implication of the Bull Minos-Cult with: "Crete...."Stricken with fear" (as I said the Early Minoans died horrible deaths). This would seem to indicate that it was the Egyptian branch of the 13 th tribe that undertook the Religious Revolution i.e. priesthood from the Jewish patriarchs. The appearance of the Sun-God Ra in icons of Crete during the Religious Revolution where men were shown raising their hands to Ra, casts great suspicion over the Grand Master of The Great White Lodge, and whether it was he and The Brotherhood who conducted the Religious Revolution against Crete? Stealing the Holy Grail with its message, cosmology and science. The Great White Lodge and Brotherhood as the highest echelons of at least one branch of Rosicrucian's dated back in descendency to the Bull-Minos cult and sons of Adam: but importantly we see here **not** a Celtic connection, but an Egyptian one and possibly a remnant of the thirteenth tribe with a connection to the 12 tribes of Israel! This seems to me to be very important, since evidently at the time of Golgotha those two groups' i.e. Celtic/Greek (13 th tribe) and Egyptian (12 tribes) were swirling in the murky waters of double agents and double cross, which was the mystery surrounding the lost genealogies of the Magdalene, who had a Greek connection. Thus it might be considered that the row between Clymer and Lewis over spurious branches of Rosicrucianism was perhaps based on this fact of two groups with similar knowledge, but one group seeking to commercialise the mysteries and another group wishing to apply the mysteries to healing. The priests of Amon (or Adam?) composed a poem in honour of Thothmes III:

> "I have come, I have given to thee to smite the land of the Syrians
> Under thy feet they lie through the length and breadth of the Od's land;
> I have made them see thy might like to a **star** revolving
> When it sheds its burning beams and drops its **dew** on the meadows.
>
> I have come, I have given to thee to **vanquish the western peoples**,
> Crete is stricken with fear, terror is reigning in Cyprus;
> Like to a great young **bull**, I have made them behold thy power,
> Fearless and quick to strike, none is so bold to resist thee.
>
> I have come, I have given to thee to conquer the folk of the marshes,
> The terror of thee has fallen over the lands of Mitanni;
> Like to a **crocodile** fierce they have beheld thee in glory;
> O monarch of fear at sea, none is so bold to approach thee.[191]
> *(Author's emphasis)*

I have already covered in considerable detail the various archaeological finds with their inherent archetypal symbology, which show that a Semitic group worshipping Ra, the Sun-God conducted a Religious Revolution in Crete, introducing drugs (opium) and Cabalistic ritual; a Semitic Order, that I have associated with the Bull-Minos Cult, Rosicrucians and to Thothmess III Grand Master of the Great White Lodge and Brotherhood, to which Crowley was attached. Obviously the fact that there are two groups involved with varying aims, means the matter is slightly complicated, but one assumes that the Druids in Scotland were 13 th tribe and Celtic/Greek connected, whilst there was another group who were 13 th tribe or descended from Adamites but presumably unlike the Tuatha de Danaan who migrated to Scotland, remained in the East and further to all intent and purposes were aligned with the 12 tribes of Israel. I have always suspected even in *The Battle of The Trees*, that at the highest level within Zionism and the secret group of the B'nai B'rith there is a very similar knowledge, to that possessed by the Druid (white) group of biblical Adamites; but with Egyptian connections through their Grand Master Thothmes III the "invisible" master of the Great White Lodge. If the official line of the COS is to be believed and Ron Hubbard was attempting to break up Crowley's branch of the O.T.O in Pasadena America by his association with Jack Parsons and the Agape Lodge, then since Crowley evidently was under the "invisible" Masters of the Cabalist Great White Lodge (and visible Masters of the Great White Brotherhood) this may account for the fact that Crowley wore a black cloak in some rituals, whereas Hubbard wore white, according to Parson's correspondence to Crowley. This certainly signifies that Crowley was not only using Cabalistic Black magic practise, but that his "invisible" Masters were probably the *Egyptian branch,* under the supreme Grand Master Thothmes III. Certainly in conducting the Religious Revolution in Crete, then some historical background must have survived in this group, which Crowley sought to further in his magical hermetic rituals. Hubbard then *may* have been under the Celtic and Druid 13 th tribe? This hypothesis, would not only answer the question as to why Scientology has been fought by France and Greece (12 tribe controlled) but why Scientology is not fought now in America or England, which must infer that those countries for the moment are 13 th tribe/Celtic/Greek connected group? This must have provided for the "special relationship", that was often spoken of in terms of British and American politics, at least until President Clinton left the scene. It would also answer why three tons of Scientology documents disappeared in France; presumably there is an active 13 th tribe in existence there. Finally it would indicate, that the push for a Federalist Europe is a 12 tribe based impetus if the previous assumptions are correct. Thothmess III as an original member of the Egyptian descendents from Adam and therefore technically biblical Adamites I assume, were evidently not white, blonde or blue-eyed as Thothmes mummy shows, thus the original stock of the 13 th tribe cannot have been white with racial characteristics of the Celts. Evidently then, whilst both Israel (12 tribes) and biblical Adamites/Druids (13 th tribe) have various psychological 'buttons' on 'keeping the race and blood pure', which has been heavily dramatized in both groups, particularly the 13 th tribe, where Hitler in his Aryan Super Race programme carried it to extreme lengths and tried evidently to eradicate the 12 tribes and the Egyptian branch: it still remains to be answered how the 13 th tribe became characterised by their blonde hair and blue eyes If not through the Celts, which may account for the blond blue-eyed Queens and mummies in Egyptian tombs, emphasising power was shared at one time which indeed may at the top of the hierarchy still be the case.

One of the jubilee obelisks of Thothmess III, which he created at Thebes, now stands in Constantinople; another is in Rome; the pair set up at Heliopolis have been given prominent sites - one in *New York* and the other on the Thames Embankment, in *London* (Twin Kings and identical goals?) Which may account for that peculiar millennium eve symbolisation in the year 2 000 of a dome in London and crystal ball (?) in New York. Thus from this last garnered piece of evidence in the interminable jigsaw puzzle, it would appear that the 'cuckoo' in the British nest, was at least at the time of the erection of the obelisk in London an Egyptian branch of Rosicrucian's. Further, there may be absolutely no difference between the Greek/Celtic branch of the 13 th tribe and its Egyptian 12 tribe affiliated counterpart, which may itself have derived from some remnant of the 13 tribe. I think it would be fair to say, that Jewish would now cover the entire upper level of the Rosicrucian's and the tribe of Judah. Thothmes III died on a significant day, that I noted in *The Battle of The Trees - 17th March* 1447 B.C. There was some indication that the significant date was being used for re-incarnation of future Grand Masters. Further Thothmes III reigned for fifty-four years meaning that his reign could have covered the Religious Revolution period in Crete c.1400 B.C., given that the exact dates for the Revolution are not sure and approximated. The main point is that the stolen data from Crete, placed The Holy Grail into hands that had no right to remain the 'man- keeper' (Guardian or Master) of such knowledge, only seeking power and wealth and hiding hitherto open knowledge. Further the Early Minoans died a really horrible death encompassed in abject terror. Thothmes III would spend his spare time carving beautiful vases no doubt tutored by Cretan artists, only to destroy the hand that fed. Cretan Seals after the Religious Revolution were to show the symbol of penis (male rood or wand) and egg (female womb) and the ultimate fusion of these symbols in the form of Hermes (God of thieves and vagabonds). It is recorded that Thothmes III also worshipped Aton (Atom?) and this cult existed at Heliopolis, which provided the obelisks for London and New York. The Aton cult at Heliopolis taught that the creator Ra the Sun God was "Shu in his Aton". Aton is the solar disk and shu is the air god, the source of "the air of life", the

Great Father (Adam?) who is the soul of the universe: Like"the Baa". Shu is also associated with the sun; the atmospheric god is manifested by lightning and fire as well as by tempest. The lightning God was one we saw in the African Palaeolithic caves, when early man really only had his shamanistic rites, which were Black Cabalistic and which he used to create fear and control, but no real science of the Grid or its record properties were understood and perhaps are not much more understood by those who believe they talk to Masters in the Black Cabalistic ritual. The Holy Grail was meant to raise mans awareness of the science of the trap, however it is perhaps significant that Hubbard designates the beginning as Inc. 1 and *Genesis* in *The Bible* starts out with the new knowledge acquired and blames Eve! Which was the justifier for committing a *prior* overt or wrong, which not only depends on Hermes theft of the Grail, but also depends on the crimes against humanity, of a select few who have always controlled humanity. The earliest and most primitive science that the Patriarchal group had, was early thoughts such as Shu is not only "air which is in the sun", but also according to Akhenaton's religion, "heat which is in Aton". In the Tell-el-Amarna poem, Aton, who creates all things: "makest the son to live in the body of his mother". Then follows a reference to "the egg":

When the chick is in the egg and is making a sound within the shell,
Thou givest it air inside it so that it may keep alive.

(*Budge's trans.*)

The small bird in the egg, sounding within the shell,
Thou givest to it breath within the egg
To give life to that which thou makest.

(*Griffith's trans.*)

When the chicklet crieth in the egg-shell,
Thou givest him breath therein, to preserve him alive.

(*Breasted's trans.*)

Not exactly the breathtaking science encompassed in the thronged stones depicting the UVG120 sphere, the armillary, the cycle of curved space time and the message of re-incarnation – the explosive 'package' of new data that came to earth c. 10 000 B.C. Some authorities identify Aton with the old Syrian god ADON. The root "AD" or "DAD" signifies "father". As "ad" becomes "at" in "Attis", it may be that as a result of habitual phonetic conditions, ADON BECAME ATON. This of course gives us a root **ADAM**, with the A substituting O in ADON. Aton was the chief of a Pantheon of Gods; he was THE ONE AND ONLY GOD. No sharing with the woman, or contest from other religions then, in effect autocracy and Theocracy. The significance of the A and O is probably

Adam as first man and the God of the Jews stated that: "I am the alpha and the omega", the *beginning and the end*: signifying the phrase in Revelations: "and the Earth shall end in fire", refers to Hermes, if not the eventual scientific prediction that the sun as an ageing star, will eventually fall from its orbit. If we assume that ADAM is synonymous with ADOMITE and DRUID, the appearance of eggs and wands (phallic member) in Minoan Seals post Religious Revolution, becomes clarified. Further the pre-occupation of the Pope Angello Roncalli, with Illuminatus ceremonies, where a woman tapped an egg with a wand, also becomes clear. This must date back to the Druids and Bull-Minos Cult, through Thothmes III and a time when the Minoan equivalent O.T. levels and Holy Grail were stolen. The Aton, says Professor Petrie: "was the only instance of a 'jealous god' in Egypt, and this worship was exclusive of all others, and claims universality". [192] We have here the real basis of a Universal Religion, within the One World Order programme and the universality of Hermes, with his janus head, that can look both ways and become male or female with resultant philosophies and goals dictated by whichever group is in power, but in reality both groups controlled at the pyramidal apex, by a Theocratic priesthood which has been constant throughout history and pre-history. As Adam Weishaupt stated, it was important to talk this way with one man and yet another way with another. The story of holly and oak, or holy one and oak royal. This is the schizoid reality of individuals, politics, secret groups and organisations that have incorporated the lie of Hermes into their ideology and philosophy: just as Hitler would claim to be a saviour, he would destroy Europe; just as Jesus claimed the universal solvent of love, he claimed to have brought a: "sword not peace"; just as my experience of Scientology and Anthroposophy was an experience of a face of two sides, with usury as one.

I noted in Cretan Seals in *The Battle of The Trees*, that a woman stood on a honeycomb mountainous structure, with wands or staves and two lions at each side. Amon-Ra, the King of the gods was another deity of the period and Amon was the son of the Great Mother deity. He became: "the husband of his mother" when the Great Father and Great Mother conceptions were **fused**. This must have brought the world the dramatization of incest, whilst Hermes apparently brought the dramatization of homosexuality and lesbianism, presumably triggered by some life event this lifetime. This process was illustrated in the triad formed by Ptah the father, Mut the mother, and Thoth the son. The principle was used in Christianity and altered to 'Father, Son and Holy Ghost', but hardly represented a truth, which Robert Graves referred to as the: "product of Latin Grammar". Where to put the woman was the dilemma she had to appear somewhere and was kept alive in 12 tribe Christianity in the form of the Virgin Mary which incorporated the Mother and child, which was to occur in the Greek icon showing the Bull-Minotaur on the lap of Pasiphae his mother: whereas she appeared as the ethereal muse of the white goddess elsewhere in the 13 th tribe. Ptah's wife Sekhet, with the head of a lioness, must have some basis for the lions in later Cretan seals and the Lion's gate at Mycenae, where the lions are the Twin Kings. As with Christianity, Amon the Great Father deity, became "king of gods", and lost his original lunar character, which was historically the woman as light on dark of the night. The fusion with the sun god of Heliopolis, which was accomplished for political purposes, made the change complete, for he became Amon-Ra, the Great representative deity of Egypt, who *combines the attributes of all other gods*. Hermes seeks to do this as combined male and female, woman locked up in his tomb!

Amon-Ra was depicted as a great bearded man, clad in a sleeveless tunic suspended from his shoulders, with the tail of an animal hanging behind. His headdress of high double plumes, with lunar and solar symbols, was coloured in sections red and blue, and red and green, as if to signify an association with the river flowing between its banks and the growth of greenery. Sometimes he is shown with Min's *ram's horns* curving downwards in a spiral round his ears, and sometimes with those of Khnumu spreading outward, with obvious symbolisation of the ram as totem beast, which glossed the earlier history of the Bull-Minos cult. He wore a *collar* as clerical? Or dog as in 'guard the secret' or perhaps the two being synonymous? Together with armlets and bracelets, presumably reflecting the snake goddesses at Knossos, who wore snakes entwined around the arms. Whether God as the old bearded man and the collar of the vicar originate from such sources I do not know, but it seems possible. There is another interesting point here, the Templars who suspiciously look like some form of thirteenth tribe, idolised Baphomet, with a ram's head and beard, which suspiciously reminds us of this particular deity and the god of the thirteenth tribe dating back to Egypt. Further rulers of Egypt later were called Amen-hotep; "Amon is satisfied" apart from four rulers called Thoth-mes, "born of Thoth". When prayers today end "Amen" surely this is a referral to the Universal god introduced into the Empire of Egypt, which at least under Thothmes III looks to be EGYPTIAN thirteenth Tribe Empire i.e. NOT GREEK. The Amon ram was an animal incarnation of the corn spirit or barley, which does have connections to the thirteenth tribe and Greek root (how about that for a great muddle!). However whether the thirteenth tribe is split into two on the basis of migrations in the early days, where one faction ended up as the Tuatha de Danaan in Ireland and eventually Scotland, the other faction remaining in the East; or whether the Egyptian faction is really just the origins of the 12 tribes, all being descended from one root or Adam is clouded, but what is certain from the finds on Crete, including the Rosettes on hats and on the Bull, that, the Rosicrucians have very early origins and that rosette is clearly seen in the Temple Asklepios in Epidaurus Greece, which was a place of healing, but governed by a secret priesthood. Further the Rosicrucian's gave one meaning of the Rose as "effusion of dew", which must have some basis in the Egyptian poem and hymn composed by the priests of Amon (Adam?) to Thothmes III.

The group of Rosicrucians or the Bull-Minos cult, who took the Holy Grail from Crete, had to hide Re-incarnation as a belief system, since the 'cult of the hero', who knew he would re-incarnate to fight another day, was potentially dangerous to any group that sought monopolistic control of religion and politics and humanity of course. Some confusion was inevitably introduced regarding the fate of the soul after death. Boats occurring in the cave of Zeus (the Psychro Cave) in Crete after the Religious Revolution, indicated that there was some land of the blessed, an isle of women, which was to occur in myth and which I covered in *The Battle of The Trees* and Crowley was to be given this sign in his communication from the Secret Chiefs; where *three* women on a boat appeared in the dream of his servant. There was a strange fusion of beliefs regarding the other world, which had never existed when the mysteries were given freely in Crete. The invention of Hermes as a sky god uniting the female and male in a transcendent third stage beyond death must have played a major part. The Chiefs and Masters, took the knowledge of Re-incarnation and used it to reap their goal and purpose over every lifetime, giving them control in each lifetime above the average man, who believed his lot was determined only by not sinning and "turning the other cheek" - pacifism - so that the Masters could control absolutely. No matter how hard it got, there was always the hope of Salvation in the next world, how you got there and past the Grid was not of course part of the teachings! And now after all these years, the Masters have the audacity to hand back a gift piecemeal, with a price tag, a gift that was not theirs to give but was stolen by Hermes god of thieves!

Strangely up until a hundred years ago, the inhabitants of Palestine still credit all the surviving works of antiquity to the "Fenish", who may be the "Fenkhu" and may hold a further connection to the Vine-man: "he who joins together" - Fenuisa Farsa, the grandson of Magog, who was the grandson of Noah and biblical Adamite or 13 th tribe. Is it any wonder that the 'cuckoo' in the British nest whether 12 or 13 played a major role in the formation of the State of Israel, with its betrayal of the Arabs. Why blame British *people* for the 'cuckoo's' wrongs? There are numerous puzzles in the Egyptian dynasties: the Priests did not revere the memory of Thothmes III, there are no folktales concerning his tyranny and impiety that have survived and has according to historical documents suffered a conspiracy of silence, however the prejudice against him remained even until Roman times. I would suggest that the conspiracy of silence must be due to the

13 th tribe background and the acquisition of knowledge from Crete at about the

same time. The Egyptian dynasties also unexpectedly carry non-Egyptian lines, where women often have blonde hair and blue eyes, such as has been suggested for Queen Tiy; one of Egypt's most notable women who has suffered conflicting views over her nationality. The Third Amenhotep, Quenn Tiy's husband, had a distinctly non-Egyptian face and his mother was the daughter of an *Aryan* King of Mitani.

Mitani was an **Aryan military aristocracy**, probably accounting for the Aryan "wave" which swept into India about the beginning of the Twelfth Egyptian Dynasty, perhaps originating the idea of Tibetan Masters, or Secret Chiefs: and I would suppose that the Chinese occupation of Tibet, the destruction of monasteries and the sequestering of old records, was really an attempt to wipe out all traces of the thirteenth tribe, which was probably why Chairman Mao referred to religion as "poison" and the strict Communist regime was an attempt to keep out the elitist thinking of the children of Adam and Noah. The indoctrination of the Chinese would certainly require a major revolution in thought to overcome, thus presumably being a major barrier to the World Order. However the lack of religion also brings with it, the unfortunate demise into Grid thinking, simply by forcing the nation into survivalist thinking along the lines of self and group. The basis of the message that arrived on Earth was that of a philosophy and as such religion or churchanity had no place in its aim, however the philosophy became the pivot of the politics of religion – metapolitics or politics of the soul. The Platonic Maxim: 'Before you can cure a man's body, you must first cure his mind and before that his soul' rightly applied to healing, would form the basis of *disease* of humanity when the mysteries that underlie the Platonic maxim were to become part of secret metapolitics. Freedom for humanity was replaced by control of humanity and The Bible I believe recognised this by stating that "a great sore" came upon the Earth, which depends on the first cut, repeated in the second cut or 'Cutting of the elm' ceremony, which Jesus re-enacted with the Magdalene, when he cut her left arm. Unfortunately too secrecy surrounding the Grail message is a major barrier to the release from the trap. Rupert Murdoch, certainly as I have discussed, is intent with the Chinese government on keeping the Falung Gong down, a sect that believes in re-incarnation. There must be some further confusion here, since Thutmose III overcame the Mitani Aryan power, which was probably not un-connected to the fact that the later "Hykos" over lordship of Egypt in what is called the Hykos period, found the: "children of Israel" settled in Egypt. Thus Thutmose III, as Grand Master of The Great White Lodge and Brotherhood, confusingly had to be working for the twelve tribes. This would make sense in the context of Aleister Crowley whose Mastership was the "invisible" Great White Lodge and who used Black Magic and Cabalistic science. This would change the game plan considerably! If Hatshepsut was ousted by Thothmes III, whom I equate with Thutmose III as one and the same personage and Grand Master of The Great White Lodge, then there must be a battle of 12 and 13 here, which may account for all records of Hatshepsut being destroyed and her mummy never being found, since she was probably of the Greek/Celtic 13 th tribe of Danaan. If we found the mummy, it might if it was blonde- haired give some proof of such a battle, since Thothmes III definitely had the usual Semitic traits.

The efforts to find out the name of the God of a particular group, was a very difficult task in history and it seems things have not changed! However given the racial characteristics of Queen Tiy and the distinctly Semitic face of Amenhotep III, then it might be interesting to look at the nature of their reign, which was marked by a court, where scholars and speculative thinkers were welcomed and to whom the crude beliefs and superstitious conventionalities associated with the worship of Amon and the practises of the worldly minded priests, had become distasteful and obsolete. Architects, artists and musicians basked in royal favour under the influence of Queen Tiy and the art of the age was as pronounced as it was beneficial. She encouraged artists to shake off still mannerisms of the schools, to study nature and appreciate its beauties of form and colour, and to draw "with their eyes on the object". Thus certain features including the power of critical observation, of the comparable O.T. levels of Crete dating to the Palaeolithic Age had not been lost. When this knowledge surfaces in periods of history, it always brings a level of high create and in this period of Egypt's history there was no exception as Egypt went through a revolution of artistic methods with its "renaissance of wonder". Just as in Crete the Early Minoan frescoes, full of life, colour and nature emerged coupled with peaceful co-existence, thus was the mark of the reign of Amentohep III and Queen Tiy, where they are shown in natural family pictures with their children as distinct from the emphasis on dynastic power of previous and future reigns. The Palace that Amenhotep constructed for Queen Tiy on the western bank at Thebes has frescoes of nature studies, with all the vivid colour of the Minoan frescoes. Over the royal thrones in this exquisitely aesthetic Palace, was a royal vulture, which compares to the vulture that abducted the nymph Thalia from Crete, shown in the red-figured vase from Nola. Zeus as a vulture abducted Ariadne with her significant ball of string, which is knowledge of the grid and the comparable O.T levels of Crete. The chequered basket in the design of the icon is also significant, being not only the archetypal symbol of the womb and Mother-Goddess, but it would become the archetypal symbol of Druids, with their wicker Osier baskets and their human sacrifices; together with further implications of Moses wicker basket and the Druid's use of Mosaic law.

The Crane was a frequent motif in Minoan art, just as the long-legged Ibis, another water foul was sacred to Egyptian Thoth the counterpart of Hermes. Hesiod stated that Cranes could be seen migrating south by October 31st of our Calendar, and returning in spring approximately February 5th. The Crane with its v-formation, is seen in Minoan Seals (H.M. 1597), at the Heraklion Museum. This particular seal shows not only four Cranes flying in v-formation, but since the Cranes migrated in the Serpent season, according to the Knossos calendar, which began about November 3rd and ended February 4th, Cranes often were shown with Serpent pattern. The seal is interesting, because it shows on several faces a geometric pattern, corresponding to the UVG120 sphere and those mysterious stones tied geometrically with thongs. Originally the significance of the Cranes was as with agricultural symbolism, to illustrate the thought and belief of the Holy Grail Message - Re-incarnation: "As I go so must I return". A message that was taken over by the thirteenth tribe with their 'scene productions' entitled 'Messiah', superimposed onto a political system of Kingship and later to provide a Universal religion allied to political goals within a World Order programme. The birth of Hermes that fused Twin Kings with Mother Goddess into one bisexual personage was another distortion of the truth that effectively removed the woman and any trace of the gift of The Holy Grail as hers. Thus at some point after the Religious Revolution and during Middle Minoan III period, the migration of the Cranes, was perceived as the going and coming of Hermes, thus finally removing the idea of Re-incarnation and re-positioning the archetypal symbols that had been utilised in the equivalent OT levels.

Classical tradition gave Hermes winged sandals and winged hat (petasos) and he is often shown with a winged caduceus, which may have a connection to the Druidic wand or rood. The rood (penis) or wand that Crowley used and signed his name as with a pictorial reference to penis as testicles as the 'A' of Aleister, represented the secrets and knowledge which were taken however the knowledge was then coupled with Black Cabalistic science applied to rituals, which were used to tap information from the Grid. Hermes, who in classical tradition was the conductor of souls to the underworld of the dead, also was connected with conducting newborn souls to earth and hence the Stork brings babies. The use of the wand as caduceus, which also was a feature of the Druids, sought by magic ritual using vibratory resonance to 'awaken' the information from the dead (Masters) and hermetic magic was the "new college of magic" that Jesus allegedly introduced and which Crowley either utilised or developed. The information that was sought was from the period of Hermes in Crete and specifically the ancient Magi or Masters who undertook the Religious Revolution.

The Aryan Celtic (?) dynasty that Queen Tiy of Egypt descended from worshipped a pantheon of gods, which included Mithras and Saint Chrysostom, writing in the early Fifth Century, and referring to the festival of the pagan Sun-god (Ra in Egypt and during the Religious Revolution in Crete) said:

> "On this day also the birthday of Christ was lately fixed at Rome in order that, while the heathens were busy with their profane ceremonies, the Christian's might perform their sacred rites undisturbed. They call this (25th December), the birthday of the Invincible One (Mithras); but who is so invincible as the Lord. They call it the Birthday of the Solar Disc: but Christ is the Sun of Righteousness".

I previously referred to the impression of a stone ring, found at Naples and belonging to the Sixth Century A.D., which evidently remembers a lost tradition and truth about the birth of Jesus. The Three Kings of Christian tradition, bringing gifts to Jesus, are in fact the ancient Trinity of three, with two Twin Kings of the Year and Hermes in the middle with his obvious wings and petasos. The birth of Jesus here is associated with Hermes and the "new college of magic" was evidently held in the hands of the 13 th tribe. Jesus as the thirteenth member of a group of twelve (disciples): the further connection of Druids and the thirteenth tribe being implied. This would account for the Celtic genealogies and the alleged descent of Jesus from his grandmother Anna and the tribe of the Tuatha de Danaan I concluded and thus accounting for the appearance of Jesus, with "orange" hair – a distinctly Celtic feature.

Greek Myth tells us that when Zeus returned to Olympus, he was so angry with the entire race of man, whom were all descendents of Pelasgus, father of Lycaon, that he sent forth a great Flood to wipe out all humanity; but one man and a woman, Deucalion and his wife Pyrrha had been warned in advance by Prometheus the Titan and having built an ark, they survived the Flood, coming to rest on the slope of Mount Parnassus. Thereupon they peopled the world anew. However the Flood failed in its purpose, and presumably *The Covenant* was broken in Biblical texts. In Greek myth some of the Parnassians who survived the Flood, wandered to Arcadia, where they revived their ancient rites, which must account for the myth of the birth of Hermes in Arcadia and presumably Black Magical Cabalistic rites, which utilised the Grid. The importance of the Religious Revolution, was that prior to The Holy Grail, the Grid was not understood, even though probably Cabalistic rituals and Shamanism have existed from the earliest of times and were responsible for the misuse of the hidden science, which precipitated some cataclysm, which may well be a Magnetic Reversal after some nuclear event.

According to Theophrastos (c. 322 B.C.). The Arcadians of his own time still sacrificed a boy to Zeus Lycaeus on Mount Lycaeum, his sacred mountain, in celebration of the festival of the New Year. Significantly the boy's entrails were mixed with the guts of sacrificed animals and served to the members of the clan of Athos, who assembled at a sacred Oak tree beside a stream. Very Druidic! Very Thirteenth Tribe and Semitic, in so far as Noah made his first sacrifice, when the Flood had ceased. Both 12 and 13 had utilised sacrifice, but the Druids had utilised human sacrifice burning many thousands in the dreaded Osier baskets, which were often crammed to capacity and were very high often in the shape of a man, presumably Hermes. Even after sacrifice of humans and animals had ceased witches were denounced, when in fact, they were mystics. The hidden science was to be kept completely hidden. The Inquisition (as I remember!) was the hunt for all remaining documents and truth regarding The Holy Grail, which was passed off as a propaganda campaign by the Catholic Church. This may have been a period when significant documents regarding the truth were lost and it seems that at the time of Jesus some new material surfaced, probably some documents from the Magdalene. Sacrifice to a cause became the substitute for actual sacrifice, where 12 versus 13 have rampaged across this earth, unknown to the many in their pursuit of "Paradise on Earth"!! At gross profit and power to themselves. It is however an illusion, since their covert goal is not to release man from the trap, but to retain their own power base and wealth. Billions who have had their bodies and minds USED, just so that the knowledge once freely given in Palaeolithic times and later in Crete, could be fused with a One World Order political system with only the dregs of truth from some Universal religion.

It is easy to see the hope of the twelve tribes, since it is written into THE PLAN - the *Book of Revelations* by St. John in the Bible and which I proposed in my first book *The Battle of The Trees.* It appears we have now reached the final pages of the 'script', and thus let us decode the 'script', at least from the point of view of **Israel and the twelve tribes**, so that the audience can at least understand the plot. Wake up audience! World War III is about to start and (Arm)- agg- hedon (The final 'Cutting of the elm' or 'arm' the "the branch" or the message or Grail from the "root" or royal dynastic line or Adam; egg the potential of the world; Addon or Adam or Adomites? And Hebrew or Hebron): Who is the egg of world potential?The twelve tribes or the thirteenth tribe? Well the 12 Tribes evidently discretely and symbolically berate the thirteenth tribe and the Greek root in *Revelations*: *9,v.1:*

> "And they had a King over them,
> Which is the angel of the bottomless pit,
> whose name in the Hebrew tongue is Abaddon

but in the Greek tongue is Apollyou"

Ab (Abaris the Chief Druid?) addon (Adom or Adam - Adomite -the thirteenth tribe?) Moreover Apollyou is Apollo the Greek Solar King, Solar Kingship of course took over from Twin Kingship and Hermes became the god, of the thirteenth tribe. The 12 tribes then, intend to elect the thirteenth tribe as the Devil. Angello Roncalli the Pope who attended the secret Illuminati ceremony with wand, woman and egg, was thirteenth tribe and a future Pope would refer to this period as the Catholic Church in possession of the Devil. The current Pope John Paul II referred to the *Book of Revelations* as **"symbolic"** having no real relevance to the end of times! But surely he should have explained the symbolism and the whole TRUTH to those who study and follow this text in their worship! As Huckleberry Finn was to remark: "You can't pray a lie".

The vision of Heaven for the 12 tribes, gives the white-haired God type vision and in *Revelations 4,6*: "And before the throne (of God) there was a sea of glass like unto crystal." Deary me, I hope that does not mean the mega-computer or UVG120 sphere -crystal! The Trumpet that sounds, (*Revelations 15 -19*), is according to the Scientology OT levels part of the "implant" or *mind control* of Inc.I where a trumpet which might gloss the term 'horn' which was symbolic of the gates of horn and the abode of the dead of the Minos cult who conducted the Religious revolution: the trumpet (or horn) sounded before the whole game for man kicked off (I would prefer the anti-matter, matter version personally with Inc. 1 as the Religious Revolution in Crete) Hubbard says "everyone" has the Inc 1 "implant"; which is understandable from the point of view of this book, since the battle of 12 and 13 has infected everyone. *Revelations* is written for the twelve tribes of Israel in which they become "the chosen ones", with the Goyim or non-Jews not part of the final exultation, except that "paradise on Earth" is created for them, which might describe a Magnetic Reversal for the twelve tribes, in so far as man would indeed start off again with a new 'script' and reconstituted earth after man has spent 36 days (according to Hubbard) stuck like a fly to the 'filaments' of the unravelled spiritual and morphogenetic bioplasma being downloaded from the Grid with the entire event and phylogenetic data (according to my own research). After which presumably the Earth will take millions of years to settle down or maybe much sooner who knows. After which "Paradise" for the MMRC case will start with presumably with a return to Earth from outer space and Day 1 plant the vine. Theatre Earth provides the stage for yet another 'production' of the 'script'.

Typically the 12 tribes and *Revelations* as is evident in *Genesis* seek to vilify the woman - ah yes its all her fault, since it was she who gave Adam the apple (Immortality - Re-incarnation and knowledge of the Grid and trap) The

Revelations text refers to: "The Great City", which "sits on seven mountaintops" and suffers a large "earthquake" to end all earthquakes. London as I have pointed out, was first called: "The City" by Rothschild who was heavily involved with the One World Order and as *On Target* pointed out [193] had proved himself a traitor to Britain over nuclear secrets. Does the Jewish One World Order hope to pull off its final part of the 'script', by allocating the earthquake to Britain? After all David Icke, did in his channelled Information? 'see' the white cliffs ("Seven Sister's?) of the southern coastline fall into the sea. The other contender of course was Crete and Knossos as the Great City of the Minoans, with the "seven mountains" perhaps signified by the seven triangles that are obtained if you apply Pythagorean geometry to the tops of the numerous mountains surrounding the Knossos site. Either way Tesla technology as I pointed out in *Alternative 4*, is capable of producing artificial earthquakes. I suspect that the reduction of Britain to a Third World status, with the purposeful policies that have run this country down, may not be entirely co-incidental: after all as I commented if you suppress a people enough (and the British are highly suppressed) they resort to Grid behaviour of survival of the fittest. Everything must fit according to the 'script' so that peoples of the world will look at BSE, foot and mouth disease, football hooliganism, racism and nod sagely and say: "Ah yes, it has all come to pass, as it was prophesied". A wonderful piece of mind control that did indeed start in Crete with the Cabal that overran Knossos and took the data, the 'cuckoo' in the British nest that owed no allegiance to the people of this country, but only to their own and the tribes of Israel. Whilst scientists currently in Britain do not know how foot and mouth disease came to be in the food chain, they are agreed that it came from *outside* the country in the form of illegal   meat imports. Since 1993, health officials and customs have been forbidden from carrying out spot checks on goods arriving from another European country – no the disease did not start in these fair Isles and I smell an unholy pie here! In the wake of the disease a study of American attitudes, commissioned by the Irish government, made "grim reading". "They don't believe there will be any food here they will be able to eat", said Northern Ireland enterprise and tourism minister. Further "They believe they can contract the disease and in some extreme cases American's think their hands and feet will fall off". Predictably "This is how *bizarre* this incident has been played in the United States. They see this place as a *diseased country* and we have a huge task to change those perceptions" (*author's emphasis*). The fact that a Jewish press and media is probably responsible for these "perceptions" (how else does Joe public learn about the so-called facts?) and the false impressions, no doubt tallies very nicely with the *Revelations* account of the 12 tribes, where the elected "Great City" is home to all "vile things". I am afraid that the British Press and media, have constantly betrayed this country, by refusing to acknowledge their code of practise and "the right to know", which as I have frequently pointed out to them, must refer to TRUTH. They would rather support the pro-Israel line and the nonsense that emits from Brussels and the World Order, than their own people and that is the truth of the matter – treason? Chris Smith, the Culture Secretary, sought to convince the world Britain is open to tourists but admitted global reports, especially in the US, were suggesting Britain was closed and the countryside "burnt to a cinder". He warned Britain was losing £100m a week but that figure could rise to as high as £250m with the peak season approaching. The British innately know that this is a small country and cannot take any great population rise, without sacrificing the health of the land, which supports its people. The objections to the rise in immigration is *not* a racial issue, but a practical cultural and economic issue of a small country already at stress point over basic provisions such as education, policing and welfare; the racial card is merely pulled it would seem by a third party, covertly seeking the destruction of this country which prevents deep issues facing this the British people from ever being intelligently discussed, including the important aspect of heritage and culture and the crisis of identity – with the question Who are we? Britain is portrayed as the "diseased" pariah in America whilst no doubt it was overlooked, that Odessa's most famous son: former state governor and now US President, George W Bush, in March 2001 let it be known that he was pulling out of global efforts to reduce the emission of greenhouse gases. Odessa as the US's most polluted state, where big business with an eye to profit disregards environmental concerns and its occupants poisoned by a petrochemical plant (*The Independent on Sunday April 1 st 2001*) would not of course be worthy of notice in the American press, who are more concerned with the 'script' as dictated by those who control that press. In June 2001 the south west of England suffered another mild earthquake, which curiously have been rare in Britain. The press followed up with the comment that England lies on prominent earth energy lines, which may well cause "the big one" (earthquake). Putting all the apocalyptic clues together, it seems more than co-incidental and I suspect that since earth energies can now be manipulated through Tesla-like secret technology that any "big one" would be more than prophetic (according to the 'script' of the World Order) – another sacrifice to the cause.

How far south things can go was illustrated by the childish use of the archetypal symbols that seems to amuse those in the know. The Janus head of Tony Blair (now Prime Minister) used in the election campaign of 1997, either a dramatization /or? Further, Tony Blair with horns on! What could that mean - Scottish Rite Masonic –United States of the West or European Union supporter? William Hague the Tory party leader is to be depicted as the 'son of Satan', by Labour in a video for the forthcoming election of 2001, designed to frighten its supporters into the polling booths but merely plays into the hands of the World Order: the politics of fear- a very low emotional level of control of a populous.

Apparently the vicious personal attack on the Conservative leader is modelled on the 1970's horror film *The Omen*. Surely though 'Son of' is a reference to Messianic thirteenth tribe? Hoping to play on the archetypal symbols then. William Hague has appeared to move towards the right corner, with his hard policies of crack downs on immigration policies and a '**No to Europe**', whilst Blair like a spinning top, has revolved his Janus head so fast, that no-one knows where he stands except on the subject of a sleazy administration, which generally typifies both groups of 12 and 13. Meanwhile those who manage the fragile ecosystems of the environment and countryside in Britain were left to explain to the dunces of the city, just what impact short-term policies have on that environment that provides enormous pleasure to the British people and visitors these Isles. However as *On Target (cited)* pointed out in their May issue, the removal of an independent national food chain in favour of the multi-nationals is very much on the Hidden Agenda. The French Revolution ran the same course. Control of money and the food supplies (by the Masons and their agents) resulted in a Revolution and that is the author's prophecy for Europe – a Third World War, unless this story is made known.

George Bush can't seem to pin the spinning top into position either. The Americans are deeply worried about a European Army and whilst Tony Blair's visit to America in 2001 appeared momentarily to quell the nerves of the American Administration, the relief was momentary since we learn that the Conservatives have been over and whispered some other story into the Administration's ear. Reading between the archetypes, I see that there is a definite confusion over the name of the god that drives Blair and Hague, with that old question "who do you serve?" i.e. 12 or 13. As I told you, this is not an easy game to find the god or name of the group. Donald Rumsfeld, a key player in Bush's administration, declared the plans for a European army, could "inject instability" into the Nato alliance and "put at risk something that is very special". Was he referring to 13 th tribe policy? This unenthusiastic response of the American administration, rather contradicts Blair's statement that Bush had agreed to support the EU rapid reaction force. Apparently Mr Rumsfeld's intervention rocked Downing Street and triggered an extraordinary response from the British Prime Minister Tony Blair as he turned on the French. For weeks Mr Blair has insisted he had convinced Mr Bush that there was no French plot to remove military planning from under Nato's wing and thus exclude the American's. Blair suddenly and extraordinarily admitted there is. In what Conservatives described as a complete U-turn, Mr Blair conceded for the first time that Paris is trying to exclude the U.S. In an interview with the Sunday Telegraph, Mr Blair said: "Well, if we don't get involved in European defence, it will happen without Britain. Then those people who really may have an agenda to destroy Nato will have control of it". The only country in the EU with such an agenda is France, which has remained outside Nato, which it resents as an American-dominated body. Blair accused the Conservatives of going to America to warn that the European Army is a French plot to destroy Nato. The problem with janus heads, is that the words and actions never quite tie up, a series of senior figures close to George Bush have expressed rising concerns at the gap between Mr Blair's rhetoric and the reality of the annexes to the EU Nice treaty signed last December (2 000). George Bush then is wondering whether Nato is going to be the primary way to keep the peace in Europe, or whether a European army signals the end of an American presence in Europe. The transatlantic rift can only mean trouble in my opinion and that possibility of a *third battle* that is recorded in past holographic events and in legend and myth. The dramatizations of the past, re-enacted on today's stage, only mean, that there is every likelihood of a repeat atomic war and another Magnetic Reversal as the terrible Twins fight it out on the world's stage.

The above edition of *On Target*[193], noted how immigration policy has affected the indigenous population of Britain and I would conclude what appears to be attempts to break the thirteenth tribe mentality in the U.K. down. If there is a racist problem in Britain, then as with the case in America it is a dramatization of both groups i.e. 12 and 13 since both were obsessed with pure bloodlines. However distinct from the dramatization of the 13 th tribe 'cuckoo' there is another issue of the culture of the British Isles. Every country in the world retains its culture, its folklore, folk dances and traditions, which have formed the psychology of the nation, but nowhere in the world other than Britain is that folk memory fought so harshly. In early tribes this anchor point of tribe memory and morals according to the elders was a very important mechanism for survival. The dispersion psychologically the British have felt, must rest upon exterior influences to break down the 13 th tribe mentality in Britain, which was really more the mentality of the 'cuckoo' in the nest. The 13 tribe or 'cuckoo' in the nest dominated British Colonialism and the British Empire. The 'cuckoo' has now vacated the nest, however the *Revelations* condemnation of the 13 th tribe now seeks to make the villain in the story the British Isles, from the point of view of the 12 tribes of Israel. The display of any national identity, which the British have unfortunately equated with 13 th tribe, brings accusations of racism and superiority. The reality is that every facet of British culture has been not co-incidentally run down together with health care and education and where standards have fallen, in line with the crisis in identity that the British feel and particularly the young. To remove the tribal folk memory and morals and then replace that with the insistence that other tribes move into an enclosed space, with their own tribal history and morals is to invite confusion and conflict according to Grid survival mechanisms. Animals in packs mark their territory and if the researcher introduced another animal pack into the territory it would prove to be a fight for survival along Darwinist lines and 'survival of the fittest'. The removal of the culture of the British and its tribal memories, without replacing that with anything other than the loose term of a "multicultural society" has in reality removed from the young a sense of belonging to anything with an anchor point. The middle classes once held the morals of the society in Britain, with its ethos of security in employment, a profession, charitable work that defined one's standing in the community and a job done well. The disappearance of the middle class, with its replacement by the Thatcher philosophy of money, power and acknowledgement to the people that "do" was meant to break down the class barriers, but in actuality there was no longer any pride in the professions or security, as everyone was replaceable and money became the new god, with the birth of the filofax 'yuppie'. Politicians no longer promoted the tribal morals and ancestry and could not be relied upon to set any standard, thus where did the standards of the tribe now come from? The aristocracy tried to keep the system in place by supporting the public school system, which bred the next generation of leaders, whilst the masses lived on short-term policies and economics that saw education, health and farming deteriorate and the ethos of hedonism and the pursuit of pleasure became the answer to the loss of long term anchor points. The manufacturing industry in Britain, it is claimed in the above edition of *On Target*, has been systematically run down for integration into Europe, along it appears with agriculture, however this might represent another facet of the *Revelations* plan. With regards to "the Great City" in the Revelations account, I refer you to page 252 of the 'script', in case you have lost the plot entirely! Where according to *Revelations 17,9* the woman pops up again (deary me the 12 tribes should learn to control their dramatizations on woman since half of mankind is womankind!) and we hear that:

"And here is the mind, which have wisdom
The seven heads are seven mountains, on
which the woman siteth..."

Since London 'sits on' or according to the map of Britain lies north of the cliffs on the south coast, i.e. the Seven Sisters (seven white cliffs) co-incidentally where the white chalk Hill Figure of the Gogmagog giant is situated, which I concluded were hermetic with Druidic and 13 th tribe undertones; then can we assume that approximately two thousand years ago when *Revelations* was written, London was going to be elected as the "The Great City", with its devastating earthquake! The thirteenth tribe always acknowledged the woman albeit grudgingly in her white or death aspect, having locked her up in the tomb of Hermes. Equally by applying Pythagorean geometry to the mountaintops around the cave of Zeus and the Minoan city of Knossos, then one obtains seven triangles ("mountain tops"). Thus who is going to be elected for sacrifice to a cause of the 12 Tribes - London or Heraklion in Crete where Knossos lies? This is certainly ridiculous and the entire finale of a 'theatre' and 'play' which has been dramatized from the start, with its Inc. 1 and Inc. 2 "implants" or the more scientific explanation that I gave as the event of a Magnetic Reversal (Inc. 2) and the Religious Revolution in Crete (Inc. 1): and all because the tribes of Israel cannot admit they are wrong. The psychotic dramatizes the computation: 'I must be right or I die'. Survival is perceived in maintaining the lie at all and every cost, since this lie would shake to the very foundations that great pyramid of power and control that has been erected on this lie. Further no religion is free from the repercussions of this lie, however some religions hold more truth than others and evidently Scientology does have a good smattering of truth in it with that inevitable Janus head.

If you feel that this is far beyond belief, then you have not seriously studied the sacrifices that have already been made to this plan, which is really a psychotic game of the MRC (magnetically reversed case). Hubbard did say that not everyone has the Inc. 2 "implant", which I referred to in my own research as the Magnetic Reversal; which means that some did not go through it, whether the MRC managed to leave in his space station or ship, thus removing himself from the implant, is not known in which case I referred to him as the MMRC (Missed Magnetically Reversed Case): equally some may have arrived after the last Magnetic Reversal. No doubt the last cycle would not have believed what was going on in the mental asylum that is earth care of the MMRC case. The psychotic apocalyptic psychology that I covered in The Cancer document and in *Alternative 4* runs on the computation "I must be right, or I die". They have so many wrongs tucked away in their mind, that if they just considered the possibility that they might be wrong, they would have to confront the entire sacrifice to a cause - who could confront the billions of people who have been murdered, tortured or duped? - The French Revolution, The Russian Revolution, The British Revolution, World Wars and the terrible outcome of Hiroshima and Nagasaki where hundreds of thousands of people were blown out of their bodies and may God truly help their souls, because to Re-incarnate after an incident like that, would have extremely bad effects - dispersal would be evident with complete dis-orientation. Probably one of the wickedest things man has done to his fellow man. Until you find the MRC's this planet will not have a minute's peace. Whilst I could decode more of *Revelations*, the point of interest to this thesis is the final referral to the battle of the 12 tribes and 13 the tribe of Judah I conclude in *Revelations 20,7-9:*

"And when the thousand years are expired,

Satan shall be loosed out of his prison, and
Shall go out to deceive the nations which
are in the four quarters of the earth,
Gog and Magog, to gather them together to battle..."

(Author's emphasis)

Although a fair bit of editing has occurred here to detract from the full meaning, the overall message is clear, that the 12 tribes of Israel are to battle with the 13th tribe of Judah and such a battle really rests on the question 'whom do you serve?' and the battle to release the mysteries and make the truth known or to continue to hide them and make Christianity the victor. And as the curtain starts to fall on this production with such marvellous dramatizations by all the actors on the stage, should we ask where the religious faction of the thirteenth tribe is? Is it behind the gates of the Church of Scientology at East Grinstead? Did Ron Hubbard come up with the hidden science himself? A genius as the COS portray, who according to Miller's Biography, which the COS tried to suppress, grew very rich and held a questionable association with the O.T.O which has never been satisfactorily explained. What is wrong with the TRUTH? Way up there at ultimate reality, where understanding occurs! If this was a fight to reveal the mysteries and take on the 12 tribes of Israel then let us hear it! Or are we all going to shrivel in fear at the might of Israel and the World Order? Well I guess there is no power or money in understanding is there. And why have *both sides* of this game including Scientology tried to suppress factual data? If Scientology hoped to combat the proposed One World Order religion of the 12 Tribes and open the mysteries, then why not admit that? Equally why do the 12 tribes persist with the story of Jesus, where not only did He manage to defy the laws of biology in birth, but the laws of physics in death. Why persist with untruths, when clearly Jesus was a man and Druid and was tutored in the mysteries: The documents are there, produce them. Why rely on the ignorance of humanity and deny man his basic freedoms, which are the right to freedom of speech, the right to choose his form of OPEN Government and the right to his own belief, whether that involves past lives and Re-incarnation or not. Why does "policy" exist which in the case of the Tibetan demonstrators quite clearly showed that these rights were being denied? Further can a man not ask questions and obtain truthful answers? - Are the Elite now so fearful of the truth that they cannot allow freedom of speech and where the cult of obedience has come to rule with no questions asked? Have they become so arrogant in their power and riches that they do not feel they are answerable to the common man, that they must suppress anyone who approaches that truth? If there is nothing to hide, then there is nothing to fear. Anyone who seeks to suppress another on the subject of truth is in fear, which according to Hubbard's *Chart of Human Evaluation* is where Communism, perversion and unethical actions lie and where people

DRAMATIZE THEIR PAST LIVES AND HISTORY. Theatre Earth as the players play on and the audience having never followed the plot from the beginning, have lost track of it, but subconsciously follow in dream-like obedience, subservient to the so-called mind control "implants" of the Religious Revolution deeply with the archetypes embedded in man's subconscious. Finally should the 13 th tribe release *their* version of *Revelations*, which differs from the Vulgate version? Or is it as I suspect that the highest level incorporates both the aims of 12 and 13 where in the lower levels the two groups are thrown together as an experiment, to see which one will achieve the Darwinian principle of: 'survival of the fittest', a game pre-determined by the resources of each group. Is Scientology unaware of this possibility and thus charge huge sums to swell their coffers, in order to combat the 12 tribes and the World Order with its huge wealth? Who can say in this covert game where only the Masters have sight of all the chess pieces? As I plug on with my miniscule resources against vast odds, with no cavalry in sight, I can assure you it is an experience that may take me a few thousand years or so to overcome. This book and what I say was always going to be ahead of its time and just how much time is available is unsure, for the final disaster of another Magnetic Reversal may come as the *Revelations* account states: "like a thief in the night". I gave my word of honour a long time ago, I believe I have fulfilled it and thus I for one do not intend to wait for the last 'Act' in this performance and cycle.

The Pelasgians of Arcadia were Pre-Hellenic (before the Greeks) tribes that inhabited not only the Peloponnese but also a large part of Greece proper. The Pre-Hellenic tribes also occupied numerous Aegean Islands, before the coming of the Greeks. Strabo wrote: "As for the Pelasgi, almost all agree, in the first place, that some ancient tribe of that name spread throughout the whole of Greece. Strabo continues by citing a number of ancient authorities who attest that the Pelasgians were the earliest inhabitants of various places in Greece and the Aegean including Mycenae, Argos, Thessaly, Epirus, Athens, the Troad, and the islands of Lesbos, Lemnos and Imbros. It has been stated that these Pelasgians, together with the Minoans of Crete provided the cultural base, which underlies Mycenaean and Trojan Civilization, and ultimately Classical Greek Civilization; the latter modified drastically by the Dorian invasions and subsequent formative period known as "the Dark Ages". What has not been recognised is the appearance of the hidden science in Crete and the Early Minoans, who were the true progenitors of the Age. Deucalion the Greek equivalent of Noah was said in myth to be the brother of Cretan Ariadne, daughter of King Minos. Since King Minos was I concluded a monarch of Solar Kingship, introduced after the Religious Revolution, then the fact that Deucalion was equated to Noah, implies a hidden truth that a dynasty was installed at Knossos, which was descended from the patriarch Noah. Politics in the form of

Solar Kingship 'wedded' to the hidden science was to form a means of implementing a One World Order. By Homer's time, after the religious Revolution, Pelasgians made up a part of Crete's rather mixed population that now longer retained the mysteries. The acquisition of this knowledge by the 12 tribes undoubtedly rendered them great power.

After the Religious Revolution, the Moon Goddess appeared as a collared bitch (dog) and the continual use of the "dog" in bardic poetry to mean "guard the secret", must have referred to these hidden events in Crete and the hidden science. The dog or bitch that hunts the (Solar) King as bull, or stag at the Solstice. In myth there was a ceremony and ritual where near Mount Lycaeum, in which an elected person, would remove their clothes and hang them on the oak tree, which was the Door to the year for the Druids and signified Royalty. The Arcadian wolf myth relates to Lycaon, son of Pelasgus, whom Hesiod called "god-like Lycaon". The myth has two layers, an inner layer derived from a Pelasgian ritual and a transparent outer layer, superimposed by later Greek Olympian religion. The name Lycaon comes from the Greek word for "wolf" and so Lycaon is a wolf-king. Mount Lycaeum, where the child sacrifice was made, is therefore "Mount Wolf". Zeus except in this Arcadian cult was never considered a Wolf-god. The sacrifice took place at a New Year festival and was intended to restore fertility to the grazing lands, thus this a god who is associated with the New Year and is also a fertility god. The name Lycaon approximates the sound of the Greek word for "light", which would be appropriate to a Wolf-god who was also a Sun god. And since one of the sons of Lycaon was called Nyctimus, which means "night" or "of the night", it appears that Zeus Lycaeus is Olympian Zeus in name only, being in fact, a solar wolf-king related to a ritual calendar. The myth reported that Zeus was angry that all descendents of Pelasgus, father of Lycaon and the whole race of man descended from Pelasgus. Lycaon as King of Arcadia had sacrificed a child to Zeus in the hope that the sacrifice would bring rain to drought stricken Arcadia, but Zeus instead caused the Flood and only Deucalion and his wife Pyrrha were saved as the equivalent of Noah in Biblical texts. The Parnassians who survived the Flood wandered to Arcadia and revived the ancient rites. The enterix or boy sacrificed even in the time of Theoprastus (c.322 B.C.) when eaten by a person dictated that he should hang his clothes on the sacred Oak, dive into the stream naked and emerge on the opposite side as a wolf. Thereupon he joined a pack and ran with the wolves. If as wolf, he refrained from eating human flesh for nine years, the legend has it that he could return to the stream at the expiration of the period, dive into it, and emerge on the other side as a man once more and could don his clothes which he left hanging on the tree. A certain Damarchos, an Arcadian, lived nine years as a wolf, regained his humanity, and thereafter won the boxing prize at the Olympic games. When Lycaon was transformed into a wolf and his sons into a pack of wolves, it was not Zeus but the Great Goddess who could perform these miracles at the solstices and she would have done so, not in anger at the sacrifice, but in acceptance of it. This is a wrong implication however, since an icon from the Shrine of the Double Axes at Knossos at the time of the Religious Revolution, (c. 1400-1100 B.C.) shows a Goddess with her hands raised to assuage the anger of Zeus at the child sacrifice. Thus as myth tells us King Minos after the Religious Revolution, regularly brought seven maidens and youths from Athens for sacrifice. Sacrifice is identifiable with both the Druids or thirteenth tribe and the twelve tribes, whom I believe took over Knossos, perhaps as Thothmes III from Egypt, with whom the Minoans had trading links with. The idea that Hermes was born in Arcadia must have some foundation in this myth. The Tuatha de Danaan were in fact from the Peloponnese in Greece, where Arcadia is situated and co-incidentally or not where the Temple of Asklepios is situated in Epidaurus, which was dedicated to healing. The painting by Poussin with its enigmatic reference to: 'Et in Arcadia Ego...' with Twin kings as shepherds looking wistfully at the tomb of the Goddess, was more fully discussed in The Battle of The Trees, however it signifies perhaps the matriarchal belief of the thirteenth tribe and its location in the Peloponnese, presumably as the Tuatha de Danaan, before patriarchal invaders forced the migrations overland to Denmark (Dan-e-m-ark) and to Ireland and Scotland.

There is also a curious folktale from the Ionian island of Zacynthos, once a part of the kingdom of Odysseus, which is known as the story of captain Thirteen:

> In the time of the Hellenes there once lived a king, who was the strongest man of his day; and the *three* hairs on his breast were so long that you could take them and twist them twice round your hand, Another king once declared war against him, and on a certain month the fighting began. At first the other King was victorious; but afterwards the strong king with his army beat the enemy and pursued them to their town. He would there and then have destroyed them all, had they not given *400,000 dollars* to his wife, who betrayed him and cut off his three hairs. This made him the weakest of all men. The enemy then took him prisoner, bound him, shut him up in a fortress, and gave him only an ounce of bread and an ounce of water a day. However, his hairs soon began to grow again. So Captain Thirteen - that was his name - and the enemy flung thirteen of his companions into a pit. As he was the last to be flung in, he fell on top of his companions and escaped death. But his enemies then *covered the pit with a mountain*. On the second day after he was thrown into the pit he found a dead bird somewhere. He stuck its wings on to his hands and flew up. He knocked his head on the mountain and sent it spinning up to the sun. He then flew further afield

and soared high into the air. But a rainstorm came on and softened the clay, with which he had stuck the feathers on. So Captain Thirteen fell into the sea. Out came the sea-god and with his *three-pronged fork* gave him such a blow that the sea turned *red* with his *blood*, and changed him into a big fish, a *dolphin*. He told him too, that he could never change back again till he found a *girl willing to marry him*. Now the sea in which the dolphin lived was of such a sort that *no ship entering it could get out again*. It so happened that a king and his daughter came that way. They got in easily enough but couldn't get out again; and so fearful a storm overtook them that their ship broke up. Nobody was saved but the princess and the king; for the dolphin took both on his back to a small *island*, and then set them ashore on the coast they had come from. The princess resolved to wed the dolphin, and to get him up to her *castle* had a *big canal* dug from the sea to it. When all was ready for the wedding, the dolphin shook off his skin and changed into a young man of gigantic strength and great beauty. He married the princess, and they lived happily ever after.[194]

This folk tale from Greece, gives no explanation as to why the hero is called "Captain Thirteen" and yet he is explicitly called this, and he also has exactly thirteen companions. If he were a Bronze Age fertility king, the answer would be, because on the third intercalated thirteenth month, where he could expect to be ritually slain. Captain Thirteen is a king, but there is the implication here from the story of Deucalion the equivalent of Noah, that he is also connected to this line of descent, as special king derived from Noah? i.e. Adamite and thirteenth tribe. Indeed the fact that the sea turns red indicates the red men from Knossos at the time of the Religious Revolution and red was a sign of royalty as in the red gemstone. In *The Battle of The Trees*, I referred to the group The Prieuré de Sion, who held a special significance to the number thirteen and at least one Grand Master, had connections with the illustration cover of *Vaincre* magazine, which showed a Hermetic knight, riding down a road, labelled 'United States of the West' (European Union) between what I concluded were political and religious aims. Here unusually then in this folk tale, we have some indication of the origins in Greece of the thirteenth tribe and the fertility king was accounted the strongest man of his people, because the manna of the tribal totem beast is vested in him. The Holy Communion is derived from the much earlier source where the tribe ate the flesh and drank the blood of the totem beast in sacrificial rites, in actual fact its very re-stimulative to such early memories and is a method of mind control. However the curious reference to three hairs, reminds us of the Druidic law of three and the old Trinity, Twin Kings and Goddess. Thus I would conclude this is not just a folk tale about a fertility king, but it has deeper import and concerns the thirteenth tribe. There is a somewhat parallel myth reported by Pausanias. In his description of Athens, Pausanias writes:

> "Behind the Lyceum is the tomb of Nisus, king of Megara, who was slain by Minos. The Athenians brought his body and buried it here. A story is told of this Nisus that he had purple hair on his head, and that he was doomed to die whenever it should be shorn. When the Cretans came into the land they carried the other cities in megaris by storm, but laid siege to Nisaea in which Nisus had taken refuge. Thereupon, it is said, the daughter of Nisus fell in love with Minos and sheared her father's hair.

Captain Thirteen is king of the waxing year, and engages in a fight with his tanist, the king of the waning year, thus they are Twin Kings. At first the other king is victorious because in the month of the summer solstice, when this takes place the sun begins to wane, but later Captain Thirteen makes a comeback after the winter solstice. However at the following summer solstice, at the zenith of his ascendance over the other king, his wife, the queen, betrays him. The American currency of 400 000 dollars is a surprise, but the amount is mythically right, being a sum divisible by four and, therefore, reflecting the four-year half-cycle of the ritual calendar. Like Nisus the way in which he is betrayed is like another mythical character Samson, his strength in his hair and she cuts the three long hairs from his chest, after which he becomes the weakest of men. This must signify that his strength lay in the Holy Grail knowledge of the old Trinity and the Grid? In the original myth, his wife will have been the moon-goddess to whom he must be sacrificed. Since his name is Captain Thirteen, the three hairs must stand for the three intercalated thirteen months in an eight -year cycle. Her "cutting" the hairs refers to the fact that the three intercalations permit her, as the moon, to catch up with him, as the sunk-king, and hence it is said to weaken him. However whilst the myth obviously gives the calendar mysteries, it would also reveal religious mysteries and the calendars were usually like alphabets governed by such mysteries.

CaptainThirteen and his companions are thrown into a pit and a mountain covers the pit. This is curious since you will remember, that Ron Hubbard gave a similar fate for Xenu, whom he said was locked up by "electronic tagging", in a mountain on Madera. In the case of Captain Thirteen, it must refer to the Mycenaean tholos type of tomb in which sacred kings were buried. These tombs shaped like a beehive were built by a three-stage process. First a great mound of earth was heaped up in the shape of a beehive. Then cut blocks of stone were put in place, using the earth as mould and temporary support. Once the domed stone structure was in place, it would be self-supporting. Then the earth was dug out from under the structure. The Bible in the *Revelations* account refers to the "angel of the bottomless pit" as being "Abaddon", which I thought was Abaris the Chief Druid and addon as Adom or Adam, Adomite, Druid, thirteenth tribe. Is it not strange that Hubbard should state that Xenu was cast into a mountain, which signifies Druid? This of course is in conjunction, with Inc. 1, which I thought referred to the Religious revolution in Crete, which was of course conducted by a Cabal, that I thought were possibly the Druids and thirteenth tribe, but the picture is clouded by Thothmes III and his Egyptian connections to the 12 tribes and thus I am afraid we are still left with the question of who stole the apples of immortality and the Holy Grail! In *The Battle of The Trees* I did state, that at the very top of Zionism was a religion that may yet be revealed! These guessing games on gods are very difficult, but it has not surpassed my observation that Scientology is no longer hampered in Britain or America, despite the powerful Jewish lobby i.e. 12 Tribes – Israel. Further in the *Revelations* account, Apollyou in Hebrew or Apollo the Sun-King in Greek, as a king comparable to the folk tale would have a tomb, described as a" bottomless pit" and in the *Revelations* account. Later covered by a mountain as per Scientology's account? The Bible may have been purposefully edited here, to remove the connection of mountain.

Further in the myth, the escape of a king's soul was through the hole at the top of the dome of his tomb, which was left open. The soul of the Cretan Talos flew off as a partridge and in the Perseus myth the king's soul escapes as winged Pegasus. He strikes the mountain sending it spinning to the sun is a reference to the tombs of sacred kings being associated with the symbol of the spiral, which was associated with the sun, but has according to the section on spirals much deeper implications of the organisation of the bioplasma vortex. But his wings fall off and he plunges into the sea, where it turns red with his blood. The mythic sense is that the sun appears to set in the western sea, and at sunset, the red rays on the horizon turn the entire sea red. This may refer to the Adamites presence in the western Isles of Scotland or Britain. He then is turned into a dolphin which is the totem beast of the sun-king and the sea he can't get out of, is the realm of the dead. The only way out is to be reborn and thus he has to find a woman who will wed him, which implies a woman to become a willing mother. The canal leading to her castle is the sexual symbol the vagina and birth canal and the castle becomes the womb or labyrinth of the Cretan Great Goddess. The Great Goddess of Bronze Age myths was always considered both mother and bride of the sacred king.

The *fig. 47,* showing a Cretan seal from mocholos of the Middle Minoan III period with octopus, sun and moon symbols, two dolphins and fertility bough was as I previously discussed a Druidic feature, that also occurred in the white chalk hill figures where the giant carried the oak club or fertility bough and identifies solar kingship. Further the fertility bough in the Seal has twenty-six leaves which is twice thirteen, with its reference again to the thirteenth month and tribe, doubled in this case since the dolphins of which there are two, are Twin Kings. The dolphin too had a large circular Eye, which I equated with the Illuminati Eye and the third eye of hermetic intelligence a sign that appeared on the One Dollar note from America, which appears as a currency to go back further, than Americans realise! The sun disc in the Seal has nineteen rays and the longer nineteen-year solar-lunar cycle may have been known to the Minoans as well as the eight-year cycle. The seal appears to be a fore-runner of the folk tale of Captain Thirteen, the dolphin-king, and the connection to Crete is not unlikely for the mythic tradition holds that the sun-god, Apollo, appeared as a dolphin to Cretan sailors and led them to Delphi, where he founded his famous oracle and made the Cretans his priests. Apollo Delphinios, Delphi, and dolphin are all derived from the Greek root "delphis" which means "the womb" and the thirteenth tribe like the Templars who held a silver head of a woman, hid a matriarchal belief as their core secret relating to the Greek mysteries and particularly Crete.

I am afraid the psychology is about to come up to speed, where you will come to understand just how clever the Masters that control Earth are. They have owned this sector of the Universe for millions and probably billions of years and they are not about to loose that control, which has been perfected to a high degree. Once again we are going to have to plough through the hokus pokus of mystical terminology that only seeks to overlay the mysteries and great increase in the power of the Masters that occurred when they sequestered the hidden science and the knowledge of the Holy Grail. I can assure you that the hokus pokus and the terminology drives one into apathy before one starts, however this is very much the confusion method of the Masters, thus we must confront these terminologies and discover what is happening in the psychological sense. The tribes of Israel did not have anything but their Black magical Cabala prior to the arrival of The Holy Grail: where that Cabala had been used to frighten man for many eons and was used to dominate and control. The shamanistic paelolithic cave paintings showing the magi on four legs and Lightening Man together with the initiation paintings give some idea of what the Masters were actually capable of, which was hardly the great civilization that they try to make out. Cabalistic ritual and knowledge may have allowed them in past cycles to develop technology and many associated advanced methods, but there was simply no religion or philosophy as such, only the adherence to Kingship and dynastic lines of despotic kings. They may even have used vacuum energies without realising the science behind their method. There was body control, but mind control only entered the scene in Crete 1 400 B.C when The Holy Grail was stolen and the archetypal symbols became imprinted on the spiritual bioplasma. The era of mind control only arrived once the Grid and its holographics were understood. The knowledge was sent to free mankind, however once in the hands of the Masters it became mind control. This was an advancement on drugs, which they have used since time immemorial within Cabalistic practise; however it seems that even the lesson of Grid holographics was to be poorly understood by the dunces, in the rush to use it to further the goal of complete World Domination.

Despite the man Aleister Crowley and his Black Cabalistic mind, he has been rather informative for the purpose of this thesis to explain just how the past holographics were accessed through the Cabalistic method of morphic resonance. These methods were obviously written down in the magical rituals, which used resonant energies and the science of morphic resonance to contact what the magician believed were spirits, or more succinctly the invisible Masters. All initiates who appeared in the public eye were controlled by Masters through the chain of the secret societies and had a part to play in the plan for World Domination. Crowley although expelled from the London Temple of the Golden Dawn secret group, nevertheless retained possession of all the rituals and by direct orders of the secret chiefs published the documents in the *Equinox: The Review of Scientific Illuminism* under the title of *The Temple of Solomon the King*. This review with the rituals was the teaching basis and the organ of his order entitled significantly enough the *Atlantean Adepts* or *The Great White Brotherhood* and closely allied to this was his *Ordo Templi Orientis* or secret group of the O.T.O. It might be concluded here, that since The Great White Brotherhood was under the direction of invisible Masters of The Great White Lodge, that Crowley in his Cabalistic rituals was seeking information from the past Atlantean magi, those who were despotic arch controllers of the pre-Flood or antediluvian period. Presumably this might define the Masters who set Hitler up to destroy Europe in a sacrificial blood bath. Crowley under his Masters created the doctrine: "Do what thou wilt, shall be the whole of the Law; Love is the Law: Love under Will". It is my opinion that such a doctrine which appeals to the ego and "I", would activate the kundalini force curled at the base of the human spine, which is considered a sexual force and when aroused forces the energy of kundalini up through the spine, opening the charkas until it reaches the crown chakra, where it connects to the Grid and past holographics through the process of morphic resonance. It is comparable to throwing a pebble into a pond creating ripples or waves that spread outwards. This uniting with the "cosmic energy", to use one of the woolly terms for the experience, is what is referred to as illumination and the opening of the third eye in the forehead. Evidently the Cabal who overran Knossos and stole the Holy Grail was practising this form of illumination on the populous as evidenced by icons where men held their hand to the position of the third eye in the forehead. This method of illumination or mind control, aided by sexual orgiastic rites so clearly portrayed on the Late Minoan seals, together with the drug opium (The Poppy Goddesses) merely connected the initiates to the Grid, which became imprinted with the archetypal symbols of the Bull-Minos phallic cult who conducted that Religious Revolution. This origin of mass mind control, I believe Hubbard picked up in the Inc. 1 Xenu incident, which was not I propose the actual beginning, but only the beginning of a method of mind control both religious and political through a World Order programme. Prior to this there was body control, however the tribes of Israel, did not have knowledge of the Grid and the holographics to pursue any programme of mind control, even though they had utilised Grid energies in their Black Cabalistic rites without understanding the science. The populous once connected to Grid holographics would then be controlled by the entire thought of past Masters including the Atlanteans.

In her *Secret Societies and Subversive Movements*, Mrs. Nesta Webster quotes an eminent neuro-psychiatrist of New York:

> "The Freud Theory is anti-Christian and subversive of organised society.... Freudism makes of the individual a machine, absolutely controlled by subconscious reflexes.... Whether conscious or unconscious, it makes for destructive effect...Not only the Freud theory of psycho-analysis, but a considerable quantity of pseudo-scientific propaganda of that type has for years been emanating from a group of German Jews who live and have their headquarters in Vienna".

Sex is a powerful survival mechanism and as I have shown in my cancer research, when the individual is under threat of survival, the conscious mind switches off and hands the 'steering wheel' to the primitive mind. This primitive mind may be nor more than the morphogenetic bioplasma or what has become The Universal mind with its holographics of survival relating to matter. The primitive mind solves loss, which is the environmental re-stimulant of non-survival, by creating high growth. The cancer tumour could be considered as a foetus and indeed in the cancer research, I show that the biochemistry of the tumour is indeed embryonic. The morphogenetic bioplasma as the primitive mind, Universal Mind or even perhaps as in Hubbard's terminology the reactive mind thus contains mechanisms of growth, survival and reproduction. This is a very clever trick by the Masters who by introducing a culture of sex into a society, restimulate the primitive mind and thus promote connection of the mind of the populace to the Grid, forming a channel for the Masters thoughts. The rise in pornography distributed through magazines, media and cinema, which is controlled by the elite under the current Masters both visible and one assumes ultimately invisible, merely reflects one method of connecting a populous to the Grid as a channel for the Masters. Women celebrities who break up with men, suddenly emblazon themselves in sexual poses all over magazines and tabloids, some of them wound up with snakes and other crouching like animals on all fours in a coitus position of submissive female. This is quite a good example of loss at work, with primitive mind full on and the sexual survival mechanism promoting irrational attempts at survival. Media then acknowledges such behaviour of the primitive as survival (since they obviously get paid for it and dubious fame) thus promoting primitive mind behaviour. The media controlled by the agents for the Masters promotes and applauds all base primitive mind behaviour, since it keeps the populace in a mind-controlled state. Drugs, dirge pop music, repetitive sounds etc all produce the same effect of connecting the young hypnotically to the Grid as a channel for the Masters. The elders of the society, who berate the young for their primitive mind behaviour, are often arrogant and egotistical in their own right, which promotes the surge of kundalini and thus the arrogant mind of the Masters becomes their persona in a dwindling cycle. The deification of humanity is another promoter of kundalini and connection to the Masters. A comparison of *The Protocols of the Elders of Zion* along with other secret group methods which I gave in the closing chapter of *The Battle of The Trees* has not been recognised as **methods of black Cabalistic ritual** promoting Kundalini and connection therefore to the Grid and Masters: the world populace is being illuminated en-masse along black magic lines. The power of illuminism lies in the awakened and perverted sex-forces uniting the mind of the individual to the mind of the Masters. I believe I mentioned at the beginning of this section, just how clever the agents for the Masters are – Satan at work: man as bee or ant in the "Universal Republic" of Judaeo-Masonry.

I have already discussed the decline in art, seen at Knossos after the Religious Revolution. Art like music has in its higher aesthetics the power to disconnect man from the Grid and thoughts of past Masters; beauty is not in the mind of Masters and thus we see art and beauty fought. I have referred to the poor quality of art that is currently raved over by the Grid controlled critics, where un-made beds, excreta, pickled animals and highly schematised art have become deified as la mode. Picasso himself admitted that his symbolic work set out "to destroy reality". This schematised and highly stylised art was to be found at Knossos, following the Religious Revolution. The Teacher taught art, since it was a useful method in the training of the eye and the power of observation. There is nothing wrong with schematised art, provided the viewer can see the mind of the person who created it. Mrs. Webster quoted a critic who wrote of a well-known Jewish artist.

> "He brings to the world of art a new gospel, a black gospel, a gospel in which everything is to be inverted and distorted. Whatsoever things are hideous, whatsoever things are of evil report, whatsoever things are sordid; if there be any unhealthiness or any degradation; think on these things."

Ugliness however is another channel for the Masters. The revolt from all restraints must see its zenith in the American Jerry Springer versions of the Roman arena, where people of generally low education are encouraged to play out their dramatizations of the primitive mind, degrading themselves as spiritual beings for the entertainment of the masses. *The Protocols of the Learned Elders of Zion*, to which I must add the obligatory 'whatever their origin', foreshadow all this in a remarkable way when they say:

> "The educated classes of the Gentiles will pride themselves in their learning, and without verifying it, they will put into practice the

knowledge obtained from science, which was dished up to them by our agents with the object of educating their minds in the direction which we require".

The Universal Mind, Darwin's theory of evolution, Freudian psycho-analysis, occult science, new age "guardians", orthodox history, political science, economics etc are all such directions controlled by the elite, including religion.

All the secret groups held political motives and Crowley was no exception in his group the O.T.O In the *19 Patriot, October 1922*, it stated:

> "We have before us, for example, a manifesto issued by the 'National Grand Lodge and mystic Temple Verita Mystica of the Ordo Templi Orientis, or Hermetic Brotherhood of Light,' dated 22 January, 1917, at Ascona, Switzerland, and signed by J. Adderley, Secretary. The manifesto announces that headquarters of the Brotherhood has been transferred to Switzerland 'since the commencement of the world War'. The ostensible object of the manifesto is to end the war and to establish a new order of Society, 'based on the principle of co-operation of all, by all'. To this end it proposes a National Congress, to be held at Ascona from the 15 th to 25 th August following, and announces that one of the attractions is to be a representation of Aleister Crowley's mystic poem 'The Ship'. The document also states that another centre of the 'O.T.O.' is New York, and we may reasonably suppose that Aleister Crowley was organising this centre during his war-visit to the U.S.A. It is at least certain that he was busy in America from 1914 onwards".

Henry Ford was to later claim that this was the period when three Jews convinced of the conspiracy of the Jews to dominate the world and Ford himself, was to have a great influence on Hitler's anti-Semitic views and therefore the future Holocaust. However it looks probable, that the 12 tribes of Israel managed to defeat Hitler against the thirteenth tribe? Which may have been a pre-determined outcome with the regeneration goal of a Federal Europe as the hidden agenda. Whilst Crowley may have considered that he was working in the best interests of the world and a proposed era of World Domination by the 12 tribes of Israel, did his Atlantean Masters through Cabalistic ritual not rule him? It is now virtually impossible to attain *The Secret Rituals of the O.T.O* together with Crowley's book *Magick*. However one passage of Crowley's work underlines the point of sexual magic that Crowley employed:

> "There is a single main definition of the object of all magical Ritual. It

is the *uniting of the microcosm with the macrocosm*. The supreme and complete Ritual is therefore the Invocation of the Holy Guardian Angel; or in the language of mysticism, union with God". (*Author's emphasis*)

High-sounding words, but which God? Since Crowley's rituals in some cases called for child sacrifice, one can only assume he was subservient to his Masters whose mind had always required sacrifice – his God was non other than the Masters, the Atlanteans and Satan. This description of magic reasonably identifies "the new college of magic" and the hermetic principle of: 'as above, so below' and the request for information by uniting the mind of the magician to the holographics of the past. The Masters whether they were Atlanteans, Old Testament Patriarchs or the Druids with their sacrificial Osier baskets or wicker men filled with human sacrificial victims always practised sacrifice as is evidenced by early Palaeolithic finds and archaeological remains usually of young children, which emphasises the use of this kind of Cabalistic black magic ritual in very early times. Such ritual was inherent in the tribes of Israel, for the first thing Noah did when the Ark landed was to commit a sacrifice. Crowley discussed the blood as the principle vehicle of prana or life force, which on the death of an animal was suddenly liberated and could be used for magical purposes. The reign of terror that descended in the aftermath of the French Revolution on the citizens of France, was only evidence of this reign of Masters, where without restraint the Republic had unleashed the battle cry "Do what thou wilt, is the whole of the law". One might consider that the sacrificial blood baths of World Wars I and II were the black magical ritual necessity of trapping life force to create some greater magical experiment, that is now appearing as the plan of the magical adepts of the 33 rd degree of Freemasonry, where the magical child of the **New Aeon** is born as European Union.

The method by which magical ritual connected the adept to the whole history of event data on Earth and the past thought forms of the Arch controllers was hardly understood in scientific terms. Eliphas Levi, in his *History of Magic* explains:

> "There is a natural composite agent, a fluid, a force, receptacle of vibrations and *images*, by the mediation of which every nervous apparatus is in secret communication together. The existence of this universal magnetic life force and the possible use of it is the great secret of practical magic; it is the wand of theurgy and the key to *black magic*" (*Author's emphasis*).

He goes on to say: "Black magic may be defined as the art of inducing artificial mania in ourselves and others". You may remember the Celts who in battle against the Greeks became hysterical and were probably subjected in that case to black magic. Religious Zealots open themselves up to the mind of the Masters by the mania of high emotion, not using their rational mind to distinguish fact from fiction, which has become the 'clappy happy' brigade of Christianity. Levi went on to say: " and by acting upon the nervous system, through a series of almost impossible exercises, it becomes a kind of living galvanic pole capable of condensing and projecting powerfully that light which *intoxicates or destroys*" (*my emphasis*). I suspect within the secret groups, the type of exercises undertaken with accompanying philosophy, can easily awaken the kundalini force with the arrogant "I" coupled with the Illuminatus Masters thought always imprinted in these groups, of the deification of man, who is a god-like superman with great powers. This is particularly dangerous, since it is a thought that is liable in morphic resonance to connect via the kundalini force directly with Grid holographics and the thoughts of past Masters: with the practical result dependent on ' think alike, act alike'. The quickest way to drive a person insane, is to tell them they are special and build up the ego and give them god-like status and without any background understanding they merely connect into the Grid vacuum energies and feel great, but they are then subject to past thoughts of the holographics embedded within the Grid. Men particularly when they reach a certain age, seek out a sexual liaison which in its emotion, will awaken the kundalini power and connect them to the Grid and they feel great momentarily since the vacuum energy is tapped, but often commit crimes against others in the process, which they show no sense of responsibility for, simply because they are under the mind of the Masters, who have no sense of right or wrong: Men or women who seek power, be that in the political or business world, or through some project, merely invite a connection to the Grid. Power and money are seen as the anti-dote to low survival and thus connect the individual to the Grid with its survival mechanisms and thoughts of the Masters. People are there to be *used* for a purpose of survival and in the case of the Masters, that survival is seen as a World Order and if the individual does not add to the purpose of self or group or the World Order, then they are spat out! Animal pack mentality and the mind of the Masters is that of an animal breighing over blood and lust for power.

The science is clear, in so far as the thoughts of Masters are imprinted on a *matter recording* concerned *only with survival*, which then incorporates Darwinian thinking and 'survival of the fittest' which knows nothing of compassion, ethics, morals, love or aiding *other* individuals or groups to survive. The secret groups become training grounds and nurseries for unwitting men and women, who become robotic and passive material instruments in the hands of the so-called "White Brothers" and the ultimate Masters or the White Lodge of Black Magicians. The decline of political morals and social group morals, could be described by this process of Grid connection and robotic or 'brain dead' individuals who only think of survival of self. Connected to the Grid, they no longer can distinguish between right and wrong or lie and truth. The Secret Government of the World - the Black Magicians, have raised the rights of man to deification level and politicians puffed up with their own self-assumed importance and ego, ignore their humble mandate to **serve** the electorate thus depriving that electorate of democratic choice on issues of importance: such is the case on the referendum issue of European Union and the euro. The loss of humility and its replacement with the cry of Crowley: "Do what thou wilt is the whole of the law", induces the ego and "I", with its Grid connections to the Masters via the kundalini sexual force. Resultant actions and behaviour are only tempered by way of education and morals with conscience, which the vast majority no longer possess. The pompous, arrogant man, swelled up with his own assumed self-importance, who constantly seeks acknowledgement for his troubles, is merely a fool and the tool of the Masters, since he daily commits wrong acts that will require him to revert the outcome of those acts, before he can even get past the first post of exit. On the karmic credit plan, such wrong acts can amount to a formidable red account after a few thousand years, all of which must be remedied according to the harm done. Man finds that fact very difficult to confront and may only realise the truth of these words, when he leaves a life and is forced to go through the life review in the death experience, which gives him the sum total of his karmic credit plan expenditure, *which includes past lives* since life is continuous. It really does not matter whether you committed a wrong a thousand years ago or yesterday, it will be there in the life review. Provided your conscience of the pure spirit does not stick on it, you can leave the first post.

Paracelsus wrote: "The Chaldeans and the Egyptians used to make images according to the constellations of the Stars and these images moved and talked, but they did not know the powers that acted in them. Such things are done by faith.... but a devilish faith supported by the desire for evil". One assumes here, that some frames or holographics in the event data of the Akashic Record, or morphogenetic bioplasma were activated or re-stimulated out of the hundreds of feet of 'film roll'. Magical ritual must have supplied the necessary method and it is easy to see how the view evolved that Masters exist in the etheric or Angels and cherubim's, who control the daily lives of men. It must have astounded these men to view such things and the concept of being watched surely must arise from the Illuminatus group who controlled all men via such Cabalistic method.

An example of necromancy was given in a *Letter on Occult Meditation, 1930* by Alice. Bailey, of New York and a theosophist and occultist:

"As you know, the Master makes a small image of the probationer, which image is stored in certain subterranean centres in the Himalayas. The image is magnetically linked with the probationer, and shows all the fluctuations of his nature. Being composed of emotional and mental matter, it pulsates with every vibration of those bodies. It shows their predominating hues, and by studying it the Master can rapidly gauge the progress made and judge when the probationer may be admitted into closer relationship...The Master, when inspecting the images works with them, and through their means effects certain results... at certain times the Master applies certain contacts to the images and via them stimulates the bodies of the pupil."

This is really the implication of black magic and voodoo, or affecting the body and mind of another from a distance. It is a method of fear and certainly if it does exist, can only work, where the mind of the individual on the receiving end is weak. People however get very worked up about this sort of thing and it is probably just a mechanism of creating fear. Alice Bailey was not merely a dupe of her Masters she was an agent of fear. Her Masters interestingly enough were the Great White Lodge, which must hark back to the Egyptian Thothmes III and the twelve tribes of Israel. The so-called "invisible" Masters has always raised the question of whether these are Masters in the etheric or a group of visible but hidden and unknown adepts, who continually re-stimulate themselves by channelling past thought and event, thus bringing that insanity to the world, through secret groups and their agents. The mysterious Brothers of the Rosy Cross designated themselves invisibles and this Fraternity was founded as I have mentioned by the enigmatic personage of Christian Rosenkreutz (born c. 1378): After his death the Brotherhood devoted themselves to the study of the secrets of nature and its hidden forces (the hidden science); their agreement did however include the cure of the sick and that *gratis*. This fraternity waited for what they called the purification of the Church, when, before the end of the world, they hoped to re-establish everything in its primitive integrity. Whether this referred to the release of the mysteries is not sure, or whether they merely refer to some Atlantean and despotic goal of a World Order. In 1614, the invisibles or Brotherhood of the Rosy Cross issued two manifestos – the *Fama Fraternitatis R.C.,* and the *Confessio Fraternitatis Rosae Crucis* in 1615 and sent them to all the learned men and Governments in Europe, inviting them to join with the Order in the universal reform. It seems evident that the magnetic nature of the vacuum as part of the hidden science was the secret of this Fraternity and the Rose-Croix degree and since that was a magical degree, it must have involved the magical rituals for accessing past holograms, event and thought. In his book, *Les Rose-Croix Lyonnais au XVIII siecle, 1929*, Paul Vulliaud goes into these manifestos, linking them with Paracelsus and Cornelius

Agrippa, Theosophy and Illuminism. Speaking of Ch. Fauvety's *Livre du Mond* (Magic of Nature) Vauulliaud wrote:

> "In a very interesting study Fauvety maintains it has to do with Magnetism. He did well in showing the importance attributed, during the time of Paracelsus, to the magnetic fluid in the Theosophico-scientific doctrines... After having observed that the followers of Paracelsus and van Helmont made a mystery of it, Fauvety adds, that the magnetic power 'might indeed according to some writers, have been the secret of the Rose-Croix, who in the sixteenth century were said to possess a universal remedy. What supports this supposition is that even the adversaries of magnetism reproached the doctors, followers of Paracelsus, with curing by magnetic processes similar to those of the Rose-Croix.' "

As I have claimed in the Cancer Report (*Appendix I*), it would not surprise me that these Freemasons at the top have their own methods of dealing with illness, which they do not make available to the public or "cattle", since to the enquiring mind that seeks to solve problems, this would be to reveal one glimpse of the source of power of the elite. It seems that many scientific minds however were captured by the Masters into the fascination of Grid holographics and the potential of the ether vacuum. Vulliaud stated that J. J. Monnier also knew that in certain lodges the initiates practised magnetism. According to Monnier, " they magnetised by divine grace (sic), by force of faith and will, through walls to great distances, from Paris even to dominica". Finally, Vulliaud concluded: "To sum up, Rosicrucianism is composed of mystic illuminism, in combination with alchemy, astrology, magnetics, and communication *with spirits*, if not with the Word itself..." (*author's emphasis*).

This lays bare the wonderful misconception that the thoughts left imprinted on the morphogenetic bioplasma were believed to be actual spirits, the Masters or "invisibles". The mind of the World Order was the mind and still is, of these so-called past Masters, who in reality re-incarnate and follow their own past thoughts! Welcome to asylum Earth! Those thoughts would undoubtedly constantly refer to the building of a World Order, since these men have been obsessed with world domination in every cycle. This goal of a World Order was expressed in Rosicrucian thinking as a goal of "rejuvenation" and is hidden in the words of the English form of the O.T.O or I.N.R.I. or Igne Natura Renovatur Integra – *the entire nature is renewed by fire*. It represents the three phases of universal generation-creation, destruction and regeneration. This is what is termed a cycle of action and since the Masters or MMRC case cannot finish a cycle of action, they never actually create their Satanic World Order, before the third battle or Armageddon in the Apocalyptic account and before they are forced to start again (Day 1 – plant the vine). In actual fact, a Magnetic Reversal periodically interrupts them, where "the seas burst their bounds" and they start the cycle again. As to the Rosa-Crux interpretation, the R.R. et A.C. ritual informs us the key to the:

> "Tomb of Osiris On-nopheris, the Justified One (illuminated), the symbolical burying-place of our Mystic founder Christian Rosenkreutz which he made to represent the Universe...is the form of the Rose and Cross, the ancient Crux Ansata, the Egyptian symbol of Life, which resumes the Life of Nature and the power hidden in the words I.N.R.I."

I assume when they refer to the God of fire, they refer to Hermes and the Hermetic principle of 'as above, so below'. I do not think that this refers to the scientific explanations and models I give, of the morphogenetic bioplasma and its double helicity in the Diablo model, since evidently they believe in spirits, however it probably refers to the Masters rule on Earth and some old Atlantean Order being re-installed as part of their insane rejuvenation plan. However after the Religious Revolution, the Rosicrucian's very definitely understood something of the Grid and its properties. Adolphe Franck, in La Kabbale, quotes Simon ben Jochai in the Zohar, speaking of the Ancient of Days, the first of the Sephiroth on the Tree of Life: "He is seated on a throne of sparks which he subjects to his will... From his head he shakes dew which awakens the dead and gives birth within them to a new life...."

This "dew" is the "Divine White Light or Brilliance" of the Rosicrucian's, the magnetic fluid of their magic. Further, it is said in the same R.R. et A.C. ritual: "Colours are forces and the signature of forces, and Child of the Children of Forces art thou, and, therefore, about the throne of the Mighty One is a rainbow of Glory and at his feet is the **Crystal** sea" (*author's emphasis*). Thus illuminism is really connection to the Grid and the Masters and here in this Rosicrucian ritual, there is even a coded referral to the UVG 120 sphere or crystal, which I believe is also referred to in Biblical texts: the rainbow of course is the electromagnetic spectrum. The mysteries of man's past, event and the thoughts of the Masters presumably formed the process of illumination in the magical degrees of the Rose-Croix, which are all Jewish, since obviously they contain Cabalistic ritual. Those mysteries formed the cup of the Grail, the part that would make money for the elilte. As Gustave Bord wrote:

> "In all times there were secret sects who claimed to understand the laws which regulate the Universe; some believed they really possessed the

ineffable secret; others, the clever ones, made their mysteries a lure for the crowd, claiming thus to dominate and lead it; at least they found the way to utilise it to their profit."

In the higher degrees such as the Rose-Croix and Kadosch, there was not only the Jewish Cabala, but also political and religious goals attached, where the idea of regeneration arose. The Jewish writer Ragon in his *Cours philosophique* (*1841*) stated:

> "As the three grades of ordinary Masonry (said Louis blanc) include a great number of men opposed by position and principles to every project of social subversion, the innovators multiplied the degrees of the mystic ladder to be climbed, they created secret lodges reserved for ardent souls; they instituted the high grades of Elus, chevalier du soleil, Rose-Croix, Stricte Observance, of Kadosch or regenerated man, mysterious sanctuaries whose doors only open to the adepts after a long series of tests, calculated to establish the progress of his revolutionary education, to prove the firmness of his faith, to try the temper of his heart. There was, in the midst of a crowd of practices, sometimes puerile, sometimes sinister, nothing which related to the ideas of freedom or equality". (*History of the French Revolution*)

The 30 th Degree, grand inquisitor, or chevalier Kadosch is the final degree of Scottish Rite Freemasonry and is also called the White and Black Eagle. I believe that it must be this level that is laid out in archetypal form on the floor of the summer Smoking Room at Cardiff Castle, Wales. The design showed political and religious goals and the "New Jerusalem" in the centre of the design as part of a world map, which I covered in *The Battle of The Trees* illustrates the political and religious goals of a Federalist Europe and World Order. Evidently at this level white (science) and black magic (wrongly applied science) are utilised. Ragon noted that the grade of Kadosch was also called "killer" and wrote the following in his *Cours d'Initiations* (*1842*):

> "Give yourself to the science of nature, study politics for the good of your fellow-creatures. Penetrate the secrets of religion and of high sciences and communicate your ideas with prudence...the initiates, therefore, studied politics and religion".

Ragon related that there were four apartments in the grade of Kadosch and in the fourth apartment or room, sits the Supreme council: "There is a cross in this sanctuary, a three-headed serpent wearing, the first a crown, the second a tiara, and the third a sword; they give him a dagger with black and white blade". The

278

cross says Ragon is the "phallic Tau". Thus there is some connection here with the Bull-Minos or phallic cabal that invaded Knossos in Crete and conducted the Religious Revolution. "The serpent represents the evil principle; its three heads are the emblem of the abuses or evil which has entered into the three high classes of society. The head of the serpent which wears a crown indicates the sovereigns, that which wears a tiara or key indicates the Popes and that which carries a sword the Army". Rosicrucianism was always a revolutionary Masonry and in the *Morning Post, 14 July, 1920, Cause of the world Unrest*, speaking of the the the 30 th grade of this Masonry it stated: "When at length the candidate is admitted into the 30 th grade, and after going through terrifying ordeals to test his obedience and secrecy, becomes a Knight Kadosch, he learns that it is no longer Adoniram (Adon-i-ram) or Hiram whose death cries for vengeance". And their catechism says:

> "Do you fully understand that this degree is not, like much of so-called Masonry, a sham that means nothing and amounts to nothing...that what you are now engaged in is real, will require the performance of duty, will exact sacrifice, will expose you to danger and that this Order means to deal with the affairs of nations, and be once more a Power in the world".

The continuing existence of Freemasonry and all secret groups is the main channel for the Masters, through which the World Order plan is continually channelled via black cabalistic practise in every cycle. This fact will always create racism, war, cruelty, sacrifice and the whole gamut of what passes as civilization on Earth in every cycle and will be that way until man can confront what I say here.

Rudolf Steiner was another agent of these higher powers who had a mission thrown on him when he was eighteen years old. Edouard Schure wrote: "He had felt at that time the irrefutable sensation of occult powers who acted behind and through him to direct him. He listened to this force and followed its warnings, because he felt himself profoundly in accord with it". That Steiner was an initiate is clear, when Schure reveals that a Master initiated Steiner at eighteen: "For they arouse, prepare, and direct those in the public eye". Rudolf Steiner's mission was to: "link together Science and religion", in what he called occult science, or to bring God into science, when in actual fact he was merely another dupe in this long plan of a World Order, bringing people's attention to the Akashic Record however. In 1890 Steiner said: "The occult powers who were directing me obliged me imperceptibly to penetrate into the then current ideas of spiritualists". In 1913, Steiner after a brief role as Secretary General of the German section of the Theosophical society founded the Anthroposophical society. Schure wrote:"By his first Master and by the Fraternity to which he was associated, Steiner belonged to another school of occultism, that is, to Western esoteric Christianity and more especially Rosicrucian initiation....". However the processes and methods used, ranging from meditation, to yoga and eurhythmy (special movements) coupled with the philosophy, opened up the kundalini force at the base of the spine and coupled with the all too familiar assumed correctness of their guru and their own deification, it is my personal experience once again that gross arrogance was the order of the day, with communistic animal pack thinking run by the elite right. The constant thoughts and images within the philosophy of a hierarchy of angels and ethers, spiritual, astral etc., with an awareness of the Akashic Record, focuses the mind into the holographics of the past together with thoughts retained on the bioplasmas. Since they are unaware of what Hubbard called Inc. 1 or what I refer to as the Religious Revolution, then clearly religion and control would go hand in hand, which was my own experience of this group. Such groups, who have so little understanding of the science of holographics and the Grid, are virtually asking to be plugged into the Masters, when they walk in "cosmic circles". Such methods were used by Crowley in his magical rituals, the "serpentine movement". Whilst the Masters understand all too well, how a man's thoughts will connect him to the Grid, the masses believe that their thoughts are totally independent of their actions!

"Processes for awakening the kundalini, whether Western or Eastern, is the same in all groups working under unknown Masters; it means that gradually the Master takes possession of the adept's mind and impresses his own will upon it, so that an advanced initiate, such as Steiner, would work under the impetus of the hidden Master and for his ends alone". [195] As the so-called Tibetan Master of Mrs. Alice Bailey, Theosophist and occultist from New York, explains, contact with the Master is recognised by peculiar vibrations: (1) at the top of the spine; (2) in the forehead (pineal gland, where the adept's kundalini unites with the Master's forces from without, it is the seat of controlled knowledge) (3) at the top of the head (pituitary body). He continues: "In time the student comes to recognise the vibration and to associate it with some particular 'Great One,' for each Master has his own vibration which impresses itself upon his pupils in a specific manner." Further cold and calculating: " a Master is only interested in a man from the point of view of his usefulness in the **group-soul** and his capacity to help. The individual is as nothing to him; he is only a part in his world revolutionary machine, to be thrown aside when no longer an asset in their game!" This aspect of the "group soul" once again defines that it is the morphogenetic bioplasma, on which these thought imprints are stored. This bioplasma carries *survival data only for the phylogenetic line of the species.* The Masters thoughts were imprinted at this level of events of matter, since the

Masters or arch controllers in history prior to the Religious Revolution, only had the ability to control bodies through despotic power. Being bodies, eating bodies, punishing bodies, controlling bodies etc., would come very far down on the emotional scale of energy and would parallel the resonant energy of matter i.e. a body. This was the mind of the Masters before the Holy Grail arrived on Earth reminding man he was his immortal spirit; thus all these past thought imprints are interdispersed with the survival mechanisms of the morphogenetic bioplasma, which relates to animals or primitive minds and *group* survival. Such a mind is not compassionate, sees no right from wrong and thus never apologises to its victims, turns a cold eye to human suffering and acts *only to protect its group* as animal. Secret groups are really in the majority if not all cases set up to keep initiates keyed into this thinking, by some aspect of the philosophy or its processes, particularly in the political goal of communism for the masses. Communism and fascism never involved choice and since choice involves a mind or thinking process, democracy is always fought along with the idea of referendum. Choice is not a luxury it is an absolute necessity as is a working democracy, otherwise if there is no choice, no thinking process, then the political system acts as another channel for the Masters. As it is said one should be very careful of which way one is going, or one is liable to end up some place else! A philosophy has only to require it is 'the only one'; or require 'no questions asked'; or require 'battle mentality'; or require 'superman status'; or require 'help only those who help our group cause' and you immediately set up a channel for the Masters.

Steiner explained: "Anthroposophy as a path of knowledge to guide the spiritual in the human being to the spiritual in the Universe". Stoddard pointed out (cited) "This was illuminism". In his book translated by Schure, *Le Mystere Chretien et les Mysteres Antiques*, Steiner wrote: "It is necessary for the soul to come out of the ordinary "I". Then it enters into a state of spiritual ecstasy, of illumination, **when it ceases to know, to think**, and to recognise in the ordinary sense of the words. For it has identified itself with the divine, they have become one..." (*Author's emphasis*). I can't think of anything more dangerous, not only is he deified, you can't become God or any other spirit for that matter, its absolute nonsense and reflects all this New Age bunkum about fusing with the Godhead and surviving for the Godhead: I am sure God can survive on His or Her own: you can't go back to the anti-matter, matter explosion or just before it, since you would not exist, it was the start of the game. Even worse here, we note a loss of Steiner's personality and by that I mean all that one has been, thought, done and known on the entire track of time. Further this fusion with the vacuum energy or ether is to fuse with the Grid and the Masters and of course you would identify. You may recall that in the UFO witness accounts the beings were mechanical and this is the mind of the Masters. Now this is the extra-ordinary thing that I noticed about groups such as this (and indeed sadly in my own experience I noted in Scientology). People would spout verbatim large tracts of their guru's thoughts and philosophy at you, but a philosophy is only there to be absorbed into your *own* thinking process in proportion to what you recognise to be true and is only as useful as it answers questions on life. You get the feeling that you are talking to a machine and when something goes wrong, as it did in my own case, you ask straightforward questions like 'Can't you see that is wrong?' and no they can't – why! Whenever I see the answer machine approach, I know there is a Master in it somewhere. Of course it can be argued that no philosophy, religion or political group is free from such, one has only to listen to a politician to know the truth of that, however I think it is probably a very good piece of advice, to be self-determined in your own thinking processes and as Jiminy Cricket said: "Always let your conscience be your guide". The problem now is that it is being filtered down from the subject of psychology, that we should become accustomed to the idea of the Universal Mind, which is another illuminatus suggestion, where people are advised to be happy as one great big fused mind, one World Order etc.

All secret groups have some political agenda and in the case of Steiner it was his "Threefold State" model that he based on the human organism. Credit to Steiner in so far as he believed that: "There is no such thing as absolute centralisation in the human organism", which he utilised in his political model to *separate* economic life, public rights, mental and spiritual life. This was a point recognised by the early colonists of America when they laid out their government. The organism in Steiner's case was headless and that is in antithesis to the illuminatus power political pyramid, laid out on the reverse side of the One Dollar note of America. The power political pyramid such as is being erected in Europe is one of the most dangerous organisations that man could employ, simply because it is yet another channel for the Masters. However Steiner rather spoilt his model, by suggesting that the economic life in the form of associations should be combined under the brotherhood. However we see the true source of Steiner's goals when he proposed a Three-fold World State, which was a World Order programme:

> "Such a close interweaving of interests will grow up, as will make territorial frontiers seem negligible in the life of mankind.... The forces to which nationalities owe their growth require for their development free mutual interaction untrammelled by any ties that grow up between respective bodies of State and the Economic Associations. And the way of achieving this is for the various national communities to develop the threefold order within their own social structures; and then their three branches can each expand its own relation with the corresponding

branches of the other communities. In this way, peoples, states, economic bodies, become grouped together in formations that are very various in shape and character; and every part of mankind becomes so linked with the other parts that each is conscious of the life of the other pulsing through its own daily interests. A league of nations is the outcome arising out of root impulses that correspond to actual realities. There will be no need to 'institute' one built solely on legal theories of right".

In similar fashion Adam Weishaupt's initiates of the Illuminati, had to take an oath swearing to help to their utmost the foundation of a Universal Republic. Steiner was also an Illuminatus and co-incidentally or not Hubbard utilised the power pyramid of the Illuminati in his organisational structure of management. However the top echelons of secret groups were always Jewish. As M. Henri de Guillebert stated:

> "The Jew looks upon himself as the sun of humanity, the male, opposed to which the other peoples are but female, manifesting and assuring the coming of the messianic era. In order to realise this sociological manifestation, the Jew organically extends his influence by means of secret societies created by him in order to spread everywhere his initiating force...(hoping to realise) the 'Universal Republic,' controlled by the God of Humanity, the Jew of the Cabala."

In terms of what I have said about two groups of Jews in this story, it is interesting to cover this point by reference to the Panacea Society, which was a secret group originating as the 'Philadelphians', a mystic sect founded in 1652, by Jane Lead. The sect was Rosicrucian illuminism, however their attitude to Jews following two advertisements, clearly defined between two groups or tribes. There appears to be some knowledge of the battle between two Jewish groups for this group had two fixed ideas: the opening of Joanna Southcott's mysterious box, in the presence of twenty-four bishops, six Jews of repute and others, and which they claimed contained the means of *saving England in the coming storm*, and bringing deliverance to Judah; the other was magnetic-healing by charged sections of linen and water. The advertisements noted this distinction of tribes:

> "Not anti-Semitism, but anti-Hamitism – The Panacea society is anxious to help the Jews (descendents of Shem) to deliver themselves from the abominable charges which bring about anti-Semitic persecution. The first thing to learn is that it is the descendents of Ham, who say they are Jews, and are not, who are, and always have been, the

enemies of God and man."   ,

"Good News for the Jews – the Prophet's promises and the Pharisaic ideals of kingdom ruled by God upon earth are on the edge of becoming FACT, for the week of 6 000 years of 6 days of 1 000 years each is rapidly closing, and the Sabbath of Rest for Israel and for Judah during the reign of the Messiah on earth is about to commence. Enquire, Panacea Society, Bedford."

Curiously they stated this:

"...will be the end of the Adamic age, which followed the Atlantean, Lemurian, and other ages, the history of which is shrouded in Mystery... God's Sabbath of Rest is the seventh thousand from Adam... (When) men will live on earth delivered from sin, sickness, and death by reason that Satan will be cast off the earth into the place prepared for him..."

This is somewhat curious to me, since in chapter one of *The Battle of The Trees*, I recounted a past life, where as a young French nobleman, I had under great duress and hot pursuit ridden through several nights of freezing wet weather across France on a horse, to get a parchment to England for safe keeping. The parchment appeared to be connected to St. John and the *Apocalypse* although I could not recall what was in the parchment, as it was in a code I no longer could remember. The one phrase I did come up with whilst in memory of this life was: "Shem son of Noah". Evidently then we are as I suspected talking about two branches of tribes from Noah, Shem and Ham. Presumably then the tribe of Judah or the thirteenth tribe in England was the Shem branch. The Panacea society in another leaflet headed "To Our Brethren of the tribe of Judah", they stated that it is for the union of Judah and Israel the world is waiting, and these Isles (the British Isles) are their place of gathering; that King George V is descended from Zedekiah, King of Judah; therefore the Hebrews have a king, a country, and because the Union Jack means, they say, the union of Jacob, they have also a national flag! They claimed that both Judaism and Christianity have sinned and that the former rejects the Son and the latter rejects the Daughter! Well there you are then the people of Britain unknowingly for thousands of years in the middle of a Jewish tribal war that still rages unknown today. The curious Joanna Southcott box is claimed as the Ark of the Testament alluded to in *Rev. Xi. 19*, called so because it contains God's Will and Testament for the British Isles! Well let us hope this is not another set up of yet another dupe, since *Revelations* I concluded was written for the 12 tribes or is it Ham? And it may well be that these fair Isles will become pre-determined proof of yet another pre-determined prophecy. 'Ah yes', they will say, 'it was all meant to be'. King

George V as a member of the tribe of Judah is an interesting one isn't it, which rather places the death of Diana Princess of Wales into the realms of suspicion as I previously mentioned, since the tribe of Judah would not want any spurious Egyptian line springing up perhaps with Ham problems arising in the future; and the 12 tribes will have no truck with goddesses, especially one's that raised the image of the British Isles, after all it might mess up the 'script'. As with the question 'Who killed the Minoans?' it is not easy to decide which group was responsible. Every death of this nature, deserves a truthful inquest however, one must remember a life was taken (accidentally or not). I am sorry to have to say I smell a pie. Finally Joanna Southgate's box or Ark can only be applied for in a time of **grave national danger**. The ark or box will prove publicly the truth of what has so long been developing privately, and also will prove the integrity of the Church, by placing before her the proof of a New Divine Revelation, before which she must bow or cease to exist.

I do not trust prophecies, since agents working for Masters, or the groups 12 and 13 invariably issue them. However there is some truth in the above statement. Cheiro, in his *Predictions*, foretells of the coming World domination by the Jews, the setting up of their kingdom in Egypt and Palestine, which is to eventuate in 1980, according to his reckoning, a reckoning that can be falsified if one recognises the danger. *Revelations* is written for the 12 tribes and obviously as I have pointed out, if these Isles have been voted for sacrifice amongst the hierarchy of secret groups working with the 12 tribes, then if there are any patriots left in these Isles they had better jump to it, since the propaganda line supporting the *Apocalypse* is rapidly if not bizarrely being pressed upon the nations of the world. In the *Berliner Zeitung* newspaper a cartoon in March 2001 showed mighty Britannia defeating the Spanish Armada, the warships of Napoleon and the battle fleet of the Nazis, only to raise the white flag as two ghost ships bearing *twin* ensigns of BSE and foot-and-mouth hove into view. *Die Zeit*, the intellectual's weekly of choice, in the same period called Britain 'The Island of Catastrophe'. Germany and America have covered articles on the grim state of Britain's public services, with *The Wall Street Journal* pointing out that 'in the land of Shakespeare and Waugh, one in five adults is functionally illiterate'. *The Chicago Sun Times* opined that Britain: " has been struck by a series of biblical plagues. A foot-and-mouth epidemic among sheep, a train crash that reduced the transport system to the tempo of a slow march, and incessant bad weather even by British standards, have all fostered a sense of apocalyptic doom among the islanders". The French traditionally we are constantly told hate the British, thus *Le Figaro in March 2001* described Britain as a "sad shambles", naming the rail service, the NHS and the crisis in the countryside as three reasons not to come here. It said: "Thousands of immigrants flood into Calais each week to get into Britain. Five years ago we might have understood why they wanted to get in so badly, but now we are wondering what they see in the place". A columnist in *Liberation* described Britain as simply "Disaster land" and another called the country "that septic isle" while others said Britain was the "sick man of Europe". *Le Monde*, the French standard bearer of anti-British sentiment, stormed: "You never hear debates about ethics or morals in Great Britain, just about saving money. It's no wonder the place is falling apart". Well I can assure the French *Le Monde*, that it was not for want of trying to raise ethical debate, as my Petition shows. However should we look to Cheiro's predictions of world (and press) domination by the 12 tribes of Israel, for the fact that not one newspaper in Britain took up my offer of submitting the cancer research to rational evaluation by a panel of *unhampered* (from the World Order by grant or position) scientists from selected disciplines? Further when I did advertise on the front page of my local paper *The Argus* the cancer report under the banner headline of '*Totally Tribal*' it was removed from the front page after the morning edition and a local department store was substituted in the evening slot, with the loss of the advertising payment! ('Do what thou wilt is the whole of the law'). There is also the question of the Petition, which I gave to every newspaper editor, The Press Complaints Commission and the Ethics office for the Association of journalists: and further, what about the alternative press, could they not have acted? As you will note, the author is a woman scientist and in Plato's Republic of Britain, women and slaves have no say! And further if you do say, you can expect the actions on the front cover of the cancer report! Thus what can I say, I have led many lives in many countries and in that respect I am international as I noted in my last page of *The Battle of The Trees*, but since I re-incarnated here, presumably for the reason of my research, I had a duty to try and help. You can take a horse (in the case of Britannia) to water, but you can't make it drink, thus I feel I must leave these fair Isles for pastures new.

Whilst it would seem that successive governments of Britain have failed in their approach to long-term policies leading to current problems, it certainly does not help matters for the Masters and the 12 tribes over there in Brussels to accuse Britain in a European report of xenophobia, racism and discrimination. The report condemned politicians and newspapers, which it said are responsible for 'particularly acute' racism against asylum seekers. It also claimed that Britain is a cradle of prejudice against Moslems, gipsies, travellers and Jews. Issued by the Strasbourg-based Council of Europe, it demanded a string of immediate reforms, including laws to give more help to asylum seekers and ease immigration restrictions. There should also be laws, it said, to stop papers publishing stories containing 'general racist assumptions and stereotypes', to ban religious discrimination and to provide large amounts of legal aid to bring racism complaints to industrial tribunals. Well that's ripe, coming from Europe's Masters, where the Holy Grail and re-incarnation has been suppressed for thousands of years. Evidently another European study published in April 2001, which showed Britain as much less racist than France or Italy was completely overlooked. The European Monitoring Centre on Racism and Xenophobia found Britons were more tolerant than most other EU nations whilst some of the most unreconstructed attitudes towards race were found in Italy This I am afraid is the problem with World Orders, not only do they become the school playground bully, intent on taking out their own particular dramatizations on their unfortunate victims, which in the case of Britain is really a tribal war between two groups or tribes of Israel, which the people of Britain appear to be trapped in the middle of: but it really does not allow a government to work rationally in the best interests of its electorate and the people that pay taxes for their services. How many immigrants for example does Israel take? Now I am all for helping people in genuine political distress, but let us first ask how much financial aid came from Brussels over the current series of disasters in Britain? It might be worthy to ask those people who pay the bills, the taxpayers, whether they require directives from Brussels as to where their money is to be spent; either in trying to get this country back on its feet, or in financing further immigration.

The point is, that if the country goes down, immigration will not be an issue will it! Whole swathes of land in the world will be unpopulated, whilst other countries will be packed to capacity, which seems ridiculous. The answer to immigration is to get rid of the World Order, for it is the Masters, who prevent the equal distribution of wealth and support despotic regimes, which force people to flee. It is the World Order that has milked the poor and continues to cream off the vast profits from sickness and suffering. It is the World Order and the Jewish dynastic roots, with its obsession with bodylines, purity of the blood and dynastic monarchical hereditary lines that has brought the world racism. It is the Masters and their agents that live in the lap of luxury, whilst dictating that man should live under communist principles that has brought the world revolution: playing with the lives of men, like pawns on their master board of pre-determined events fulfilling their prophecies, towards that goal that they have always sought - World Domination. Theatre Earth is a 'script' of a **TRIBAL WAR** between the tribes of Judah the thirteenth tribe and the remaining twelve tribes of Israel derived from two sons of Noah Shem and Ham? Nowhere is this truer than in the British Isles. However in THE BEGINNING THE HOLY GRAIL HAD NOTHING WHATSOEVER TO DO WITH THIS TRIBAL WAR. The events at Knossos 1 400 B.C. saw the Holy Grail knowledge taken and the tribal war then involved the woman in the story. The recognition of the son by one group and the daughter by another group has merely prevented knowledge of the trap reaching mankind, as the terrible twins play out their incessant hidden agenda in the field of politics and religion on Earth.

In *fifth chapter of the book of Genesis* are found the statistics of the ages of the antediluvian patriarchs. Adam considered to be the first man lived 930 years: Seth, the second Patriarch lived 912 years; Enos 905 years; Cainan, 910 years; Mahalaleel, 895 years; Jared, 962 years; Enoch, 365 years; Methuselah, 969 years; Lamech the ninth patriarch lived 777 years; whilst Noah lived 950 years. *Genesis* tells that Cain and Seth were born in 4969 B.C and 4924 B.C respectively and upon maturity became the progenitors of two distinct races, isolated from one another known as Cainites and Sethites, they developed totally different life-styles. Record tells us that Cain lived in the land called nod, meaning 'place of exile'. *Genesis* mentions the land where he settled did not 'yield her strength', but there is no further information concerning the early years except that in c. 4784 B.C a son Enoch was born. Sometime between this date and Cain's death in 405 B.C, Cain gathered his descendents together and built a city called Enoch City, named after his first son. This city would require the development of a higher order of mathematics, the manipulation of building materials and knowledge of architecture. Little is know of the descendents of Cain other that the sequences of descent given in *Chapter IV of Genesis.*

Names were given which reflected the status or character, or major events in the lives of these men, thus from the names of the Cainites one can perceive a little information. The name Enoch means 'devoted, the initiated (into secret learning) or a teacher, with the implication that Enoch was a master of the Black Cabala and is mentioned obliquely in secret group history as the 'Enochian Keys'. The fact that Cain named his city after Enoch, suggests that the city was not just a political centre but also a 'religious' one of sorts. Enoch as high priest in one assumes a city run by a Theocracy, or initiated priesthood. Irad, the son of Enoch was born c.4599 B.C thus three generations ruled Enoch City. Irad means 'a townsman, a Prince of the city'. Mehujael was the son of Irad c. 4415 B.C and his name meant 'smitten of God' and thus one assumes he was struck down by some disease or disaster as a punishment. Nethusael was next in line born 4367 B.C and his name indicates, was 'a great man before God'. Lamech, the son of Methusael, was born approximately 4180 B.C and died 3403 B.C. The history of his father Methusael indicates some mixing of the two races for a while, for some specific but unnamed purpose, however overall the Cainites and Sethites appear to have developed as separate races. However immediately after the races had intermingled the account indicates that open lawlessness was common. Lamech not only means 'a strong young man, or hero', but the record shows he was a murderer and the first polygamist mentioned and with the arrival of Tubalcain (3860 B.C) who was a son of Lamech by one of his wives (Zillah), technology entered the antediluvian world and *Genesis 4:22* calls Tubalcain "an instructor of every artificer in brass and iron".

In 1968, Dr Koriut Megurchian of theSoviet Union unearthed what is considered to the oldest large-scale metallurgical factory in the world, at Medzamor, in the old Soviet Armenia. Here, 4500 years ago, an unknown prehistoric people worked with over 200 furnaces, producing an assortment of vases, knives, spearhead, rings bracelets, etc. The use of copper, lead, zinc, iron, gold, tin, manganese and fourteen kinds of bronze was evident. The most out-of-place discovery which I mentioned earlier in the book, was several pairs of tweezers made from steel, taken from layers dating back before the first millennium B.C. As with the footprints of giant man, found alongside the dinosaur footprint in the Paluxy riverbed, these sorts of facts are hidden in order to not upset the lie of Darwinian evolution. The steel was later found to be of exceptionally high grade, and the discovery was verified by scientific organizations in the Soviet Union, the United States, Britain, France and Germany. French journalist Jean Vidal, reporting in Science et vie of July 1969, expressed the belief that these finds point to an unknown period of technological development. 'Medzamor,' he wrote: "was founded by the wise men of earlier civilizations. They possessed knowledge they had acquired during a remote age unknown to us that deserves to be called scientific and industrial". What makes the Medamor metallurgical site interesting is that it is within fifteen miles of Mount Ararat, the alleged landing site of the survivors of the Flood.[196-198] However we have increasingly come to recognise, that such knowledge whilst it could have been handed down from Noah and the antediluvian Patriarchs, is also likely in addition, to have been channelled from the Grid, since Palaeolithic finds exhibit the' umbrella' shapes that is indicative of the Grid.

Seth was born about 4924 B.C and he is not known as either a city dweller or a city builder, but seemed to have lived quietly on the fertile soil provided by the four rivers mentioned in early records. Something happened to undermine the physical well being of the Sethites, for his son, born in approximately 4819 B.C carried the name Enos, which means 'mortal weak mankind'. The Hebrew Aggadah comments that during Enos' lifetime, faces of men became more apelike. This may have been a war of a nuclear type, which the Indian epics speak of in veiled terms, where the survivors may have been forced to occupy the bodies of more ape-like forms as a regression. There is certainly something amiss in the chronology of the Biblical accounts of dates and the Flood as I have previously referred to. However we do know that Methusela (4367 B.C), Lamech (4180 B.C) and Noah (3998) son of Lamech were all Sethites. The dates however given in Biblical texts may not be accurate and may purposefully hide the occurrence of the last great Magnetic Reversal that wiped the dinosaurs from the face of the earth. Spiritual intervention occurred on Earth c. 10 000 B.C and no Magnetic Reversal or great Flood has occurred during this period, thus there has to be a discrepancy in the Biblical dates, which purposefully hides up some unpalatable facts, for which reason the Nag Hamaadi scrolls have been refused scrutiny by scholars, as they may indeed give a different record of events, particularly over the story of Noah's Ark. Noah's sons importantly however, were Shem, Ham and Japeth and Noah was said to be a Sethite and his sons comprised the eleventh generation from Adam. Whether the Panacea society tried to draw a distinction between these sons of Shem and Ham, must rest upon the use of the Black Cabala. The descendents of Noah in Chapters 10 and 11 of *Genesis* become divided into nations and races, with the result that the common background is lost. Hindu records speak of a highly destructive war waged with the possibility of nuclear weapons, soon after the Flood. Further *Genesis 11* records how the generations following Noah, suddenly show a huge decrease in life spans from more than 900 years to approximately 100 years. This is a very large clue that a Magnetic Reversal co-incided with the Flood and the age of the dinosaurs and mythical giants, who appear to be none other than the Patriarchs and the human race before the Flood and a Magnetic Reversal. Many world myths and religions remember these events. In Guatemala the ancient Mayas recorded in their sacred book, the *Popol Vuh*, that the "first men" possessed tremendous knowledge: "They were able to know all, and they examined the four corners, the four points of *the arch of the sky* and the round face of the earth' [199] *(Author's emphasis)*. What is this other than channelling using Black Cabalistic methods and the "arch" paralleling the curious 'umbrella' shapes of the secret caves of the magicians. The ancient Chinese also recognized that before them were "giants" and "Men twice as tall as us", who once inhabited the "realm of delight" but lost it by not living "by laws of virtue". [200]

Many fragments of technological know-how of unknown origin have surfaced over the years and like the Knossos site, have usually been ignored by modern science, because not only do they represent a mystery, but also grants and **policy** determine academic research. I would suggest that policy has determined the enormous amount of data that has been omitted from explanation of icons in museums. On *page 292* of *The White Goddess*, Robert Graves refers to this criminal under use of museums with regard to the description and labelling of artefacts. I have made the same condemnation in the under use of the Knossos site and given that I see the Religious Revolution in Crete as the basis of Hubbard's Inc. 1 and mind control, then these observations are not entirely co-incidental! However the hidden policy that undoubtedly exists, which mirrors that of the state of 'no cure' for cancer is one that requires the 'reality' of the World Order to remain in place unquestioned. No part of the hidden science, or its long history and usurary in the secret groups together with the background to the patriarchs as Black Cabalistic magicians, with their prophecies of world events must be revealed; otherwise that precarious pack of cards of Babel and the World Order, will come tumbling down. Philo of Alexandria (c. 30 B.C – 40 A.D) wrote: "By reason of the constant and repeated destructions by water and fire, the later generations did not receive from the former the memory of the order and sequence of events". Plato in the *Timaeus*, recorded what Egyptian priests had told his ancestor, Solon: "There have been and there will be again many destructions of mankind", and when civilization is destroyed, "you have to begin all over again as children". The problem has been, that in each cycle the World Order, to fit their own purposes, has edited all previous events and further channelling has enforced the will of the Masters.

The Sumerians who are thought to have founded the first civilization after the Flood (*Gen.10:8 – 12*) also recognized a pre-Flood civilization antedating their own. In 1922, the Weld-Blundell Expedition, excavating at Larsa, a few miles north of Abraham's city of Ur, discovered what is now called the Weld Prism, held at the Ashmolean Museum in Oxford UK. The Prism contains a history written by a scribe named Nur-Ninsubur in approximately 2100 B.C. In his account he records the list of ten pre-Flood kings and ends his writing with the sad words: " and the Flood overthrew the land". The date is very early and may co-incide with a Flood, but not a Magnetic Reversal and the major catastrophe. The Sumerians and later the Babylonians and Assyrians further recognized the pre-Flood era as the source of superior literature. Whilst fragmentary details are handed down, the great purges of knowledge and books in the past, such as the one carried out by the Emperor Ch'in Shih Huang Ti of China, who caused all historical books to be burned in 212 B.C, have left gaps one assumes in the knowledge of secret groups. Leo Iaurus sent 300 000 books to be burnt in the eighth century and the annihilation of manuscripts and books during the period of the Inquisition in the middle Ages, must have seen many manuscripts including Black Cabalistic rites burnt, which presumably was an attempt to stop the use of the Grid and appears to be behind, the burning of the library of Alexandria.

After the Second World War, the discovery of the Dead Sea Scrolls created a sensation among Biblical scholars, for these documents, dating back to the second century B.C, agreed remarkably with a Biblical manuscript known as the *Masoretic Text* of AD 10. The discovery in 1975 of the Eblite Tablets at Tel Mardiqh in Syria was also to create excitement, since they dated back to 2 300 B.C. It is evident however from the academic stranglehold by Jewish authorities placed on these texts, which no doubt offer a varying reality from the World Order 'reality' that there was no intention of releasing the full texts. In *The Battle of The Trees*, I give some account of the Nag Hamaadi scrolls that show a completely different story of Jesus and Magdalene and despite the fact that these documents are of comparable antiquity to Biblical Gospels they are ignored. It seems that a vast storehouse of knowledge was lost over the years, but in my own conclusions I believe there was a project among the World Order to reclaim such knowledge, which co-incided with the rapid technological advance that occurred in the 1960's, presumably when the realisation dawned of Magnetic Reversals and the need to develop a space programme, to secure the survival of a chosen few. The longevity of life on planet Earth, in the cycle preceding the last Magnetic Reversal had lead to man's belief, that he was his immortal body and Spiritual intervention c. 10 000 B.C was to remind man of his immortal soul and the fact that: "they don't stand a chance", without the intervention of knowledge that would free man from the trap, including the requirement to pay up his karma of past lives, which is really continuous existence punctuated every 70-80 years in this cycle by loss of a body, due to the prevailing electro-magnetic cycle.

Electricity may have played a vital role in the Ark and may even have accounted for the demise of the last cycle, where odd electrical artefacts have been found. *Genesis 8:6* records the Hebrew word Challon or 'opening' referring to the window through which Noah released birds from the Ark. In another reference however, the word tsohar is used to translate as 'window' but it does not mean that at all, since where it is used twenty two times in the Old Testament, it means 'a brightness, a brilliance, the light of the noonday sun'; or something that 'glistens, glitters or shines'. Many Jewish scholars of the traditional school identify tsohar as 'a light, which has its origin in a shining crystal'. What is this but some form of utilisation of the vacuum energy, or free energy! Further Hebrew tradition has described the tsohar as an enormous gem or pearl that Noah hung from the rafters of the Ark and which illuminated the Ark. This however, sounds very much like the Cabalistic secret of perpetually burning lamps and some form or method of tapping the zero point energy. King Solomon may have utilised the secrets of this light source in 1 000 B.C. An ancient Jewish manuscript entitled: *The Queen of Sheba and her only son Menyelek* (*trans. By Sir E.A. Wallis Budge*), contains the statement: "Now the House of Solomon the King was illuminated as by day, or in his wisdom he had made shining pearls which were like unto the sun, the moon and the stars in the **roof** of his house" (the "roof" as 'umbrella' of Palaeolithic art, the dome or crystal?) However, since the Palaeolithic wall painting of the 'Missionary Woman', indicated that she wore a string of pearls then one cannot be sure how much of this knowledge was taken from Spiritual intervention and how much was known in the last cycle. It seems probable however, that the concept of free energy may have been a new addition through Spiritual intervention, which may have sought to prevent the old cycle of destruction through the repetition of technology which brought about the demise of the last cycle. Solomon once wrote: "there is no new thing under the sun. Is there any thing, whereof it may be said, see, this is new? It hath been already of old time which was before us" *(Ecc, 1: 9-10)*. The historian Josephus Goriondes related how Alexander the Great wrote to his teacher during the conquest of Persia telling him that an island located off the coast of India, was inhabited by men who ate raw fish and spoke in a language similar to Greek. They believed at one time prior to the Flood, Cainan the great-grandson of Adam, was entombed on the island with a high tower over his sepulchre and anyone who approached the tomb was struck dead by a flash of lightening, discharged from the top of the tower.

S. N. Kramer in his book *History Begins at Summer*, quoted a fragment of Sumerian text that spoke of: "Ziusudra, the King, the preserver of the seed of mankind" and how he constructed a: "huge boat which was tossed about", in a flood that overwhelmed the land. Ziusudra is identical to Berosus Xisuthros and the older Sumerian Utna pishtion. The Sumerian text also mentions that in preparation of Ziusudra's "huge boat", the hero Utu brought: "his rays (of the sun) into the boat, in order to give it light". Utu corresponds to Ubarat-Utu (in the Weld-Bundell Sumerian list, quoted initially in this book) who was the eighth king of the ten pre-Flood rulers and counterpart of Biblical Methuselah. Thus this king may have given Noah some secret of the ever-burning lamps and one assumes methods for tapping the zero point energy or electricity. The root word of chemistry – chemia – is attributed to Khem, the ancient name for the land of Egypt or the land of Kham, derived perhaps from a fusion of Ham and King? Thus it would seem, that Ham or his branch of the Israelites might have been Black Cabalists. This priesthood may have indeed remained in Egypt and since the pyramids appear there, it seems possible that they were using anti-gravity Grid anomalies to build these structures: and indeed it may have been this priesthood that overthrew the 13 th tribe who carried out the Religious Revolution in Crete; presumably it was this priesthood of Thothmes III or the Grand Master of the Great White Lodge who installed the Semitic religion at Knossos.

The Hebrew monarchy of Egypt is well documented in *The Bible* from Solomon's alliance with Pharaoh Sheshonk (Shisak) related in *I Kings, iii,1 and I Kings,ix, 16*; to the decline of the priest kings who were driven from Thebes and founded theocracy in the Nubian colony, which became known as Ethiopia and from where the oracle of Amon controlled the affairs of State. In time the Ethiopian kingdom became strong enough to control a large part of Upper Egypt and Thebes. Shabaka, the first pharaoh of the Ethiopian (Twenty-Fifth) Dynasty, ruled over all Egypt and is believed to have been the biblical: "So, King of Egypt"

(*2 Kings, xvii,* 4). Taharka, the third and last Ethiopian Pharaoh whose mother was black, is referred to in *The Bible* as Tirhakah (*Isaiah xxxvii, 9*) and amongst others allied himself with Hezekiah, king of Judah. Isaiah, a statesman and scholar was not party to the alliance between Egypt and the tribe of Judah. The new god of Thebes Amon, or Amen, arose in Egypt and the earliest reference to him appears in the pyramid of the famous King Unas of the fifth Dynasty, where he and his consort are included among the primeval gods associated with NU – "the fathers and the mothers", who were in "the deep" at the beginning. I previously mentioned that the Chinese word for "ship" is a combination of the symbols for "mouth" and "eight", which suggests that the Ark was a boat that carried eight persons. The Chinese regard Nu-wah as their ancestor and hero and quite possibly Nu-wah could represent Noah, or New World. The ancestor of the Chinese and early Chinese history further supports the idea of a Noachian involvement in the birth of China. Is it any wonder that the Chinese, threw religion out of China! Dominated as it is by tribal wars of the Jews.

Amon was thought to signify: "The Hidden One" and he concealed his "soul" and his "name", like the giant who hid his "soul in an egg". The curse in *Revelations i*s on frogs *Revelations 16,13-14*:

> "And I saw three unclean Spirits like frogs come out of the mouth of the dragon and out of the mouth of the beast and out of the mouth of the false prophet. For they are the Spirits of devils, working miracles which go forth unto the kings of the Earth and the whole world, to gather them to battle of that great day of God Almighty".

This curse I previously concluded, was the curse of the Twelve Tribes against the thirteenth tribe, for utilizing Akashic Record knowledge? Whilst the twelve tribes presumably accepted *The Covenant*, is really directed at the group who took over Knossos, or at least the group who acknowledged some role for the woman. The twelve Tribes of course throughout the Biblical prophesy vilify the woman and evidently do not want to loose control of the Grid and their own Black Cabalistic practices, evidently laid out in the Old Testament of their patriarchs! However as I have often repeated both sets or groups i.e. the twelve tribes and the thirteenth tribe have both utilized the Grid knowledge and mixed The Holy Grail, irreversibly with the history of the Jews, with their eternal mixing and borrowing from sources, until they have both produced a very fine muddle of the message and The Holy Grail. There is not one religion that has not been touched by this story. However either *The Bible* has been so heavily edited, that the priests have irreparably mixed up the story line, or it was always considered that Judah should be part of the "chosen ones", for *Revelation 7, 5-8*, deliberately includes the thirteenth tribe of Judah to be amongst the chosen ones of earth for salvation, the rest being the other so-called twelve tribes - one missing but never mind the odd inconsistency!

Amon was represented in various forms (1) As an **ape** (2) as a lion (3) as a **frog-headed man** accompanied by Ament, his serpent-headed female counterpart and (4) as a serpent-headed man, while his consort is cat-headed and (5) as a man god with royal sceptre in hand and the symbol of life (ankh) in the other and (6) as a ram-headed man. The connection of frog to Amon Ra and the curse in *Revelations*, with the clue of Ape, must refer to the Sethites, whilst the curse can only come from the descendents of Ham and thus the twelve tribes of Israel. The growing disaffection with Christianity in Britain must surely reflect the nature of covert politics in this country, where the 13 th tribe of Judah, is at war with the 12 tribes of Israel. Further the ape is shown in the late Minoan Fresco at the time of the Religious Revolution, which indicates that the downfall of the Early Minoans first came by stealing The Holy Grail from the woman by the thirteenth tribe and then in all probability the thirteenth tribe was overthrown by a priesthood representing the 12 tribes of Israel and the Ham branch of Noah; whilst the monkey illustrated together with the red men of Knossos the 13 tribe and Judah or the branch of Shem I conclude. However what a sorry tale that the woman and The Holy Grail was dragged into a tribal war, when her purpose was to set up a system of education in the comparable OT levels, to free man from the trap: the knowledge thereafter was be withdrawn into the secret confines of the 13 th tribe and later commercialised and sold at profit?

Thebes is believed to have been derived from the goddess' name, the female article "T", being placed before "Ape"; Tap or Tape was pronounced Thebai by the Greeks, who had a town of that name (Budge's *Gods of the Egyptians*). The sacred name of the city was Nu or Nu-Amon, again giving some line of descent I assume from Noah. However importantly it seems that the priests of Amon, abused their knowledge, for they utilized Grid knowledge to strengthen their power by the ability to prophesy. Thus it would seem that neither group wanted the woman on the scene, since the twelve tribes made use of the **B**lack Cabala for methods of power and profit and the 13 th tribe utilized the Grid and Cabalistic channeling in order to further their reputation as foretellers of future events, which also gave them great power. A good deal of trickery was evidently indulged in, we gather, since the god signified his assent to an expressed wish by nodding his head, or selected a suitable leader of men by extending his arm! Neither group could give the elixir back to man, both used the cup of power and wealth to achieve their own ends of hereditary monarchy or power and wealth; and both groups used their knowledge to control religion.

The cult of Amon also employed the bull as a war god and it was significant that the Bull-Minos phallic cult that entered Knossos, not only brought with them the Bull motif, but also weapons such as helmets and swords. The war god Mentu as bull was fused with Horus and he appears in human form wearing a bull's tail with head of hawk, surmounted by a sun disc or rosette! Thus the Order of the Rose and World Order once again can be traced back to the Cabal that overran Knossos, prior to the 12 tribes who finally ran out the thirteenth tribe and admist the shambles the Holy Grail stolen! Between Amon's double plumes appeared the sun disc and whilst the *Prince* fresco at Knossos still retains its red skin character and plume, Sir Arthur Evans from Oxford, who was the chief archaeologist of the site, may have airbrushed the rosette out. Evidently the Greeks in requesting back the Elgin marbles feel that some part of their history has been sequestered and used by the 13 th tribe and the Elgin marbles have become a focus for that grievance: however the loss of The Holy Grail has yet to be grieved over or the role of the woman! The Late Minoan seals also show a bull-headed man, which was another symbolism of Amon Ra and he often carried bow and arrows, a club and a knife, all of which have featured in archetypal symbolism of the World Order, in the reverse side of the One dollar note, Cardiff Castle and Hercules with his club and Hitlers Nazi SS regalia of knife respectively. Can we not see at least in this, a common thread of not only a World Order, but the stages of destruction and construction that the World Order have forced upon the World and particularly Europe.

Amon was linked with the great sun god in the Eleventh Dynasty i.e. as Amon Ra, which was the god that I perceived was at the back of the Religious Revolution in Crete, where icons showed figures with hands raised to Ra. This god ultimately rose to position of National god, whilst his cult became the most powerful in Egypt. Amon's wife was Mut, whose name signifies "the Mother" and evidently the mere mention of the phrase " The Father is the Mother" from *Isaiah* by Pope John Paul I (Albino Luciani) led to his premature death and some say murder, presumably by the 12 tribes of Israel, whereupon he was replaced by the current communistic Pope, who no doubt was a man of the 12 tribes of Israel. It was to Mut that Amenhotep III, the father of Akenaton, erected the magnificent temple at Karnak, with its great avenue of ram-headed Sphinxes. One thing is certain the woman as muse, certainly gave men inspiration to achieve in the fields of art and architecture as was the case with Queen Tiy, where the family became an important issue together with art. The concept of the Great Mother and the mother-goddess-and-son, which was illustrated at Knossos, with the Minotaur man-bull seated on his mother Pasiphae knee, is an enduring archetypal symbol that was utilized in the Maddona and child pose of Jesus and Mary. The twelve tribes had to place the woman somewhere, thus they gave the position to the Mother of the Divine male child! The Goddess, which archaelogists equate with the early belief of the female as the origin of the world and life as Mother Earth Goddess, has far greater unknown and secret implications, which were held by both groups. The male however disliked the idea of power in a woman and thus elevated himself as self-begotten as the "Great Father" and in some twist of mind of the secret groups, he also became "husband of his mother", which no doubt led to all sorts of wonderful karma! The confusion created by the two groups in the field of religion was phenomenal! There is no doubt, that channeling also allowed the tribes of Israel through their cabalistic rites to gain headway into influencing the order of the day. In one Egyptain papyrus of the Ramessid period, the Pharaoh said: "Let a great magician who is learned in the mysteries be brought before me". Such mysteries were held by a male priesthood, thus it is inevitable that *Revelations* should come up with the curse on woman and the thirteenth tribe, just as it started out in *Genesis* with blaming the woman, for its own Black Cabalistic practices, that had been passed down from the pre-Flood patriarchs! The woman represented a severe threat to the power of the 12 tribes and only survived in the 13 th tribe as a muse, which as was the case of Hitler created the justification for the cause of a tribal war between 12 and 13, which had nothing whatsoever to do with The Holy Grail. The priesthoods would periodically unite and dis-unite and in the period of Hatshepsut and Thothmes II there was a period of conflict. Thothmes II was a priest of the temple of Amon, as I have covered, and either married Hatshepsut or her daughter in order to achieve power as pharaoh.

What is evident, is that the tribes of Israel appear firstly in the Black Sea region and the Beth-Luis-Nion alphabet was said by Graves to have first appeared in this region. Historically speaking the area was occupied in the seventh to tenth centuries A.D by the Khazar Empire, which played a significant role of political destinies in the area. Yakubi a ninth century Arab historian traces the origin of the Khazers back to Japheth, the third son of Noah. The tribes of Shem and Ham however are more difficult to trace, but it appears that the Tuatha de Danaan of Greece were possibly the tribe of Shem, who on invasion of Greece by patriarchal invaders, migrated to The British Isles in the second Millenium B.C. The priesthood of Ham however appear to have installed themselves in Egypt. There is not a religion in the world that remains untouched by this story, with some misunderstanding on the truth. The Indian *Mahabharata* also reveals this intricate connection to the 13 th tribe and the mark of the woman in the story. In this account the ape-god Hanuman, which may be an altered Nu – man or man of Noah combined with Ham as the other son of Noah; opened his sleepy red eyes, signifying the red men of Knossos and the root of Adam, together with royalty. Hanuman on opening his eyes states: "Sick am I, but I was slumbering sweetly, why hast thou awakened me so rudely?" Bhima the raconteur of the epic asks: "Who art thou that hath assumed the form of an ape; art thou a god, or a spirit, or a demon?" Interestingly then the idea of body regression after some cataclysmic event is inferred and indicates the tribe of Shem who were said at one time, to have become more ape-like after some unspecified event, presumably either a Magnetic Reversal, or a nuclear event, reminding one of the wizened carvings of the Toltecs, portraying men who looked as though they had tumors or radiation poisoning. Hunuman states: "At that Age the universe was not as it is now. Thou canst not behold the form I erstwhile had…In Krita Yuga there was one state of things and in the Tetra Yuga another; greater change came with Dwapara Yuga, and in the present Yuga there is **lessening** and I am not what I have been" *(author's emphasis)*. He goes on to say: "the gods, the saints and all things that are, have been changed. I have conformed with the tendency of the present age and the influence of Time". The "lessening" I conclude, is the referral to loss of life span and size and the giant nature, which must refer to a Magnetic Reversal that also saw the demise of the dinosaurs. Bhima then asked the ape-god about the various ages of man and Hunuman replied:

> "The Krita Yuga (Perfect Age) was so named because there was but one religion, and all men were saintly: therefore they were not required to perform religious ceremonies. Holiness never grew less, and the people did not decrease. There were no gods in the Krita Yuga, and there were no demons or Yakshas, and no Rakshasas or Nagas. Men neither bought nor sold; there were no poor and no rich; there was no need to labor, because all that men required was obtained by the power of will; the chief virtue was the abandonment of all worldly desires. The Krita Yuga was without disease; there was no lessening with the years; there was no hatred, or vanity, or evil thought whatsoever no sorrow, no fear. All mankind could attain to supreme blessedness. The Universal soul was Narayana: he was White; he was the refuge of all and was sought for by all; the identification of self with a universal soul was the whole religion of the Perfect Age. In the Treta Yuga sacrifices began, and the world Soul became Red; virtue lessened a quarter. Mankind sought truth and performed religious ceremonies; they obtained what they desired by giving and by doing. In the Dwapara Yuga the aspect of the world soul was Yellow: religion lessen one-half. The Veda, which was one in the Krita Yuga, was divided into four parts and although some had knowledge of the four Vedas, others knew but three or one. Mind lessened, Truth declined, and there came desire and diseases and calamities; because of these men had to undergo penances. It was a decadent Age by reason of the prevalence of sin. In the Kali Yuga the world Soul is Black in hue: it is the Iron Age; only one quarter of virtue remained. The world is afflicted, men turn to wickedness; disease cometh; all creatures degenerate; contrary effects are obtained by performing holy rites; change passeth over all things, and even those

who live through many yugas must change also".

Thus here we have the Indian equivalent to Atlantis and the assumption that all was well with the Atlantean method of rule, which was despotic kings. Thus the propaganda line that has been exerted is to make the patriarchs the progenitors of an ideal age in the past. However spiritual intervention came to release mankind from the trap and whilst it is evident that men were good and bad, it is doubtful whether those who controlled humanity were ever good. Having spoken thus, Hanuman bade Bhima to turn back, but Bhima said: "I cannot leave thee until I have gazed upon thy former shape". Then Hunuman favored his brother, and assumed his vast body; he grew till he was high as the Vindhya mountain: he was like to a great golden peak with splendor equal to the sun, and he said: "I can assume even greater height and bulk by reason of mine own power".

Hunuman is however matriarchal since we learn that he gathered the Celestial lotuses for his queen by the side of a lake. In this tale we discover the ancient Indo-European myth regarding the earth's primitive races. The first age is the White Age, the second is the Red Age, the third the yellow Age, and the fourth, the present kali Yuga, is the Black or Iron Age.

Hesiod, the Greek poet, in his *Works and Days*, divided the mythical history of Greece similarly, but the order of the Ages was different; the first was the golden Age (yellow); the second was the Silver Age (white); the third was the Bronze Age (red); the fourth was the Age of heroes; and the fifth was the Age in which Hesiod lived - the Iron (black) Age. The fourth Age is evidently a late interpolation. Authorities consider that the Heroic Age did not belong to the original scheme. In the Greek Golden Age men lived like the gods under the rule of Kronos; they never suffered the ills of old age, nor lost their strength; they feasted continually, and enjoyed peace and security. The whole world prospered. When this race passed away they became beneficent spirits who watched over mankind and distributed riches! In the silver Age mankind were inferior; children reared up for a century, and died soon afterwards; sacrifice and worship was neglected. In the end Zeus, son of Kronos, destroyed the Silver Race. However although not related here the silver race was an attempt to free man. In the Bronze Age mankind sprang from the ash and they were endowed with great strength, and worked in bronze and had bronze houses: iron was unknown. But Bronze Age men were takers of life, and at length Black Death removed them all to Hades.

In *Le Cycle Mythologique Irlandais et la Mythologie Celtique*, the late Professor D'Arbois de Jubainville has shown that these Ages are also a feature of Celtic

(Irish) mythology. Their order, however, differs from those in Greek, but is of special interest to note that they are arranged in exactly the same color order as those given in the *Mahabharata*. The first Celtic Age is that of Partholon, which Jubainville identified with the silver Age (white); the second is Nemed's, the Bronze Age (red); the third is the **Tuatha de Danaan**, the Golden Age (yellow); and the fourth is the Age of the dark Milesians, called after their divine ancestor Mile, son of Beli, the god of night and death. The Irish claim descent from the Milesians. Now the interesting fact emerges here, that Professor D'Arbois de Jubainville considered that the differences between the Irish and Greek versions of the ancient doctrine were due in part to the developments that Irish legend received after the introduction of Christianity; there are however, he showed, striking affinities. The Tuatha de Danann, for instance, like the "Golden Race" of the Greeks, **became invisible**, and shared the dominion of the world with men, "sometimes coming to help them, sometimes disputing with them the pleasures of life" (*my emphasis*). This idea of the invisibles, secret Masters in the etheric and such organizations as the Great White Lodge; must refer to the White Age and the successive attempts to channel information. However as we saw in Crowley's rites, those Masters were not the gods that led impeccable lives, for Crowley was often asked for sacrifices. It is easy to see that real Masters of the age, may have purposely given out this information, to encourage men to believe that invisible Masters were ordering things, when in fact it was a mere dupe's method of making men comply with the true Masters who although secret were very much visible on Earth! These prophesies and propaganda data have it appears been put out by the diktat machine over a very long period. Just as the encyclopaedists or intellectuals preceded the French Revolution, with their ideas of 'equality, liberty and fraternity', thus giving impetus for the forthcoming planned revolution, then the idea of invisible Masters was surely taken up by many men, who must have been convinced that channeled information was indeed from the Masters, as opposed to www-com/grid. Like the early Christian annalists of Ireland, the Indian Brahmans appear to have utilized the legends, which were afloat among the people. Both in the Greek and Celtic (Irish) myths the people of the Silver Age are distinguished for their folly; however in the Indian silver or White Age the people were so perfect and holy that it was not necessary for them to perform religious ceremonies; they simply uttered the mystic word "Om".

There are many interesting points of resemblance between certain of the Irish and Indian legends. We are informed, for instance, of the Celtic St. Finnen (from Fenuisa Farsa or Fennish – the vine man that joins together and related to Magog and Noah?), who fasted like a Brahman, so to compel a pagan sage, Tuan Maccarell, to reveal the ancient history of Ireland. Some of these ancient Bardic histories are given by Graves in *The White Goddess* and in part I have quoted such as Gwion's poem, where he states he was in the Ark. This perpetual linking of Noah to Ireland and Scotland is also repeated when Tuan Mac Carell assured St. Finnen, "in the presence of witnesses", that he remembered all that happened in Ireland during the period of 1 500 years covered by his various incarnations. He states he fled to Ireland with the followers of Cesara, granddaughter of Noah to escape the flood. One of the long-lived Indian sages was named Markandeya and he gives some indication of the repeated cycles when he states that after the universe is dissolved, all Creation is renewed, and the cycle of the four Ages begins again with Krita Yuga. "A cycle of the Yugas comprises twelve thousand divine years. A full thousand of such cycles constitute a Day of Brahma". At the end of each Day of Brahma comes "Universal Destruction". Thus as I suspected the World Order has created cycles of destruction and construction, which covers the French and Russian revolutions and Two World Wars in all probability! Once again the secret priesthoods use these sort of esoteric writings in all times, to convince man that it was all inevitable and that is also the point of the prophesy and this is really very evil, for it is a method of despotic control, which was and is the mind of the arch controllers. The glorious days in the beginning I am afraid, were always tainted by the arch controllers, be they priests of Israel or Atlantis.

Markandeya goes on to say that the world grows extremely sinful at the close of the last Kali Yuga of the Day of Brahama, however is that not all part of the plan as set out in *The Protocols of Zion* discussed in the last chapter of *The Battle of The Trees* and also set forth in that prophesy of the Twelve tribes ie. *Revelations*! Drugs, sex, control of publishing and media to print all manner of lies, distractions of a hedonistic society, crime etc.; this was all predicted and moreover planned one concludes. The necessary destruction, before that World Order of the Rose and a uiversal political and religious kingdom is brought to fruition, however there will be no white age, or peace, since it is run by the very despotic Masters who have brought each cycle to its Magnetic Reversal close. As Markandeya points out, in the closing age Brahmans abstain from prayer and meditation, and men degenerate and beasts of prey increase. The earth is ravaged by fire, cows give little milk, fruit trees no longer blossom, and the world of men becomes filled wth sin and immorality. Then the earth is swept by fire and heavy rains fall until the forests and mountains are covered over by the rising flood. All the winds pass away; they are absorbed by the Lotus floating on the breast of the waters, in which the Creator sleeps; the whole Universe is a dark expanse of water. What is this but the cyclical event of a Magnetic Reversal that the MMRC case dramatizes, producing world events in repeats of past cycles that only add to the precipitation of a catastrophe in the present. Would such a cycle be inevitable, if man had developed technologies to mesh with Nature's pattern, instead of challenging it? If instead of electricity, some other form of power had been used: if man in his greed had not ransacked the Earth.

The winged or solar disc in Hittite inscriptions appeared in Nazi iconography and even as an emblem of the Royal air Force in Britain reflecting the 13 th tribe! I am sure many ex-servicemen and women in Britain, who fought Hitler in The Battle of Britain, will be dismayed that the war appears to have been a planned cycle of destruction, before construction (of a Federal European Super State) and the possibility that it was all just a tribal war, that was managed at the top by the Masters! Recent attempts by media (as controlled agents) to portray the Royal air Force in elitist terms and denigrate that, is merely the 12 tribes once again attacking the infrastructure of culture of the British that is evidently unknown to the majority and has had a large input from the 13 th tribe into its class-conscious culture. The Hittite inscriptions with winged disc emblems are interesting, since the central portion of one seems to be composed of two crescents underneath a disk, which is also divided like a crescent. Above the emblem there appears the symbol of sanctitiy, the divided oval or theta! Which was to make its appearance not only in Scientology, but also in the Finglesham buckle (*Plate 19*) and the divided oval as the two opposing pyramids as a sign of Freemasonry. In another instance of the disk, the center of the winged emblem is shown as a rosette. Whilst the World Order may seek that perfect Age of the white period and equate that with race, it is no doubt the reason why the World Order treats the Third World as its dustbin and a profit making machine, with no concern whatsoever for its abuses and encroachments.

On Target has been particularly voiciferous on the subject of British culture, raising the standards of moral debate; in the February 2001 issue [201] the following enigma that has constantly puzzled British political observers arose:

> "...Whenever one examines those forces at play both domestically or in a much wider, global context, the Jewish factor, particularly as encapsulated in the Power of *Organized*, Political, Zionist Jewry, come disproportionately into play in the pattern of names and organizations. This has its focus in the pivotal role of the State of Israel and runs in a thread through all elements of the global Power Play. Advertising and the Mass Communications Media are identifiably largely under the same influences, hence the relentless bombardment of Nazi-German, "Fascist" and holocaust themes; yet a relative dearth of any corresponding coverage of **British** heroism and the **British** wartime experience except, for example, in terms of denigration such as the *class* background of Royal Air force pilots. One cannot but be concerned at the repercussions of this situation on oridinary Jewish people who have no part in this scenario..."

The 'cuckoo' has long been in the British nest, where even the heroism of British Air Force pilots of World War II, must be tainted by this tribal war, never mind that they went up exhausted in their Spitfires day after day to fight The Battle of Britain, many giving their lives in this most secret of wars. The Masters of the twelve tribes of Israel seeking their pound of *Revelations* flesh against the 13 th tribe? Whilst the poor Jew and Briton stand in the middle, each persecuted in their own way. British culture however is not dependent on the 13 th tribe until one brings up the Empire, class system, elitist organizations and all things that emanated from the mind that believes it was superior and chosen in some odd way and forced politics and social organization in this country down that path: being 'British' unfortunately has become associated in the mind of the twelve tribes, with being thirteenth tribe. It remains to be seen whether the true spirit of the British people lies within the soul of the Air Force pilots and all those who **fought for freedom** during World War II, where the true soul of a Celtic warrior nation was embodied in Churchill's words: "Never in the history of human conflict has so much been owed to so few". I do not want to get into the political arguments of monarchy versus republican government, but unfortunately many people who identify that wrong path of elitism with British culture, are not only merely dismissing the whole philosophy of British people north and south of the Thames and London; but they play into the hands of the 12 tribe Masters who will seek to break this country, if they have not already done so. Tribal enmities run deep. Further Martin Short in his book *Inside the Brotherhood* wrote of the infiltration of Freemasonry (Jewish) into all sectors of British society including the police, the armed forces, and the law including Judges etc. *On Target* in the above edition noted that: "powerful pro-Semitic influences in the domestic corridors of Power is such that we read that the (British) Metropolitan Police Commissioner, no less, has "launched" the Anne Frank Memorial Awards, to be granted for "deeds of outstanding courage". Worse still, in an educational environment of officially sanctioned Holocaust brainwashing, the nominations are to come from children in the United Kingdom. So whatever has become of British heroes"? Well I trust here the position is clear, one might just as well fly the flag of David over Britain, or the flag of Jacob as the Panacea society suggested, indeed why not fly the Red Star of David over Europe and at least call a spade in truth a spade, rather than dupe billions of people, with some insane esoteric cycle of Ages, or destruction and construction cycles, which will only end in a Third World War, based as it is on a dramatization of the past cycles by the MMRC case.

Unfortunately too, the 'cuckoo' with its 13 th tribe "messianology", has made Britain a stronghold of Christianity and thus it was always going to be difficult to get my research past the multitude who dramatize some aspect of 13 th or 12 tribe mentality as the front cover of the Cancer Report illustrates. The fight against Feminism in the U.K. with the perception that the seeds of Feminism split the Anglican Church around the world, with objections to the consecration of women in the United Kingdom by the year 2008 on the grounds of Theology, is to deny the origins of Christianity and the fact that the male Trinity is as Robert Graves pointed out, a product of Latin grammar. The ancient Trinity even though it was a downgrade of the Holy Grail, did at least have the woman in the story: thus those who fight Feminism merely ascent to the 12 tribe mentality and the Jewish Daily Prayer, which is a disgraceful piece of sexism. No doubt that the World Order has sought to direct the militant branch of Feminism: however sexism is really a channel for the Masters and support for a World Order, based on the sexist and Zionist club of Freemasonry and the Jewish horror of the woman's power. The Feminist movement has been a great diluter of the Master's power and in my opinion has not been vociferous enough, as women all over the world are severely repressed by the tribal mentality of both thirteenth and twelve tribes. Ask any single woman and parent after divorce, about the mentality of friends who happily desert her, since they perceive she no longer has any power (without the male) and is therefore of no further *use* to them! The mind of the Masters works on a daily basis through seemingly non-causal events. Further professional women including scientists, are continually hampered by sexist attitudes of where true power lies (in the male) and female science is likely to be ignored on such basis, which I covered as a point of issue in the *Appendix to Alternative 4*.One has only to view the overtly male political line up of Ministerial Government and Brussels hierarchy, to see just how far the tribal mentality has dominated world politics (and religion) and therefore the lives of billions. The reason the Church does not woman back in the story, is that they are afraid to confront the transgression of God's will on Earth and the theft of the apples of immortality along with The Holy Grail, with the instigation of mind control c. 1 400 B.C in Crete and what Hubbard terms Inc.1.

The mind of the World Order is perpetuated through its policies and 'Think Tanks' of various organizations and the 'experts', who act as unwitting conduits for the Masters. C.H. Douglas pointed out foot and mouth disease had occurred in the U.K at various times in the past with cases numbering 99 in 1939; 160 in 1940; 264 in 1941; and 670 approx. in 1942, with another outbreak in the 1960's. One lady, a member of a family with a long hereditary experience of cattle breading in the U.K., but with no interest to serve but that of farmers, claimed not only in 1942 to have a cure, but to have demonstrated it beyond any possibility of refutation. The ministry of Agriculture was not even interested and refused reasonable facilities for a demonstration, where the policy of wholesale slaughter was followed, without even looking at a possible solution. I might compare this scenario, not only to the crisis of foot and mouth disease that broke out in Britain recently (February 2001), but also to the author's cancer research.

In reply to my research on cancer dating from 1989, the author received a letter from the Department of the NHS (National Health Service) Cancer Policy Unit, explaining how hard they were looking for answers, whilst ignoring the one I had presented for evaluation! I wrote back to say, that if ever they tire of looking for an answer, they should contact me, since at least I did have *an* answer if not *the* answer! The **hidden policy** here is that there is no acceptance of any *outside* solutions (and preferably no solutions from the inside) and definitely no solutions that threaten to reveal one tip of the iceberg, which I present in this book, which would ultimately threaten the World Order 'reality'. Outside the system is dangerous, since the future policy makers and the mattoids and stooges who run the World Order for the Masters, are picked from schools, elitist universities and institutions that would have already brainwashed them sufficiently to act as robotic conduits. Unfortunately as a female scientist and presenting female science I had a twin dramatization to fight!

The elite universities are renown for selecting individuals who will be groomed for high positions in the World Order Theatre, in return for power, protection, money and acknowledgement. The state of no cure for cancer, as was evidently the case for the (female) outsider with a possible solution to foot and mouth disease, is more the result of *policy of a philosophy*, enforced by a World Order with severe dramatizations on the subject of woman. As Douglas was to state: "It does not require much imagination to see that the type of mind which regards mass slaughter of cattle as the least troublesome way in which to deal with a curable disease is the same type of mind, which regards the mass liquidation of millions of Russian farmers as the easiest way to stamp out collective farming". Douglas was of course referring to the Russian Revolution and Bolshevism. The words are still true today. I might however apply his words to that of cancer victims and I have been sincerely amazed just how far people will go, not to print any facet of the research, even as a *possible* solution or evaluation along the lines I suggested (evaluation by *independent* scientists), or even the one line of a scientific reference! (*Appendix I*). How hard do these dramatizing individuals fight in order *not* to tell the cancer victim that there may be a *possible* solution, even to the extent that alternative press will not even release the details of a scientific reference! May God truly help their souls, for that is one hell of an overt. The posing of solutions are *rational* efforts of the rational mind to solve problems, however the mind of the World Order, does not want a solution to problems, if that affects his balance sheet of profits from human suffering, or the mystery maintained at profit The World Order evidently has its own 'solutions' to population control, in the form of destruction and mass sacrifice, followed by construction of World Orders, followed by mass destruction – working in cycles: the cancer patient represents only profit – illness is BIG BUSINESS to the Masters. The posing of solutions merely represents a threat to the Masters and all those who stand either to maintain a position of power, or make a profit from maintaining the mystery, whether that be UFO's, crop circles, cancer, politics, religion or any aspect of this story. The real story, which is the story of one's *own soul*, is evidently lacking in profit and power. However, if a man or woman wishes to stay and experience the greatest show on Earth – a Magnetic Reversal, that is up to them.

"Another technique that is well-understood" according to Andrew Rugg-Gunn, M.B., F.R.C.S., "by those who are more interested in getting what they want than in allowing others to have their own way is the technique of controlling the agenda. This technique operates in all sorts of "democratic" associations, from the state down. It is one of the chief methods of defeating democracy at source and the larger the association the easier it is to work it. It is, like all effective techniques simple; it consists simply in arranging things where the voters are asked to choose between two or more methods of attaining a certain objective and in taking care that they are not allowed to vote on the *desirability* of that objective… the choice between 'being boiled or hanged'". Whilst the author was referring to the field of medicine, which undoubtedly has come under the control philosophy of the Masters, it also applies to European Union, where the desirability of the outcome is no longer questioned or voted upon! "Control of the Agenda technique is often accompanied by the 'Trust Your Leaders' technique. All that amounts to is; Look here, leave this to us. We'll get you to where we think it is good for you to go; there just isn't time to find out whether that is where you would like to go." This Technique is often accompanied by references to the "urgency" of the situation and this has been the case with Europe and the politics of fear that have been employed - what happens if everyone else joins up to a European Federal Super State and our country is left out in the cold (trade market)! Further there is a HIDDEN AGENDA AND POLICY IN EUROPE that is not known, which makes an absolute mockery of democracy apart from truth. Switzerland and Norway are not part of Europe and neither country has suffered as a result. European Union has nothing to do with trade, but it has everything to do with POWER and the HIDDEN PHILOSOPHY which UNDERPINS AGENDA AND POLICY.

In the above reference the author gives a method for defeating the agenda: "It is necessary to discover the fundamental **policy** which is to be implemented by the **method** for which you are asked to vote, and to discuss and vote on the **policy**. **If you are not permitted to discuss and vote on policy, you can always refuse to vote at all**. Whenever you are asked to vote on anything, you should analyse the motion carefully. The first question to ask is: "**What is the result that this proposal would secure, if carried out**"? The second is: "**Do I want the result**"? The Third is: "Does this motion give me any choice concerning the result"? The fourth is: "what is the method suggested to get hat result"? The fifth is: "who will be empowered to carry out that method, and is he a person who wants the same result as I want?" *(my emphasis)*

Defeating the agenda of Europe, sex, crime, drugs and the whole gamut of World Order policy, must be aimed at **source**, by **directing questions at policy** and for this reason I sought to confront The House of Commons and British Parliament, with the questions laid out in my Petition and specifically, **who** today is making the policy in Europe and whether that policy is still governed by the secret groups who have always sought a Federal EuropeanSuper State, dating back to at least the time of the French Revolution. As I have moved on in my research, there is now another question based on this book and that question must ask whether a tribal war is being played out, manipulating politics and religion in an **agreed upon policy** of a World Order with a universal communistic political system, in tandem with a universal religion: is man merely the pawn in a chess game set up 1 400 B.C where mind control was instigated during the Religious Revolution in Crete! Removing truth and the power to vote on **real alternatives** rather than the 'boiled or hanged' alternatives, has been the foremost reason for the decline in democracy and the active part and interest taken by the electorate in politics. Man is all too willing, to pass the reigns of power to those who have hidden agendas and policies and it is up to every single citizen to question those policies which govern matters of great importance in the welfare of their country and humanity. Should the Christian also question what I say here - is it true? And was Golgotha planned as I conclude? It would seem that this is a matter of great importance to man and perhaps Christians should question their leaders on this point, although I am not sure they would obtain a truthful reply, or the documents that prove the events of the Crucifixion, which are undoubtedly locked away somewhere. What does it matter? Let the World Order control this section of the universe, for it is they who will experience the Magnetic Reversal and when the sun as an ageing star, finally gives out, then they will play their games of control in the dark. It is only important, to find one's own exit out.

There is a long Biblical history on the tribal wars between Israel and Judah, which throughout history has remained a hidden agenda dictating policy in various countries. After Solomon died in biblical history the kingdom of his son Rehoboam was restricted to Judah, Benjamin, Moab and Edom. Oddly enough in *Solomon's song vi, 4* only "ten tribes" of Israel are mentioned ruled over by Jeroboam; however there were continual religious wars between Rehoboam and Jeroboam (*Chronicles xii, 15*) and what is clear is that there was not only the persistence of secret priesthoods in directing secret politics, but the continual dispute over whether these priesthoods were acting as God or claiming to be God, in their arrogant assumption that they were chosen through their knowledge, to direct mankind. Jeroboam who established the religion of the Canaanites: "made gods and molten images" and was condemned by the prophet Elijah who declared: "The Lord shall smite Israel, as a reed is shaken in the water; and he shall root up Israel, as a reed is shaken in the water; and he shall root up Israel out of this good land, which he gave to their fathers, and shall scatter them beyond the river, because they have made their groves, provoking the Lord to anger. And he shall give Israel up because of the sins of Heroboam, who did sin and who made Israel to sin" (*I Kings XIV, 1-20*). The mention of the word "grove" is the minimal amount of information that could have been left after editing, to make any sense of the condemnation. However the "grove" refers to the secret priesthoods, who like the Essenes existed in communities covered by high hedges to keep prying eyes out. These secret communities invariably employed the Tree Alphabet and the Beth-Luis-Nion alphabet, which I used in *The Battle of The Trees* to decode many mysteries attached to the Holy Grail. These alphabets brought the world the art of secrecy and uniformity of purpose in these secret Jewish priesthoods, where the religious mysteries were locked into the alphabets, only understood by the priests as humanity forgot the story of what had happened.

If the tribes of Israel continually utilized these secret priesthoods and the hidden science and alphabets, to gain power and control, then the tribe of Judah was no better, for Rehoboam similarly: "did evil in the sight of the Lord"; his subjects "also built them high places and images and groves on every hill, and under every green tree" (*I Kings XIV, 21-3*). Once again this not only refers to the secret alphabets and religious mysteries, but also the magnetic energies of the hidden science are also implied with the reference to "hill", which the Druids as 13 th tribe and Judah utilized in Britain. Further as I covered in *The Battle of The Trees*, Jesus was tutored in these mysteries and the Tree Alphabet as a Jewish priest, or Druid I have concluded for the 13 th tribe; whom he betrayed in favor of the 12 tribes of Israel, causing The Templars to spit on the cross and refer to Jesus as "the thief on the cross". This was a reference to the stolen genealogies of the Magdalene. It was the thirteenth tribe of Judah, which brought the world the science of "messianology" and more specifically the Rosicrucian's at Rose-Croix and Kadosch Knight level in ascent from the Druids. The arrogance of secret groups and specifically Freemasonry in their assumption of god-like powers and the committal of the ultimate sin of *claiming to be God* was evidently the sin of Rehoboam who: "Humbled himself, the wrath of the Lord then turned from him, that he would not destroy him altogether: and also in Judah things went well" (2 *Chronicles xii, 1-12*) The idea of "humbling" presumably covers the abstinence of use of the hidden science as Black Cabalistic science utilized in prophecy and miracles waithin secret groups and priesthoods, to control religion and politics in order to direct the course of humanity. The tribal conflicts of Judah and Israel are well documented in *The Bible* (I *Kings xv, 25-6; 2 Chronicles xiv, 1-6; I Kings, xv 6-7, 8-9, 20-2; I Kings xvi 9-10, 5-8, 21-2; 2 Chronicles xviii, 1-2; 2 Chronicles xxii, 10-12; 2 Chronicles xxiii 1-17*). Whilst man believes that such tribal conflicts are over and long gone, that it would seem is not the case, as this very Jewish tribal conflict and its squabbles over the Holy Grail and the woman, have spilled out onto the Earth's stage, both groups having written the 'script' for all humanity to follow.

The appearance of the cherub in Hubbard's Inc. 1, which I equate with the Religious Revolution in Crete in the Bronze Age, was mentioned in the first chapter of *Ezekiel* and clearly a calendar beast. There are four parts which represent the 'four New Years' of Jewish tradition: Lion for spring; Eagle for summer; man for autumn, the principle New Year; and ox for the winter, the Judean ploughing season. *Ezekiel* identifies this cherub with a fiery wheel, which is the wheel of the solar year, perhaps so plainly and covertly displayed in London, as a Ferris wheel or 'The London Eye' of the Illuminati. Moreover each cherub of the four stations of the year is a wheel of the Solar God of fire (Hermes) and his chariot, which as another archetypal symbol was displayed in Hubbard's Inc. 1. The appearance of the cherubs to *Ezekiel* was summarized as their work as it were, was as a wheel in the middle of a wheel and has become proverbial for its unintelligibility, but it does make calendar sense. Each wheel of God's chariot is the annual cycle, or wheel, of the four seasons; and the chariot's arrival inaugurated a cycle, or wheel, of four years. Every year, in fact, wheels within a four-year wheel, from the beginning to the end of time: and the Eternal Charioteer is the God of Israel! The color of the cherubim was Apollonian amber, as the man, they served. The cherubs could be ministers of Hyperborean Apollo, the sun god whose sacred jewel was amber and it was this God that was honored among the Druids and the 13 th tribe of Judah. Amber also reflected the color of honey, the product of the slave drones and must reflect the obsession of the Illuminati (and Rosicrucian's who took over Knossos), with the idea of ant heaps and bee- hives, controlled by that one signal from the top! You may remember not only the Queen on her hive and mountain in iconographic seals of the Late Minoan period after the Religious Revolution, but the appearance of the omphalos the navel of the world with its bee relief, in Britain and in Greece (*The Battle of The Trees*). Further icons from Knossos, showed men with their hands to the third eye (of illumination) and the appearance of the rosette, has to form the basis of the conclusion that the group or very probably the 13 th tribe who overran Knossos and took the Holy Grail, was the phallic bull-Minos cult, who would in ascendancy form the Rosicrucian's and Illuminati with their political and religious goal of a Universal Kingdom or World Order. This group however may have long held aspirations of total domination and control, since in the Paleolithic caves of France were found the coral, magnetic iron ore and the curious 'umbrella' drawings. Thus whilst both groups had some knowledge of Grid properties in their cabalistic practices, it was not until they took over the knowledge at Knossos, did they realize the full potential of channeling Grid holographics and past events, thus giving them the power of prophesy of future events.

Each golden spoke of the wheel significantly ended in the leg of a calf and the golden calf was the sacred beast of the god, who according to King Jeroboam had brought Israel out of Egypt. That the sun wheel has implications to the Grid is clear, as it is recorded that a student who recognized the meaning of harshmal (amber – 'hasmal' is modern Hebrew for electricity, which as a word is derived from the Greek word for amber) and discussed it imprudently was blasted by lightening (*Haggada, 13,b*). For this reason according to the Mishnah, the Maaseh Merkabah ('work of the chariot') might not be taught to anyone unless he were not only wise, but able to deduce knowledge through wisdom ('gnosis') of his own and no one else might be present during the teaching and further: "he who speaks of the things which are before, behind, above and below, it were better that he had never been born". Thus a warning, to keep away from the secrets hidden in the Merkabah and presumably concerning the worlds and cycles that have gone before, the methods of channeling the Grid and the whole gamut of secret politics and religion! It was stated that in the "fullness of time Ezekiel will come again and unlock for Israel the chambers of the Merkabah" (*Cant. Rabbah, I, 4*) and thus the Grid holographics of the past. The belief that the exposition of the Merkabah mystery might cause Jehovah to appear evidently meant the end of times. However, it seems rather pertinent to me at least that we do lay these matters in the open, since as Dr. Becker (twice a Nobel Prize nominee) stated a Magnetic Reversal has already started! Which might just account for the bizarre and erratic weather experienced worldwide. Thus it might be pertinent to forget about tribal wars and concentrate on the karma (wrongs of this life and past lives) to be paid as the necessary first stage of moving out past the Grid and trap.

The cherub with the turning wheel guards the Paradise of Celtic legend, for according to *Genesis II, 24*, cherubs were stationed at the east Gate of Eden and were armed with: "the whirling sword of Jehovah" – the one with which according to *Isaiah (xxvii, 1)* Jehovah killed the Dragon. The paradise of Ezekiel's vision is a well –watered garden at the base of a hill, significantly enough and which may imply Judah. The Seraphs, or 'fiery serpent's' associated with cherubs in their guardian duties, are another way of expressing the sacred spirals carved as a warning on the gate of the *sacred enclosure or grove* and the cherubs distinguished separately are according to Graves likely to have been swastikas, or fire wheels: and the appearance of the archetypal trieskelion or swastika in the Late Minoan period or Religious Revolution in Crete was to identify not only the 13 th tribe of Judah, but also provides us with some background to Hitler and Hubbard's Inc.1 which he associated with mind control. That the cherubim should be viewed in the experience of regression into the Inc. 1 event of Hubbard's O.T. levels, seems along with the other archetypes of horn (gates of horn and the abode of the dead and as Bull-Minos of the phallic cult that took over Knossos and The Holy Grail); chariot (as the god of Hermes) as totally logical in terms of mind control, which the incident was perceived as; where the arch controller was Xenu. The hotch potch of archetypal symbols viewed in Inc. 1 is not as has been supposed, for it is a story where the equivalent OT levels were taken, presumably by the 13 th tribe and the woman was fought. No doubt the 12 tribes or another priesthood hoping to obliterate the 13 th tribe achieved the final sack of Knossos. However there is no doubt, that not only has the Holy Grail been used against its purpose of freeing humanity, but it has long since been locked up in the tomb, with a series of male Messiahs and the god of Hermes. The "new college of magic" instigated by Jesus was evidently the ability of the Masters to utilize the UVG 120 sphere or crystal to predict future events and prophecy with the God of the *Revelations* mystery sitting in power over the "crystal" or Grid, indicating triumph of the twelve tribes. The curious thong-wrapped stones from Crete show the knowledge that was obtained, in Crete during the Religious Revolution, was indeed knowledge of the Grid. Thus the secret Jewish priesthoods, whether from the twelve tribes or the thirteenth tribe, through the various secret groups of Freemasonry, the Bildbergers and the whole plethora or red, 'divine' men who comprise the secret government of the world, were able to covertly manipulate both religion and politics on this basis that they were God and the irony of it is, that they dismissed that there was indeed a higher source: the fatal flaw in both groups was to deny that higher and true source from whence The Holy Grail issued.

Ezekiel's king was Zedekiah of Judah a descendent of Solomon and it would seem that he too committed the same crime as the King of Tyre, which was the ultimate sin of claiming to be God, which must not only refer to the misuse of the hidden science and Grid holographics, but the personal flawed characteristics of ego, pride, arrogance and vice in the persuit of personal power and wealth, with the dismissal of a higher source. Zedekiah did not head the warning laid down and died blind and in chains as the last king of Judah. It may well be, that Judah then decided to reframe its power pyramidal apex, by utilizing the tiered structure of the Brotherhood or early Masonic groups, where the ruling apex was a Theocracy or initiated priesthood, presumably with both political and religious aspirations as is the case of the Knight Kadosch in the Rosicrucian's. The King of Tyre and presumably a twelve- tribe society were then also wiped out fulfilling a prophecy naturally! However it seems that the resulting Theocracy of the 13 th tribe and the organization of political Zionism which forms the aspirations of Israel, still have not learnt their lesson of claiming to be God and writing the eternal 'scripts' for humanity to follow in the wake of the "chosen ones", whose claim is based on the withholding of knowledge from humanity.

Fig. 34 illustrated a Cretan seal from Mochlos of the Middle Minoan III period, which must be post Religious Revolution and shows an octopus, sun and moon symbols, two dolphins and the fertility bough; however I also perceive a system of circles or wheels. There are four large and two small wheels and the large four wheels must refer to the Ages of the World; which implies that the goal of the World Order was incorporated within the prophecy of *Ezekiel* ultimately inclusive of the manipulation of cycles of destruction and construction in world wars and revolutions. The four calendar beasts of Ezekiel's vision   included man, lion, eagle and ox; however the original four beasts of the Knossos calendar that ruled the entire year were the Bull, Lion, Serpent and Eagle. *Ezekiel* specifically kept the woman out of the story, by substituting man. The two smaller circles one suspects are the solar kings or two holy Messiah's who would fullfil the *Ezekiel* vision and if one was Jesus, then we await the second cycle of the science of 'messianology' as a very thirteenth tribe cycle. In my final conclusion I must on the basis of the accumulative evidence point to the 13 th tribe as the Cabal that stole the Holy Grail, since here in the seal there is every indication of the link to *Ezekiel* and thus the 13 th tribe.

Returning to Ezekiel's vision and the reference to "ring" and "wheel" symbols. He saw: "one wheel upon the earth by the living creatures, with his four faces. The appearance of the wheels and their work was like unto their appearance and their work was as it were a wheel in the middle of a wheel...As for their rings, they were so high that they were dreadful; and their rings were full of eyes round about them four. And when the living creatures went, the wheels went by them; and when the living creatures were lifted up from the earth, the wheels were lifted up. Whithersoever the spirit was to go, they went, thither was their spirit to go; and the wheels were lifted up over against them; for the spirit of the living creature was in the wheels" (as the soul of the Egyptian god was in the sun disk or sun egg): "**And the likeness of the firmament upon the heads of the living creature was as the color of terrible crystal, stretched forth over their heads above**...And when they went I heard the noise of their wings, like the noise of great waters, as the voice of the almighty, the voice of speech, as the noise of an host; when they stood they let down their wings.." (*Ezekiel, I, 15-28)* I have strongly emphasized part of this quotation, since obviously here there is the origin of Hermetic philosophy or 'as above, so below' and this clearly refers in my opinion to the control of the UVG120 sphere on man below. Putting together the decoding of this seal, with the "rings" or "wheels" of Ezekiel's vision, the Cretan thong-wrapped stones, the Illuminatus eye of the dolphin, the octopus with its arms outstretched over the Earth and the rosette with previous evidence in this book; then quite clearly here we have the start of a **system of mind control** and the goal of a **universal political and religious kingdom** in the form of the **Rosicrucian's and Illuminati**. This type of World Order, with a universal political kingdom based on world socialism or communism, allied to a Rosicrucian goal of a universal religion is clearly displayed on the reverse of the One Dollar note from America and is also displayed on the floor of the Summer Smoking Room from Cardiff castle Wales, U.K. the question becomes, whether that is a goal of the twelve tribes of Israel *and* the thirteenth tribe, or whether that goal is that of the thirteenth tribe alone i.e. Judah. There is the possibility that whilst in the lower echelons of secret groups, there may be a pre-determined dichotomy and apparency of battle between the two groups, in the highest echelon and known only to a handful of men, there is every intention of combining both in the aims of Israel and Judah, fulfilling the messianic dream and the Feast of Tabernacles of the eventual triumph of the Jews irrespective of tribe. Ah yes, after all the cycles of destruction and construction, they will have given man the Holy Grail! Whether that hope lies in Scientology is anyone's guess, however I cannot see any other group on the Earth's stage that holds the mysteries.

Another description of the cherubs' states: "Their whole body, and their backs, and their hands, and their wings, and the wheels, were full of eyes (stars?) About, even the wheels that they four had. As for the wheels, it was cried unto them in my hearing, O wheel!" – or, according to a marginal rendering, "they were called in my hearing, wheel, or Gilgal," i.e. move round…"And the cherubim's were lifted up." (*Ezekiel, x, 11-5*). It seems then that channeling had produced the idea that the god was within the wheel or UVG120 sphere or crystal and this notion also appears again in *Revelations*, where God has crystal laid at His feet. The original Semitic belief, which was overlayed at Knossos, was that the deity was incorporated within the stone pillar. The Assyrians believed evidently much the same thing and saw a feather-robed figure, which the wheels enclosed. His trident-headed arrow resembles, as has been suggested, a lightening symbol. This represents some use of the Grid in Cabalistic ritual, which Moses apparently was cognizant of, when he caused thundering and lightening on Mount Sinai, when producing the *Ten Commandments*; after which he descended the Mountain his face being horribly burnt, which implied some radiation effect. However importantly this sign of lightening was also meant to convey the idea of God's word. Ezekiel's references are suggestive in this connection. When the cherubs "ran and returned" they had "the appearance of a flash of lightening", and "the noise of their wings" resembled "the noise of great waters", which must obliquely refer to the Flood and God's wrath at man's wickedness, if not channeled information on past events.

In the Indian epic, the *Mahabharata*, the revolving ring or wheel protects the Soma or ambrosia of the gods, on which their existence depends! Thus the elixir or knowledge of The Holy Grail and the Grid and its Akashic Record not only provided a profitable little earner for the priesthood, but it aided them to control politics and religion, through the power of prophesy. This was an easy one to run – the priesthood arranges for one of its agents to make a prophecy regarding some future event that the priesthood were arranging within their cycles and when the event happens, they pointed to the prophesy and put it down to God's will! There is an inevitability that is set up wherebye people accept the pre-determined event! In the Indian epic, the eagle giant Garuda sets forth to steal the soma or the elixir of the Grail and the gods, fully armed, gather round to protect their life-giving drink. Garuda approaches: "darkening the worlds by the dust raised by the hurricane of his wings". The celestials: "overwhelmed by the dust", swoon away. Garuda afterwards assumes a fiery shape, then looks: "like masses of black clouds", and in the end its body becomes golden and bright "as the rays of the sun". The Soma is protected by fire, which the bird quenches after: "drinking in many rivers" with the numerous mouths it has assumed. Then Garuda finds that right above the Soma is: "a wheel of steel, keen edged, and sharp as a razor, revolving incessantly. That fierce instrument, of the luster of the blazing sun and of terrible form, was devised by the gods for cutting to pieces all robbers of the Soma". The Persian god Ahura Mazda hovers above the king in sculptured representations of that high dignitary, enclosed in a winged wheel, or disk, like Ashur, grasping a ring in one hand, the other being lifted up as if blessing those who adore him! Shamash, the Babylonian sun god; Ishtar, the goddess of heaven; and other Babylonian deities carried rings as the Egyptian gods carried the ankh, the symbol of liFe. Shamash was also depicted sitting on his throne in a pillar-supported pavilion, in front of which is a sun wheel. **A star symbol** and threefold rippling "water rays" form the spokes of the wheel. All this sounds very Judah, very thirteenth tribe, with Hermes as baetyllic pillar incorporating twin Kings and Goddess as the three-fold ancient Trinity. However is this not also the Star of David and the Jewish national flag!

In Hittite inscriptions there are interesting winged emblems; the central portion of one seems to be composed of two crescents underneath a disk (which is also divided like a crescent). Above the emblem there appear the symbol of sanctity (the divided oval or the theta sign) and the hieroglyph, which Professor Sayce interprets as the name of the god Sandes. In another instance the center of the winged emblem may be seen to be a *rosette*. Above, two dots follow the name

Sandes, and a human arm bent in adoration is by the side. Professor Garstang studied these symbolisms and significantly enough studied further inscriptions in rocky points or hilltops and 'Sanes' or Sanda was identical with Sandon of Tarsus, who links with the Babylonian Tammuz. Sandon's animal significantly was the lion, and he also carried the **double axe**. Thus here we have more evidence for the beliefs of the Cabal that took over Knossos overlaying the knowledge of the Holy Grail and manipulating the archetypal symbols in the re-positioning era. Significantly too, bearing in mind the appearance of Hercules at Cardiff Castle in the tiled murals, which I believed together with the floor design was representative of the history of Scottish Rite Freemasonry or Rosicrucianism, then Sandon links to Hercules and Melkarth. All the younger gods, who displaced the elder gods as one year displaced another, were deities of fertility, battle, lightening, fire, and the sun. In Scotland it was believed that on the morning of May Day (Beltane) the rising sun revolved three times. This signified the old Trinity, which included Goddess or the woman in the story and the younger god was a spring sun god and fire god. Great bonfires were lit to strengthen him, or as a ceremony of riddance, the old year was burned out. Indeed the British without a clue why, lit bonfires or beacons on government instigation (policy!) at the start of the Millennium! Such arrogance of deceit in the blatant display of 13 th tribe celebrations unbeknown to the British is astounding even by secret group standards: not to be outdone by New York in the New Year's Eve or millennium (2 000) celebrations, with their Illuminatus Crystal!

Well now that we have decided Britain's history, can songs like 'Land of Hope and Glory' 'Rule Brittania' etc., be restored along with that good old nationalistic bash in the Last night of the Proms? Let the Air Force keep their solar disc and wings, since you can take the mystery out of the history, but you can't take history out of the mystery. You cannot deny a people its cultural history on the basis of a tribal war of two tribal factions or the messianic dream of the Jews, since the history of a nation is an anchor point (*The Cancer Report*). If you remove anchor points you destabilize individuals and nations and without replacing that anchor point by anything other that miles of rules and regulations from Brussels, I am afraid it will only result in a country loosing its 'hearth'. The Greeks admire their history along with the French and all other nations, but Britain is being unfairly singled out, presumably for retribution as victim to a World Order with Israel and the Twelve Tribes and the thirteenth tribe at its core. There is also the possibility, that both the tribes at the very top of their secret group power structure not only **work in unison** but also are willing to sacrifice Britain, just as the Jews were sacrificed in the Holocaust.Whilst the dramatizing thirteenth tribe die-hards in Britain hold up the thirteenth tribe elitist Institutions as the soul of the country, they merely sell the country down the river of the muddy past. The future of Britain lies in understanding its history and carving out a new direction, where all regardless of race colour or birth, can achieve. If man is to achieve, then the 'dumbing down' of the masses must cease, civilization will only be achieved by way of education and spiritual awareness. No one said you could not re-write the 'script' and like the Phoenix be RE-BORN! And perhaps Britain will be the first to send out that message to the world, which would undoubtedly clear her international karma of the past. If personal karma is little understood, then International karma is hardly understood at all, but it is very important.

Let us take the *Ten Commandments* in *The Bible*, which really refer to the reduction of survival of others. "Thou shall not kill" and if one transgresses that Law, then one imprints the action very strongly on another's holographic memory bank. However as we have seen the Grid or morphogenetic bioplasma stores any *changes in the survival of matter* and thus the event will be recorded there. Whether there is such a thing as Hubbard's 'Reactive Mind', or whether that mind is just the Universal Mind or vast holographic computer banks of the Grid, which control the individual on the basis of his or her *past* holographics, when the individual no longer uses his or her mind as a rational being is unsure, however what is certain, is that those holographics are connected with the holograpahics of others. A person tries to leave through the Grid and is prevented in the 'life review', if they confront holographics of their past which cause the spirit as pure conscience to 'stick' on the confusion of energy created. *They elect to come back* and sort out the confusion they created, however the problem is, you have to find THE EXACT SOUL THAT YOU HARMED and undo the confusion. A man or woman who is too proud and arrogant to go to the person he or she has harmed and apologize and ask what he or she can do, to make that harm turn to good purpose (which must rest on increasing the survival of the other(s) in proportion to the harm or lack of survival created) is a fool: for in many hundreds or even thousands of years he or she will search for that soul, to make good the harm and that is indeed very time consuming if one makes a habit of reducing the survival of others! The man or woman who repeats this karma on an international scale by creating wars or lies, has reduced survival to such a degree that they have no hope of undoing all the confusion created in the holographics of all those involved and thus the only chance they have of getting past the Grid, is to do something highly survival for a very large number of people. This is the problem of the MMRC case, he is stuck simply because he cannot create that amount of survival, because he is a fixture of non-survival in virtually everyone's holographic banks! The mind of the MMRC case is stuck up there in www-com/grid controlling Theatre Earth, purely in terms of the survival of the matter (material wealth and power). You will never get the MMRC case to recognize that he or she has harmed, simply because if they admitted they were wrong, they would have to confront the entirety of their own memory banks and that would be too much loss or non-survival. Lies are permitted, since truth is a solution they cannot confront, as truth in its highest order is ULTIMATE REALITY. A Magnetic Reversal is merely part of the cycles and wheels of Ezekiel that the MMRC case created to explain away his own abberation.

EXISTING POLICY

The Holy Grail brought to Earth c. 10 000 B.C was meant for all, it contained the message of Re-incarnation and knowledge of the Grid and a cosmology, which was to enable man to be released from the trap. There was no policy attached, no connection to tribes of Israel, kingship or secret groups and the mysteries of the equivalent O.T. levels were given freely in Crete. It would appear that the Bull-Minos cult, which I relate to the Druids (or their precursors as some Egyptian priesthood) and the 13 th tribe of Judah took over the knowledge in a Religious Revolution and then attempted to write the woman out of the story. The final sack of Knossos may have been conducted by patriarchal tribes who wished to wipe out the 13 th tribe who had built up the Minoan Civilization: but at the base of that civilization was not the tribes of Israel but the Holy Grail that had been sequestered: the message of Re-incarnation was utilized by Kingship and the secret groups, whilst installing the idea of total death on the populous. Today in Freemasonry the third degree ritual requires the candidate to act the part of Hiram Abiff. He is symbolically slain, then brought to life again. Grand Lodge denies this is a resurrection rite in any sense, yet many Masonic writers claim it is. ; J.S.M. Ward states that Adonis is the true model for Hiram Abiff. Mackey a respected Masonic scholar stated:

> "Take for instance, the Hiramic legend of the third degree. Of what importance is it to the disciple of Masonry whether it is true or false? All he wants to know is its internal significance; and when he learns that it is intended to illustrate the doctrine of the *immortality of the soul*, he is content with that interpretation" (*Author's emphasis*).

Martin Short in his book *Inside the Brotherhood* stated: "If, despite what Grand Lodge is now saying, Freemasonry does have a doctrine dealing with the soul's immortality, and illustrated by a resurrection rite, this would disturb Christians who hold that only belief in Christ's resurrection can bring immortality". However what Christians do not realize, is that the very basis of Christianity lies within the earliest religious mysteries, which not only sought to hide the The Holy Grail, but also the role of the woman. Successive plans of the eternal "wheels" that have moved politics and religion on this planet, have made a very complex story indeed of a message sent to Earth and meant for all. Freemasonry whilst evidently hiding the role of the woman, within in its secret degrees, where only those at the top realize the true significance, has a policy of not allowing women into the Brotherhood and yet immortalizes the Goddess in their rites, which only portrays that they never really had any true reality on this story or the knowledge; otherwise they would realize that they can't present the Holy Grail as their gift to mankind, be that in the form of Christianity or Scientology, whilst hoping to skip over the last 10 000 years as a justification for their cause, which has more to do with the cause of Israel than the cause of humanity.

The connection of Hiramic legend to Solomon in Freemasonry probably stems from the fact that Solomon learnt his secrets from Byblos, Adonis, the god of Byblos, who was often shown in the company of the horned Moon-goddess Isis, or Hathor, or Astartate; once again harking back to the Bull-Minos cult and Crete. It seems the crime of stealing the Grail never rested easy with Israel or Judah and it was hoped perhaps one day to return the knowledge to mankind, presumably at the inevitable price and within an Illuminatus organization that would allow them to retain control and power over it. The Jews knew Byblos as Gebal and it was the Byblians who helped Solomon to build his Temple. This is mentioned in *I Kings, v, 18*, although in the Authorized Version 'the men of Gebal' is purposefully mistranslated as 'stone quarters': "And Solomon's builders and Hiram's builders did hew the stones, and the men of Gebal; so they prepared timber and stones to build the house". The reason for the mistranslation of 'Gebal' which means 'mountain height', must be the possibility of detection of the 13 th tribe of Judah, who used mountains as places of electro-magnetic activity to conduct their rites: however as I have pointed out, if Solomon obtained his knowledge from Judah, then they were the Cabal who stole the Holy Grail. The wisdom of Byblos whilst viewed as Jewish wisdom, with Byblos giving rise to the Greek word for 'book' (and the English word Bible); was derived from Spiritual intervention. Byblos was compared by that sexist prophet *Ezekiel*, with Hiram's Tyre (*Ezekiel, xxvii, 8-9*) and Tyre significantly enough was an early Cretan trading center. It was from the early Cretans that the tribes of Israel took their knowledge. Solomon certainly built his temple in the Aegean style, closely resembling that of the Great Goddess at Hierapolis, described by Lucian in his *De Dea Syria*. Interestingly also there was a Danaan colony close to Byblos, dating from the fourteenth century B.C., which roughly co-incides with the Religious Revolution in Crete: the Danaans I assume were none other than the tribe of Judah who wandered down from the Black Sea region and into Greece in the Peloponnese presumably learning the secrets of the Grail, which were once given freely; and eventually this tribe as the Tuatha de Danaan migrated to the Brtish Isles. There is no doubt that the history of the Jews is complex, however the Calebites interpreted 'Adam' as the Semitic word Edom ('red') and the original hero at Hebron was the Danaan Adanos or Adamas or Admastos, 'the unconquerable', or the 'Inexorable', a Homeric epithet of Hades, **borrowed from the Death Goddess his mother**. This borrowing aspect of the Jews, as will be noted from the appearance of the 'red men' in the Prince fresco at Knossos, was the desire to take anything of value in terms of power that could be used by them to further their goal of total domination of man and the Earth. Such domination rests upon the psychological history prior to a Magnetic

Reversal, where total domination through despotic kinghood was the policy of the day and the antediluvian monarchs: despite the message of The Holy Grail, those who had always retained power, just could not let that go: after all it is probable that they have retained such power on Earth through numerous cycles, to the extent where it has become in a psychological sense obsessive. The Holy Grail inexorably became mixed with the history of the Jews, where every propaganda line has sought to eradicate the woman from the story.

Plate 22 shows what is probably an early Antelope King, which illustrates the concept of control and kingship prior to the emergence of The Holy Grail. The antlers or tines in all probablility represented the Black Cabala and the Tree of Life. Importantly the idea of semen or the bodyline as the progenitor of the tribe is illustrated, along with the implied obsession with tribal bloodlines. Such ideas of purity of the blood by inter-tribal marriage and divine kingship, are deeply imbedded in the psyche of the priesthood of the Jews and were to surface as the Aryan super race programme in their worst enemies the Nazi's, in what appears to have been a tribal war of 12 and 13; although as I have suggested, this war may have been orchestrated by a unity at the top, in order to create a pre-determined outcome of World War II and the destruction of Europe, paving the way for a World Order and a Federalist Super State of Europe. This idea of tribal bloodlines was to be imprinted on The Holy Grail and became the cup or material wealth and power (Rex mundi) that was to be had from the elixir (knowledge). The message of Re-incarnation was transferred to Kingship and only kings and the initiates of secret groups would possess the power of resurrection; portrayed in Christianity as the resurrection of Jesus (as a solar king) and the Second Coming.

The knowledge of the Grid meant to free humanity, was bound up with Black Cabalistic practice whereby the secret groups or initiates sought past Grid holographics, believing they were in contact with past Masters or tribe progenitors as spirits. The Grid and the science I produce here, was simply not understood. Machpelah was an oracular cave cut from rock and was the sepulcher of Abraham; Caleb also went there, to consult presumably with the spirits or progenitors of the race. The editor of *Genesis*, describes it as the sepulcher of Jacob (*Genesis xxiii, 19; xxv, 9; l, 13*) and in *Genesis xxxv, 29*, it is implied that Isaac was also buried there. This statement regarding Jacob is contradicted in *Genesis L, 11*, where it is said that he was buried in Abel-Mizraim. Moreover, Isaac originally lived at Beer-Lahai-Roi (*Genesis xxiv, 62; xxv, 11*) which means 'the well of the Antelope's Jawbone' and if Isaac was a Boibalos, or Antelope King, his prophetic jawbone, like the singing head of Bran in Celtic legend, seems to indicate some oracular method of consulting the spirit of this ancestor, presumably by Cabalistic ritual. Jaw bones were the rule in oracular shrines and were usually stored there, with the hero's naval string or umbilical cord, which would give its name to the well; there was a sacred cave nearby, which eventually became a Christian chapel, just as I discovered a Christian chapel exists near the cave of Zeus in Crete. It is perhaps little wonder that man has been continually trapped in the Magnetic cycles, where the kings would in each cycle through their Black Cabalistic practice consult the Grid and what was believed to be actual spirits, when in fact they were merely picking up past holograms of event and thought, which dictated policy or the 'script' in every cycle!

Jesus was held to have fulfilled the prophecy of the *110 th Psalm*: "Jehovah has sworn and will not repent; thou art a priest forever after the order of Melchizedek". This is enlarged upon in St. paul's Epistle to the Hebrews. Melchizedek (*Genesis xiv, 18-20*) was the sacred iking of Salem who welcomed Abraham to Canaan ('Abraham' in this sense being the far-travelled tribe that came down into Palestine from Armenia at the close of the third Millennium B.C.) and who 'had neither father nor mother'. Salem is generally taken to mean Jerusalem and was also a priest to the Supreme God. There is a record in the Talmud of a heretical sect of Jews, called Melchizedekians, who frequented Hebron to worship the body and probably consult the spirit of Adam. Thus not only can we assum that Cabalistic ritual was utilized, but that Jesus is indicated as an Adomite and an initiate of a priesthood; further in this particular priesthood it appears that it is necessary to show divinity by having no father or mother in the biological sense. Adam had no father or mother; Moses was a foundling and therefore had no visible father or mother; and Jesus in his alleged miraculous virgin birth had no mother and therefore no father. Certainly it is odd, that Hubbard tried very hard to write his own parents out of the story and the COS tried to ban Russell Miller's autobiography of Hubbard, which details the long-suffering nature of his parents and replace that in official COS data, with a parallel to the story of the precocious Jesus. Thus there is an attempt in Biblical texts to identify Melchizedek's kingship with that of Adam and it was the 'red men' or Adomites of the 13 th tribe who stole the Holy Grail from Crete, along with healing knowledge. The Calebites as Adomites was to connect with the original hero at Hebron as Danaan or Adamos and it was this root that 'borrowed' from the goddess his mother, just as Jesus would utilize the Greek root of the Magdalene and her knowledge, where I claim the genealogies were also stolen. Melchizedek's lack of a mother not only mirrors the story of Moses, but also of Cretan Zeus and Jesus, where in each case the boy is removed from his mother as soon as he is born and he passes under the care of tutors. This is a transitional stage from matriarchy to patriarchy and as a stage is inherent in the icons from Knossos during the Religious Revolution, which show a transition from matriarchy to patriarchy and the eradication of the woman.

321

Cretan Zeus as the murals at Cardiff Castle show, was suckled by the goat Amalthea, thus showing the absence of the mother. This certainly had implications within the secret groups, who only ever portrayed one half of the story to the initiate and the other side of the story before my research, has never been heard; for which reason women are not allowed to enter Freemasonry, which must be the only sexist club to survive equal opportunity legislation, by reason of the fact that a large overt against the woman is hidden within its rituals: further I suspect that homosexuality is inherent in some form at the top as part of the Hermetic principle and no doubt a woman would find that and the control of humanity unacceptable. An all male priesthood is responsible for initiation, thus anyone who is destined to become the visible oracular head or jawbone of the World Order is brainwashed into the mind of the Masters and such indoctrination forms the policy of the World Order – as a case of 'like begets like'. In the Eleusian mysteries the Divine Child was carried by Shepherds, not by his mother or nurse and this was evident in the paintings of Poussin discussed in *The Battle of The Trees*.

In the Sethian heresy given in Ethiopian *Legends of our Lady Mary*, translated by Bridge, the Gnostic theory gives Hannah (Danaan or Anna?) as the mother of the virgin Mary, who was one of a triad of sisters, of which the other two were another Mary and Sophia (wisdom). There were also three Mary's who constantly surrounded Jesus and whence the phrase 'Three Hail Mary's' originates? According to Ethiopian legend the Virgin first came down into the body of Seth, 'shinning like a white pearl'; this must give some background to the 'Missionary Woman' in the Paleolithic cave paintings, with her string of pearls. The Virgin it is claimed successively: "entered Enos, Cainan…Jared, Enoch, Methuselah, Hamech, Noah …Abraham, Isaac, Jacob…David, Solomon and Joachim". What is this, but the idea of divine kingship repeating the old idea of the *semen* creating the line of the race or tribe, now superimposed with the stolen knowledge of the Holy Grail with its message of Re-incarnation whereby the re-incarnated spirit is now responsible for the spiritual line! Thus the Jews used the Holy Grail for themselves, to create these stories and passed it off to mankind as the mark of a "chosen race"! The white pearl and the white dove became equated and was considered the Spirit of Life; which probably accounts for the Cabalistic Tree of Life found at Knossos, with the epiphany of the dove in its branch or apex. "The white pearl was mentioned for its purity and the white bird because Mary's soul existed aforetime with the Ancient of Days…Thus bird and pearl are alike and equal: from the body of Mary, the pearl, the white bird of the Spirit then entered into Jesus at the Baptism".

The entire policy of the world has been virtually governed by the desire of the Jews to place the Holy Grail, into their own history, claiming the gift for themselves; that has certainly meant, that the patriarchal priests and secret groups have had to exert a policy, that would prevent one edge of this story being uncovered and has dominated grants for academic research, museum explanations of icons, academic scrutiny of documents such as the *Dead Sea Scrolls*, which tell a completely different story from the official line of *The Bible*. Importantly then, this policy of maintaining the lid on the pie, has even made its presence felt in publishing and media and ultimately politics and religion on this planet. Whilst *The Bible* denies Re-incarnation, it may have been vastly edited to remove such beliefs. Alternative religious texts, that are unlikely to be read by the masses, show quite a different story where in the so-called Sethian heresy; Jesus is viewed as an *incarnation* of Seth. The Bible does in some vague instances still carry some indication of this where it is said of John the Baptist "He is Elijah come again"; however for the main, all traces of the Holy Grail have been wiped out, however as this book shows, there are still sufficient references to illustrate the true meaning. Thus whilst the Masters appear to have cornered the message of Re-incarnation for themselves, at the present time of writing there is a World Order policy that supports any belief, provided that it does not allow anyone to claim a past life spiritual identity and woe betide anyone who in the communistic World Order claims to be anything – for beingness in spirit is cornered as a market by the "chosen ones".

Rhea whose philosophy was: 'as I go, so must I return' (Re-incarnation), was the Goddess of Crete and in some texts is shown as the mother of Zeus, thus illustrating the *root of knowledge*. This however has been largely hidden, however certain bardic poetry reveals such secrets as the Welsh poet Gwion, indentifed Eve in *The Bible* as Rhea and hints that she brought forth thirty children in all and then the Divine child Seth. Once again we see that the Jews borrowed heavily from the Greek root. Why thirty children? – Doubtless because the 'reign of Saturn' lasted thirty days and culminated with the mid-winter feast which afterwards became Yule, or Christmas and the birth of the new Eon brought forth by the holy Messiah as divine male Sun Kings, which was the mission of Jesus.

I have already discussed what I believe the policy is towards the British Isles and such policy by Israel may have been in evidence for quite some time. Graves in *The White Goddess*, quotes the poem of Gwion called *Yr Awdil Vraith, ('Diversified Song')* and the poem either has remarkable prophetic ability, or was written by one knowledgeable in the policy of Israel and the "wheels" of destruction and construction in the creation of a World Order as Illuminatus and Rosicrucian. That policy is also laid out it would seem in the 'script' or prophecy of *Revelations* specifically written for the twelve tribes against the thirteenth tribe: these prophecies seem to be non other than World Order policy dating back thousands of years and which were in all probability part of the 'script' or plan that is still utilized today and which must fit exactly with the Jews and their history. According to Gwion:

Oh! What misery,
Through extreme of woe,
Prophecy will show
On Troia's race!

A chain-wearing serpent,
The pitiless hawk
With winged weapons,
From Germany.

Loegria and Britain
She will overrun,
From Lychlyn sea-shore
To the Severn.

Then will the Britons
As prisoners be
By strangers swayed
from Saxony.

Their Lord they will praise,
Their speech they will keep.
Their land they will loose,
Except wild Wales.

Till some change shall come,
After long penance,
When shall be made equal
the pride of birth.

Britons then shall have
Their land and their crown,
And the stranger swarm
Shall vanish away.

All the angel's words,
As to peace and war,
Will thus be fulfilled
To Britain's race.

Graves attributes the source of the poem to the Essenes who existed in the time of Jesus and yet here in this poem there appears to be a predicted war with Germany! Which further places that war according to the poem on the doorstep of Israel or the thirteenth tribe, or as I have proposed by a unity at the top! However the author of the poem is evidently writing this from the perspective of the twelve tribes, for it is obvious that the overrun of Britain in the poem, attempts to dominate the 13 th tribe of Judah. The Essenes I concluded were a secret group set up in two- tiered hierarchy, presumably Druid or Rosicurucian in the upper tier, whilst exhibiting communistic doctrines of the 12 tribes in the lower levels. The statement in the poem that "when shall be made equal, the pride of Birth", indicates that ultimately as I concluded, there is to be a joining of the twelve tribes and the thirteenth tribe within the World Order plan: Rosicrucian and Illiminatus doctrine must therefore in the highest echelon of both hierarchy's cover the World Order plan and policy. One must ask then, whether Britain it being bowed presently to break 'her' pride, only to be absorbed in to the Jewish tribal hierarchy and World Order at a later date!

Gwion explains that the books from which he derived his wisdom, were originally brought to Adam of Hebron, by the angel Raphael, thus effectively and covertly hiding the source of the knowledge and Spiritual intervention 10 000 B.C. In *Tobit* and *The Book of Enoch*, Raphael is described as the angel of healing and must have been the chief patron of the therapeutic Essenses; however the holy Grail that was stolen had healing knowledge incorporated into it and the Mary Magdalene I maintain before her murder in France, just north of Marseilles, which was a Greek colony, was healing using this knowledge, which involved the third part of the Platonic Maxim and Re-incarnation (the soul): 'Before you can cure a man's body, you must cure his mind and before that his soul'. The Mary Magdalene had simply fallen foul of the World Order policy with respect to Re-incarnation, which was one mystery of the Holy Grail, which was to be kept hidden from the masses. Whether the World Order finally in one of their "wheels" or cycles envisages releasing the Holy Grail mysteries, as *their gift* to humanity and which will incorporate healing of the mind and soul; is a question that I have raised with respect to Scientology. That the Jews envisage the Holy Grail as their gift is evident from Gwion's poem:

"The concealed books
From Emmanuel's hands
Were brought by Raphael
As Adam's gift".

A case of "ghusts of laughter the moon stir", to quote Robert Graves, however a comedy it may have turned into, which would be extremely funny, if it were not for the very Greek tragedy and the fate of billions of souls locked into a Magnetic Reversal. Emmanuel refers to Isaiah's prophecy of the birth of the Divine child from a Virgin i.e. Jesus as Hercules. In an Egyptian magical papyrous published by Parthay in 1866, a close connection between the Druid-like instruction into the meaning of musical sounds as an earlier form of the cosmic keyboard with the causes of the birth and decay of herbs, trees and bodies, shows a parallel to Essene mysticism and Pythagorean cults which are echoed in the following lines:

> "Come foremost angel of great Zeus IAO (Raphael)
> And those too, Michael, who holdest heaven (rule the planets)
> And Gabriel thou, the archangel from Olympus".

It is interesting that in the above, the angel of knowledge is placed with Zeus and therefore in Crete, at the time of the Religious Revolution, when the Holy Grail was stolen. Gabriel was the Hebrew counterpart of Hermes, the official herald and mystagogue of mount Olympus; but who was in fact the god of the Religious Revolution, with the removal of the woman from the story. The significance of the use of Hermes as the new god, was that he had a Janus head, with a face of two sides; one was matriarchal and the tribe of Judah and the other was patriarchal and the twelve tribes of Israel. Thus depending on which way the World Order wished to take their policy, together with political and religious manipulation, determined which side of the face was used within the secret groups set up with pre-determined purpose and outcome according to the 'script'. However both sides of the Janus head of Hermes were covered by one cap, the petasos and as I suspect, there is a unity of purpose in the highest and secret echelons of the World Order of Rosicrucian Illuminati: and Greece in her evident policy today in support of Israel over Judah and the policy against Re-incarnation, may yet experience the face of two sides with usurer as one.

There were two mysterious Orders of the Essenes, the Sampsonians and the Helicaeans, who were adepts in the calendar mysteries and were named after Samson the sun-hero and the Helix or cosmic circle. The latter were I suspect initiated into a higher tiered Order or level and the mysteries of the Grid and the spiral. Whether Jesus was initiated into the Essenes and into what Order, i.e. whether 12 or 13 is based on his obvious knowledge of the Tree alphabet, which was Druidic. The Nag Hamaadi scrolls repeat an alleged phrase of Jesus and how he had "fooled them", referring to the 13 th tribe I concluded, which indicated perhaps that the Essenes were specifically set up by the 13 th tribe and Jesus did no such thing, for he too may have been duped. However *I Corinthians, xv, 24-25* relates how St. Paul claimed that Jesus had vanquished the Galation Jews and presumably the 13 th tribe, by claiming that Jesus Christ alone mediates with the Father: this rather implies, that there was an effort to stop channeling, or at least the hold of the 13 th tribe on politics and religion and their quest for a Celtic Commonwealth equivalent to European Union. However this does not support the alleged statement of Jesus in the Alexandrian text, where he supports the God Hermes and states that he came to destroy the "works of the female" as a good Jew naturally! Thus Christianity more than anything pushed the Holy Grail underground, as the *Underground Stream* (of wisdom) associated with the river Alpheus in Greece, to be used by the Jews within their secret groups; working towards the day of so-called healing, when they would deign to give back to mankind a gift claimed as their own and at a price – the arrogance is breathtaking in its ignorance, for they may have trapped billions of souls here including themselves!

Gabriel equated with Hermes and the Herne Giant in Britain was equated with Thoth in one aspect in Egypt and in another aspect was the dog-headed Anubis and his face was depicted interestingly enough as sometimes fair and sometimes black, thus depicting the nature of the ultimate hierarchy as Hermetic and sometimes acting as the thirteenth tribe and sometimes acting for the 12 tribes of Israel; but always acting in a pre-determined outcome towards a World Order. In Egypt, Thoth was sometimes portrayed as an ape and the monkeys or apes were portrayed at Knossos in one fresco dating to the Religious Revolution and it was you will remember the ape that was associated with the Sethites; and Seth was said to be a prior incarnation of Moses and Jesus. The ape was a sacred animal, which also identified Celestial Hercules who was portrayed in the summer Smoking Room floor at Cardiff Castle. The floor I concluded depicted Scottish Rite Freemasonry or more specifically Rosicrucian Illuminism and a plan for a World Order, incorporating both religious and political aims. Celestial Hercules was identified with Thoth the inventor of letters and was a sun-god, worshipped as a god of eloquence, god of healing and god of fertility and prophecy and whom the Greeks worshipped as 'assigner of titles' as ruler of the Zodiac and this type of Hercules was worshipped by the Druids as Omega sun-face. Thus there is a long line of connection through Adam, Noah, Seth, ape, Religious Revolution, Hermes, Hercules, Gabriel and Thoth with the ultimate conclusion, that there is a long history of such connection in relation to the World Order plan and the secret groups of Jewish origin, that have guided that plan. Finally Hermes as ogma sun-face was the inventor of the Ogham alphabet and the Boibel-Loth alphabet that with the Beth-Luis-Nion alphabet brought the world of secrecy and the hiding of religious mysteries including the history of what had happened to the Grail, within those alphabets. Only the initiated, could have acess to what had gone before and obviously such knowledge gave them power; as it is said: 'He who controls the past, controls the present and he who controls the present controls the future". If man is doomed to a Magnetic Cycle, then it is because the patriarchs through the secret groups have always controlled history and the truth: which as a policy has ensured that only one group on Earth, ever had the right of reply to inaccuracies.

The Boibel-Loth alphabet contains many approximations to biblical names taken from *Genesis* and *Exodus* which are names concerned with Sinai, Southern Judea and the Edomite Dead Sea region: this region is where the Essene communities were settled about 150 B.C to 132 A.D. The Essenes appear to have been an offshoot of the therapeutae, or healers, an ascetic Jewish sect settled by Lake Mareotis in Egypt and like the later Druids, believed in the return of pure souls to the sun. The Essenes wore line garments and this arose in the case of the tribe of Jews described as those from Shem who are associated with Britain, in the case of the curious Diana Southcott box of the Panacea society. These Jews avoided animal sacrifices, practiced divination, mediatated within magic circles and were expert in the knowledge of healing plants and precious stones and were thought to have been under the philosophic influence of Pythagoras, who was an ascetic pupil of Abaris, the Hyperborean. Abaris was in all probabliltiy a Druid and Diodorus's famous quotation from the historian Hecateus (sixth century B.C) places Abaris and the Hyeprboreans in Britain, remarking on the Druid Temple of Stonehenge on Salisbury plain: "In this island, there is a magnificiant temple, of round form". The close connection to the Greeks was also noted: "The Hyperboreans use a peculiar dialect, and have a remarkable attachment to the Greeks, especially to the Athenians and the Delains, deducing their friendship from remote periods. It is related that some Greeks formerly visited the Hyperboreans... and also that in ancient times Abaris, coming from the Hyperboreans into Greece, renewed their family intercourse with the Delians". The connection to Greece however was through the stolen Holy Grail and the Tuatha de Danaan. It was said that Pythagoras was instructed by the Dactyls in Crete into the mysteries and in another quotation, Pythagoras was said to have been instructed by Abaris. However if the 13 th tribe or Bull-Minos cult were also the Druids, then this connection is clear. The Bronze Age people who imported the Egyptain beeds into Salisbury Plain, from Akhenation's short-lived capital, the City of the Sun c. 1350 B.C were contemporary with those in early Bronze Age Crete, who whilst giving their mysteries away freely, were surely duped and the Holy Grail stolen. Whilst Pythagoras was credited with the theory of the transmigration of souls, which Hitler followed, it was later credited to Indian sources, although it has not been credited to its true source and Spiritual intervention 10 000 B.C.

The Irish *Book of Ballymore* contains a manual of cryptography, which reflects the increasing complexity that the secret groups placed on language, with only the initiates now knowing the religious mysteries intricately tied up in them. The

Irish initiate had to master one hundred and fifty cipher alphabets and we know that the Druids never wrote anything down, but it took nineteen years of initiation to become a full-fledged Druid. A passage from the *Mabinogion* again shows that Britain was intricately tied to the thirteenth tribe: "The Thirteen Precious Things, The Thirteen Kingly Jewels, The Thirteen Wonders of Britain". This number was also to be encoded into the the British Beth-Luis-Nion alphabet, which I used with Ogham script in *The Battle of The Trees*, to decode a number of mysteries attached to the Holy Grail, which in this complex story has lead me to this research and the final decoding of the secret agenda and policy of international politics and religion. The continual connections between British myth, legend and archetypal symbols connect the thirteenth tribe continually with the Bronze Age Minoans. The comparison of Stonehenge and New Grange barrow in Ireland originally occupied by the Tuatha de Danaan Father-god bears a connection to the labrynth as womb in Crete as a place of re-birth, for solar kings. It has not always been safe to write such matters as this down and therefore the battle is often recorded in veiled terms in myth, legend and folklore.

The Druidic Tree Alphabet that was allied to the groves appears to have evolved in the Black Sea area, which points to the tribe of the Tuatha de Danaan or at least the thirteenth tribe being originally placed in this area, only latterly wandering to Greece and the Peloponnese and thence after patriarchal invaders drove them out, traveling to the British Isles. In Crete, Greece and the Eastern Mediterranean in general, sacred trees were formalized as pillars and it was these Semitic pillars that I identified in the Religious Revolution period at Knossos. Further the figure-of-8 that appeared in iconography in association with this period was a number sacred not only to the calendar and the years of rule of a Twin King, but was much favoured by the Pythagoreans, who formed one aspect of Druidic philosophy. The number 8 referred to the new name of God incorporated into the patriarchal religion. However for the Druids and Hyperboreans, the Lord of the seven-day week was OAOUEIY or in Roman letters JIEVOAO. However notably this is a 7 letter name and therefore is matriarchal! The new name of god in the cross over from matriarchal to patriarchal religion was said to have been invented by Mercury, who I identify with Hermes who was the god of the Religious Revolution and the new name of God was JEHVOVAO. It would make perfect sense that Thoth, Hermes or Mercury invented the 8-letter name of God, since the word (of God) was seen as the 'Eight-fold City of Light', and in which for the Gnostics, Jesus Christ was said to dwell. This guessing the name of the God was quite an effort in the past as this book shows; however one might predict here that the real name of the god of Israel is matriarchal and not patriarchal, where it is envisaged that some new healing religion will emerge – Scientology? Scholars, priests and magicians in the past played this guessing game of the 'Blessed Name of the Holy one of Israel', but it appears that it was the intention of Israel to give back the woman's gift to humanity as their own! Rupert Murdoch once stated that the: "Pope will write for me". How he could make such a statement, if the Pope was not aware of the name of the god of Israel, is anyone's guess!

The appearance of Antlers at New Grange barrow associated with a matriarchal religion of the Tuatha de Danaaan, harks back to the classical icon of the Minotaur as divine child seated on his mother Pasiphae's knee. The Goddes and her semi-divine son of the King, was to become part of the science of 'messianology' of the thirteenth tribe; where the Goddess as the woman in the story would be honoured grudgingly as source and mother in myth and legend, but in practice would be ousted from any political or religious group, where she might give the true story away, such is the case of Freemasonry. Significantly in Arcadia, the mythological birthplace of Hermes, the semi-divine Son wore antlers. Thus the concept of Mother-and-son in Christianity has a long and manipulated history within the secret groups and is particularly unique to the thirteenth tribe of Judah. This really reflects the hidden agenda and goal of Israel and the advent of the messianic era, celebrated at the Feast of Tabernacles. Originally the flag of Europe had fifteen stars on it and that really reflects the religious goal, not only of Israel, but the religious goal of a Federal Europe. Fifteen is not only a number implied in iconography at Cardiff Castle, but on the map at the center of the Summer Smoking room floor design is marked, Jerusalem. Since this floor I concluded was an archetypal representation of a Rosicrucian and Illuminatus plan for a World Order, then Jerusalem flgures strongly in that. The ecstatic fifteenth, the full-moon climax of the Song of Ascents at Jerusalem belongs with advent of the messianic age and the Feast of Tabernacles. Further Cardiff castle features strongly celestial Hercules in the tiled murals and in *The Battle of The Trees*, I decoded a secret on Hercules sword – the apple cut lengthways to reveal Curoi's soul, which much really represent the weapon with which the World Order hope to triumph. That weapon of course relates to the Holy Grail stolen in Crete. The apple is the sidonian (i.e. Cretan) apple, which once again harks back to Re-incarnation and the apples of immortality, which the woman originally used as a teaching tool, to explain curved space time, to Bronze Age man – not an easy task one might imagine! The apple on Hercules sword at Cardiff Castle, had five dots on it, which not only represented the pentad of vowels in the secret British Beth-Luis-Nion alphabet, but it was a female number. The apple was first cultivated by the Cretans and significantly grew on the shores of the Black Sea, which is where I thought that the Tuatha de Danaan or thirteenth tribe originated. The 'British' Beth-Luis-Nion alphabet is also thought by Graves to have originated in the Black Sea area.

The ritual of Tabernacles, which I have previously mentioned earlier in this book, was taken over by the Hebrews with other rites in honour of the Moon-goddess or the woman. The Feast began on the first new moon of the year, and the quince or apple season. The Feast it seems was also intricately linked to the Beth-Luis-Nion alphabet and where both willow and apple are associated with the number fifteen, especially sacred to the Moon-goddess, which corresponds to the number of strokes in the Ogham-finger alphabet. The Feast of Tabernacles saw the Levites sing the fiteen Songs of Ascent, attributed to King David, as they stood on the fifteen steps leading up from the women's court to the court of Israel. The number also figures in Solomon's house with its significant numerical architecture: being built on the three rows of cedar pillars, signifying the old Trinity of Twin Kings and Goddess; fifteen to a row, and fifty cubits long by 30 cubits wide. Well if it is hoped after 10 000 years of lies and manipulation, that Israel will now give back that which was once given freely to all mankind, as Israel's gift to humanity (at a price naturally), then I am afraid that the Cabala has inexorably mixed up the truth and therefore also the method of exit. As I have indicated, I have concluded a very different interpretation of Hubbard's Inc.1 and Inc. 2. – Inc.1 in my thesis being the Religious Revolution in Crete and the theft of the Holy Grail; and Inc.2 being a Magnetic Rerversal: one has to get these things right, since one's exit depends on it, I am afraid.

The appearance of the Partridge in the frescos of Knossos, again at the time of the Religious Revolution, is significant. The so-called *Partridge Fresco*, with partridges shown as mirror opposites among veined pebbles of the sea-shore looking remarkabley like those archetypal eggs, is obviously a symbol of the Twin Kings and the first downgrade of removing the woman in the story and substituting kingship (**ownership**) into the knowledge of the Holy Grail. This was also the time when the bisexual god Hermes evolved hoping to combine the woman and man into one personage. The mythical connections of the partridge and cock to the religious mysteries was played out in the story of the Crucifixion, where the cock crowed three times, to signify the betrayal by Judas. However this is merely the imprinting of the hidden archetypes and as I suspected whilst Jesus supported the god Hermes and the 13 th tribe, he appears to have been betrayed himself by the thirteenth tribe and Judas who must be a gloss for Judah. The cock partridge according to Pliny was unusual since: " In no other animal is there any such susceptibility, in sexual fealings"; and when the female sits on her eggs the cocks relieve their emotions by practicing sodomy. Alistair Crowley utilized this form of sexual magic in his Cabalistic rites and evidently the "new college of magic" instigated at the time of Jesus was some form of sexual magic, which provided morphic resonance with the holographics of the Religious Revolution and the god of Hermes. I have no answer as to whether Hubbard obtained his data for Inc.1 through Crowley, or

Cabalistic practice; however what is clear at least in my own research is that Inc.1 is not the beginning, but only the beginning of **mind control** and the Religious Revolution in Crete, which suppressed the Holy Grail and the knowledge. However if one looks at Hubbard's *Chart of Human Evaluation* (in his book *The Science of Survival*) with emotions and behavior charted on a scale of energy, then one perceives that sexually deviant practice occurs at the low emotional states and gives some clue to the mind that conducted the Religious Revolution. That level of behavior is also associated with communism and fascism and thus easily equates with the goal of mind control that the Cabal who stole the Holy Grail sought, in total world domination. The Celts curiously enough were quoted in history and previously mentioned as: liking young boys more". I am afraid this is one more dramatization of the 13 th tribe and the attempt to keep woman out of the story and if the thirteenth tribe or the twelve tribes were given a solution by the woman, you can bet your bottom dramatization that they would send boys to check that out and do their utmost to keep the woman out of the story, which I am afraid is the policy in Britain where 13 th tribe dramatizations are locked full on!

It seems that the partridge cult was superimposed by the phallic Bull-Minos cult and this dramatization of sodomy must have its history back in Sodom and Gomorrah or some low emotional behaviour and psychology of the past. Once again this dramatization was overlaid on the Holy Grail and the hobbling cok-partridge was later transformed into a dance honouring the Moon-goddess. Pasiphae, the cow in heat, mother and lover of the sun-hero, the bull-headed Minos. This was an absolute horror that the tribes of Israel inflicted on the world and the Holly Grail and goodness knows how many overts this created as man dramatized this memory. The spirally danced Troy-game is still remembered in folk dance in Crete and as Homer once remarked: "Daedalus in Cnossos one contrived a dancing floor for the fair haired Ariadne". How homosexual practice could honour the woman, is best explained by the mind that invented such a ridiculous dramatization! The maze pattern has been shown to represent 'Spiral Castle' or 'Troy Town', where the sacred Sun-king goes after the death and from which if he is lucky, he returns: again indicating Re-incarnation for sacred kings.

Protestant churches are divided between liberal theology and fundamentalism, but the Vatican authorities have made up their minds on the problem. They encourage two trends (or is it tribes and the Janus head of Hermes?) of thought to co-exist within the church: the authoritarian, paternal, which secures the priest's hold on his congregation, steering them away from the entire background to Christianity, which lies in the story here and alternative texts (other than The Bible), myth, legend and folklore let alone history! However, the Vatican knows only too well the story of Israel and the hidden role of the woman, who has always been denied her rightful gift and is only acknowledged in order to give religion its romantic glow, which is utilized in the Madonna and child. This really does not matter very much or indeed who the gift belonged to, unless one wanted to exit and thus the church and its leaders can keep their secrets and their story and stick with the ageing star and sun and presumably pride and arrogance will prevent them from ever issuing the true story: however there was never a truer word written than the Biblical text: "You won't get out of that place, until you have paid up the last coin, of least value". The woman is remembered as an immemorial obsession inextricably linked to the tribes of Israel and the secret groups and is fixed deeply into the racial memory of religion. Her game however was never the cup of power or conflict, it was only a message and knowledge and I must refer to Graves and another memorable line: " It is easier for her to play man's game a little while longer, until the situation grows too absurd and uncomfortable for complaisance. The Vatican waits watchfully".

If such absurdity is recognised in the field of religion, which has evolved on the history of the Masters and of Israel, the Hebrews and the persistant battles of 12 and 13 rather than the history of truth; where *The Bible* is considered a book of authority by those who have no understanding of the hidden archetypal symbolisms, or the hidden science; then such absurdity is also recognised in the field of science. Professor Lancelot Hogben noted in the *Conway Memorial Lecture of 1949* entitled *The New Authoritarianism,* that scientific research has become so complicated and demands such enormous apparatus that only the State or immensely rich patrons can pay for it; which means that a disinterested search for knowledge and truth is cramped by the demand for results or solutions that will justify the expense and in the case of truth which is the goal of science, no solutions are required under World Order policy. What 'The New Authoritarianism' really requires in religion, politics and science, is an adherance to the policy of the World Order and a **state of no cure** in respect of the Platonic Maxim: 'before you can cure a man's body, you must cure his mind and before that his soul'. The cancer patient is just another Holocaust victim a statistic in the eternal "wheels" of Israel and the battle of 12 and 13, or the Masters in their obsessional persuit of total domination in the form of a World Order. Every sacrifice and victim will be justified as the means to the end or cause of Israel and the One World Order and the advent of the Messianic Age - a time of healing, a gift from Israel naturally. The 'experts', be they religious, scientists or the army of technical administrators and civil servants - all as mindlessly driven robots support the great edifice of absurdity that requires obedience to the policy or diktat churned out by the Masters and the elite club of Rosicrucian Illuminati. Everyone in the edifice has some vested interest to maintain, be that readership of a magazine, a newspaper, church pews filled, or salaries and pensions paid. No one has a vested interest in truth and yet without truth or reality there is no escape from the trap and the eternal "wheel". Surely though if the Masters, the elite clubs of the secret societies had the answers, then they would have exited from the trap before now would they not, instead of depending on an ancient destabilized star – the sun, to support their holographics of the past and their so-called inivisible Masters, who have dictated the policy on this planet for billions of years. Surely they will know the keys to exit and the truth of the crab, so wrongly portrayed on the tiled mural at Cardiff Castle; and surely they will lead mankind out of the trap. The ageing and ridiculous sun-god together with the ridiculous sun-kings and the hereditary lines of the "chosen ones" will no doubt save all those who would not give lip service to an alternative account or the truth; and when the sun expires, then surely all those who have followed such ridiculous notions, with no use of their own mind, can follow the ridiculous games of the Masters in the dark and what a game of hell that will be. Man will not be able to exit the trap even if the crystal or Grid is destroyed with the electro-magnetic spectrum, since he will have a thousand and one connections to matter, via his past holographics and the real game in anti-matter will be denied him. Unfortunately man prefers the comfort of religions provided by the Masters and bows to the dramatizing   majority – it takes courage to stand alone.

There is now no free field of science, even the non-commercial benevolent institutions like the Nuffield foundation, is as high handed as any Treasury controlled government department. I was refused a grant for my research and the resolution of the Platonic Maxim: 'before you can cure a man's body, you must cure his mind and before that his soul'. The request for a grant from all the major funding bodies I approached, was bound to be turned down, on the basis of policy which dictates that no solution to the predicament of planet Earth is wanted; it runs according to the 'script' and it has been run that way for millions or billions of years where the policy is: 'Don't meddle with the script'. Quite possibly there lies the ultimate absurdity of the Masters and all those who follow them. I am afraid that the robots who follow the Masters, rather than seeing that action together with the total bankruptcy on behalf of the author in following this research, as total survival, view that action as non-survival, simply because in their conditioned and brainwashed minds, answers come from the Masters, male, orthodox, inside the establishment and from a position of power – World Order. The World Order do not have to do much along this line, for man in his Grid controlled state is perfectly capable of *being* the World Order in action and thought! The reaction to the research is not one of rationality as the front cover of the Cancer Report illustrates. I suspect that it is the equivalent of a female in a group of monkeys offering suggestions to the dominant male, on how to run his tribe! This theme was taken up in the *Appendix to Alternative 4.*

To quote another memorable line of Graves: " the organizer in fact, seated on Zeus's throne, is beginning to find his ministers obstructive, his courtiers boring, his regalia tawdry, his quasi-royal responsibilities irksome, and the system of government breaking down from over-organization: he regrets having enlarged the realm to such absurd proportions and given his uncle Pluto and his half brother Mercury a share in the regency, yet dares not quarrel with these unreliable wretches for fear of worse to come, or even attempts to re-write the constitution with their help. The goddess smiles grimly at his predicament". There are so many lies now, with so many involved and the very foundations of so-called civilization, that no doubt the Masters would rather hold on to their psychotic thought: '**I must be right or I die**', than admit the truth. Certainly this is a very Greek tragedy and a very sad 'script' and policy, where the Masters would rather take billions through a Magnetic Reversal and trap them for all eternity, than admit to the truth: and man would rather follow the 'script' than take the courage to support an alternative policy of truth. **The World Order policy is - no solution to the Platonic Maxim: 'before you can cure a man's body, you must cure his mind and before that his soul', for the solution requires ultimate reality, which is truth.** No doubt the World Order intends to bring about a solution to the Platonic Maxim as their own gift, however the MMRC case just can't finish a cycle of action and is frequently interrupted by Magnetic Cycles and the 'Paradise' that he seeks, is really encompassed as the Beginning, where it's a case of Day1 – plant the vine; and he can re-run the entire 'script' again! Next time however there will be no help.

The existing policy denies UFO incidents, simply because any research into this area would reveal the information I gave in *Alternative 4*, together with on-going experiments into tapping the zero-point energy. Further the Akashic Record stands to be revealed, with its connection to all that I say in this book. Further still, secret weaponry being developed towards mind control including the HAARP and GWEN programmes in America would also come under scrutiny. I believe that Dr. Becker, who was twice nominated for a Nobel Prize, lost his job in a university over his warnings against such programmes and mind control capability of the populous. This attack on scientists who have sought to reveal any corner of the web of secrecy have in the past as the Appendix shows lost their positions, grants or have been attacked and ridiculed and in some cases have been imprisoned or murdered for their research.

The new Vehicle-Mounted Active Denial System (V-MADS) has been nicknamed the People Zapper because it is designed to be used against large crowds of civilians. This new form of non-leathal weapon poses a threat and method of side-stepping arms and humanitarian agreements and could undermine the terms of specific conventions. The whole idea of developing specific wapons for use against civilians by armed forces is at odds with the current law. Despite this weapon has been developed in America, there is no reason to believe that it will not have also been produced in Europe. Peter Herby who works for the legal team at the Red Cross in Geneva, which achieved an international ban on laser-powered weapons designed to blind people stated recently: " Armed forces should not be engaged in policing duties. Troops are constrained by specific conflict laws while police, who may well be armed, are subject to domestic and human rights laws". For the smart among you, it will be realized that not only is Europe forming its own army but police force also and where will control emanate from? Not from individual countries but from the power that runs European Union. This is the fatal flaw and policy, in so far as government and human rights issues are slowly being placed beyond the law and into the hands of the elite. This policy of 'Do what thou wilst is the whole of the law', is the mind of the World Order, which will rule by force and this is the entire danger of globalisation and   the formation of a World Order. It has to be noted that in the reign of terror in France during the French Revolution, the leaders turned on the citizens of France! The V-MADS weapon predictably works by harnassing electro-magnetic power to fire an ivisible pulse of energy at light speed towards a target. In effect like microwave radiation it fries the flesh to one 64 th of an inch and causes water molecules under the skin to vibrate violently, which effectively causes horrible pain and causes a person to flee the area. Whilst this weapon has been described as safe and humane Richard Lloyd of Landmine Action, the leading British charity campaigning against anti-personnel mines said: "So-called non lethal weapons are potential killers. No one knows the long-term effect of microwave radiation on eyes or internal organs. We are afraid that these new weapons will be deployed indiscrimately and that innocent civilians will be injured or maimed.... these weapons are not the solution to long-term peace". Indeed not, but then the 'script' and policy on Earth has never written peace into the lines, simply because the MMRC case and the Masters have controlled policy and the script for a very long time, even in this cycle recounted in the *Old Testament* and further recounted in the Indian Epics where previous cycles speak of wars that produced a large catastrophe: of course it is a matter of foregone conclusion that the catastrophe will be repeated, since man is incapable of challenging the Masters and as my own case proves, even those you try to help in the avoidance of a Third World War, will dramatize their own psychological case where in low emotional tones of the Grid and primitive mind, you will find yourself as I did, on the run for 15 years! Do I regret it? No of course not, since in order to leave or exit, you have to be at peace with your own conscience, to get through 'the life review' and know that you did everything that was within your power.

CHANGING THE SCRIPT AND POLICY

If you put only two chemicals (A and B) into a test tube and only chemical C is present at the end of the experiment, then you could say with some certainty that C was the result of combining A plus B.The problem in the author's research, is the broad base of subjects I have had to cover and the time span over which these events occurred. It is complicated by the fact, that secret groups use so many front groups and hide their tracks so well; it is impossible to identify all those present in the 'test tube'! However in this particular story I would say with some certainty that the groups 12 and 13 or the twelve tribes of Israel and the lost thirteenth tribe have caused many of the 'reactions' or events in the 'test tube' of Earth. Further, metaphysics and parapsychology has been so poorly researched (not a co-incidence I might add), that I have had to spend a great deal of time and thought developing models for the mechanisms of such phenomena as the UFO and crop circles, past lives etc. This mechanism was discussed in *Alternative 4* and again outlined here as *The Onion-Ring Model.* Any individual can pick up past events, retained in holographic form in the geometry of space with extended psychic ability and the brain or field of the mind, acting as a dipole radio-receiver. Certain fluxes of energy through the system can also dislodge these holographics and again the brain or mind field, acting as dipole-radio receiver picks up the past holographic content which accounts for the UFO experience in its natural form. There is however a complex interplay, when these holograms are picked up either in the UFO experience, channeling, or seership which in the latter two cases actively through Cabalistic method and ritual create morphic resonance, that is likely to re-stimulate the holographics of the past event, with the goal of obtaining information. The complex interplay is what a scientist would call a variable in the system. This means that if for instance you had one picture or holograph and you asked three people of different backgrounds, ages, sex, nationality, religion, job, and education, to interpret that holograph, you would get a story that has a central hologram as common to all three, but the details of the story would differ. Thus the variables are the types given above, but must also include past lives of individuals and *personal experience*, together with the *goals of the spirit*.

Once the Grail became mixed up with the twelve and thirteenth tribes, politics was inevitable and of course to follow the Grail, one had to fight on one side or the other, depending on the times and what was perceived as moral or just for that time. The Mary Magdalene evidently tried to make a compromise of the truth, by hitching up the Grail to the power of the time and marry a Solar King who aimed at holy one or holly and oak royal: the plan was dashed, since oak royal won the day with its goal of money and power, which saw the elixir or belief and knowledge go underground again: the effort to get the mysteries above ground was dashed along with the hope for that millennium. I don't know how many readers will   feel a sense of bitter betrayal at this point, but I can assure you, it is no more than was felt 2 000 years ago, by those who experienced the events at Golgotha. I may have spoilt your day, but rather that, than spoil your eternity. Which reminds me of a significant dream I had. I was sitting in a beautiful meadow and making food from the very flowers. I heard a terrible stampeding sound and as I looked from my quiet observation point, I saw olive-skinned people like a heard of stampeded cattle plunging over a cliff face, it was horrific and all I could do was to watch. One man came over to me and asked me what I was doing, I said: "sit awhile and I will tell you many things": so he sat and when I   had finished, he jumped up and shouted: "you have spoilt my day!" He ran and jumped over the cliff with the others and it made me sad, but somehow I thought it was inevitable. Was it the cliff of Europe? With the Freemasons and twelve tribes or perhaps now a combined twelve and thirteenth tribe, stampeding their victims and "slaves" into a dark chasm from which there is no return, since European legislation is binding and final; until that fateful day when the 'script' arrives at the third battle, which determines the final act and the curtain comes down, on yet another production of Theatre Earth. Or was it more that I saw the Greeks as olive-skinned people, being stampeded into some form of betrayal?

I cannot give concrete conclusions but only broad questions that need to be looked at, as a matter of urgency as quite clearly the transatlantic rift between America and Europe, could spell a Third World War, as the secret groups dramatize the entire holographics of the past and repeat that past which may be identified in so many myths, legends and in the Indian Epics where a third battle is so well reported: apart from nuclear fission reactions found in Europe and America that have yet to be explained. Despite this, there is sufficient evidence that has accumulated in all my three books, which need to be assessed in total, rather than individually, including the Cancer Report; to form a framework or overall viewpoint, which I proffer as part of freedom of speech and religious belief. You may not agree with my conclusions, but that is your own choice and right to your own opinions. There is however sufficient evidence in my first book *The Battle of The Trees*, to show that European Union was never evolved through the process of democratic vote. It is ludicrous for the British Home Office to state to me, that a Referendum on Europe has taken place, implying from the use of the word referendum, that the people had all the facts on which to make a judgment. The definition of a referendum is: 'the submission of an issue of public importance to the direct vote of the electorate'. Further the definition of vote is: 'an indication of choice, opinion, or will on a question of public importance,' etc. How can one express a vote, opinion or choice, when one has only a limited view of the facts and where the majority of facts are withheld? The limitation of choice to no choice, is a method of the Masters as fascism or communism and as such acts as a channel for those Masters on the reverse hermetic principle: 'as below, so above'. The whole of hermetic philosophy is a channel for the Masters and the illuminatus power pyramid that is utilized in World Order politics and religion, is merely another channel. The possibility of a few insane individuals at the top of the power pyramid, controlling the world according to their view of 'reality' is the REALITY OF INSANITY. The ability to ask questions is always denied, since questions and the requirement for rational answers, challenges the policy and mind of the World Order and its sanity. How do you get round the 'London Eye', the dome and the string of bonfires or beacons in the New Year's celebrations in Britain! I really would like to hear the answer. The insanity is evident, in so far as millions of pounds of taxpayers' money were spent on the dome, with no apparent sense or use for such a large dramatization. When the world wakes up it might look around at the insanity caused on a much larger scale by the dramatizing World Order and perceive that a Federal Europe run by a few power hungry drones, is no more than a recipe for a disaster in the making – which is based more on how to challenge the power of the United States.

The facts in my first book quite clearly show, that the goal of secret groups since the time of The French Revolution at least has been a: "United States of the West", or a Federal Europe and therefore European Union was formed on **a hidden agenda and policy** rather than democratic referendum. Further Geoffrey Dobbs in his booklet (cited) - *Correction Needed - There was No Referendum on Joining the EEC*, made the position quite clear. A Federal Super State, was conceived in the same cradle as the idea of a Universal Political and Religious Kingdom or World Order, together with the covert and occult nature of the French and Russian Revolutions which eradicated monarchy; and World War II which has yet to be fully revealed, invites the question as to whether a universality of religious belief will follow political integration of nation states, together with the nature of that religion. *The Daily Mail (July 8 2000)* reported *Evangelist Hague -Tory leader seeks Christian TV stations and a boost for marriage*: "William Hague was given a standing ovation by black church leaders yesterday after he demanded tax benefits for married couples and called on the Government to allow national Christian TV and radio stations". -Allellulya! And certainly wonderful for Christians, whilst 'dissidents' presumably can expect a great deal more of the events pictorially covered on the front cover of *The Second Millennium Working Report into Cancer*. Hague added: "What message are we sending about standards on television when we allow the law to discriminate against Christian TV and radio stations?" Either William Hague the Conservative opposition leader in the U.K. is remarkably un-informed or he is deliberately pulling the Christian card along with Tony Blair for electoral mileage. Is this not the case of 'boiled or hanged'? Where there are no real electoral alternatives to the policy of the World Order: and of course they are not un-informed and it is certainly lame for Margaret Thatcher a previous Conservative Prime Minister of Britain, to claim that she now regrets her position of encouraging European integration, when she cannot have been un-informed of this particular story to some extent. However, as politicians incredibly admit, they did not even bother to read the Maastricht treaty before signing away the trust and freedom of the democratic electorate. Treason?

How many times in history have men and women warned of a conspiracy, before they were labeled as anti-Semitic? The Book of *Isaiah 17; 14* states: "And behold at evening tide trouble; and before the morning he is not. This is the portion of them that spoil us and the lot of them that rob us". Eustace Mullins (cited) wrote:

> " Five men rule the world. This Council of Five consists of Baron Guy de Rothschild, Evelyn de Rothschild, George Pratt Shultz, Roberta Roosa (from Bush's family firm of Brown Brothers Harriman) and one vacancy at this writing".

That was in 1984 and whilst there appears to be a pyramidal apex of power and wealth, that is only a fraction of the true battle and story, which is the *battle for man's soul*. Mullins's went on to say that:

> "The World Order rules through a simple technique, Divide and Conquer (divide et impera), natural or unnatural division among people, every occasion for hatred or greed, is exploited and exacerbated to the limit. The polarization of racial and ethnic groups in the U.S. is accelerated by a flood of government decrees, originating in the foundation "studies", which are designed solely to set American against American. Only in this way can the world Order maintain its iron grip on the daily lives of the people. The World Order also rules by the principle of "1984" – no groups of two or more people are allowed to gather unless the world Order has a representative present. If you start a club of dandelion fanciers, the Order will send someone who will be quietly helpful, avoid taking the front position, and who will offer to pay the rent of a meeting place or the printing of the minutes. In more radical groups, the Order's representative will be the first to suggest dynamiting a building, assassinating an official, or other violent action".

340

Not only does this reflect the use of the Janus head of Hermes (a face of two sides) and the 12 tribes and 13 th tribe, but it is the psychology of the Magnetic Reversal, where constant recourse to past Masters and the Grid through channeling, which retains a memory of the reversal, precipitates a particular psychology of duality, which expresses itself in a diverse manner e.g. in philosophical dualism (good and evil). Is it any wonder that the World Order has always employed duality ('Good and Evil', black and white, communism versus fascism, East versus West etc.) when such duality is merely the product of their particular psychology? Every human being always has the choice of whether to act as the primitive, irrational and Universal Mind of survival, or as his immortal and spiritual self. The mind of the World Order through perpetual attention placed on survival and the Grid by channelling and adherence to the dogma of the past, merely plugs into www-com/grid and past holographics. Humanity as it is called in the lowest ranges and using only his/her primitive mind enjoys a good victim when he/she sees one and enjoys nothing better than to savage that victim dramatizing the Masters!

The fact is that all the secret groups in history that pushed forward plans for a political World Order and religion, employed initiates from Steiner, Blavatsky, Fourier and Crowley to modern initiates in groups such as the Bilderbergers, Freemasonry, B'nai B'rith etc. We know that in the past, initiates were under the control of Masters and acknowledged the group of invisibles in The Great White Lodge, there is no reason to believe that things have changed, for if there is one sure datum of the mind of the elite, it is their dogmatic following of the 'script'. All secret groups at some level are now linked to this system of Masters and esoteric men who have channeled information and have filtered that down as *policy* via the channeling method to initiates and through the dogma of religion. Mrs. Bailey stated that the Secret Government is a: "Hierarchy of Light, Elder Brothers with the King Snat Kumara living in Shamballa a mystical or mythical center in the Gobi desert". It's never up the road in South London; no.23 to be precise in X road is it! That is the whole point, without specific references you can't trace it down and find the real source or identity of the *visible* Masters, for which reason I have asked the question is Scientology a secret group? for Hubbard did not reference his work and being a realistic scientist I have a problem with the genius explanation. There is no doubt that Scientology has helped and I have never known anyone say that the knowledge was not incredibly enlightening and useful to him or her – it is compelling stuff! However, I like to know where my path or journey leads and to be sure that I am not following a path that may have the wrong sign on it. I abhor lies and I have made it my philosophy that when I see a lie, I pack up my bag and leave. Scientology may or may not be the best game on the planet, however I for one would like my questions answered, before I make a decision on that one.

Another good rule I employ is to leave, when I see the cold eye of Illuminism and no conscience, again like Jiminy cricket: 'Always let your conscience be your guide', I pack up my bag and leave. When I was told to: "Help the more able first", by a senior Scientologist with regard to cancer, then it was time to pack up and leave and when they took no interest in the law case I fought in London in support of freedom of belief, there was a strong indicator to me, that all was not what it seemed.

Further the World Order borrows constantly and always places source at its own throne, thus note well what I have said in this book and the research, for at some point in the near future you will see just how, when and where they will use it, twist it about and spew out another version to suit their own agenda. The World Order mind mirrors the Grid mind of the Masters and the Darwinian concept of survival (of the fittest) in so far as it acts along primitive mind survival mechanisms, taking all that is useful for its *own or minor group* survival and by claiming source, it can in its own mind increase its own survival. The World Order like the Grid or crystal has developed its own sentience and acts as a machine bent on survival. This is a grand mistake, for actually by decreasing the survival of others you create a thousand and one strings in the holographic banks monitoring survival of individuals and matter, which will trap you as a Spirit, in the 'life review' as you try to exit. If you see groups suddenly change policy, *without detailing truth*, then do not be fooled, into believing that is anything but an attempt to secure survival and bring one more twist in the tail of the lie.

Mrs. Bailey informed that: "at the head of all great organizations will be found either a Master or initiate", which must reflect the words of the Jewish writer, Dr. Angelo Rapport in his book *The Pioneers of the Russian Revolution*:

> "There was not a political organization in the vast Empire which was not influenced by the Jews or directed by them; the Social Democrats, the Revolutionary Socialist Parties, the Polish Socialist Party, all counted Jews among their directors; Plehve was perhaps right when he said that the combat for political emancipation in Russia and the Jewish question were practically identical".

In Cheiro's World Predictions, he made the prediction that is true today for European Union:

> "From 1980.... will, in my opinion, see the restoration of the Twelve Tribes of Israel as the dominant power in the world...Another law giver, like Moses, will arise ...and so in the end through this 'despised race' universal peace will be established".

This is almost certainly unfair to the Jews as a people for they like the British, have had no inkling of the power games that have been played by the secret priesthoods: but the Jewish people can like the British ask questions and demand truthful answers. That Cheiro was talking about the European Court of Justice as the ultimate "law giver", which sits in secret making up its laws and which govern Europe is questionable. The appearance of a European army and police force must have been another branch of the plan, which has never ceased to exist since at least the time of The French Revolution and I would maintain Bronze Age Crete, but which, has never been known to the public. This would certainly account for the irrational bile that emits from Europe towards the British Isles and the perceived archenemy of Judah and Shem? That of course leaves the descendents of Ham somewhere in this, which only leaves them at the top of the power pyramid in Europe, which bodes ill for peace. The first laws of Europe were laid out at Gortyn in Crete, which dates back to the Religious Revolution conducted by the secret Cabal. Whilst it has been difficult to decide which group conducted this Revolution it appears that the woman was betrayed by the thirteenth tribe and the final fall of Knossos came when the 12 tribes wiped out the 13 th tribe. This betrayal of the woman is a constant feature of the thirteenth tribe and arose in the story of the Magdalene and rests upon the initial overt of Crete and the truth of the beginning. As the Magdalene prophecied: "There will be no peace on this Earth until the cut is healed".

If you ask me whether the Cabalists and Masons at the top of Europe know they are following a 'script', the answer is emphatically NO! Just as the man in the insane asylum does not know he is insane. It is in the hands of these men, millions of Europeans are willing to divest power, which will end in a third battle and war, since the MMRC case not only works in cycles of destruction and construction, but cannot finish a cycle of action, based on the experience of the Magnetic Reversal. No, European Union will not end in peace, only war and destruction, before the curtain comes down and the whole cycle starts again – Day1. Plant the vine. I have continually looked around the European stage for a significant group, who are fighting a Federal Europe. Whilst Sir James Goldsmith may have represented some 13 th tribe interest which could only have been answered by himself, he curiously developed cancer and died shortly after his attempt at a Referendum party. William Hague the conservative leader has made noises on an anti-Europe campaign, but hardly the truth is being offered. The dual nature of the World Order which I have commented on with regard to individuals and groups may rely on the ability of groups 12 and 13 to act in unison at the top, where only a handful of men know the true policy and goal, whilst dichotomy is retained further down the power pyramid based on the Hermetic god. The Hermetic god allows either left or right path to be followed and in this way it follows Hegelian dialectics, the dialectic of materialism, which regards to the World as Power, and the World as Reality. **It denies all other powers and all other realities**. How far this 'reality' is maintained depends on the extent to which that power can brainwash entire populations. It depends on how effectively it can control media, publishing and any free communication line that would allow another reality to emerge. So firmly have the populace and even the so-called free lines of communication been brainwashed into the Christian ethic of not upsetting anyone's viewpoint, that freedom of speech is denied on the grounds that a variant viewpoint might trouble the sensibilities of readers: when in actual fact they have merely bowed to the World Order ethic of not troubling the master pattern, 'script' or indeed the Masters themselves. If the dissident shouts: "hey what about errors in pages x, y, z, of the script!" You would get the reply "Don't meddle with the script, we've been doing this production for billions of years!" The fact is, whilst the 'script' is written from a majority viewpoint along Darwinian principles of he who wins, gets to write the 'script', it is not survivalist for spiritual man. As Ghandi said: "Even if you are in a minority of one, the truth is still the truth".

"No two individuals are exactly alike" and "all organisms exhibit variation" are biological clichés expressing the most obvious feature of living organisms. Individuals exhibit biological variation of hair color, eye color, and the overwhelming number of possible combinations, which produces biological individuality. Individuals within the same species e.g. Homo sapiens may differ as a consequence of either heredity or environment. However, only the differences inherited by the next generation are of importance to evolution. Genetic variation is under the control of genes within the human population pool. The combinations of these genes with thousands of others result in the formation of distinctly individual human beings. The idea of natural selection as the guiding force of evolution was the principal contribution of Charles Darwin to evolutionary theory. Darwin's original concept of selection was somewhat unsophisticated and negative and was applicable to individuals rather than to populations, but his recognition of this essential principle provided the key to understanding evolutionary processes. Darwin saw the process of *evolution as a struggle for* existence between individual organisms. Since all species produce many more offspring than survive, he concluded that the total environment eliminated those individuals least fitted for survival and encouraged the survival of the fittest. The environment thus acted as a selective force, sorting out those variants best adapted to the particular environmental circumstances. Natural selection at its simplest is the impact of any factor in the total environment of an organism that tends to produce systematic genetic change from one generation to the next. Natural selection brings about evolutionary change by favoring differential reproduction of genes and differential reproduction of genes produces change in gene frequency from one generation to the next. Natural selection or environmental factors does not produce genetic change, but once genetic change has occurred (by mutation and recombination) it acts to encourage some genes over others.

This is the position with the body of man or the phylogenetic line. The morphogenetic bioplasma I maintain records the master genetic pattern along with event in the environment. There is a complete record if you like of changes in environment and genetic changes that accompanied that environmental change. Thus any change in the environment over a prolonged period on Earth, would along these lines I propose have some influence over which genes are selected in the master pattern, which determines the body tri-partite energy field of the embryo. However what appears to be printed is a *majority* change and significant events in terms of the environment. A Magnetic Reversal would undoubtedly be recorded somewhere and may provide the master pattern with the opportunity to recombine the 'filaments' corresponding to the master DNA blue-print in response to a majority non-survival message. I have already spoken of the increased electro-magnetic input from new technology and computers, which must interface with the master pattern. The question becomes how the pattern is changed in response to that overload input. The invention of 'new' electronic technology that may have easily been channeled off past records may stand to repeat that past, along with any environmental catastrophe. There is also the question of how far repeating on the earth plane holographics of the past, serves to re-stimulate holographics of the master pattern thus precipitating events of that master pattern including environmental catastrophes. As the master magicians through their Cabalistic ritual constantly re-stimulate the thoughts of past Masters and past events, then as they seek to impose the channeled philosophy, policy and technology of the past Masters on the world, man can only walk as a sleepwalker to his fate of a repeat of past catastrophes. Further conflict in the environment whilst acting as a selector for genetic evolution along Grid lines, is *not* a selector of spiritual evolution. Whilst many people believe that conflict is necessary to create spiritual evolution it is actually a *deterent*, since man focuses on survival thus plugging him into Grid survival and the survival of matter. Spiritual evolution can only evolve in an environment free from the worry of survival and concerns of matter. To see the truth of this statement look around you at the world and see how far man has spiritually developed under the Masters – that is the truth and reality of just how wrong the Masters are and how wrong man is to support them. To suggest another way, where everyone is freed from hunger and the threat of disease and educated to a high level, is to suggest that man changes the 'script'.

The most noticeable point in World Order thinking is the reaction to natural selection and the *individuality* of human beings. Britain has long fought genius in these Isles, simply because in the mind of the 'cuckoo' and the "chosen ones" there is no room for the individual or genius who threatens the superiority of the chosen race. Race being a major psychological button of the World Order, which appears to rest on their own origins and race and the migrations in early history. Abberative programmes such as the Klu-Klux-Klan and the Aryan Super Race programme are mere dramatizations of this psychology. However the Hegelian dialectic of the World Order reality as the *only* reality, must stem from this complete dramatization of the past holographic record and their insistence in present time of re-stimulating those past holographics with Cabalistic rituals, which not only tap into the past holographics, but through that ritual and ceremony re-stimulate their own personal past life memories. This becomes a dwindling cycle where the sick man gets sicker. The ' reality' for the Masters is the past, they are still fighting a battle and goal **back there on the time track**, which they carry forward into present time. All insanity of the World Order can be placed at the door of this mechanism. A World Order of political and religious domination is not rational to ordinary men and women who mostly perceive it with suspicion as an organization of absolute power, but are not prepared to challenge it, by allowing the dissident to speak, such is the control of the Grid. The politics of fascism or communism suit the World Order since they do not allow a variant reality to emerge, to challenge the diktat of the World Order and the press subservient and controlled by that World Order, do not challenge the 'reality' as they have become the 'reality'. As the **Ethics** office for the National Association of Journalists in Britain told me: "We have no power to force newspaper editors to print, what they have no wish to print" – even if it is the truth? The battle for the mind is another part or facet of maintaining the World Order 'reality'. All religious groups tell you 'don't look over there its too dangerous'. I was quite irritated when a senior Scientologist, who one expects to be way up the emotional and liberal scale, blacked out references to OT material before she gave me a copy of the *Time* magazine article that blasted Scientology. This is certainly communist ideology of control of the mind, where censorship is the rule of the day, as even now China sets up 'gateways' on the Internet, which determines what the Chinese can view. The implication is there, that man cannot decide for himself, what is true or not and such decisions require observation from a large number of viewpoints, until one can determine in one's own mind, the actual reality or truth. Publications that go along with the idea, of not printing dissident viewpoints merely agree with communist World Order brainwashing and policy handed down from the Masters. In fact it is the **individual** who controls *spiritual evolution* and not the World Order or their methods of thesis and anti-thesis. The method of ACCELERATED EVOLUTION through conflict, employing cycles of destruction and regeneration by the Cabalists of the World is a DRAMATIZATION OF THE MAGNETIC REVERSAL CYCLE! They justify the blood sacrifices of wars and revolution and conflict, in their own minds, by believing that they are helping humanity to evolve along the Darwinian principle of 'survival of the fittest', where the old, sick and disabled are chaff and husks, spat out since they are of no further use to the World Order programme. The method of organizing conflicting groups and then throwing those groups together on the world stage just as animals are forced to evolve from conflict is merely to apply the morphogenetic survival mechanisms of animals to man as a body. Man however is a spiritual being with a mind, to deny a man his mind and thinking process, allows the World Order to control man as both his mind and his body. The arch controllers have never ceased in methods of body control, but mind control as Hubbard gave in his Inc. 1 originated in Bronze Age Crete where the World Order took over the Holy Grail and developed a policy that would retain control of the Grail, using the power for themselves and employing politics and religion as methods of mind control.

The World Order functions on the principle of duality, which must result from the hermetic god and ultimately a Magnetic Reversal, where the hermetic principle of: 'as above so below', is most suited to the channeling methods of the Cabalistic Jewish priests, who install the mind of the Master Hermes or the gods of Sirius on the world. The Janus head of two sides, that can speak one way and then another, throwing thesis and anti-thesis together for a pre-determined outcome towards the goal of the Masters. I have noted in research that secret groups and individuals, are contacted by the Masters in such a manner, where opposing groups of thesis and anti-thesis or 12 and 13 are set up with pre-determined outcomes. The battle of 12 and 13 or THE TRIBAL WAR has formed the basis of such warring dualism of good and evil in the world, where no doubt the pain, sacrifice and suffering is justified in that phrase 'THE END JUSTIFIES THE MEANS', which is the calling card of the World Order, all revolutions, wars and sacrifices to a cause, which is the cause of the Masters and total control. Ah yes! The messianic era and the Feast of Tabernacles that will wash away all the pain and suffering, where the "chosen ones" will sit down to their boiled and pickled woman, after their labors of Hercules, so portrayed in the wall murals at Cardiff Castle as Knights Kadosch of Rosicrucian Illuminism: but it will not wash away the lies and betrayal and those stolen apples of immortality along with the Holy Grail at least not in my book of truth. To quote that immortal poem by the master poet Robert Graves in *The White Goddess*:

> "Gusts of laughter the Moon stir
> That her Bassarids now bed
> With the unnoble usurer
> While an ignorant pale priest
> Rides the beast with a man's head
> To her long - omitted feast".

The World Order finances and organizes one group and then organizes and finances its anti-thesis in order to create a pre-determined outcome. The cold war of Russia and America was formulated on such a basis, since both sets of scientists, as records will show, were sharing information throughout the cold war. I suggested that whilst Solar Kingship was set up to become the political arm of a Theocratic priesthood, later when the function of Solar Monarchy had outlived its use, the French and Russian Revolutions were financed and set into motion, by anti-thesis groups in order to create a pre-determined outcome of removal of Monarchy creating a step closer towards European Union. The World Order in all likelihood also created this pre-determined outcome in the case of World War II, where Hitler was a mere puppet, in the chess game set up by the World Order. It has been noted by political commentators in the past, that at the top, there appears to be a cohesion or unity between Russia and the west, which reflects the World Order ability to move to the right or left according whether the philosophy of groups 12 or 13 are utilized. There is every indication that the two in all probability act in unison where at the top no doubt there is a belief and justification that they are regulating the balance of the world as deified gods and the "chosen ones". People are dispensable in this World Order 'reality' and they are only there to be USED and when of no further use, simply spat out like chaffs. The mind of the World Order is usurious, where the control of money and the world banking system is of course a major concern of the World Order in maintaining their 'reality'.

One of the most influential conspirators was Walter Rathenau of Germany. He greeted the First World War ecstatically as the golden opportunity to establish world socialism. Rathenau wrote: "In Days to Come", 1929, "No part of the world is now closed to us. No material tasks are beyond our powers. All the treasures of earth are within our grasp. No thought remains hidden. Every undertaking can be put to the task and realized. The fertilizing distribution of the possession of the world is our task. We must discover the force that will effect and up and down movement of the masses". In *The New Society, 1921* Rathenau wrote: "A far reaching policy of socialization is necessary and urgent. The goal of the world revolution upon which we have entered, means in its material aspects the melting of all society into one". This was the "leveling" effect, which was a key goal of the conspirators, the Illuminati and many other branches of the World Order. This leveling through communism would become the dictum or diktat of the universal god of Hermes who was a jealous god requiring only one reality that of the World Order when he stated: "thou shall have no other God but me". The World Order identified in their minds as God controlling the chessboard and even believing that they could control Nature's laws with their eternal meddling, which I discussed in *Alternative 4* as the HAARP and GWEN programmes. The deification of humanity would allow the kudndalini force to connect man to the Grid holographics of past Masters, just as the Priests of the World Order are through their own identification as God connected to those holographics. The individual who could still think standing on his or her feet, who consciously remained unconnected to the Grid was to be fought, no questions asked and a policy of harassment and censure for all those who did not conform to the psychotic duality that was Hermes 'reality'. Everyone "on message" for the World Order programme, which is no more than a complete dramatization of the past and a dramatization that appears very real to the insane that promote it and those who mindlessly follow it to their unenviable fate.

It is interesting how the World Order and money markets spectacularly misjudged the Internet and dot. Com. companies. The Internet in some respects mirrors the Grid or crystal – www-com/grid with its capacity for information. The Internet however, was about *sharing* information, which is comparable to the Grid and its survival mechanisms. However whereas the Grid or UVG120 crystal is concerned with MATERIAL SURVIVAL OR THE SURVIVAL OF MATTER, the Internet has often provided information and products free of charge, which can be downloaded. Bill Gates and Microsoft definitely made tremendous profits for helping to give birth to the computer age, but each upside has its downside and the contribution towards a Magnetic Reversal must be considered. Thus in this brief moment in time, a door of knowledge and communication has opened, which could travel the globe and challenge the World Order and the Grid: that door will not remain open for long and man should grasp this brief moment in time.

The realization of the goals set out in *The Protocols of the Learned Elders of Zion*, does not require a discussion on who wrote the Protocols and whether it was a Jewish conspiracy for world domination, which evidently appears to be the case, based on the facts of this book: or whether it was a goal of the white imperialists, since the tribes of 13 and 12 may be synonymous in the goals at the top. One has only to look into the observable world or the obvious, to see the World Order plan being finalised in its details. The oligarchy owe no allegiance to any nation or to any philosophy of life as Mullins stated:

> "These people were a biological throwback in the continuing development of humanity. They were persons who were unable to become productive members of any society, and who could exist only by maintaining a parasitic attachment upon a host. Incredibly, they seized upon this striking difference as a sign that they had been chosen to rule all of mankind! Initially no more than a harmless illusion, this self-deception was transformed into an evidence of "superiority". Their biological uniqueness, their committal to a parasitic mode of life, became their principle advantage in attaining their goals. They set up

techniques of immediately recognizing each other in any part of the world. They resolved to act always cohesively as well-trained determined phalanx against their unwitting opposition. They made full use of their qualities of non-allegiance and nonalignment, which was actually enmity, undying hatred towards all nations, races and creeds of host peoples who tolerated their presence. This freedom from all loyalties and moral codes of the kinds which governed all other groups gave them an enormous tactical advantage over those whom they planned to enslave and destroy"

Their allegiance I would conclude from this book, only depended on the superiority of those who had survived a Magnetic Reversal and Flood, with the secrets of the hidden science, along with new information that they had stolen during the time of the Religious Revolution in Crete. Prior to the Flood and the last Magnetic Reversal as in all previous cycles, there had been virtually no opposition to their despotism and power (although the Indian epics speak of a war between two kings). The ability to utilize the Black Cabala and magical rites had lowered man to the emotional level of the Arch controller – fear. The attempts to sequester the Holy Grail with its message of Re-incarnation, knowledge and cosmology and importantly the trap of the Grid meant that a concept of duality as opposing goals of male and female were united in the god of Hermes, who best fitted the methodology employed along with the apparent duality of the tribes 12 and 13. The camouflage of confusion created by the game of guessing an individual's or group's God, was really the method of cleverly camouflaging the enemy, whilst the World Order I suspect was really controlled and directed at the highest level by both groups acting in unison. I have outlined such confusion, in trying to decide which group 12 or 13 invaded Knossos and took the Grail. In actual fact, in the past one fought on one side or the other, with the possibility that ultimately you were being used and sacrificed in a World Order game, with a pre-determined outcome. Thus went Golgotha.

The parasite of mistletoe, that the Druids regularly lopped from the oak royal, signified no more than the "branch" which was the Holy Grail message of Re-incarnation, which was to be subservient to the royal oak, the dynastic and monetary power of the elitist groups of 12 and 13. The knowledge, which represented power to tap holographics from the Grid that was taken in Crete, during the Religious Revolution, created a new power that could be USED. **Treason**, or the betrayal one one's sovereign, country, or group incorporating any treachery or betrayal of the goal or aims or laws of the group or nation, is a former crime that has now vanished, because national loyalties no longer exist and the majority of groups have sold their aims down the river of gold to the World Order. Laws are made to be adhered to, just as purposes must be adhered to e.g. the goal of science is to discover truth and a scientist should not sell that goal short in response to the World Order goal of control and no questions asked. Science poses questions and uses the rational mind to solve them. Find out *that you are* a scientist and you will find the goal of *truth*. Find out *that you are* a <u>British politician</u> and you will find your goal is to *serve* the <u>British</u> electorate. Find out *that you are* a lawyer and your goal is to uphold the law and truth. Find out *that you are* a body and your goal is the survival of matter. Find out *that your are* - a mind and your goal is the resolution of problems. Find out *that you are* a spirit and your entire goal lies in anti-matter and the reverse of matter postulates (goals).

The woman was viewed as the parasite and where the elite finally believed that the gift and knowledge was theirs to give, deciding how and when and for how much, man would receive back a gift that was given to him c. 10 000 B.C. The elite tried to combine holly (holy one) and oak (royal) in one personage, thus denying the truth and reality. This became their own warped sense of 'reality', where the knowledge and hidden science created the arrogant assumption that they were in some way "chosen": Just as the Essenes a communistic group was in all probability set up by the World Order elite or 12 and 13, then the duality of the group, was expressed in its tiered layers. The higher tier as servants to the Brotherhood of a rich powerful and politically right group, whilst the 12 tribes and their communistic principles ostensibly controlled the lower group or tier and masses. This duality is seen in virtually all secret groups that are controlled by the World Order. Such duality always leads to a confusion of aims and goals and despite the rhetoric, there will be no freedom for man within that group, since the goal of the World Order is *not one of freedom for humanity*. The goal of the World Order is *destruction* and although they are not consciously aware of that goal, they create destruction constantly and chaos. They follow mindlessly the 'script' of the past. Channeling and crystal seer ship together with Cabalistic ritual has created the so-called "invisible" masters who are no more than a visible (if you could identify them) or real powerful group who are insane and follow the Akashic Record of past Masters, which are thoughts in all probability of their own or past incarnations! The controlling group has no national loyalties other than perhaps Israel or the secret group which holds the goals of the World Order, since the group exists outside those boundaries and employs the cry of Crowley: "Do what thou wilt is the whole of the Law". They are beyond the law and accountability and their great arrogance and contempt for humanity is all the more, because man will not challenge them, he simply fails to ask questions and keep on asking those questions until they are answered. A man will constantly seek to evade truth if he believes he has a vested interest in a lie, which he perceives as survival either for self, or group. This however is the matter universe and it is not survivalist for spiritual goals.

There is no freedom, no peace and no achievement of spiritual goals in the lie, since it is the 'out reality' of the World Order: the false reality that runs the world today. There will be no understanding for man, no release from the trap unless a few or many are prepared to ask those questions and **get them answered**.

The conspirators knew that their parasitic way of life would not be long endured by any host. They had to set up a program to subdue and overcome all governments, all religious creeds, all group loyalties, and replace them with their own World Order reality, which would allow any type of perversion, as long as the host peoples tolerated the presence of the parasite. The culture of sex, drugs, crime, the abandonment of monogamous life, the abandonment of children and cruelty to children with the gratification of sexual desires would all be tolerated, provided there was no challenge to the controlling elite. The darkest days of Atlantis or the New Atlantis has arrived, with the dark beings that have always remained in control, now dramatizing full on, their past and the holographics that they had for so long re-stimulated by their perpetual use of channeling, seer ship and Cabalistic Black Magic ritual. They merely selected the master 'gene' (holographic of the past) from the master pattern that contained not only event data, but thought also. Such Grid control was conveyed to the masses in the form of the "new morality" and "see how far you can take it", where man became a "slave" to the Masters, just as they became a slave to their past holographics and the Grid of animal behavior, retained in the morphogenetic bioplasma of event and phylogenetic data: There was no spiritual life in the days of Atlantis, it was pure despotic rule. Thus the assumption that Inc.1 which I equated with the Religious Revolution in Crete c. 1 400 B.C. as the beginning, is incorrect. In fact it was the beginning only of a battle for the Holy Grail and man's soul on Earth and thus the intensity of energy in the battle became imprinted as holographics on a higher and more finely graded energy that I termed the spiritual bioplasma. I was not the beginning, only the beginning of a duality where male and female were conjoined as the god Hermes. The surfacing of the 'Underground Stream' (of wisdom) in renaissance periods in history was only the woman trying to escape from her jailer in the tomb of Hermes overseen by the Cabal.

The "new morality" and "liberation through drugs and sex", merely plugged man into holographics of the past, where the World Order had perpetually used sex and drugs to access certain Grid holographics, which mainly occurred in Atlantis and were dramatized in Crete at the time of the Religious Revolution. Thus man in having re-stimulated the Grid or morphogenetic holograms would be directed by Grid behavior - man as animal driven by Darwinian evolution of conflict and survival of the fittest. Man as his body only, controlled by the morphogenetic and phylogenetic mechanisms that govern the survival of bodies and matter. Since man's mind was no longer used, vestigial through non-use as man sat glued to his telly and read his daily dose of propaganda, he went about his daily business in the hive, relying on the 'reality' of the World Order. After all, if what I say here was true, then man reasons he would have read it in his *Sun* newspaper or seen it on the telly. As for the soul, well man as Christian knew that one day Jesus would come and sort out all the mess and in the interim, he had only to go about and impress Christianity on others, which would presumably buy him or her their ticket out from a Magnetic Reversal! Whilst the Scientologists believed that ethics was a loose term that did not apply when anyone shouted the words: "Group Survival!" Which as a method is co-incidentally or not the method of Israel when under threat – "To your tents Oh Israel!" Whether Scientologists can grapple the subject back into their own hands and decide which Bulletins came from where and adhere to their goal of *healing humanity?* Is a question once again only they can answer, by going back to their aims and the truth of their own history.

Man is merely the host on which the parasite of the World Order exists. The parasite is always smaller and weaker than the host on which it lives and further the parasite always disguises itself and its aim in order to carry out its parasitic mission. As soon as you start to question any facet of this story, you have the label of anti-Semitic hung on you, but this is not the case, but merely a method to stop questions being asked. The struggle between parasite and host followed the laws of evolution and the aim of the parasite is not to entirely destroy the host, since itself would no longer find its sustenance, no its aim was to live quietly bleeding off the life force of the host. Since the parasite of the World Order lives according to the past holographics of the Grid and past thought forms of the Arch controllers, it went into agreement to protect the Grid as the master-controlling pattern. The Black Cabala merely utilised the Grid, but until new knowledge arrived on earth c. 10 000 B.C. the World Order had no idea of the possibilities. That knowledge was meant for all humanity, however the World Order took control of it, since once again they saw the Grid as a method of power and money. I was reluctant to even write this book, since the dilemma arose that whatever was said, would be picked up and *used* by the World Order and man would probably shrug his shoulders and go back to his 'telly'. Whilst some wondered whether my two prior books should have been edited, there was no recognition, of the battle that was fought with the Grid and Master pattern, no comprehension of the forces involved and the practical manifestations in the physical-matter world. **EVERY** SINGLE THOUGHT AND TASK WAS FOUGHT I can assure you that it has been a pyrrhic victory, in so far as the victory of this conclusion and my own experience are as great as those I have defeated. However I gave my word of honour a long time ago and whilst we prefer to believe in past lives, simply because we periodically drop a body every eighty years or so, the fact is that the spirit is continuous and a word of honour given thousands of years ago, is still one's word of honour today. I believe that I have now fulfilled that word. If anyone intends to leave a position or post, then they write up that post for the next person who may (be foolish enough) take the job. I have stood on this post for a very long time, but now intend to leave and thus have written up the entire post.

If man had stuck with the OT levels in Palaeolithic times, I am sure that ladder upwards and out would have materialised, however the reason man did not follow that route, was his own inability to confront reality as opposed to the 'reality' of the World Order. He found it comfortable and after all, he had experienced it all before and he was used to the MRC case and a One World Order; anyway this was the 'script' that had been followed for billions of years and the sun was still there and this was still a beautiful world apart from the crime, drugs, immorality, sexual deviance, rape, armed robbery, incest, child molestation, ethnic cleansing, arson, murder, and slavery. No, it was not such a bad world and better the basement with the rats, than a world of anti-matter in the upper floors and library of a house that he had forgotten. I am reminded of the *Tales of Beelzebub to his Grandson* by Gurdjieff who told of an alien who visited Earth in a space ship – **Karnak** and wondered in awe at the goings on this planet and could only view it with a sense of humour. I can sympathise with that and named the charity set up in the hope of providing a centre and research centre after that idea. The *Natural World Order*, which is based on the laws of the universe, has been replaced on Earth by the unnatural World Order of the parasite, who is run by www-com/grid or the crystal of past holoraphics. Any attempt to dislodge the parasite, is denounced as conspiracy theory, or anti-Semitism, racist or the full gamut of defence reactions installed by the World Order as Mullin's stated: "Another law of nature is that the parasite, not only by sucking off the life sustenance of the host, but also by altering its life cycle, will inevitably kill the host". This process is called "the decline and fall of civilization". Thus went the Early Minoans and the comparable OT levels. The natural life cycle and spiritual cycle of man would be to evolve into a higher state, however the cycle of the MRC case or MMRC case (Missed Magnetic Reversal Case) is one of not being able to finish a cycle of action. The end of the cycle to him is loss of sustenance from the host, after all if man were to be released from the trap, what would happen to him? There would be no more superiority, no more game for him, no more control and no more power. He will do everything within his power to keep man chained to the trap of www-com/grid As if to emphasise the point, when I tried to type www-com/grid then it immediately at least on my computer, came up with mauve type, underlined and reverting me to programme it asked whom the server was! For a joke I wrote www-com/grid and then the computer help line asked if I wanted to write a new script – YES PLEASE!

GOD GENES

Hermes Trismegistos, the Thrice-Great Master Geomancer of Earth, with his Smagdarine Emerald Tablets, the keys to Gaia's (Earth's) energy body has become the god of the World Order. Hermes however was the god of the Religious Revolution and great lie of Crete. The ancient magus lies behind all concepts of the Planetary Grid and is represented as the god's messenger to Earth, later passing his flame of mastery, to the Archangel Michael with his initiatory sword. The Hebrews claimed that Michael was the keeper of the secrets of the Relations between Heaven and Earth – geomancy. The Grid is being promoted within the Brotherhood as the foremost and paramount spiritual phenomenon on Earth, however it was not Hermes who brought the secrets and The holy Grail to Earth: Hermes was the product of a revolution that tried to hide the truth and the role of the woman. I have spent considerable time in this book, giving evidence for the case of the stolen apples of immortality and The Holy Grail message, which was taken along with a whole cosmology and knowledge of the Grid. The Grid is not a spiritual phenomenon, but a vile trap and prison. The problem has been that so much information has been channelled from the Grid and mixed up with portions of the truth, that The Grail has become virtually inseparable from the history of the Hebrews and the tribes of Israel and occult, with the deification of Adam and the condemnation placed on the woman, which is merely justification for having committed a wrong in the beginning. Channelled information will favourably give the viewpoint of the Masters and it is this knowledge that is now appearing once again on the cutting edge of New Age esoteric knowledge. This knowledge gets mixed up with just enough science, to dupe people into connecting with the Grid. Further when people meet seers or occult channellers they are impressed with predictions of the future and apparent knowledge of someone's past and the energy these people exude. Hitler created the same sort of hypnotic mesmerism with his energy channelled from the vacuum by opening the crown chakra. I have found it increasingly difficult to retain control of my research and notice already how ideas have been taken and mixed up with some insanity! Thus I will only place this final warning before leaving, since I personally have no intention of staying for a Magnetic Reversal and thus this is in effect a write up of my post, which I have held for some considerable time.

Spiritual intervention c. 10 000 B.C brought information to this planet and that information was sequestered very early on by the Masters or patriarchal priests. Undoubtedly they had knowledge of the Grid and had used that knowledge to retain power even in the antediluvian era: however the attempt to connect the Elohim who allegedly brought the domes to Earth, with Adam and a spiritual intelligence together with giants, is not accurate from my own view. The specific information that arrived was to remind man of his immortal *soul*, forgotten during the last cycle, where giants existed due to different gravitational conditions of the magnetic cycle and where longevity had led man to believe he was his immortal *body*. Specific information on the Grid and the manner in which the Grid controlled man was also sent, however the Masters who had long controlled humanity, had no desire to loose that control and thus sequestered the knowledge for themselves.

The Earth as a dynamically changing fly-wheel or gyro spinning at about 1 000 miles per hour spin rate, has a correctional balance system and if it were not for the 20 movable locking points or "vile vortices", or the Earth Grid Magnetic Reversal anomalies, the Earth would tear itself apart. According to Richard Lefors Clark (cited) the Earth's magnetic poles do not completely shift (reverse or flip) in correctional balancing, only the Earth's Bloch wall magnetic reversal anomalies move positions in the northern and southern hemispheres to balance the Earth. Lefors Clark places the so-called deluge and glacier phenomena some 10 -15 000 years ago, when the Bloch wall anomalies were much further north. The reversals caused massive ocean/sea tides and levitation effects accompanied by dramatic weather changes. I have already pointed to the reversal of the Earth's magnetic field, as providing a relationship to vast species extinctions during such periods and those who support the beauty of such reversals as part of Nature's correctional system, have not looked at the larger picture and what I say in this book – beauty for man as a spiritual being, it is not! Dr. Becker at the Lamont conference (cited) proposed that reversals could be accompanied by major changes in the ELF frequencies of the magnetic field micro pulsations, which would have produced behavioural changes that reduced the survival of the more advanced species. More recently, Dr. Abraham Liboff of Oakland University has proposed that these frequency alterations could have influenced reproduction and produced defective offspring, which might account for the deformed wooden carvings produced on Easter Island, in some memory of the survivors of either this reversal, or an atomic war, which may have caused the Sethites to regress to ape-like form. In *The Second Millennium Working report on Cancer* that covered the author's research, I gave a whole section on the effects of varying ELF's on behaviour and biochemistry. There is every reason to believe that thought processes and memory retain these reversal events, which was given as a theory for the MRC case, or the Masters who have always retained control of this planet.

Fig.33 illustrated the die-outs of species during magnetic field reversals and these die-outs prove that evolution was not simply a random event, but has in the past been driven by changes in the Earth's natural magnetic field, as well as by the abnormal fields resulting from overuse of electro-magnetic energy for power and communications. According to the geological times of major reversals, the last major reversal was in the Triassic and cretaceous periods of Earth's history and this would indicate that for the past 25 000 years Earth has been free of geological disturbances and a reversal. The attempts in Biblical history, to place Noah's Ark in a more recent time in some cases as early as c. 3 000 B.C is certainly at odds with the scientific evidence of geological catastrophe. The attempts to confuse dates and history along with the suppression of religious texts such as the Nag Hamaadi scrolls; with suppression of artifices in archaeology that do not fit in with the World Order enforced reality of Darwinian evolution as a slow grinding ascent from primitive forms, is perpetrated at such a high level that one can only view such suppression as an ongoing policy which seeks to silence any attempt to research this whole area along with the hidden science: Such policy has been supported by a controlled media, publishing and throughout the academic system by way of controlled grants indeed I believe Dr. Becker lost his University position, despite the fact that he was twice nominated for a Nobel Prize. This is a standard method of the World Order in silencing any independent scientific opinion, which might challenge the government's 'experts' who always toe the official policy line. In 1998 Hungarian-born Dr Arpad Pusztai revealed the connection between genetically modified (G.M.) potato and cancer in rats. This was not the "politically correct" scientific line for a Government that was busy conspiring, along with its masters in the United States Administration, and the World Trade Organisation, to sell out the electorate in favour of the biotechnology giant Monsanto, Novartis and the rest of the Agri-Chemical conglomerates with proposals to approve the introduction of potentially dangerous and untested G.M. methods in Agriculture. Not only did Pusztai abruptly lose his job with the Rowett Research Institute in Scotland, 19 superficially impressive authorities were wheeled forth to discredit his research in a joint letter to the press. Of these, only four appeared to have qualifications remotely appropriate to Pusztai's work, a further three were beholden to vested commercial interests, and another had no scientific qualifications at all. If anything Dr Pusztai's work confirms my own theories here, that meddling with the genetics disrupts the biofield and tunes the etheric DNA and primitive survival mind into a growth=survival mode, which creates the cancer growth or tumour. The World Order and their 'experts' have no understanding of the mechanisms of the primitive mind, since they are run by it! Such a mind is incapable of my suggestion of sitting around a board- room table for a week with independent scientists, free to access the cancer research I have proposed, without fear of losing their professional position or grants. In order to complete this research I have had to forego both, which I can assure you is an absolutely bankrupting position.

It might be suggested that since Dr. Becker warned that freedom from a

Magnetic Reversal is not assured that there was an attempt to silence him particularly as he stated: " The evidence is that we are in the initial stages of a reversal", which might account for the dramatic changes in global weather: further Dr. Becker has warned about the mind control capabilities of the GWEN (Ground Wave Emergency Network) and alleged defence system in America that could be used for mind control of all Americans. A similar capability is being developed in Britain under the cover of police transmitters, which are to be erected country-wide and which *against all independent scientific advice* will operate in the very low frequency bands, which in *Part I* of the author's research and *The Second Millennium Working Report into Cancer* she provided scientific evidence for the affect of this band on biological systems including behavioural and genetic changes. Cyclic cataclysm is known at some high level and it was during the author's research into UFO's and her second book *Alternative 4*, that she started to pick up this story with the book and TV programme *Alternative 3*, where in the 1970's an eminent American scientist had warned of dramatic changes in weather to come, before he too was silenced by the American equivalent of the Official Secrets Act. A psycho-civilised society or mind controlled society (*Alternative 4*), which the author claimed was the World Order final solution to control of mankind through Tesla related technology, has finally revealed itself in this book, as a dramatization of past Grid holographics in a repeat cycle of all that have gone before.

The eleven-year solar cycle is approaching a peak and all indices show that his cycle is stronger and more disturbed than any that has previously been measured. Recently solar flairs only just missed Earth and as Dr. Becker pointed out: "However, the problem may very well be academic, we may have unwittingly produced the equivalent of the greatest reversal ever through our global use of electromagnetic energy. A natural magnetic reversal takes thousands of years to occur. It appears likely that the biological effects of reversal are due to changes in the frequency spectrum of the micro pulsations and we have produced far more than the equivalent change in frequencies in the last fifty years alone". It is not inconceivable that technology existed in pre-flood races which utilised Grid energy lines and anti-gravitational anomalies, which might form the foundation of myths and legends, such as the Indian epic *The Mahabharata*, which spoke of flying machines or 'Vinmas' and significantly **a war between two opposing kingships**: such a war may have been nuclear or the last reversal may simply have been natural, however metallurgical works were making steel near the place that Noah's Ark came to rest and one might conclude that any technological expertise was simply carried through a magnetic reversal, along with those who appear to have missed that reversal in some manner– the MMRC case (the missed Magnetic Reversal Case). I will return to the two opposing kingships in the last section of this book and its existence today which WILL create a Third World War, if you do not stop it and expose this story.

In *Alternative 4*, I formed *The Onion Ring model*, to describe the manner in which past holographics impinge onto the mind in present time, in the natural UFO experience: such a mechanism would identify the event as a metaphysical experience, or current time recognition of an **event that occurred in the past**. The suppression of UFO research, again exhibits policy of the World Order, in so far as the Grid and its Akashic library is involved and thus this is another area of research that has been suppressed and the media utilised to ridicule such research: ridicule is just another method of the World Order along with non grant status, refusal of publication, attack by law or dismissal from academic position. Bruce Cathie (cited) and other UFO researchers were able to recognise a pattern of UFO sightings, which enabled Cathie to formulate the Grid pattern. Whilst Cathie has on this evidence predicted that "an intelligence" lies behind the UFO phenomenon that intelligence does not necessarily indicate a present intelligence, neither does it indicate that the intelligence is benign, it is in fact malign and thought of the past Masters. It is likely that Grid anomalies of anti-gravitation were not only used in the building of megalithic sites and the pyramids, but it appears from such epics as the *Mahabharata* that Grid lines may have been used in antediluvian flight, which might be proven by the odd archaeological artefacts that indicate **scaled** models of aircraft and which have been purposefully not exhibited in museums. This misrepresentation of data or omission of explanation of museum exhibits is a disgraceful under use of educational facilities and even worse, is part of the deliberate alteration of archaeological remains. I have compared original archaeological photographs of the Knossos frescos in the period of the 1930's to the actual frescos in Crete at the Heraklion museum and the red colour of the Prince fresco is definitely paler! The red men of course depicted the thirteenth tribe and royal status.

UFO research utilising the genius of men like Tesla and Schauberger has been ongoing since the time of the Nazi's and undoubtedly after the War, the German scientists who went to America, took that research with them. Scientists and researchers who are aware of the Grid and the vacuum energy are at a loss to explain why such knowledge has not been used to provide free energy which would have revolutionised the communications and transport sectors, however the Syndicate or business elite of the World Order, find no profit in free energy, despite the fact that by use of electricity as Dr. Becker pointed out, we may have already precipitated the most catastrophic reversal yet. To recognise the Grid however would require a recognition of the religious mysteries and whilst one group hopes to slowly drip-feed the mysteries to mankind, is it not a case of too little and too late? Had the Holy Grail not been stolen, things would have worked out very differently for man and civilization and he would not be here at the end, with the possibility of being trapped by the holographics.

The secret alphabets such as the Beth-Luis-Nion not only originated with the secret patriarchal priesthood of the tribes of Israel, probably the thirteenth tribe; but also contained the religious mysteries together it would seem with mysteries relating to the Grid. Such mysteries were not only encoded in the meaning of the trees in the Tree Alphabet, but numerical values in the Gematria and Cabala were utilised also. There are 72 letters in the Beth-Luis-Nion alphabet and that figure would arise as the three-day (3 X 24 hours) resurrection period of Jesus, who was tutored in the mysteries and particularly the Tree Alphabet as I discussed in *The Battle of The Trees*. The cycle of matter and anti-matter with its two complete revolutions (720 degrees) of 360 degrees was to make its appearance in the figure-of-8 design at Knossos in the Religious Revolution period and the scroll design noticeably in The Queen's Chamber at Knossos in its 'Broken 8' design was meant to convey the concept of: 'Into a life and out of a life' – Re-incarnation. However there is a deeper mystery that was taken by the Cabal who conducted the religious Revolution, which I will explain shortly. The god of the alphabet controlled the year and it was a fatal flaw in the thinking of the elite, to assume that they controlled everything and therefore believed themselves to be gods. The condemnation of the Jews by God in *The Bible* rests upon this point. The Gematria and the alphabets are coded into *The Bible* along with what is left of the religious mysteries after severe editing and omission of facts. Cathie calculated that the harmonic of the speed of light in free space had a value of 144, which multiplied by 1 000 gives another magical number of 144 000 of the tribes of Israel that would be saved in the future Apocalypse as "the chosen ones". Further the "rainbow" (as electromagnetic spectrum) and "crystal" (Grid) is also referred to a number of times obliquely in *The Bible* and with reference to God in the Book of *Revelations*! The sun god of Aton or the sun god Jesus evidently encompassed the power that originated with the sun and spread that power, as was the case with Christianity throughout the living world as the 8-arm tentacle octopus shown clearly in the Marine Vase from the Religious Revolution period in Crete. The original Tree alphabet had 15 trees that ruled the whole year, reflected in the original flag of Europe, which had 15 stars. The idea that the God was in the crystal or sun will be explained in the last section of this book with reference to Hermes and the Sirius A and B Stars.

The cabal, who stole the Holy Grail in Crete, failed to understand how the Grid worked or the anti-matter cycle and matter cycle, but they did however apply such knowledge to their Cabalistic practices. Ivan T. Sanderson proposed that the ten "vile vortices" were areas of gravitational anomalies[201] and Nicholas R. Nelson in his book *Paradox* [203] believes that the vortex areas are entrances to other dimensions and that such "doors" to other dimensions account for the strange disappearances and vanishings e.g. in the Bermuda triangle. The description of Jesus in semi-transparent form, able to pass through walls along with the connection to the significant number of 72, implies the anti-matter cycle of 720 degrees long with ruler ship of the whole year by Masters and it also implies etheric Masters such as those on Sirius and the GWL (Great White Lodge). If there was an attempt here by the ignorant priests to connect Jesus with anti-matter and another dimension as Heaven or home of the Masters on the GWL of Sirius, then it was poorly done from a scientific viewpoint: for there is no perception by our physical senses of the anti-matter cycle, viewing events as we do from the point of view of the matter cycle alone. Jesus could not have an anti-matter body since if he had dematerialised into anti-matter as is being suggested, then that would have caused an atomic explosion to wipe out the entire Middle East at least! The concept of the anti-world has been completely misunderstood by the Brotherhood, however this idea of another realm, anti-world, anti-matter cycle, heaven or whatever etheric term that was employed, has given rise to the idea that Masters do in fact live in this realm and are directing humanity. This surely has given rise to the myths and legends that surround the end of the cycle, when "Monsters" come marching over the "rainbow bridge" at the end of things and presumably when there is another magnetic reversal and the giants once again descend as gods to Earth. How far this idea has penetrated into secret group beliefs can only be guessed at, but I would remark that this is Black Cabalistic significance that was not originally part of the Grail. I have already described in detail how channelling gives the impression of actual spirits in the etheric layer, due to the properties of the Crystal or Grid which stores archetypal symbols as elements of thought. The Universal Mind, which I equate with the Grid, Akashic Record or great library in the sky or in my own terms the primitive mind or morphogenetic bioplasma is a mind of survival and undoubtedly contains all data on past events relating to the survival of the matter cycle. This may describe Hubbard's so-called reactive mind, which records events relating to non-survival.

In his book *The Keys of Enoch* by Dr. J. J. Hurtak, the author produces a metalinguistic code document of linguistic cybernetic information and predicts areas of artificial (above) and natural (below) time warp areas used for contact by the Brotherhood. This appears to me, to be another case of channelling from specific Grid energy points, presumably above areas such as hills and mountains, or places of high energy activity of the Grid and which are likely as areas, to contain the past thoughts of Masters who utilised cabalistic practice to access what they thought were the past Masters: a case of the sick man getting sicker! Cathie found that the harmonic of light has a definite relationship with the geometry of a circle and the mathematics and geometry of the Grid were utilised by Pythagoras, who was indeed initiated by the Dactyls in Crete, who I assume were the ascendants of the cabal who conducted the Religious Revolution: Pythagoras was also said to have been initiated by the Arch Druid Abaris, thus providing one more connection to the thirteenth tribe. The Rosicrucian's have long been aware of the Grid and the mathematical and geometric significances and presumably the connection, which Cathie found i.e. the Grid lattice is tuned harmonically to twice the speed of light. The significance of this fact may have been part of the alleged Philadelphia experiment where perhaps it was hoped that a vast distance could be covered by altering the very structure of space itself by altering the space-time geometric matrix, as a method of achieving space travel. Cathie pointed out that the way to do this was to alter the matter and anti-matter cycle and time (which is itself a geometric as Einstein postulated). The ball of string, which Ariadne gave to Theseus in myth to find his way in and out of the labyrinth to kill the Minotaur in Crete and which although prominently displayed in classical icon (*Fig. 27*), is not commented upon; is undoubtedly another referral to the Grid. The Earth as a huge magnet and dynamo, wound with magnetic lines of force as it coils is rather like a ball of string. The lines of force of the magnetic field form a lattice, or grid pattern, due to the spin of the planetary body, thus the analogy to the ball of string takes on new significance and again is part of the knowledge taken in Crete and which originally formed part of the equivalent Palaeolithic OT level equivalent! Gravity however which controls the matter cycle, is manifest within the Grid at the points where the lines of force cross and where a small vortex is created drawing matter into it. There are trillions of such vortices and matter is drawn towards the gravitational field, just as water is drawn down the plughole of the bath. This brings us to the bath-shaped sarcophagi of the Early Minoans before the Semitic Religious Revolution, where the 'tubs' were re-placed by square-shaped sarcophagi imitating the god of the Semitic stone pillar.

The dead were originally laid in the foetal position (awaiting re-birth) on sand and seashells connected to the woman and the sea. The 'tubs' of the Early Minoans however were flat-bottom trapezoids with elliptic curved rims along with the implication of curved-space-time. Sir Arthur Evans the archaeologist from Oxford, who excavated the Knossos site, unfortunately described the 'tubs' not as burial urns but as "lustral" bath-tubs! thus was born the Disneyland of the Knossos site and which has only aided the secrecy surrounding it. Gravity and the constant flow downward through the vortices has catastrophic effects, in so far as the perpetual DNA etheric imprint is permanently stamped on the body and pattern of man, along with the thought processes contained in the Grid or crystal of the past. Man evidently feels comfortable with the familiar pattern and cycle, enough to constantly support the World Order and prevent anyone with an alternative viewpoint and 'script' from challenging that – so be it, man is stuck with his cycle. You can only challenge the World Order with the hidden science and logic - that is what the World Order fears most, since when you confront the insane with their own insanity, they completely cave in, since you have removed **their perception of reality**!

Cathie maintained that matter is formed in the positive stage or pulse as waves of electrons travel in a spiral motion through space: whereas the anti-matter cycle is created in the negative pulse, with each spiral constituting a 360-degree circle or pulse. The speed of light is the product of the period between each pulse of physical matter. The double cycle of 720 degrees can also be described in the figure-of-8, which features in Scottish stones as the 'spectacle design' and in the Knossos site. Our consciousness can only perceive the matter-cycle pulse and by analogy if you took a film roll with event frames recorded, then each event frame would represent a single pulse of the matter cycle. The secret of The Grail that was never understood, is that whilst a recording of the matter-cycle occurs, there is also a recording of the anti-matter cycle, but that may be likened to a corresponding or parallel film roll or even the period of the finish of one frame and the next. In other words there is a recording of the matter cycle **and** the anti-matter cycle, although the body with its material and physical senses cannot detect the anti-matter cycle only the matter cycle. The Grid and our own primitive memory banks merely record the matter cycle, since the Grid is only concerned with the cycle and survival of matter. Whether the anti-matter cycle is the anti-world or parallel universe and the existence of our 'Twin' or doppelganger as a recording of anti-world event, or whether the anti-world is the spiritual recording of events is only relevant in the Death Experience. In the 'Life Review' at death one not only faces in the first stage of the review the event record of the matter cycle, but in the next stage one faces a record of the **spiritual review** or events of the anti-matter cycle. If one persisted in maintaining survival for self or small group (family) only in a life or the event cycle of Earth, then the actions and thoughts may be survivalist in terms of a matter cycle and the Grid, but may be very non-survivalist in terms of the anti-matter or spiritual recording. Conscience arises when one compares the two in the 'Life Review': could you have done more; could you have helped more; could you and did you etc. Religion actually causes a great many non-survivalist frames on the anti-matter roll of film, since every religion believes it has the entire truth and through its converts seeks to impress that truth on others, however in so doing a religion may suppress a greater truth and thus the convert in the spiritual review, will see just how well or how badly he or she did in terms of survival of a spirit and on the basis of that review, will trap or release themselves. My own story is one of complete non-survival in terms of the matter cycle, but then truth (ultimate reality of the spirit) was never a part of that cycle and my attempt to resolve the Platonic maxim through my research has pre-determined that I should resolve an anti-matter cycle: thus I have worked for some time in the anti-matter cycle, which I am afraid is so poorly understood that the research was bound to fall foul of all those who work in matter cycles of money, power, ego and the full dramatization of Grid holographics of past matter cycles. The World Order dramatizes past Grid holographics of the matter cycle and the individuals who either comprise or aid the World Order now have so many recordings of non survival in the anti-matter cycle of the spirit that it would be impossible to rectify, unless they resolved what Hubbard termed the basic incident: this is the first incident in one of many and in this case would refer to the truth of what happened to the Holy Grail. The Brotherhood seek to retain the World Order survival, reality and policy of the matter cycle at all costs; a reality that is out-reality and non-survival to the anti-matter cycle and the survival of the spirit.

Irrespective of Hubbard's background, he has to be applauded in classifying Inc.1 with mind control, even though he terms that incident the beginning, which varies with my own assertion that it was only the beginning of mind control through religion. Prior to spiritual intervention c. 10 000 B.C man had forgotten about the anti-cycle and was deeply enmeshed in the matter cycle only. There was no religion as such, since the Masters were concerned with body control only and the use of Cabalistic science in maintaining power. The Religious Revolution of Crete saw the introduction of the god Hermes and the keys to Hermes Geomancy, which are now being exhibited as spiritual evolution! "All is Infinite mind, which is the fundamental reality and the womb of all universes"; "whatever is below is like unto that which is Above and whatever is Above is like that which is Below, to accomplish the miracles of The One"; "Nothing rests, everything moves and vibrates"; "Everything has its tides and its rise and fall, its equal pendulum swings to the right and to the left, its peaks and troughs"; "Every effect has its cause, every cause has its effect, all proceeding by Law, never by chance and Everything has its masculine and feminine aspects".[204] Such is Hermes thinking, which contains enough of the Grail inevitably mixed up with other significances by that borrowing bee! The inclusion of the Universal Mind is a clever trick and 'Above' and 'Below' control via the Grid and World Order and the channelled thoughts of past Masters; with The One as in the Oneness so openly and yet covertly displayed on the reverse side of the One- dollar note of America. Hermes has been deified and yet nowhere is there a greater lie and injustice.

The Grid is not some abstract theory, it is a reality that impinges daily on behaviour and thinking of mankind, maintained as a connection through the policy and methods of the World Order in denying any other reality to the matter cycle and orthodox policy on religion and politics. The cunning methods of connecting mans thinking to the Grid and past holographics requires a policy of no conscience, no questions asked coupled with of course no questions answered. The Grid appears to have a sentience or thought process, since it does indeed contain thought as a waveform of matter only: thus imprinted thought is at the level of controlling bodies, punishing bodies and the full gamut of the World Order method. New Age publishing has been cleverly utilised by the World Order, where channelled information with World Order significances has been interdispersed with the Holy Grail, paralleling secret group methods of giving the initiate just enough truth, so that he or she will overlook the pyramidal control policy and agenda written into the text.

Hubbard described Inc.2 as an "implant", which contains hundreds of frames virtually identical to modern times, including Hollywood! However is this not a Magnetic Reversal, where man is downloaded with all event data of the matter cycle of Earth – the Akashic Record? However whether you accept Hubbard's explanation or the author's, the conclusion remains identical, in so far as man receives a complete matter cycle 'script' and when Day.1 – Plant the vine arrives again, he will surely read his 'script' from the beginning, including a crucified man holograph that occurs in Inc. 2. This is a 'groundhog day' too far for me, I am off and leave you with the truth of the events of Golgotha and a great deal more that has occurred on my post, whilst I have held it! What is more you can bet your bottom 'script' of matter cycle, that now Hubbard and all that high emotion of the battle of Scientology has imprinted itself on the matter cycle holographics, then no doubt in the next cycle men and women in naval uniforms will appear, with ships and all those times when the Scientologists hit the matter cycle hard (World Order) and that cycle hit back on the **subject of survival**: and sure enough there has been a very large battle in the matter cycle with regards to Scientology as the American government waged an all out attack for twenty five years. This current cycle however was completely unique, in so far as spiritual intervention occurred and there are frames in the matter cycle that have not occurred before. The appearance of the cross or man crucified in Hubbard's Inc.2 or what I conclude is the down-loaded holographics in a Magnetic Reversal, does not automatically mean that this holographic comes from the last cycle or antediluvian period (pre Magnetic Reversal), it could be a holographic from this period retained in Grid crystal memory.

Man must be well and truly asleep if not comatose, if he believes that the Patriarchs or some secret group is guiding humanity through some spiritual experiment for mans' greater good, which is the general hype that is emerging from (manipulated) New Age sources, with that Hermes at the helm! Take a look around the planet and how much spiritual guidance do you see at work? Personally I prefer to listen to Dr. Becker and the scientists who have warned of the start of another Magnetic Reversal and I prefer to trust my own knowledge and knowingness, thus I personally have decided to go for the exit using the keys, which I have worked out from the science after straightening up all karma of past lives. No doubt everyone has their own viewpoint and beliefs on exit (or salvation) and will follow their religious beliefs accordingly: as I have warned I am not sure there will be another chance on exit, simply because the sun is an ageing star and will at some point collapse, so I trust the choice you make according to your beliefs is an informed one. Man has come to maturity and the mature do not depend on Mother or Father, but their own judgement; magnetic cycles are a horrible fact of the matter cycle, but true none-the-less and if one hopes to survive as a spiritual being for all eternity in a matter cycle, that would indeed be a vision of hell. If man cannot confront the Grid, he cannot confront mind control or the Masters and Hubbard's remark: " that which you will not or cannot handle, will handle you", is very true.

Dome information has been linked to the Gematria and Adam and I cannot see how such information was obtained if not from channelling, since this is pre-history and therefore not recorded in any *written* text. The fact that the domes allegedly appeared as energy centres, connected with hills and mountains strongly indicates the Druids and the thirteenth tribe, perhaps as I have noted accounting for that curious Dome in London, along with the London (Illuminatus?) Eye. Further the information on Domes spoke of the "Captain" of the Domes or the major energy centre, which again has oblique connections to 'Captain Thirteen', or the thirteenth member of a group of twelve, thus indicating once again the thirteenth tribe. I have however warned of the problem in channelling, where you pull down one or two frames in a whole 'roll of film' and the probability of mixing information from earlier times to later times or the question of space-time reality. The Domes or energy centres were attributed to the Elohim with connections to Adam, however phrases such as "spinning wheel" matrix applied to the description of the method by which the light energy from Dome centres was distributed, reminds one very strongly of the visions of *Ezekiel* and may well apply to the method of control or domination via thought from the Grid. It must be questioned how *Ezekiel* himself obtained his information and whether that information was obtained by channelling. These Dome energy centres importantly became marked by ancient monuments with stone circles, major temples, barrows, stone chambers and by single standing stones and eventually by churches: this implies religious control or mind control through such positioning, where Grid points above those areas would retain information of the past. The fact that the master Dome or the Grid's umbilicus cord in popular mythology was called King Arthur's Round Table of Camelot and Arthur was the thirteenth member of a group of twelve, has further implications to control of the Grid by the thirteenth tribe. Dome centres as places of high consciousness and meditation with inter-dimensional transport of awareness through the domed exit points in the House of the God's, once again implies interdimensional 'doors' and the more practical and scientific implication of channelling thoughts from past Masters at those points. The House of the Gods for the Tuatha de Danaan, was the Celtic barrow of New Grange and it is stated that many visited the House to seek an audience with the Gods of the Tuatha de Danaan, which again implies channelling; just as in all probability the oracle of Delphi, was placed at a significant Grid point for such purposes. It is also claimed that the Domes supplied a meditatively acquired insight into the "planetary thought matrix" which according to some descriptions is akin to a "holographic library" in the energy field of each Dome, which implies channelling once again. Significantly Moses who was revered in Mosaic Law by the Druids and the thirteenth tribe, received the Pentateuch, or Torah Or, on Mt. Sinai, which was a prominent sacred domed mountain and therefore channelling point to the Masters.

The Domes numbered 1746 and in the mystical science of the Cabala with its mathematical language of gematria, is a combined primary solar (666) and lunar (1080) number. This again refers back to the Religious Revolution in Crete and the absorption of the woman and The Holy Grail, into the political and religious control of man through the god Hermes and solar Kingship. The condemnation in *The Bible* on "the Beast" or "666" must surely refer to the Bull-Minos cult ("the Beast") and the fact that it is: "a man's number" refers to Solar Kingship, Apolloyou or Apollo and the initiation of mind control that originated when The Holy Grail or God's word was stolen. The absorption of the woman and man into the next transcendent stage beyond death in the figure of Hermes further removed the Holy Grail and divinity from the power of Kingship, into the hands of the pale priests and the tribes of Israel. This is certainly the explanation I would maintain for Hubbard denoting his Inc.1 with its archetypal symbols (of horn - gates of horn – the abode of the dead and Bull-Minos cult; cherubim and chariot of Hermes) as the beginning. **It was not the beginning**, only the beginning of mind control through the new found knowledge that was stolen and which incorporated Grid explanation and the philosophy or belief in Re-incarnation, which is followed by the Freemasons, whilst the philosophy of 'ashes to ashes, dust to dust' has been forced through Christianity on the populous, with only one resurrection for non-Brotherhood humanity at the time of judgement. The Apocalypse not only condemns Apollo the sun king, but also places a condemnation on the dragon which implies the twelve Oroboric Grid lines which are referred to as "dragon lines", and the coiling nature of the lines as the "Orboros serpent", which again occurs in archetypal symbolism in the Apocalypse. There are also three minor lines, ordinarily denominated by the qualities of male, female and neutral, which again has implications of woman and man (sun king) combined as the neutral bisexual transcendent third of Hermes. The Domes have two vertical light cords, one gold and one silver, which relate to the archetypal significant colours of male and female as gold and silver respectively. These cords are referred to in Ecclesiastes as: "the silver cord, the thread that binds all the selves in the human being with the divine". The divine presumably referring to the sun god or the Masters presence in the Grid! This really underlines once again how it was believed that channelling was thought to provide some contact with the Masters who were resident in some etheric world (The Great White Lodge on Sirius) directing man from 'Above' and making man in their image as 'Below' according to the Hermetic keys and the Hermetic god. A wonderful theatre of madness run by www-com/grid!

The Oboric Grid contains 15 great circles which really supplied the sightings of the UFO phenomena and as I have mentioned the original flag of Europe had 15 stars, which really comprises the UVG120 sphere or in Bethe Hagen's and William Becker's terminology "Earth Star". The crystal geometry of the Grid encompassing the five Platonic solids, illustrated by the thong-wrapped stones from Crete: with 120 equal-sized triangles (or 10 hexagons, or 30 diamonds) with 62 interaction points. Given that Pythagoras was initiated by the Dactyls in Crete who were ascendants of the Bull-Minos cult in all probability and the Cabal that conducted the Religious Revolution, then the connection of Pythagoras to the tutor Abaris the Arch Druid further supplies a connection to the thirteenth tribe. Is it not curious given that Secret group Grand Masters such as Weishuapt the original founder of the Illuminati, were obsessed with anti heaps and beehives; that one should find not only the omphalos with its bee design in England and Greece, but also in the Palaeolithic caves in the similar form of a *social colony* of coral along with honeycomb and magnetic iron-pyrites. The honeycomb which made an appearance in the Religious Revolution in Crete, with the Goddess on a honeycomb mountain, with two lions (Twin Kings) at her sides, was a transient stage of thought in the Religious Revolution, where the woman and the Grail knowledge was fused with solar kingship and the mountain undoubtedly depicts the Druids and the thirteenth tribe. Further the honeycomb of the bee, consists of individual unit 'cells' of a six-sided nature, which must have provided some historical background to the Gematria of "666" as a mans number, with the implication of control of the hive or humanity via the Grid and solar kingship, or as it may be now from one God-gene frequency or signal!

Whilst the woman tried to explain the holographics of the Grid and its structure to man, as a crystal which could amplify and project thought forms and act as a library carrying a record of past events that would only re-occur in the future and which man would experience as his immortal soul; those who had always retained control of Earth could only think of the immense power and profit such knowledge would acquire for them. Free energy, burning lamps forever without apparent power source and the power of prophecy which would impress man who had no inkling of the hidden science, or the Grid. The curious umbrella shapes that occurred in Palaeolithic caves was part of the secret doctrine to initiates even at that early date, following spiritual intervention c. 10 000 B.C. It was however the mixing of the Grail with Black Cabalistic science by the Masters of these secret groups that proved fatal as channelling. Channelling only provided thoughts of the past and not as was believed, Masters who currently lived in the etheric layer or Great White Lodge; it was through this fatal ignorance, together with the interpretation of holographics by the seer, who was invariably an a berated priest that man followed all that had gone before: leading him asleep to his inevitable fate of another Magnetic Reversal through the misuse of the hidden science. The Magnetic Reversal would stamp man again with the etheric DNA primitive evolutionary record of the matter cycle and according to Hubbard's Inc. 2 which I equate with a Magnetic Reversal, mans' soul would stick to the "electro-magnetic ribbon" receiving 36 days of "implants" from the arch controllers in Hubbard's terminology. However this was another fatal error on the part of Hubbard, in so far as he did not recognise the significance of Inc.2. and what I perceive as a Magnetic Reversal. Whilst presumably NASA are aware of the forthcoming event and seek a safe haven for "the chosen ones" with the banks of DNA for each species in a project of Noah's Ark, can we be certain that such an event has not occurred before and was recorded as the Biblical Noah's Ark? However the anti-matter cycle or recording supplies man with a conscience and as long as he has maintained a policy of survival of the fittest in the matter cycle, he will be tied by a thousand and one strings to that cycle and cannot exit: in so far as each time he created non-survival for another he also created a standard frame in his anti-matter cycle 'roll of film' (the spiritual recording) against which he will judge himself in the Death Experience or 'Life Review'. Thus one can see just how important it is to correct past life (continuous existence) karma of the matter cycle, creating a Diablo of balance between the two 'film rolls' or two records of matter (mind and body) to anti-matter (spirit). Unfortunately the more power in the matter cycle you acquired, the greater arc the interconnective consequences of non-survival created for others in the matter cycle: material power is not without grave karmic consequences, although I am sure politicians never loose sleep on it. Man might escape a Magnetic Reversal on Earth via some space station, but then he will not escape the matter cycle Universe or enter the anti-matter cycle or parallel universe, whilst he has a mismatched balance on his two 'film rolls' and a conscience in the spirit. Further and finally you must find the exact harmonic of that which has been harmed and no two people have identical harmonics, thus you must find the **actual identity** you harmed and reverse the matter-cycle of non-survival created! This certainly would have been a somewhat less formidable task 10 000 B.C. but has it gone too far? Further was man not lazy in his acceptance of a World Order, despite the injustice he perceived in that Order. The 144 000 who are saved in Biblical texts and who stand on Mt. Zion with the Lamb (Christ) each has the Name of God, written on their foreheads which corresponds to the third eye or the 7 th chakra, which is associated with the seat of illumination, the power of prophecy, connection to the Grid and the 7th Tarot Card of Hermes with his chariot (*Fig. 16*) and the 'script' of *Revelations*: Hermes the god of the Religious Revolution and mind control. The condemnation of woman by the tribes of Israel has been a lasting justification for having condemned man to another cycle and Magnetic Reversal and the original and basic overt committed by the sequestering of a message and knowledge originally sent by a higher source of compassion and love, to help humanity. It wasn't *her* fault for as we are told: "666" is a *"mans number"*, which can be traced back to the origins of mind control through politics and religion, the Religious Revolution in Crete. The Universal Kingdom or combined political and religious goals of the World Order displayed on the reverse side of the one dollar note of America and in the *Vaincre* magazine illustration surrounding the formation of European Union, will not bring peace only a third battle or World War III. As the Mary Magdalene so accurately stated: "There will be no peace on this Earth until the cut is healed". My withering comment to the World Order is to look again at the Crab Mural at Cardiff Castle and you will perceive you did   not understand the lesson!

The number 72 not only finds all the previous explained significances, including the length of stave in the Long Man Hill figure in Britain but also again is curiously represented in the radiating lines of steel infrastructure of the Millennium Dome in London, which cannot be *again* co-incidental! The number represents completion (of the cycle) not only in the ancient Beth-Luis-Nion alphabet of 72 characters, but in the 72-hour resurrection period of Jesus and has some significance in terms of sound and musical resonance. In the book *Healing Codes for the Biological Apocalypse* [205] the authors refer to the word "Selah" as a musical term meaning to "sprout" give rise to life and indicate the term as being found seventy one times in the King James Bible. The term "Higgaion" is used once and the two are interchangeable as seen in *Psalm 9:16*. The term Higgaion means "a deep sound". Many hymns and chants contain secret sounds and resonances, which find some tuning fork with the Grid and vacuum matrix. The term God or "Yah Vah" in Hebrew means to "breath is to exist". We have already seen that this life giving breath was inferred in the prayer to Aton in Egypt and there were also many deep breathers in the Nazi party. God's Covenant, involves the importance of oxygen carrying blood, which being red, has evidently been made to parallel royal or chosen blood in some dramatised significance by the elite! The hymn to Saint John found in the Apocrypha referred to a process of enlightenment of the masses to optimal spiritual potential by washing away guilt, originated by the Church; thus one assumes that some future revelation is on store, hoping to right the wrong of thousands of years or do the World Order hope to bypass all the lies by implanting a specific gene frequency in man? It appears that according to the Covenant and the coded implications that "144 000" spiritually enlightened people are believed to be able to bring about a transformation of the planet to a Godly state according to *Revelation 7:*4. The magical number according to the 'script' is to be comprised of "*all* the tribes of the children of Israel" (Author's emphasis): although evidently the belief centres on this magical number as "the people chosen by God" *(their* God), or according to Revelation 7:3 as the "servants of God" who: "were sealed" with "the seal of the living God", the implication is that the required Godly state is through magnetic resonance and the combination of "Selah" occurring 71 times and "Higgaion" occurring once in the King James Bible, which in addition gives the magical number of 72. The above authors however make an interesting connection, when they note the appearance of the word "Higgaion" in reference three times in *Psalm 9:16*; *Ps. 19:14*; and *Ps. 92:3* but only once in *Psalm 9:16*. It is missing from *Psalm 19:14* –"Let the words of my mouth and the meditation of my head, be acceptable in thy sight, O Lord, my strength (Hebrew rock); and my redeemer (cross referenced to *Isaiah 44:6*)". According to Webster's dictionary the term "rock" (or "strength") derives from "back and forth in, or as if in, a cradle", which must have some hidden meaning to the Mother Goddess and further "to cause to shake violently". However Webster's also refers to: "popular music usually played on electronically amplified instruments", and "a large mass of stone" such as a "**rock crystal**". Here we have the connection of the magical cycle of completion of 72, to the term "deep sound" and the Grid as crystal, with the further implication of the Goddess. This must lead us back once again to the Religious Revolution in Crete and the knowledge that was taken as part of the Holy Grail. This would certainly make sense of the Semitic appearance of the stone pillars in Crete, where the God was envisaged as a spirit within that pillar and after The Holy Grail knowledge was taken, the God was transferred to the crystal and the belief that the Masters could speak to initiates: however as I have discussed, through channelling it was evidently believed that the Masters existed within the vacuum matrix or some other etheric world and at some point these Masters were viewed as God and the visible Masters on Earth, through control of religion and politics, finally viewed themselves as gods or God. What does this all mean? Does it mean that by some all encompassing resonant signal or "deep sound" created by 144 000, that man will be tuned into the Grid, the Masters or what is believed in the insane mind of those who run this planet – God as (UVG 120 crystal transmitter of) the Masters on the Great White Lodge of Sirius, which is the God of Revelations (His feet on a sea "of crystal")! The authors of the *Healing Codes or the Biological Apocalypse* also show that the six-tone musical scale is encoded into *Numbers* and indicate that the electro-magnetic frequencies of importance were encoded in modern Torahs and Bibles. These frequencies also carry Pythagorean number significance and Plichta (cited) also uncovered some aspect of this in atomic configurations, with particular interest on numbers 3,6 and 9. The number three as I have commented is an intricate code represented by a frequency or resonance that not only controls the three-layered or tri-partite energy biofield which forms the shape of the animal (head thorax and abdomen) but also holds significance as a frequency within the physical structure of DNA, within the cell. Since I have posed the theory that the etheric master pattern of DNA, which must merely be a resonant frequency pattern in space, governs the physical DNA in the body then the frequency representing the numerical significance of 3 is of fundamental importance.

On Target[206] pointed out that the British Government had budgeted over £15 000 000 to sponsor investment in the U.K by Life Science companies, including Monsanto and Du Pont the major companies researching genetic modification of species. In an article in *The Guardian* (*17 th Sept. 1998*) it was noted that: "Firms involved in genetically modified (G.M.), food have met government officials or ministers 81 times since Labour was elected. Monsanto visited the agriculture and environment departments 22 times, while Zeneca held 31 meetings with officials and ministers". Three months later articles appeared in the *Independent on Sunday* ("exposed: Labour's real aim on G.M food") and in *The Daily Telegraph* ("Ministers manipulated G.M debate") along with *The Times* ("No. 10 to set up secret team to back G.M foods"). These articles demonstrated that the Government was secretly planning to manipulate public opinion and in an extract from *The Times*:

> "A secret unit has been established by Downing Street to win over the British public to gene altered crops and foods, a leaked Cabinet office letter reveals. There are even damaging suggestions that ministers have "leant" on the Government's most senior Scientific and medical advisers to give the impression that G.M crop and food production has a clean bill of health".

As *On Target* commented this was: "primarily a party-political issue", once again however I perceive a hidden policy at work and agenda. This policy is not however restricted to Britain, it is a world wide policy which is now being utilised to impress genetically altered crops on humanity and particularly the Third World! Such a policy is also at the heart of Europe, for in another report in *The Mail on Sunday* ("caught in the web of gene food giant", *21 st February,*

1999) it was reported that in May, 1998, the official country residence of the Foreign Secretary, Robin Cook, had been loaned for a two-day conference of politicians from Great Britain, France and Germany and that the occasion had been largely sponsored and organised by Monsanto. *On Target* courageously once again could be relied upon, to draw the web of connections including Lord Sainsbury and his connections to "two lucrative Biotechnology companies, Diatech and Innotech and his Gatsby Trust, which funds research grants" and "all operations with links back to the B.B.S.R.C. funded John Innes Centre (that is, funded by the Minister!) and in turn with connections to Du Pont and Zeneca".

Mysteriously Robin Cook, created quite a furore in the British press in April with a comment that the British were not a race and further suggested that an Indian dish Tikka Masala should be described as the National dish over the family roast meat and vegetables and Yorkshire pudding with lashings of gravy, which has been enjoyed traditionally on Sunday by families gathered around the table for essentially a family meal. Curiously too, the British farming industry, with its potential for self-sufficiency, has been hit by one crisis after another, particularly the BSE and foot and mouth diseases, causing widespread hardship and eminent bankruptcy for many farmers. The possibility of controlling the food chain and the inclusion of GM food into that chain is not only a problem in the U.K but as *On Target* reported in the above issue, India and many nations are being targeted: "Multinational agrochemical corporations are pressurising poor farmers into replacing local crops with their genetically engineered and expensive ones". Indeed a report in *The Financial Times* (*16th March, 1999*) reported in the above issue of *On Target*, in an article entitled "*Genetic engineering will not feed hungry, say Africans*" it was reported that:

> "Gene technologies would destroy diversity, local knowledge and sustainable agricultural systems that have been developed for millennia, and will undermine their capacity to feed their populations. Significantly *African countries* are also wary of increasing dependence on developed countries and multinational corporations as a result of the introduction of genetically modified crops of particular concern is the development by Monsanto of technology that will make seeds *self-destruct* after one season" (*author's emphasis*).

This certainly reminds us of the wheat famine in Egypt under Joseph discussed earlier in this book and also the control of grain into Paris by the Freemasons, which instigated the French Revolution among a duped people: but the self destruct gene has greater implications for a World Order that is committed to a policy of population reduction, according to a tight and specified schedule.

Further articles (*Financial Times, letters, 2nd March 1999*) and in the same year *The Independent on Sunday* followed the same theme of virtual blackmail tactics in forcing nations to accept genetically modified food. The Prince of Wales (Charles) in Britain, once again could be relied upon to take the rational and ethical view, in a leading article in *The Daily Telegraph* headed: "seeds of disaster...the genetic modification of crops is taking mankind into realms that belong to God, and God alone". The term "Frankenstein foods" was coined and headlines such as: "Is G.M the new astrology?" and "Alien Seed?" with "How Green is my trolley" certainly begs the question, whether a genetically modified populous with a 'God gene' with a resonant frequency permanently hitching man's consciousness to the Grid, is the manner in which the Elite perceive that a more Godly society will prevail – which would certainly identify the Elite as completely off *their* trolley (insane)! Can this really be the fulfilment of the World Order idea of "accelerated evolution"! Dear me back to the classroom boys, for the retread of misunderstoods on the Grid and its method of entrapment, given in class lesson c. 10 000 B.C. This really underlines the parallel I drew to the Religious Revolution in Crete c. 1 400 B.C to Hubbard's explanation of Xenu, the beginning of mind control. Surely, it is not believed that some resonant frequency or "deep sound" emitted by an artificially inserted gene resonance in the food chain, can connect man to the Grid, crystal, Masters and ultimately the God of Revelations! You really couldn't make it up could you? I did note in *Alternative 4* however that some origins of this research may (and probably was) carried out on unsuspecting UFO witnesses, who had their biofields tampered with via beamed frequencies. Are we merely to suppose that profit is the entire purpose of G.M food, or are we to conclude that religion is always the justification behind policy and politics as Hitler himself pointed out when he referred to religion as the basis of politics. As The Prince of Wales asked: "What sort of world do we want to live in?" and "If something goes wrong with a G.M crop, who will be held responsible?" however the Elite or the secret groups who have always secretly governed this planet, have always acted beyond accountability and responsibility and according to myth and legend were the culprits behind the demise of the last cycle, which ended in a third war or battle and a cataclysm. Never mind on with Day1 – Plant the vine and 'groundhog day'!

On Target in its *Part I Series*[207] referred to a review by Tuula E. Tuormaa on the "Betrayal of Trust" which appeared in the *November-December 1998* edition of *The Ecologist* and which outlined the grip of the pharmaceutical industry over medical education, medical journals, academic research grants and its influence over governments, which as a point I have long bashed the pulpit box on, with regard to Cancer research and the power of the Medical Syndicate in the fields of mind and body – to no avail in the last 15 years. In 1989 I stood outside South

Kensington tube station in Sloane Square with a stand hoping to educate anyone who would stop to listen, on the dangers of the genetically modified Frostban gene in strawberries, which was the major push period for G.M research. I am afraid people could not foresee the consequences then and still cannot see the ultimate consequences of allowing the Syndicate to operate with all encompassing power to do as they please. The connection of pharmaceutical industries through the interlocking network of policy control, is not only covered by Section 118 of the Medicines Act of 1960, which involves the Official Secrets Act, which prevents the industry from coming under public scrutiny, but also prevents scrutiny of important individuals among drug regulatory authorities who have close ties in other regulatory sectors. These pharmaceutical companies are also part of the growing G.M web of common interests, directorships and funding bodies, which has effectively in the past controlled the medical profession. Just as the Chemical Syndicate has taken control of the mind and body through the policy of a Therapeutic State, dependent on drugs and vaccines to cure all known ills both mental and physical, then it must follow that not only does Genetic Engineering stand to be the key to the exploitation, expansion and eventual monopoly of food supplies, but predictably it would seem that such technology seeks to cure the soul and the final part of the Platonic Maxim: 'Before you can cure a man's body, you must first cure his mind and before that his soul'. The World Order have simply followed the Hermetic God and principle through to its illogical and insane conclusion of 'as above, so below'; where the cure of a man's soul will be sought in the 'God gene' and connection to the Grid, crystal and God of Revelations care of the 144 000 "chosen ones" or magical adepts: the ultimate solution for humanity in control of mind, body and soul through the master geomancer Hermes, with man permanently trapped by Hermes and the World Order – at a good profit naturally! The life-blood or "oxygenated blood" of 'Yah-Vah' being International Finance Capitalism.

The suggestion of the terminator gene, which caused uproar and which probably now has gone underground in secret group ops research, is interesting. The sound vibration rates for creation (and destruction) are intricately tied into coded religious texts. The pale priests who have commanded the knowledge from early times have, inevitably through secret groups and particularly Rosicrucian laboratories, passed relevant data to key research scientists, who have merely added to the armoury of the World Order, in return for fame or money in the alleged pursuit of science and truth – some betrayal of humanity! It is no wonder that science is littered with the names of men and women, who fell foul of the World Order, when they tried on an independent basis, to research the hidden science. Men like Upton Knuth and Armstrong, who were broadcasting resonant frequencies in crop pest control; also Wilhelm Reich and Nikola Tesla, both of whom researched resonant energies and had their research taken by the FBI.

Some scientists have mysteriously died or allegedly committed suicide and the World Order justifies wars, revolutions and murders under the heading of 'sacrifice to a cause' – the cause of the case of the MRC.

There are now in existence resonant frequencies for the majority of pathogenic bacteria (and viruses?) and theoretically one has only to broadcast such frequencies to simulate attack by the bacterium. Upton Knuth and Armstrong were conducting similar research in protecting crops from pests, until the World Order forced the research to closure. Man is vulnerable to any resonant frequency that is aimed at his biofield, which can alter physiology, mood, behaviour and thinking accordingly. The potential to use this biofield in a full scale programme of mind and body control of a populous was discussed in *Alternative 4*, with the possibility that illegal testing of technology on the biofield of individuals in UFO witness accounts had already occurred and had been passed off as a UFO experience. The human biofield and its chakras are a composite of colours and therefore specific frequencies, closely related to the electro-magnetic spectrum and sympathetic vibration. In an essay entitled '*Scale of the Forces in Octaves*', Keely provided a technical explanation of the relationship between octaves of healing and tones of light. Each colour is represented not only by a frequency, but also a musical note and frequency. Theoretically by beaming a certain resonant frequency, musical note or colour at an individual's biofield, then one could affect different chakras and the associated physiology, mood, thinking and behaviour. If you open the third eye or crown chakra then the mind is susceptible to any thought that is placed in the environment, including ordinary means of written text. Initiates in secret groups who open this chakra should be very careful what philosophy and thoughts they read when they open the crown chakra, which occurs on a free flow of energy through the body. Initiates will often 'parrot' everything they have been told or given to read, for this reason. Pythagoras used music to alter mood and emotion and Ekhart a secret group initiate stated: "Follow Hitler, but it was I that called the tune", which could only have referred to the secret use of tonal emotional scales and colours which Hitler prominently employed in his speeches and rallies. Hubbard curiously enough drafted *The Human Chart of Evaluation*, in his book The *Science of Survival*, which gives a scale of behaviour and physiology according to a scale of energy. The chart is a highly workable and observable and whilst Hubbard relates the chart to the mind, he never gives a source for the chart, other than his own genius. The Cosmic Keyboard chart in secret group Rosicrucian knowledge has some parallel foundation either co-incidentally or not!

I have already given the Nazis as a secret group of initiates with access to resonant frequency knowledge and there was some question over whether Hitler was using a psychic to channel information from the Grid. Henry Kissinger a prominent member of the Bilderbergers, often described as 'The Secret Government of the World', was a Nelson Rockefeller associate and he himself was a chief administrator in Germany facilitating 'Operation Paperclip', which referred to the transfer of key scientific and other personnel to America after World War II. I have already outlined significant anti-gravity research by Schauberger and it was such knowledge as this that was transferred. It was Kissinger in 1968 under Richard Nixon, who promoted biological warfare as an alternative to nuclear weapons; however his patron John D Rockefeller with John Foster and Allen Dulles, created I.G. Farben, Germany's leading industrial organisation prior to World War II. Farben was con-incidentally never bombed during the war, proving the secret nature of this war, since Farben was the obvious bombing target for the allies. Farben's top executives were Hitler's highest- ranking SS officers and at the end of the war, escaped with Nazi loot, which was worth millions. The Vatican has been implied in their escape along with the Military Order of Malta (SMOM), which is linked to the Prieure de Sion, the secret group who I concluded were Judah (13 th tribe) initiates and possibly Rosicrucian's, dating back in some form to the Bull-Minos cult or Druids. It was Kissinger who in a National Security Memorandum 2000, called for depopulation of the Third World. Kissinger was later to be knighted by Queen Elizabeth II at Windsor Castle in Britain! The authors of the *Healing Codes for a Biological Apocalypse* (cited) give an impressive and horrendous story of the possibility that a Third World depopulation programme, was linked to the appearance of man-made plagues such as AIDS and BSE. In *The Second Millennium Working Report into Cancer* I quoted in 1989 research by NAVS (National Anti-Vivisection Society U.K.) which claimed that AIDS was produced in the laboratory, as a product of cancer research into viruses that jumped the species barrier developing new characteristics in the process. The authors claim that the AIDS epidemic is man-made and to boot, the CJD (human form of mad cow disease or Creutzfeldt-Jacob disease), stealth viruses, CFIDS (chronic fatigue immune dysfunction), hepatitis B,

E. Coli, Alzheimer's, Spiroplasmas and mycoplasmas are intricately tied up in this story; and further produce the all too familiar chain of big business links, government, research and development which created the chain of horror which is steadily decreasing population numbers. The further link to the cover up on the Gulf War Syndrome and the contaminated vaccines given as 'cocktails' to serving military personnel in the Gulf, provides the authors with a conclusion that: "the mycoplasma germ(s) contaminating the experimental AIDS vaccine, given to the troops, may have been intentionally developed and administered". The authors state: " In this political milieu – given the evolution of a New World Order by largely secret agents, and a history of genocidal practices involving "dispensable" populations – Gulf War Syndrome is reconcilable". They go on to say: " The U.S military, generally comprised of nationalistic, sovereign-thinking, patriotic individuals who pledged to kill and died to defend the U.S Constitution against all foreign and domestic enemies, represented a risk to the evolving New World Order. Thus, the military need to be culled, largely killed, defunded, "defanged" and demoralised – roughly where it stands today". The mention of the word "domestic" rather mirrors the position of treason that has gone unchallenged in Britain, where having no Constitution has been a huge error in allowing a gradual erosion of any values, standards and sovereignty. The position of the military in America as clarified here, must represent a similar phenomenon in Britain along with the added erosion of the British identity and extinction of a self-sufficient food chain in farming. These things are not unconnected, but refer to a hidden agenda and policy that has gone unchallenged. The military as with agriculture in Britain is undergoing a policy of demoralisation, thus effectively removing any challenge that these sectors might provide to the World Order. Further European armies and police forces that will come into being will be loyal to the Federal European Super State and not to any one country. The feminist cause has been totally manipulated to turn it into one of ridicule, by breast implants being given to women soldiers on tax-payers money; also in an article in *The Daily Mail 2nd May 2001* 'A soldier's torment –seargent went AWOL to face his homosexuality', causes a division of the army on its opinions of such matters as homosexuality. An army is principally a fighting force and not the counsellor's chair, thus to produce *any* division in an army or loss of morale, is to *invite* **treason**. These worries with the cutbacks of 1.2 billion pounds for equipment, caused Col. Bob Stewart, DSO former Commander of The British Forces in Bosnia to write in the *Daily Mail May 2nd 2001 'Why I'm ashamed of the Army now'*. He stated:

> "Once the envy of the world, the British Armed Forces are in danger of becoming a laughing stock. What could be more absurd than the Ministry of Defence policy of providing free cosmetic surgery to serving personnel? Yesterday it emerged that 12 women have been given implants at the taxpayers' expense, four men have had sex change treatment and at least ten members of the Services have had liposuction. You really couldn't make it up, could you?"

Whilst enormous amounts of money are spent on defending a country from without, man has yet to realise that his true enemy has always acted from *within,* where power lies in the secret policies governing religion and politics, with the ultimate enemy of mind control. The demoralisation of the army and farmers is a hidden policy and agenda that is being implemented at the very highest level.

One very interesting fact emerged from the book *Healing Codes for the*

Biological Apocalypse (cited), which ties in with the author's research in an extra-ordinary way. The authors discuss prions, which are crystal like proteins, which create disease and which the authors claim may have resulted from secret research. A review of an article (*May 30 th 1997*) in the journal *Cell* stated: "New type of DNA free inheritance in yeast is spread by a mad cow mechanism". Researchers at the university of Chicago's Howard Hughs Medical Institute, reported that: "a protein molecule able to transmit a genetic trait, without DNA or RNA in yeast is able to string itself together in long fibres much like those found in the brain in "mad cow" and human Creutzfeldt-Jacob diseases". This is certainly unusual, since it is considered impossible for any inheritance to occur, without DNA or RNA (Ribonucleic Acid) having been transferred. Research shows that the normal protein in the brain in such diseases becomes "twisted" and then corrupted when other "healthy molecules of the same protein do likewise in a process by analogy to the "seeding of a crystal". In other words the protein or prion grows as the protein molecules spin together as fibres, recruiting other molecules, in much the same way as a crystal grows. This unusual form of hereditary and protein growth is implicated not only in mad cow disease (BSE or Bovine Spongiform Encephalopathy), but in scrapie a disease affecting sheep and also the human form of mad cow disease (CJD) and unusually in the disease of Kuru, which affects the cannibal tribes of Papua New Guinea.

Mark Rogers, from the department of Zoology at the Biotechnology centre at University College in Dublin Ireland wrote:

> "The term 'prion' was coined by Stanley B. Pruisner of the University of California School of Medicine at San Francisco in 1982 to distinguish the infectious agent that causes scrapie in sheep, Creutzfeldt-Jacob disease (CJD) in humans and Bovine Spongiform encephalopathy (BSE) in cattle from other, more typical infectious agents. The prion hypothesis postulates that these diseases are caused not by a conventional virus or bacterium, but by a protein that has adopted an abnormal form".

Rogers also comments that prion proteins have been manufactured in laboratories using E. Coli bacteria "**altered through recombinant DNA techniques**". Prion research ominously has been produced through genetic engineering and from the point of view of this book and the author's cancer research, it is significant that in alleged prion related diseases, the abnormal crystal-like protein growth occurs mainly in nervous tissue i.e. nerves and particularly the brain. Nervous tissue however significantly has lost the ability of cell division and growth through specialisation. Normally cells can grow and replace old cells in the process of cell division, however nerve cells have become so specialised in their function that they no longer divide and grow. I will return to this point, but the authors of the *Healing Codes for the Biological Apocalypse* remain sceptical and questioning of the connection of prion research to the University of Chicago, built with Rockefeller money and from where Gallo who first identified the AIDS virus graduated.

I have commented previously that so-called dramatic breakthroughs in science have not been unconnected to secret group knowledge. Newton and a number of scientists who have made their mark in history had associations with secret group knowledge and particularly Rosicrucianism. It is unusual to say the least that some World Order (Rockefeller funded) laboratories were apparently researching protein-crystal growths and prions before the plagues of this century swept throughout the world. However in glancing over prion research, it seems to the author that the protein in the absence of any central and directing DNA or even the master etheric DNA code or pattern appears to align itself and grow according to the pattern of the Grid or crystal as UVG 120 sphere. I have already discussed how the physical DNA in the cell of animals including man or Homo sapiens can act as transmitter and receiver and may indeed connect with a master DNA pattern according to morphic resonance. The DNA pattern in Homo sapiens would exhibit a particular resonant frequency that is uniquely different from say sheep DNA or cattle DNA or frog DNA. The expression of the DNA in any particular living organism would depend entirely on its unique frequency. I have suggested that the long length of frog DNA must represent the very long history of this species, as having survived Magnetic Reversals, due to its ability to live on land and in water, a feature that gives the Amphibian a great deal of adaptability, which favours evolutionary survival. Further I have also referred to the human embryo in its development recapitulating phylogenetic ontogeny. In other words as the embryo grows, it starts off looking like a tadpole or the Amphibians, with gill-like slits reminiscent of fish and only as it grows and contributes more cells containing DNA to the morphic resonant signal, which transmits and receives signals to the master etheric DNA pattern, will the embryo grow according to the pattern of Homo sapiens or man. However one cannot dismiss that each human embryo appears to travel the path of the phylogenetic history of Homo sapiens from fish. It might be inferred that the master etheric DNA contains all codes for all species in one gigantic pattern, which may resemble the double helicity of the physical DNA by way of vortex filament patterns. The part of the master pattern that is ultimately transmitted to the growing embryo must depend on the signal received from the species DNA. In other words human DNA will send a signal 'human DNA' and will receive its stamp or orders from the master DNA pattern and 'gene' coding form man accordingly. If you could imagine a large strip coded a to z in the etheric or vacuum pattern, then 'gene a' for example might resonate at the frequency of frog or amphibian DNA; 'gene b' might resonate at the frequency of fish etc. **Thus the individual and sum total of gene frequencies in the human genetic code is of fundamental importance in governance by the etheric Master pattern DNA, which codes for man.**

If this is so, then let us consider the implications of genetically modified species, will for example a genetically altered embryo send the same signal? Indeed if homo sapiens through the food chain imbibes all manner of odd genes or even some 'God gene' care of the World Order, what will the master DNA pattern make of it? After all I have proposed that the master pattern or DNA is concerned with *survival* and on that point does not miss a trick (even one care of the World Order)! I think it is ridiculous to take on a master pattern, that has evolved over billions of years to ensure survival of body lines and believe that by tinkering with the genetics of a body line on Earth that it will not have some major and catastrophic effect; Let us consider the effects of cannibalism or the Kuru disease in the tribes of Papua New Guinea. According to Hubbard's *Know to Mystery Scale* (and expanded form of the *Chart of Human Evaluation*) eating (human) bodies, being (human) bodies and controlling (human) bodies is very far down the level of spiritual and body survival. At that level the spiritual being has left control of a body to the primitive mind and the morphogenetic bioplasma where survival problems (in the absence of the primitive 'fright and flight' response i.e. threat = fight or threat = run away) are solved according to the author's cancer research along the lines of threat = growth=survival. The Grid or Universal primitive mind solves survival problems according to survival of bodies. It is certainly interesting that kuru disease and mad cow disease in humans should centre in the nervous tissue and brain, since as I have explained this tissue is incapable of growth. The proteins or prions however appear to take on the crystal-like characteristic of growth, perhaps reflecting the primitive mind survival mechanism of growth=survival. Cattle do not normally eat animals, they are herbivores (plant eaters) and thus the animal-based feed that cattle were forced to eat, which produced (along with organo-phosphates?) BSE must have had some basis in this mechanism of the primitive mind. In other words the message from cattle to the master DNA code for that species was definitely one of non-survival (cattle eating animals). Thus the growth=survival mechanism would have been triggered. The conveyance of infected proteins to humans through the food chain and the production of the human form of mad cow disease (CJD) would exist as a time bomb, in so far as this protein would only start to grow as a crystal-like growth when the individual carrier dropped on the emotional scale of non-survival, to the point where the primitive mind clicked on. Thus once the spiritual being is suppressed on the scale of survival, then the primitive mind with its own survival mechanisms can not only create cancer, but can trigger abnormal protein or prion growth in non-dividing brain or neural tissue, according to the crystal pattern I would propose. I suspect that neurological diseases such as MS or multiple sclerosis may have a similar pattern of abnormal protein in conjunction with nervous tissue. Also, one cannot dismiss the role of the chakras and biofield in pulling energy down from the vacuum, which helps to retain a high psychological state and integrity of the biofield and organ system. Thus the happier one remains and the higher psychological state of the individual may be a greater predictor of health than the various time bombs laid into the system, via the primitive mind or DNA survival mechanisms.

Once the World Order start to meddle with the DNA however, the predictor may well fall into the category of those who do not carry artificial genes have a better chance of survival! The cohesion of prion proteins or filaments in many respects I would conclude parallels cancer growth or the primitive mind equation of growth=survival: in the case of cancer it is an embryonic growth and biochemistry. The differentiation between physical and emotional loss is a critical factor in the mechanism underpinning the embryonic biochemistry (Cancer Report by the Author). Prions or proteins without nucleic acid (DNA or RNA) would certainly as chemicals simply align to the Grid as crystal and its morphic resonant pattern, which must have represented very early forms of life on this planet and even social colonies like coral or bees and ants who exhibit primitive mind social cohesion survival behaviour! The collection of prions in the brain also would seem to be the position of maximum correspondence via morphic resonance with the Grid and since proteins are formed as result of DNA coding, some connection with the master Grid pattern may still be retained. In summary the biblical plagues of the Apocalypse may not only be man-made to give confirmation of the 'script' *(Revelations)* – as the audience nods sagely and says "ah yes it is God's work come to pass", but it must provide the ultimate justification of the World Order in connecting man forcibly to Grid harmonics and the God of the Apocalypse and the chosen 144 000. It is certainly curious as the authors of the *Healing Codes of the Biological Apocalypse* point out, that ongoing research into diseases like Kuru, which were funded in laboratories connected to World Order names, was ongoing in the 1960's when such research would certainly only apply to a minority of Papua New Guinea tribes, which the World Order would not have the faintest interest in, unless there was some application. Why the World Health Organisation (with its own inevitable links) should have funded such studies into cannibalism can only be viewed from the fact that in the 1960's the Rockefellers who also had links to the United Nations and World Bank funded the World Health Organisation. According to the authors:

"Laurence Rockefeller was, in fact, chairman of the Memorial Sloan-Kettering Cancer Centre, and a trustee for the Sloane Foundation, at the time their researchers supplied Robert Gallo (the alleged 1984 AIDS virus –HIV discoverer), with the reagents he needed to develop viruses that were descriptively and functional to HIV. Both the Sloan Foundation and the Rockefellers were heavily connected with, and major shareholders of the Merck pharmaceutical company".

Today as Africa is fast becoming de-populated by AIDS, the pharmaceutical companies who produce AIDS drugs have declined to relinquish "intellectual copyright" on such drugs, to allow Third World countries to produce the drugs at a fraction of the cost. Apparently biblical plagues are vastly profitable, which illustrates with what contempt the World Order actually holds God, having manipulated the prophetic Apocalypse so often at profit that evidently no longer believe in God other than their Masters and the UVG120 crystal.

The definitions of words in Webster's dictionary, is fascinating for the connections posed and the manner in which significant biblical words relate back to the Religious Revolution. I have many times in this book referred to the manner in which religious mysteries were secreted into the alphabets and only those with a view of the overall picture would fully understand these connections. The words derived from "APO" e.g. Apocalypse cross reference with "CRYPT". The definition of crypt curiously is also referred to as "crystalline", which not only according to the authors of the *Healing Codes of the Biological Apocalypse* refers to prions and the crystal like proteins of the biblical plagues, but also finds oblique referral to the UVG 120 sphere or crystal and the Grid. Further the Greek mystery and tragedy outlined in this book, must find a secret explanation in the world "APOCRYPHA" and significantly in the "APOCALYPSE" definition it reads "fr. Apo - + kalyptein to cover – more at Hell (13c)". Hell presumably as life under the Lords of the crystal and a Magnetic Reversal. Significantly also "HELL" cross references to "HEIR" which is Middle English term, referring to entitlement (property, hereditary, rank, title, office, throne); and the original overt act in the Religious Revolution, was to hitch the Holy Grail to a royal blood line (King Minos) overseen by an initiated priesthood, giving undue and dramatizing importance to the "oxygenating blood", or red blood that was associated with royal divinity, so clearly seen in the "red men of Knossos" after the revolution. The bloodline and obsession with hereditary lines can only have emerged from Elite thinking and which has been a pre-occupation of both Nazis and Jews. The word "DIAL" also finds a cross reference and is obviously related to sun-dial and the sun god: however "DIAL" can also be defined as "a device that may be operated to make electrical connections or to regulate the operation of a machine <a radio~> <a

telephone~>, which begs the new question and inclusion of whether that includes www.com/grid? The mega-computer that controls humanity via the primitive mind. The definitions of "JET" in Webster's and the second definition of 2: something issuing as if in a jet < talk poured from her in a brilliant ~ - Time>; can only refer to Minoan Crete and the Goddess or woman in the story. The authors of the Healing Codes of the Biological Apocalypse significantly noticed that the definition of the word "JETTISON" refers to "a voluntary sacrifice of cargo to lighten a ship's load in time of distress", which the authors refer back to the World depopulation programme; however the idea of 'ship' and Noah is also cross-connected in early languages, as I have shown. The idea of survival of the elite few in a ship in a period of cataclysm, is indeed where we started this book, along with the idea of 'sacrifice to a cause' and 'survival of the fittest', which is World Order thinking along primitive phylogenetic Grid mechanisms – so much for the 'spiritually aware' and the trust man places in them!

Secret biological weapons such as those developed by the Russian Academy of Science's Ehglehardt Institute of Molecular Biology in Moscow have already developed nineteen "biological microchip" inventions that contain "chemical compounds" that could analyse, affect, or attack "biological targets" including DNA sequences: and DNA itself is up for commercial grabs under the Human Genome project, which aims to map the entire set of human chromosomes by the year 2005 and which must present another updated version or dramatization of Hubbard's Latrus and the Lambda Life project of body control coupled with the Xenu mind control in Incident 1 (or the Religious Revolution in Crete, whoever you believe). You can bet your bottom dramatization though that man will sit an argue the finer elements of this story, whilst the World Order gets along with business as usual! Once the World Order controls human DNA, you can kiss freedom and sanity goodbye. The Human genome project is seen not only as the birth of a multi billion pound industry, but has profound implications for humanity and yet typically, no overall ethical body has been elected to control or oversee those implications or the research and once again no barriers to the World Order playing God, have been set in motion, particularly as the Rockefeller and Alfred P. Sloan Foundations are right up there in the funding of such projects.

How far the prophetic Apocalypse has been manipulated to create war and revolution, plagues and weather patterns to give it authenticity and create the ultimate justification as the 'script' written by God and not the gods of Earth, is questionable in proportion to the manipulative hold of the World Order over the events of history and scientific research. *Joel 2:2* and *Revelations* refers to the triumph of the Lords of the crystal and the author can only ponder with incredulity the idiocy of these louts, if they believe that one major sound resonation or 'God gene' will suddenly turn humanity into a godly (read mind and body controlled) society. *Revelations* as I have pointed out, is written for the 12 tribes of Israel and predictably the woman and the 13 th tribe are vilified; and where the "chosen ones" as the 12 tribes of Israel are "sealed" in *Revelations 14: 10-12*, whilst another alleged destructive "sealing" occurs related to the "mark of the Beast" presumably indicating the beast of Bull-Minos cult and the 13 th tribe together with the final battle against Gogmagog, Apollo and the sun kings. The venom appears to point directly at the 'cuckoo's nest' – Britain, which accounts for all those so-called Biblical plagues and the policy of treason within this country: and just as the Jew in Israel has nothing to do with this story, neither has the Britton: this battle is far beyond the average man and woman in both countries, it is a battle of secret politics and religion of an elite who are willing to sacrifice the pawns as no doubt the Holocaust will eventually prove, if it was fully investigated. The groups 12 and 13 have dominated all countries of Earth and all peoples, Britain however I suspect is going to be sacrificed to this cause of the Lords of the crystal and no doubt when London was first coined "the city" (by Rothschild) it fitted very nicely into the prophetic terminology of the "Great City", which suffers an earthquake of devastating proportions. The woman however is reserved for the worst venom, since she always thwarted the World Order in its plans and wrongfully she was locked up with the 13 th tribe as Hermes after the Religious Revolution. The Apocalypse refers to "harlot churches", that teach false doctrine, which must beg the question of how the Patriarchs obtained their knowledge, if not through use of the hidden science, the crystal and channelling following their 'Spiritual Masters' or more succinctly their own thoughts from the past!

The 144 000 are allegedly without fault, and are spared the "Mark of the Beast", once again referring to the Bull-Minos cult and the knowledge that was stolen and which was manipulated and used against its purpose. However it appears that there is a lack of knowledge in both groups 12 and 13 (those terrible Twins), with regard to the Grid, history and science. The 144 000 will proclaim the accuracy of the scriptures and according to *Rev: 7: 9-11* will win the battle of the Apocalypse leading everyone into heaven, or as I maintain a Magnetic Reversal or Hubbard's Inc.2, with just a bit more confusion on the channelling line next time. Is Dr. Becker (twice a Nobel Prize nominee) wrong in stating that a Magnetic Reversal has already started, which might just account for the erratic weather and so-called global warming? Is the entirety of what I say here, just another dupe line or can it be, that this is the truth and man is incapable of confronting the fact that the party is over and its time to grow up and take responsibility for future generations in the hope that there will still be enough time for man to clear his karma and leave? Or has it gone too far? Is man capable of thinking this through, without the predictable propaganda against anything, including solutions, which threaten to reveal one tiny edge of this story?

Is it not significant that the definition of genesis, which is the title of Moses' first book in *The Bible* entitled *Genesis,* is defined in Webster's dictionary as:

> **Gen-e-sis** ...[L, fr. Gk, fr. Gignesthai to be born – more at KIN] (ca. 1604): the origin or coming into being of something.

Not only do we see a Greek origin (which cross references with Hubbard's misunderstanding that Inc.1 or in my own explanation the Religious Revolution in Crete was the beginning – which it was not), but also 'birth' or the The Cycle of Eternal Return may be implied. Further there is another reference here to "KIN".

> **Genesis** n [Gk]: the mainly narrative first book of canonical Jewish and Christian Scriptures – see BIBLE table.

> **Gene-splicing** ... n (ca. 1978): any of various techniques by which recombinant DNA is produced and made to function in an organism.

Interestingly the above being derived from "gen-" which Webster's records as:

> **gen**....[perh. Fr. General information] (1940) chiefly Brit: information 2a

> **¹gen-** or **geno-** *comb from* [Gk genos birth, race, king – more at KIN] 1: race, genocide. 2: genus: king < genotype>

> **²gen-** or **geno-** *comb from*: gene <genome>

> **-gen** also **gene** n *comb from* [F – gene, fr. Gk – genes born; akin to Gk genos birth] 1: producer < androgen> 2: one that is (so) produced <cultigen>

Whilst the obvious connections of genetic engineering are made, there is here the key connection of KIN, RACE, KING, and ANDROGEN along with BIRTH. This certainly points one back to the Religious Revolution and the Greek origins of many of these root words. Androgen means having any of several steroids that promote development of male sexual characteristics and the Bull-Minos cult who I concluded conducted the Religious Revolution, was a phallic cult and further in Biblical texts "the Beast" as Bull-Minos I would conclude was related to "666" and a "man's number": however as I have pointed out the Book of *Revelations* was written by the 12 tribes against the 13 th tribe and this is predictable. The use of "race", "kin" and "king" also appear to refer to Adamites, Semitic tribes and solar monarchy, which was introduced after the Religious Revolution. The word "androgynous" in the Botanical sense refers to having male and female flowers in the same inflorescence or in a second definition refers to a hermaphrodite or an organism having male and female parts, which brings us back to Hermes the god of the Religious Revolution, the beginning according to Hubbard's Inc. 1 which I conclude was not the beginning, but just the beginning of **mind control** and further brings us back to the androgynous nature of the Millennium icon in the U.K! (*Plate 3*) Incidentally "android" in science fiction, is a robot resembling a human being, which must be the ultimate conclusion of genetic engineering. However it is interesting that all this should equate to *Genesis* and the beginning according to Biblical texts and the tribes of Israel! To gain the truth however one has to go before this and the arrival of the Holy Grail on Earth. The British origin of "gen" is another interesting connection to "race", "king", "kin" and "geno" (genotype, gene etc) with implications of the 13th tribe. Further does "kin" connect to Keltoi (Minoan) and kilted men, both in the description of the Cretans after the Religious Revolution and in Scotland as discussed earlier in this book? The idea of "race" or "chosen ones" and the purity of the royal bloodline ("king" and "kin") were certainly inherent in the beliefs of the elite of both groups 12 and 13.

Whilst I have explained "gene-splicing" (*Fig. 43*) in the physical DNA as the manner in which DNA re-combines to throw up new evolutionary forms, I have referred to the possibility that the 'filaments' of the master DNA pattern in the etheric recombine during a Magnetic Reversal. Hubbard's so-called Inc. 2 which he refers to as "implant" is according to my own account here, a Magnetic Reversal, where the entire contents and event record of the Akashic Record or morphogenetic and spiritual bioplasmas as holographic 'frames' are downloaded into the memory banks of mans soul memory. One might be able to equate those 'frames' of events, which cover survival and event record, to the genes of the physical DNA. I have discussed the likelihood during a Magnetic Reversal of those frames being inter-spliced, such that the event record in mans' soul memory is now no longer in logical sequence. By analogy a pack of cards in suit and number order, represents the ordered events of planet Earth, but during a Magnetic Reversal the coiled 'filaments' of electro-magnetic energy (or some form of energy) containing the ordered pack are disrupted and the card deck randomly shuffled and downloaded into the spirit's memory banks. Xenu or Yatrus may have been past controllers, but that does not place them in present time (unless they re-incarnated). Also I referred to X and Y (Xenu and Yatrus) as co-incidentally symbols for the male and female genes used in biology with male and female hormones produced from those X and Y genes. The recombination event possibility during a Magnetic Reversal then requires a greater power of analytical ability to solve; thus the Grid is not only a prison, it evolves one to a higher analytical state in order to solve the data which it holds as the master mega computer or www-com/grid. One could never solve that 'rubric cube', from the viewpoint of matter or the matter cycle of survival and I have had to approach this from the point of view of a spiritual cycle, which in my own case was not survivalist from the point of view of matter, but from the point of view of a spirit it is total survival and through this research I discovered the route out or exit from the maze. I did suggest in *Alternative 4*, that the MRC case or MMRC case (Magnetically Reversed, or Missed Magnetically Reversed case - depending on whether he experienced or missed a Magnetic Reversal), originally tried to control man from the viewpoint of the master DNA or Genetic Code in the etheric and on arrival on Earth, became the *effect of what he had caused* or his own experiment. The obsession of the World Order with genetics and genetic engineering would then, be a complete dramatization of the past and therefore the psychological case of the MRC. They know somewhere in their befuddled memory that genetics has something to do with entrapment, however as I have noted in the introduction, this is insanity of a high order and I doubt whether they actually know they are dramatizing their past: in fact they do not, just as the insane do not know they are insane: they can only see profit and control and their original goal of mind and body control as a method of realising such profit and power. It is highly likely that they actually believe that they are helping humanity. They hold the psychotic computation: 'I must be right or I die' – there is no chance of them actually realising that they are insane. The trouble is they are very clever psychotics and you won't find them in the local psychiatric hospital. The Earth as one big Theatre (or asylum), with the key players as psychotics playing out the 'script' according to the way it has always been played out and written down in *Revelations*, which becomes the psychological justification –God's will.

The trillions of **vortices** inherent in the structure of the UVG120 crystal or Grid at intersection points, may pattern energy in a coil reminiscent of the DNA molecule shown by Crick and Watson to have a double helix coiled or vortical structure, which may represent the model for the morphogenetic bioplasma that I formulated. The double helix is then, coiled in a manner that not only reflects the coiling of the physical DNA, but also is analogous to the coil of the television set or radio. In explaining just how UFO witnesses experience pictures or holographics from the past, then this model of a master DNA etheric mega-computer or the Akashic Record (of past events) provides one solution.

The physical DNA molecule, acting as a resonant coil, transmits and receives information from the Grid in the form of holographics of past events, together with thought as I have proposed. I have given substantial background scientific data to the effects of electro-magnetic frequencies on biological systems including genes and DNA in *The Second Millennium Working Report into Cancer*. **DNA actually exhibits resonance along with genes and electro-magnetic frequency ranges alter that resonance**. Changes in polarity and surface properties of proteins, also covered in that report, in response to changes in electro-magnetic frequencies, may also provide the background to prions and abnormal protein formation in certain neurological diseases. The author has demonstrated in her own research that thought and memories can significantly change the human biofield colour and shape, which can be monitored as the thought occurs, on a computer screen! Thought may be a significant predictor of which genes or frequencies at any one time are activated. In other words if you entertain thoughts of malice, jealousy, greed or negative emotions, how far does this alter the biofield and the transmitting and receiving properties of DNA? More importantly would such thoughts not register as part of the primitive mind, concerned with survival and would these thoughts not encourage behaviour and psychology associated with that mind – the Universal Mind, which carries thoughts of the Masters! It has long been known in cancer research and homeopathic medicine that positive thinking can affect the course of disease. This concept of two-way transmission from the etheric morphogenetic bioplasma, primitive mind or Universal Mind then gives some understanding of that mechanism. Negative thoughts would only register in the primitive mind memory banks and any solution would be irrational to a spiritual mind e.g. a cancer growth, but it is entirely rational to the primitive mind and its own solutions based on phylogenetic solutions and computations of: threat of non survival= growth=survival. In dismissing negative thoughts and steering clear of the 'ugly brigade', who live according to selfish primitive mind survival mechanisms based on self and at best family group, then one steers clear of the primitive mind. Association with people or projects that create high survival for humanity and spiritual beings is a great predictor of health and happiness! If anyone reduces your survival, then that person is well in the Grid controlled range and is accumulating spiritual karma that will not allow them to exit. Exit is a tough process!

The Second Millennium Working Report into Cancer discusses the diurnal rhythms which have governed mans evolutionary body. The authors of *The Healing Codes for the Biological Apocalypse* (cited) comment on how the clock was altered and thus I conclude some interruption of these rhythms inevitably occurred. The alteration of calendars to maximise this interruption of rhythm is another major factor in disease, more fully explained in the section on EMF's in the cancer report. Further the differentiation of body tissues into various forms e.g. heart muscle (cardiac), muscle tissue (somatic), liver, kidneys etc., is controlled by the tri-partite energy field or the L-field of Burr, which governs the development of the embryo. I have already noted that the field is susceptible to drugs e.g. thalidomide, but the early embryo shows recapitulation of past evolutionary forms in its development. It appears then that the DNA in the physical body not only determines the species e.g. Homo sapiens, Amphibians and fish etc., but the L-field or tri-partite biofield has some function in determining that capitulation of ancestral evolutionary form (recapitulation of phylogenetic ontogeny). I would propose that the 'tune' or music of frequencies played by the master code or DNA in the etheric carries a resonant frequency that translates into a pattern of energy in the physical body in the embryonic stage. As the embryo develops the 'tune' changes and with stronger signals from the accumulating physical DNA in the growing embryo, the specific 'genes' or frequencies of the master DNA code are activated, which determines that the embryo grows into Homo sapiens and not a frog or fish. Thus the mega-computer is the hard drive of the computer and the cells with the physical DNA are the software, the data is simply downloaded. Alteration of Grid frequencies that are normally controlled by electro-magnetic radiation from the sun could in effect alter the L-field of the individual and also determine which sections of the DNA are read or translated. It is not inconceivable that an artificially inserted gene (or gene sequence) through the food chain, with a specific frequency could be tuned into a specific man-made frequency applied through the Grid, such that any individual with that artificial gene would be potentially controlled by a man-made source. This idea although it occurred to the author in the production of the Cancer Report back in 1989 whilst researching effects of EMF's on genes and biological systems, has evolved through *Alternative 4* and this current work, which more fully defines why there can be no answer to cancer – it would simply reveal the whole hidden science, together with the hidden agenda and policy.

One can easily perceive in this, the possibility of playing around with Grid energies to activate certain genes in the physical DNA or inserting specific gene frequencies by artificial means such as genetic engineering. DNA in the physical cell is the main receiver and transmitter of information and thus the possibility of control through genetic research, has vast implications. I have already discussed in *Alternative 4*, just how the biofield may be controlled and the possibility of illicit research in the manipulated UFO experience. De-population programmes can also be carried out using this information and again in the cancer report I gave specific frequencies, which cause cell death through termination of cell division and replication of DNA. All information is carried by the DNA and which sequence at anyone time that is utilised, depends on which genes are activated. The onset of puberty is marked by some activation of X and Y chromosomes and teenagers notoriously exhibit selfish behaviour that finds a curious link of thought with the masters and my observation that Xenu and Yatrus the master controllers strongly remind one of the X (male) and Y (female) chromosomes. Curious in so far as Hubbard links Xenu in Inc.1 to mind control and Yatrus to body control. In terms of evolution the development of the mind over body has determined how successful a species will become in grappling with predators and the environment. It might be concluded that Grid controlled beings are merely controlled by Grid holographics of the past and therefore primitive survival mechanisms, which creates predatory patterns in their psychology and behaviour, corresponding to the lowest levels of anger, hostility, fear, grief and apathy in Hubbard's *Chart of Human Evaluation*. The MRC case or the World Order priesthood however, have access to the religious mysteries, now locked into secret alphabets, language and secret group knowledge; this undoubtedly enables such people to become master predators and parasites, since such people are not only not controlled by Inc.1 in Hubbard's terminology or the Religious Revolution in Crete in my own terminology, but it also enables them to fully act out Inc.2 or the Magnetic Reversal holographics thus creating a 'script' that they are not actually aware of, just as man is not aware of. There is no conscience, since by now they have come to believe that they were the progenitors, race and genius that created the knowledge. In effect they now believe they own the hidden science, which irrationally computes in their own insane minds as owning hidden knowledge=owning man= superior or chosen. This of course gives rise to ideas of "chosen ones" and the godly 144 000 that will presumably through some god gene, connect man to their God – Hermes the master geomancer and controller of the Grid. Insane? - You bet they are! Man however feels very comfortable with this insanity, since the majority are Grid controlled by the primitive mind and holographics of the past and provided they own a piece of territory of earth and no-one enters that territory or interferes with the 'reality' of their world, they are content to allow the parasite of World Order, secret politics and religion, World Bank and the pale priests of Europe get along with it. After all it's all very familiar and they have seen it all before and its just sort of predictable. Third World War? – Oh probably, but what can you do? Asks apathy and Grid controlled man.

The lethal prions that are now a basis for major neurological diseases act as crystals and crystals may indeed have formed the very basis of life on Earth. Crystals store information and transmit and receive through resonance and also have the ability to **self-replicate**. The World Order has persistently maintained the primitive mind survival mechanism of GROWTH. Growth has been observed as International Finance Capitalism, conglomerate and Global business growth supported by the Darwinian principle of evolution – 'Survival of the Fittest'. It might be posed that such thoughts have continually activated certain genes or gene sequences in proportion to the strength of the transmission signal. As man descends more deeply into matter, past holographics and thoughts of past masters where sacrifice and predatory thoughts were foremost, would it be surprising if other species and even primitive crystal early life forms started to make a re-appearance, as these energies activate their gene sequences or the UVG 120 crystal itself organises such crystal-like life forms? As animals are forced into abnormal food chains of cannibalism would this not indicate to the etheric DNA or master pattern, that the past holographics are now current? The change in the overall biofield frequency (and the DNA frequency) of cattle fed sheep remains or offal, must surely create quite a different resonance for the entire animal and the appearance of prions or proteins in abnormal and crystalline form, may be merely a response by the master pattern – not as DNA but as UVG120 sphere or crystal. In effect the master DNA pattern no longer recognises the frequency DNA of the species, in the case of BSE – cattle. The new Biblical plagues may indeed be placed at the door of World Order funded research laboratories as suggested, but neither can one dismiss that man is by his thought processes and actions re-stimulating the appearance of early crystalline life forms and the early world of bacteria and simple organisms that man has not co-existed with in his current body form and therefore finds no immunity recognition of. The super bugs may be just another result of mans inability to confront the World Order as that Order suppresses man backwards in time to periods of GROWTH and where now cancer prevails as the experience of emotional and spiritual loss through that Order is 'solved' by the Grid or primitive mind, which cannot compute physical loss with emotional loss. Emotional loss (job, relationship, home etc.) was not part of the primitive mind data. The World Order may be busy manipulating the Apocalypse to bring about their own religious end, but are they quite sure they really understand their God (the Grid) and the workings of their own mind and their unenviable fate. Genetic engineering and the super-bugs may simply relay the increasing frequency message to the Grid that time has reverted to the beginning and the epoch of the bugs, who may well once again become the dominant life form on Earth, as depopulation provides an ever weakened DNA resonance to the master DNA blue-print.

THE ONE SLIT WORLD

Physics experiments that set out to observe the behaviour of electrons, throw up certain puzzles in quantum theory. Unobserved electrons behave as waves of probability, but when the physicist attempts to observe the electron it becomes a solid particle! The famous two-slit experiment in physics tells us that when two holes are provided for electrons to pass through from a source such as a crystal, the electrons behave as a wave (energy) and create interference patterns. If however you only provide one hole or slit, through which the electron can pass it behaves as a particle (matter) Not only are we an inseparable part of the pattern and not mere external observers, but the collapse of the wave function of the electron as soon as we attempt to observe it, may underline the limitations of our senses to observe the greater interactive pattern. The very act of wishing to have something to observe, may create the solidity of matter, together with the limitations of our physical senses, which cannot perceive the energy dance or the 'tune' that is being played. The inability to perceive the anti-matter 'film roll' or the spiritual recording, which occurs between every frame and parallel to the frame of every matter cycle event, does not mean that it does not exist. That recording is truly the trap, when in the spirit we view our totality of thought and action in the matter cycle during the 'Life Review' as a spirit after death (of a physical body) and compare that to the standard of the spiritual ' film roll' and what we **should** have done. Obviously unless you know major wrong deeds in past lives, these too as recordings on a **continuous** 'film roll' will play a major part and deciding factor in exit. Pity the man or woman who does not know of the past and threatens the survival of others in the present. Survival actions and thought to a spirit are totally different from that of survival of a body in the matter cycle.

Quantum theory is based upon the supposition that if there is more than one possible way in which an event can occur, then unless we actually observe the details of the event itself, the outcome we observe will be the sum of the probabilities of all the various possibilities having *actually* occurred. This explains precognition and the realisation of future events. The electron unobserved is a wave of interconnections and interactions reflecting the vacuum patterning of energy, but when observed becomes a solid unit or particle with no apparent interconnections. Because we cannot see the interconnections and the energy pattern we assume that it does not exist. The recordings of the matter cycle are the frames of the 'film roll' you observed with your senses. Grid controlled man looks around him and believes what he sees is 'reality': his house, his car, his new extension are all very real in the matter world. Even a man who has access to past lives and has a greater spiritual dimension may view his matter 'film roll' of past events and believe that is 'reality', however not until he can view his spiritual 'film roll' which extends beyond Earth, will that man come to have some perspective on true reality. Past lives recalling the matter cycle, usually revolve around deaths and loss of body parts or some aspect of loss in the material world and therefore times when survival was threatened in terms of that world. Whether an electron behaves as a wave or matter, depends on the two different ways of observing energy – from a material or spiritual point of view. If you viewed the matter cycle from the point of view of a spirit you would 'see' a vast energy pattern of which you are a part. If however you view the matter cycle from the point of view of a body, you will see very solid objects and the more engrossed a man is in the matter cycle and run by www-com/grid then the more solid is his 'reality'. In this pattern of energy of vacuum and grid sits the spirit and convinces himself that he is *separate* from the pattern – a player in the orchestra, but refusing to recognise his instrument. The withdrawal of the alternative viewpoint of Re-incarnation in the Religious Revolution, initiated mind control, simply because it removed by analogy the two-slit hole through which the electron passes. One policy, one viewpoint or one hole controlled by the World Order elite, meant that matter became just that bit more solid: particularly as ownership of matter became the sole goal. Ultimately the World Order became the *sole viewpoint*, policy and 'reality' and the true or actual reality became withdrawn into the hidden science, such that the masters had a greater control over it. The web of interconnecting energy and hence the trap was forgotten.

Whilst the reactive, primitive or Universal Mind is a recording of your interaction as matter or a body, within the pattern of energy of the matter cycle; there is another recording based on spiritual interaction or lack of it! The electron as wave and interference pattern can only exist when there are two holes through which it can pass. Likewise man will only come to understand the energy pattern, when he allows more than one policy, viewpoint or reality to exist. The 360-degree circle (cycle) of the electron, also exhibits a figure-of-8 pattern and 720-degree cycle, which as the magical number of 72 was controlled by the secret priesthood. In effect, the elite has controlled the anti-matter cycle and the spiritual viewpoint of reality. Some indication of this anti-matter cycle and its control was given by the appearance of Jesus after the events of Golgotha at his resurrection and in the period of 72 hours or three days. This concept of other realms has existed in all cultures and the majority of world myths and legends: the idea of gods or beings in some other unearthly dimension. Channelling however has led to this miss-guided viewpoint that an anti-matter cycle exists in the same universe as a matter cycle – the two are mutually exclusive: and channelled information is now so intricately tied to the body of esoteric knowledge through people like Blavatsky, Steiner and Crowley, together with new emergent knowledge in the New Age literature, indelibly imprinted with channelled information, that it may be impossible to separate that channelled information from truth – although I have attempted it here. This is also true of religious texts and in all this channelled information you will find the view of super-human masters controlling humanity. This is really extended into the World Order viewpoint.

There is no doubt that men and women (the sex of the body is immaterial) as *degraded spiritual beings* have continually controlled humanity and that a World Order is their aim. Many people however have reasonably questioned just how the World Order or the few can control the many and humanity, so aptly illustrated on the reverse side of the One-dollar note of America (**One** out of many). The Masters through **policy and the one slit reality**, merely have to keep man in a perceived state of non-survival and prevent any differing viewpoint or reality from emerging, to produce a Grid controlled populous. By keeping man low down on the psychological, emotional and behavioural scale, they manage effectively to keep man tuned to the Universal Mind, primitive mind or Hubbard's reactive mind. Man fights man on the Darwinian principle of 'Survival of the Fittest' and where 'sacrifice to a cause' feeds the sacrificial memories of the Masters. The elite merely make use of man's greed, jealously, laziness, ignorance and the full gamut of behaviour described in Hubbard's *Chart of Human Evaluation* from 2.5 – 0 on the descending energy scale. Hubbard stated that in these low tones "help equals betrayal" and woe betide you, if you try to help anyone at this level – they will betray you, they will turn on you like an animal in the pack that sniffs out any other member of the pack which poses a threat to their perceived authority, control and survival. The World Order is just a method of politically and religiously creating a one-slit reality – the viewpoint of the Masters or "guardians", even though that viewpoint is insane and psychotic. The World Order own the media, but what of the alternative press, could they not have published the mechanism of cancer (*Appendix 1*) – even as a *proposed* solution? The world of power however is all male country in the primitive mind, simply because evolution has dictated the strongest (which now translates as the most predatory or richest) male runs the pack, as evidenced by a glance at the world's leaders. The World Order had only to apply policy dictated by the few in groups such as the secret Masonic groups, restricting money flow through the World Bank and other such institutions, to create that signal of non-survival and bingo! Man connects to the Grid and **man himself** does the rest! The media promotes people who are dumb, egoists, criminals or 'experts' of the World Order and in effect puts out a strong message to mankind that the way to survive (in the matter cycle) is to either to follow Darwinian principles of 'Survival of the Fittest' (leader of the pack) or toe the line with the leader of the pack (the World Order) and be "On Message" (from the Grid and Masters). I believe that *Revelations* referred to the fact that "no-one could buy or sell in those days" without the sign on his forehead – opening of the third eye or crown chakra to the Grid and Masters! If you are Grid controlled, you will receive media coverage and even payment for criminal acts and the public receives the message that Grid man fares better in the material world than those who are spiritual.

Drugs, sexual obsession, hedonism, repetitive beat 'pop' music all creates the comatose state that facilitate connection to the primitive mind with its survival mechanisms. Man **himself** blocked other viewpoints, the two-slit viewpoint and the alternative reality, through his dogmatic and robotic adherence to World Order instigated religion and viewpoints, with the trail of out-realities that are inherent within that, together with his reactive mind dramatizations of past lives. It was quite a surprise to see just how many fought even a *proposed* solution to cancer! The World Order grew in power and wealth in proportion to the dictates of the survival mechanism of the primitive mind: GROW=SURVIVAL. Those who could not grow in response to survival threat merely grew tumours and developed diseases and became the victims of the new super bugs of the past. The cancer within humanity and society is GROWTH and the cycle continues, whilst the World Order as the leading players play on. The power pyramidal system of government where power is concentrated in a few at the top is a reflection of the primitive tribal mind displayed by both groups 12 and 13 throughout history. It would never occur to mankind to demand or form political parties comprising individuals who have **proven track records of spiritual development**. In *Alternative 4 (pg. 358)* I gave two systems of government, one a Constitutional Republic which was envisaged by the Founding Fathers of America, where **power was widely diffused** and a dictatorship impossible; the other was a system of Democratic Socialism where every facet of power is governed by policy from an executive (the One), which is the Illuminati power pyramid that is currently employed in International politics and globalisation. The problem has been that the power apex is not the one people imagine, it is a clique of very few powerful and rich men or multi-national companies, who dictate hidden agenda and policy through secret groups and politics. The policy of world 'reality' and the one viewpoint emits from that apex and thus any Illuminatus system that concentrates power in an apical point is a system of the Masters. As I have pointed out earlier, GM technology is not a democratic policy of governments or the will of the people (as most people are opposed to it), but a policy and hidden agenda of powerful Biotechnology companies that interlink through the pharmaceutical industry. Media, politicians, bankers, lawyers and accountants at the top of the pile are mattoid stooges to that policy and agenda, rewarded as dogs from the Masters table – pity the man and his fate. The World Order 'reality' and policy then filters down through many sub-branches such as the grant or university system, medicine and education. A scientist when faced with authenticating policy, in return for rewards from the elite, publication and funding of his research, which will pay his mortgage and family's food bills and hence survival, will choose the primitive mind of survival; for the other root I can assure you is bankruptcy and battle all the way, with loss of apparent professional credibility. However Quantum theory is a description of *physical reality* (matter) and if there is an ultimate policy of the World Order, then it is to maintain that 'reality' at all costs: the Grid forever. The World Order has merely to retain its own 'experts' and its own publishing houses and media channels, which filter down policy and 'reality' to the masses, in order to prevent any alternative reality from emerging – and God forbid being researched and funded! The French Revolution was set into motion by the encyclopaedists, the intellectuals who laid the groundwork of intellectual revolution, by creating such ideas as 'equality, liberty and fraternity', parroted by the masses during the revolution. *The Protocols of the Learned Elders of Zion*, indeed outlined such methods as the creation of mattoid mouthpieces that would bring down to the masses whatever information the Masters deemed necessary for the epoch or "wheel" within the cycle. I suspect the introduction of the idea that a Universal Mind is a spiritual mind, emanates from such sources, along with the idea that the Patriarchs were working for the good of humanity, which has filtered its way into New Age literature I note.

God knows what philosophical and quasi scientific augments created in World Order funded laboratories persuade scientists to sell their souls to the Masters, apart from financial or survival concerns. You can bet your bottom dramatization that any policy on de-population even through cancer, or DNA manipulation, will find its justification along with Capitalist market growth, in some aspect of the hidden science. Incidentally de-population was a consideration of Hubbard's arch controller – Xenu, who is probably through Re-incarnation still with us! What I present here in this thesis is a very different viewpoint from the World Order and even standard religious texts however as Ghandi was to note: "Even if you are in a minority of one, the truth is still the truth". Einstein in his relativity theory realized that we couldn't talk about space without implicating time and vice versa. He realized that there is no absolute frame of reference by which to judge space and time, because everything, including the observer exists within space and time. The observer cannot get outside of space and time in order to be a truly independent observer. The Einsteinian concept of space and time, results in the concept of a space-time continuum where gravity is due to a curvature of that space-time. The Grid however as we have noted, causes gravitational anomalies and as far as we know Einstein did not mention the Grid, although anti-gravity effects on the moon passed everyone's notice! Relativity theory does recognise the non-absolute nature of any space-time co-ordinates, thus what we observe of space and time are relative to **where we are in space and time, relative to what we are observing**. It might according to World Order 'reality' seem unbelievable to say that I witnessed the events of Golgotha – **I was there**. What initially seemed contrary to any previous orthodox account became explained as I pursued answers to questions that the account raised. Why on earth would Jesus take genealogies of the Mary Magdalene? What had genealogies got to do with the events of Golgotha? And so on. The best observation point from the point of view of reality is to BE THERE! If you have been there enough times, you get more reality on events of history and have no need to resort to channelling. If a person states your account is not correct the question becomes – 'why, were you there'? Second hand data is never an observation point – you have to **be there to know** and believe you me, tiring it is, to keep up with every trick of the World Order, watching and waiting for that ultimate slip up, so that you can squeeze that alternative or two-slit viewpoint through!

In light of warnings here on a Magnetic Reversal it is interesting to refer back to the Fatima Miracle discussed in *Alternative 4*. The woman who appeared to several children and ultimately created an energy effect witnessed by thousands, has been claimed by the Catholic Church as the Virgin Mary. That is one viewpoint, but the woman takes on a new significance and an alternative viewpoint in this thesis. The woman in the Fatima miracle claimed that unless man turned to peace, a great disaster would befall man. In another vision in 1962 now known as the Garabandal case, there was also a prediction that a great schism would occur in the Catholic Church where: "cardinal would oppose cardinal and bishop would oppose bishop". Significantly in both cases of the Fatima miracle and the Garabandal case, the vision of the woman appeared to children as the future generation. In the latter case in 1962 the children who witnessed the miracle gave a vision of disaster, where in a state of shock and terror they saw the world engulfed by fire. In the first vision of Fatima a young boy appeared as the "angel of peace" and was in later visions followed by a woman, who predicted the end of the First World War, and prophesied a revolution would occur in Russia. Further, the woman spoke of a Second World War under a Pope Pius XI and indeed 22 years later the event came to pass under that Pope's reign. The woman initially appeared headless, with a clap of thunder preceding the apparition, which indicates some electro-magnetic effect. Curiously the Garabandal apparition in the 60's occurred in the Cantabrian Mountains in North West Spain and in Palaeolithic times, this area and its people portrayed some knowledge of the Grid in the execution of cave paintings. It may be significant that in the Garabandal case the apparition again started with a brilliant orb of white light and in the light appeared the figure of a boy, dressed in a blue robe. He had jet black eyes set in a face of dark complexion. Conchita one of the children who witnessed the apparition significantly stated that it seemed as: "though it was the face of a child it seemed to have the strength of a giant within it". Thus once again we see the UFO witness phenomenon, in so far as several thought forms are interconnected via one or two frames of the past, thus relying on the witness to interpret those frames. Here, we may have that complex thought of boy enterix or sacrificial victim, giant, 13 th tribe and black as black cabalistic ritual – giant referring to those who had survived a magnetic reversal. Significantly and contrary to the Fatima miracle, which I believe was a true apparition, the Garabandal case witnesses stated that the apparition had declared he was Michael the Archangel. Thus whilst the Fatima miracle was I believe a true apparition, I believe the Garabandal case was past holographics impinging according to either 'The Onion Ring Model' of the UFO experience, or this was a deliberate manipulation by the 13 th tribe. The boy in the Garabandal case appeared significantly with another boy (Twin Kings) and a "beautiful woman" indicating the ancient Trinity of Minoan Crete and the relationship to the 13 th tribe. The Archangel Michael was of course interchangeable with Adam. The girl between the two boys wore a robe of white and blue, which were the death colours of Minoan Crete, however she significantly carried a baby, reminding one of the Bull-Minotaur on his mother's knee and the pose of the Virgin and Christ child. The Holy Grail however was sent to teach the children.

The witnesses to the Garabandal case over the period of 1961-1965 numbered two thousand, however there were an alleged 70 000 witnesses at the Fatima miracle. During the apparition of the Garabandal case, the children significantly became so heavy that the strongest men in the village could not lift them, indicating some gravitational property of the Grid and the implied impingement of holographics by Grid activation. The children also spoke in languages during the apparition, even though they normally spoke only in Spanish and often recited *Greek* prayers, again indicating that this area may have been a secret group centre, which as presumably 13 th tribe carried significant knowledge on the Religious Revolution in Crete. The Garabandal female apparition made two further predictions, the first concerned a supernatural event in which everything in the world would emit light for a short period of time and this "event of light", would precede an imminent disaster, and would awaken the conscience of humanity. I can only perceive that this is a warning of a Magnetic Reversal. The woman in the Fatima miracle tried to impart the same message, when in a spectacular show of energy witnesses believed the **sun would fall to earth**. It is significant that in the Fatima miracle, the boy who initially appeared prior to the apparition of the woman did so in an oak tree. I have already discussed the significance of the oak in relation to the Druidic Tree Alphabet, royalty and the 13 th tribe who used young boys as a sacrificial victim and presumably forms of ritual related to their god, bisexual Hermes. The groves of trees were placed at significant electro-magnetic sites and thus the Fatima miracle was I conclude a metaphysical apparition based on the model of 'The Onion Ring' I gave in *Alternative 4*.

In 1968 a woman also appeared on the roof of an orthodox Coptic church in Egypt at Zeitoun. Churches as I have explained, are often built on significant ancient energy centres and thus would be prime places for natural holographic or UFO type events. The woman at Zeitoun appeared with a luminous bird hovering above her head, which signifies the epiphany of the Goddess in Minoan Crete. The woman once again appeared with a baby and in one hand carried an olive branch; again a boy occasionally joined her. The woman of course was locked up in the tomb with the 13 th tribe from an early time and thus the appearance of the boy may signify the odd frames in this story overlaid upon one another, which the witness has to interpret. The child witnesses having being taught along orthodox religious lines, would undoubtedly refer to the woman as the Virgin Mary, but this is not the case. However the message the woman left was clear, it was in all cases a call for peace and a warning of disaster. The Mary Magdalene was to give a prophecy that reflected this message, when she stated:

"There will be no peace on this Earth, until the cut is healed"

BOHEMIAN GROVE AND "SHAPE-SHIFTING REPTILES"

Each Age has had its Adepts, initiates privy to the mysteries; they were known as the Magi, the Masters, the Mahatmas, the Illumined Ones, the Rishis and the Great White Brotherhood. They have been Hindus, Buddhists, and esoteric Christians, pagans, Sufis, Zoroastrians and members of all religions throughout the ages. However two groups (12 and 13) always formed the uppermost and secret hierarchy and the "hidden hand" that moves politics and power on this planet. At the apex, it is highly likely that one group moves both 12 and 13 and plays the two in duality, with man as dispensible pawn. In this cycle they took knowledge they had no right to and have used it for their own profit and empowerment, in a cycle of mind control dating back to the Religious Revolution. More recently, the Masters have been presented as Extra-Terrestrials and the idea that this extra-terrestrial hierarchy is directing mankind along a path of enlightenment. It is true that spiritual intervention – extra-terrestrial if you like (if you must use that now overworked term with World Order significances overlaid), did occur c. 10 000 B.C. and that intervention brought with it the Holy Grail, or knowledge meant for **mankind**. Those who took this knowledge, researched it to greater degrees and now parts of this expanded knowledge have been leaked piecemeal, at various times into New Age literature. Invariably though as I have discussed, this knowledge finds a link with the patriarchs in some form and therefore only serves the ends of the group who now seek applause for 'their' gift to humanity.

Each age of Adepts and initiates privy to the Mysteries, believes that by releasing this knowledge piecemeal that they are superior and "the guardians", leading humanity onwards towards *their* own view of enlightenment. We are now living in the so-called 'Kali Yuga' or Black Age as the Hindus call it: an age of gross materialism and little spirituality - the age of Horus. The half-Christianised Egyptians identified Christ with Horus, son of Osiris and spoke of the Saviour as the young avenger in the "legend of the winged disc", which swept down the Nile Valley driving the devil (Set) out of Egypt. As early Gaelic converts said: "Christ is my Druid" and those of the land of the pharaohs appeared to have declared similarly: "Christ is my Horus". As Jesus declared he had come "to bring a sword and "not peace", which was at odds with his pacific role, although understandable in the battle of 12 and 13. I have commented at length on how Christianity was a planned affair, with much double agent secrecy and indeed Christianity drove Re-incarnation underground, as the 'Underground Stream' (of wisdom). Egypt appears to have been a sequence of battles and compromises of groups 12 and 13 accounting for the various Pharaoh's carrying different racial characteristics along with their Queens (*Plate 21 and 22*). The purity of royal or Masters bloodline has been overlooked in Anthropology and *Plate 23* (*'The Antelope King'*) illustrates the idea of bloodline, semen or seed as the progenitor of the race or tribe, with the implication of a seed or bloodline from the Patriarchs. This idea may well have given rise to the phallic Bull-Minos cult, with ideas of supremacy of strength and again the importance of relaying that strength in the Darwinian thought of 'Survival of the Fittest': however royalty and the "red men" of Knossos was always associated with that line.

The seeker after Truth is confronted with a maze of sects, cults, religions and theories and yet the path a man follows will depend to a large extent on which past lives, he chooses to dramatize at any one time. The individual, who wishes to exit, will play all existences at once and reverse all karma, although it is an experience that will drive you to the edge! However time is not in abundance now in this cycle and had the Holy Grail not been stolen, then man would not be here at the end, ruled by the insane with another Magnetic Reversal already underway. There have been attempts and movements in the past to challenge the World Order e.g. the hippie and the 60s – 70s student movements, however in each case the World Order hijacked the movement, just as they will hijack the movement against the World Order this time, as they have tried to hijack the UFO phenomenon (*Alternative 4*). Professor Timothy Leary who promoted drugs to youth by constant media exposure in the 60s 'pop culture', created the manipulated connection to illumination through drugs ('drop in and drop out'): Indian gurus and the idea of guiding Masters also arose. Dr. John Coleman in *Conspirator's Hierarchy: The Story of The Committee of 300* refers to Mick Jagger and The Beatles pop groups and the Tavistock group. The true message of the 60s and 70s, which aimed at the World Order (although it was not recognised in that way) was covered up as a youth revolution in clothes, pop music, drugs and enlightenment together with sexual promiscuity, all of which connected the young to the Grid and the Masters – a whole generation duped. Joan Biaz was later to state of Bob Dylan, he "wrote about revolution, but never participated in one" and in fact the youth not knowing the real target, rebelled and revolted against their parents, the family, education and teachers and in fact played into the hands of the Masters. The *intellectual movement* of the 60s and 70s was never allowed to speak, just as the recent (*May 2001*) television programme in Britain (*Channel 4*) on 'The World Order' based on a book by John Ronson called *Them*, never interviewed the most obvious heavyweight intellectuals who write against the World Order, such as the Editor of *On Target* Col B.S. Turner, C.Eng., F.I. Mech.E. who would run intellectual rings around politicians and individuals subservient towards that hierarchy; and more importantly would ask questions that would defy the flippant and dismissive answers given by those who work within the secret machinations of power and who provided a gloss of sanctimonious whitewash for Ronson's programme and lightweight questions, which leads one to wonder, whether it was not a put up job. The World Order are getting very clever with psychology these days and as I have noted are now a disinformation line in New Age literature.

The policy of the hierarchy weakened the moral fibre of the nation state, demoralized workers in the labour class by creating mass unemployment, where jobs dwindled due to the post war industrial zero growth policies introduced by the Club of Rome, after which demoralized and discouraged workers resorted to alcohol and drugs. Youth were encouraged through pop culture to take drugs and rebel against the status quo, eventually undermining the family unit, which was also attacked by various laws and policies of The World Order. Coleman claimed in his book that the Tavistock Institute were ordered by the Committee of 300 to prepare a blueprint as to how all this might be achieved and Tavistock directed Stanford Research to undertake the work under the direction of Professor Willis Harmon. This work later became known as: "The Aquarian Conspiracy", marked by the musical "Hair" in London, with its much-publicised nudity and now famous song 'The Age of Aquarius'. The Age of Aquarius follows the Age of Horus, in secret group mysteries, where it is believed that man must trace the hard labyrinthine way to fulfilment and no doubt, through the labyrinthine path of New Age literature! The Age of Horus and horrors of the French and Russian Revolutions, World War I and II, was followed by the 60s and 70s culture and the growth of the alternative movement, with its labyrinthine therapies, cults, religions and sects. All this is hardly co-incidental! The driving force of World Revolution and politics is really the occult mysteries.

The manipulation of politics and world conflict was justified as the Age of Horus and the necessity for man to pass through this period, in order to evolve – "accelerated evolution" as the World Order term it. The "sacrifice to the cause" – another well worn method of the World Order, would ultimately achieve the plan and goal that has never ceased to exist – a Universal Kingdom with religious and political control – which **is** the World Order plan. The left reverse side of the One-dollar note of America shows the Illuminatus political goal, but the right side shows the Rosicrucian (Scottish Rite?) goal of religion. Meanwhile in a policy of population control, the Third World became the dumping ground of the Syndicate's drugs, whilst reducing immunity of the population and coupled with famine and disease, white supremacist policy effectively de-populated vast areas of The Third World. According to Coleman the Committee commissioned Cyrus Vance to produce a paper on this subject of genocide produced under the title of the "*Global 200 report*", which was approved by President Carter or and on behalf of U.S. Government and accepted by Edwin Murkie, then Secretary of State. Under the terms of that report, the population of the United States is to be reduced by 100 million by the year 2050. Only a war could produce that figure, or disablement of the X and Y genes through genetic technology (enter the controversial terminator gene?) Goodness knows what the Master DNA pattern will make of that – will it assume that survival is threatened (since reproduction is a major factor in survival to the primitive mind) and instigate its own mechanisms of survival on the computation that the species has failed and recombination is necessary or more growth! A world spinning out of control on the irrational computation of growth at all and every cost, to enable survival. What indeed will the Master blueprint make of pigs now inserted with cow genes, or pigs inserted with human DNA and to be used as spare body parts for medical conditions in humans! This is pure dramatization of Hubbard's Xenu character, whose concern was de-population and mind control, with body control according to Hubbard as part of Yatrus' goals. Why consider that the Master or Arch controllers are not still with us along with the Sorcerers apprentices! Man in his ignorance playing God.

The prolific appearance of occult groups and sects, which arose from the time of the French Revolution, which was occult and Masonic driven, was in preparation for the Age of Aquarius. The decline in sanity may be placed at this door, since virtually all sects and cults and occult knowledge was channelled from the Masters and the Grid and interdispersed with just enough wisdom and truth from elsewhere, to make it believable! I have already explained the gross miss understanding of the earthly Masters, in their belief that they were talking to Etheric Masters, when in fact they were drawing down **past** events from the UVG 120 crystal or Grid! This has the effect of confusing space-time reality and the World Order insanity is based on their inability to distinguish space-time: 'was it then, or is it now?' They have lost the entire ball-game, since they are stuck back there in the past and bring forward into present time, not only the goals of the past (World Order) but the occult beliefs, which centre on the Religious Revolution at Knossos, overlaid onto the supremacy of the Jewish Patriarchs from Noah and Adam and the pre-flood Atlanteans. Man looks around his world and sees that genetic technology is insane, he sees control of the money system as insane, he sees a European Federal Super state and a World Order as insane and he sees the pretence at democracy as insane: but he dare not question the lunatics who run the asylum! Man allows the policy: '**One** out of many' and the Jewish Patriarchal God (Sirius) and Hermes with the justification from Adam of: 'Many out of **One**': so pertinently phrased on the One dollar note of America - all along Hermetic lines of: 'as above so below'. The arch controllers just keep reading their 'script' from the lines *they wrote* (Re-incarnation and past lives) lines dictated from past Masters or in actuality past events from the Grid! Is it any wonder that genetic cloning, technology and manipulation of DNA has again arisen, as it arose in the programme of eugenics and the Aryan super-race and as it arises obliquely and indirectly in the Jewish policy of intermarriage. Is it any wonder that atomic weapons and electronics again made their appearance – well if you must follow the 'script' or Akashic record of the past, then a Magnetic Reversal follows as sure as night follows day and before Day 1 –plant the vine and the players again take up their 'script' once again dramatizing all that has gone before –'groundhog day indeed'!

The books of Madame Blavatsky (H.P.B) such as *The Secret Doctrine* have influenced a whole generation of occultists, together with the works of Annie Besant, her successor. The classic *Ancient Wisdom*, by Besant and *Telepathy*, by another Theosophical lady Alice. A. Bailey plundered Grid Akashic Record or channelled information, claiming they were directed by either earthly, or etheric Masters (read One World Order). There is no doubt that such books in their time were just as astounding as the piecemeal information on the hidden science, which appears from World Order Rosicrucian sources today. Rudolf Steiner and his Anthroposophy movement, along with the above Theosophical initiates promoted the idea of advanced beings, traditionally known as the 'Masters of Wisdom', who comprise the occult or, as yet, hidden 'Hierarchy' overshadowing and supposedly guiding all evolution and therefore humanity on this planet. One has only to glance around the world, to see that such 'guidance' is utter nonsense! It was Rudolf Steiner who promoted the Akashic Record and set into motion a whole era of channelling. The idea is that these so-called Masters, have not only mastered themselves and have developed super-human skills and through such development granted them god-like status and mandate to lead mankind on through the various *planned* ages of Horus and Aquarius! Dr. Becker has stated that a Magnetic Reversal has already started, so let us see if they can stand before Nature's Laws and stop it! Evidently Hubbard's Inc.2, which I equate with a Magnetic Reversal shows that man has witnessed this event before. However we do not know if the "chosen ones", on the appearance of a great sign in the sky and impending event, took off in their space-ships until earth was once again ready for Day 1 – plant the vine. The MRC (magnetically reversed) or MMRC case (missed Magnetic Reversal case) depends on whether the arch controllers went through the event or not.

The Bailey books were written on behalf of the Hierarchy, just as Steiner was a 'tool' in the hands of the same hierarchy as was Besant and Blavatsky. Bailey's Treatise on *The Seven Rays*, talks of the 'antahkarana' or 'the rainbow bridge' as though it was some kind of spiritual phenomenon and yet myth and legend speak of "monsters" marching over that bridge at the end! The rainbow of course is part of the "great sign" in the sky that the book of *Revelations* speaks of at the end. This of course is the dramatic light effect, which is not only seen in LSD experiences (which must hook the mind up to these past holographics of a

Magnetic Reversal) but is the sign of an impending Magnetic Reversal. Alice Bailey's books contain the teachings of the Tibetan Master, Dwhal Khul (DK) and whether or not he was tied with the Great White Brotherhood (GWB) of Masters, Initiates, Disciples and Aspirants and the whole line dating back to Egypt, can only be questioned.

I do not know how David Icke came up with his "shape-shifting" reptile idea in *The Biggest Secret*, of the British Royals as blood sucking reptiles in their spare time, but to quote Mr. Icke: "The Queen: I've seen her sacrifice people and eat their flesh" (*Fortean Times Dec. 1999 issue 129 UK*). This sounds like channelled information, since I cannot see how else he could "see her"; and if David Icke ever discussed my theory of reptiles and the MRC case (issued in 1996 and which he sent for) over the phone or with placed World Order agents, then perhaps some of the 'synchronicities' that Ivan Fraser spoke of in his article '*David Icke Arizona Wilder Credo Mutwa and The Biggest Secret*' (The Truth Campaign @ truth.free serve.co.uk, www.vegan.swinternet.co.uk/truth campaign.htlm (*49 Trevor Terrace, North Shields, Tyne and Wear NE 30 2DF, UK*) make sense. However if you channel information, not only are you your own worst enemy, but you simply go down the insane route of the World Order with out-space-time reality – 'Was it then, or is it now?' Further if you channel information, then you stand to develop the ego, open the crown chakra and be a mere tool in the hands of the Masters and an agent of disinformation.

As I have explained when you channel, you obtain single frame composite holographs of the past, which the channeller must then as seer or transcriber of the Akashic Record, place those holographs into a coherent story. How the channeller does so, very much depends on their past lives and time track record of understanding. The best way to view an event is TO BE THERE! If you were not there, then you rely on second hand observation points, which is not an observation point of actuality. If you were there on enough occasions you have something of a true observation point (actuality). Past life hatreds of monarchy, victimisation by bloodthirsty rites of the 13 th tribe or even membership of the two groups (12 and 13) would colour the interpretation of the holographics! The problem arises of 'Was it then, or is it now?' Prince Charles has worked against World Revolution let us look at his track record: 1. Supported the Bristol Clinic for alternative Cancer care in the 80's 2. Spoke out against modern methods of medical care in support of alternative health care and challenged the BMA (British Medical association) 3. Evidently believes in past lives and has asked to be Defender of Faiths on becoming king as opposed to Defender of the Faith (Church of England). 4.Refused (against protocol) to attend a State Banquet for China's President and has met the Dalai Lama (holds a belief in Re-incarnation) 5. Has supported farmers and survival of the British countryside, during the Foot and Mouth crisis in spring of 2000 6. Has spoken out over genetic engineering asking, "what world do we want?" This is the reality and whilst I am not supporting monarchy or a Republic, I merely point to the reality and the 'now'. However monarchy has been a part of this story from very early times; and during the Religious Revolution in Crete, the tacking on of a monarchical system (King Minos) to the Holy Grail, was a secret cult or group affair, with the Bull-Minos cult, who definitely had links to the 13 th tribe or Druids and who did in fact conduct blood rituals and sacrifice. However there is a huge story and history in between current monarchy and the history through thousands of years, although current monarchy in Britain must know the background, to some extent Two and two do not make five in the analytical mind. I will return to this idea of "shape-shifting" in its true context in a moment, as we must first get a better grasp of the historical secret and occult groups and the emanation from ' **the One out of many**'.

There has been an attack on British monarchy orchestrated from a central directive, which started to emerge with publication of secret tapes of private telephone conversations. The death of the late Princess Diana has thrown up some curious connections to significances of The Holy Grail, including the curious memorial garden, which is being proposed for the site in St. Albans in Hertfordshire U.K. The garden co-incidentally or not, like the Millennium Dome in London and the Millennium "Eye" (a ferris wheel) shows archetypal significances relating to the story of the 13th tribe. The current case of the butler Paul Burrell who is alleged to have in his possession items from the late Princess Diana's estate is another curious and extraordinary twist in the tale. The listed items appear so trivial in many cases that it is a wonder that St. James's Palace did not stop a proposed prosecution, particularly as the butler was described by the late Princess Diana as her "rock" and over a long period of employment, might be expected to retain some mimentos. Princess Diana's family through her brother Earl Spencer made it quite clear at the funeral that there was enmity between the House of Windsor and the Spencers as he referred to the closer ties of the bloodline. St. James's palace did indeed question the wisdom of an Old Bailey trial, which would bring to media forefront once again old wounds, but were allegedly outmanoeuvered by Diana's sister Lady Sarah McCorquodale who is to become the main witness at the trial. Her appearance shows how seriously she views the allegations as executor of Diana's will, although she is strongly supported by Earl Spencer. According to *The Mail on Sunday* (*August 9th 2001*) Diana's sister is said: "to have grown tired of Burrell's self-appointed role as keeper of the Princess of Wales memory". This may be associated with the indecisiveness of Her Majesty Queen Elizabeth as to the protocol required in the wake of Diana's death, which allegedly heard one courtier pointedly remark in response to such indeciveness: "Do you want her brought home in a Harrods van". Whilst obvious enmity between the two families of Windsor and Spencer exists, British Intelligence MI6 significantly began the investigation into Burrell. It seems that MI6 pressurised the police at a high level, when it seemed Scotland Yard (the police headquarters in London) might cave in to wishes expressed from Prince Charles's base at St James's Palace for the case to be quietly dropped. Princess Diana made it quite clear before her death that she did not want Prince Charles to become King, the line instead passing to her son Prince William. The Spencers by persuing this case may only play into higher hands, since Lady Sarah's role is in sharp contrast to that of St James's Palace, which has been anxious to avoid a potentially embarrassing court case. Some of the reasons are not hard to fathom. For the heir to the throne to be involved in any way with this court case would hardly be good for his image and undoubtedly certain factions of the media would be utilised to question once again the fitness of the heir to become King. Prince Charles however, given the limitations of his position has proved to be a significant voice against the World Order plan and was almost certainly a major contrubuter to the current battle against GM food. The World Order is opportunist and works by the principle of "divide and conquer", if the battle between the Spencers and Windsors can be used as a platform for a greater purpose, then the Spencers might take time to pause and ask the question that Prince Charles asked: "What kind of world do we want?" The answer to that can only be decided on democratic vote based on all the facts and not covert manipulation or personal vendettas.The battle of the Wales's should have ended with the death of Diana, but I strongly suspect as with past history of the Grail story, it will create a myth and will become a divisive tool for many years to come, such is the use of the Grail and its complicated story through history. The list of 342 items including an item labelled "lady's black cloth bag, yellow metal chain, containing chewing gum and 2p piece" appear in most cases to have more in common with those everything-must-go army surplus advertisements or closing day sales, than valuable items in the estate of a Princess. The question of whether the butler did it, seems to be a minor detail in the purpose of this trial, rather like the insignificant retired bank manager who by taping private conversations rocked the monarchy and disappeared, strangely never heard of again: like the bright white flash in the tunnel, the linked bank account of the driver of Diana's car, the white Fiat Uno and its apparent journey in close proximity to the British Embassy. If Diana could speak from the grave, she would not be asking whether the butler did it.

More recently the Masters, have been presented as Extra-Terrestrials and the idea that this extra-terrestrial hierarchy is directing mankind along a path of enlightenment. However as I have noted in my second book, this idea of extra-terrestrials and UFOs is slowly being linked to a Jewish or Apocalyptic hierarchy and orientals, which reflect both groups 12 and 13 and the inevitable hierarchy. Paid agents as writers also continually disseminate World Order dictates and create disinformation, which is now rife in New Age literature, just as the encyclopaedists of the World Order paved the intellectual revolution which preceded the French Revolution, where the citizens parroted the cry: "Liberty Equality and Fraternity" (Brotherhood) written in the Lodges and as I illustrated is central to the Scottish Rite Masonic beliefs, which may now fuel Europe, with its legislation of Human Rights (not that it aided the numerous violations in the author's case!) Each Age of Adepts and initiates, privy to the Mysteries, believes by releasing such Mysteries piecemeal on the orders of the Masters he is superior to the common man, leading him onwards as the guru. The danger of ego cannot be underestimated! We are now living in the Kali Yuga or Black Age as the Hindus call it. An age of gross materialism and little spirituality: in Western terminology it is the Age of Horus. The seeker after Truth is confronted with a maze of sects, cults, and religions and yet the path a man follows, will depend to a large extent on which past life he chooses to dramatize at any one particular time and those who now fight the World Order are tied in some way in all likelihood to either group 13 or 12 or indeed both. If you do not know you're past lives, you stand to dramatize or repeat those lives and past battles. It might have been pertinent to accuse the past World Order of the Druids as "blood sucking", since they practiced cannibalistic rites, but it is out space-time reality to make the same accusation today, since sacrifice has evolved into World Order de-population policies and wars, which satisfy the hunger of 'blood lust' as part of the primitive mind, Universal Mind and Hubbard's reactive mind or in the authors terminology the morphogenetic bioplasma.

The books of Grace Cooke, who was connected to the GWB (Great White Brotherhood), were also delivered through mediumship and channelled the teachings of the Master 'White Eagle'. There is no doubt that these sort of books as with the good Reverend Owen recounted previously, desired to help humanity and much of that is interdispersed with the channelled information, which therefore *sounds* spiritual: one must look closely however at what is being said, in between the beautiful prose. Krishnamurti was indeed in our own time a good soul, but he was however connected to The Theosophical movement and his classic *At the Feet of the Master*, did promote Theosophism and the Master K.H. or Master Kuthumi. Admirably however Krishnamurti declined the role of world Teacher, which the Theosophical movement were pressing upon him. I quote his true message at the beginning of this book. The mistaken great humanity of the Masters lies in the goodness of men like Krishnamurti, who imprinted their own soul. The White Eagle books may be full of blessings and speak to heart and head, but this is truly the Age of the head and the need to think logically. No artificial gene frequency of the World Order can redress the suffering in one's

Fig.49 Gizeh and Masonic Symbolisation

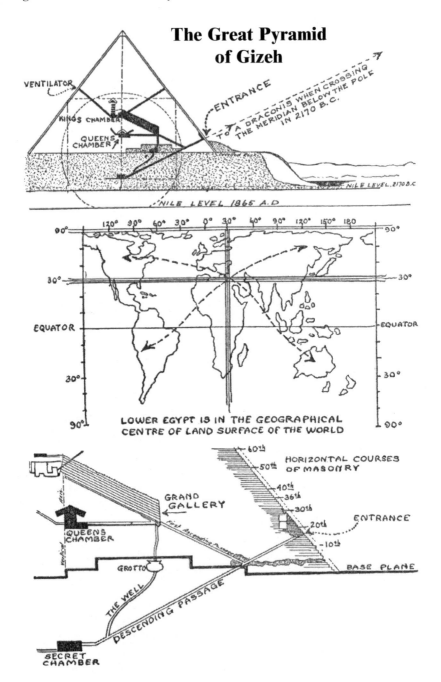

The Great Pyramid of Gizeh

VENTILATOR

KINGS CHAMBER

QUEENS CHAMBER

ENTRANCE

TO A DRACONIS WHEN CROSSING THE MERIDIAN BELOW THE POLE IN 2170 B.C.

NILE LEVEL 2170 B.C.

NILE LEVEL 1865 A.D.

LOWER EGYPT IS IN THE GEOGRAPHICAL CENTRE OF LAND SURFACE OF THE WORLD

HORIZONTAL COURSES OF MASONRY

GRAND GALLERY

QUEENS CHAMBER

GROTTO

THE WELL

DESCENDING PASSAGE

ENTRANCE

BASE PLANE

SECRET CHAMBER

soul from the accumulative past and the age of Horus – the deceit, lies, blood and pain in incessant wars and revolutions. The White Eagle books appear to promote this idea of the necessity of suffering before some greater Age will be revealed:

> "Something has to be undergone before the soul is open to receive truth – maybe a great sorrow or great joy must be experienced. Something has to crack the shell or break the crust" (*The Living Word of St. John: White Eagle Publishing Trust, 1979*).

Two words here indicate a more secret hand at work -the use of the word "shell" (Goddess connected to the sea, egg of the Phallic cult and before that Akhenaton of Egypt in the hymn of the egg) and "crust" (bardic poetry and use of " pie", referred to by secret groups at the time of the French Revolution and coined as "to pie" by Robert Graves as to make a pie and put a secret inside and cover with a crust – refer to Greek letter Pi in *The Battle of The Trees)*. Notably the reference refers to the "Word" of St. John (13th tribe/ Rosicrucian/Druid/ Bull-Minos) who was imbedded in the World Order plan as the Book of *Revelations* illustrates.

One cannot deny there is a truth in it, however would the sorrow have existed, without the World Order and their promotion of the selfishness of humanity with its animal-like 'qualities'? Does one need to experience pain, before one can know joy? Pain or sorrow, is merely a method of driving man into apathy, such that after great pain e.g. World Wars I and II, the World Order can gain acceptance from a populous in apathy for their own plans e.g. European Union. How far manipulated religious wars on this planet seek the same end of apathy and the goal of a Universal Religion must also be questioned. Further it is a justification for having continually committed a wrong: a man cannot accept he has wronged and therefore seeks to explain it by degrading the terminal he has wronged. The controllers took knowledge, hid it and used it; they Re-incarnated each time to use and acquire more of that knowledge, thus came the view that they were superior or "the guardians". However in so doing, not only did they confine man to ignorance of his real existence, but such ignorance meant that on Re-incarnation they were not drawn back into the secret groups or the knowledge and thus in effect lagged a great deal behind and descended into the unreal world of pain and suffering. The World Order justify this, by deeming it is necessary for man to know this world, before he can develop and therefore justify the Ages which have been planned. In this manner the World Order saw themselves as gods and the quick jump to becoming God was only a small step; where man was controlled by a hierarchy of "guardians", ascending from the Patriarchs – naturally!

The main symbol of the White Eagle Lodge was a six-pointed star, which is a Jewish sign. The GWB works in synchronous ways, which devotees perceive as links between the inner and outer worlds and which I perceive as holographic interconnections within the past Grid holographics. A person chooses a book or path and suddenly as if by magic a person is introduced to them, or a book they needed suddenly appears by some perceived synchronicity. The web of matrix energy of the vacuum and the patterning of energy in the past holographics of the Akashic Record however holds people together in that past and when you choose a particular role in a past life to play in present time then you can expect the whole 'cast' of the prior production to appear! You have no idea how many personnel of the era of Golgotha and Jerusalem I have met this lifetime, since I decided to go back and sort out the events of Golgotha – many if not all dramatizing heavily some aspect of that! It is very dangerous to work in World Order country without knowing your past lives, since it is a highly re-stimulative area and you stand to repeat your karmic path of the past and follow the identical holographic 'script' if you are not absolutely aware of WHO you are (the accumulation of all of your existence and time track). The World Order are stuck in past life personalities and goals and that is the insanity – they simply bring forward to present time their old goals and personalities to be played out in present time. They are e.g. Druids or Patriarchs or Grand Masters back there and bring that forward, utilising secret group history to maintain a false sense of reality. This fact is quite discernable in Masonic symbolic ritual and the Bohemian Grove ceremony, which I will come to. It is well known in psychology that a group will enforce one another's reality to the point where they can no longer see actuality.

The GWL (Great White Lodge) which I discussed as an ethereal or spiritual hierarchy, but which in fact as I propose is past holographic thought channelled by the Masters on Earth as the GWB or the Masonic magicians have 'guided' humanity – and that is the sorry truth of it. The Bailey books stress a link with the Dog Star (or in reverse God star) of the star Sirius and Egyptian archaeology often portrays the dog, which also appeared in the Revolution period of Minoan Crete! The dog in Bardic poetry was a gloss for: "guard the secret". There is no doubt that the Egyptian Initiates, left their Semitic hallmark on the Religious Revolution, but those initiates must have been the Bull-Minos phallic cult or had some connections to the parent or Masters in the UK at that time – The Druids. The connection to Sirius depends on this idea of extra-terrestrial intervention and the Masters. The hierarchy of our planet is said to maintain regular contact with an even greater hierarchy, which comprises the GWL on Sirius and is an idea that runs through many of the teachings of the occult texts. It is an idea that dominated the architecture of the pyramids (*Fig. 49*). Occult writers under the direction of the World Order; have continually stressed the link between earth and the star-sun system of the past – Sirius. In the Master White eagle's words:

> "You cannot see the silent watchers who watch over you during your earthly journey, and you do not understand how closely you are cared for, how you are guided" (*"Wisdom From White Eagle"*, *White Eagle Publishing Trust 1974*).

This old idea of the all-seeing eye of Horus and Jehoveh and the World Order also occurs at the top of the pyramid on the reverse side of the One-dollar note of America, with the implication that occult Masters are at the top of power pyramidal politics. There is a classic confusion here, in so far as there were TWO extra-terrestrial landings on this Earth: and possibly THREE if you include the APPARENT LANDING of the MMRC case (i.e. those who missed the last Magnetic Reversal in a space-ship? And returned thus giving the *appearance* of landing for a fist time). I have already covered the case of the MRC – the fallen Angel or Lucifer – "666" who originally came to Earth. The third and questionable landing of Noah and the Ark, which might have been a space-ship descending after a Magnetic Reversal, may have been the case and was confused with the spiritual intervention that brought the Holy Grail to Earth c. 10 000 B.C. I have covered the sudden appearance of civilization including the appearance of startling Art of the Neolithic period, very different Art from the Masters, in so far as one Art depicted great observation (reality) and beauty and the other was highly schematised or stylised and indicated the Cabalistic Tree of Life and magical shamans. The rise of Egypt and the Minoan civilization show a thought that was interpreted two completely different ways. The Masters have purposefully hidden spiritual intervention c.10 000 B.C claiming the Holy Grail for themselves and depicting themselves as the owner of the 'gift'. They rounded up all documents, controlled all communication lines and stole all the hereditary lines (genealogies) of the safe hands that tried to hold the Grail. They have tried to obliterate and confuse archaeological finds, dates and religious texts, editing and adding texts or mistranslating and purposefully restricting the freedom and right of science to discover Truth. Every attempt has been made to associate The Holy Grail with the Masters and the line of Noah and Adam. The dualistic battle of good and evil was born of the attempt to recover the Grail from the Masters. Mind Control in the field of religion was instigated at Knossos during the Religious Revolution and corresponds I conclude to Inc.1 of Hubbard's Space Opera. The curse on the woman was the battle of the Lucifer to hide his evil actions. The MRC case cannot confront the fact he has harmed and therefore tried to degrade the terminal (woman) he wronged, in taking the Holy Grail and offering it piecemeal as 'his gift' to humanity, whilst making a profit from it. The memory is brought forward in present time and he keeps woman out of his secret groups and defers her to the lowest rung of society, in

the hope that she will remain ignorant (of his deeds). The World Order is still the ,
phallic Bull-Minos cult.

In 1974 Robert Temple published *The Sirius Mystery*. Temple was an American
scholar of Sanskrit and oriental studies. The book recounted how two highly
respected French Anthropologists lived with the Dogon people of the Republic
of Mali in West Africa for more than 20 years and eventually unveiled the
Dogon's belief that they were civilised by beings from outer space, from the star
system of Sirius. Significantly the Dogon called their tutors "Nommus" and
have ever since worshipped them as the monitor of the Universe, the "father" of
mankind and the "guardians" of its spiritual principles. This of course smacks of
One World Order, Patriarchs, Atlanteans, Adam and the controllers of mankind
from Hubbard's Inc.1 or the author's proposal of a Religious Revolution in
Crete. The Dogon according to Temple knew that Sirius had a companion star
(Sirius B) that was invisible to the naked eye and was not known to our
astronomers until the middle of the nineteenth Century and not described
properly until the 1920's and photographed in 1970. The two anthropologists
(Griaule and Dieterlen) published their findings in 1950, which were then made
available to a larger public by Robert Temple in 1976. The Roswell UFO
incident occurred roughly in the same period of early publication, together with
the increased media coverage in popular magazines of UFO's. Could this all
have been co-incidental, I think not and further, the Sirius connection had long
been taught in occult circles including certain factions of Rosicrucian's. Here we
have the swirling underground battle of the two spiritual interventions and the
MRC case, trying to pinpoint himself as the guardian of mankind!

Ronald Story, who attempted to demolish the Space-Gods 'cult' referred to
Gruaule and Dieterlen in his work and pointed out that the two Anthropologists
had stated that Nommo had descended to earth on a gigantic arch, and that 'He'
manifested himself in the "rainbow" which is referred to as the "path of
Nommo". The Arch of course holds significance in Freemasonry as the Arch
degree and is a high Order: also myth and legend tell us that "monsters" arrive
over the "rainbow bridge" at the end! Thus was all this just a piece of
disinformation from the World Order, swinging mankind round to the idea of
Adam and the Patriarchs as gods from outer space with special powers! No
doubt "ghusts of laughter, the Moon would stir". Blavatsky's *Secret Doctrine*,
states that the Dog Star (Sirius), was the star of Mercury or 'Budha' and like the
Dogon, she stated (wrongfully) that it was called the Great Instructor of
Mankind. We must not forget that Blavatsky was using channelled information
and admitted she was under a Master: Alice Bailey also furthered this doctrine,
in 1922 under *Initiation, Human and Solar*, where Sirius was emphasised as a
cosmological influence:

"All that can be done in dealing with this profound subject is to enumerate briefly some of the cosmic influences, which definitely affect our Earth and produce results in the consciousness of men everywhere, and which, during the process of initiation, bring about certain specific phenomena. First and foremost is the energy or force emanating from the Sun Sirius. If it might be so expressed, the energy of thought, or mind force, in its totality, reaches the solar system from a distant cosmic centre via Sirius. Sirius acts as the transmitter, or the focalising centre, whence emanate those influences, which produce self-consciousness in man" (*Initiation, Human and Solar – Lucis 1977*).

It is impossible to say whether Hubbard's Inc.1 controller Xenu was or is based on Sirius, or whether mind control and Masters thoughts are relayed via the sun to Earth through the UVG120 crystal as receiver and transmitter: or whether the Brotherhood regularly channels information from such Masters, or thoughts imprinted on the UVG120 crystal; however there must be something here, for Bailey states that Sirius is a **"transmitter"**. Who is to say whether the MRC originally came from there before he fiddled about with the DNA etheric code (or Master DNA pattern) and became trapped by his own meddling and has forever tried to get back – currently dramatizing his past in the field of biotechnology and cloning. You can bet your bottom dramatization that some scientists in the space programme are working for the World Order on it (paid for by the "fools" mankind or the taxpayer of course). A. Bailey in *A Treatise on Cosmic Fire* was to give psychological results of the influence of Sirius, which was also given in *Esoteric Psychology* (*vol.1 of the Seven Rays Treatise*). In *Alternative 4*, I reported one UFO witness account that warned of a powerful group with immense "psychology" that existed on Earth. As a well worn 'General' I instinctively knew that my own path would have to be trod alone, for one cannot risk outside "synchronicities" and certainly at least twice (apart from the experiences in Greece), I was the attempted subject of such psychological attack, which was identical to methods laid out in *Microwave Harassment and Mind-Control Experimentation* (*communication by Julianne Mc Kinney, Director Electronic Surveillance Project Association of National Security Alumni Silver Spring, Maryland*): I gave the method by which the biofield could be manipulated in *Alternative 4*. Bailey stated in Esoteric Psychology:

"We have practically no effects on our parent system, the reflex action is so slight as to be negligible, but very definite effects are felt in our system through causes arising in Sirius"
(*A Treatise on Cosmic Fire – Lucis 1972*).

It is impossible to say, whether Hubbard's Xenu character is associated with Sirius, or whether there is a very real science in this, in so far as Xenu and Yatrus as I have commented, could be the X and Y chromosomes. The male chromosome and consequently the male hormone testosterone could provide a 'tuning fork' or receiver properties that co-incide with transmitter signals from the UVG120 crystal and/or its receiving properties from Sirius and consequently Masters thoughts: as I have commented, men have some peculiar computation that goes round in their heads of:

man=sexual prowess=success=power=money=control=head of pack=survival.

This appears to be an X chromosome function, whilst women who utilise the body and more cunning methods of control are Y operated and such descriptions mirror the characters of Xenu and Yatrus in Hubbard's Space Opera. *The Bible* does warn that "666" is "a man's number": and man again for some peculiar reason, always finds it necessary to prove his prowess through sexual activity, ego or kundalini power, which might account for the 'Messiah syndrome' and the virtually all-male political power scene (apart from "no secret to a woman"!). The phallic Bull-Minos cult has left its mark on the world even today. It is conceivable that the morphic resonance of these genes actually tune to some specific frequency that transmits from Sirius through our Sun and the UVG120 crystal; it is for this reason, coupled with the World Order policy of population and populous control that one should stop all genetic tinkering now. This might sound like science fiction, however I have in my possession a chart from Rosicrucian laboratories (which of course is copyrighted), but which shows resonance of elements in the Periodic Table of Elements, sounds and sensory imput resonance, various colours and bands of the spectrum of light and other resonant energies together with significant Pythagorean numerical systems. It is extremely probable that the psychology and human sensory resonance systems, have been researched according to that chart and I can only envisage what other astounding research they have hidden and which is not known – perhaps DNA band frequencies? In Britain a police communications frequency using thousands of transmitters is being set up, which will act in the very low frequency range, rather similar to the GWEN system in America, which scientists have warned has a mind and body control possibility. I have given the low frequency significances in terms of biological function in *Part I* of the Cancer report (*The Second Millennium Working Report into Cancer*) and that research shows that reproduction and chromosome function is affected by alterations in the low frequency band, which curiously not only ties in with this thesis of population control, but also psychology. Despite scientists have warned of using the low frequency band, this has been tacitly ignored – why! Europe now is to have not only its own army, but also police force and one can only perceive the nature of the reign of the World Order in the pipeline. The media, whilst railing against genetic engineering has yet to challenge the World Order insanity on the principle of the "Right to Know" (The Truth). One should never underestimate "666" as Bailey stated:

> "Only once has such a Being visited our system. The effect of such a visit as that of the Avatar from Sirius is seen as the sum total of civilization and culture, viewing these from the standpoint of the centre systems and in one flash of time".

Bailey therefore shows the classic muddle over which was the Spiritual intervention and which was the channelled word from her Masters, who were the World Order Masters and *their* visit to Earth. The problem is that the mind classifies data according to subject data and heading e.g. a dog bite at 3 years old, is classified by the mind with a dog bite at 30 years old. The two incidents are separate, but the mind classifies them under one heading. There have been two so-called extra-terrestrial interventions (one good and one bad) but the mind will classify the two together: further the World Order have continually muddled the two, hoping to hide the true spiritual intervention and the source of The Holy Grail, which they have claimed as 'their' gift to humanity: in much the same way that they have tried to hide the natural UFO phenomenon by the manipulated version – clever fellow our "666". This has given rise to dualistic philosophy and the battle between good and evil. Alice Bailey was later to reveal that she received her teachings *telepathically* from the Tibetan master whose name was later admitted to be Djwhal Khul (DK) the Master who also co-incidentally helped Madame Blavatsky, who gave the world racial doctrine, utilised by the Nazis in their eugenics and Aryan super-race ideology against the Jews. In 1934, D.K. had stated that he lived in a *physical body*, on the borders of Tibet and presided over a large group of Tibetan Lamas. Jung the famous psychologist who promoted the "collective unconscious" or the Universal Primitive mind and who placed everything at the door of sex and therefore was a conscious or unconscious World Order initiate, suggested that the Tibetan teacher was Bailey's "higher self", however D.K sent parcels from India to Bailey and thus would seem to be a physical Master. Dr. Douglas Baker was another esoteric writer who claimed that Sirius is to the Sun what Venus is to Earth, which I interpret as data imprinted on holographics of the Grid and further Baker claims that Sirius is the "Head Centre in The One". The opening of the third eye and its appearance in icons of the religious Revolution period in Crete, including the Mochlos seal with the eye of the dolphin and man with hand held to middle of forehead, may indeed have this meaning, along with the significance of opening the crown chakra to Sirius and the Masters (or the holographics of thought). Survival psychology was however recognised by D.K, when he warned that influential and potent forces are pouring in from the stars Betelgeuse Sirius and in *Esoteric Psychology* (*vol. 2 of the treatise on the Seven Rays*) he stated they produce a stimulating of the heart centre (Betelgeuse) and the head centre (Sirius). It is a fact that if you work with the head centre for too long, you will suffer from the loss of your heart and compassion, which is why The Holy Grail was employed in the field of healing or care, where compassion and the heart is essential. No one should fight the World Order, unless they retain a line to the heart and compassion, for you will end up with the thoughts of the Masters and a cold heart. A. Bailey's *Initiation, Human and Solar*, explained that in addition to the force from Sirius:

> "Another type of energy reaches man from the Pleiades, passing through the Venusian scheme to us, just as the Sirian energy passes through Saturnian's. It seems to stimulate the heart centre".

Earth however is hurtling through space and one simply does not know what in fact the crystal is picking up from planets or galaxies that precede Earth. Further, A. Bailey's *A Treatise on Cosmic Fire*, says that in the present manifestation, the Masters are more closely concerned with: ".... the Pleiades and their influence via the Sun and in relation to our planet via Venus". Grace Cook also received her messages from the Master White Eagle, by the method of mediumship. The Master of the White Eagle revealed how "God" sent messengers, from the spirit world and other planets to reveal the "vision glorious" to man and give him the key to the mysteries of life: however it seems again here that the Brotherhood has been muddled with the spiritual intervention c. 10 000 B.C. The White Eagle Master maintains that "God-men" have come from various planets to Earth, and that beings from outer space will come again and "bring happiness to Earth people" (*Wisdom from White Eagle, White Eagle Publishing Trust 1974*). Not if the "monsters", march over the "rainbow bridge"! However this idea of Masters visiting Earth was part of Dome theory, which appears to be displayed in the London Dome and Millennium icon – who says that the Freemasons have no control over politics! That little dramatization just cost the British taxpayer millions of pounds! I have covered earlier the idea that 'gods' populated this Earth prior to a cataclysm, with giants who remain in folk legend, myth and archaeology, including the Toltecs, who appear to provide further background to the New Year celebrations in New York and London and the ushering in of a new Aeon. Grace Cooke in her *The Illuminated Ones*, states that the White Eagle Himself, was instructed by a Master, the "Wise Knight" which obliquely refers one assumes to the Knight Kadosh level of Freemasonry! This wise knight usually appeared in a purple cloak and played a key role in the hierarchy of the Masters as outlined by Alice Bailey in *Initiation, Human and Solar* and *The Externalisation of the Hierarchy*. Even the word "Externalisation" gives some sense of groups set up as fronts for the goal of high ranking Masons at any one particular time in the 'wheels' of their plans.

The purple cloak was mentioned by Desmond Leslie and George Adamski in: *Flying Saucers have Landed*. Adamski stated that he had been taken to a meeting of a cosmic council on Saturn, where he was given a robe to wear, like each of the council's delegates. Significantly he stated that the robe had a rose embroidered on it. Either Adamski had a 'flash back' of his own time track, or he experienced some past holographic of a cosmic council meeting i.e. a holographic from the past, which he picked up by the brain acting as a dipole radio receiver. The third alternative was that his biofield was manipulated in the manner I suggest in *Alternative 4*. If it was a natural 'flash back' or holographics, then the World Order would not care for such a hologram to be in the public domain and Adamski, did meet a premature and suspicious death. The Rose of course is a Rosicrucian emblem and in Eileen Buckle's book *The Scorpion Mystery*, she revealed that on the day of Adamaski's death a man named Ernest Bryant, who resided in South Devon, made a UFO contact. He stated how he was taken on a tour of a saucer, during which he noticed a purple coloured robe, with a rose embroidered on the sleeve. Ron Hubbard was to state that he was millions or trillions of years ago part of some cosmic council and Aleister Crowley was to go on to state a similar experience and both directly, or indirectly were connected with the secret group the O.T.O. with its World Order hierarchy connections: although as I have pointed out, there is much in fighting in the Rosicrucian's and we cannot be sure of who "sent" Ron Hubbard into the O.T.O. Hubbard however, who was not a man who would be poetically inclined, did write a poem on the rose. It is anybody's guess whether Hubbard individually went against the World Order of mind control and tried to help humanity, thus inviting the vicious attacks, or whether he was part of some Rosicrucian group who hoped to take on the World Order, or whether he was set up, so on his death the organisation would be taken over; or finally whether he sold out to the World Order for money – there are any number of possibilities here, but one thing is sure, Hubbard was economical with the truth and his sources and to do that in a Church is quite unforgivable although it would seem not uncommon in other churches; the case of Jesus is another point in unforgivable question. If only man realised that his **entire eternity is at stake** and whether or not he will ever be free of this trap. I have however at least cleared up in this book, the appearance of the Rose in Crete at the time of mind control and the Religious Revolution, which Hubbard also recognised as mind control, although he curiously labels it the beginning and Inc.1. As I have stated the beginning was not in Crete, it was the original atomic explosion of matter and anti-matter, which may have been muddled with atomic explosions on the time track (and mind filing system) thus causing those who perpetually remain stuck in the Religious Revolution (The World Order) to dramatize atomic explosions and create nuclear war as a consequence: for this reason alone, the end cycle of the MRC case is atomic war – a Third World War. I repeat that Hubbard's Inc.1 was not the beginning; it was only the beginning of mind control in religion grafted to politics.

Adamski described his meetings with a Master in the book *Inside the Space Ships*, where he was told mankind had not yet learned to live in peace and brotherhood and that selfishness precluded man from the life of extra-terrestrials. One cannot argue that this is true in respect of selfishness and only illustrates that man is conditioned by his primitive Universal Mind and the mechanism of survival for **self** (and at most his immediate family although that has gone by the roadside). Pity the man or woman who holds that philosophy, for they will witness the greatest show on Earth – a Magnetic Reversal – keeping your head down will not like the ostrich with its head in the sand make the problem go away.

Dr. George Hunt Williamson was one of the witnesses at the time of Adamski's alleged first meeting with a Venusian and apart from the curiosity of Adamski's name, which seems mighty fortuitous Dr. Hunt Williamson went on to write of the Sirius connection in his book *Other Tongues – Other Flesh*. He stated that the "Sons of God" came to earth and made wives of ape creatures and the progeny was antediluvian man: there may be some truth in this and explain Adamski's death. The migrants he claimed arrived on Earth during the middle division of the Tertiary period known as the Miocene epoch. Significantly this bi-passes the age of Reptiles who were at their peak c. 165 - 205 million years ago in the Jurassic period: whereas the Miocene period is c. 30 million years ago, after the appearance of mammals in the Oligocene (c. 40 million years ago). However it is *before cultural man* who is thought to have arisen 2 million years ago in the Pleistocene period. The dinosaurs were wiped from the stage at the time of a major Magnetic Reversal and the stage set for mammals, thus Adamski's witness places this so-called extra-terrestrial arrival of the "Sons of God" in the pre-flood or antediluvian era although long before cultural man was thought to have arisen. .Jesus was to become a Son of God, with super-human powers and as I have pointed out was tutored somewhere within the labyrinth. Thus according to Williamson, man descended from a race of 'angels' or ET's, who mixed with "beasts". Once again we have some confusion here over which intervention occurred when and who came from where. The appearance of the Bull-Minotaur as man-beast, must have portrayed this thought of the 'gods' uniting with man: where the Cycle of Eternal Return (Re-incarnation) was manipulated by the Bull-Minos cult who conducted the Religious Revolution, into the idea of *their* return to Sirius or some such immortality as "sons of God"!

Dr. Paul Brunton in his book *A Hermit in the Himalayas* refers to the importance the Egyptians placed on Sirius and he stated that the star is definitely connected with super-human beings – "the silent watchers". Once again the all-seeing eye is implied. I have covered the Jewish background to Uri Geller's UFO experiences in *Alternative 4*, which may well have been manipulated and involved the scientist Dr. Andrija Puharich, who brought Geller to America. The idea of super-human powers was the outcome of this and there was I concluded an apocalyptic group in the background who were evidently Jewish. Krishnamurti (K) was to speak of his meeting with the 'King of the world', Sanat Kumara (in Hindu) and told how the silver star had flashed over SK's head and that the star was just a part of Him. K. Also claimed that in an out of body experience he saw the Buddha and the Master K.H. K's order was the Order of the Star in the East and Sirius has been equated with a silver star and the GWB: further K was attached to the Theosophical Society who tried to claim that he was the world Teacher, which he declined. The White Eagle Lodge was descended from the French Polaire Brotherhood, whose symbol was also a silver star according the Lodge's first book: also according to Grace Cooke's daughter Joan Hodgson in the Stella Polaris Lodge magazine, the year that K closed down the Order of the Star within the Theosophical society, a mysterious message arrived from the Far East, to form the Polaire Brotherhood in France. The English Lodge of the Polaire was called The White Eagle Lodge, with some connection to the Chevalier Rose-Croix and thus the Rosicrucian's.

David Anrias who wrote *Through the Eyes of the Masters* in 1947, worked with Annie Besant in India and was also associated with the White Lodge. He described how dark spiritual forces were menacing mankind and the necessity of reinforcing the White Lodge with more highly evolved beings associated with Sirius, which sounds like magical rituals 'calling' spirits, when in fact one is merely activating holograms retained on the Akashic Record or Grid/crystal. Besant of course did channel material. According to Besant and
 Lead beater, both Theosophists, it was Krishnamurti who originally took down the precepts, which were later issued as *The Voice of the Silence*, by Blavatsky. The book once again emphasised the Sirius connection or the "flaming star". Krishnamurti had some association with the Buddhist sage Asanga and the Aryasanga took Buddhist teachings to Tibet and became on incarnation the Master D.K, the Tibetan teacher of Alice Bailey and Blavatsky and was allegedly the spokesman of the Masters affiliated to the GWL on Sirius (non earthly spirits)! Thus there is a long line here from Masters on Sirius or channelled information, to the Theosophists who influenced a whole generation of occultists and secret groups including the Nazis – who I concluded were 13th tribe influenced! Although I did question whether the 12 and 13th tribes acted in unison at the very top, since the Apoclyptic Revelation specifically mentions "all

the tribes of Israel".

Leadbeater who has written Masonic articles in his *Lives of Alcyone*, quotes Sirius in connection with a number of past lives and the Sirius connection not only occurs in Freemasonry, but in the division of some order of Rosicrucian's. When an initiate joins the Masonic GWB (earthly) it is for eternity, implying that despite Freemasonry holds *The Bible* as a holy text, they do in fact believe in Re-incarnation and Sirius is seen as the "Star of Initiation" where each brother is approved by "Lord of the World". Paul Mevryl deciphered an inscription at the head of a cross in the foothills of the Pyrenees discussed by Fulcanelli in his book *The Mystery of the Cathedrals*. The inscription read OCRUXAVES PESUNICA, which Mevryl suggested was an anagram of the Latin phrase ORCUS AVE PUSE CANIS which in English reads 'Lord of the Dead, Hail, down from Dog'. The Egyptians referred to Osiris as the Lord of Sirius as well as Lord of the Dead, the dark god. Sirius A and B may be referred to, when the Egyptian terms of Lord of the day AND night sun, Lord of the two Earths and Lord of the two Lands were used. Sirius B cannot be seen with the naked eye and Mevryl calls Sirius the Son behind the Sun i.e. invisible. The dog appeared in (Late) Cretan iconography at the time of the Religious Revolution, with the monkey fresco occurring in earlier iconography, which I have cross-referenced with some cataclysm that occurred which saw the Sethites regress to ape-like form. The mention of two lands and stars may even initially have been a referral to the two interventions, trying to separate the two i.e. the Sethites and Cainites? It seems to me that the early Neolithic cave paintings showing perhaps the ancestral root memory of the origins of that particular cult or race as an anthropomorphic or semi-reptilian figure (*Plate 11*), presumably derived from Cabalistic ritual as a form of channelling, or some verbal tribal memory of root racial types, was exchanged for the story of true spiritual intervention c. 10 000 B.C. In other words the Masters (Sirius) as the cult or race descended to earth, thereafter tried to erase that memory and conducted the Religious Revolution in Crete. Spiritual intervention c.10 000 B.C displayed what had happened in a Magnetic Reversal and explained the background! Thus the World Order or the MRC case then took over the story of spiritual intervention and laid it upon his own history, this is why there is a confusion of thought, which is further misinterpreted by channelling and which has infected virtually the whole of occult (secret) group knowledge.

The pre-historic cave engravings of La Marche, situated near the village of Lussac-Les-Chateaux in Western France, break all the conventions of Paleolithic art and the orthdox story of man deriving through a slow process of evolution from ape and one phylogenetic line or form. The engravings are a mass of hairline scratches and from the start, it was clear that the subjects of the carvings were not the ordinary designs of Ice Age art. Breuil one archaelogist of the site was particularly struck, by the four or five extraordinary male profiles. The profiles (*Fig.50*) definitely showed what appeared to be different racial types. Stephane Lwoff the main excavator of the site, was struck by the dozens of strange human faces and figures intertwined with animal outlines or apparently meaningless random lines and scribbles. Many painstaking years of observation produced a gallery of fifty-seven isolated heads. The main difference exhibited, is the muzzle-like or protruding jaw and nose line of some, compared to the up turned and snub nose of others: however none of the faces resemble the ape-man of the orthodox view of descent of man. Bearded men ocurr in some engravings and moustaches also appear perhaps with some Bull-Minos (handle-bar moustache) implied. Lwoff's original drawings showed details of costumes and hats, already referred to earlier in this book and although the drawings have been replaced with more 'accurate' sketches, it is admitted even in the 'accurate' descriptions that a dozen hats and one head band exist, together with belts and bracelests! This really cuts the evolutionary time-scale to shreds. Further, a number of women occur without heads and this suggests not mere co-incidence but a belief of some sort and perhaps the idea of the oracular head (head of an oracle or 'god' of a tribe that was kept after the person was deceased). In *fig.50*, the most striking head is the one at top left, which bears a great resemblance to the anthropomorphic or 'reptilian head'. Archaelogists have noted that for some obscure reason artists of cave paintings were reluctant to depict human forms and animal engravings are far more common. This fact makes the La Marche engravings significant and implies that there was some censorship or fear here. Just as genetics and racial types together with research, has become taboo after the Nazis then it may be that there was some secret veiled in racial types even at this early stage. Even more obscure, is the fact that unrealistic bestialised forms are almost as numerous in cave and mobile art as are the realistic types. Caves however, had significance in terms of spiritual ancestry, which the Druids evidently recognised in their practice of utilising caves (and mountains) as significant electro-magnetic sites. The early Semitic stone pillars, which also made their appearance in Crete at the time of the Religious Revolution, depicted the belief that the ancestor or god of the tribe was embedded in the rock or stone: thus one perceives that these anthropomorphic forms are meant to describe spiritual and body ancestry. Indeed one of the strange "marriage certificates" from La Marche appears to indicate the spirit of a woman entering a (female?) person in some attitude of prayer or religious position, implying that someone at La Marche may have been trying to explain some of this story to the tribe there!

It might be argued, that the Sethites and Cainites produced two racially distinct forms or indeed the "sons of God" and ape-men. However let us suppose for one moment the MRC case did in fact miss a Magnetic Reversal, by removing himself via a space-ship to some remote place (MMRC) and then returned, when the apocalypse or Flood was over: would he not have saved his **body** or **phylogenetic line**? I have already discussed that the Holy Grail was sent to earth to guide man from the trap of the Grid, but it also was sent to remind man that he was not his body, a thought that had arisen from the very long mortality rates of bodies prior to a Magnetic Reversal and mentioned in *The Bible*, where the patriarchs lived hundreds of years. It seems that the Atlantean Masters may have sought to save their bodies, but only recognised that they were their immortal spirits, after spiritual intervention had reminded them! They then used that information for their own ends! In my research dating back to 1995, I suggested that the MRC case developed from Reptilian or Amphibian lines and was co-existent with the dinosaurs in the pre Flood era which may be given some credence by *Plate I*: and further that these men were giants under very different gravitational conditions which allowed the enormous sizes of dinosaurs to exist, which could not survive today under the present gravitational level. The question becomes whether the head at top left of *Fig. 50* was the racial type descended from those who missed the Magnetic Reversal and returned in an apparent landing thus creating that facial type? Further are the anthropomorphic cave engravings of reptilian like creatures a tribal memory of ancestry or just a representation of the totem beast as crocodile or lizard – *Plate 24*? Since totem beasts were chosen to mark some special character of the tribe, it might be asked why they chose that particular form. Further the idea that male gods came to Earth and mated with female ape-like forms may be further questioned by the appearance of some of these disturbing anthropomorphic figures with breasts and beards, which implies there were either two sexes to this racial type or they were asexual. The archaeologist Magin Berenguer has suggested that they represent a "racial caricature" of Homo sapiens and a genuinely bestial Neanderthal man, co-existent with cave artists: however it is evident that even at this stage, man was cognisant of his ancestry in some form of related history or tribal memory. The ancestral spirit is probably depicted by the appearance in cave art of various totem beasts of the tribe or more specifically the tribal leaders. The appearance of the bull (or bision) in feint outline in *Plate 13* of the *Rock Panel* showing impressionistic horses and the mysterious mauve hands in the Aurignacian to late Magdalenian stage, may attempt to show the totem beast (as bull) or tribal ancestry of the group retained by the tribal leaders and depicted in certain cave art. *Plate 13* also shows the 'Strange Composite Beast' and a late Aurignacian techniqe from Lascaux (Dordogne) France. Thus we gain some idea of the ascendency of secret groups, Masters and the totem beast of the tribe as representative of that. The feint outline of the Bull indicates that this is a *past* totem beast or tribal ancestry memory of the new or then current horse cult. I assume that the totem beast was chosen to remind the tribe of the physical or racial attributes of the group – the muzzle nose being significant and its relation to the reptilian type facial characteristics of the head (top left) in *Fig.50*, together with the anthropomorphic reptilian or beast like form in *Plate 11*.

Fig.50   **A small selection of heads from La Marche**
     drawn for comparison at the same scale and
     orientation (said to be 14 000 years old or more)

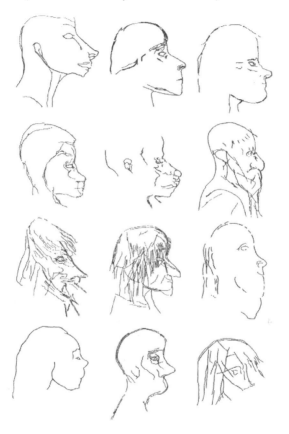

Plate 24 shows a Goanna (lizard) with eggs, which is an aboriginal bark painting of the Ungarinyin tribe. This has some connection to later Egyptian philosophy of Akhenaton and the idea of the egg and oxygenation and further with the dot like appearance or lizard skin, may have some connection to the curious system of Paleolithic art of engraving with dots, which were usually depicted as red, which further finds connection with the royal (oxygenating or life-giving blood) line and "red men of Knossos" and the oxygenating blood theory of the Egyptians and curiously relates back to a reptile – the crocodile with its muzzle shape snout and eggs. The Antelope King in *Plate 23* also shows this curious

system of dots and one can only perceive that the semen or seed collected in that depiction (presumably as the progenitor of the tribe or race) relates to the dots that cover the King's body. The dots must represent some tribal or ancestral memory of the root of that tribe, which by connection also relates to the muzzle head shape, the Bull-Minos cult, the Egyptian sun cult, the horse cult, the mauve hands, the anthropomorphic figures or reptilian (lizard) like depictions in cave art and significantly birds. Further the dots may find significance in the inscriptions of Col. Koor (*Fig.51*) where the dot-like engravings eminating from an umbrella shape (The Sky – or Grid?) presumably represent rain and the Flood, with connections to the dynastic line of Noah (Magog and Fenuisa Farsa and the 'gods' or Danaans who were tutored in Greece?). Why standard accounts have chosen to name *Plate 23* as the "Antelope King" is curious since there appear to be no antlers present, although the king does possess the beaked or muzzle-shape face, with a red body depicting royalty and further bulls are present and far from being Rhodesian 'Bushman Art', as it is labelled it appears to have some connection with the phallic bull cult, dating back to the lizard or reptile cult.

There is a very distinct memory on the time track of the regressive (past life) memory of man of birds and being eaten: thus the proposal of a species or racial line of the MRC case evolving through the reptilian line of reptiles and birds (Jurassic) and thus through a predatory line, which survived as a racial and tribal memory in the group of muzzle-shaped men that presumably survived a Magnetic Reversal, is not so outrageous and science fiction as it seems: although another explanation may be offered as *Plate1*. If there has been a significant cover up on the dates of the Flood and Noah's Ark, together with the obvious cover up on Magnetic Reversals and the demise of the dinosaurs, it may be that man or antediluvian man was co-existent with the dinosaurs suggested by the Paluxy footprints (*Plate.1*). If as I further suggested men survived a Magnetic Reversal in their **bodies**, which would mean that they took off from Earth (Noah's Ark?) before the cataclysm, then obviously those bodies would be of enormous dimensions, giving rise to the myths that gods descended and mated with female (ape-like forms) and that there were two races of giants and normal-sized men. This was evident in the Toltec history, which made a mysterious entry into the background of the Millennium Dome in London for the year 2000 celebrations. The anthropomorphous reptilian-like forms in cave art are sparse, which would suggest few such survivors or limited tribal memory (presumably retained by the Cabal or hierarchy), further they may depict the ancestral body form of the antedilivians. After the demise of the dinosaurs and reptiles presumably through that reversal, the stage of Earth was set for the mammals and therefore the apes. It is important to recognise however that the spirit of man was forced to re-incarnate into such forms. The souls who were stuck to the "electronic ribbon" and fully downloaded (Hubbard's Inc.2 or as the author states in her research, a Magnetic Reversal) would have had to re-incarnate into the ape line as the most advanced form of body at that time, although they may conceivably have re-incarnated into earlier mammal forms.

I have discussed the possibility that the Ark came to rest in Armenia where the pre-historic metallurgy site was discovered. Russian colonel Alexander A. Koor submitted a sketch of archaeological sites in the region to the *Sacred History Research Expedition* in 1946. It showed the archaeological sites still to be explored in the region of mount Ararat, but curiously the ark-searching expeditions neglected these sites. Further in *Fig. 51* Col. Koor submitted sketches and notes of some inscriptions he discovered in the region, whilst he was on army duty in the Ararat region around the beginning of World War II and copied many inscriptions found there. It cannot be entirely coincidental, that two pyramids or Sirius A and B (?) were depicted. The dots appear, which here seems to signify rain from an 'umbrella' shape (the Arch?): he also refers to Magog and Gog stating that the pictorial signs: "give me an accurate explanation of the origin of the words Magog, Gog, etc. (*Ezekiel 38:2 and 39:1*) This explanation also upholds the truth and accuracy of *Chapter 10* and of *Genesis*. In short, the words Magog, Gog are words of the **Sumerian** tongue, which shows the ancient origin of the words. Jews incorporated the words through the Assiro-Babylonians. The word Magog consists of two words: The word MA is a pictorial sign which is (picture inserted) and in cuneiform: (picture inserted). It means: (1) "origin, (2) "the seeds of the waters (FLOOD)". Thus the seed or semen of the Antelope King may have merely been denoted as the markings on his body and as royalty accounting for the red dots in cave paintings. Thus the demise and battle of the two kings in antediluvian times, perhaps covered in the Indian epics, appear to have carried on with monarchical lines *after* the Flood. This system of Twin Kings or two Kings was to be disastrously grafted onto the Holy Grail message of re-incarnation and the warning of another cataclysm, along with the science which was stolen and the message transferred to kingship only (immortality of sacred kings). Koor states that the word GOG has a pictorial sign (which looks like a snouted head?) and gives another cuneiform picture of the word. Koor also states that GOG or the signs of that signify: "the World of God" or "by the Word of God", but also "*thrown*" or "*banished by God*": the two pyramids and the mention of "God" (or Dog?) cannot be entirely without connection and this account, is surely as Koor points out, amazingly co-incidental with Biblical texts (*Gospel of St. John: chapter i, v.1-3*). Koor further states: "The word GOG is met with in the text "Ishtar", from the library of the Temple Ishtar in Nipur, and also in the text of "7 tablets of the Creation of the World" (part 6, p.11)". Also "Pictorial sign (picture of the two pyramids) is read: TO KOOR and means: to come to rest on mountains" or "peak". Cuneiform (picture inserted) means, mountain (inserted river?) (Koora or Kura) ". This may have some background to Kroomata or Cromat and "Men-keeper" already covered. Further "Pictorial sign (picture inserted of tomb like figure) is read: TOOB and means: "to fill earth". (TUB-AL) (picture inserted)". "Pictorial sign (picture inserted) is read E-GA and means: "the flood, night descended from upon". "The signs: (pictures inserted) they may be translated as follows: "These thrown by God, by waters came to rest on the mountains when the night and the waters (flood) descended from upon the earth..." and "Since these four pictorial signs alone, through the centuries, were well preserved from two or more lines of damaged inscriptions (possibly by earthquakes), I copied only the four signs. The place where these signs are inscribed is called "Karada". (m.b. Kara-dagh) Which does have some root connection in Abra-ca-dabra or Abra (Abraham?) - ka (soul or place of landing?) dagda or dag(h) or dad (father?).

Sacred History Research Expedition

FIRST MESSAGE FROM THE ARARAT REGION

By Col. Alexander A. Koor

Some inscriptions of Karada (Kara-dagh?)

Some inscriptions which I found and copied in the year 1915 in the region of Mt. Ararat:

1.................................?

2.................................?

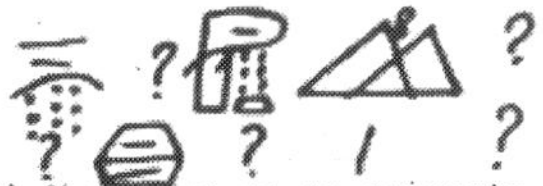

I translated the pictorial signs and they give me an accurate explan-ation of the origin of the words KAGOG, GOG, etc. (Ezekiel 38:2 and 39:1) This explanation also upholds the truth and accuracy of Chapter 10 and of Genesis. In short, the words Magog, Gog are words of the Sumerian tongue, which shows the ancient origin of the words. Jews incorporated the words through the Assiro-Babylonians. The word KAGOG consists of two words: MA and GOG.

The word MA is a pictorial sign which is   and in cuneiform:

It means: (1) "origin, (2) "the seeds of the waters (FLOOD)".

The word GOG, his pictorial sign is   and in cuneiform:

It means: (1) "the Word of GOD" or "by the Word of God."

        (2) "thrown" or "banished by God."

Having two meanings:

Pictorial sign   -"originating from (by) the Word of God" and "the seeds of the waters (FLOOD), thrown by GOD," are both amazingly coin-cidental with BIBLE texts. Noah came in Mt. Ararat's region with the Flood, that is, with the waters. Likewise, the first meaning: "Originating with the Word of God", is upheld in Chapter 1, Verses 1, 2, 3, The Gospel of St. John.

The word GOG is met with in the text "Ishtar", from the library of the temple Ishtar in Nipur, and also in the text of "7 tablets of the Crea-tion of the World", part 6, p. 11. For linguistical disbelievers of Ancient Ball "Sumerians", pictorial signs, as proof.

Pictorial sign   is read : TO KOOR and means: to come to rest on mountains" or "p=ax". Cuneiform   KOOR" means, mountain. (Koora or Kura.)

Pictorial sign   is read: TOOB and means: "to filled earth." (TUB-AL).

    Cuneiform:

Pictorial sign   is read E-GA and means : "the flood, night descended from upon."

The signs:

they may be translated as follows: "These thrown by God, by waters came to rest on the mountains when the night and the waters (flood) descended from upon the earth......."

Since these four pictorial signs alone, through the centuries, were well preserved from two or more lines of damaged inscriptions (possibly by earthquakes), I copied only the four signs. The place where these signs are inscribed is called "Karada". (m. b. Kara-dagh).

Fig.51 **First Message from the Ararat Region by Col Alexander A. Koor**
The Sacred History Research Expedition 1946

If a body did survive as a bodyline (phylogenetic) on Earth (after a Magnetic reversal) that bodyline would hold a genetic memory of that line. I have noted that the human embryo appears to recapitulate phylogeny i.e. it passes through a fish or 'tadpole' like form with 'gill slits' during its development with an obvious tale. The Amphibians are the most likely group to have survived a Magnetic Reversal and Flood, simply because they can exist on land or water: however if the giants or hierarchy of the antediluvians did miss the Magnetic Reversal, then obviously they would have brought back a body line to Earth that would have a complete genetic record of the past and that genetic record (DNA) **would still find a connection to the Master pattern** or etheric DNA. It must be assumed that inter-mating occurred, as is claimed by the occultists and that perhaps the left top head in La Marche engravings is a record of this intergenetic mating in early form, with reptilian-like traits still observable. Hubbard speaks of the "**genetic entity**", which is: "a beingness not dissimilar to the thetan (Spirit) which has carried forward and developed the body from its earliest moments, along the evolutionary line of earth and which, through experience, necessity and natural selection, has employed the counter-efforts of the environment to fashion an organism of the type best fitted for survival, limited only by the abilities of the genetic entity". The goal of the genetic entity is survival on a much grosser plane of materiality". (*Scn 8-8008, p.8*). Further he states: "Formerly referred to as the somatic mind. It has no real personality; it is not the "I" of the body. This is the "mind" of an animal, a dog or a cat or a cow". (*HOM, pp.13-14*). "That entity which is carrying along through time, that is making the body through the time stream, through the action of sex and so forth". (*5410C10D*). It may be that the genetic entity is the primitive mind or tri-partitie energy (3-layered) somatic energy that surrounds the *body* and relates to the old embryonic layers (ectoderm, mesoderm and endoderm). This mind as I have pointed out not only shapes the body according the Dr. H. Burr's 'jelly mould' theory, but I have equated this primitive mind, with the Universal Mind or the Akashic Record or www-com/grid. In other words this mind or the body in the absence of a thinking mind (the remaining auric layers constituting the 7-layered auric system?) and a spritual "I" computes and resolves problems relating to survival through the primitive survivalist mechanisms, based on Darwinian principles of 'survival of the fittest', or the Grid phylogenetic memory. This is the mind of the World Order computing on Growth=survival. The idea of purity of bloodlines may have simply conserved the DNA from the reptilian type or MRC case in 'undiluted' form (through inter-marriage): thus in effect this 'undiluted' DNA would find a connection with the sections of the Master pattern or DNA and events on the Akashic Record that relate to this earlier line, carrying with it thoughts of the Masters. It may be for this reason that Hitler tried to kill of the bodyline or genetics of the Jews and develop his Aryan super-race programme. There is no doubt that Hitler had some inkling of the crystal or Grid, since he followed the theories of Hans Horbiger who proposed the 'World Ice Theory', which saw the Earth as innermost to layers of crystal or ice:

> "I shall construct...an observatory in which will be represented the three great cosmological conceptions of history –those of Ptolemy, Copernicus and Horbiger. (*Adolph Hitler - 28 April 1942*)

However obviously these theories were insane, since genetics and DNA is now homogeniously mixed. However I do agree with Hubbard, in his assessment of the Anti Social Personality and the characteristics he presented of that case, which may be part and parcel of the MRC case. Hubbard recognised that this personality represented a minute fraction of humanity, but infected 22% with abberated thinking. Hubbard also recognised that this personality causes much of the upset on this planet and in his twelve traits of this personalty he curiously mentions that they: "cannot finish a cycle of action". I have certainly noticed these traits in the MRC case and particularly that last trait, where the end of the cycle I propose translates to the MRC case as the beginning. He simply cannot finish the cycle, since to him it means a Magnetic Reversal.

The World Order however had only to implement policies, which threaten survival and man becomes run by the primitive mind (Hubbard's reactive mind?) or www-com/grid and **the past**, with its animal-like computations and abberative behaviour, which Hubbard charts in his *Chart of Human Evaluation* (below 2.0 on the energy scale) in his book *The Science of Survival*. As I have pointed out, this primitive mind equates loss (of body part) with emotional loss (relationships, financial, death etc.): the primitive mind cannot distinguish between the two. As man becomes more and more stressed in his environment, worried and confused, then he switches to the primitive mind and www-com/grid - hence the rise in insanity among Homo sapiens. Hubbard himself did not appear to make these connections to the Grid or the entire history, including the Religious Revolution, which the author equates with Hubbard's Inc.1 and which Hubbard curiously refers to as the beginning, although it was only the beginning of mind control allied to secret group politics and World Order goals. Hubbard did however recognise the importance of running loss out of the primitive mind, in order to maintain and achieve a healthier and happier state (if not sanity) through his thesis and procedure of *Dianetics* (*Dianetics the Modern Science of Mental Health*): such losses also relate to past lives. The bodyline the author concludes does have holographic memories of a Magnetic Reversal, which appear to be re-stimulative and LSD may activate these holographs. Finally the body itself in its biochemistry curiously has many optical isomeric chemicals, which display mirror image symmetry and have completely different properties; which might enable continuity of life under Magnetic Reversals. The World Order are solidly connected to the Grid and the past holographics and constantly re-stimulate themselves by studying the ancient background and following thoughts channelled down from the Grid and past Masters. Hitler or the secret groups behind him, may have based their eugenics programmes on this knowledge and the attempt to kill of the Jews may also have had its origins in Blavatsky's racial root doctrines – the body lines now are so well genetically homogenised that such programmes are certainly racist, as opposed to scientific. Further a spirit can re-incarnate into any body, as I point out in *The Battle of The Trees*, "I" has been many nationalities (bodies).

Plate 25 shows a bird-like man from a cave on Pellaegrino overlooking Palermo in western Scicily, where notoriously the organisation of the Scicilian Brotherhood or Maffia descended, presumably not without some tribal memory! The bird as owl will shortly be discussed in terms of Bohemian Grove ceremonies, but here in this cave painting, man is illustrating his totem beast or tribal memory and a spiritual form as bird. In *Plate 26 a* scene is depicted from Lascaux in France, where there appears to be a dead person and where the totem beast ancestry of the tribe as bird and bull is shown: once again we see the connection of tribal ancestry or more specifically the blood line, where the totem beast or beaked bird is chosen for some specific reason and connection to the ancestors. The Bull may have been chosen for its muzzle shape character and strength, which by calamitous referral was overlaid onto the Holy Grail during the Religious Revolution in Crete c.1400 B.C. Further the dead or prostrate man has an obvious phallic depiction. *Plate 27* clearly shows a man in a Bulls mask and headress of Palaeolithic times, which must represent the Bull-Minos phallic cult and the familiar muzzle that has now replaced the reptilian-like form and the face underneath, although not as clearly pronounced as the La Marche head, is still very muzzle-shaped. This cult evidently present in France in the Palaeolithic period and clearly shown in *Plate 14* at the Trois Freres site in France as Bull-man, evidently also displayed its tribal ancestry from the reptilian anthropomorphic form not only in Derbyshire in England, but in Northern spain *Plate 11*. The Shaman like figure in *Plate 8*, with deer's antlers, must also depict some ancestral line of the World Order or MRC case hierarchy of the time and the antlers as symbolic presumably of the Cabalastic Tree of Life (black cabala and magic?) which was basically a hierarchy descended from the MRC case or the Masters. This Tree of Life was to eventually appear at Knossos, with the bird of epiphany of the Goddess (in her death aspect as dove) portrayed in its branches! In other words the Bull-Minos, Egyptian Sirius link or Ra the Sun god, dating back to the Reptilian-like ancestor? took over the gift from Spiritual intervention c. 10 000 B.C. and mixed that intervention (and knowledge) up with their own monarchical line from the patriarchs with various and innumerable significances relating to the knowledge and symbols within the secret group hierarchy: and now try to represent the knowledge and gift as their own! The Shaman at Trois Freres is no more than the Antelope King or the Bull-Man or the phallic cult that overran the early Minoans and stole The Holy Grail from the true God (if you must use that term) or true Spiritual intervention. The various totem beasts only serve to show **the forms (or shapes)** that the World Order has taken and its true ancestral or body line from those who survived a Magnetic Reversal and gave rise to a specific race, whilst evidently another group did survive and I do not discount that the two groups of the Sethites and Cainites were representatives of the two groups, where the Sethites went through some form of ape-like regression due to either atomic warfare or more likely a Magnetic Reversal and had to Re-incarnate into an ape-like mammalian form after that reversal. Certainly the ape is well represented, together with the reptilian form in Palaeolithic cave paintings as *Plate 15* illustrates and curiously at the Knossos site the Minoan Frescoes show monkeys: and perhaps this line came from the Sethites who had tried prior to a Magnetic Reversal to fight the MRC case or Sirius invaders (Xenu or Yatrus according to Hubbard?) and thus accounting for the ancient Indian epics such as the *Mahabharata* which speaks of a war of **two kings**, prior to a cataclysm and also speaks of flying machines.

Only nine anthropomorphic forms exist in the whole of Palaeolithic art and six of these are only from two caves: les Trois Freres and Le Cabillou. Thus the line of ancestry from these forms or the knowledge of the totem beast ancestor was not widely spread or known and one might consider such caves as those of the secret cabal that ran this planet – World Order. The Lascaux site is a shaft about five metres deep and the pit is located at one end of a small chamber with a **dome-shaped** ceiling, thus giving some background to the 'umbrella shapes' (or "cup" in Palaeolithic art). The 'umbrella' or Grid on inversion and the Hermetic principle of 'as above so below', becomes a cup, thus presumably giving rise to the myth of the Holy Grail cup: the cup holding an elixier that I covered in *The Battle of The Trees*, which connected with **knowledge and immortality**. Hermes the great geomancer or holder of the keys to the Grid and the Hidden Science drank from the cup of knowledge as did the Masters, denying that "soma" or the drink of the gods to mankind. The atmosphere at Lascaux reminds one of a small vaulted chapel in a cathedral and evidently also reminds one of the domes of the Elohim and that Dome in London. The man in the Lascaux engraving also shows a prominent phallus, which cross connects with the Bull-Minos cult and birds and the curious appearance of the cabalistic Tree of Life at Knossos. In Lascaux, the bull or bison is disembowelled and there is also a rhinoceros with six dots under its tail, which may provide the "666" ancestry and connection to Pythagorean numerical mysteries, apart from the cabalistic (shamanistic and Black magic ritual) connection to the Tree of Life. The

Lascaux cave dates from c. 15 000 B.C and thus the heads depicted at La Marche and thus occurs before proposed Spiritual intervention (c. 10 000 B.C) and as I have stated the religion as such on this planet before that intervention, was based on the black Cabala, which has woven its way through secret groups, without any true comprehension of the science of the UVG120 crystal. Further in about twenty caves throughout South-west France and northern Spain, there are dozens of painted hand impressions and in one or two caves, these stencilled hands form the main works of art, but usually they are inconspicuous. In the cave of Maltravieso in northern Spain, the hands appear and in the caves of Tibiram and Gargas in France.These hands may signify the ancient Druidic finger-signalling alphabet (*The Battle of The Trees*). Fifty per cent of these cave paintings show the total loss of the upper joints of all four fingers, but the thumbs remain in tact. The thumb, according to the finger-signalling alphabet of the Druids contained the Tree alphabetic significances of "A" (Ailm – a female tree) "M", (Muin or the vine which the Danaans carried northward from Greece as the emblem of the 'vine-man who draws together – Fenuisa Farsa or the grandson of Magog, who was grandson of Noah) "H" (the unlucky tree or Uath -13 th tribe?) and "B" (Beth or female and first tree). *Fig.52* shows the hands with apparent mutilation, which hold significance on the ancestral line of the 13 th tribe as Bull-Minos cult and horse cult (*Plate 13*). I do not deny that the 13 th tribe in holding the woman in reverence, did originate as the monkey fresco at Knossos may indicate from the ape-like form or Sethites and those who may have tried to fight the MRC case; but whatever case for righteousness they may have held, this has now been inextricably linked with the Masters, occult, grid channelled information and a great deal in the way of nonsense and untruth.

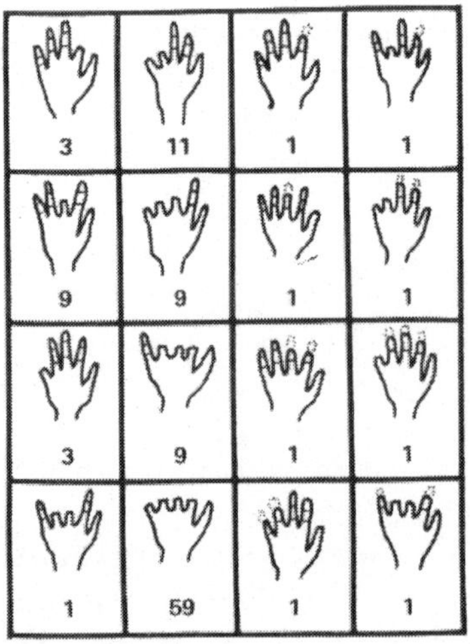

Fig.52 **A chart showing the alleged finger mutations At Gargas.**
Compare to Druidic finger signalling alphabet (The Battle of The Trees)

Nenri Breuil – the 'pope of prehistory'

(1877-1961) was to famously label the woman in *Plate16* as the 'white lady' in 1947. He also stated that she was a Caucasian visitor – Cretans or Minoans –from the Mediterranean area. This idea that Southern African art could be attributed to 'foreigners' fitted the common misconception at that time that the Bushmen were too 'primitive' to have produced this type of of rock art, seen in South Africa. A certain Colonel Imker Hoogenhout, Smuts's administrator of the territory, declared on seeing Breuil's copy of the art: "This is no bushman painting: this is Great Art". In an evident cover up the famous White Lady of Namibia, with curiously an unattributed date (naturally) was finally (defaced?) attribured as a male, with penis! The fact that she is carrying a bow and arrow, which is attributed to "male equipment", almost certainly depicts a cover up. Furhter, the fact that the arrow has five feathers each side (equates dove or bird of epiphany) and five being a female number, with bow as crescent moon and she is carrying a white lily, evidently must be air-brushed out for political reasons. This ignoral of significant archaeology is no more than has occured at Nasca in Peru, where the ground drawings or geoglyphs comparable to British hill figures, clearly viewed from the air show images of birds, a monkey, a spider and whales! The whale of course occurs in the central design of the Summer Smoking room floor at Cardiff Castle (*The Battle of The Trees*). The whale was one of three royal 'fish' of Britain and another was the porpoise whose skins made the covering for the Ark of the Covenant. The whale was allegedly the first living thing created by Jehovah and the fish-taboo in *Leviticus*, was total in Britain and curiously enough among the Egyptian priesthood, again indicating the attachment through patriartchal ancestry between the two. There were also bird-taboos and evidently these were totem beasts, or ancestral tribal memories and therefore protected. The story of Noah's Ark has been attributed to myth derived from an Asianic icon in which the Spirit of the Solar Year is shown in a moon-ship, going through his habitual New Year changes –bull, lion, snake and so on; and the story of the Whale from a similar icon showing the same Spirit being swallowed at the end of the year by the Moon-and-Sea-goddess, represented by a sea monster. The she-monster Tiamat who, in early Babylonian mythology, swallowed the Sun-god Marduk and was used by the author of the Book of Jonah to symbolize the power of the wicked city, mother of harlots, that swallowed and then spewed up the Jews. The Hebrew prophets knew Tiamat as the Moon-and-Sea-goddess Rahab, but rejected her as the mistress of all fleshly corruptions; which is why in the ascetic Apocalypse the faithful are promised 'No more sea' – which has more to do with the Flood and the Covenant and a promise made to God. Significantly the animals at Nasca are found amidst geometric shapes and trapezoids, which I commented were the shape (flat bottomed trapezoid) of the Early Minoan bath-type (sea) sarcophagi, in which the dead were buried in foetal position, among sea shells (awaiting re-birth or the gift of re-incarnation through the Great Goddess?): there are also numerous straight lines, which some believe are ceremonial pathways, but which equally could be electro-magnetic or ley lines of Earth energy corresponding to anti-gravitational anomalies, which could have formed the scientific basis of the accounts of flying machines in the Indian epics. The enormous hill figure of the monkey at Nasca significantly has a tail wound in a cosmic circle design, which might explain the Phaestos disc of circular design found in Crete in the Minoan period (*Alternative 4*). It has been suggested that these lines provided ceremonial pathways, in much the same way as the New Age fad is to walk in cosmic circles! The innumerable grid-like designs were also found engraved in rock shelters in the Fontaine-bleau region, south of Paris with no date attached to them (*Plate 28*). These grid designs also occur in painted pebbles from Le Mas d'Azil along with egg-shapes with zigzag designs, thus showing a continuity of ideas and secret groups of the World Order or hierarchy that survived the Flood.

The deserts of the American southwest also show the abstract patterns, which may represent some form of Grid knowledge. On the northern plains of North America, prehistoric inhabitants constructed what are described as "medicine wheels" using stones to form the patterns. This however relates to the the 'wheel of life', discussed earlier, since these "wheels" quite clearly show the radiating spokes as does that Millennium Eye in London as did presumably the chariot of Hermes (and the chariot of the Egyptians and Romans). Some believe these designs are 5 500 years old. An aerial view of the desert near Blythe California (United States) also shows a similar hill figure as that in Britain (Long Man of Wilmington) and is a giant figure with arms outstretched although off-road vehicle tracks have erased what may be the staves, comparable to Long Man. The figure is 29 metres from head to toe and although it has been passed off as a "representation of evil" clearly here is a connection of 13th tribe and Druid to America presumably long before Columbus arrived! This presumably provides some background to the "special relationship" of America to Britain. The array of facial characteristics that were illustrated in the La Marche engravings (thought to be more than 14 000 years old), were also to crop up as clay figurines from Butmir near Sarajevo, Bosnia (up to 7 000 years ago). These figurines are said to have "neatly combed hair" which dismisses the fact that the hair either shows the dot like design (12 tribes), or the zigzag design, which arose in Early Minoan Crete and on the early Kamares pottery, along with the crane design in Minoan seals and the migration of birds ('as I go, so must I return'). I have to say that the incised zigzag heads have a variety of shapes, some resembling the La Marche heads and some retaining what looks like the beaky-head or muzzle reptilian type and others with decidedly Asiatic features. Clearly a great deal of archaeology has suffered from a veil of silence and the orthodox hand that dictates man came from monkey or ape –quietly ignoring the La Marche heads and a great deal more!

The cross that Mevryl deciphered as 'Lords of the Dead, Hail down from Dog', could also be represented in cyclical symbolic form as OCRUX (a cross in a circle) and this quadrisected circle appeared in iconography from Crete again during the Religious Revolution of mind control, connected to Rosicrucians and Bull-Minos cult/Druids and Thothmess III the Master of the GWL on Sirius (The 'wheel of life' p. 84 *Alternative 4*) but it is also displayed at Cardiff Castle in the Summer Smoking Room Floor design (which is quadrisected), with connections to Westminster Abbey in London! (*The Battle of the Trees*). The readings then curiously become 'CYCLIC DESTRUCTION, HAIL DOWN FROM DOG' and 'Lord of Sirius, Hail down from Dog': Thus were the thirteenth tribe (and some sector of Rosicrucians) who evidently favoured the woman, trying to warn of the Sirius connection and the Masters who did not come from the ape line of Seth, but the reptilian or muzzle-shaped facial line? Certainly the monkey fresco at Knossos appears to indicate the ape line and one might conclude that the 13 th tribe was connected to the woman and then overtaken in a Religious Revolution by Thothmess III and the Sirius connection or the 12 tribes? This cyclic destruction may be explained in cyclical Apocalypses (thus enabling one to prophesy!) and the Magnetic Reversal cycles. One might even perceive that the "monsters" who march over "the rainbow bridge" at the end are the Masters from Sirius and the reptilian line. Further, there was that curious account of the Philadelphia experiment and alleged attempts to manipulate space-time and a ship through another dimension. This begs the question of whether some experiment of sorts and similar to the goal of the Philadelphia experiment occured back on the track of time, where the magicians became locked into some other dimension and await return after another Magnetic Reversal. Indeed it might be, that these magicians have been represented as the scientists of their day and as the progenitors of modern science. It might be further believed that these Masters came from Sirius and now reside in the Etheric Great White Lodge; whatever the case, this sort of thinking has been deeply embedded in the occult. The fact that Hubbard places Xenu in a mountain on Madeira however "electronically tagged" and Revelations refers to the "bottomless pit", both provide connections to the significant electro-magnetic and cabalistic rites of magicians. The problem I believe is that the MRC case on Earth has convinced initiates by his cunning, that the so-called Masters are benevolent, when in fact they are malign. Indeed since the GWB have channelled their information, then they have picked up holographics and thought from the crystal in their belief it was the GWL or Sirius Masters! Indeed Mervyl speculates that the inscription could be some form of warning of a cyclic destruction, which will come from the Sirius Star system. The cross is curiously situated in the region called Henday or 'end-day'! Further at Cardiff Castle there is a black Madonna (Isis?) on the roof and Doris

Lessing has also referred to the star Canopus, who was also the god Osiris, who was in an ever-changing relationship with Isis with whom Lessing equates with Sirius. She also refers to the fact that al-Sufi, an Arabian astronomer of the tenth century; spoke of Canopus of the constellation Argo, which is associated with Noah's Ark! And also forms the background to the quest for the Golden Fleece and the Argonauts in myth. Thus was the Ark a space ship that returned after a Magnetic Reversal, or is it that the MRC case originally came from Sirius (perhaps Hubbard's Xenu character?) or both of these alternatives?

The Koran also appears to make a warning regarding the Lord of Sirius:

> "And that He it is the Lord of Sirius. This is a warner of the warners of
> old....
> THE THREATENED HOUR IS NIGH...
> and laugh and not weep.
> Which ye amuse yourselves?
> Rather prostrate yourselves before Allah and
> Serve Him".
> (*The Koran – The Star*)

One cannot say that man has not had enough warning! Ascended Masters, Surya and Cuzio are said to exist on Sirius and it is ominous that the GWB is now a part of the culture, history and religion of America! Is it realy case that European Union is yet another quest in the tribal differences of 12 and 13, which can only end according to the 'script' as it did in the past and as I predict will happen in the not so distant future – in a THIRD WORLD WAR OR A BATTLE OF TWO KINGS AS IN **THE PAST** ANTEDILUVIAN ERA. Are the high initiates of Europe and America merely dramatizing their own past lives and like the Dome in London and the crystal in New York, or genetic biotechnology and cloning force that lunacy on mankind? The MRC case back there still fighting his battle of two kings and bringing that forward into present time, along with his battle to rule the world and prove he is the "chosen one" or the presenter of the gift to mankind. Daft? No deadly serious I am afraid and if you could get into the mind of the earthly Masters who are running things on Earth, you would see a weird world from the eyes of the predator. The huge blue eagle is now a part of occult symbolism occurring on the One-dollar note and as part of AMORC symbols. There are references in the Summit Lighthouse GWB book, to a Judgement Hall on the God Star, where twenty-four Elders render judgement in a court of the Sacred Fire. This is confused in so far as the judgement of 'Lucifer' is emphasised in the organisation's *Vials of the Seven Last Plagues* and adds that the "wicked" are to be delivered into the hands of the legions from Sirius: however as I have discussed the plagues of the Apocalypse may have more to do

438

with the attempt to manipulate the Apocalypse and reduce population numbers. Not all groups are convinced that Sirius was a God Star, in 1923 Aleister Crowley in a lyric referred to the hideous hate and heat of Sirius although he too confused matters by his allegiance to both groups and to neither!

In the white magic text *A Treatise on Cosmic Fire*, Dwhal Khul the Master of Alice Bailey warns her that black magic is based on the degradation of sex and the creative function. White magic he claimed is based on the transmutation of the creative faculty into higher creative thought. The black magician utilises energy in the lower three chakra centres (the sex organs, the spleen and solar plexus). Black magicians operate under six great entities and Crowley utilised AIWASS as one of his spirit guides (holographics). These entities also have significance as "666" in *The Bible*, with whom Crowley identified himself ("The Beast") and shaped his initial A as male genitalia, which leads one back to the phallic Bull-Minos cult and Hermes. Crowley was a complex puzzle and may have acted as a double agent, just to satisfy his own craving for magic and knowledge. He claimed control of access to the Argenteum Astrum, which is the Order of the Silver Star or Sirius, whilst decrying its hatred! Crowley's so-called Master or AIWASS had a mission to inaugurate the Aeon of Force and Fire and since he was actually channelling holographics from the Religious Revolution, then naturally he would have come across holographic thought related to control through a World Order! World War II was to follow, which paved the way for the World Order and European Union! The World Order believe and have justified the Age of Horus as a necessary cycle before they can implement *The Protocols of Zion* and their idea of an aeon of Truth and Justice! It is this latter aeon of Truth and Justice when the World Order will introduce *their* religion and no doubt Truth will not include the events and battles of 12 and 13 or the theft of the apples of immortality – after all its 'their' gift to mankind!

I have already covered the Golden Dawn group set up by MacGregor Mathers and connected to the Theosophical Society as the outer order of the GWB and Rudolf Steiner as an initiate connected to higher Orders. Mathers was also a member of the Rosae Rubeae et Aureae Crucis (Red Rose and the Golden Cross) which was the second Order of the GWB. The Third and inner Order was the Silver Star or Argenteum Astrum, which might account for that curious 8-pointed star of the Millennium icon in the UK! (*Plate3*) with the earlier Festival of Britain logo of 1955 with its particularly hermetic depiction and the quadrisected star: or the Marine vase at Knossos, with its eight-armed octopus as World Order. It might also account for that curious Star (?) on the 7-linked staff of Gog (and Magog) destroyed in the Blitz in London (1940): further the 'chain' is a 7-knotted wand of Brahminism with links to the Druid wand. I have already discussed the star of Mercury (Hermes) occurring over the Christ child in an icon from Greece, where the three kings are in Greek dress, with a central figure of Hermes, three being Druidic thus indicating the background to Jesus. How far this star fits in with the Dog Star of Sirius, must arise from the new college of magic that arose from the knowledge obtained of the Grid in Crete, at the time of the Religious Revolution, with Hermes and the face of two sides an agreement of both groups 12 and 13 to carve the world up on their joint chessboard, creating apparent conflict, but only with the ultimate goal of joining as the 'script' dictates in the Book of *Revelations* where "all the tribes of Israel", participate in the feast of their victory and apparent gift to mankind. Presumably they have no intention of telling the truth of just how they acquired that gift and the lies they have woven to prove that the gift was theirs to give.

Crowley's infamous Book of the Law, *Liber Al vel Legis*, was actually another channelled dictation from the Masters, or holographics from the past as I conclude. This book not only became the 'Holy Book' of the Argenteum Astrum whose Silver Star is Sirius, but the O.T.O was the Order of the Temple of the Rising Star (Sirius) and thus the O.T.O was really headed up by the GWB and the GWL (or masters on Sirius). This might account for Hubbard breaking up Crowley's group and concluding that Inc.1 was an "implant" or thought from the Masters on Sirius? However since Crowley was channelling his information hermetically from AIWASS as I have covered, all the symbols of the Religious Revolution were being channelled and thus the thoughts of the Masters. It may be that Scientology has worked out that those who come marching over the "rainbow bridge" will be "monsters" and not divine Masters? I do not have any information of that, so I cannot say what they believe ultimately in their highest Order or OT (Operating Thetan –spiritual) level, although the mere fact that they are trying to heal the mind is an indication that they do not go along with the World Order? Goodness knows one never likes to pass any judgement on those who are helping, so I reserve judgement until I receive a truthful answer over Hubbard's past, sources and connection to the O.T.O., together with other matters: however I do find any form of secrecy abhorrent – particularly in a Church! However no church appears to be free of this story.

Kenneth Grant the occultist, refers in his book *Outside the Circles of Time*, to the incoming influence of the Aeon of Maat or the era of Truth and Justice, which is mentioned in the Book of *Revelations* by St. John as: "the truth shall set you free". However according to Grant it is the *Egyptian* Goddess, who symbolises Truth and Justice! The truth of the matter is that justice if it occurs, must go back to Greece! Is it any wonder that they rounded up the Magdalene's *Greek* genealogies! The Egyptian line is very important to presumably the 12 tribes who had a long history in Egypt, which might provide more background as to why Princess Diana met her death with Dodi Al-Fayed who was Egyptian.

Grant calls the aeon of Horus disintegration and the coming of the aeon of Maat as re-integration, but the cataclysm that has long been warned against – a Magnetic Reversal is one of total chaos and disintegration. Libra (balance, scales and justice) is a sign of the coming aeon. According to Crowley, the Tarot card 'Adjustment' represents the goddess Maat, with the sign of Libra ruled by Venus. The 8 th Hebrew letter (Heth) and the eighth Tarot card *(Fig.17)* have already been covered. Crowley referred to Maat or the goddess of justice as the Double-Wanded one and must refer to either the Twin Kings (13 th tribe) or groups 12 *and* 13. Perhaps it is that after causing chaos on this planet, they now intend to shake hands and cease their covert mongering to create wars as the third party, bringing forth an aeon of peace, truth and justice – however, the MRC case is simply not capable of it and betrayal will lie afoot. I really can't see them telling the truth on this one! In *The Battle of The Trees*, I referred to a split in the secret groups in the 80's, which looked very much like a split of political and religious aim, with the Prieure de Sion holding the religious aim. The Prieure de Sion was a group, that held the number 13 in great reverence and thus one considers that the religious aim is a 13th tribe affair, whilst the 12 tribes hold the political aim of the World Order – the world carved up between the terrible Twins, with the Goddess presumably locked up in some Egyptian or Hermetic tomb! Crowley appears to refer obliquely to this and the plan for a new aeon:

> "For **two** things are done and a **third** thing is begun. Isis and Osiris are given over to **incest** and adultery. Horus leaps up armed from the **womb of his mother**. Harpocrates his twin is **hidden within him**. **SET is his holy covenant, that he shall display in the great day of M.A.A.T.**, that is being interpreted the **Master of the Temple of A.A.** whose name is Truth" (*Author's emphasis*).

> (A.A = Argenteum Astrum Temple or Temple of the East –Sirius)

I read this as the groups 12 and 13 creating the Age of Horus via "incest" (collusion) and the reference to Isis and Osiris must be the marriage of two different racial types in Egyptian dynasties (12 th tribe providing King and 13 th tribe providing the blonde haired Queen). The reference to "womb" and "mother", is obviously a reference to Crete and the labyrinth and the Goddess who is the "third" and the Twin Kings the "two" and also by implication both groups 12 and 13. However the most interesting reference is that Set and the Covenant are "hidden within him", implying that Crowley may have always known the secret of the end and presumably the final betrayal of unlucky 13, where the 'Trojan Horse' of the World Order, finally reveals the true colours and the 12 tribes with their Sirius connection. One can only see the setting up of

Britain as the apocalyptic Nation by foreign press in the Spring of 2000 following a series of disasters including the running down of vital services and agricultural crises as the ongoing plan of the 12 tribes against the 13 th tribe and the 'script' of the Apocalypse according to *Revelations*: that 'script' being manipulated by the 12 tribes of Israel and as Crowley implicates the Sirius connection. As I suspected from double agent capers in the past, there is a **Third World War on the way** once this double cross destroys the balance and the terrible Twins fight it out, on the world's stage, presumably with nuclear weapons, before the curtain comes down on the players (and the audience applaud the God or Dog Star Sirius and the Masters) with a Magnetic Reversal and off they go again – Day1. Plant the vine. If there is one thing that the MRC case cannot do, it is finish a cycle of action! He will never *ever* bring peace to this Earth – it's just not in his psychology. The Old Testament is littered with his double crosses against his 'brother', which may be a code for 12 and 13. This is obviously good news for Christians, since they will be proven right and applauded by the World Order and who is to say that the 12 tribes will not arrange the Second Coming, after all technology now can create holographics of whole armies, to confuse the enemy on the battle field – fantastic but absolutely true (I have lost the newspaper reference). The Dog or God Star will have won and the Illuminati will take control as the "monsters" come marching over that "rainbow bridge". Hardly "Paradise" for man, but presumably paradise for the Masters, who can get along with another World Order.

The "wheels" of fortune have however lined the coffers of the MRC case and the elite of The World Order and since they were able to prophesy which move came next on their chessboard, the profits were huge. The White Eagle Lodge, spoke of the years of fire marking the transition from the Age of Pisces and orthodox Christianity to that of Aquarius and the Golden Age of Brotherhood (Grace Cooke's *Illumined Ones*): sure enough you won't be able to "sell in those days", according to Biblical texts, unless you bear the mark on the forehead, which presumably refers to the third eye, Sirius and the Masters. Crowley in his *Confessions* said that the Age of Horus was explained by the secret chiefs as the **destruction of civilization** and as we look around the world, has man not allowed the World Order, full reign to do so - by not lifting the voice of descent and by following the tune of the World Order, indulging in an obscene frenzied era of selfishness with all the excesses of hedonistic pleasure, greed, avarice and cruelty of sacrifice to a cause; whilst children were starving, uneducated, homeless and died of disease and the unforgettable picture of an old woman left to die in a gutter in a war zone – dignity of age denied her: a nurse in Russia dying of gangerene with only her torso left after her body was blown apart by bombs from warring factions: men women and children trying to gain a living and life (sleeping and eating) on top of a rubbish tip in Manilla. There have been so many disgusting pictures world-wide including another unforgettable picture of a child running screaming with napalm burns during the Vietnam War (that Kissinger a Bilderberger, has recently been accused of prolonging and thus committing genocide) that one should fill the Dome in London with them, along with the 'rogues gallery' of those who allowed it to happen, least future generations forget what life is on Planet Earth under a World Order and the Masters – no future generation should forget what genocide and cruelty has occurred in the Age of Horus and perhaps they will look in astonishment that man could fall to such a depraved level, whilst **allowing** a World Order to reign. One would rather write the truth and die with one soul in tact, than admit surrender to such grotesque violations of the spiritual world. The age of Horus all of which was planned has marked the entire collapse of humanitarianism, ethics and morals and this plan was certainly evident in the notorious *Protocols of the Learned Elders of Zion*, although the authorship has been disputed (*The Battle of The Trees*).

In Crowley's *Magick in Theory and Practice*, he stated in 1911, there was a magical operation of importance – the initiation of a new aeon. The whole planet would be bathed in blood on the utterance of a word according to Crowley – whose word he did not say! The Great War (World War I) he stated had to be fought since the bloody sacrifice was necessary to proclaim Horus as Lord of the aeon – insane! But there you are that is the mind of the World Order and the MRC case. In 1936 Crowley stated that the world was stricken with madness and added: "on every side we are confronted by evidence of insanity, which is sweeping across the world like a pestilence. Murder and terror in Soviet Russia; concentration camps and persecution in Germany; war fever and blood lust in Italy and Japan; civil war in Spain; economic crisis in USA; recurrent strikes and labour discontent in France – there is no corner of the Globe untouched!" Crowley seems to have overlooked that channelling from the Masters had something to do with it and man was simply following a 'script' that had been enacted on the world's dark stage before the last Apocalypse. It was channelled information that was perceived as the Masters, who proclaimed the need for war and the earthly Masters who wrote the story line around the holographics. Chapter 3 of *The Book of the Law* was so repugnant that even Crowley objected to it – but that was the mind of the channelled Masters or holographics of the past and Crowley admitted that many parts of the channelled information were unintelligible. Hitler was to paraphrase *The Book of the Law* and the excesses of Nazi Germany was the full reign of the Masters. Hitler as I have covered was obsessed with the occult and may through the mysterious woman at Berchtsgaden, have channelled information regularly for himself, even though he was warned against black magic (channelling). Alice Bailey quoted her real life teacher D.K on the subject of obsession, which enslaved Hitler, as it enslaves many occultists and anyone who is obsessed with channelled information:

"In the case of obsession, the evil force enslaves the personality and which in the majority of cases, is but a shell of this, Hitler is a case in point" (*Alice Bailey Lucis 1972*).

Crowley's group of the O.T.O claimed descent from the Knights Templar. Kenneth Grant maintains that there was a loosely knit Hermetic Brotherhood of Light which he alleges included Eliphas Levi (a magician whom Crowley claimed as a past life) and Rudolf Steiner. Eliphas Levi was to pronounce at the time of the French Revolution, that a Universal Kingdom would come (political and religious) and that it would be had by those: "with the keys to the East". East immediately gives the clue of the Dog Star and keys presumably are the magical rituals necessary to contact the GWL or Brotherhood on Sirius. Grant maintains that it was this Brotherhood of Light, which was the springboard of the O.T.O. The third order of the O.T.O was however the G.W.B. who retained the Sirius Egyptian connection i.e It was as I have discussed Theodor Reuss who described the O.T.O as the Ancient Order of Oriental Templars (Ordo Templi Orientis) and added: "otherwise: The Hermetic Brotherhood of Light". Karl Kellner was the Austrian adept who was the first to reveal that the true name of the Hermetic Brotherhood was the O.T.O and it was also Kellner who carried on the Illuminati system as the O.T.O. In 1880 Leopold Engel and associates set up a re-formed Illuminati allegedly modelled on the tradition of Adam Weishaupt's eighteenth century organisation and which is said to have included Rudolf Steiner, who was related to one of the original Bavarian Illuminati and several Grand Orient Masons.The Hermetic Brotherhood of Light, however must have had some connection to Rosicrucian's if not a branch or group of it. The split in the O.T.O., which created the various warring factions that I previously covered, occurred in 1925. The German occultist – Karl Germer, supported Crowley and the other factions were headed by Eugen Grosche (of the Brotherhood of Saxern) and Heinrich Tranker who was diametrically opposed to Crowley and this warring descent may or may not provide an answer to the question of who sent Hubbard into the O.T.O to break up black magic. The picture is far from clear, since there has always been a lot of in-fighting in the O.T.O with the various factions at odds over the commercialisation of the mysteries, however the battle against Scientology appears to have ceased curiously in the UK and America. Karl Germer allegedly gave the O.T.O charter to a Brazilian called Marcello Motta who now claimed to be the sole authoriser of O.T.O and Argenteum Astrum organisations. The latter of course is the etheric Sirius Masters connection! Let us suppose that Hubbard failed to agree with the divine Masters and the World Order, would that not have created a hell of a battle to gain control of Scientology and Hubbard's powerful technology of the mind –Dianetics? Hubbard was certainly against mind control; however as I mentioned, the subject of Scientology could have gone one of two ways: either a force against the World Order, or a manipulated World Order religion (the latter is a "condition of treason" in Scientology parlance). I think the breakaway group *Phoenix* are very correct to demand answers to their questions that were covered earlier and any Scientologist who believes Scientology was exempt from World Order control is living in an out-reality or 'cuckoo land'. The Vatican has suffered from political interference for hundreds of years: as Rupert Murdoch the media mogul and "Sun King" once stated: "The Pope will write for me".

Mr. Motta also produced the *Equinox* and the *Oriflame* which first publicised the O.T.O in c.1904 and was also the official organ of the Berlin Grand Lodge of the United Grand Council of Rites of the Ancient and Accepted Scottish Rite of 33 degrees, of the Ancient Primitive Rite of Memphis of 95 degrees and the Egyptian Rite of Misraim of 90 degrees. All these degrees are World Order linked and thus the O.T.O was and is connected to the World Order and specifically the Scottish branch, which I maintain holds the keys to the future world religion and presumably the 'gift' after all these years is salvation at a price. Cardiff Castle, which I covered in *The Battle of The Trees*, had a map at the centre of the Summer Smoking Room floor, which clearly displayed **Jerusalem** and the World Order plan for a political and religious Hermetic Kingdom. They may find however that the betrayal will come from Sirius! This group evidently held its origins in the Bull-Minos Druid cult and the Religious Revolution in Crete. Scottish rite Freemasonry held the Greek connection and thus it is explained why Scientology and Dianetics organisations should be thrown out of Greece when the author was there, since I believe the Greek government has a policy against the 13 th tribe although Prince Charles does spent a yearly week retreat at a Greek monastery. Now you begin to realise why this book would tax the mind of a computer – convoluted does not describe the trail! The possibility is there, to follow the Sirius (Egyptian) or Hermes (Greek) path within the secret groups (a face of two sides – or the Janus head of Hermes) and evidently America must be Sirius I conclude, from details of the Bohemian Grove ceremony, which I will cover shortly. Britain must be Hermetic (Greek connection but related to monarchy and the Twin Kings) and certainly the ex-Greek royal family came to Britain after they were ousted. This policy against the thirteenth tribe may or may not account for the apparent non-action of the Greek government on the 17 th September terroist organisation. The Greeks however are whistling in the wind, if they think that their country is not the jewel in this particular crown, which may come from Sirius and not Hermes! Although one can never be certain in this game, of where the knife will come from! However as Golgotha showed, the betrayal will come. If the British people are betrayed, a great more betrayal will come, since this is an international and karmic responsibility.

Reuss in 1917 proclaimed that the O.T.O possessed the one right Key to all the mysteries as well as the secret knowledge of all oriental orders, which can only imply the hidden science. Well presumably they know about the crab then! The World Order is Illuminatus in its political aim, but the religious aim is obviously Rosicrucian but there is an ongoing conflict it would seem between the Greek and Egyptian (Hermes and Sirius) backgrounds and beliefs and presumably the long enmity of 12 and 13 despite the requirement of *Revelations*, that ALL tribes of Israel are honoured at the end. Crowley I believe re-discovered Hermetic magic and opened up the background to the Religious Revolution in Crete, although since the information was channelled through AIWASS and the Grid, it obviously only held one side of the story – the Bull-Minos cult and presumably Thothmess III or the Master who looks to be the culprit of the stolen apples, with some link obviously to the 13th tribe and Druids – the true story of Spiritual intervention, never appeared on the channelled record except as various warnings of the woman that re-appeared in some UFO incidents and the Fatima miracle. Crowley in developing the Tantric or sexual rites of the O.T.O evidently hit upon the right **musical key** or *morphic resonance* to bring down holographics and information from the **phallic** Bull-Minos cult. The Knights Templar appeared to practice some rituals described as black magic, but probably some form of Crowley's rites, which may have given them information on the same period. These magical rites may have been taken from the Temple in Jerusalem: at any rate the Templars obviously had something of importance and were to join with the Scottish Freemasons in one of the "strangest marriages" of secret groups ever to occur. They evidently knew of the events of Golgotha and openly spat on the cross and called Christ "the thief on the cross" – perhaps referring to the stolen genealogies of a Greek nature. Crowley signed his initial with the sign of male genitalia, thus obliquely identifying himself with the Bull-Minos cult and Hermes, utilising Hermetic magic. The situation is confused since Blavatsky not only railed against Tantric or sexual "black" magic, but explained that 'Budh' was a name signifying not only the sun as a source of regeneration, but also a male organ; which appears to place her in Bull-Minos territory, along with her acknowledged Masters.

The Knights Templar were said to possess an arcane science, which I assume is some part of The Holy Grail or the hidden science and undoubtedly were accused at their trial of homosexual practices, which indicated Hermetic Tantric or "black" magic. However as I have explained it was a method without current technology of bringing down the holographics or information from the Akashic Record or UVG120 crystal. The rise in technology since the 60's depended on the intensive research undertaken on the hidden science and resonance where many famous scientists (including the Los Alamos atomic bomb team?) were part of the Rosicrucian laboratories. Evidently the arcane science rites or knowledge that the Templars had went into the Rosicrucian's and Scottish Rite Freemasonry, who also held the mysteries of Crete and the Bull-Minos cult. Blavatsky in Isis *Unveiled* (1877) stated that since the destruction of The Templars, no lodge in Europe or America knew anything worth concealing until presumably Crowley re-discovered the rites to pull the holographics down and the O.T.O then held such knowledge. Significantly The Templars held meetings once every thirteen years on Malta, thus signifying 13th tribe. The Beth-Luis-Nion alphabet of the Druids had 13 consonants and five vowels (17 letters) and the secret group of The Prieure de Sion, which I discussed in *The Battle of The Trees* and earlier here, held the number 13 in significance. At least one Grand Master (who produced the *Vaincre* illustration *Fig. 48*) was connected to plans for European Union, or the religious goal of European Union. Thus originally the religious goal centred on the Greek connection and the mysteries, but it would appear that America holds the Egyptian connection, thus one can only foresee a war here eventually, if not sooner. The agreed upon peace between ALL the tirbes of Israel according to *Revelations* and the plan for a new Aeon, will always end in betrayal, since the highest initiates within the secret groups are dramatizing their past.

The Prieure de Sion also had links with Christian Democratic parties of Europe, various movements dedicated to European unity, royalist cliques, neo-chivalric orders, and Freemasonry sects, the CIA, the Knights of Malta and the Vatican. The British Royal family (the Windsor's) visit the Church of the Mary Magdalene, when they go to Balmoral Castle in Scotland, for their annual Christmas vacation: further I believe that Queen Elizabeth II is a member of the Knights of Malta. The knights of Malta cross fertilize through the complex network of education, intelligence networks, religion, media, military, politics and various think tanks e.g. William Buckley a Knight of Malta is also a member of the Council on Foreign Relations and Frank Shakespeare was a U.S. Ambassador to the Vatican and also President of CBS Television Services and Vice Chairman of RRO General. Shakespeare joined ultra-rightist Paul Weyrich when the former became Chairman of the Board of Trustees of Weyrich's Heritage Foundation and Weyrich travelled to Moscow to help the Soviets establish a "democratic" system of government. The Heritage group also brought karl Von Hapsburg to America as a speaker. The Hapsburg dynasty is the primary force behind the Pan European Movement. Two CIA Directors have been Knights of Malta. The Sovereign Military Order of the Knights of Malta comprises an elite power able to depose world leaders and entire governments at will. They can also create governments as apparently can the secret Order behind the Bohemian Grove ceremony, despite claims to the contrary.

The Secret Kirkwall scroll fortuitously recently discovered found hanging in a

Masonic Lodge in the Orkeney Islands in Scotland UK where it has laid unnoticed allegedly for three centuries is said to contain ancient Freemason and Templar symbols of great significance. It is curious that the scroll should suddenly find an entrance in the media (*The Times of London owned by the "sun-king"and media mogul Rupert Murdoch*) Allegedly the Masonic Lodge in Orkney was unaware (pull the other leg!) of the importance of the 15th Century scroll until Andrew Sinclair Cambridge (naturally) History don, whilst researching the ancestors of the St. Clair Earls of Orkney and his ancestral line, who were connected with the Grail (Bull-Minos cult!) just happened to come upon the scroll. The St. Clair Earls of Orkney were associated with the Knights Templar and to save Andrew Sinclair the trouble of bringing out a book let me refer to *The Battle of The Trees* and the symbols of the scroll:

> Arch of Masonry –Grid umbrella or UVG120 crystal.
> Two supporting upright pillars with arch forming lintel across (hermetic) Twin Kings –tomb of Solar King.
> Square Semitic pillar in central position with symbolic chequer pattern base (Minoan basket and Moses connection) sign of the womb, labyrinth and Bull-Minos cult who introduced Hermes as the god of the Religious Revolution – dispensing with the woman and stealing the knowledge!
> 4 quarters of the quadrant design on central pillar of Hermes (the Herm). The four aeons.
> Male and female each side of the pillar in the centre indicating Hermes and the woman now locked up with Hermes, who stole the 'gift' and hopes to present it as his own in the World Order religion. A star either Mercury (Hermes) or Sirius hangs in the sky.

Once again in *The Times* (*23.7.000*) our old 'Sun King' Rupert Murdoch's organ of the World Order and financed initially by Jews according to *On Target*, covered an article *Legend of the Minoans is a Racist Myth*: decrying the work of Sir. Arthur Evans who was the Oxford archaeologist who it is claimed altered iconographic evidence of the Knossos site in Crete. As I pointed out in *The Battle of The Trees* and here, there has been a significant cover up of the site and the true history of events – not surprisingly! The article covered a book by Sandy Mac Gilliuray an established Canadian archaeologist which debunks the idea of Kings at the Minoan site and idea promoted by Arthur Evans: the latter sounds very much like 13th tribe even to the point where he was a suppressed homosexual and in later life convicted of gross indecency. This all sounds like another propaganda battle of 12 and 13, with the 13 th tribe attempting to hide the secrets of Knossos and thus the disinformation line of Evans, whilst still maintaining Knossos with royal connections: whilst the 12 tribes (Communistic

448

and to which Murdoch despite being ultra-rich subscribes) decry the 13 th for its racism and monarchy and underplay the importance of the Greek connection, presumably in favour of their God Star and Masters on Sirius. Such is world politics and religion under the Twins! *The Times* newspaper for the first time in its long history, under Murdoch ownership, in June 2001 and the run up to the British elections supported Tony Blair (pro-Europe) which rather underlines just where Murdoch stands and presumably answers the question of why he refused to print an article the author submitted 'Who Killed the Minoans?' stating that he had "no control over editorial" when the author complained that the British people were being misled and stood to become the victims of a World Order plan.

AMORC The *American* Rosicrucian organisation has connections in Southern France and traces its ancestry back to the survivors of Atlantis and the Egyptian ruler Thutmose III (1501 –1447 B.C) who I conclude was the thief who stole the Holy Grail and was contemporary at circa the time of the Religious Revolution (1400B.C). Who exactly moved tons of Scientology documents in the court case in France, might provide some more clues and connections in this story! Certainly the Egyptian link is all there in archaeological finds in Crete at the time of the Religious Revolution, including the dog (Sirius) displayed in one icon.

Thutmose III is acknowledged as the first Master of an organised Brotherhood of learning (GWB) – but as you will remember he ousted Hatshesput and where indeed was he tutored? – was it not with the Early Minoans, from whom he stole the Grail and then murdered, conducting a Religious Revolution and thereafter signing his own name to the gift of spiritual intervention c. 10 000 B.C. The thief who would defy the true spiritual source and made himself a god and God: a thought that has dominated all initiates whether from 12 or 13. However there is the pressing problem of the two distinct races from Cain and Seth, the Cainites and Sethites who developed totally different life-styles. There is another pressing problem of the Tuatha de Danaan who were the 'gods' of the Celts – where did they get their tutorage from if not from Greece? – and was Fenuisa Farsa the 'vine-man who draws together' (a second organised Brotherhood) not the grandson of Magog who was grandson of Noah? It was this group who probably wandered from the Black Sea region into Greece: thus there appears to be a great secret revealed here: there were obviously at least **two groups on Earth** or two races which might account for Homo sapiens appearing amongst the Neanderthals or a bodily regressed race after the Magnetic Reversal, as opposed to the muzzle-like or reptialian type. However it seems that one group was the MRC case, which tried to control and manipulate the DNA field and the other group presumably had always fought them. One of these descended to Earth as the fallen 'Lucifer' from some planet or Star system and this has been confused with perhaps Noah, who may have used technology to survive the Flood and then *appeared to land* as 'extra-terrestrials'. Thus one could quite easily see the confusion here, over who exactly was the Cainite and who Sethite, since the races presumably at some point were not distinguishable. Further in my past life account mentioned in *Chapter 1* of *The Battle of The Trees* I mentioned "Shem son of Noah", although goodness knows how this fits into the story. However some ideology of this separateness of race must have come down through secret doctrine (Blavatsky's root racial doctrine) and the various groups, which consequently displayed itself in both the Jewish practice on inter-marriage and the Aryan super-race programme. When a third and true Spiritual intervention occurred c. 10 000 B.C it was drawn into the battle of 12 and 13. Thus you would be mistaken to believe that this was a sexist battle of male and female: the answer lies in the fact that a maiden always carried The Grail, since she would not be drawn into the battle of 12 and 13, or their secret groups and channelling. The Holy Grail carried a message that was open and not distorted by channelling with a warning and that message, was irrespective of which group a man or woman belonged to, race, creed or colour - it was meant for humanity. The Magdalene rightly prophesied that: "There will be no peace on this Earth until the cut is healed", as she was betrayed by the face of two sides (12 and 13). Her message is clear that until the two groups make peace there will be no peace. However as I have pointed out in that oblique reference by Aleister Crowley, there is betrayal afoot in the World Order and there will ALWAYS be betrayal, since the MRC case – the Lucifer will simply not allow his own wrong doings to be healed by past life regression.

There is allegedly a cartouche or seal, which appears on the obelisk of Thutmose III erected in the Temple at Karnak. It represents creation or beginning and includes the infamous point in the circle of the Illuminati and the scarab beetle. The point in the circle forms the Law of Three and the Druids and 13 th tribe used this Law as the Triangle within the circle. The law of three has Pythagorean and ancient Trinity implications (Mother Goddess and Twin Kings). As I have pointed out the ancient Trinity was not the beginning, but only the beginning of mind control. The Rosicrucian's claim that Master K.H, re-incarnated as Thutmose III and this might convince some, but if Thutmose III of Egypt (Sirius connection) stole the Grail and the information on Re-incarnation, then this might have been a subtle plan of his, which would aid his rise to political power and the overthrow of Hateshput. We know that KH was known as "Men-keeper" and no one had much to say about him after his death, which is unusual – presumably the Brotherhood was wielding fear even then, which may account for the lack of human portrayals in Palaeolithic cave art. The aeon of Maat (truth and justice) presumably is to be derived from Master KH or Thutmose III who presumably is now in the GWL on Sirius! Kroomata or Kai-Ra-Au-Meta that becomes Cro(maat) a Rosicrucian word which means Truth! Who indeed was to assign early advanced type man as Cro-mag-non - Cromagon or Cro (Cromaat) – mag (Magog) – non (name)! The Pharaoh Akhnatum, whose earlier name was Amenhotep IV, studied at Heliopolis, where Jesus is claimed to have studied and later developed the mystery schools of Thutmose III. Amenhotep IV may have had very different racial characteristics from Amenhotep III (*Plate 23*). That being so the Buddhist influences in the teachings of Jesus, did not come from Thutmose III (who stole the Grail?) or indeed Heliopolis, they came from spiritual intervention and The Holy Grail c. 10 000 B.C.. Jesus in the Alexandrian text quoted earlier, which appears to be Hermetic, railed against the woman, just as the Jews today and the Freemasons are all sexist in their exclusion of women, simply because they really could not confront the original sin of stealing the Holy Grail and hiding the Goddess, who was at least in their beliefs the third part of the ancient Trinity. The Alexandrian text refers to the "two becoming one" and thus to the joining of 12 and 13 in peace, however He (Jesus) was to betray I concluded group 13 in favour of the 12 tribes and further stole the Greek genealogies. Akhnaton significantly denied all other gods (sources of the Holy Grail) and claimed there was only ONE GOD – the Universal deity symbolised by the sun-disc and the God or Dog Star (Sirius and the GWL). It was Akhnaton who became the first alleged Grand Master, of the first great Brotherhood of learning. However as I have pointed out, Hermes is the God of the World Order and evidently some agreement between the two groups (12 and 13) has been concocted for the realisation od the final act of the 'script' – *Revelations*. In 1617 *Symbola Aureae Menseae* a book on Alchemy by Count Michael Maier, Sir Francis Bacon's deputy on the continent referred to the Egyptian Hermes Trismegistos, The Thrice-Great, as the Lord of Maat. Since the World Order's next great aeon is that of Maat – Truth and Justice, fulfilling the 'script' (*Revelations*), then as I suspected we can see The Feast of Tabernacles of the Jews and great sighs from all those in the World Order, who after a healthy profit, much sacrifice, innumerable lies and lots of conflict – finally give 'their gift' back to humanity – probably at a price and then only available to the wealthy and not the "useless eaters". It may have occured to you that no church has ever confronted the World Order, followed by the question – why? The answer lies in the fact that no church is free from this story and no church (other than a recent comendable statement from the Church of England over the ressurection) has ever questioned one point of this story, despite the fact that all beliefs and churches are tied to this story.

In *Legacy of the Gods* Robert Charroux states that the Sirius calendar is more than 6200 years old. Significantly the Egyptian civilization only started 8-9 000 years ago and if the Masters and those who survived the flood, were so gifted as 'gods', why did it take so long to get a civilization up and running? When I talk of civilization I do not mean palaces, gold and purple clothes and Babylon. The differences in Palaeolithic art have already been referred to, together with the impetus behind the Minoan Civilization, which was not Masters from 12 or 13, but spiritual intervention c. 10 000 B.C. Group 13 may have used the Spritual impetus to create the early Minoan civilization, which was then destroyed in the Religious Revolution by Thothmess III but the original impetus came from neither. Things only started to shape up on planet Earth c. 10 000 B.C and this of course has led to the immense cover up on archaeological finds and dates e.g. when Noah's Ark came to rest, Magnetic Reversals and the wipe out of species including the dinosaurs, including the Dead Sea Scrolls and the background to so-called miracles, which utilised the hidden science. Charroux in *Masters of the World* refers to the fact that during the last century, archaeologists discovered a number of gold tablets in the Gobi desert (etheric base of Shambhalla according to Alice Bailey) that told the history of mankind before the deluge or cataclysm. Charroux stated that the tablets told of Masters of the World who came "from the sky" and identified them as astronauts from Venus and the Star Sirius. Where exactly are these tablets? I certainly can find no reference to them. According to Dr. Douglas Baker the predictions of the modern American seer Edgar Cayce, including geological catastrophes, were given *in a trance* from the Master D.K and his predictions of the discoveries at the Gizah pyramid in 1998 were forecast by Nostradamus to occur one year later. However since the Masters and World Order work according to strict dates, plans and cycles according to their eternal 'script', then it is quite understandable that these things run to time! However when they do, the audience as with the current manipulated world scene compared to the book of *Revelations*, exclaims 'See! It is all happening as God said', well actually it was as the World Order said, or as the 'script' dictated from the last production on Earth.

Uri Geller who was attached to an Apocalyptic group (*Alternative 4*); once wrote a poem which referred to the wind growing yellow, the coming of the red when the purple turned to green and rainbow colours approached – on a day in which the skies opened up forming a hole. Geller wrote this in a trance and said that it seemed to describe a catastrophe and this curiously reminds one of the myths and legends which recount that the god looked through "a hole in the sky". The whole poem Geller felt, pointed to something so extreme, that the people of Earth had to **evacuate the planet** (did he mean the MRC case or Apocalyptic group that run the World Order today?). This certainly might provide one varying account of the proposal the author made, of one group leaving Earth to avoid a Magnetic Reversal and apparently landing again as gods. Since Geller was attached to an Apocalyptic group which in *Alternative 4* I concluded had to be Jewish, then evidently here we are looking at the proposal I made earlier, of some group or "chosen ones" who exited prior to the Magnetic

Reversal and then presumably returned giving rise to the extra-terrestrial or gods from the sky belief or Noah's Ark, which became muddled with the original arrival of the Fallen Angel or Lucifer from Sirius i.e. the two etra-terrestrial, Twin Kings or Sethite and Cainite groups! Thus here we have the origins of the muddle of two landings or extra-terrestrials, but the third intervention from a spiritual (good) source c. 10 000 B.C. was not understood or recognised. Stuart Holyroyd (another fortitudinous name – Holyrood?) who worked with Geller's scientist friends Puharich, stated in his book *Prelude to the Landing on Planet Earth*, that initiates of Earth always recognised the validity of the Book of *Revelations* – well quite! since it is the 'script' and has been validated by Freemasons along with St. John who was the patron saint of Lord Bute who had the Summer Smoking Room Floor at Cardiff Castle made, with its plans for a universal political and religious kingdom! Significantly however Holyroyd states that not all groups on Earth believe the space Brothers or Masters are coming to save the planet, some feel that they are coming to control it, which is what I believe Scientology feels is the case, although I have no evidence for what they believe in their ultimate order or OT level (8 at the last count).

The Master Rakoczi transmission (channelling) quoted in a book *The Magic of Findhorn*, by Paul Hawken (1975) referred to the Scottish Findhorn new Age community. The transmission as with the UFO warnings (past holographics of thought) warned that **time is growing short** and emotional imbalance, instability and hatred is bringing the world closer to a cataclysm. I have always felt that is the case, it was virtually a done deal after the betrayal at Golgotha, but there is now through that betrayal very little time left, indeed Dr. Becker has stated that the Magnetic Reversal has already started and even according to the 'script', *Revelations*, the signs are there with the MRC case playing his final scene and that oh so close final betrayal that will see the world plunged into a third nuclear war, through man's declining insanity. That war would undoubtedly be enough to tip a full-blown Magnetic Reversal.

It is against this background that I will review the hot topic of Bohemian Grove. This is a wooded site in California America, where a ceremony takes place that has for the past hundred years or so involved prominent men including past Presidents Reagan, Nixon and Bush and future Presidents! This implies that American politics are fixed from this group or more realistically the group behind it. Kissinger a prominent name in the World Order and Bilderberger group has also attended: and if the author is correct with regards to the Bilderbergers as part of 13 th tribe, would tend to indicate that the Bohemian Grove ceremony is a 13th and 12 tribe tribe affair, further implying that groups 12 and 13 are united at the top i.e. "all the tribes of Israel", according to the 'scipt' of *Revelations*.The group of exclusive all males (Masonic) has claimed that the ceremony and stage theatre produced is merely light- hearted relief from having (like Hercules) to run the world and affairs of state. From what I can gather from recent video footage, a group of men get together, urinate up trees like dogs and watch some theatre production, where a huge owl forms the backdrop of the stage, whilst some form of man-made enterix (sacrificial victim of child's age?) is placed on what looks remarkably like a Druid type alter and someone shouts "Fools!" three times. I suspect you have already noted some archetypal symbols, but in case you have not, then a few are noted for you. Three is Druidic, along with the parallel of the owl to the wicker man of the Druids, which was used as the sacrificial osier or wicker basket with connotations to Minoan Crete. In *The Battle of The Trees*, I explained the leech or psychic finger of the Druidic finger- signalling alphabet (the index finger) as referring to the "fools finger" and the requirement of demons to answer difficult questions. This finger as I have shown appears prominently in the painting by Guercino (c. 1618) which bears the significant phrase 'Et in Arcadia Ego', referring to the mythical birthplace of Hermes. Hermes however is not only the God of the World Order and the Religious Revolution of Crete; he was **born in Crete** from the Bull-Minos cult. Here we have then, significant symbolism relating to the coming of the World Religion and World Order Universal political and religious kingdom – the aeon of Maat, which has gone through many cycles and is to now enter the age of alleged Truth and Justice (Maat) as in Cro(maat) a Rosicrucian term relating to the era of truth and justice. Thus the gods of Earth take a bit of light relief from the twelve labours of Hercules so prominently displayed on the wall tile mural battling with the crab, at Cardiff Castle! "Fools!" repeated *three* times in each stage line evidently refers to Hermes as Twin Kings and Mother Goddess (The ancient Trinity). The Druids of course used sacrificial victims to the wicker-man, just as on the introduction of a hereditary monarchy (king Minos) into Crete, to placate the Goddess, seven maidens and youths were brought from Athens in myth, to satisfy the Bull-Minos or Minotaur. Originally one Twin King was replaced (sacrificed) by his Tanist the Twin King of the New Year according to the agricultural cycles to embody the Goddess in her message and that of Rhea the ancient Goddess of Crete: 'As I go so must I return'. The 'swinging icon' (*Fig.5*), the tides, the agricultural cycles and the migration of cranes on the Cretan seal (seen as the coming and going of Hermes) all conveyed that message. However the Bull-Minos cult stole the message of Re-incarnation and transferred it to hereditary monarchy, such that one Twin King was slain and re-appeared as his Twin to continue rule – his immortality the gift of Her, the Great Goddess. This obviously was a degraded form of The Holy Grail, which had nothing to do with Kings (12 or 13), sacrifice or hereditary monarchy, however eventually the king did not much like being sacrificed at the end of the agricultural year, so he changed it to nine years and eventually the nineteen year cycle to maintain hereditary, patriarchal rule. Thus the idea of sacrifice (symbolic) at Bohemian Grove not only parallels some symbolic resurrection ceremonies in Freemasonry, but more importantly relates to the Druids, the 13 th tribe and the Minoans, which evidently the World Order believe, was a civilization that centred on their Master from Sirius; or Noah back to Adam! There is also the curiosity of men urinating all over the place that gives one the idea of dogs and the Sirius connection, apart from the white phallic fireworks (with stars) that are released at the end of the theatre of Bohemian Grove, recalling the phallic Bull-Minos cult.

The enormous owl however, provides the biggest clue. *Fig.53* illustrates a comparison of Celtic and Minoan motifs: the origin of the swastika c. 1400 B.C and the figure-of-8 all appear, but what is of interest, is the scroll design of the Minoans. I have already explained the scroll that also appears at New Grange barrow in Ireland and in the Queen's Room at Knossos, as a motif that depicts the Cycle of Eternal Return, the thought that overlaid the Holy Grail message of Re-incarnation (which was the impetus behind the Minoan civilization) and became immortality for the Masters and Solar kings of the World Order. This cycle took on religious and political significance that was not intended and became applied to the resurrection and immortality of solar kings only, as with Jesus. The cycle also became part of the various cyclic aeons that were planned and the "wheels" or cycles associated with the World Order plan in denying man the knowledge, with the justification that man had to develop and tread the hard labyrinthine path, which of course the Masters created for man at a profit - naturally. The Masters, who had always controlled Earth, just could not envisage giving man such knowledge, which would free man from the trap of the Masters. They devised their cycles always of course, with the *intention* of giving the knowledge back at some point, but from their hand and as 'their' gift to humanity. Such intention of course is over-ruled by the evil intentions of the MRC case, in so far as he would never be able to complete the cycle, since he himself is trapped here through many such cycles and karma. The MRC case would always unknown to himself and others who support him, create delays, until of course he has to leave in his space ship or Ark and take the genetic codes with him (all living things of Earth or the two by two – male and female or X and Y chromosomes) with the justification that he is of course the "guardian" saving future humanity. He would not worry whether man gets stuck like a fly in the web of 36 days of "implants" as Hubbard relates in Inc.2 or what I refer to as a Magnetic Reversal, where the entire contents of the Akashic Record or mega computer www-com/grid is downloaded into man's spiritual memory banks and the whole cycle starts again, after the MRC lands –Day 1. Plant the vine, or hereditary kingship and "chosen one" or "guardian" mentality.

Fig. 53 **Decorative motifs and symbols**

Figs 1 to 8: Minoan and Celtic patterns compared. The treatment in different

areas of motifs, which were probably of common origin, is of special interest. Nubers 7 and 8 are identical. Fig.9: The equal-limbed Cretan cross. Fig.10. The swashtika (swastika) symbol –cross with arms bent (compare to the evolution of the cross and crux ansata). Figs 11 and 12: Celtic knot developed from swashtika by connecting points of bent arms by curves – single treatment (point to point) in 11 and double treatment with swashtika reversed (inner curves corner to elbow and outer curves point to point) in 12. Figs.13 to 17: Religious Symbols with figure-of-8 shield and cosmic circle represented and crossed arrows; figure 14: could represent a 'door' into another dimenstion? Or key hole? With significance on Eliphas Levi's comment of a Universal Kingdom being had by those with the "keys to the East" or keys to the hidden science and Grid? The 8-form shield was to feature at Knossos and in Mycenae (sun-kings). Fig.15: is said to be a Cretan "deity" on a seal. Fig. 16: Scoto-Celtic "spectacle" symbol shown upright as on standing stone and Fig.17: Scoto-Celtic "crescent and arrow" symbol but also 'umbrella' or Grid And Illuminatus eye?

The Minoan symbol of the Cycle of Eternal Return is highly stylised in *Fig. 53*, but it is the figure of the Bull-Minos with its horns representing the 'gates of horn' or the abode of the dead, which the deceased passes through to join with Her the Great Goddess, whose gift it is of his re-birth or Re-incarnation. I discussed in *The Battle of The Trees*, just how the symbols of The Teacher were manipulated and transferred to the Bull-Minos cult and this is an example, where the scroll which initially meant: 'into a life and out of it' (Re-incarnation) was covertly altered and transferred to Bull-Mionos cult significance.This thought was applied to the Twin Kings and as one died the King or his Twin was born as the spirit of the New Year: how far this thought then became spirit of the new year or aeon of the World Order plan, applied to the four quarters of the year or the totem beasts of man, bull, lion and eagle of the Beth-Luis-Nion calendar and the full gamut of overlaid Semitic significances that were never intended in The Holy Grail, can only be guessed at, in relation to Ezekiel's vision, where he deliberately left the woman out of the story! The earthly Masters of the GWB could eventually unite with the Masters in the etheric, of the GWL on Sirius who would eventually again in a Cycle of Eternal Return appear on Earth. This is the Greek tragedy of The Holy Grail and the method by which a message of Re-incarnation for all humanity was taken and used in some insanity of the World Order priesthood. The MRC case simply took the Holy Grail and applied it to his own psychological case! I suspect the manipulated (World Order) bilateral brain appearance that became the standard format for representing extra-terrestrial heads, originates with the eternal symbols of Twin Kingship or groups 12 and 13 and Bull-Minos (two horns) – which demonstrates how far 'south', the mind of the MRC case can go, with his games of significance – apart from

Freemasonry ritual and the Bohemian Grove ceremony, which as Alan Jones (anti-World Order fighter) commented was a disturbing ceremony, when you consider that the attendees are either past Presidents or future Presidents of one of the most powerful nations on earth. However both the Minoan and the Celtic design of the Cycle of Eternal Return in *Fig. 53* both strongly indicate the owl and hark back to the wisdom of the Masters.

The owl as such does not appear in Minoan iconography, but again the bird of the Goddess or her epiphany as the dove, was later manipulated through the egg connection, goose or crane and even the duck or swan: white of course was the Goddess in her death aspect (killed off by 12 and 13): **in her silver aspect her message and warning were immortal**. In icons of the Religious Revolution period the dove is manipulated and occurs in the Cabalistic Tree of Life! The owl however makes an appearance in Indian myth as a messenger of death. In Vedic legend "the land of the fathers", was a shining Paradise where two kings (naturally) – Varunae and Yama sit below a tree (with oblique implications of the Druidic Tree alphabet and the oak tree of royalty) where Yama a form of Mithra plays on a flute and drinks the soma of the Celestials, where soma gives immortality. Yama's messengers were the pigeon and the owl and he also had two brindled watchdogs, each with four eyes, thus there is a Sirius connection here with two dogs implying Sirius A and B and also two tribes of 12 and 13 with four eyes representing the four corners of the Earth. There is also a connection of the Twin Kings and the observance that Sirius B cannot be seen with the naked eye, only Sirius A. This then has implications of the 'Trojan Horse' or betrayal that Crowley obliquely spoke of and the World Order who once they have implemented a universal political system, which is more or less complete coupled with a monetary system, will instigate a world war rather than a world religion and peace: there will be at the last moment, a grand betrayal as the Koran appears to warn of and this will lead to a third world war and the end of the cycle – repeating the last cycle and the war of two kings – 12 and 13.

The idea of exclusivity of re-incarnation was implied in Vedic legend:

> Fear not to pass the guards –
> The Four-eyed brindled dogs – that watch for the departed.

The bardic poetic gloss of dog is: 'guard the secret' and evidently refers to the Dog Star Sirius and the Masters or the hermetic connection of Mercury (the star of Hermes). The fact that dog and owl occur together in Vedic legend implies not only the unity of both (12 and 13), but their separateness and must refer to Bull-Minos cult and Sirius with the Master Thothmess III or KH the Master now on Sirius (GWL) as the connection. The Brotherhood would become immortal, but immortality would be given to man at a price. The idea of the Dog Star as the White Lodge of Judgement by some cosmic council also arises in oblique form:

"Return unto thy home, o Soul! Thy sin and shame
leave thou behind on earth; assume a shining form
Thine Ancient shape- refined and from all taint set free.
(*Sir. M. Monier Williams trans.*)

Yama equated with the owl was "the finisher" as Kritana; and "he who ends life" as Antaka; also "King of righteousness" as Yama the judge: and as Samann "the leveller". Thus not only do we sense the end of the cycle in the Bohemian Grove ceremony, but also the completion of the plan in a Universal religious political and religious kingdom. Thus the World Order are working up towards their Egyptian Dog Star and Bull-Minos cult view of Maat or the era of truth and justice. Yama was significantly "the wielder of the rod or mace", strongly reminding one of the Druid rood or wand. Yama had a noose with him with which to bind souls, and compares to the Hangman card (*Fig.54*) of the Tarot pack and the 12th Hebrew letter (lamed). In *The Battle of The Trees* I discussed the Minoan seals, which showed Twin Kings with heal raised signifying a solar king or royalty. Jesus was allegedly laim and Noah was allegedly bitten and lamed by a lion. This also relates to that curious ceremony enacted at Gisors entitled 'the cutting of the elm' and in one sense was re-enacted with the cut to the Mary Magdalene's arm made by Jesus with his sword. There is also an oblique reference to this in the crab mural at Cardiff Castle where drops of 'blood' arise from the cut by sword to the left claw of the crab, which has another under laid meaning. The arm became the sign of expansive movement and whilst the Magdalene envisaged an expansive spiritual movement based on The Holy Grail and Re-incarnation and healing, the World Order had their own view of the nature of expansion and growth in International Finance Capitalism and a global economy – and so it came to pass, coupled with a world religion of Christianity. The Hebrew letter (lamed) and the Hangman Tarot refer to all ideas of **extension and expansion**, of possession and as a last sign, it is the image of the power derived from elevation. Astronomically the lamed letter corresponds with the Zodiacal sign of the balance – justice: thus it would seem the owl in the mind of the World Order, is a fitting epiphany of the ancient trinity and the Bull-Minos cult and the ushering in of the age of Maat, with its world religion and political system with the Masters in total control of growth and expansion (a global economy). However one cannot ignore that the owl is also a Bull-Minos and retains the stolen Holy Grail, which will presumably emerge as the universal religion. The 12th Arcanum Tarot fills the centre between the 6th Arcanum (wisdom or owl) and the 15th (Fatality). Significantly the World Order seems to have forgotten that this Tarot serves as an example to the presumptuous and the requirement for the absolute submission which the human owes to the true Divine source – the source of spiritual intervention c. 10 000 B.C which is not Sirius A or B or 12 and 13, I am afraid!

Fig. 54 **The Hangman - 12th Tarot Card**

Hieroglyphically the Lamed or 12th Hebrew letter designates the arm – sign of expansive movement. Applies to all ideas of extension, of occupation, of possession. Image of power derived from elevation. Divine expansion in humanity is produced by prophets and revelation, and inspires the idea of the revealed law: punishment for those who violate it and elevation for he who understands it. Hands tied behind the back and the fold of his arms forms the base of a reversed triangle, of which his head forms the point. His right leg crosses his left and forms a cross.

In the hermetic grades of the Rosy Cross (18th degree of the Freemasonry of Scotland) one of the signs of recognition consists in crossing the legs as in the Hanged man and thus the Tarot pack has great significance in Freemasonry along with the Hebrew letters. The Seventeenth card of the Tarot pack is the The

Stars corresponding to the 17th Hebrew letter (Phe) which expresses the same hieroglyphic meaning as the Beth (2nd card of the Tarot) and signifies mouth, which reminds one of the Chinese character of mouth with its referral to Noah as I have covered: it also represents speech (*Fig. 55*) Speech presumably in one sense is the Word or Logos and the Masters both of the GWB and the etheric Masters of the GWL on Sirius: but in another sense one side of this story has never been allowed to speak, whilst the World Order and its lackeys always controlled all the communication lines. The Word however as we have seen was channelled via the UVG120 crystal! And thus the Logos or Word, is the thoughts of past Masters either here on Earth or transmitted through the crystal from goodness knows where, if not Sirius as Earth hurtles through space. Astronomically this 17th letter and Tarot corresponds to Mercury (Hermes) and Hermes had the best traffic with money, as you may note from a comparison of the Hendekaglyphs (system) of the various beliefs. Hermes was associated with riches and evidently then, the god of the World Order. Hermes you will remember had the face of two sides (a Janus head) and thus through conflict, prophecy and betrayal, great wealth could be had. Hermes is also the god of speech and significantly of scientific or commercial diffusion, the god of universal exchange between beings and all worlds – well that accounts for the connection of Mercury (Hermes) to Sirius then! Phe is also a double letter which would indicate Sirius A and B, which again demonstrates not only the groups 12 and 13 and the creation of conflict, but also Sirius B is hidden or Hermes is hidden behind Sirius (A). This might all sound terribly inconsequential and esoteric, but believe you me, the insane Masters of this world have run this planet on such significances and thus end up at Bohemian Grove where past and future Presidents are only too happy to play out these games. In the Stars Tarot, the woman connected to the sea pours **two cups** of water of universal life and seven (female Pythagorean significance) stars are surmounted by one brilliant one (compare Mercury in the Greek icon of the birth of the Divine child) presumably Sirius star which was seen as the brightest star. The implication once again, is of the joining of the tribes of Israel or 12 and 13 (Twin Kings) either side of the Goddess (the female in the card), thus referring back to the ancient Trinity, Minoan Crete and Twin Kings and Mother Goddess. This Trinity is the basis of two extra-terrestrial landings and apparent landing, making the third, by those who survived a Magnetic Reversal by removing themselves from Earth. The butterfly clearly shown is a symbol of immortality as a soul that survives the body, taking us back to Minoan Crete. The body in this Tarot is only seen as a place of trial (the ephemeral flower of the Goddess in Crete as the Lily) and according to the World Order the 17th Tarot is the courage to bear these trials, which they cause!

Fig. 55 **The Stars or 17th Hebrew letter of the Tarot**

Signifies immortality – hope and the force, which dispenses the essence of life – no destruction is final everything is eternal and immortal in God. The fall is not irreparable. The idea of Rhea the Goddess of Crete: 'As I go so must I return' and the philosophy that there is continual renewal after destruction.

THE STARS.

Such thoughts however were transferred from The Holy Grail and spiritual intervention, as the gift to humanity, to those who had survived the Magnetic Reversal and took it upon themselves to believe that this message, its hope and the science was their own! It was their *intention* to give it back to humanity at some point, but not before they squeezed mankind like a lemon for profit and placed themselves in a position of elevated material power and assumption of spiritual power – the 'gods' or "guardians". The true God or spiritual power, was fuming with wrath in the Heavens – hence the condemnation of the Jews in *The Bible* as "God's chosen people"! Why did they not give the knowledge to man? Surely any spiritual being would have done so; the argument and justification for having withheld the knowledge and keys to the trap, which promotes the idea that man must tread a hard path to enlightenment, would not be accepted by way of mitigation in the greater court of a man's own conscience in the death experience; when he will be forced to reap on Earth what he has sown and he will have a prime seat for the greatest show of light on Earth (a Magnetic Reversal)! When the sun as an ageing star finally explodes, no doubt he can play his theatre in the dark or seek another planet with some bug life form into which he will be forced to re-incarnate just to have a viewpoint in the material universe – some game and some jsutice!

The singing birds are all singing spirits in India as in Europe. The language of the birds is the language of the spirits and the owl in Egypt hooted as Egyptian ghosts. Homer's ghosts twittered like bats. In parallel in the Scottish Highlands the spirits of the dead sometimes appear as birds and fairies. In the Assyrian legend of Ishtar the souls of the dead in Hades: "are like birds covered with feathers". The Bohemian Grove ceremony significantly is not only set in a cedar wood (with connotations to the Ark) but beside water with implications of the Apocalypse and flood and also Re-incarnation, with Goddess connected to the sea and tides and the Cycle of Eternal Return – 'as I go, so must I return'. The Indian epics make numerous references to semi-divine beings that haunt streams, lakes and forests. In Assyrian and Babylonian myth and legend the ghosts of the dead and male and female demons were birds. When the owl raised its melancholy voice in the darkness the listener heard the spirit of a departed mother crying for her child. In his *Arabia Deserta (vol.i, p.305)* Doughty relates Arab women and children mock the cries of the owl as one explained to him: "It is a wailfull woman seeking her lost child; she has become this forlorn bird". Certainly the 'child' The Holy Grail was lost and along with it the hope for all children.

The Bible with reference to the Babylonian civilization and originally Akkad included the cities of Babylon, Cutha, Kish, Akkad and Sippar and north of Babylonia proper was Semitic Opis. Why should Hermes be born in Arcadia in Greece? When he was the product of a Religious Revolution in Crete, driven from Egypt and the East. In fact Akkadians came from Akkad, but this was in Babylonia or the East. The curse in *Revelations*, which is placed on the harlot and Babylon, is very carefully switched from Babylon and the Patriarchal Masters to the woman! The Book of *Revelations* however is written for the 12 tribes, against the 13 th tribe and thus the woman is railed, since there are crimes against her (in psychology this mechanism is called justification). Babylon in the East was a place of immense wealth and luxurious palaces with kings and in biblical reference the kings of Elam tried to imitate the splendours of Babylonian courts in the latter days of Esther and Haman and Mordecai:

> "White, green, and blue hangings, fastened
> With cords of fine linen and purple to silver
> Rings and pillars of marble, the beds were of
> Gold and silver, upon a pavement of red
> And blue and white and black marble
> (*Esther, I, 6*)

The curse of the Hebrew prophet claimed:

"Babylon, the glory of kingdoms,
the beauty of the Chaldeans excellency, shall be as when God
overthrew Sodom and Gomorrah,
It shall never be inhabited;
 neither shall the Shepherds make their fold there.
But wild beasts of the desert shall lie there;
And their houses shall be full of doleful creatures;
And owls shall dwell there, and satyrs shall dance there.
And the wild beasts of the islands shall cry in their desolate houses and
Dragons in their pleasant palaces"
(*Isaiah, xiii, 19-22*)   (*Author's emphasis*)

The Book of *Revelations* has cleverly tied the woman in with Babylon and presumably the 13 tribe, dating back to Minoan Crete, deflecting the curse from the Masters and materialism to the woman (and the 13 th tribe)! *Stern* magazine (*May 2000*) from the nerve centre of Europe (Germany) took twelve pages (co-incidentally or not!) to cover the "apocalyptic" state of Britain running through the railway, health, farming and other crises such as BSE and Foot and Mouth disease. Further Alisteir Crowley who seems to have been remarkably well informed on World Order plans and final betrayals, prophesied that when the Devil's chimney a piece of cliff line not far from the Seven Sisters or seven white cliffs of the southern coastline of Britain (with significance to "7 mountain tops" in the Revelations account) fell into the sea, a great disaster would befall Eastbourne (a town not far distant from the Seven Sisters). Significantly amongst all the propaganda (generated by the 12 tribes?) of apocalyptic Britain, the devils chimney did drop into the sea in this year (2000) after virtually six months of non-stop rain.

The Ng or Reed month in the Druidic Beth-Luis-Nion alphabet is the month when the terrible roar of breakers and the snarling noise of pebbles is heard on the Atlantic seaboard, which filled the heart with terror. In Ireland the roaring of the sea was held to be prophetic of a king's death. The warning also came with the harsh cry of the screech owl. Thus the sense of end or Apocalyptic is imparted with the owl, which is vocal on moonlight nights, with all the significances to the Goddess in her white death aspect. Owls are the messengers of death as goddess Hectate in Greece. However the labyrinth of the Great Goddess in Crete was a burial place and not a palace of kings as the archaeologist Evans was to have us believe. The dead were buried among seashells in bath-shaped sarcophagi awaiting re-birth in the early Minoan period. After the Religious Revolution the sarcophagus was replaced with the square-shaped Semitic kind, with pictures of sacrifice reflecting the square of the Beth-Luis-Nion alphabet (*Fig.19*). The owl was a messenger of death as Hectate, Athene or Persephone from whom, as the supreme source of prophecy, they derive their reputation for wisdom. With reference to the Moon or the 18th Tarot of the pack (*Fig. 55*), it signifies the **AIM AND THE END**. Thus as the World Order finalise their plans and the finale of fireworks (resembling remarkably white foam and phallic symbolism of the Bull-Minos cult) went up at the Bohemian Grove ceremony, then there are a plethora of symbols and meanings all relating to **the finalisation of a plan**. In one sense they are paying tribute to their ancestral spirit form or totem beast of Bull-Minos cult and the beliefs of immortality and the Cycle of Eternal Return, with homage to the Dog Star (Sirius A) but with homage evidently to the hidden Sirius B or the star of Mercury and Hermes related to the phallic Bull-Minos cult and the ancient Trinity of Goddess and Twin Kings, with the bird or owl as was noted in Palaeolithic art as a precursor of the Bull-Minos cult. The ceremony is conducted under the Moon (at night) and by water in a wood, signifying the aim, end and the Moon as owl and cycle, or a final term, a secession and yet division and aim as the 18 th Tarot and the Hebrew Letter (Tzaddi). Tzaddi corresponds astronomically with the zodiacal sign of water and the spring of life as Aquarius (the water carrier – or underground stream of wisdom). This water theme was displayed in the symbolic art of Guercino and Poussin discussed in *The Battle of The Trees*.

Fig.56 **The Moon and 18 th Tarot Card**

Fig.57 **The World Tarot - twenty-first Tarot Card**

(Note the calendar beasts of bull and lion of the Beth-Luis Nion alphabet and the angel, with bird of epiphany of Goddess)

Fig. 58 **The Fool or 21 st Hebrew letter (shin) of the Tarot**

Arrow, object or aim seen on right hand side of reverse of One-dollar note of America as symbol of arrows and religious aim of World Order. Vibration from one pole to the other, with an unstable point of equilibrium in the centre (12 and 13 tribe games! – compare Diablo and reality in Fig. 1!) Shin is a sign of relative duration and the movement relating to it; whilst the Samech expresses cyclic movement and absolute duration (World Order idea of cycles and immortality of group and aim) this is an unnumbered card of the Tarot ("no-one knows the hour" of the end of the cycle according to Revelations). Appears to concern the "fool's cap" which could mean the Petasos of Hermes? The fool pays no attention to the dog that bites his leg as he trundles along his way with his bundle on his shoulder (World Order aim?): a symbol of the Flesh and of its gratification. The matter of the world attains the maximum of its material progression signifies the animal kingdom. In the Bohemian Grove ceremony appears to relate to 13 th tribe ("Fools" shouted three times reflecting ancient Trinity of Goddess and Twin Kings). Also St. Paul referred to "Fools" as "stupid Galatians" –Celts and Druidic? Old religion. The significance of "flesh" and sacrifice is implied. The card has no number presumably since it is the secret or lost 13th tribe. Thus Bohemian Grove ceremony and its members are 12 tribes (Israel) the author concludes.

The boys then up at Bohemian Grove are *not the top order* or hand that moves. The fact that Ronald Reagan was present must signify that this can't be the top group! This group evidently believe that the two groups 12 and 13 have joined and that all will be well on Earth under the age of Maat and Truth and Justice. Evidently the 13 th tribe (European Union?) may believe the same thing (although a call for a centralised army bodes ill), however neither group have learnt from the past and the betrayal of Grand Orient Freemasonry, which the author covered earlier and in *The Battle of The Trees,* with regard to the French Revolution. Further *The Bible* is full of quotes of one brother betraying another (Brotherhood and the two groups). I believe they think they are doing the right thing, but ignorance is no excuse when you get sucked up for your 36 days of "implants" or downloading from the Grid and entire Akashic Record as the MRC case and the Masters once again take control of planet Earth. It is **individual eternity at stake**, which they might consider whilst urinating up a tree. This story was never a game it was always deadly serious – deadly serious. There is no safety in numbers, thus the **individual** must decide.

The material world is the last point that the spirit can reach; it can descend no lower than the Age of Horus, which is where man is today. The Tarot of Moon shows the boundary of fields and the drops of blood represent the descent of the spirit into matter. As Hercules in the crab mural at Cardiff Castle, cuts the crabs claw, it shows blood. A path sprinkled with drops of blood loses itself in the horizon. The dog and the wolf appear and howl at the moon as the owl hoots. Finally I come to David Icke's "shape-shifting reptiles" and if you can bear with me, I will tell you one more tale. The Greek legend that the God Dionysus placed the Asses in the Sign of Cancer ('the crab') suggests that Dionysus who visited Egypt and was entertained by Proteus King of Pharos was Osiris, brother of the Hyksos god Typhon, alias Set. The Hyksos people, non-Semitic pastorals, coming from Armenia (where the Ark of Noah is supposed to have landed) or beyond, pressed down through Cappadocia, Syria and Palestine into Egypt about the year 1780 B.C. Curiously they managed to establish themselves in Northern Egypt with their capital at Pelusium, on the Canopic arm of the Nile Delta, and their acceptance can only be accounted for by an alliance with the Byblians of Phoenicia. Byblos was a protectorate of Egypt and was called the 'land of Negu' ('Trees') from which the Egyptians imported timber, and a cylinder seal of the Old Empire shows Adonis, the God of Byblos, in the company of **the horned Moon-goddess Isis**, or Hathor, or Astarte. The Byblians with the Cretans managed the Egyptian carrying trade, since significantly the Egyptians hated the sea! The fact that the Byblians honoured a goddess as Isis, means that they had some matriarchal influence and the date is prior to the Religious Revolution. Further the Druids held the ancient Tree alphabet and thus this whole period looks remarkably like the infusion into an area of a group who eventually conducted the Religious Revolution. Proteus the oracular Old Man of the Sea, was King of pharos and lived in a cave and in legend had **the power of changing his shape**, like Merddin (Merlin who was connected to King Arthur in British folk lore as magician and therefore 13 th tribe) and Dionysus, Atabyrius, Llew Llaw, Periclymenus and all Sun-heroes of the same sort.

Evidently Proteus and Osiris were regarded as the same person. There were a number of Proetus characters and one of them was Arcadian, which must have been the confusion over the birth of Hermes in Arcadia. Significantly the island of Pharos was connected with the numbers five and seventy-two, which have all the previous significances I outlined including the anti-matter and matter cycle of 720 degrees and the attempt to place the dematerialisation of Jesus into this 3 day or 72 hour period, along with the number of letters in the secret alphabet, 72 languages and priests at the tower of Babel, which was the first attempt at a World Order in the post flood era. Thus Proteus was some early form of Druid or 13 th tribe and the Jews of Alexandria used to visit the island for an annual (five-day?) festival, the excuse for which was that the five Books of Moses had been miraculously translated there into Greek by seventy-two doctors of the Law ('the Septuagint') who had worked for seventy-two days on them. Proteus or the priest-king of Pharos may have married Sarah, the goddess mother of the

'Abraham' tribe that visited Egypt at the close of the third millennium. Thus the shape-changing Proteus has some connection to the 13 th tribe and Druids I conclude, but also significantly with Egypt.

In the myth of Llew Llaw Gyffes he was a Divine Child and born of a virgin which sounds very druidic! This follows the same course as the story of Jesus. Significantly Gwydion creates Llew's wife Blodeuwedd from the blossom of oak and other trees. Blodeuwedd's fingers are "whiter than the ninth wave of the sea", which connects her with the nine-year cycle of monarchy and Crete as Moon Goddess (the nineteen year cycle was purely patriarchal): Blodeuwedd betrays Llew and she is punished and turned into an Owl by Gwydion the magician. This signifies a betrayal of the 13 th tribe and the Minoan Crete line and she is transformed into the **owl and its connection with Sirius**. This according to Graves is a patriarchal interference, since she was an owl thousands of years before Gwydion was born and the same Owl that occurs on the coins of Athens as the symbol of Athene, the goddess of Wisdom, the same owl that gave its name to Adam's first wife Lilith (Lily of Crete and the goddess?) and as Annis (Anna grandmother of Jesus and 13 th tribe – Danu or Dan and the Tuatha de Danaan/ Druid) the Blue Hag (Picts of Britain - the ancient tribe with their blue stained bodies and 'goggle' eyes or cosmic circle and Cretan labyrinth) sucks the blood of children in primitive British folk-lore. This is evidently conveys the idea that Blodeuwedd is 13 th tribe and there is a poem about Bodeuwedd the Owl by Davydd ap Gwilym, in which she swears by St. David (Royal Davidic line of Anna and Jesus) that she is daughter of the Lord of Mona and equal in dignity to Meirchion himself. Thus she is calling herself a 'Daughter of Proteus', who was Jewish in some way, connected to the 13th tribe and also could change his shape, as could Meirchion. Thus Bodeuwedd is aligning herself with the old bloody and sacrificial line of the Druidic religion, which is connected all the way back to the Bull-Minos cult. The Roman Paulinus in Anglesey suppressed the Druids, after the events of the crucifixion in A.D.68 as I have covered. Llew Llaw could also **change his name with the seasons**. Dylan the Fish is his New Year name and in some accounts significantly Dylan and Llew are twins; Llew Llaw the Lion is his Spring-Summer name; his Autumn name is withheld for reasons of bardic security and in mid-Winter he is the Eagle or nant y Llew: this is evidently a referral to the Beth-Luis-Nion alphabet and the seasons covered by totem beasts.

The old idea of betrayal by the woman actually is not betrayal by the woman, but betrayal by the 13 th tribe and there was a betrayal of a woman in Crete as the Mary Magdalene was betrayed. Sampson was betrayed by Delilah and the name 'Samson' means 'of the sun' and 'Dan'- his tribe - 13 th tribe. Sampson also killed a lion with his bare hands and the first swarm of bees emitted from its carcass. There are a number of versions of the Blodeuwedd story but in the Cuchulain version she is named Blathnat and extracts the secret of her husband's soul (King Curoi) hidden in an apple. This apple can be cut only with his own sword. This is the secret story that is engraved on the sword of Hercules at Cardiff Castle as it cuts the crabs claw, however they have obviously missed out on truth here and a completely different story – never mind boys you can't win them all! Significantly once the secret is known the husband looses his strength. Thus this is the story of 12 and 13 again. The husband cries out: "No secret to a woman, no jewel to slaves!" and for that reason Freemasonry does not allow women into its hierarchy, for fear she will once again cut his strength into two and reveal his secret and give it to the slaves (humanity): The fact that this is karma and will always come out this way, on the basis of the original betrayal of man to humanity and the source of The Holy Grail and which places the curse on woman in *Genesis*, has been perpetuated by the Jewish Brotherhood. All genius emits from male painters, scientists and philosophers etc. from the Brotherhood and as I have shown in the case of scientists from the Rosicrucian laboratories, they are given quite a head start in Atlanta's race! Many of these myths are propaganda for both 12 and 13 and according to the source group (male or female or 12th and 13th tribes respectively) ends up betraying one or the other, reflecting the two sides displayed in the political battle of the Grail legends (*The Battle of The Trees*). Hopefully you the reader now realise that this battle of 12 and 13 has teinted a great deal of history, myth and legend, religion and politics on planet Earth.

Shape changing or name changing reminds one of the *Song of Amergin*, some of which I quoted earlier, but the full version is in *The White Goddess (p.205)* by Robert Graves. "I am the wind of the sea", "ox", "stag", "salmon", "lake", "hill", "battle-waging spear" etc. This is really a 'pied' (secret or coded) bardic poem that Graves de-coded according to the Druidic Tree alphabet and the alphabets I used in *The Battle of The Trees*, to decode many mysteries attached to the Holy Grail. The fact that Proteus and Llaw Llaw could change their shapes and were connected to the 13 th tribe, Druids and magic, does not mean they *actually* changed shape! As with the representation of totem beasts in Palaeolithic art, the bull, reptilian anthropomorphous figure, bird, crocodile, giraffe, horse, fish etc. are all changes of shape, but denote the various and on-going line and secret group continuity of a World Order hierarchy that has never ceased to exist through its secret groups or 'shapes' and forms. It is just a method of the World Order as I have covered in this final section, of setting up different secret groups with different names and apparent 'shape' or identity, concealing the **source** from which they have come and therefore whether they are Hermetic or Sirius i.e.13 th tribe or 12 tribes and thus concealing *the hand that moves all secret groups*. Evidently also there is an attempt to hide the original shape, which existed as some racial type with a muzzle-shaped snout and is perhaps portrayed in the La Marche cave engravings and the reptilian-type figures. It looks from where I am sitting that D. Icke may have channelled or someone channelled this information, since I can't quite understand how he could, according to *The Fortean Times* article "see" Queen Elizabeth II in the act of sucking blood! These appear to be transposed thoughts (holographic), which have been connected into a story line that is out-reality or out space-time reality. The World Order through their seers and magicians as I have illustrated have channelled a great deal of material from the UVG120 crystal or Grid and have come up with some pretty wild stuff that has confused man and also directed him as a method of disinformation. As I have pointed out the holographics are there and how the story is woven, rather depends on the past lives and the personality of the one that weaves it. Hitler was warned about the 'easy wins' and the moral of the story is to do it the hard way, rely on your own past life memories and double check those memories with actuality, or history even though that process may take you years and years. The World Order have now based their entire ideology on channelled material - take a look around the world and see what insanity and madness it has produced, even to the point where last year, one terrorist group were hacking off children's hands with machetes in some dramatization presumably of finger mutilation and Grid Akashic Record! The Age of Horus must end, it is time for the Age of **reason and intellect** and importantly the Age for the Whole Truth and Nothing but the Truth, for there may or may not be little time left – no one "knows the hour" (*Revelations*) It is easy to prophesy when you know this story and thus I prophesy to you that unless this story is told, there will be a third world war created by the two groups (two kings) and all that has gone before will be repeated.

A recent programme on British television (*Channel 4 'The World Order'*) based on a book "*Them*" by John Ronson who was the presenter, included David Icke and "shape-shifting reptiles" theory, which unfortunately had a negative effect – coincidental or not! According to the programme however, *Spotlight* magazine and their arch sleuth (Jim Tucker) on the trail of the Bilderberger secret group, had noted that a recent meeting of the Bildberger's included Monsanto representatives, a large pharmaceutical company, the usual Kissinger, Rockefeller, J. Heinz of the baked bean company and Rothschild along with other prominent politicians, industrialists and financiers including Peter Mandleson (who planned the archetypal rise to power of Tony Blair (Labour Party) the current Prime Minister of Britain). The symbol of New Labour party is *the rose* and Mandleson oversaw the Dome project in London, although it was not his inception: and the Millennium icon, with its hermetic quality with all the significances of Knossos and 13th tribe (*Plate 3*). The ADL (Anti Defamation League) with connection to the B'nai B'nrith (who rounded up all of Comyns

Beaumont's books on Scotland as The Holy Land) have accused *Spotlight* magazine of being anti-semitic. However the Bilderberger group is not noted for its Jewish membership, however this does not disclude that they may be in fact 13th tribe and Rosicrucians. Significantly the Bilderbergers have been noted for their royal members and whilst the Secretary General of the group Martin Taylor (Chairman of W.H. Smith books) tried to paint the group as a discussion group of world (Order?) policy, rather than the instigator of it, it has to be noted that Tony Blair was an attendee before his rise to power. Dennis Healey a past politician and Minister of Defence in Britain and founding member of the group, not only displayed open arrogance and rudeness on camera whilst being interviewed for the programme, but mentioned a "single community" and stated of the group: "It's what happens in the world – whats wrong with that!" It is however this kind of attitude and acceptance of the secret world of politics and religion (and now genetic technology – why should Monsanto be there?) that has created a very precarious position for mankind, through men who in all times, have held that exact same attitude and have viewed themselves as the 'movers and shakers' or gods, who would become God. There are numerous condemnations of this assumption in religious texts: the assumption was that there is no God (if you must use that term) or Higher Spiritual Source – how wrong they were.

As the author closes this final warning, Lionel Jospin the French Premier unveiled his vison of an 'economic government' imposing harmonised taxes across Europe and called for closer integration of the community's economic management, with a unified legal system and a centralised European constitution, with a "social treaty" imposing more workers rights, all run by a "federation of nation states". This is proof of the goal of a Federal European super-state, if not Rosicrucian or Scottish Rite goals? Indeed M. Jospin said he wanted to see the community turned into a "European federation of nation States". In what looks like a push towards Maat, or the aeon of Truth and Justice M. Jospin stated that: "Working conditions must be harmonised upwards. There must be a special focus on information to employees and their involvement in the life of companies, as well as on lay-offs, the struggle against job insecurity and wage policies". He also wanted a European Constitution, with the Charter of Fundamental Rights at its heart: the charter will boost the right to strike. Further the legal harmonisation, which proposes a European public prosecutor's office, is another part of central policy directive. The average man looks at this and says – well that seems to be good and he can't understand what all the fuss on Europe is about, other than the fact he does not like any central authority telling him what to do (he has had too much of it on the track of time from a World Order!). However the mere fact that Brussels, desires military affairs run from there with obvious forthcoming conflict with NATO and America; together

472

with a European police force, should send warning bells off in anyone's head! EUROPEAN UNION IS NOT ABOUT TRADE, IT IS ABOUT POWER AND A POLICY BASED ON A PHILOSOPHY OF SECRET GROUPS who have persued this goal of a European Federal Super State, at least since the time of the French Revolution and according to the thesis here, thousands of years prior – EUROPEAN UNION IS A DOCTRINE OR BELIEF SYSTEM. On defence matters M. Jospin said that the European (military) rapid reaction force should be bolstered by a "centralised military doctrine". Not only is 'doctrine' a word, which refers to beliefs! One perceives in all this not an era of Truth and Justice but CONFLICT AND WAR! Significantly M. Jospin called for a unified "European position" on what he called America's controversial anti-missile shield initiative (electro-magnetic): which would certainly prevent Mr Blair from pledging support for the system and thereby damage what the press call the "special relationship" of Britain with America (which can only infer 12 or13). What you are witnessing on the world's political stage is a square up of groups 12 and 13 and as sure as night follows day, THERE WILL BE A THIRD WORLD WAR, SINCE THIS IS A COMPLETE DRAMATIZATION OF ALL THAT HAS GONE BEFORE and a war of two kings, neither can one be certain that the weapons used will not tip the balance on a Magnetic Reversal, in which case man will receive his "36 days" of downloading from www-com/grid and he can look forward to Day.1 Plant the vine and the beginning again – not "Paradise" but a very black world run by the Masters. As you have noted this is my resignation from the post I have held for some time, I hope that you make it out!

TWO JERUSALEMS

Sir Henry Mahon, the British High Commissioner for Egypt, in 1915 sent a series of letters to Sheriff Hussein of Mecca in the name of the British Government, promising the Arabs their independence if they would fight on the side of the allies in the war against the Old Ottoman Empire. As a result of these promises Arabs who remained under the dominion of the Turkish Empire and necessitated them to fight for the Turks throughout the first stages of the war, entered the war on the side of the Allies. The Jews had different ideas however and that of the old plan of a Zionist Palestine. As early as January 25th 1915 the Baron Edmond de Rothschild and a Russian co-religionist approached Lord Bertie over what he considered "an absurd scheme". A scheme apparently supported by Liberals and with the approval among others of Mr Lloyd George then Prime Minister of Britain. The "absurd scheme" was for the formation of Palestine into an Israelite State under the protectorate of England, France or Russia, preferably England. Despite objections to the scheme the Zionists pursued it and a leading Conservative Statesman finally championed it. On November 2nd 1917, Mr (later Lord) Balfour penned his signature to the Balfour declaration, as it is known, in a letter to Lord Rothschild stating:

> "His Majesty's Government view with favour the establishment in Palestine, of a National home for the Jewish people, and will use their best endeavours to facilitate the achievement of his object, it being clearly understood that nothing shall be done which may prejudice the civil and religious rights of existing non-Jewish communities in Palestine or the rights and political status enjoyed by Jews in any other country".

This pledge was totally incompatible with the pledge given two years earlier to the Arabs. If Palestine was to become an independent State it was not within the power of Great Britain to offer that to the Jews, the offer if there was to be any, should have come from the Arabs. The Mac Mahon pledge was therefore totally contravened in that it clearly stated:

> "Subject to the above modifications Great Britain is prepared to recognise and support the independence of the Arabs within the territories included in the limits and boundaries proposed by the Sheriff of Mecca".

The British Government later contended that Palestine was part of the territory excluded, which was described as "portions of Syria lying to the West of the

474

districts of Damascus, Homs, Hama and Aleppo". This obviously did not include Palestine. The Mac Mahon correspondence was never published by the coalition Government however a book entitled *The Palestine Deception* by Mr J M Jeffries of the Daily Mail published in 1922, helped with other accounts to bring the matter to light. Curiously subsequent governments did not rectify this discreditable incident and the incessant wars in the Middle East can be traced back to this most curious if not "absurd scheme". The incident was again raised in the House of Commons in the thirties when Mr Morris, Liberal Member for Cardigan said:

> "Undoubtedly definite promises were made to the Arabs...we know that the Balfour Declaration had been printed, although we do not know what it means, but the Mac Mahon correspondence has not been published. Why not? The present government, like the previous Governments, have always declined to publish the Mac Mahon correspondence".

Mr Seymour Cocks, Labour Member for Broxtowe spoke to the same effect:

> "When during the war we wanted the warlike assistance of the Arabs, we pledged ourselves to give them their independence. I know that successive Governments have said that pledge was not definite, and that they have shielded themselves behind successive correspondence... It is quire certain in my opinion that the Arabs were promised independence".

The Arabs did not find out about the Balfour Declaration until 1918 and in order to minimise the Arab fears on November 7th 1918; Lord Allenby then in command of the British Army in Palestine, had the following Proclamation posted up in every village throughout the country:

> "The war.. is to assure the complete and final liberation of the people so long oppressed by the Turks and the establishment of National Governments and administration deriving their authority from the initiative and free desire of the native population. They are far from wishing to impose any form of Government on the people against their will".

At the time 90% of the population were Arabs in Palestine and thus this statement was a clear indication that if the British left Palestine, then the administration would fall to the Arabs. Despite this, the Zionists pressed ahead with the "absurd scheme" and the Zionist Organisation planned a draft before the Peace Conference on February 7th 1919, the way having been prepared through America during the Presidency of Wilson. The Jewish Menorah Journal in America in its issue of February 1928 stated:

> "The objective was not merely to maintain the esteem and willing co-operation of President Wilson himself, but to permeate every avenue of his administration and the whole British Service in this country, with a friendly understanding of Zionism, so there was no fear of the outcome of the Peace Conference."

It has never been understood why so many Jews should have surrounded the British Government in the past, however I trust the background is laid bare here. Mr Lloyd George a past Prime Minister whose immediate associates were largely composed of leading Jews and Zionists, found himself under considerable pressure over a homeland for the Jews: " the high contracting parties should recognise the historic title of the Jews to Palestine". Thus the claim of the Jews to an independent state of Israel was being claimed on Biblical legitimacy. This did not prevent Article 22 of the Covenant of the League of Nations stating:

> "Certain communities formerly belonging to the Turkish Empire have reached a stage of development where their assistance as independent nations can be provisionally recognised subject to the rendering of administrative advice and assistance by a Mandatory until such times as they are able to stand alone. The wishes of these Communities must be a principal consideration in the selection of the Mandatory".

The Arabs of Palestine were given the right to administer their own country though provisionally under a Mandatory power. At the San Remo Conference of the Allies in April 1920 the Mandate for Palestine and Mesopotamia was given to Great Britain and it was decided that the Balfour Declaration should be included in the Mandate for Palestine; a complete reversal of the plan incorporated in Article 22 of the covenant of the League of Nations, and also in conflict with Article 20, which stated:

> "The members of he league severally agree that this Covenant is accepted as abrogating all obligations of understandings inter se which are inconsistent with the terms thereof, and solemnly undertake that they will not hereafter enter into any engagement inconsistent with the terms thereof. In case any member of the League shall, before becoming a member of the League, have undertaken any obligations inconsistent with the terms of this covenant, it shall be the duty of such member to take immediate steps to procure its release from such obligations".

476

The Balfour Declaration having been made before Great Britain became a member of the league and being inconsistent with Article 22 of the Covenant should therefore have been considered abrogated. The League of Nations violated the Covenant when on July 24th 1922, it confirmed the Draft Mandate, which included the Balfour Declaration drawn up on January 5th 1921, and was not endorsed by Parliament. It was pointed out: "The Mandate never received the Parliamentary sanction of Great Britain, the only Parliamentary expression of opinion being that of the House of Lords, which voted against it". Thus the outcome of this was that the Arabs having fought with the Allies found that the land had been offered as a national home to an alien   race – the Jews. The first of many conflicts in the area as a direct result of this arose in Palestine when in the spring of 1919-20 the Arabs revolted and this culminated in the Jaffa riots of May 1921. If the Zionists had wanted to promote a peaceful co-existence with the Arabs, then it would have been more advisable to keep a low and diplomatic profile, however Zionists chose to fuel the antagonism when Dr Weizmann head of the Zionist Federation in America stated in an address delivered on September 21st 1919 that:

> "We said we desired to create in Palestine such conditions, political and economical and administrative that in a given time, as short as possible, Palestine should become as Jewish as England is English or America is American".

On a recent television programme I heard one Jewish woman complaining that the British or French would not like their country to be taken over by people from another country! This shows the extent to which the background to Palestine has been obliterated in media, such that man fights man and becomes a tool to the World Order. Further c. 1919 Dr Eder, Chairman of the Zionist Commission in Jerusalem stated:

> "There can be only one national home in Palestine and that is a Jewish one, and no equality of partnership between Jews and Arabs, but a Jewish predominance as soon as the members of that race are sufficiently increased".

Very naturally this aroused anger in the Arabs and the Colonial Office for Great Britain issued statements in June of 1922, hoping to play down these comments and others by the 'smudging over' of statements: they (the Colonial Office), would "draw attention to the fact that the terms of the Declaration referred to, do not contemplate that Palestine as a whole should be converted into a Jewish national home, but that such a home should be founded in Palestine". Exactly where the British (or the 13th tribe?) intended the Jews to make their home within

Palestine was left undefined, thus creating confusion and ultimately conflict. If one was being kind, one might describe it as a monumental 'cock up', however that appears to be far too generous and one might perceive the hand of the World Order behind all of this. In fact the Jews rapidly not only populated the area, but also became prominent in positions of power. Sir William Joynson-Hicks (later Lord Brentford) spoke of these violations of rights when he stated:

> "The Arabs decline with the utmost determination to come under Jewish rule. They see a High Commissioner a Jew, his private Secretary a Jew, the head and second of the legal department...Jews, the head of the contract department a Jew and many more, we are denying to the Arabs the right of self-determination".

The Jews at that time were not united on the question of Zionism (political branch of Jewry), indeed before the conflict had started, the Arab and Jew had lived in the area together peacefully. The large influx of Jewish immigrants and violation of Arab rights however was to become a major factor in further upset and ultimately the wars in the area. The Zionist also acquired large tracts of land in Palestine, thus depriving the Arab of his livelihood, when Arab farmers had tilled the land for centuries and now found themselves evicted from their own land. Large commercial concerns became Zionist owned and monopolies became a direct method of oppression e.g. in 1929 The Dead Sea Concession with its vast mineral wealth was given to the Russian Jew, Moise Novomeisky.

Thus against a background of World Revolution involving The British Revolution, The French Revolution and Russian Revolution, all of which were directed by secret groups and were not as is generally believed the will of the people; comes that curious Declaration of Balfour, who was surrounded by names generally associated with the World Order, such as Rothschild. There is no doubt that the Jews as extensively covered by the historian Nesta Webster (cited) were tied up very intricately in these Revolutions. When in 1930 The Shaw Report and The Hope Simpson Report together with two white papers issued by the Labour Government in Britain on their policy in Palestine were published, a picture of the flagrant abuse of Arab rights emerged: 29.4% of the rural Arab families in the villages became landless and the economic depression was attributed to the high level of immigration. The Labour Government's stated intention of reviewing immigration laws, were greeted with outrage from the Jews the world over who spoke of "British betrayal". In fact the Zionist plan was to outnumber by immigration the Arabs and thus possess the land. The Labour Government inexplicably backed down and a Conservative paper warned of: "setting the powerful international force of Jewry against us". This may well have been a referral to the ultimate secret hand that moves groups 12 and 13, or those who had directed the Revolutions towards their own ends. The notorious document The *Protocols of the Learned Elders of Zion* was in circulation and which allegedly outlined the goal of a Jewish secret hierarchy to rule the world. Whilst the Protocols were hotly debated in fact many of the points or goals in the Protocols have materialised. Theodor Herzl the founder of political Zionism stated in 1897, following the French Revolution in Europe that:" It may take five years or fifty years, but the Jewish state is a fact now". On November 29th 1947, the United Nations General Assembly passed Resolution 181 (ii), which called for the partition of Palestine and the creation of a Jewish State. Public sympathy was at an all time high as the details of the Holocaust emerged, co-incidentally or not.

The birth of Israel did not end the problems of the Jews who considered their survival as threatened in the 50's and 60's and developed the "periphery plan" for survival amongst the emerging independent Arab States, which involved Israel forming allegiances with countries bordering or on the periphery of the Arab states in The Middle East, e.g. Turkey, Ethiopia and Iran. This strategy over the years meant ties with factions seeking protection as a minority among the Arab Moslem world e.g. Phalangists in Lebanon, royalists in Yemen, rebels in Southern Sudan and Kurds in Iraq, the Lebanese Maronites and the Druze, who were seeking independence. Often the United States became Israel's biggest ally and acted in concert or behind the scenes through the CIA. Israeli policy was one of intervention in inter-Arab conflicts preventing Arab unity and stability, channelling the Arab energies away from Israel into internal rivalries, this preventing an Arab coalition against Israel; allowing her to develop a military fighting machine and ultimately nuclear weapons. Israel supported right wing regimes and was opposed to any decolonisation, which might shift the power from the right wing (World Order and 12 and 13) to the left. This policy resulted in the invasions of Egypt in October 1956 a joint operation of France, Britain and Israel in an attempt to destroy the radical Nasser regime. The Nationalization of the Suez canal by Egypt in a final act of Independence, meant regional colonial powers took steps to reverse that in the so called Suez Crisis, Israel was a willing partner and Ben Gurion himself spoke of "the Third Kingdom of Israel" and vowed never to return Sinai to Egypt. After the Khomeni regime took over Iran, Israel who once was the ally of the Shah continued supplying arms to the regime. The U.S. gave its full approval in order that a channel of arms to the Iranian military could be kept open and aid Iran in the war against Iraq in 1980. Iraq was an Arab enemy and the U.S. became directly involved in 1985 and 1986 with the sale of arms, which led to a major political crisis in the United States. The Iran Contra affair as it was known, referred to Israel's connection with the Islamic Republic of Iran and sale of arms continued by Israel despite the disclosures – business as usual. According to one

Israeli expert, there were forces in Israel that were interested in strengthening not only Iran, but all radical forces in the Middle East, to prevent a peace settlement which was a strategic disadvantage to Israel. Here we have a sad truth about the causation of wars and conflict, there is always a *third party* often hidden, which *promotes* conflict to realise their own ends. God's chosen people - the Israeli's, in fact had a great deal to do with much of the conflict in the Middle East during the past decades as part of her foreign periphery policy. Israel would survive, but at what cost? Further Israel entered the Third World legitimacy fight, hoping to outmanoeuvre the Arabs, falsely presenting herself as a young developing nation with David Ben Gurion as the Gandhi or Nkrumah, what was omitted was that Israel had been created through the dispossession of the native population and thus her colonial background omitted. The political programme of Zionism towards Jewish Imperialism has always sought refuge behind the accusation of anti-Semitism. After the Holocaust, it became impossible to question the policy of the Jews, particularly where justifications are sought in biblical texts. As Gandhi was to accurately comment in the late 30's when diagnosing the problems in Palestine as between Jews as settlers and Arabs as natives, he stated unequivocally that Palestine belonged to the Arab natives and that their rights took precedence over any other claims, he further stated:" The cry for the national home for the Jews does not have much appeal to me. The sanctions for it are sought in The Bible and the tenacity with which the Jews have hankered after a return to Palestine. Why should they not, like other peoples of the Earth, make their country their home where they are born and where they earn their livelihood? Palestine belongs to the Arabs in the sense that England belongs to the English and France to the French. It is wrong and inhuman to impose the Jews on the Arabs. What is going on in Palestine today cannot be justified by a moral code of conduct".

In fact Israel supported right wing regimes even though those regimes such as in Guatemala, Nicaragua and El Salvador were utterly despotic. Israeli intelligence advisers stationed in El Salvador in the 70's and 80's worked with the notorious ANSEAL death squads in the setting up of computerised intelligence systems similar to the one in Guatemala where guerrilla sources claimed the computerised systems monitored 80% of the population, providing names for the right wing death squads. This is a matter of history and the Israeli involvement, was confirmed by Matityahu Peled in the Knesset in 1985. Israel was to further support Gjarcia Meza the leader of the Junta and representative of the cocaine dealers when he came to power in Bolivia in 1950. Through this policy of maintaining right wing regimes and preventing decolonialisation, Israel supported the survival of the white regime in Rhodesia and helped in substantial ways, including counter insurgency operations in the 70's. This policy was also extended to south Africa and when Balthazar Johannes ("John")

Vorster the Prime Minister of the Republic of south Africa visited Israel in April 1976, he was taken to the compulsory first stop of any dignitary, the Holocaust memorial in Jerusalem. As a Nazi collaborator, according to Israeli Law, he should have been arrested once he put foot on Israeli soil, he was instead warmly received. Israel played a crucial role in the survival of the apartheid regime in South Africa and the Beast of Soweto Rooi 'Rus' Swarepoel the Chief Interrogator of the 1964 Rivonia Trial that put ANC leader Nelson Mandela and others in prison for life and founder of Kaevoet the notorious Namibian Counterinsurgency unit, was an honoured and welcome visitor to Israel in the 1970's. One American journalist described the special link the Israelis had with the South African Afrikaners: "To Afrikaners, the parallels are as obvious as they are embarrassing to the Israelis, they (the Israelis) are essentially a white Europeanised people who have carved their own nation out of a land inhabited by hostile non-European majorities that would destroy the two nations if the Afrikaners and the Israeli listened to the United Nations or world opinions. Their religions are similar, each being a 'chosen people'". In fact both America and Israel profited by arm sales through world conflicts and whilst Israel survived, there is no doubt that the setting up of a State of Israel in 1947 was part of the battles of 12 and 13.

The Jews see their justification in claiming Israel in Deut: 3:18, where God's command to the Israelites was to go in and possess the land. However it is significant that the floor of the Summer Smoking Room at Cardiff Castle depicting a plan for a Universal and Religious political kingdom, illustrated Jerusalem as part of the centre map. This floor was laid in the 19th century and was I concluded *Scottish* Rite Freemasonry and presumably 13th tribe. There is a hymn dating to the Victorian period of Britain, where a line reads: "And was Jerusalem builded here in England's green and pleasant land.." This must refer to *Scotland as the Holy Land* and presumably accounts for the Zionist organisation of the B'nai B'nrith rounding up all the books by Comyns Beaumont, which state that Scotland in Britain is the true Holy Land: further 'Jerusalem' appears in the map at the centre of The Summer Smoking room floor design at Cardiff Castle Wales, which I concluded was Scottish Rite Freemasonry and a plan for A World Order, which included Europe. There is said to be another version of the prophetic Apocalypse, which differs from the vulgate (*The Battle of The Trees*) and must I assume refer to the variant version of the end of times, according to the 13th tribe: where presumably Britain is Jerusalem and the land of the family of Jesus. Surprisingly the hymn "Jerusalem" was not allowed in a church wedding ceremony in 2001 by the local vicar who stated it was "too nationalistic". Thus the idea emerges of *two Jerusalem's* and the inevitable two secret groups of 12 tribes (Palestine as the Holy Land) and the 13 th tribe (Scotland as the holy Land). One perceives a manipulated duality in this and the seeds of future conflict with two prophecies, two tribes and two kings – but one future world war. I also strongly suspect that New Age literature is being manipulated, such that elements of the story are emerging and one group if not the top group that pulls strings on both 12 and 13 has already determined which script they will follow. The Jews and Britons appear to be somewhat the victims in this story, which is encoded into The Bible.

It is claimed that the Arabs have no scriptural claim over Jerusalem, whereas the Jews claim their authority for ownership of Jerusalem in Palestine in Biblical texts. In *Zechariah 12:2-3*, God or the patriarchal God of the Jews states: "Behold I will make Jerusalem a cup of trembling unto all the people round about when they shall be in siege both against Judah and against Jerusalem". It is not absolutely clear (at least to the author), which Jerusalem is being referred to here! The text goes on to state: " and in that day I will make Jerusalem a burdensome stone for all people: all that burden themselves with it shall be cut to pieces, though all the people of the earth be gathered together against it". As always the twin-bladed axe, which referred to the Twin Kings, could as in myth cut both ways here. However it appears to the author that the two groups of 12 and 13 far from joining in peace appear to be battling out some private battle once again, on the chessboard and politics of earth following a prophecy. A ruler in *Ezekiel 38/39* is prophesied to lead this alliance of nations against Israel or Britain again one cannot be sure: "The word of the Lord came to me, son of man, set your face **against Gog and the land of Magog**, the chief prince of (Rosh – Russia) Meshech and Tubal and prophesy against him and say, Thus says the Lord God; behold **I am against you O Gog**, Chief prince of (Rosh) Mesheck and Tubal; I will put hooks in your jaws, and bring you forth and all your army...Persia, Ethiopia, Libya, Gomer (Europe), Togarmah...and I will bring you upon the mountains of Israel ...You shall fall upon the mountains of Israel, you and all that is with you" (*Author's emphasis*). The reference to "hooks in your jaws" however indicates the fish and the connection of the Goddess to the sea; the Jews were promised: "no more sea" and thus this is the 12th tribe version against the 13th tribe.

I have already pointed out that Gog and GogMagog is specifically related to the 13th tribe and Britain and here we see an illusive threat from the 12 tribes, who evidently mean to betray the 13th tribe, whilst the Britton sits in the middle of the augment, not knowing as with the Israeli people anything about this particular battle. What does a Biblical prophecy matter, the still unconvinced might ask? – It matters since the Third Party Law states that contrary to popular belief, it takes three to make an argument or war and the top group that pulls strings on both 12 and 13 will decide which way the prophecy will go. **This battle will result in a nuclear war and the 'script' is the biblical prophesy and plan being followed**

to the letter. The question becomes which of the two 'scripts' or prophecies is the top group following? One cannot deny that the 'script' *is* followed, after all the State of Israel was founded on the 'script'. In The Bible, there are three geographical areas relating to the prophecies about the return of Christ: Israel, Russia and Europe. President Clinton failed to achieve a new agreement with President Putin in Russia and destabilisation of the Middle East has also occurred in the death of President Hafez al-Assad of Syria, where his son Bashar will need time to establish his authority, which may be under threat. Former president Assad hindered a peace agreement between Israel and the Palestinians by his insistence that Israel return Golan and all the territory captured in 1967. Lebanon is still virtually controlled by Syria and Israel and the Palestinians (Arafat) are still further from peace now Clinton has gone, with escalating tension between the two sides. Into this volatile pot comes Saddam Hussein of Iraq, who despite the genocide policy of U.S. and British air-raids calls the USA the Great Satan, meanwhile thousands of Iraqi children are dying. Saddam Hussein's real venom is against Israel and he recognises that there is growing international support for action to resolve the crisis of Israel's "occupation" of Jerusalem and control of the West Bank territory taken in the 1967 war. Yaser Arafat has Parkinson's disease and will not be in control of the Palestinians much longer and it may be that the next leader will take a harder view, which can only be based on the ongoing atrocities in the region by both sides. The Palestinians may call for a Palestinian State with Jerusalem as its capital, although escalation of conflict between the two sides this year (2001) only reflects the ongoing tragedy. The proposed site of the Parliament building for the Palestinian State is in the east Jerusalem suburb, Abu Dis, only half a mile from the Temple area (Dome of the Rock).

Into this volatile pot place those magicians at the head of the World Order on both sides (12 and 13) who rabidly follow the religious texts and quote them to provide the justification for aggressive world politics. Each side bent on its own realisation of the prophecies and each one trying to outwit the other in the most secret of games. However as I have pointed out, this 'script' has been written and followed before as man disappears down the same route and its inevitable consequences. According to 'script' or *Ezekiel 38* and his wheels or cycles, where he tried to keep the woman out of the story, the King of the North attacks Israel. Some might interpret this as Russia and some might return to *The Old Testament*, where the King of the North was Syria (Assyria). However that might have been so in the last production of Planet Theatre Earth, but this cycle is unique; in so far as the Bull-Minos cult stole The Holy Grail. Thus in this cycle, the King of the North may well be European Union, or 13th tribe. The other Twin King is of course the 12 tribes and Israel. It might be questioned whether the bombardment of Iraq is due to some prophecy or other, where

Saddam Hussein in his alleged weapons of destruction programme, hopes to fulfil the prophecy against Israel: tricky times at the end of the 'script', just before the curtain comes down, with everyone vying for Messiaship, including the alternative fraternity! Excuse me if I stick a stiletto and silver high heel into this large pie, which appears to be one way of resolving the last Act, after all there are some who would like to get to "Paradise on Earth" and sit on the beach and get some fun!

Returning to the Indian epics and the war of two kings, it occurs that the two kings or groups have fought this battle for chosen one status before and the mention of Jerusalem as the place which God has chosen, surely dwindles into the psychotic cycle on both sides of 'I must be right or I die'. Can't they both be right? – apparently not, they would rather drag this world to the final curtain, than admit they were following a 'script' that has absolutely no relevance to the majority audience, or the reality out on the street. A 'script' that for the main has been channelled from the GWL or etheric Masters and where the UVG120 crystal is even acknowledged as lying at the feet of God in the Revelations text, which is the 'script'! The cult who stole the Holy Grail never understood the lesson they were being taught they only saw power and wealth along with control through manipulation of the Grid. Instead of recognising the Grid as a trap they channelled off past events and labelled them prophecies for future events, which the audience then saw as God's fulfilment of promises: Here lies the insanity! These guys are still back there fighting a game of kings, which in this cycle has taken significances of The Holy Grail, which was never intended to be locked up in this battle. Whilst the Arabs and the Jews fight it out, there is a real cause for concern that this battle for Jerusalem will provide the final justification for all out nuclear war, or a war of two kings. The most humanitarian and unimaginable gift that the Arabs and Jews could give to humanity would be peace - otherwise they both become dupes to a higher power that has sought to destroy humanity.

The patriarchal God of the 12 tribes Himself stated that as long as the sun and moon (coded terms for 13 th tribe) endured, Israel will never cease to be a nation before Him – *Jeremiah 31: 35-36*. Thus whilst Christians and Messianic Jews look forward to a Third World War or Armageddon and the fulfilment of the prophecies or 'script' including *Jeremiah 16* and *Ezekiel 38*, one can only reach the few, who realise that there was always going to be a much bigger story at the end, and that end is by no means a certainty of "Paradise". If one had to endure the next cycle, it will be *extremely tough* and will not be "Paradise", but hell under the "monsters", that march over that "rainbow bridge" – a Magnetic Reversal. The Christians and Messianic Jews must not be saddled with guilt, for this was a very complex story and unless you had followed it, through the endless convoluted trails of 'shape-shifting' deception, then it would not have been discernable – cunning fellow "666". The only way he will win is to set man against man in war, reflecting the dualistic battle of two kings and the duality inherent in his own mind resulting from a Magnetic Reversal; thus it is for that reason alone man must find peace: and in *The Battle of The Trees*, there were quite a few documents that referred to "Peace" as part of The Holy Grail, apart from the warnings of the Fatima Miracle.

G. W. Bush as the new President of America has threatened a major downgrading of American relations with Europe, where he declared in June 2001 that the number of annual U.S. – EU summits would be halved. Amid growing strains in the Atlantic Alliance he unilaterally decided that one of the twice-yearly meetings between the President and European leaders should be cancelled. This would not be merely Bush's decision, no - this is made at a much higher level and is the exact scenario of non-communication and miss-understanding created by non-communication and third party conflict that the anti-Christ works so well in, achieving his own goals and his ultimate goal of an all-out nuclear war. President Bush's administration is already at odds with European leaders over the proposed Euro Army, his dumping of the Kyoto agreement on the environment and his plan for a 'Son of Star Wars' missile defence, which even by implication has religious connotations. The new rebuff to Europe heightened fears that the main focus of American foreign policy and military firepower will switch to Asia and the Pacific thus undermining the traditional link with Europe. Meanwhile it cannot be co-incidence that Europe is forming its own army and this squaring up of two kings is really just another religious battle in the war of 12 and 13 the terrible Twin Kings. Asia of course was another land mass mentioned by name at the centre of the summer smoking room floor design at Cardiff Castle. Whilst Bush and his superiors no doubt maintain that a new defence strategy is required to shield America and its allies from nuclear attack by "rogue states" is this not a discrete reference to a Federal United States of Europe, or European Union? The recent manipulated event with China was a mere illusion one assumes to create the atmosphere and politics of fear, that such a defence system is required. Once again we see just how petty these twin kings are and their attempts to keep this battle secret – after all if this game was known, what power is left to them.

The EU Ambassadors in Washington claimed that the downgrading of EU relations with America was a case of 'By doing less, we'll do it better', which sounds like a phrase of our cunning fellow "666" in fact its a recipe for disaster, where low communication inevitably leads to misunderstandings. Ivo Daalder, who was President Clinton's director of European affairs, warned that a marked shift in relations is being prepared by the White House. President Bush would not alone make that decision; it comes from some hidden and secret group who , are deciding the agenda and policy. One EU Ambassador to the U.S., warned of damaging repercussions for Nato and stated: "unless presented with great care, this decision to move to one summit a year could meet with an unfortunate reaction in Europe". "Arnaud de Borchgrave, is currently the Chief Executive of United Press International. He is journalist with editorial appointments on *Newsweek, Insight* magazine and the *Washington Times*, which is controlled by the Unification Church of Dr Sun myung Moon. De Borchgrave has extensive experience of Indo-China, the Congo, North Africa, the Middle East and Europe. He was educated in the United Kingdom, he is a cousin of the Belgian Rothschild's, a friend of Dr Henry Kissinger, and he served in the Royal Navy from 1942-46. He is also a member of the Council on Foreign Relations (C.F.R.), and moves in those obscure, smoky circles connected with the Special Operations Executive (S.O.E.), the K.G.B and Mossad. He is a senior adviser to the Centre for Strategic and International Studies. He is associated with the hard Right Wing Israeli politician Ariel Sharon through Dr Joseph Churba, who's international Security Council, is also sponsored by Dr Sun Myung Moon. Arnaud de Borchegrave is therefore well qualified to assess the growing problems that face the United States at the centre of World power, when even its own borders are no longer sacrosanct against the on-going process of Globalisation. The following text has been adapted from what Arnaud de Borchegrave wrote on the 11th September 2000, under the title "Opposition to U.S. Imperialism Growing Worldwide":

> Is the United States emerging as a de facto world government and the rest of the world as the opposition party? Sounds nuts, but that is how a growing number of world leaders are beginning to see their roles as they search for ways to counter-balance American omnipotence and omnipresence. When the soviet empire imploded and the United States emerged victorious from a four-decade Cold War, Washington assumed that the whole world was applauding. But behind the cheers were countless millions of disappointed militants throughout the developing world, and not an insignificant number in the developed world as well. They laid low through most of the 1990s and they are now crawling out of the woodwork. There is much for the 43rd President to ponder.

The French are not alone in warning about the dangers of the "hyper power", as they refer to the world's only superpower. France is crafting a new ideology that is designed to spearhead a covert global opposition movement to United States hegemony" (*On Target Vol. 30 No. 12 2nd December, 2000*).

The above issue of *On Target* went on to say: " There are two different opposition groups. The "Official Opposition" consists of France, Russia, China, and several European Union members only too willing to let France do the running. They resist the colossus of Washington, for example, by opposing and then breaching sanctions against Iraq; engaging in competitive diplomacy in the Balkans and the Middle East; weakening united States control of the international financial system; undermining America's global crusade for democracy (sic!) and the economic "neo-liberalism" of the Anglo-Saxon world. The second opposition is a blend of neo-Marxism and the autocratic regimes of the developing world: Iraq, Iran, Libya, Cuba, Venezuela and their silent admirers. From the Battle for Seattle in November, 1999 (on the occasion of the World Trade Organisation Conference) to similar cyber-organized demonstrations and riots against the International Monetary Fund (I.M.F.), and the World Bank in Washington and Prague; to the visit of Venezuelan strongman Hugo Chavez to Baghdad, the first head of state to confer with Saddam Hussein since the end of the Gulf War 10 years ago. To Castro's state visit to Venezuela to anoint Chavez as his successor as Latin America's trouble-maker in chief, the common thread is a worldwide movement against what they perceive to be America's winner-take-all strategy".

This development of anti-Americanism is just too predictable to be anything other than policy that is filtered down from the super-elite, the unelected Masters or the so-called 'Hidden Government of the World'. It is this elite that has throughout the ages controlled ruling bodies and national governments and their electorates, who were stripped of meaningful control over their own destinies and the environment. The United Nations, the World Bank and International Monetary Fund (I.M.F.) are policy makers, spawned after the 1939-45 war, and about which the electorate is encouraged to know very little. The same mix of international power brokers who control policy are found as attendees of such groups as The World Economic Forum at Davos, in Switzerland, the Round Table network, the Mont Pelerin Society, also Swiss-based, the Aspen Institute, in Colorado, North America, the Centre for Policy Studies, the Ditchley Foundation, the British Atlantic Committee, the Council on Foreign Relations (C.F.R.), the Royal Institute of International Affairs (R.I.I.A.), the Trilateral Commission and the Bilderberg Group. Despite that men such as Peter Mandelson, who was the architect of New Labour (Socialist political party in the U.K.) rise to power with Tony Blair becoming Prime Minister are members of the Bilderberger group, no questions are answered on precisely what role these secret groups play in defining policy within the globalisation plan.

Lord Carrington and Lord (Denis) Healey are founder members of The Bilderberg group along with members such as Sir Edward heath, the late Enoch Powell (a recognised racist), Margaret Thatcher, the late john Smith (past leader of the labour party in the U.K.), the current Chancellor in the U.K. Gordon

Brown, past Prime Minister William Hague and even Bill Clinton past President of the United States, was given the 'look over' before his election. The pro-European Kenneth Clark as potential leader of the British Conservative party in the U.K. is thought to have taken over from Lord Healey is a regular participant. However questions in Parliament concerning the nature of the Bilderberg group have been continually rebuffed. I have proposed in this thesis that the group is essentially 13th tribe, with its Greek background and further proposed that Bohemian Grove members (including the current President of America G.W. Bush) are twelfth tribe with an Egyptian background. This is a recipe for a disaster in the making! All secret groups act on the interlocking "circles" or concentric rings, so prominently displayed in Greek archaeological remains and at Cardiff Castle Wales U.K. The plan for a world order with a political and religious system is portrayed at the centre of the Floor design at the castle and thus it would be naive and foolish to disclaim that religion is still not a pivotal justification in this battle of two sides. Indeed the One Dollar note of America displays both political and religious aims on the left and right sides of the obverse side of the note, presumably with left (political and Communistic) and right (religious and 13th tribe) holding their own significance.

Monsanto the 'Life Science' multi-national company, represented at a past Bilderberger meeting is more evidence of the power of the multinational conglomerates the Transnational Corporations (T.N.C.S) and the corporate Global Power Brokers, the Establishment Elite and their ability to pull strings on national Governments and their policies. The influence extends nationally and internationally through boardrooms of the banking systems and multinational conglomerates and encompasses all profitable fields including the Pharmaceutical industry, chemical and agri-chemical industries, through to the research institutions and funding companies of Biotechnology, right into government circles, such that in the case of genetically modified food, it can be pressed on the electorate despite people have persistently made it clear that they do not want genetically modified food. If the West has little power to resist governments that no longer listen to the electorate, then the Third World, held in the pincers of the predatory World Order have very little chance of not succumbing to economic pressure to accept this altered food. Pressure has emerged from the United States to impose hormone treated American beef and genetically modified agricultural produce on a reluctant European market. The major "Life sciences" companies with interest in food, agriculture, pharmaceuticals and biotechnology are Du Pont and Monsanto in the United States, Bayer and Hoechst in Germany, Novartis in Switzerland, Rhone-Poulenc in France, and I.C.I spin-off Zeneca (now Zeneca-Astra), in the U.K. In 1999 the Bilderberg meeting, held in Portugal, was attended again by two American directors of Goldman Sachs, the Chief Executive Officer of Novartis, and James

D. Wolfensohn. The 1997 list of members of the Rockefeller's Trilateral Commission included two united states directors of the British Government-linked Goldman Sachs, directors of the food, grain and seed conglomerates Archer Daniels Midland, and Cargill, the editor of The Economist, owned by Evelyn de Rothschild, John Roper of the Royal Institute of International Affairs (R.I.I.A.), Peter Sutherland of British Petroleum and Goldman Sachs, formerly of G.A.T.T and the World Trade Organisation, and British Government Ministers Lord Gilbert of Dudley, Minister for Defence Procurement, and Lord Simon of Highbury, formerly of British Petroleum and Goldman Sachs, and also linked to the R.I.I.A. The 1998 meeting of the Bilderberg Group, held at the Turnberry Hotel in Scotland, was attended by the Group Chief Executive of British Petroleum, the Secretary of State for Defence, George Robertson (U.K.) and the Secretary-General of Nato (interestingly enough, twelve months before the *planned* campaign in the Balkans), Peter Sutherland, the Chief Executive Officer of Novartis, and James D. Wofensohn of the World Bank. The 1999 Sir Jonathon Porritt of Forum for the Future, Robert Shapiro of Monsanto and Peter Mandelson British Minister Without Portfolio attended the Bilderberg meeting and as the 'weakest link' in this chain inevitably connects to the Millennium Dome and Icon in Britain, with all its significances of 13th tribe. It is now widely accepted that moves to depose Prime Minister Margaret Thatcher began after the 1989 Bilderberg meeting as a consequence of her anti-European "Bruges" speech. As *On Target* pointed out "Those who have observed the almost fanatical determination of Prime Minister Blair to force the pace of the unilateral and illegal United States-Nato campaign in the Balkans, his determination to enforce a settlement in Ireland against all the portents, his obsessive association with United States President Clinton, and his equally determined attempts to enforce acceptance of Genetic Engineering, may fairly wonder if he has been in some way psychologically or mentally 'programmed'". However it appears that the programme or hidden agenda here of the Bilderberg group is really the war of two kings or 13th and 12 tribes, with the new President of America being obviously not a member of Clinton's old group. More warning bells! China proposed a treaty in June 2001 to ban weapons in space because of what it called the imminent danger from U.S. missile defence plans. However as sure as night follows day the MRC case will if allowed, cause a Third World War on this Planet, simply because he has no space-time reality – he is still fighting a war back then – a war of two kings, which he has brought forward into present time and which he plays out with Theatre Earth as his stage: unless man recognises this story he stands to become the audience to the greatest show on Earth – a Magnetic Reversal, where he will be downloaded with the entire events of Planet Earth from www-com/grid before sitting down once again to Act. I: Plant the vine - a story of two kings.

Lawmakers in the U.S. backed President George Bush in August 2001 by approving a sweeping ban on human cloning. Why then should Britain legalise cloning and in doing so become the pariah of the civilised world? The answer may lie in the meetings of the Bilderberger group and its inclusion of Life Science company Monsanto representatives and prominent New Labour "Prince of Darkness" – Peter Mandleson credited with the rise of New Labour and Tony Blair to power. The legislation on cloning was not even accorded the dignity of an Act of Parliament, but was smuggled through as an amendment to a statutory instrument, without proper debate. Having rammed it through the Commons last December and the Lords in January, Tony Blair was quite indifferent to the dismay it provoked throughout Europe and America. Whilst the rest of the world saw this as a giant leap towards the dehumanising of mankind and Britain was widely accused of excluding herself from European civilization, is this not a similar world reaction to the Foot and Mouth crises and BSE, which was laid at the door of Britain? France under President Chirac called for an international ban on all human cloning and other European nations are to follow suite. Tony Blair with his wife Cherie are allegedly professed Christians and yet divorce those beliefs from actions subordinated to political and economic considerations, which may well have more to do with orders from above and the "hidden hand that moves" or the 'face of two sides' than the spinning top and head of Tony Blair. Arguments that morality must not be permitted to inhibit research or the evolving front of science are mere justifications for what the author perceives as a policy directive from above. That policy directive may have been cloaked as the political and economic advantages for Britain in staying at the forefront of world science, however the author smells a large pie and betrayal here. The majority of Britons find it abhorrent that the creation of hundreds of thousands of embryos purely for experimentation since the human Fertilisation and Embryology Act 1990 and yet as with the subject of abortion in Britain this issue has hardly warranted public debate. The Warnock Committee was persuaded to rule in favour of embryo research on the basis of cost-benefit advances in medicine, which were perceived as justification for cannibalistic dismemberment of the unborn for the benefit of providing sick adults with spare parts. There would be no objection to taking a cell from the adult or even cells from the growing adult as a child for cloning purposes and then storing such material for their OWN use: however there is every objection to USING ANOTHER to supply spare body parts. The truth is that there have been few, if any, medical advances as a result of a decade of such experiments, let alone practical benefits for patients. An enquiry into the Foot and Mouth crisis in Britain has been denied, just as a debate on cloning has been denied, to avoid ostensibly an embarrassing audit, however in reality this is merely another facet of the 'no questions asked, or answered' with regard to POLICY. The arguments for cloning like the arguments for culling animals in the Foot and Mouth crisis have been forwarded by 'experts' and scientists who for the main represent either government (policy) or large commercial interests including the Life Science companies in the case of cloning. The British political, medical and pharmaceutical establishments presented a united front to the public in Britain, who no longer care about political issues as was witnessed in the last political poll, where more than a third of the country did not vote. The Archbishops of Canterbury and York, the Cardinal Archbishops of Westminster and Glasgow, Evangelicals and Baptists, Free Church and Greek Orthodox spokesmen, the Chief Rabbi, leaders of the Moslems and Sikhs all requested a meeting with Prime Minister Tony Blair, but were ignored four times in their request.

The Oxford philosopher Professor Sir Michael Dummett is on record as stating that the strongest objection to cloning is the possibility of the creation of a Western elite, genetically perfected, which could lord it over the rest of humanity. Such a programme not only existed with the Nazi eugenics programme, but as I have pointed out the Nazi party it appears were puppeted by an Elite, who pulled strings on Europeans with the final goal of a World Order and a Federal Europe in mind: further that Elite has for millennia believed in their own god-like rightness and superiority. The mind of the World Order finds no moral quarrel with the idea of usurious sacrifice of the individual, to a cause and justified as a means to the end. When the lies of history are revealed, the World Wars, Revolutions and even the Holocaust may be proven to have reaped their horror under such thinking (incidentally my experience of Scientology was based on such thinking). Daniel Johnson as associate editor of *The Daily Telegraph* wrote in *The Spectator (July 2001)*:

> "Only in Britain do politicians suppose that it is 'utilitarian' to sacrifice the individual for some notional social end. Can it be right that, to satisfy the **primeval urge of a self-selected elite to see their genes perpetuated**, the entire natural order should be inverted? And so the British, despite their instinctive revulsion for human cloning, acquiesce in our sordid isolation. We are indeed leading the world; leading it in an unheard-of abdication of responsibility, the hubris of inhumanity. The present generation has no right to exploit the next, merely to prolong it own longevity. The selfish gene has become a selfish genie, now too late to rebottle. Britain is the laboratory in which posterity is sacrificed for the **illusion of immortality**" (*author's emphasis*).

It would be wrong however to assume that the British people have any say in this matter, just as it would be wrong to assume that the average Jew in Israel has any say in policy (dramatization) determined by a World Order. Embryo research is merely with genetic cloning, religious wars and revolutions a dramatization of the past of the MRC case where actual sacrifice including children occurred. The story goes back at least to the use of the interrex or

491

sacrificial child victim to maintain the rule of a solar king in Greece at the time of the Religious Revolution, where the belief and truth of immortality or re-incarnation was lost and absorbed into the secret groups principally of the 13th tribe. The longevity and giant-like stature of *the body* in a prior magnetic cycle and subsequent loss of spiritual awareness of man as his **immortal spirit** transferred the aberration to hereditary monarchy, blood-lines and the self-perpetuation of an elite through a genetic line. The aberration that presented itself in Minoan Greece and which saw The Holy Grail message (re-incarnation/immortality of the spirit) and knowledge of the trap and hidden science withdrawn into the secret groups of the Elite was itself also a dramatization of an earlier incident where the master blue-print or genetic code was I propose manipulated by a group outside of earth, who subsequently 'fell' to Earth and became subject to their own trap. It is debatable whether Noah's Ark carried the genetic codes of all species, however we must assume that some code is intended, since it would have been impossible to take this story literally – no boat could provide the capacity for a "two by two" of every species. Are British politicians bent on dragging their countrymen and women into the dramatization of their Masters and a games condition from which they are unable to escape, since even the right of Petition has been denied? Further the actions of politicians and New Labour is certainly playing into the hands of an Elite governed by the twelve tribes, who may yet nominate Britain as "The Great City" of the *Revelations* account according to the eternal 'script': where "unlucky thirteen" must surely derive from the number of times the 13th tribe tried to seize power and were thwarted by the twelve tribes.

It is perfectly ridiculous to claim that European Union was the outcome of democratic vote, as the Foreign and Commonwealth Office claimed as they tried to fob off the Petition to the British Parliament I presented in 1997. Just after the 1939-45 war, the pamphlet Design for Europe, emerged and the globalisation plan it has been claimed was started with Lord Milner's' Round Table Groups at the beginning of the Twentieth Century, when it was believed by the Establishment Elite that the British Imperial ideal would benefit the world as a whole. Professor Carroll Quigley (The Anglo-American Establishment: Books in Focus, Inc., 1981) has written that Colonel Edward Mandel House and the English round Table members were the power behind American President Woodrow "Wilson and founded the royal Institute of International Affairs (R.I.I.A) after the Versailles Peace Conference in 1919. The American Council on Foreign Relations (C.F.R.) followed a year later, which created an Anglo-American Elite, which continued to work for a New World Order and the end of the Nation state. However in my own research I have proposed that the World Order plan emerged at least in the time of the French Revolution and that revolution along with the Russian revolution and both World Wars, were merely cogs in the greater plan that originally was envisaged in Bronze Age Greece. This plan has monstrously woven its way throughout history, along with the secret politics and groups who have promoted it –"the hidden hand that moves" as it was referred to at the time of the French Revolution (*The Battle of The Trees*). I have argued that the very nature of the Versailles Treaty was bound to provide the injustice for Germany where a puppet (Hitler), could be manipulated by the Elite to create a Second World War, as one step closer to completing a World Order, with European Union as the obvious outcome of World War II. Once again the people duped as the Germans were rallied around that old justification of sacrifice to cause, which operates in all religious wars and revolutions.

In 1939-40, the R.I.I.A commissioned a series of studies that were published as World Order Papers. Hilaire du Berrier, in his September 1989 Newsletter, wrote of deep American involvement in order to establish European Union out of which were to come the Bilderberg Group and the Treaty of Rome. Professor Quigley was one of the few among the ruling Elite, who believed that the people should be told of these plans for World Government and wrote *Tragedy and Hope – as a History of the World in our Time*, as an effort to inform man of these plans. Federal Europe was to be part of a pattern of global economic blocs and the roots of this plan not only lay in the Internationalism of Karl Marx, but I conclude in a communistic ideal, run by a rich and powerful elite, driven by knowledge and a philosophy derived from the belief in god-like powers of the Masters. The slippery trail of this plan, the hidden agenda and policy of the Elite who drive both 12 and 13 at the apex is usually displayed in the ongoing wars, revolutions and in the case of Britain recently the ongoing disasters of British farming, with the B.S.E and Foot and Mouth disasters. These disasters may not be disasters at all, but more as with other significant world events, the outcome of deliberate policy and a hidden agenda. The agricultural crisis in Britain was deliberately suppressed by media and any cursory glance at the boards of media, will show an interlocking network of interests that are evident in all areas from politics to business. It is curious that on the 8th and 16th of April, 2001, *The Express on Sunday*, ran a story that a phial of the Foot and Mouth virus had vanished from the centre for Applied Microbiology Research (C.A.M.R.) at Porton Down, in the U.K. *On Target* pointed out:

> "Foot and Mouth Disease outbreaks and relentless extermination, have followed a remarkably coincident pattern with protected tourist areas of outstanding natural beauty, in Cumbria, the Brecon area of Wales, and Devon. The Christian group, Cutting Edge Ministries, in the United States, has stated that these areas also conform to those designated for "rewilding" – the return to nature, under the United nations Biosphere Plan (*Osmanczyk, Edmund Jan: The Encyclopaedia of The United*

Nations and International Agreements. Taylor and Francis, 1985)".

The above edition of *On Target* (*Vol. 30 No. 23 and 24 May 2001*) further reported that the Seventh Report White Paper of the Environment, Transport and Regional Affairs Committee, stated that: "The role of rural England as the food provider for the nation is **no longer an essential one**". Christopher Gill, R.D., M.P., wrote in March 2001:

> "Another complication is the fact that even though in terms of agriculture he is the highest elected person in the land, our Minister is positively prevented from using his own judgement anyway because so many of these matters require the specific agreement of our so-called European 'partners': speaking of which the suspicion is growing that there is a 'done deal' within the community of European Ministers whereby British Agriculture must be phased out so that we come to rely upon other parts of the European continent for our food and upon Tourism for our income. Is it really so fanciful to believe that the Foot and Mouth epidemic has been deliberately mismanaged to inflict maximum carnage and the greatest economic damage?"

The role of a Jewish conspiracy in The World Order plan has been noted by many authors including, the highly respected works of Nesta Webster (cited) and *On Target* provided a further background, particularly in *Vol.30 No.s 15,16, 19 and 20*. The control of the press and publishing is just one facet of the conspiracy to maintain the World Order Plan. What has gone unnoticed here however, is the backlash against Britain from abroad engineered in a principally Jewish controlled media, which has displayed Britain as the "Apocalyptic" country. Whether this will suffice as the final justification of fulfilling the Apocalyptic prophesy of *Revelations*, with Rothschild's "The City" (London) designated as "The Great City" in the Apocalyptic account and therefore a victory of the 12 tribes against the 13th tribe; must also be considered in the context of growing anti-Americanism and the likelihood that the psychotic mind of the MRC case and the Elite of the World Order, is building with chess-like precision and mindless primitive mind repetition of UVG120 crystal holographics his final victory of a Third World War (Armageddon) as a complete dramatization of his psychological case and his past in a war of two Kings. As the final curtain is about to fall on this production of Theatre Earth, it might be a miracle if the audience was to wake up and demand Truth and Justice, before man is once again downloaded with the entire holographics and past in a magnetic reversal (Hubbard's incident II?), with just a little bit more complexity added, challenging man or woman to solve the crystal and the psychotic mind of The World Order – never again, I am off!

ACTUAL INCIDENT ONE

Peter Moon in his book *Pyramids of Montauk Explorations in Consciousness* (*P. Moon and P.B.Nichols – Sky Books New York*) claimed that Brookham National Laboratories on Long Island New York was a research establishment which aimed to couple computer technology with sophisticated radio equipment in some form of mind control experimentation, with the ultimate aim of transferring human thoughts to esoteric crystal radio receivers and from there into a computer. I referred to the cluster ray complex of computers developed in America with fantastic memory capacity in *Alternative 4*, posing the question as to whether some mind control project was intent on storing all human thought: which might be termed the holographics of the Grid; neither can the possibility be dismissed that Grid memory is being preserved elsewhere (another planet) in the event of an electro-magnetic catastrophe on this one. It seems likely however, that the belief in Maters or extra-terrestrials in some etheric or anti world still exists as a misunderstanding in occult circles, deriving from the black occult magicians ritual of contacting spirits. Men like Aleister Crowley evidently believed their "Guardians" were spirits directing the magician through their knowledge: this book will come as a severe disappointment to the black magicians no doubt, along with the World Order, who evidently are tied up with this nonsense. This idea is presumably the background to the Great White Lodge (GWL) with its etheric Masters who direct a more earthly group, or the Great White brotherhood (GWB). The reality is more that the Grid is directing matters and past thought is a property of Grid crystal memory storage and the manner in which holographics appear to be stored under a general heading or 'filing system' producing composite holographics. It is these **composite holographics** that the magician has tapped into, whilst having no understanding of what he is actually doing. These composite holographics are also the basis of the *natural* UFO experience.

P. Moon also claimed that secret research was being conducted at Camp Hero, a derelict Air force Station at Montauk Point, Long Island, New York. This locale was chosen Moon claimed, since it housed a huge Sage radar antenna that emitted a frequency of approximately: 400-425 Megahertz, coincidentally the same band used to enter the consciousness of the human mind. Also at the site was evidence of a particle accelerator, but I will return to this. I have asserted in this book that the vast technological advances made in the immediate decades after World War II and particularly in the 1960's, were made mainly due to Nazi research and occult channelling of past technology from the Grid. A leister Crowley was deeply involved and according to Moon visited Montauk Point in 1918; further, many Nazi researchers went to America after the war (Operation Paper Clip). Jack Parsons as head of the O.T.O Lodge in Pasadena, connected to

Ron Hubbard and Aleister Crowley, was an extremely talented rocket scientist and is regarded as one of the leading researchers into the early rocket programme. Hubbard's *Chart of Human Evaluation* whilst he claimed it was his own genius and research, may or may not, have held some relation to past knowledge and the Tree of Life/chakra energies. Personally, I have always considered some of the policies of Scientology extremely hard and somewhat reminiscent of Illuminatus thinking ("Fair Game"): one demand of the breakaway group from Scientology (Phoenix) requested that only materials issued by Ron Hubbard constitute the subject of Scientology and this must stem from some doubt as to who is actually in charge of Scientology technology now. Even so, this does not answer the question of Hubbard's sources, as Hubbard unlike the method of the scientist and the cause of truth, has not entered any definitive source other than vague and vast tracts of history e.g. Babylonian or the illusive Commander 'Snake' Thompson.

In the 1960's however a great many psychics tramped through the offices of the CIA. The occult have been, since Einstein formulated the theory of relativity, obsessed with the idea of warping space-time and utilising time travel. The idea of portals or doors to other dimensions has long interested the occult, since they continually obsessed on the question of the true origins of the Masters. Einstein himself a Zionist, was in some way connected indirectly to research that evidently troubled him and perhaps the Philadelphia Experiment, which allegedly teleported a ship (the SS Eldgridge) from one place to another, along with its crew. Science has proved teleportation of large objects impossible and whilst myth surrounds this experiment, it is obvious there was some experiment here, with the use of extra-ordinary large magnets, but that the transference of the ship did not occur. Jack Parsons was a devotee of the Goddess and on several occasions tried to invoke the Goddess of Babalon who he claimed on one occasion commanded him to write in mystical communication, couched in picturesque biblical terminology and this became the *Book of Babalon*. Russell Miller (cited) claimed that Ron Hubbard, Parsons and Marjore Cameron took part in an invocation of the scarlet woman Babalon, with Hubbard as the: " scribe of the message from the astral world". The description of the ceremony is far from the reasons that the COS site for Hubbard's association with Jack Parsons and Hubbard's alleged attempt to break up black magic in America. People get very 'twitchy' when you mention 'black magic', but I hope that in this book, you will realise that this is an ancient ritualistic and shamanistic method of channelling information from the Grid and the past. The fact that 'black magic' is associated with evil purpose, merely derives from the fact that many have used Grid information, throughout history to obtain power, wealth and control, or for those recognising the cyclical nature – the power of prophecy is a good method of religious manipulation and as good as money in the bank.

Moon claimed that the Montauk site had been associated with a description of birds flying in frenetic circles, which is an indication of a distortion of the Grid vortices and electromagnetic fields, which determine bird flight and migration patterns and according to my own model in *Alternative 4* creates natural crop circles: this would further identify the use of the particle accelerator at the site and the possible manipulation of the significant Grid vortex point at Montauk. Further, Moon confirmed the connection between the Montauk site technology and the Sieman's Corporation of New Jersey (with past Nazi connections), through the Cardion Corporation, which it purchased in the 1990's.Norman Scott according to Moon was an influential lobbyist on Capitol Hill and had just completed a documentary about Montauk, when he ended up with a mysterious heart ailment and then dropped the investigation. Moon gives a very interesting history to the Montauk site and its significant location for the native Montauk tribe, who were denied not only Native American status, but also the rights to reclaim their land. It appears to me, that the Montauk Indians may have held significant data within their language relating to the thirteenth trive and the comparable Cerne-like giant hill figure found in America, which parallels the Cerne white chalk hill figure in the U.K although curiously and obviously no connection has ever been made. Indeed there were originally 13 tribes and the tribal system was governed in each tribe by a chieftan, which must remotely resemble the Celtic organisation. The plot thickens when we read that attempts were made to mix the bloodline of the Montauks (intermarriage with black) thus removing (in the mind of the World Order) the pure bloodline and connection to the 13th tribe, I assume: preventing any future claim to the bloodline of the GWB or GWL and the 13th tribe. The Chieftan's sons formed a powerful organisation of "The Four Federated Brothers" and Dr. Trumbell gives the entymology of the word Montauk as derived from "manatuck" a name frequently bestowed on a high hill or land denoting "a place for seeing (or to be seen) far off". This must find a connection with the word "seer" or one who channels (information) and further finds connection with the Druids and 13th tribe through hill, which was utilised for seership purposes with close connection to a Grid vortex point, or anti-gravity anomaly which determines the geography of the land, causing uprisings. Small pyramnids according to Moon were found and photographed at the Montauk site on Long Island in 1911, however those structures curiously (or not) no longer exist.

George Pharaoh (with significant surname) was allegedly the last chief of the Montauk Indians (1798), who spoke his native dialect. Thomas Jefferson (a past President of the United States) was a Freemason and allegedly received the Great Seal of The United States from the Freemasons. This seal is virtually replicated on the One Dollar note of America with its datum 'out of many come one' and 'out of one come many' (illustrating the principle of Adam, the power pyramid and communism run by an elitist priethood). Jefferson took the trouble of recording the entire vocabularly and the alphabet of the Montauk tribe, presumably realising that many secrets are hidden within the alphabets of languages. The pharaohs of Egypt according to Edgar Cayce the psychic appeared at Atlantis and the hidden science I have concluded was encoded into some languages and alphabets. The 'babble' at Babel (Tower of Babel in biblical texts) and the creation of 72 languages, rests on the purpose of initiates to withdraw the secrets from common language spoken by the "vulgar" (uneducated) and the retention of the secrets in alphabets only meant for those priests in 'the know': the Tree alphabet (*The Battle of the Trees*) and Ogham script, were secret alphabets of the Druids and in whaich, many of the religious mysteries are tied up. Moon stated that the Montauk language was known as Vril, an ancient Atlantean tongue and this has connection to the Vril society, underlying the Nazis secret occult system. Bulwater Lytton also referred to Vril in his book *The Coming Race*, which became Nazi propaganda and was applied to the Nazi super race programme. Vril is supposed to derive from Enochian language, with its own grammar and syntax: the Enochian keys were allegedly able to unlock the mysteries and Universal Laws. The most talented physicists today are apparently searching for the Enochian keys, although I will return to this point later.

There are further links of the Native Americans and Montauk tribe, with the 13th tribe and the U.K. Atlas in Greek myth was the father of the Pleiades also known as the Seven Sisters, which figure in the creation legends of almost all primitive tribes. The Native Americans believe that they were descended from the Pleiades and the Cerne giant white chalk hill figure in the U.K. is situated not far from the seven white chalk cliffs on the South coast of England, known locally as the Seven Sisters. It is these cliffs, which I have discussed in relation to the prophetic Apocalypse of the 12 tribes and the *Revelations* account of the end of times; with London quite possibly elected as "The Great City" (derived from Roshchild's first coining of the term as "The City"!) which could be described as "sitting on seven mountain tops" (*Revelations*) or in fact the Seven Sisters white chalk cliffs. This would of course fit in with the 12 tribes account of the end of times, as written in the biblical book of *Revelations* against the 13th tribe, but is only I *emphasise* a secret group agenda against a group that has long occupied and controlled the British people. I cannot deny however that this group (13th tribe) has not shaped the ruling British psyche (bloodlines, aristocracy, class system), in the same way that the 12 tribes and Cabala have shaped the psyche of the Jew. The Holy Grail and its message, along with the knowledge was always the victim of both groups, in the same way that now it may be impossible for the world to differentiate between those groups and people who have no idea of this battle. It is very easy for some to place the Jew or Briton into the same hell's cooking pot and identify ordinary people with either a Jewish plan for world domination, or the British goal of a bloodline, aristocracy and Empire: in each case if you involve ordinary people in this battle, you merely ascent to the World Order plan. If you are going to fight the World Order, then do not make ordinary people the victim, seek those who through the network of interrelated directorships and groups pull the strings and you will find them DIRECTING POLICY. You can only challenge a World Order through its policy and groups who either keep that policy in place or define such policy; and not through people who are innocently drawn into this battle by virtue of place of birth. There is however always the admonishment of those who support World Order thinking be that through the belief in the Jews as the "chosen people" or the support of an aristocratic system, which judges a man or woman on the circumstances of their birth (bloodline), rather than their spiritual or ability status.

Alternative 3 (1970's) of which my book *Alternative 4* was an extension, allegedly uncovered a plan of Space agencies in America, to populate Mars in the advent of some predicted catastrophe on Earth. Mars has always been a basis of speculation of alien occupation, through the mysterious alleged pyramids or 'face', which scientists dismiss as tricks of light. According to Moon, there is some Grid energy link between Mars and Montauk, with some maintaining that the geology of Montauk on Long Island New York, as part of a different land mass to America, with implications that it once formed the continent or island of Atlantis. This connection is furthered by Moon, when he quotes James Aldridge's book *Cairo Biography of a City,* explaining that Cairo or 'Al-kahir' means Mars. There is a persistent legend of alien invaders, which extends from the cataclysm theory of Sirius, which forced the aliens to colonise Mars and when that planet became subject to environmental storms, the aliens came to Earth. The confusion I have discussed between an actual and apparent landing (of "gods" or aliens) may indeed rest upon this point. If the original aliens came from Mars, via Sirius then that would have represented the original landing; however the story of Noah's Ark may represent an apparent landing, where the occupants 'landed' after a magnetic reversal on planet Earth, having saved significant past knowledge along with perhaps the genetic codes of all species as male and female ("two by two" according to the biblical story). It might be remarked that the story of Noah has deep implications, not only in terms of the X and Y (female and male chromosomes) but also with the retention of *past . knowledge*. If Noah's Ark were indeed a space ship, then it would be understandable how alien invasion has been confused with an apparent landing. Spiritual intervention c. 10 000 B.C. should not be confused with either, it was an independent act of help.

The interest of occult groups in the anti-matter world stems from the desire to know where Spiritual help came from and the confusion of this intervention, with the alien landings and apparent landing of Noah's Ark. It appears that occultists for many years have confused Hermes and the Greek connection, with the 13th tribe, since they were not aware of the *separate origins* of the 13 th tribe and Spiritual intervention. Knossos was not the beginning, only another chapter in the Holy Grail story. Crowley seemed to be obsessed with the magical knowledge of Hermes and in his biography on page 361, mentioned Ludovic Cameron as wanting to revive the Celtic nations: Hitler himself paraphrased tracts of Crowley's *Book of the Law* in *Mein Kampf* and Hitler's Aryan Super Race programme reflected the ideal of a ruling hierarcy, which the Nazis hoped to become.

Art and literature were also deeply tied into this story and *Mac Beth* by Shakespeare is not only a literal translation of the Cabala, but Mac Beth according to Peter Ellis (cited) was a High King of Scotland (and presumably 13th tribe/Druidic) with also presumably a high command of the Cabala and mysteries of the stolen Holy Grail. Ellis places the Celts originally in India and I have already discussed the caste hierarchal system in India, along with the comparable hierarchal sytem of Brhamanism, together with the migration of the Celts to Egypt under the leadership of Niul, who then married the Pharaoh's daughter Scota, who gave Scotland in the U.K. its name. The Pharaoh was Rameses II and his connections to the GWL and GWB and the cabal who invaded Knossos and stole the Holy Grail have also been discussed. The connection of 'Beth' with 'Mc.' denoting 'clan of' must surely find cross reference to the first letter of the Beth-Luis Nion alphabet, discussed more fully in *The Battle of The Trees*; as the first letter or 'first born' of the alphabet of the Druids, once again signifying the connection to Adam and 13th tribe. The Egyptian connection through the Montauks and 13th tribe also finds curious connection to the proposal of an ultimate group, which sought a "Universal Kingdom" or political and religious World Order, by uniting the 12 tribes and 13th tribe, in so far as the Pharaoh united the upper and lower Nile, symbolic of the upward (spiritual) and downward (material) pointing triangles reflected in the Great Seal of the United States of America and the Star of David. Th Davidic line is 13th tribe and notably Moses (who was adopted into the House of Egypt) was to notably lead the "children of Israel" out of Egypt, sweeping down the Levant ark and killing all those who worshipped the golden calf (13th tribe –bull Minotaur?); although receiving his commandments by some utilisation of the hidden science significantly on a hill, with Druid implications! This was a fine old web of cross and double cross, between the tribes.

The word Pharaoh means "great house" and entymologically derives from the Greek and Persian words "Magos" and "maz" respectively. The implication of house of Magog, the grandson of Noah is indicated with connections to "Gog" and "Magog" together with the extrapolation to the Twin King statues at the Guildhall in London, with one statue bearing the Mongolian slant-eyes; which turned up in the *manipulated* UFO phemomenon as the 'three men in black' (with slant eyes): also implied in the three kings story at the birth of Jesus, which in an early icon (illustrated) from Naples had Greek connections to Hermes and Mercury (13th tribe), before the World Order dusted the tracks! UFO witness accounts which involved these men in black who came in threes (with implications of Mother Goddess and Twin Kings) also included a description of the slant eyes and was I concluded a manipulated event trying to confuse the natural UFO phenomenon, with origins of aliens and 13th tribe. The World Order in other words tried by such manipulated events, not only to confuse the real source of the natural UFO phenomenon (the Grid) but attempted to connect the UFO phenomenon to aliens, Masters and ultimately a Jewish group (Uri Geller's experience), Tibet and one concludes the 13th tribe. I have covered the fact that many significant occultists over the past two centuries, who have influenced alternative circles and are inherent in World Order thinking, allegedly received their direction from Masters in the East or Tibet/Mongolia. "House" is derived from the Indo-European word "skeu" or "keu" meaning "to hide" and it was the secrets of the past, including the hidden science and Grid, which the Masters hoped to hide along with their plans for a World Order: indeed many occultists such as Blavatsky claimed Tibetan Masters as their inspiration.

The octahedron is a geometric of the Grid and is a shape that occurs in Freemasonry symbolism and which Peter Moon described as the shape of the Delta-T atenna at Montauk. If 33 tetrahedrons are laid end to end, they form the comparable helical structure of DNA, the hereditary genetic material in the cells of man. I have already stated that the DNA forms a 'tuning fork' link with the Grid and thus the geometric shape of the antenna perhaps indicates some form of receiving property and the attempts to channel information from the Grid in the 1990's (when Moon's book was written). The visit of Crowley to the site of Montauk however indicates Crowley's attempts to either communicate with perceived Masters or his attempts to channel significant information from the Grid, which provides the background for the antenna at Montauk. If as I propose the whole of the past and genetic record is laid on the Grid or UVG120 crystal, then the goal of Crowley and the antenna, was to tap into the record of the past, believing presumably that this was another dimension or anti-world of the Masters! There is said to be a secret underground chamber which I illustrated on the Great pyramid of Gizeh, which stores all the records of the past: any such records would have been sequestered by the World Order, but it seems that Crowley believed and presumably was successful in channelling information from the Grid and therefore tapping into this record, through Hermetic magic.

The tetrahedron and the way it evolves from the dot and circle, is not only occult knowledge within the Rosicrucians, but also appears in the Illuminati (*The Battle of The Trees*). Adam wishaupt the founder of the Illuminati, indicated to his student "Philo" that there was a great secret in the dot and circle, which is based on the symbolism of the One Dollar note of America and the intimate relationship of the political goal of the left (communism and Illuminati) to the right (Rosicrucianism and religious 13th tribe): it is for this reason that I have questioned the Illuminatus power pyramid of Europe. The dot and circle is also indicative of St. John's Gospel in so far as: "In the beginning was the word (dot) and the word was with God" (as the dot unfolds to give the circle, which is governed as in the Summer Smoking Room floor of Cardiff Castle and Scottish Rite Freemasonry, by the four quadrants or T-shaped cross of Taur or the Bull-Minos cult).

Tahuti, the god of wisdom, learning and magic was usually portrayed as a dog or ape and both these symbols turned up in the Knossos Religious Revolution c. 1400 B.C. and which I have concluded may be the basis of Hubbard's Inc.I. The Greeks identified Tahuti as Thoth and also Hermes, the Romans called him Mercury and the Hebrews knew him as Enoch. The keys to Enoch were not so much the keys to Hermes, as the keys to spiritual intervention and the basis of the beliefs of the Early Minoans, before the Religious Revolution and the theft of the Holy Grail. Hermes was alleged to have been born in Arcadia in the Perlopnnese in Greece, and I was in Greece (1993 –5), when pyramids predating the Egyptian were discovered (*The Battle of The Trees*); this however is a fabrication of the truth and the fact that Hermes was born of the Religious Revolution in Crete.Tahuti as Hermes was credited with the building of the pyramid of creation, the tetrahedron and the quadrisected circle, however once again Hermes stole the information in the form of the cabal who entered Crete and conducted a Religious Revoloution forcing The Holy Grail, together with its message (of re-incarnation) and knowledge of the trap and Grid underground into the "stream" of secret group knowledge, thereafter only available to the initiates, who came to believe that they were the sole originators of the Grail! In fact The Grail was present on Earth from c. 10 000 B.C and was also evident in Africa and among the Montauk Indians, to the obvious discontent of white supremacists trying to maintain a *white* bloodline.

Tahuti as with Hermes in myth was the sacred bridge between this dimension or world and another world of the spirit. Hermes and therefore Tahuti, was the improvision of the pale priests and cabal who overran Knossos, to erase the true guardianship of The Holy Grail and wipe the woman from the story. Professor George Hunt Williamson was a professor of archaeology at the University of Colarado in the 1940's, who supported the legend that a Martian colony initially settled Earth and were called the elder Race or Elohim (first born). I have already covered the Elohim and their domes, along with *that* Dome in London and the "Eye" as apart of the covert Millennium celebrations in the U.K., along with the crystal ball in New York. The professor lost his job, which underlines the control of the World Order over academic institutions and free speech, together with the right to an opinion. The mysterious archaeological artefacts I have discussed, cannot be explained by orthodox accounts of evolution and the idea that man evolved from a primordial 'soup'. UFO witness accounts that I discussed in *Alternative 4*, spoke of "**mechanical beings**", with robotic voices and "drop down" or mechanical jaws; together with accounts of little men or aliens who continually were to be found tinkering with their aircraft, or space ships, which indicated a mechanical nature. I have explained how these stored holographs or **memories of the past** as in the UFO witness acconts, become dislodged from the electromagnetic vortex of the Grid and impinge on the witness, with the brain acting as a dipole radio receiver ('The Onion-Ring Model'): further the hologram is a **composite** picture of the past and is not only classified according to subject heading, but also contains past thoughts, which become **superimposed** on one another according to subject heading. If for example, I take a dog bite at 3 million B.C. then that will be classified along with a dog bite in 2001; the only thing to distinguish the two are the **space-time co-ordinates** of each incident. If David Icke cannot distinguish between then and now, it is a reflection of the problem of the Grid (and channelling) and the superimposition of holographs i.e. reptiles may have formed the bodyline to the World Order and may have utilised monarchy along the way, but the space time co-ordinates of each event, will classify it as an individual incident under a general heading or file numbering system. To take a composite holograph channelled from the Grid and then fuse all space-time coordinates into one story line, is to walk down the same path of insanity as a World Order, who cannot distinguish between co-ordinates of space time, the past and present; the World Order is still back there fighting an old battle. Let us take the example of evolution of the alien species on this planet; perhaps they did arrive in a space craft, perhaps they were mechanical beings and perhaps they were evolved through a reptilian line: in the holographic storage system of the Grid, one might expect to find some superimposition of the various historical holgraphics under a general heading of 'alien evolution' IF, THAT LINE BROUGHT ITS OWN BODY LINE AND GENETICS TO EARTH. UFO witness accounts which describe men tinkering with space craft (mechanical), drop down jaws (mechanical and possibly carnivorous) along with curious composite animals with orange eyes and bird-like wings with shuffling gate, might indeed indicate a composite picture of the alien evolutionary past and character. As I wrote this incident up I had a flash of the World Order's attempt to explain this book and their futile excuse of 'well that was all in the past and this is now', so watch out for that one, it simply is not true! A battle that is engrained in Grid memory drives such a battle.

The holographics of the (natural) UFO witness accounts all point to the arrival of space ships on Earth, with MECHANICAL BEINGS. Whilst the "drop down jaw" of the witness accounts may portray this character of the aliens, it might also relate to the history or evolution of the skull, in this case of the alien line through perhaps the carnivores. The unhingeing mechanism of the "drop down jaw" may be a sign of the predator or carnivore, which has a completely different jaw action from the herbivore (plant eater). The unhingeing mechanism allows prey to be held e.g. the snake or reptile; whereas in the herbivore the movement is from side to side e.g. the rabbit, as the cellulose in plant material is broken down in a grinding action. Placing this clue alongside the composite man-animal UFO witness holographs, where beings with a strange shuffling gate, orange eyes and bird like wings were observed, then it appears that the composite holograph from the Grid details the evolutionary body line of perhaps the alien, through reptile/bird and man. Fish have also appeared in UFO witness accounts and the modern emerging consensus is that mans body line may have evolved through this route, which I discussed in *Alternative 4*. The recapitulation of phylogeny (the major group or phylum) in the embryology of the human foetus may be exemplified in the gill-like slits, which emerge at a certain stage in development, indicating further perhaps that some master code is being read off sequentially, presumably accounting for Harold Burr's 'jelly moulds' (the electromagnetic shape into which the matter of the body is 'poured').

In respect to the early evolution of mammals, the same situation exists where animals which dominated the land in the later Permian and early Triassic Periods before the dinosaurs appeared, were the mammal-like reptiles or therapsids, which in both their skulls and teeth were almost halfway between the typical reptiles and primitive mammals. Many of the smaller reptiles in the group ancestral to dinosaurs and crocodiles (which features in secret group totem beast history) could have provided the route from which the birds arose, walking exclusively on their hind legs. The UFO witness account of a man-animal with "shuffling gate" (indicative of a change in posture and hip and limb placements) and "orange eyes" with "stumpy wings" could have described this early emergence from reptiles on four legs to bird-like creatures half bird and half reptile walking on two legs. In *Alternative 4* I reproduced a picture of Archaeopteryx, which is thought to be just such a 'missing link' (fossilised form between bird and reptile) and in its facial appearance and top body (minus the tail) could be mistaken for the curious 'Amorphous figures' in Neolithic cave art, with the obvious reptilian or snout-like nature, which may account for the myths of "monsters appearing over the rainbow bridge", which presumably refs to body line of the aliens after a magnetic reversal, but I will return to this point later. Some of the mammal reptiles exhibited forelimbs with quite well developed 'fingers'.

At around 36 million years ago, in the Oligocene Period, the modern mammals appeared with the spread of anthropoid apes 25 million years ago in the Miocene Epoch. Clearly the mammal-reptile would have to have some genetic similiarity to a mate or evolving ape form, in order to produce viable offspring from mating. If animals were far too separated genetically (e.g. cow and giraffe) no viable offspring would result, even if mating were possible. The ancient myths of gods mating with man, presumably have some historical foundation in this long distant past, where the reptilian/mammalian genetic form mated with the anthropoid ape form and perhaps explains the array of faces found at La Marche. The common genetic link would presumably be the mammalian genes. This may indeed account for the change of archetypal significance from the crocadile, egg and dots on the body of the king in Neolithic cave art in Africa. Is it not curious that a terrible dramatization of the aliens has occured there in recent times, with 'animals' (guerrilla fighters) cutting of limbs and fingers of children! Neanderthal man may have represented some regressive survival form in Europe of a line that was not included in a mating or breeding programme. It might be inferred now since the bloodlines are well and truly mixed that we all, in the darkest recesses of our primitive (body line) minds, find some connection with the sexual excitement of the alien mind as it hunted its victim and prey as a carnivore and predator: the dream of flying and its sexual interpretation presumably is a body line memory of flight and predatory reptilian/bird memory. The willingness of man to descend into the depths of this mind is frequently displayed by those who relish having a victim to worry, hunt or villify (the most vunerable in society sufficing to these cowards). Amphibia, reptiles and Aves (birds) are related categories or classes and there is in the *Book of Revelations* a condemnation on "frogs" and presumably either refers to the use of a hallucinogenic drug, or indeed this line of evolution. The first terrestrial class of vertebrates (with backbone) essential for movement on land and the beginnings of the upright gait, were the reptiles which laid eggs and it appears that the egg was not only a prominent feature in the earliest Egyptain science and philosophy (the egg breathing life and Aton etc.) it featured in Neolithic cave art and the reptilian dot-like appearance of the Neolithic king was presumably a representation of body-line and the alien/reptile – with Divine status implied. The dot of course came to be dramatized in all sorts of ways in the secret group knowledge including Illuminatus; and the egg was dramatized at Knossos in the seals already discussed. Further a recent Pope was to be found tapping an egg with a wand in a secret Illuminatus ceremony, later that era would be described by the Catholic Church as one in which Satan took over the Church: and yet the

Pope did not deem it necessary to reveal at least what the Catholic Church knew of this story! The burning question in my mind is whether the Illuminati took over other Churches including Scientology, or whether in the case of Scientology they were engaged through Hubbard in a 25 year battle with the American government and presumably the Illuminati: only Scientology can answer that one.

S. Romer an eminent paleontologist stated: "Primitive Paleozoic reptiles and some of the earliest amphibians were so similar in their skeleton that it is almost impossible to tell when we have crossed the boundary between two classes". Thus the condemnation on frogs in *The Bible* may have a foundation in this reptilian/amphibian line. It is impossible to say whether secret research resulted in the allegations of sights of "greys" or small alien-type grey figures, which is now part of UFO history of the 1990's. There may have been some secret research attempt of genetically back-crossing compatable F1 hybrids to the parental species. This sequence of events in genetic research of hybridisation, back crossing, and stabilisation of back cross types by selection is known as introregression. The fact that the "greys" were alleged to have had the typical and now archetypal double-bumped (each side of the skull) alien-type appearance indicates some form of transgressive segregation, where the desired result is the **amplification of a particular characteristic trait of the parent**. The possibilities of genetic research aligned to any idea of a super-race are inevitable, whilst occult and secret groups control research direction. If a magnetic cataclysm as perhaps the Flood in biblical accounts indicates, occured to wipe out the dinosaurs in the Cretaceous Period of the Mesozoic era, then prior to that, mammal-like reptiles in the Triassic epoch (220 million years ago) would have been dominant. The MRC case or alien who left Earth taking his records with him (and body) to avoid such a cataclysm, would have returned thus perhaps accounting for the idea of space ships and mythical accounts of "monsters" arriving "over the rainbow bridge"; or indeed 'gods' mating with man: as opposed to the myth of an Ark. Further it would have been impossible for the Ark to carry "two by two" of every species in male and female pairs, unless it was the genes (DNA or genetic code of X and Y forms) that were stored, indicating the Ark may be an analogy to a high technology ship –space ship or not. The important point is that if the alien left in a body, which he perceived as his immortal self, due to the long mortality rates under differing electro-magnetic conditions, then he would indeed have returned with that body and genetic line following the reversal. This bodyline appears to be indicated in Neolithic art and the cave paintings of La Marche and in the curious 'Anthropomorphous figures' in Neolithic caves, which have a courious reptilian quality. Most orders of mammals originated after the cataclysm in the Paleocene epoch 65 million years ago, which is the era generally agreed that wiped out the dinoasaurs, the world's stage cleared for an entirely new group of animals – the mammals and apes.

If a population is isolated genetically for long enough and then mates with members of a foreign population, fewer vigorous offspring are produced which are fertile: consequently mutations or gene combinations which favour mating between individuals of the same species will have a positive selective value and will spread through the population. The isolation of a group or population is one method of creating different species. If a species were re-introduced after a long period of isolation, there would be a fertility drop with sterile progeny. Hybridisation or crossing pure lines which differ by a single gene, as in the experiements of Gregor Mendel, has greater definition to the evolutionist where crossing of populations having different adaptive gene complexes. Such populations may be either different races or subspecies of the same species or different species separated by variously developed isolating mechanisms. Rate of population growth is determined by many factors including homogeneity of the gene pool. Today there are billions of humans and each mating is capable of producing a viable offspring, but if a large proportion of the population were inserted with a different gene sequence, it would theoretically be comparable to the isolating mechanism and would create infertile or sterile offspring. Whether the World Order have decided to cull population numbers, through such genetic programmes and GM modified food, is an interesting proposal given Hubbard's Space Opera and the claim that population control was an incident on the track of time, which would imply that the current obsession with GM food and cloning, is merely a complete dramatization by the World Order of the past incident – back there still running a control of population/ slave species programme! The World Order in their white supremacist attitude, have notably dumped this GM food on the Third World, with the justification that it will reduce famine, even though that is a premise without any rational foundation. Once the World Order control seed supplies and agriculture comes under a few large multi-national concerns, then they effectively could control reproduction and the genetic line, which must at least set alarm bells off. Further, there is no assurance that private eneterprise (The World Order) will not patent and control the genetic code, once the Genetic Codon project is complete! More dramatized horrors to come.

The Rhesus factor is usually attached to male genes and hybrid sterility due to abnormal gonad development is very common in animals, particularly the testes of the male. We know that male sperm counts have been dropping in recent years, although research has not determined why. Sterility can occur not only through genetic separation of the species e.g. the cow and elephant but also through abnormal reproductive development. The former example is segregation sterility and the latter development sterility: there is also sterility due to isolation of populations as discussed. Cloning could create abnormal embryos or genic disharmony, through uncoordinated rates of various processes, which normally form an integrated sequence in the development of the embryo. The obsession of secret groups with bloodlines must also raise the question of whether the dramatized incident will assert itself once again in a super race programme. Geographic segregation is usually needed before reproductive isolation and the origin of a distinct species can occur. I have already discussed the idea of Masters, the Tibetan Seven Rays of light monastery and the obsession of Blavatsky with distinct races, which she admits came from her Masters. The Jews and Aryans had similar views on maintaining bloodlines and bloodline obsession must hark back to this ancient memory of the alien bodyline and the desire not to mate with that line. This incident seems to have greatly affected the psychology, resulting in the warped idea of racism on today's world stage. It is not inconceivable that some bloodline has been retained in some secret group somewhere, perhaps some isolated monastery: neither is it inconceivable that the "King of the World" referred to in the notorious *Protocols of Zion*, will be a hybrid or regressed line, retained by geographical isolation of the genetic line – sympatric species. Allopatric populations, which do not undergo this isolation, are quite different from sympatric populations. There was some indication (*The Battle of The Trees*) that some pure bloodline existed in the Merovingians and the line of David. It is difficult to understand fully the mind of the World Order and its incomprehensible and irrational lines of thought, but it has occurred to me, that a body line (Homo Sapiens with presumably its mixed genetics from ape and alien) with an entered selector e.g. specific gene insertion could in theory over time separate the two genetics. Another possibility is once again the creation of an FI hybrid that is weak or sterile having resulted from a cross between parents with a gene difference. This progeny will go on to create another generation (F2 progeny) further weakened and sterile through this genic disharmony of the parents. Animals and plants are particularly susceptible to genic disharmony in the first division or cleavage mitosis in the fertilized egg; for which reason genetic cloning could produce embryos which will grow to adulthood, but may be sterile and the obvious implication from the occult point of view is the development of a sterile slave species, governed by a super-race presumably the aliens breeding through a hierarchal caste system as was employed in India and the Aryan super race project of Hitler.

The fact that the Grid appears to retain memories in pictorial form, or 3-D holographics including THOUGHT must depend on the *geometrical conformation* of the Grid and its interconnectiveness. It is perhaps significant that early writing is in pictorial form – hieroglyphics and the ancient Greek alphabets I replicated in *The Battle of The Trees*, where the beehive (communistic) was associated with the Greek letter Pi or ? which finds association with the idea of secrecy ('to pie' – to place a secret in concealment) and also finds connection to the pyramid, which is such a prominent symbol of a World Order built on secrecy, technology, elitism and materialism, as opposed to its ORIGINAL MEANING OF **SPIRITUAL HIERARCHY**. Thus the aliens who appeared to come from Sirius and from there to Mars and Earth appear to have been a TECHNOLOGICALLY MINDED group and this is a crucial point, which helps us to understand the current madness in the world and the obsession with technology, where the logical, linear and list forming mind is valued more than the spiritual mind and its ability to interconnect. The aliens were technologically evolved, but were not however spiritually evolved and Spiritual intervention c. 10 000 B.C came to redress that fact. Spiritual intervention was not technologically evolved in the sense of the MATTER UNIVERSE; they were however spiritually evolved in terms of the ANTI MATTER UNIVERSE.

Professor George Hunt Williamson was a professor of archaeology at the University of Colorado in the 1940's who supported the legend of a Martian colony initially settled on Earth, who were called the Elder Race or Elohim (first born). The professor lost his job, which underlines the control of the World Order over academic institutions, freedom of speech along with opinion. The mysterious artefacts that I have produced showing ancient batteries etc are not indicative of the orthodox account of evolution, from the primordial 'soup', through to the ape and man. There appears to be this distinction of ape line and reptilian line, which was to surface in the mysterious decline of the Sethites, or ape form dating back to a certain son of Noah. The Knossos frescoes show monkeys in the Early Minoan period and there appears to be a distinction once again being made between the two lines. The alien was co-existent with the dinosaurs thus perhaps accounting for the huge footprint (*Plate I*). Professor Hunt Williamson claimed that the "scrolls" of the Elohim were actually geometric symbols "etched" into crystals – no wonder he lost his job at the University! H.G Wells referred to a "crystal library" in his book *Time Machine* and one wonders which particular group he belonged to! Interestingly the professor claimed he learnt about the crystals in the Andes (Tibet) through the original Monastery of The Seven Rays. This again smacks of the Masters, GWL and GWB and the 13th tribe, and further the professor claimed that the Elohim migrated to Earth from Mars having derived from Sirius or the God/Dog star that features so prominently in the architecture of the pyramids. The professor was to go on to claim that Tibetan records dated back 450 000 years and the oldest at possibly over a million years old. If true then obviously not only must the records be electro magnetically recorded in crystals or some form of non eroding system, but those records would have had to be removed from Earth in a magnetic reversal, or the memory would have been wiped out in such a magnetic event. The return of the records and the aliens, must account for the arrival of gods in myth: seen as gods no doubt for their technological or Cabalistic knowledge, which must have seemed like the magic of the gods to the primitive Homo sapiens and illustrated in shamanistic cave paintings and 'Lightening man'.

The arrival of The Holy Grail, its spiritual message of re-incarnation (long forgotten in the obsession of saving body lines and knowledge) along with the warning of the trap of the Grid, was not predictably viewed in a spiritual manner by the aliens, who being technically evolved and elitist, seized the knowledge for themselves, revelling in the technical possibilities of the Grid for control, power and wealth and being generally interested in the mechanics. The Early Minoans or true Cretans th EteoCretans were being tutored by Spiritual intervention, before Knossos or the group was overrun and the knowledge or Holy Grail stolen. The aliens did not truly understand or comprehend the spiritual message and the Cycle of Eternal Return to them was to become successive returns to complete World Orders and maintain bodylines. I was interested to note the zigzag 'light on dark' pattern in the early Minoan pottery or Kamares ware, which reflects the zigzag patterning of UFO incidents and I conclude the successive spirals of the vortex Grid phenomena. The natives in the Andes who drew maps of Mars on their pottery particularly struck professor Hunt Williamson. I also noticed the ellipsoid rim of the Early Minoan 'bath' sarcophagi, where the dead were buried among sea-shells and sand, in the foetal position, awaiting re-birth I concluded, through the Great Goddess's gift of immortality and her connection to the sea and tides 'as I go, so shall I return' (Re-incarnation). The spiral shells in some manner illustrating the vortex to another world perhaps and the ellipsoid/trapezoid sarcophagus perhaps illustrating curved space-time. Further the appearance of icons at Knossos at the time of the Religious Revolution, which saw the theft of The Holy Grail, showed a man with one hand held to the central position of the forehead. This is the position of the third eye, or crown chakra, which appeared to be displayed in some cave art paintings of the Neolithic period, where the head in one stylised painting showed a funnel-shaped head, which I deduced was the opening of the crown chakra or third eye and connection to the Grid for purposes of channelling and illumination, through Cabalistic ritual.

The standard depiction of the alien or ET brain is bilateral (two bumps either side) or bi-lobed. The right eye controls the analytical, intellectual, linear or analogical left side of the brain, and the left eye controls the right side of the brain or intuitive creative aspect. The opening of the third eye or initiation is aimed at connecting the two. This opening of the third eye is called "illumination" and the group of Illuminati presumably have this goal in mind, which as a point is illustrated on the reverse side of the One Dollar note of America, where the Illuminatus political system is on the left and the religious or creative Rosicrucian goal on the right, with its implications of left and right politics, communism and fascism or elitism. Only the elite would have access to the Holy Grail and the knowledge, only the elite could re-incarnate to continue with their development, with access to the mysteries; and usually the elite of Illuminism were and are signed up in the elite universities, thus ensuring the policy of elitism was furthered. The aliens however did not bring The Holy Grail to Earth and in stealing The Holy Grail, merely and pointedly applied it only to the matter universe, technology and growth, dismissing the wider implications and spiritual warnings. The consequence on Earth is as it has always been, growth of technology and obsession with mechanics and materialism over spiritual growth.

The pituitary gland at the base of the brain is a master hormonal gland and not only releases hormones, but those hormones control other hormones in the body, principally the sexual hormones which cover survival in terms of behavioural psychology and reproduction. The mere act of opening the third eye and crown chakra and the subsequent change in hormone levels, particularly the sex hormones, acts as a direct conduit of energy or kundalini sexual energy to and from the base of the spine and sexuality to the Grid (and past occult thoughts of Masters): the primitive mind therefore without education acting under ego or personality, is likely to direct the individual along primitive mind mechanisms, which relate to survival principally of self and at most group, dismissing spiritual direction. The cult of the personality personified by Hollywood is curiously enough part of what Hubbard calls Inc.2 or the alien implants and which I conclude is merely a downloading of Grid holographics. The World Order had only to force man into the low survival levels, whereby the primitive mind 'switches on' and the Darwinian datum of 'survival of the fittest' would emerge and which as a datum complies with World Order policy. Many have asked how the One (World Order) can control so many and the answer lies in the primitive phylogeny of evolution and the tribal or group mechanisms of the primitive mind, with subservience of less powerful (strong) individuals in a group, to the leader: after all a female in the group is not supposed to question the top male – hence my failed Petition to Parliament and long search for help. It never ceases to amaze me how quickly people decide what is right or wrong based on Darwinian principles ('what's in it for me, or my group' socially or financially and subservience to a dominant hierarchy). Man maintains his niche in this hierarchal tribal 'pecking order' and automatically selects victims on this basis – women and slaves and the old at the bottom! It is very sad indeed that the anti-Capitalist groups, environmental groups and even churches all have their own group agendas and really do not want anyone to interfere with their own hierarchy/agenda which merely reflects World Order thinking. This hierarchal domination with one male or a select group of males, at the top is not a spiritual organisation, whereas democracy (one man, one women, one vote) is.

Aleister Crowley the black magician, by incorporating sexual magic, merely sought to work the reverse process of creating a sexual rush of hormones and psychic attitudes, all of which create altered auric or electro-magnetic fields, which can then open the crown chakra, whereby certain Grid connections via mutual resonance could occur; thus retrieving information or holographics, which Crowley thought were actual spirits or Masters! Female and male sex hormones, X and Y chromosomes and Hermes (as bisexual and transcendent third who resulted from the Religious Revolution) are all implied in the magic of Crowley as he attempted to contact knowledge relating to The Holy Grail, the woman and ultimately the secrets to be had, which evidently may have been lost to The World Order and Crowley dug up. The emergence of sexual or orgiastic rites at Knossos at the time of the Religious Revolution, were dramatized in the Roman Arena, where man took great delight in the then current prey or victims – the Christians; which was a spiritual versus materialistic battle or Grail versus aliens or World Order and early Christians often believed in re-incarnation. "The Seven Seals" in the Apocalyptic Revelations account refer to the seven charkas in the body and the final seal must refer to the crown chakra and the ultimate release of the Tree of Life and knowledge: which interestingly enough takes us back to the cyclical beginning and Genesis (Day 1. – plant the vine!). This must as a point surely reflect the psychology of the MRC case, who cannot finish a cycle of action, merely because he usually gets to the end and precipitates, or is overcome by a magnetic reversal, thus pushing down the ladder to the beginning where he must start again. The MRC case has thus become obsessive in his game, of building his Atlantis. We are told that when the last seal is broken, then the kingdom of God is revealed, and presumably the choice remains, of whether we choose The Holy Grail and the Spiritual message, or go the sheep route, of accepting a hierarchal elitist system headed for explosive growth consequences – a magnetic reversal, which Dr. Becker maintains has already started. Presumably one might find some argument here for the battle of Armageddon in *Revelations* (if one lived by the 'script') however it seems to me, that there is a scientific basis for such prophecy; which might distil into the simple choice of whether or not man can accept the history of this planet and   more pertinently what exactly will he DO about it. If you refer to the cancer report, I pointed out that 'doing' is rather an important factor in deciding whether or not a tumour or growth can be stopped. For all those who have fought the World Order and globalisation and wonder why you do it, then the answer is in seeking freedom for others, you gain your own.

The Knossos site after the Religious Revolution is an important glimpse into the mind of the World Order. The cabal that stole the Holy Grail were not only jealous of the creativity of Spiritual intervention but also, sought to take over the Grail and masquerade themselves as the progenitors of the knowledge. Prior the Religious Revolution there was a high level of creativity in the Early Minoans, producing what are still considered to be some of the world's greatest works of art. The Early Minoans had developed a shipping fleet for trade with Egypt and of course this is presumably the direction from which the cabal came and must find some connection to the 13th tribe Druids in England. This connection has been evolved in this book, through the Rosicrucian's and the Order of the Rose, along with the hidden science and Grail knowledge. The knowledge and hidden science of the Grid has undoubtedly been fully researched as one might expect of the mechanical beings. Creativity is however something that was always missing in the aliens and the decline in creative art at Knossos after the Religious Revolution, was indicative of the absence of Spiritual intervention. Magdalenian Period cave art suddenly appeared from nowhere and in the case of the 'Eland' and other works quite clearly illustrated the sudden appearance of a highly creative input, which in the case of the 'Eland' cave painting actually captured the very soul of the animal. There was a 3-dimensional quality in this creative art, which was not to be found in the shamanistic cave paintings or the stylised art of Knossos after the Religious Revolution. I am not seeking to compare art styles today since symbolic art can be highly creative, I merely point out that the creative 3-dimensional art portrayed attempts to teach man not only the art of observation, but also depiction of spiritual reality. It might be considered that the artist was attempting to connect man to a spiritual and aesthetic world that had long been forgotten, through the experience of the sacrificial and murderous mind of a World Order – where fear prevailed. Further the art of observation in science is not very different from art itself and one might speculate that a lesson in observing the obvious was being taught. The artist who looses sight of science does not loose his spirituality, but the scientist who looses sight of art stands to be drawn into the mechanistic thinking of aliens and thus the scientist must take great care with his soul. The art of the symbol or stylised art was directed at certain hidden significances, which were only discernable to those in the know. Just as Picasso attempted to destroy reality with his art, then Salvador Dali in his painting *Persistence du Memoire* (*Fig. 100 The Battle of The Trees*) and other paintings clearly symbolised secret meanings. The woman long acted as muse to painters and clearly in the works of Poussin and Guercino shown in *The Battle of the Trees*, there is once again a hidden story of The Holy Grail. There is in Neolithic cave paintings a clear difference in art styles and the shamanistic art that was found in the Pyrenees is very different from the paintings found in Africa.

Peter Moon (cited) stated that the blood lineage that emerged from the locality of ancient Baal was the same as the Gaelic races that settled in the Pyrenees, St. Angeles and Italy. The depiction of totem beasts in cave art in the Pyrenees was I concluded the various 'shape-shifting' secret groups through which the World Order has worked, thus defying identity and dusting the tracks. Moon also stated that 60-90% of the Gaelic peoples have Rh negative blood. "Rh" stands for Rhesus monkey. If your blood is Rh positive it means that your genetic line is akin to the Rhesus monkey and presumably the ape ancestry. Moon stated: "Without the rhesus monkey factor, there is no logical reason to assume that the genetics of these people must have originated from Earth. The message in all this is clear: the Gaelic race and/or whoever has Rh-negative blood may well have descended from ancient Martians". Well the bloodlines are now so homogeneous that if you have Rh negative blood it certainly would not describe your purpose as a *spirit*: having said that the body line definitely carries memories of its own and what Hubbard defined as the Genetic Entity.

It might be surmised that the secret group behind Hitler utilised various genetic theories noted in Blavatsky's work and applied them to the Jews. The Thule and Vril society and Haushofer who was a clever initiate played their part in Nazi ideology and Rudolf Hess was indeed a pupil under Haushofer at the University of Munich. Hess was to make that inexplicable flight to Scotland during the war, which must have centred on his belief that the British had misunderstood Hitler and his ideology, which must find some connection to the 13th tribe. Rudolf Steiner headed the esoteric branch of the Thule society and the exoteric branch consisted of industrialists and bankers, signifying the close association of International Finance Capitalism and the occult. Aleister Crowley who was deeply involved in occult circles connected to the Nazi's was to write his *Book of the Law* based on an experience in the Great Pyramid where he slept with his wife Rose. The whole experience had an odd effect upon her and it was she who was to show Crowley and image of Horus in the personage of Ra-Hour-Khuit or K.H.Ra, with its connections to the Masters, GWL and GWB at the Cairo museum. The museum mount for the piece was labelled "666" and Crowley would spend the rest of his life trying to understand the experience. Crowley used AIWASS as his guardian and spirit guide, to provide information that became *The Book of the Law*. The incident was to lead Crowley to declare that the Equinox of the gods had arrived and a new epoch in human history had begun on March 19th 1904. AIWASS identified as some aspect of Horus, or according to this book more accurately as composite thought holographics including Hermes and the Religious Revolution conducted it would seem by the great Egyptian initiate K.H. Ra. AIWASS revealed that he was "the inspired fourth-speaker of Mentu", where Mentu is a form of Horus, with respect to the planet Mars. Hitler prominently utilised the colour red (of Mars and war) with black (occult) in his rallies and flags. Hours continually identified himself as the god of war and stated:

> "3. Now let it be first understood that I am a god of war and of vengeance. I shall deal hardly with them. 4. Choose ye an island! 5. Fortify it! 6. Dung it about with enginery of war! 7. I will give you a war-engine 8. With it ye shall smite the peoples; and none shall stand before you".

Crowley later inferred the "island" was England and the matter was *a military secret*. Then he referred to the English war engine as probably foreshadowing a Great War, where Horus would triumph completely. Further AIWASS (Horus) stated:

> "I am the warrior Lord of the Forties: the Eighties cower before me, and are abased. I will bring you to victory and joy: I will be at your arms in battle and ye shall delight to slay. Success is your proof; courage is your armour; go on, in my strength; and ye shall turn not back for any!"

Whilst Crowley assumed he was talking to a spirit guide and was dealing with present time, I am afraid in this text, we see how the occult has pulled man down a route of insanity, by confusing space-time co-oridinates – the then (past) and the now. I have explained fully how composite holographs and thought can be channelled and each may have as a past incident and thought, its own space-time co-ordinates. Further I have explained how the spiritual goals and past life experience of the seer or channeller can 'flavour' the story when those space-time incidents are given in one story line. Aleister Crowley admitted that in a past life long ago, that he was a member of a council of twelve, deciding the affairs of men: such goals do not die with a body and one can assume that Crowley was fulfilling a goal and purpose of control. He also admitted that he was Eliphas Levi in a past incarnation, an occultist magician around the cradle of the French Revolution, which was the start of the push to eradicate Europe's monarchies and create a World Order, which is coming to fruition in our own times with European Union. It was Levi who 'prophesied' that a "Universal Kingdom", would arise (religious and political World Order) and that it would be had by those with "the keys to the east", which must refer to the hidden science, Enochian keys and the whole of the Hermetically channelled information and technology. Crowley was thus bound to imprint *his* goals upon any information received or channelled. The reference to "island" may refer to Atlantis and I have suggested that Atlantis may have been Crete, in so far as a Religious Revolution occurred here, The Holy Grail was stolen (the Enochian

Key equivalent) and a system of mind and body control emerged. Further after the Religious Revolution, icons of war with helmets and swordsappeared, the emphasis was on a war-like influence; and that influence or cabal headed presumably by the puppet king Minos in myth (Ariadne and Theseus) conducted sacrifice. This all points to an alien influence and the great weapon would of course have been the information relating to atomic structure, or Grid technology.

The use of the phrase "engine of war", is also interesting, since this appears in ancient Greek texts already referred to ("vile engine was his name") and was connected to the Bull-Minos cult, 'Stauros' or Star and Tauros (bull) and Crowley was indeed a member of the Argentum Asteris (A A) or Silver Star (Sirius), which must represent not only the Illuminati, but Mercury (as Hermes), a silver-like metal that runs together like quick-silver which is an old term for Mercury; with the Brotherhood implied (run together). Hermes was the product of the Religious Revolution, where the truth and the woman were cleverly hidden in the bisexual and transcendent third of Hermes as Twin Kings and Goddess in *one* personage. Re-incarnation as the message was also hidden and further I have equated Hubbard's Inc.1 and mind control with the Religious Revolution incident. This incident however occurred 1 4000 B.C. The important point is I conclude that Crowley tapped or channelled into Grid holographics in this incident, believing that he was gaining a *present time* message from a spiritual guide. Following the Religious Revolution evidently this information ended up in the hands of the Druids and 13th tribe in Britain presumably through the Egyptian cabal, if not one and the same? The "vile engine" in Greek texts was also connected to the 'T' or Tau-shaped cross (and thus 'pyr' or pyramid and fire); signifying not only 13th tribe, but also the link to Sirius and the aliens. Deary me, the aliens as the saviour of mankind and the knowledge *their* gift! What however did they do with the Holy Grail? – why they kept it to themselves and utilised it in the greatest plan of mind control, through religion and politics, generating thousands of years of lies and pies! -The pupil who could not acknowledge the gift from a greater *spiritual* hierarchy and paraded himself as genius and originator. Crowley in his channelling uses that term: "and ye shall *not turn back* for any" (*author's emphasis*). This phrase turns up in *The Bible* in the story of Lot, who was turned into a pillar of salt for looking back and it also turns up symbolically in the 'Harvesters vase' at Knossos following the Religious Revolution, where priests (?) or harvesters are laughing and mocking someone who looks back and trips. The pillar of salt refers to the sea and there is some indication that the implication here, is 'don't look back to the Goddess' and the spiritual message, but look forward to the patriarchal priesthood and the new religion, which will become the 'reapers' of men – grim reaper more like! Crowley also talks about the "eighties" and "forties" and projects his channelled information into the form of a prophecy for those times in *the future*. This is again a great misunderstanding of Grid holographics, in so far as the 'eights' and 'fours' were also evident at Knossos, after the Religious Revolution. The figure-of-8 not only appeared on shields and in the Queen's chamber, but it turns up in Celtic motifs and also on standing stones in Scotland as the 'spectacle' design. This I concluded not only holds implications of the path an electron takes in orbital around a nucleus, but is also connected to the 720^0 circle or 2×360^0 and the diabolo of anti-matter and matter and indeed Cathie's (cited) wave form of the electron. Could Crowley more accurately have interpreted his holographic information as "Lord" of the "eights and fours", which would describe the cabal who stole The Holy Grail from Crete? Crowely merely took a *past event* – the Religious Revolution of mind control and brought that forward into present time projecting it into a future plan or prophecy, which suited his own spiritual goals and that of the secret Order of initiates to which he belonged, principally Illuminatus. One might conclude that the blood bath in Europe with World Wars I and II, were really the result of men acting out in present time a **past** incident. This is really the psychotic mind of a World Order and the perfect illustration of great ignorance of how the Grid works, which has no doubt created the worst excesses and repeats of the carnivorous and blood-thirsty past of the alien line, with its requirement for sacrifice and blood to quell the primitive mind. I trust you will understand how prophecies work and how they are manipulated in psychotic minds, to control others, be that through body control and sacrifice or mind control, which requires twisting and hiding the truth into a pack of lies, which is then fed to humanity and children as part of their programming (education). By tapping into the Grid, you merely receive the Masters thoughts and version of this story, since the Grid merely records survival in terms of matter and mechanics. The aliens it appears have learnt nothing in 10 000 years since The Holy Grail arrived on Earth, they have little creativity and the expression of that character is played out on the world's stage continually, where the man who creates, who works a 9-5 job and produces something (creates) is fed upon by a group of parasites who make money from that creation. The second plank of Marxism was introduced at Knossos after the Religious Revolution – taxation and today the globalisation plan where 'fat cats' feed from the creativity of others, is merely a reflection of the inability of the alien to create.

The alien is jealous of another's ability to create (something out of nothing) and the artist is particularly vunerable to this type, where the creative work is seen as something to be covertly destroyed. The alien decries genius in any other than those *he* directs, for which reason he surrounds himself by 'experts' who are under *his* control: indeed many scientists in history appear connected to the secret groups including Newton. Another method of the alien is to take others creativity and assign his own name to it, without giving one reference or acknowledgement to his sources and their own particular genius. The only future ability and rehabilitation a man has is through his ability to create. The anti-capitalist movement, whilst I decry violence has in fact created an impulse of reflection or thought, on which way the world is headed, thus create can have many facets. In one conversation with an anti-capitalist group and in answer to my question, as a long supporter of the peace movement: "Why the violence in protest?" he retorted: "its the only way the b....... will listen". This is very true for the alien views life from the observation point of matter and force and I guess the anti-capitalist movement decided to out-create the alien on the subject of force, but it is not an answer: one should out-create him on the subject of all that is spiritual and the hippies called for 'love'. In fact the anti-capitalists got themselves on to the front page of newspapers throughout the world, through sheer creation of force and yet, they were tutored by those who tried intellectually to expose the World Order. The young have many things to learn and one thing that they do not realise is that you can never win a battle on force alone it must be coupled with an intellectual revolution and **a goal**. The World Order have understood this point very well from the time of the French Revolution, where the phrase 'Liberty Equality and Fraternity' was issued by the encyclopaedists of the Masonic Lodges, long before it was parroted by the French on the streets of Paris, believing they had made it up! The student revolution of the 1970's which saw Paris grind to a halt, was almost prophetic in so far as the students stated: "Parliament has become a theatre and so we are taking over theatres and making them into parliaments". If there was an appointment with fate in the 1970's where student revolts worldwide and the hippie peace movement occupied newspaper columns, then it was missed simply because force was not coupled with an understanding of the mind of the World Order and the immensity of lies that have occurred; neither was there a concerted goal whereby governments would be forced to tell the **truth** on the globalisation plan. The media have always deliberately suppressed the alternative viewpoint and promoted their Masters and owners goals as the propaganda line. Further I often see Col. Barry Turner's ideas (researcher and writer of *On Target*) utilised in mild manner, but never once have the press (or politicians) given him acknowledged credit or interviewed this man, simply because they dare not! The one thing the World Order does not want is a platform of opinion and speech, from the highly informed and impressively intelligent. The young perceive the last generation as the source of their problems and do not wish to employ the wisdom of those who have seen it all before on the world's stage. The sadest thing is to see groups who believe that any one person or group can fight this movement, the 'Messiah syndrome'- in fact the only way to fight the World Order, is to form a cohesive group, which cuts across individual agendas (including religion) and presents a *united front*.

518

Man however in his egocentricity cannot apparently cohere to bring about "Paradise on Earth", even though the World Order works on the principle of cohesion and like quick-silver, join forces when threatened. The response to the student revolts of the 1970's, which shook the World Order, was to remove student grants, forcing students to take out hefty loans, thus the student could no longer afford the luxury of protest.

Crowley through the Vril an Thule societies had extensive contact with the O.T.O and Crowley's aim was to tap into the Hall of Records, which many thought was located in the secret chamber below the Great Pyramid of Gizeh. Hubbard curiously was to claim some illuminating experience, where all knowledge was laid out like a 'smorgasboard'. It is certainly curious that Crowley's first experience, which governed his life, took place at the Great Pyramid. At one point Crowley contacted a spirit called LAM. This is somewhat coincidental with Hubbard's Space Opera and his description of the Life or Lambda project, for the control of bodies, which you can further reference in L. Kin's book (cited) or in Hubbard's O.T. materials. Presumably Crowley was contacting some information on the Lambda poject and the O.T.O allegedly founded the cult of LAM, in order to use the egg, as an astral form of travel. Crowley as I have previously described in one occult session, was told by his guide: "It's all in the egg", which identifies the secret group history of the alien, through the crocodile reptilian line, Knossos and up to the Pope who conducted an Illuminatus ceremony in New York, with egg and wand. The aliens therefore were only interested in creating a mind and body controlled populous and Crowley by utilising the egg, was to bring down the thoughts of the Masters right through the whole line of holographics from the crocodile to Knossos.

Jack Parsons head of the O.T.O Lodge in Pasadena California, sought to invoke the goddess of Babalon, thus bringing an end to the age of Yuga or Kali, the black age. He was devoted to the Goddess and evidently sought her mind and thoughts in his rituals. The symbol that Parsons used was the seven pointed star, with the angles of calcium carbonate crystals (51.5°) which reflect not only the angles ineherent at the pyramid of Gizeh but also gypsum or calcium carbonate (white chalk) was used to cover pyramids and the whole site of Knossos; and also was found covering the barrows of New Grange in Ireland, which I concluded were connected to the Danaans and the whole line from Magog, the great grandson of Noah. Thus the egg and the significance of white (chalk) or gypsum reffered back to the incident 1400 B.C. the Religious Revolution and the theft of The Holy Grail. Unfortuantely it seems that whilst indeed a battle of alien and Spiritual intervention occurred in Crete, the occultists were merely tapping into or channelling one side of the story, that of the Masters who stole The Holy Grail: thus in fact not following the Goddess or Spiritual intervention, but taking the egg and the line of the Masters as their truth. Peter Moon claimed in his book (cited) that Ron Hubbard and Marjorie Cameron were present in the Babalon working and that it changed them forever, curiously creating a brief paralysis in Hubbard to the right side, which conspicuously resembles the right side tremor that Hitler developed. If I were to propose a solution to this, it would be that they had contacted the incident at Knossos (the Religious Revolution) where the creative (right side brain) and left (mechanical) were united in illumination of the third eye. If one channelled information from the Grid, then the information would illuminate, but it would only illuminate from the mechanical or Masters point of view: in effect you would cause a dichotomy of the brain. If Hitler reguarily channelled information, perhaps through the mysterious woman at Berchtasgaden, then he would have caused a dichotomy activating only one side of the brain. Hermes was created by the cabal who stole the Grail, thus hiding the entire incident, which was only a beginning for mind and body control and the attempts to create a Universal Kingdom (political and religious) based upon the desire of the elitist aliens to become the progenitors of such knowledge, with the gift of The Holy Grail as theirs. It is my conclusion that the Illuminatus hard thinking inherent in many secret groups has been coupled with The Holy Grail message of Re-incarnation along with Grid knowledge, which has lead to the behaviour and thinking of initiates – which is almost split thinking in the sense that one perceives much that is good and much that is bad in such groups. It is in effect schizoid or bilateral brain thinking, with the attempts of the aliens to link creativity and spirituality with mechanical thinking: secret groups therefore can often go one of two ways and such groups can either save or entrap- only your own conscience will guide you. Crowley and Parsons may have been devoted to the Goddess and The Holy Grail; however Spiritual intervention never utilised Grid or channelled knowledge, since it was realised that any interference with the Grid, inevitably placed information on the Grid, which could and would be used by the aliens. Crowley made the mistake of channelling from the Grid and contacting the egg symbol as a means of entry into the hologram; he was however merely utilising a symbol of the occult and alien Religious Revolution, which would if contacted bring down the entire hologram of the Masters and the incident at Knossos and prior mind and body control events of the composite hologram. In effect although he believed he was working for the Goddess, he was in fact a dupe of the Masters and their plan for a World Order: this plan was evidently furthered by Crowley when he influenced Hitler through *The Book of the Law*, which was paraphrased by Hitler and England would become a mere dramatization of the island of Crete: once again confusing in space-time the incident of the Great City of Atlantis, with Crete and London (and perhaps NewYork as Long Island and Montauk Point), under the subject heading of islands and it would seem control. The consequences were two World Wars and a furtherance of the 'script', which is merely a repetition of the past and Grid holographics or <u>www-com.world</u> wide grid and the outcome is really decided by those initiates who may have already elected their victim, with regards to the "Great City" of the Apocalyptic *Revelations* account; dependent more on whether version 12 or 13 is the desired outcome of the aliens and whether they have nominated Crete that beautiful orbit in the Moon of Greece, or Rothschild's "City" of London.This is indeed the source of mans insanity. Both Crete and London are vunerable, since Crete sits on a pedestal in the ocean and London sits on the electro magnetic fault lines that run from the Seven Sisters (white chalk cliffs) on the south coast; both are susceptible to electro-magnetic disturbance and Tesla technology, which is capable of *producing earthquakes* (manmade): further both nations have been used in this theatre of Earth.

Hitler may have fought for the Goddess, utilizing the womb or labrynth of Knossos as the basis of the swastika; however what information he received from presumably the psychic in residence at Berchatasgaden, if not the 13th tribe intiates that surrounded him, must define the course of his particular battle and other occultists like Crowley and Parsons, who in channelling information merely became dupes to the past and Masters. Curiously although Jack Parsons fell from grace in the O.T.O he never fell out with the Argentum Asteris (A A), Silver Star, Illuminati, Mercury or Hermes. Crowley's guardian spirit AIWASS and Mentu, were froms of Horus and therefore connected to the aliens. It might be questioned whether Hubbard took on the Illuminati but never falling foul of the O.T.O. in attempting to release the mysteries and spring man from the trap he believed was created by implants, but which I have given a different interpretation of here. If Hubbard fought a 25-year battle with the Illuminati, then it must be questioned what happened within the Church after his death. There were rumopurs that Jack Parsons was head of, if not a prominent Member of the CIA and their headquarters in Langley has that curious reference to St. John: "The truth shall set you free". Crowley and Parsons were Illuminati members and it was inevitable that any release of the mysteries that perhaps Hubbard sought, would result in a battle for control. If scientologists are hard pushed to survive economically on a 10% commission fee, then I suggest that they study the accounts of Scientology and the policy of the apex; for everyone should be paid a decent wage rather than commission, in order to survive: otherwise you will invoke the primitive mind and survival of self or group, regardless of the sacrifice of another's soul – which was my horrendous experience and as such is the policy of the Masters in 'sacrifice to a cause' and surely negates the message of The Holy Grail and its purpose here on Earth, where every individual soul is important. People who choose to work on a spiritual line have a right to support themselves and their families, but if you put money on a spiritual line, you had better make sure it is ethical.

Crowley's aim was to set in motion occult forces that would illuminate all by the end of the century: however by restimulating holographics of the Religious Revolution, setting into motion all connected holographics, he would have pulled down the entire composite holgraphics on the subject of mind and body control. The rapid rise of the age of Horus played out on the world's stage since World War I, with incessant violence, wars, uncontrolled averice, greed, secrecy, globalisation, unethical actions, cloning, GM modification of food, secret weapons utilising electro-magnetic fields and the whole gamut of so called 'civilization' is the result. How easily man fell for that old trick of telling people not to question policy, for the makers of such policy including religious dogma, are 'saving the planet'. The key to freedom lay not in blind acceptance, but in the ability to question and the right of free speech. You can beat a man to a pulp and yet, he will not further your cause, but if you tell a man he is saving the planet he will work for your cause until he drops. Encourage him to believe that yours is the ONLY solution and ask him to overlook 'collateral damage' in the sacrifice for a cause and he will accept such sacrifice of individuals or permit unethical actions as the justification. Scientists, who are experts in a mechanical field or the matter energy space-time universe, are very susceptible to such auguments. In *Alternative 4* (*Appendix 1*) I commented on the use of the physicists in the Los Alamos atomic bomb project and the justification that a bomb would stop the war with Japan. Some physicists after Nagasaki and Hiroshima were horrified to learn that the bomb was to be rattled to bring Russia into line and one physicist when reflecting on why they continued said: "**We did not stop to think**". The same comment could be made of today's scientists who have not considered the implications and consequences of their research. Scientists from my own experience do not know very much if anything about the World Order or the occult and make no connections between these fields and their own field. The classical education has gone by the board and the early age at which one specialises and the intensity of the subject knowledge, coupled with hours at work, really mean that for most scientists there is no time to study such connections. Further man driven by his ego prefers the easy route of becoming a highly paid 'expert' with a good home, respected in his field, his children in good schools, a good pension and in the case of scientists that means not making any waves that would rock the 'gravy train' of grants, salaries and position; which are invariably controlled by the Chemical Syndicate in some form or other. Further if you stand out on theories, which do not fit into orthodox established viewpoints, you must run the gauntlet of ridicule and professional suicide, orchestrated by primitive minds subservient to the dominant tribal hierarchy. The problem is new thought is always fought, since there is always some form of personal investment in maintaining the mystery.

The occult became obsessed with the idea of Masters in some etheric world, which they believed was anti-matter. Whether like the Elohim, who were said to have arrived and then left, or whether the aliens are still trapped here, in body form now indistinguishable, is the question I have posed: however what is clear, is that science has been unknowingly harnassed to the occult. The idea of anti-matter was utilised in the biblical description of Jesus after His death, where He shimmered and walked through a wall and then ascended. The Phailadelphia Experiment, was reported by witnesses in much the same fashion with the crew of th SS Eldridge shimmering through walls. Whilst one accepts that some form of experiment did occur at Philadelphia, with which Einstein was indirectly connected to, science tells us today that teleportation of large objects is impossible. The use of the particle accelearator which Moon claimed at Montauk point, together with Crowley's visit to the area and the whole connection of Montauk to the 13th trribe as I have proposed, really underlines the connection of physics to occult research and goals. Was it believed that the significant vortex point at Montauk was a 'door' to another world? Was information being channelled?

George Smoot is a highly talented astrophysicist and no doubt picked up no inclination that he was working on 'The Holy Grail' of physics and further had no reason to question the curious interests of his project leader Charles orth. Alvarez, or Luie as he was known. Luie was best known for helping to develop the ridiculous (to my mind) theory that the dinosaurs were blasted into extinction when a giant asteroid or comet collided with Earth, 65 million years ago. Not only has this theory been taken up and pushed by the powers that be, but it also prevents data from other sources emerging co-incidentally or not. The radiolarian population data, which I have already discussed, with the curious finding that the magnetic components of these small fossilised sea creatures suddenly reversed at this time, has not received any notice. Luie may not have known much about Radiolarians and since various inter-disciplinary conferences are never in my experience as a scientist organised, then how would he have known? Any scientific theory is only as good as it ties up all observable data, thus Luie's theory was not a good one, unable to answer all the odd artefacts in archaeology or zoology, let alone the Neolithic cave paintings etc. However this theory has become the orthodox explanation and yet it is only a theory: but it does prevent other theories like the one I present here from emerging – however Luie became the 'expert'. Luie was a legendary figure in physics and was the winner of the 1968 Nobel Prize for physics and significantly he was born in 1912, the son of a famed newspaper columnist Dr. Walker Alavarez of the Mayo Clinic and Luie was to work on the Manhattan or Los Alamos atomic bomb project. Luie further investigated the Kennedy assassination, concluding (against all evidence) that the "one bullet, one gunman" theory was basically sound: he also significantly studied the Egyptian pyramids and with such a background one might consider he was aptly suited to work as project manager in the search for antimatter. Luie allegedly initiated the project in the 1960's with the NASA-funded High-Altitude Particle Physics Experiment (HAPPE, inauspiciously pronounced 'happy'). HAPPE was initiated as a precaution or a way to continue particle physics research, should congress stop funding the construction of new, larger particle accelerators and ultimately the search for anti-matter. NASA I have long suspected has with perhaps agencies such as the Goddard Space Centre (aptly named – Dog/God!) certain connections to occult knowledge. Congress funded the Fermilab accelerator, which is now conducting experiments to produce antimatter! Have the physicists 'stop to think', that if there is no antimatter in this Universe, then perhaps that is the way it is intended, otherwise there might not be anything left to observe as anti-matter and matter do not exactly mix well! *Alternative 4* also discussed the possibility that space research was directed at looking for a safe haven, in the event of a cataclysmic catastrophe on Earth – Noah's Ark: which the reader will note is a dramatization of the past cycle.

Once again this summer (late August 2001) a rash of crop circles appeared in wheat fields across Hampshire in the U.K. In *Alternative 4*, I commented on the DNA similarity of these intricate patterns, which appear curiously enough on the borders of Wiltshire and the location of the significant Grid point beneath which Stonehenge the Druidic Apollonian temple was built. This year crop circle enthusiasts describe the patterns as among the most spectacular examples yet of a mystery that has been going on for 25 years. One pattern made up of hundreds of individual circles appears to show a face in its 3D effect. The binary message in the second formation allegedly includes digits from one to 10 and the formulae for sugar and DNA. In fact sugar or glucose is a 6 -carbon atom *ring* and the first pattern resembles a honeycomb of a beehive! It is claimed that the crop circle binary pattern is recognised as a pattern transmitted as a radio message in the direction of a star cluster in 1974 from the world's largest radio telescope in Puerto Rico. NASA apparently beamed this message into deep space in the 1970's in an attempt to contact alien civilisations! The beam was allegedly aimed at a star cluster M13, some 25 000 light-years from Earth, as part of NASA's Search for Extraterrestrial Intelligence (SETI) project. Which DNA code used is not mentioned, or whether Sirius figured in this attempted contact, however it seems to be overlooked that any radio message would not reach the M13 star cluster for more than 20 000 years and therefore it seems that the message in the 70s', may have been captured by the Grid geometry as a binary code and beamed back as a holographic by dislodging it artificially from the Grid; which emphasises my question over what effect and consequences, will binary TV transmissions have on the Grid? It cannot be argued that NASA is not in the forefront of occult associated research and once again we find the link of the Druids, 13th tribe, Rosicrucians and UFO manipulation. Next they will beaming down the Second Coming and no doubt many will fall for it!

Paul Dirac proposed the existence of antimatter in 1929 and as I have covered in a previous section concluded that when matter is created from energy, an equal amount of anti-matter is also created. For every proton (positive particle in the nucleus of an atom) there should be an antiproton, for every neutron an antineutron, for every electron a positron and so on. *The New York Times* was quick to pick up this theory in its *September 10, 1930* issue: *'Scientists acclaim new Atomic Theory'*. In 1932 Carl Anderson of the California Institute of Technology detected the first antimatter particle – the positron or anti matter particle of the electron. Dirac had been proven correct and won a Nobel Prize in 1933, as did Anderson in 1936. However the one detection, placed serious doubt on whether this was the result of cosmic radiation and was in fact produced by such interference, as opposed to coming to Earth from some antimatter star (or world). In the 1950's a particle accelerator called the bevatron was built at Lawrence Berkely Laboratory, with sufficient energy to generate its own antimatter. In 1955, Emilo Segre, Owen Chamberlain, Clyde Weigand and Thomas Ypsilaritis ran an experiment at the bevatron, in which high energy protons collided with target protons, producing pairs of protons and antiprotons – a quarter of a century after Dirac's prediction. In 1947 during the run up to the antimatter experiments and following nuclear bomb detonations, there were a rash of UFO phenomena; with witnesses claiming mechanical aliens abducted them. Place into this experimental pot, the magic of Aleister Crowley pulling down holographics of the technology and information in past holographics and Hitler's development of craft utilizing the Grid in the 1930's and it appears that the past holgraphics were restimulated and it is difficult to decide whether Crowley's magic initiated control via the Grid, or all these experiments disrupted the Grid pulling down the holographics (which came first – the chicken or egg?): however it seems certain that from this point, man was on a path to repeating his past actions and catastrophes exacerbated by the advent and spread of electrical gadgets. The method, by which the holographics impinged on witnesses, was described in 'The Onion Ring Model' in *Alternative 4*.

The physicists reasoned that if experiemental 'little bangs' simulated in the particle accelerators could simulate the symmetrical conversion of energy into particles of matter and anti matter, then the 'Big Bang' or the start of the Universe, must have had a similar outcome i.e. production of matter and anti matter. Segre and Chamberlain shared the 1959 Nobel Prize for their work; however the question became if half the material universe is comprised of anti matter then where is it? For there is no significant amount of anti matter on Earth or in the rest of the solar system. The idea of causality in physics whereby the existence of an anti particle is required for every elementary particle is a precept that cause precedes effect. It is not obvious that this would be true as special relativity tells us that moving different observers could see things happen in reverse order – were there not mirror pairs of particles and antiparticles. In a restricted sense, anti particles moving backwards in time behave like particles moving forwards in time and particles moving backwards in time are equivalent to antiparticles moving forward in time. This exchange is a space-time mirror symmetry and I am drawn back to my theory of the diabolo of matter and antimatter and the separation of the two in what I term the first Incident (which differs from hubbard's version and his Inc.1 which I place as the Religious Revolution at Knossos and the start of mind and body control). Why is it, that regressive accounts have not allowed a memory of this matter/antimatter incident or the true beginning? – the answer may well be that Hubbard claimed *everyone* has Inc.1 (I can't find it) however let us assume that the forgettor phrase "Don't look back" was a major mind control implant or imprint, which occured at the time of The Religious Revolution and which has prevented the ability to remember or *go before* the incident; then everyone that has Inc.1 Or Hubbard's Inc.1 would be unable to go before that incident, or remember the actual Inc. 1 which is the matter/antimatter explosion. Some have claimed that the story of Lot in *The Bible* is descriptive of a *nuclear incident* and the phrase "don't look back" is once again evident. UFO witness accounts of abductions speak of being shown atomic blasts and there is certainly a connection of aliens to atomic blasts and perhaps the long battle of two kings: it may well be that an atomic war of two kings perhaps spoken of in the Indian epics precipitated an electro-magnetic reversal and man as his soul was swept up into days of terrific storms and downloaded with the entire Grid holographics at that point, which may prevent him from locating the actual first incident. More regressive research needs to be carried out, to find out the connection of atomic bomb blasts, to the forgettor phrase 'Don't look back'.

One might conclude that the physicists in trying to loacate anti matter, have bypassed this command phrase ('don't look back'), but they are still approaching memory by a mechanical means. Let us suppose the memory would entail separation of matter and antimatter in the firmament at the very beginning, in the first trillionth of a second, which created spirits (ourselves) – then what exactly is a spirit (the I of existence) and what is our purpose?

I will return to this in one moment but the diabolo of mirror image symmetrical halves (which could be portayed as the double axe symbol of Knossos which represented the idea of one Twin King dying by one blade as the other was re-born!) of anti matter and matter moving away from one another in expanding matter and antimatter universes gives us the idea of time and change of space-time coordinates, which is time relative to observation point. If you stand at a point A and something moves away from you to a point B, you have the fealing that time has passed, because B will occupy different space-time coordinates as it moves away, relative to your observation point (A). It is not inconceivable that one universe e.g. matter moving in one direction and the other anti matter universe moving in another direction holds relative time according to observation point and from where you view this movement. Let us say that from the point of observation of an antimatter universe, I concluded the matter universe was moving backwards in time and by conclusion the antimatter universe was moving forwards in time; I would also consider that the beings in the matter universe were travelling backwards. Equally a being in the matter universe might consider they are moving forward and the beings in an antimatter universe are moving backwards. Beings in the anti matter universe might view beings in the matter universe as backward and being heavily emersed in gravity and the mechanics of matter – mechanical beings. In fact mechanical beings probably think very differently from anti matter beings, they think in lists and downward spiralling concentric and condensing realities under the influence of gravity and spin of atomic particles. Beings of the antimatter universe probably think in expanding and outward interconnectiveness and these thoughts may well be determined by the spin of the particles. Once again I am drawn to my intuitive use of the 'suck down' and 'suck up' movements of the diabolo I produced in *Alternative 4*. The most pronounced character trait of the alien or MRC case is his inability to distinguish morally, ethically or spiritually, right from wrong: the case of human embryo cloning is a case in point. In my own experience I have been amazed that certain groups have no concept of right from wrong along with numerous individuals. To a mechanical being or those who operate on primitive mind lines however, right and wrong are only subjective standards in relation to survival of self and at most group – 'what's in it for me?' Every day man is asked to make ethical decisions of right from wrong and yet the first question he often asks is 'how does this affect *me*?' The material or matter universe is subject to the laws of entropy and decay and man having committed his spirit to the matter universe, has developed obsessive mechanisms for retaining growth and survivalist mechanisms as the answer to entropy – growth at all costs is the aliens answer to entropy and the laws that govern the matter universe. He also obsesses on the subject of control and the need to know all laws governing quantum mechanics, which he believes determines survival in the matter universe. The World Order as a phenomenon of growth could be considered as the adaption of psychological method of coping with the laws of the matter universe.

Swedish physicist Alfuen observed in the 1960's that there can be no anti matter in the sun for: "If the sun consisted of antimatter it would emit antimatter plasma, or antiplasma and this would travel toward Earth where the aurorae would then glow at a thousand times their present luminosity". This must have put paid to the occult and secret beliefs of the return of pure spirits to the antiworld and sun, which may have provided the background to the sun god; and the idea of the black sun of the Nazi's as anti-matter. Occult beliefs based on the idea that man *in his body* can cross into an anti-world finds some basis in the description of Jesus after the Crucifixion (drawn up at a later date by those who sought to promote ideas of the anti-world and Masters) and the crew of the SS Eldridge in the Philadelphia experiment, which underlines how little those occult groups and ultimately the aliens have learnt from Spiritual intervention, the warning and message. The body and bloodline and the requirement of saving bodies and knowledge, has totally ignored the truth and purpose of The Holy Grail and the fact that it is only **a spirit** that can traverse the trap of the Grid, providing that there is no conscience on the antimatter 'film roll' or deeds and thoughts together with considerations of energy in the matter universe. The Christian religion and others have little to say about the soul after death, other than there is some form of judgement, which I have explained as the comparison of 'film rolls' and the requirement to return (Re-incarnate) if conscience exists. The galaxies are receding in all directions from a matter, anti-matter explosion. Alfuen curiously enough in 1966 stated:

> "If someone were to claim that *Sirius*, the brightest fixed star in our firmament, consists of anti-matter and not (ordinary matter), we would not have any tenable argument to demolish his claim, were Sirius to consist of anti-matter it would have exactly the same appearance and emit the very same spectrum as if it consisted of ordinary matter. The space around *Sirius* must then contain anti-matter, but this may be separated from the oridinary matter in the space around us by a thin Leidenfrost layer, which we are poorly equipped to detect" (*Author's emphasis*).

Why exactly Alfuen chose the example of Sirius with its deep occult connection is unclear although it is the basis of occult beliefs in the origin of the Masters (mechanical aliens I conclude). Alfuen's theory attracted a lot of attention in the late 1960's, which co-incided with the time that psychics tramped through the offices of the CIA. If Alfuen was correct in the statement that stars like Sirius could be made of anti-matter, then clearly at least some of the stream of particles that constantly shower Earth, would be anti-matter. Whilst Carl Anderson at Cal.Tech in 1932 detected an anti-matter particle, it did not indicate its source as anit-matter and may have been a fluke of cosmic interaction. George Smoot and his colleagues however found no evidence for anti-matter in this universe and published their findings in *Nature* and *The Astrophysical Journal, Physical Review Letters in 1975*. The American Insitute of Physics recognised the research as one of thw world's twelve outstanding physics experiments of 1973: thus the search for anti-matter seemed to grind to a halt. The Russian physicist Andrei Sakharov in 1967 proposed a theory, which basically stated that in the beginning after the 'Big Bang' a slight excess of matter over anti-matter was produced and then matter and antimatter particles self-anhilated in a cataclysmic release of energy leaving the slight excess of matter, thus the universe is somewhat of a fluke. Apart from Einstein's comment: "God doesn't play dice" this theory would violate two "givens" of particle physics 1. The conservation of baryon number, which is a statement that energy is always converted into equal amounts of matter and anti-matter and there can be no net production or net loss of baryons (matter) over antibaryons (anti-matter) in any reaction. 2. CP symmetry, which states that the chemical and physical reactions of matter and antimatter are identical. It is my consideration of this however, which leads me to the conclusion that anti-matter and matter must resemble biochemical isomers (mirror image chemicals), which are similar in properties however they rotate the plane of polarized light in different directions – which might account for the different spins and 'suck up' and 'suck down' effect of the two diabolo halves or matter and anti-matter: gravity is a major consideration.

Pakistani physicist Abdos Salmen at the University of Texas and Weinberg from Harvard in the 1960's attempted to show that the two "givens" were violated in conditions of the 'Big Bang' or beginning of the universe and utilised what are known as GUTs or Grand Unified Theories. These physicists argued that in the unimaginable temperature of the first instant of the universe (10^{-34} seconds, or one ten millionth of a trillionth of a trillionth of a second after the 'Big Bang') the weak, strong and electro-magnetic forces which behave differently in the universe as we experience it, were essentially the same and operated in the same way on particles and according to GUT theorists, baryon (matter) number will not be conserved. This theory argues that matter in that early moment behaves slightly differently from anti-matter, which according to my own conclusions would be correct. However into this firmament, I have placed the 'birth' of the Spirit. Let us assume that in that first moment, you and your doppleganger (your anti-self) danced the game of Life as matter and anti-matter. 'I am matter' and 'I am anti-matter' as you changed viewpoints dancing two and fro with great joy and rhythm between particles and antiparticles; but shortly afterwards you individuated and became OBSERVATION POINT ON BOTH   - '**I AM**' (viewpoint on matter and antimatter). The purpose of the Spirit might then be defined in terms of *remaining observation point on both matter (mechanical) and anti-matter (spiritual) energy*; thus explaining why aesthetic art was being taught in the Neolithic period along with Grid mechanics – the scientist and artist combined. This conclusion or formation of observation point (over matter and antimatter) may have then **caused the separation of the two universes**, in much the same way as in the two-slit experiment of physics an electron can be a particle or wave, depending on the *presence of the observor (you)*! The question is whether some Spirits chose to BECOME the viewpoint of matter or anti-matter. Let us say that you never got to the conclusion 'I AM', but stopped at 'I am matter', or 'I am anti-matter'; then as a Spirit you would move accordingly into a matter or anti-matter world. The curious belief that the Spirit of some god was inherent in a stone, which was the belief displayed in Semitic stone pillar worship found in stones at Knossos after the Religious Revolution; and which also displayed the double axe symbol; was famously as a belief to be illustrated in the otherwise incomprehensible start to the epic Hollywood film of '2201' (with monkeys gibbering around a stone pillar). The idea must have incorporated one of man deriving or evolving from matter and a primordial 'soup', which is the popular evolutionist theory of Darwin, along with its datum: 'Survival of the Fittest'; thus promoting mechanical views, the matter universe and the absence of a Spirit: Spiritual intervention came to redress this thinking. Whether or not the mechanical beings have ever known an anti-matter world and have somehow become trapped in a matter universe along with spiritual humanity, or whether Hubbard's Space Opera, which describes how arch controllers or Masters trapped souls into 'small boxes' and brought them here is correct, is open to opinion. The outcome however is that those who *became matter* and resided in this universe, lost viewpoint on the spiritual and anti-matter world as *The Bible* states it would be easier to pass a camel through the *eye* of a needle than for the rich man to enter the gates of Heaven: actually its not riches that do you in, it is how you use those riches and in fact the belief that spiritual beings must be poor, is merely a propaganda twist of the Masters, since as we all know without money, you cannot in the material world achieve a spiritual purpose now, since even an advertisement and publication of books independently requires money. The aliens or mechanical beings always had a vast experience of matter, however they could not create and this shortcoming was indeed the source of enmity and jealousy towards Spiritual intervention.

Physicists continually ponder the question of the singularity or the infinitely condensed state of the universe before the 'Big Bang'; comparable according to British mathematician Roger Penrose to the collapse of a star into a black hole as an infinite contraction of matter compressed into a region of zero volume with a density of matter and curvature of space time as infinite: however since the Spirit or who we are was not yet observation point and therefore was not 'born' before the matter/antimatter explosion, there seems little point in pondering it, or the argument of whether a Divine Being set up the game, or whether the universe is just a recursive 'donut' (comprised of diabolos expanding outwards forming the edge of the donut ring) with the centre of the 'donut' the point of balance between all diabolos with matter and ant-imatter worlds, or whether the 'donut' centre is ultimate observation point for some Divine Being. The game *is* observation point and the ability to remain observation point, thus retaining the ability to play with matter and anti-matter: the Spirit of Fatima appeared to be able to do just that. The SCC or super conducting collider will test baryogenesis, the production of the excess of matter over anti-matter by the year 2005, although the experiment in attempting to create the first incident on the time track, will not evidently include a consideration of inherent observation point; and what effect observation of the experiment (by souls of physicists) will have is unclear. As the physicists follow their own Holy Grail, and theories of the first incident, they are really using mechanics to bi-pass spiritual memory and regression. If physicists do not like the idea of time having a beginning, it is because they dislike the implication of Divine intervention and have not considered a greater spiritual world, which cannot be observed from the viewpoint of matter. If there were large regions of anti-matter in our galaxy, we would expect to observe large quantities of radiation from borders between the regions of matter and anti-matter where particles would be colliding with their anti-particles annihilating each other, giving rise to high-energy radiation. There is no direct evidence as to whether the matter in other galaxies is made of protons and neutrons or of antiprotons and antineutrons.

GUTs or Grand Unified Theories allow quarks to change into antielectrons at high energy; they also allow the reverse process of antiquarks turning into electrons and electrons and antielectrons turning into antiquarks and quarks. It is argued that there was a time in the very early universe when it was so hot that the particle energies would have been high enough for these transformations to occur and according to the diabolo theory I produce here, with Spirit as viewpoint that would be correct. Up until 1956 it was believed that the laws of physics obeyed each of three separate symmetries called C, P and T. I have referred to CP symmetry, but again here C means that the laws are the same for particles and antiparticles: P means the laws are the same for any situation and its mirror image (which could be a diabolo). Under P presumably a particle spinning in the right-handed direction would obey the same laws as a particle spinning in a left-handed direction. This would not apply to biochemical isomers where as I point out, each mirror image isomer has different properties including the rotation of the plane of polarized light: further I have proposed that thought in the two worlds (matter and anti-matter) is different. How much the Early Minoans under tutorage knew of these facts is fascinating to guess, since the spiral motif at Knossos is virtually a left and right handed spin motional direction and also appears at New Grange barrow in Ireland, which again was a burial place for the dead and was I concluded connected to the Danaans or 'gods' from Greece. Were they implying that the Spirit departs to some anti-matter or spiritual world, to be re-born? Further the figure-of-8 design on the sheild at Knossos and in the Queen's chamber, along with the 'spectacle' design on standing stones in Scotland has some connective symbolisation with this idea of electon spins and anti-world diabolo. The symmetry T means that if you reverse the direction of motion of all particlesand antiparticles, the system should go back to what it was at earlier times, in other words the laws are the same in the forward and backward directions of time. However the matter universe has the problem of spin and gravity, whereas the anti-matter universe has a different spin and is not built on the principle of mechanics or gravity. There is a mathematical theorem, which says that any theory that obeys quantum mechanics and relativity, must always obey the combined symmetry CPT. In other words, the universe would have to behave the same if one replaced particles by antiparticles and took the mirror image. Cronin and Fitch showed that if one replaces particles by antiparticles and takes the mirror image, but *does not reverse the direction of time*, then the universe does **not** behave the same. The pointed question that some people ask, as to why they need to regress or **go back**, to past life incidents is perhaps answered by this theorem and unless you go back, it would not be possible to exit from the material universe – there lies the trap! The laws of physics must change, if one *reverses the direction of time* – they do not obey the symmetry T. In fact the whole of my own research has been a regression in time through incidents and space-time co-ordinates, constantly leading me backwards and as you have read this book, then you should have reversed the motion of time as *observation point*; but you must not rely on anyone's account, you must have the courage to find out your *own truth*. According to the laws of science there is no distinction between past and future: it is stated that the laws of science do not change under the combination of operations (or symmetries) known as C, P and T and yet the anti-matter world works very differently in terms of spiritual awareness and anti-gravity/spin must be a major consideration. Life it is claimed would be the same for inhabitants of another planet who were both mirror images of us and who were made of anti-matter rather than matter. Spiritual intervention however shows that those who came to tutor man thought very differently and probably would have split their sides laughing at Theatre Earth, unless they had not perceived that it was a very *Greek tragedy*.

SEPTEMBER 11

On September 11 2001, two of three hijacked commercial airliners were piloted by Islamic fundamentalists into the Twin Towers of the Trade Centre in New York and a third into the Pentagon in Washington. The hope for world peace and sanity was lost on September 11. Donald Rumsfield, the American defence secretary, stated that terrorism was " a cancer on the human condition and we intend to oppose it wherever it is". The response to the 'disease' of terrorism paralleled the response of medical orthodoxy to the case of cancer – cut, burn and poison; the desperate

situation requires desperate measures, where growth of the 'cancer' or Islamic fundamentalism would be attributed to rogue units out of control. The underlying mechanism and the Platonic maxim; 'before you can cure a man's body, you must first cure his mind and before that his soul' will not be considered as with the case of cancer as the real cause of the disease. The symptoms of 'cancerous' growth in Afghanistan would be "relentlessly" blasted by weapons, in response to the attack in New York on the Twin Towers of the World Trade centre and the Pentagon, the former the symbol of capitalist growth and the latter the sign of military growth. The choice of the *Twin* (King?) Towers, is in itself curious for its symbolism.

Osama bin Laden gave a chillingly final interview to *al-Jazeera* Arab television channel in 1998. The full transcript was printed in *The Sunday Telegraph Oct 7th* 2001. In one excerpt from the interview OBL stated: "There are *two sides* to this conflict, the international crusaders and the Jewish Zionist alliance headed by America, Britain and Israel. The second party is the Islamic world" (author's emphasis). Here quite clearly is a fundamental cause and a war of two kings, which I had predicted throughout this book and prior to 9/11. It should be remembered however that the American CIA (Central Intelligence Agency) created OBL allegedly in response to, but in truth in a manipulated invasion of Afghanistan by Russia; thus the dramatization and conflict may be sourced to this point. Neither can one dismiss the possibility of planted agents within Arab groups deliberately fuelling conflict, by transmitting false data, for Bill Clinton was reported in *The Guardian* (*Jan 26th 2002*) as stating: "In Pakistan, the main reason that all those madrassas (religious schools) were not teaching maths but promoting such ludicrous notions as America and Israel brought dinosaurs back to Earth to kill Muslims, is that the Pakistanis ran out of money in the 1980's to support their schools". Thus it seems there has been an underground and secret vein of knowledge and pre-history of man falsified for a pre-determined goal of conflict, by a third party.

The Indian epics spoke of the distinct racial characteristics of two warring kings and even throughout the current cycle on Earth, there have been crusading wars between Islam and Christianity. Such a war I have concluded in this book may have occurred in a past magnetic cycle, where I presume the war concerned **power and kingship**, rather than religion. The unique feature of this cycle is religion and the case of the stolen Holy Grail, however the real and repeat cause of the cycle is a war of power and control of resources. The war of the hour, we are told, is against "global terrorism", so declared President Bush in his speech to Congress on September 20 and repeated by Tony Blair in his oration to his Party (New Labour) Conference (Oct. 2001). This is not the case – in every war, the first casualty is said to be truth. In this one, our politicians have not even begun to admit to what this war is really about.

I have previously explained in this book the method by which groups are often set up by the real power brokers in the thesis anti-thesis method, whereby it is hoped that through supply of funds or weapons the outcome of power in any one region can be predicted. The CIA and other intelligence agencies have acted in this manner in the past. Any plot always has its sub plots and any terrorist outrage is often not as simple as defined in the press. The CIA played a role in the early 1970's to foment and support armed Kurdish rebellion in Iraq, presumably as a method of destabilising Iraq and Hitlerizing Saddam Hussein. The CIA, in league with the Shah of Iran, provided $16,000,000 in arms and other supplies to the Kurds, leading to Iraqi capitulation to the Shah in 1975. Five years later, in 1980, Iraq invaded Iran to redress the C.I.A. – assisted humiliation of 1975 beginning an eight-year war that cost a million lives. These events as precursors of the Gulf War and today's demonisation of Sadam Hussein were commented on by Mr David Pidcock, co-founder of the Islamic Party of Britain and The Institute of Rational Economics who had privy to a 47-page document compiled by the late Dr Kitty Little. In this it was argued that in 1975 George Bush Senior and Dr Henry Kissinger (Bilderberger) had devised a strategy to seize control of Arab oil resources, to displace the indigenous Arab population and to resettle parts of the region with immigrant Soviet Jews. They had a clear inference for a further expansion of the

State of Israel. The Gulf War of 1991 was to be used to achieve this. David Pidock submitted Dr Little's paper to The Hon. James E. Atkins, United States Ambassador to Saudi Arabia from 1973-1975, and an expert on the Middle East. His reply, dated 20th February 1998 was extremely significant; here is an extract:

> "In early 1975 some twelve articles appeared in American newspapers and magazines on "How we can solve our economic problems". The basic idea was that we would occupy the Arab oil fields from Kuwait to Dubai (not Iraq), expel the indigenous populations, "not more than 2 million", bring in Texan and Oklahoma oil men who would produce the oil. ...It was clear that the articles came from a single "deep background" briefing. I assumed it was given by some idiot in the Pentagon or the C.I.A. (Central Intelligence Agency), and said on American television that "anyone who proposes solving our domestic problems in this manner is a madman, a criminal or an agent of the Soviet Union"...Subsequently several of those who were present at the briefing revealed that Henry Kissinger was the one who gave it.... Kissinger was not amused and my diplomatic career was terminated shortly thereafter...The Zionists at the Versailles Conference (1919) presented a map of Eretz Israel; its borders would include all of Palestine, all of southern Lebanon up to Sidon, all of southern Syria, not just the Golan, including the entire Jebel Druze, and all of inhabitable Trans-Jordan. The Herut Party (now part of the Likud (of Ariel Sharon), uses as its logo this map superimposed by an arm carrying a rifle and the word "Kahk" – only thus. This concept has never been disavowed by Herut-Likud....The late Rabbi Kahane said that within three months of his becoming defence minister, Israel will be "free" of its Arab population – by this he meant Arabs in Israel as well as those in the occupied territories. And the main area of settlement of these Arabs would be **Iraq**, with its adequate land, water and oil. Even Kahane never talked about Israel occupying Iraq". (*On Target Vol.31 Nos. 18 &19 March 2002*).

In fact Kissinger is a Bilderberg member, a group that I have concluded is 13th tribe, and in descendent can be traced as Druid, Rosicrucian, Bull-Minos and presumably bird and stag cult to Noah and Adamites in one phallic and continuous line complete with World Order aspirations and rule by an elite. In any war as Nesta Websta proved in her works (cited) and the case of the French Revolution, there is always a **third and hidden party** present in any war or revolution. History has proven that war or revolution on a major scale invariably also has a predetermined plan and goal. I have put forward the conclusion in this book that the French and Russian revolutions were a method of removing monarchy paving the way for two

World Wars, which ultimately paved the way for European Union and decline of British power. At the centre of the concentric circle design of the Summer Smoking Room Floor at Cardiff castle was a map where "Jerusalem", "Asia", "Australia" and "Europe" are clearly defined. I concluded that not only was this a plan for a "Universal Kingdom" (religious and political) but also questioned which "Jerusalem" was being indicated (Jerusalem in the middle East or Jerusalem in the U.K Scotland). Quite possibly the New Jerusalem in light of the above comments would become a great slice of the Middle East. I also noted coincidently that the secret Bilderberg group met in Scotland in 1999, significantly at the beginning of the new millennium and asked whether a plan to complete the World Order was set into motion and what exactly would such a plan consist of, if not the plan laid out on the Summer Smoking Room Floor at Cardiff Castle (Scottish Rite Freemasonry/Rosicrucian) and control of Asia?

The altering political stage post September 11 mirrors quite accurately the map on the floor at Cardiff castle, where "Asia" is indicated alongside "Europe". The "war on terrorism" therefore seems just another cog and justified means to an end, in the wheel of sacrifice to a cause - the World Order plan. However as American troops build up in Asia, there is another adjacent world power – China, which does not appear on that floor design that could either eventually become foe or ally (in any communistic plan) for a World Order. Most of the biggest Chinese companies on the Fortune list are in the same energy and petrochemical sectors that control the Bush Administration international agenda, from Kyoto to Kazakhstan. Money and power and the old Bull-Minos phallic cult, will not allow any competition to their own 'own all' philosophy. This is no more than recognition of Kissinger's outline of American foreign policy and the domination of those who conflicted with US unilateral interests. *The Quadrennial Defence Review* identified Asia as "emerging as a region susceptible to large scale military competition", with a "volatile mix of rising and declining regional powers". China is one of the former and without mentioning China by name the Pentagon warned "a military competitor with a formidable resource base will emerge in the region"; adding that the lower "density of US basing" in this "critical region" places a premium on securing additional forces in Hawaii and formidable military guarantees backed with hardware, for Taiwan, which is regarded as a rebel province.

Andrew Murray author of *Flashpoint: World War III (Pluto)* in a study of post Cold War international conflict noted: " But long before September 11, Asia was already seen as the centre of post-cold war competition and China as the main potential rival for commercial and strategic influence over the Continent and its emerging markets". Further "The Pentagon's Quadrennial Defence Review attracted little attention when it was published shortly after the attacks on the World Trade Centre.

However this official policy document, the first of the second Bush presidency, identified north-east Asia, and the East Asian littoral as "critical areas" for US interests, which must not be allowed to fall under "hostile domination". The US already maintains 40 000 troops in South Korea and similar number in Japan and Soviet Central Asia. The significance of the new US presence goes well beyond even the signal importance of Exxon- Mobil's share price and the securing of oil supplies.

Eastern Europe along with Central Asia are of great importance in the battle of multinational interests to tap and supply (at enormous profit) the 'black gold' that lubricates the cogs of the vast grinding machine, run by mechanical beings who in many cycles have taken control over the Earth's resources and reduced man to a **slave state**, where grinding efficiency of the machine, is a mere reflection of the mind that has always dictated events and wars on this planet, a point that appears frequently in myth and legends of the past and which I concluded is held in holographic memory (UFO witness reports) within the Grid or UVG120 crystal. Indeed wherever the mechanical being is in control, it is noticeable how he sucks the life force and joy out of any creation and game – witness the change in art style at Knossos after the Religious Revolution c. 1400 BC and witness too the introduction of implements of war and sorcery (in Zeus's cave). The lack of life force again was so evident in marked comparison of artistic styles of these beings to Magdalenian art with its striking life force and aesthetics. The 'own all' policy was applied to the mysteries held by the early Minoans, where knowledge of the Grid and whole cosmology was sequestered by the Bull-Minos cult. The sequestering of this knowledge has been the major and decisive factor, which has led to man following the same worn out path of prior cycles, with its inevitable consequences – the catastrophe. It was noted after many Scientologists that personally knew Hubbard were forced out of the Church of Scientology in the early 80's during the 'cull', that the entire life force disappeared from Scientology, where it became a machine rather than a joyful game, once again indicative of control by mechanical beings. Life is no longer a game for the majority, but a work to live and live to work first dynamic survival 'game', where the rich constantly as multinational corporations or countries exploit the poor as cannon fodder for wars, or slaves to the machine of profit and growth supporting the apex of puppeteers.

On Target (*vol. 31 September 2001*) published what the media and religious leaders have stayed silent on – the battle for 'black gold' – oil:

> "The ultimate objective is the centralisation of world Power per se; as seen in the drive for globalisation. The strategy to achieve this included control of the world's natural resources, with particular reference to oil, without which the entire fabric of western society would grind to a halt.

The operational level of this process therefore involves control of those countries where these deposits are located. This involves control of the Balance of Power in the Middle East and the Balance of Power between Russian interests, those of Christian and Islamic States of the former U.S.S.R and the control of those peripheral countries with a potential influence on the security and movement of oil...The Balance of Global Power, with its emphasis on oil and the common organic "life blood" of Money Power, has divided the world sharply between the predominantly Christian nations of the West, with a powerful undercurrent of Political Zionism and the mainly Islamic countries".

I have noted how secret groups such as the Bilderbergers and the Bohemian Grove group appear to vet future world leaders, presumably with this geo-political balance in mind even manipulating the American elections to ensure their man was in the White House. Third Party influence in the causation of wars and revolutions has gone unreported in the media, whilst inaccurate causation such as Human Rights is widely covered. As *On Target* pointed out "Human Rights" and the exploitation of the "authority" of the "United Nations simply become very malleable factors in the hands of those who wield Power". Intervention in the Balkans, on the grounds of "Human Rights" certainly clouded the real issue and the battle for resources and balance of Power. Bosnia was just such another case where "for multinational corporations working alongside NATO, one of the most important rewards will be the construction of a trans-Balkan pipeline to bring oil from the Caspian Sea region to Europe".

William Ramsay, United States Deputy Assistant Secretary of State for Energy Sanctions and Commodities, claiming that Caspian oil is crucial to the world energy Balance of Power over the next 25 years, has revealed that: "there already exists a kind of outline of a new Silk Road running through the Caucasus and beyond the Caspian. We think oil and gas pipelines, roads, railways and fibre optics can make this 21st century Silk Road and superhighway linking Europe and Central Asia" Afghanistan is central to this "superhighway" and further "The European Union, the United States government and a gang of multinational Corporations (including BP Amoco, Exxon, Unocal, Caterpillar, Halliburton-Brown and Root and Mitsubishi, are using all the military, political and economic tools at their disposal to destroy and recreate the infrastructure and economy of South Eastern Europe in their own image".

Every twist in the war on terrorism seems to place one more foot in the Asia – Pacific region, from the former USSR to the Philippines, which is now under threat from 'sheriff' Bush. One of the lasting consequences of the war could be what amounts to a military encirclement of China, with the possibility that "two warring civilizations" will not be Islam versus Christianity, but east versus west as two superpowers size up. Neither can one dismiss the ongoing antagonism of the secret groups in Europe to US bullyboy tactics and America's unilateral policy, along with the worrying development of a European army. Thus is must be asked whether the World Order plan seen I propose on the floor of Cardiff castle, with its Rosicrucian and specifically Scottish Rite Freemasonry sources, meant for China to become a part of the World Order – world communism run by the far right and rich elite: the slave state of the Masters and the hive of mankind, as an efficient machine run by none other than the mechanical beings or MMRC case. The invaders from Sirius via Mars making man (even cloned and robotic man) in their own image – but as miniscule cogs of course in the quantum mechanical universe of matter. Unfortunately who would believe it; man has so far been removed from the truth that it is beyond his reality, or even intention to bother to read and attempt to understand what has been given to him in this cycle. Indeed I await anyone who can say GOT THAT! (Duplication of a communication).

US Bases are rapidly being set up in Uzbekistan, Kyrgyzstan and elsewhere in the once Soviet Central Asia. Britain has according to that "special relationship" which appears based on secret Rosicrucian alliances and plans, also promised support in the Philippines despite the fact that the Abu Sayyaf Muslim guerrilla movement there only numbers 500 fighters. Thus once again the "war on terrorism" may be a mere pretext for protecting and exploiting oil supplies by vested interests. The question becomes which "Jerusalem" also portrayed on the floor of Cardiff Castle is indicated as central to the World Order plan of a political and religious kingdom? If the political kingdom is defined by vested interests and secret groups (money and power) one cannot expect a religious goal to be free from such influences. Indeed Rupert Murdoch the media mogul had a particular part to play in suppressing the Falung Gong in China, who hold a belief in Re-incarnation and Chi (life force). The support of New Labour (Tony Blair's government) in the United Kingdom for creationist schools, mirroring a similar development in the US cannot merely be co-incidental. Whether such a movement is being centrally directed to re-educate man into accepting a race of men descended from Adam through Noah and Abraham directed the course of civilization and evolution, rather than Darwinian evolution, can only be guessed at; but it seems somewhat predictable for the Bull-Minos cult and its Rosicrucian descendents to claim source, rather than admit the message and knowledge was stolen c.1400 B.C during the Religious Revolution in Crete: and earlier than that in *the first cut* c. 10 000 BC. It seems predictable that they would eventually either try to give the stolen apples back to man as *their* gift or remove the knowledge from the masses and only sell the stolen apples to the "more able" at vast profit.

The Daily Telegraph Sept. 28 2001, reported that the attack in New York has in one sense, suited the European Commission. Those with a federalist agenda have taken deliberate advantage of it to pursue aims and ambitions that they had before: "They even anticipated the usefulness of an attack along these lines; five years ago, the Commission drafted a forward planning report which said: "It will be difficult to achieve political union without there being the perception of an external political threat. A terrorist outrage would contribute to the perception of an external political threat". I have in this book stated that the aftermath of World War II created the exact milieu into which the concept of European Union could be introduced as a peaceful trading community. The denials that European Union would ever become federalist with its own police force, army and intelligence bureau (Europol) were being denied as late as 2000 and yet the deceit with which this plan has forged ahead is breathtaking for its arrogance and ignoral of the right of *informed* democracy and referendum.

The pointed finger (aimed at the tomb of Hermes) and the requirement to answer difficult questions (even Petition Questions!) was the secret symbolism I decoded behind the painting *Les Bergers d'Arcadia by Poussin c. 1640-42 (The Battle of The Trees)*. The use of symbolism to replace the written word, thus ensuring that any message is only understood by those with access to the 'keys'/ symbols, means that security is ensured; a point which the Druids may have recognised by using symbols and never committing any of the details of their nineteen year training to written word. As Tony Blair appeared to fulfil the Messianic function of the right (Rosicrucian symbolism of the one dollar note of America) whilst Bush fulfilled the Illuminist and political power pyramid left side (of the note); one might be forgiven in raising one's eyebrow at an editorial in *The Times* newspaper (Rupert Murdoch's stable). The article '*Looking After Britain*' (*January 2002*) pointed out that whilst Tony Blair was entitled to bang the drum for Britain's role in world affairs, it does not mean: "we have a **magic wand** to wave their problems away. Nor should Mr Blair "**over-egg**" our so-called "pivotal role in world affairs" (author's emphasis!). One might almost consider whether Murdoch's masters and International bank rollers had just shot a warning over Blair's bows – to 'cool it' on the religious kingdom goal. What a co-incidence, along with the depiction of Murdoch some time ago in *The Mirror* newspaper complete with (bull?) horns, traditionally a symbol of Satan (Bull-Minos cult) and with pointed finger! Further Murdoch was referred to as "The Sun King" in an article by *The Express* newspaper. In any war there are always codes to crack and I felt some sympathy with the code breakers at Bletchley Park (U.K) who decoded the enigma code during World War II, as I sat through many nights at my desk in Crete.

The least martial assembly that Churchill had probably ever addressed at Bletchley consisted of mathematicians, librarians, Egyptologists, musicologists, museum curators, classicists, chess players, historians, cross word and puzzle addicts and of course the unique and brilliant Alan Turing the mathematician who designed and built Collosus which was to become the basis of modern computers. Churchill was to famously comment: "Well you don't look dangerous". The same might be said of the codes I broke in *The Battle of The Trees* and some people criticised unable to understand, my emphasis on the Greek base! The contempt for learning for learning's sake has reached its apex under New Labour political/educational policy in the U.K. There is poetry in science, but I am afraid you will not obtain a grant to find it! An ability to understand the six-patfugue in Bach's Musikalischis upfer was invaluable in seeing the hidden pattern in a line of Kriegsmarine cipher. In 1940 Alan Turing and his colleagues demonstrated pure maths was not an irrelevant subject, when it provided the intellectual impetus, which led to the refinement of the code-breaking machine Colossus. I seem to remember that in one UFO incident related in *Alternative 4*, that the witness was told to: "study these ruins" – and many a hot day and night I did so with the Knossos site and at the Heraklion museum in Crete along with many other intrepid expeditions. Certain dreams (recognition of spiritual knowingness) also indicated the work was of the utmost importance and amazingly, as I wrote (at breakneck speed – hence the lack of editing) the dreams changed, as if I was re-writing the end of the 'script'! The soul journey is a curiously wonderful and yet awesomely responsible experience.

The terrorist attacks have allowed other measures to be introduced without discussion. An intelligence service (Europol) has emerged in Europe along with no doubt justification for the European police force long in the pipeline. National police forces must now provide "any relevant information" about terrorists. Europol does not have an unblemished record and serious allegations have been made involving corruption in the computer department, where secrets are stored. National governments will have virtually no control over Europol and it is uncertain whether views of personnel held by that intelligence agency will mirror those of national governments. Anti-globalisation protestors may in future be marked as "terrorists" along with any dissident who challenges secret group **policies**. I have within this book long predicted that this would happen. Violence as anti-globalist protestors should have intelligently realised, only plays into the hands of those they hope to defeat and is no answer for peace on earth. Europol will develop into a European version of the FBI (the U.S Federal Bureau of Investigation) and will simultaneously start to become a version of the European Central Intelligence Agency. All this from an alleged European trading community! This will be an extra-ordinary concentration of power in the hands of one organisation and moreover, similar moves in America are now removing the democratic accountability that both the FBI and the CIA owed to Congress, although the CIA has always underneath in its labyrinth proved to be a loose and unaccountable cannon, as third party and with curious connections to the 13th tribe Rosicrucians.

"Terrorism" will henceforth have a wide definition and involve an action involving intimidation designed to alter the political, social or economic structure of the country – secret group policy. *The Daily Telegraph (Sept. 28 2001)* asked whether "we are seeing a major extension of EU police and judicial power that is in danger of being nodded through without any national debate about whether it is desirable". It seems also that in the aftermath of September 11 the British government are not only willing to return to the blasphemy laws of the 19th Century, but also David Blunkett (British Home Secretary) attempted to resurrect the Inquisition against those who retain a variant philosophy and religious viewpoint. There are already in place in Britain laws, that cover violent action and terrorism and thus the question as to why any further change was required, is answered by the fact that no edge of this secret must be exposed. For any civil libertarians, even the racial hatred legislation was objectionable because it contravened what seemed a fundamental principle of English law – deeds or direct incitement to unlawful action should be punished not thoughts. As I predicted in 1996 it will become unlawful to even produce a variant history and academic treatise, which questions the events of the crucifixion or the almost supernatural accounts of religious texts. However even a senior figure in the Church of England stated of the resurrection: "we can't be sure".

The fantastical stories of religion deserve to be subjected to the objective scrutiny of the scientific eye and truth. The purpose of science is not to ridicule or harbour a desire to stir up hatred; the purpose of science is merely to discover truth. Science has always stood on the threshold of blasphemy and one of the biggest barriers to the freedom of science is religion, since science seeks truth, which apparently religion (or those that manipulate it) does not. No religion held the entire truth, although all religions hold part of the truth, the path or spiritual journey an individual takes is entirely personal preference and responsibility, for which reason I fought for the freedom of belief in a court of law in 1989 – and won.

It must be asked whether Roger Penrose and Stephen Hawking both eminent British academic physicist/mathematicians in their research between 1965-1970 could be considered either terrorists or heretics. They showed that according to general relativity, there must be a singularity of infinite density and space-time curvature within a black hole, rather like the big bang at the beginning of time. Einstein's general theory of relativity, on its own, predicted that space-time began at the big bang singularity and would come to an end either at the big crunch singularity (if the whole universe re-collapsed), or at a singularity inside a black hole (if a local region, such as a star, were to collapse). Stephen Hawking pointed out that the Catholic Church had made a bad mistake with Galileo, when it tried to lay down the law on a question of science, declaring that the sun went round the earth. Hawking attended a conference on cosmology organised by the Jesuits in the Vatican in the 1970's, having decided to invite a number of experts to advise it on cosmology. At the end of the conference the Pope told the delegates it was all right to study the evolution of the universe after the big bang, but they should not enquire into the big bang itself because that was the moment of creation and therefore the work of God. Hawking narrowly missed his inquisitional moment, when the Pope evidently missed Hawking's talk at the conference, where he proposed the possibility that space-time was finite but had no boundary, which meant that it had no beginning, no moment of creation, to quote Hawking: "I had no desire to share the fate of Galileo"!

To question the alpha and omega (the beginning and end) is indeed to invite the wrath of Europol, the thought police and whatever other inquisitional agency that the World Order has currently come up with. The curious referral of Tony Blair to being with America at the start or beginning and the promise to be with them to the end, had implications at least to the author (the alpha and the omega or the full continuity of secret Rosicrucian groups?), although presumably he was referring to September 11. Indeed another 'Messiah' appears to have entered stage left (or is it right?) – Prime Minister Tony Blair in the U.K. By page five of Tony Blair's speech to the Labour Party Conference (Oct. 2001) the greater part of Britain's Armed Forces were earmarked for battle across the globe: to quote Jesus "I have come to bring a sword not peace". The 'healer' by the end of his speech had more or less solved planet Earth utilising a resounding 21 mentions of "justice": social justice at home, injustice of oppressive regimes and the justice that international terrorists face. "Community" was close behind with 14 mentions (close enough to communism to warrant concern) and two references to "war" (although "seize, "strike" "risk" "courage" "danger" "fear" and "duty" along with "victory" and "defeat" were used repeatedly). "*Blood*" (hereditary?) was mentioned *five* times "fight" came up four times and "battle" three times: further Mr. Blair pledged four times to defeat things (including "climate change") and "Good and Evil" occurred and low and behold "truth" came up significantly and co-incidentally five times (a symbol of entry into the new Aeon or gate to the New Year - vowels of the Druidic Ogham script alphabet). Huge emphasis was given to the word "new" and "new world" (mirrored by the public use of the phrase World Order, first coined by the last President Bush senior). I believe it was *The Daily Telegraph* that first reported that half the speech had been written some months' prior, which half they did not state. There was "new beginning", "new situation", "new relationship" and "new life" along with phrases like "turning point" and "globalisation"/ "global" significantly used eight times (a patriarchal symbol corresponding to the figure-of-eight). All this delivered in almost religious or Evangelical tones!

Co-incidentally you will remember that I 'prophesied' in this book that the Rosicrucian's were heading towards the age of maat or justice of the eighth Tarot card after the age of Horus or war: the author can see nothing "new" in fact it seems rather old as World Orders go. The re-statement of the over-used British election slogan about "the many not the few" is to the author just another way of interpreting the obverse side of the One dollar note with its Hermetic philosophy of 'out of the many come the one' (or 'out of the one come the many'), which was illustrated by the power pyramidal apex of the Illuminatus (political) power pyramid of the left, with the Rosicrucian religious aim on the right of the obverse side of the note. The matriarchal and patriarchal dichotomy of religion, was perhaps obliquely illustrated by the Editor of *The Daily Telegraph* (*Oct 3rd, 2001*) when he stated that the Prime Minister used this context to seize a probably unique chance to "**dramatise**" what he called his (Tony Blair's) "governing idea". "The combination of toughness in response to threat and compassion in response to suffering was presented as the Blairite approach to domestic policy and to the entire world" (*author's emphasis*). Well the Editor of *The Daily Telegraph* said it not me! However since the Floor of the Summer Smoking Room Floor (Rose Croix and Scottish Rite Freemasonry) does not mention China, a betrayal could be afoot.

The events of September 11 not only created the opportunity to push suppressive legislation and justify thought police, but it also provided an opportunity to push through the Euro and another hike on the Second Plank of Marxism (taxes in the U.K) all under the veil of fear and threat of war. Millions of personal e-mails, other internet information and telephone records are to be made accessible to the police and intelligence services in a move that has been denounced by critics as one of the most wide-ranging extensions of state power over private information. Plans being drawn up by Europol, the police and intelligence arm of the European Union will propose that telephone and internet firms retain millions of pieces of data-including details of visits to internet chat rooms, and of calls made on mobile phones and text messages. This significant change in the control over private information is being worked out **in secret** and brings reality to significant World Order statements made some years ago, where a "more controlled and directed" psycho civilised society was being predicted if not planned. The computer E-mass systems I discussed in *Alternative 4,* which were being developed almost a decade previously, certainly were capable with their file page that could reach into the ionosphere of carrying that volume of data or even the entire Akashic record. The events now occurring on the world's theatre stage are not in response to the events of September 11, but were planned many decades if not centuries earlier.

Another facet of the aftermath of September 11 was the indication that NATO will become no more than a cog in a vast global machine under the absolute control of Washington. European States that had claimed some right to be "consulted" by the White House before the launch of any retaliatory strikes were given short shrift by Paul Wolfowitz U.S Deputy Defence Secretary. Britain's role in the preparations for the "war on terrorism" appear so intimately interwoven with the U.S Defence Department and through that "special relationship" which Israel has recently also claimed with America (Hebrew Daily – Oct. - *Yedioth Ahronot*), that the NATO structure is almost superfluous. As in Operation Desert Storm in 1991, which deliberately destroyed the infrastructure of Iraq (*On Target Vol. 31 Nos. 18 & 19 and Vol. 31 Nos. 20 & 21*) the talk-up for aggressive military action by the United states, is surrounded by secret group names among the so-called "hawks"; Assistant Defence Secretary Paul Wolfowitz and Defence Adviser Richard N. Perle are both Bilderbergers, which I have concluded is the 13th tribe with its goals of a Universal Religious and Political kingdom dating back to the Bull-Minos cult.

As if to justify the loss of liberties and freedoms at the time of David Blunkett's (British Home Secretary) bill, the newspapers co-incidentally ran "evidence" of a posed threat to the nation (UK) 'Bin Laden in plot to bomb City – Terror blueprint for attack on London (*The Observer 16th Dec. 2001*) "Chilling plans for a devastating bomb attack on the City of London have been discovered in a terrorist base in Aghanistan". *On Target* magazine (cited) in its issues from 9/11 onwards have repeatedly warned of accepting the media's version of "evidence" pointing to the broader political perspective of the battle for oil. *The Guardian* (*Dec. 22nd 2001*) reported "New terror threat to Britain" co-incidentally in the same period. Whilst undoubtedly this aided Blunkett's legislation placing the British into fear (along with Israelis and Americans) "Security Services deliver stark warning of risk to the UK, including nuclear and chemical attack", fear is always a method along with the threat of external attack of creating an unquestioning adherence to central policy. There is also a possibility that such threats mirror the secret war of two groups on this earth, particularly the Revelations condemnation of "Gog" and the thirteenth tribe. However to attack *any* nation is to merely play into the hands of "666".

President Bush immediately post 9/11 was careful to be photographed talking to his senior Cabinet officials or Secretary of State Colin Powell, Defence Secretary Donald Rumsfield, Attorney-General John Ashcroft and Vice President Dick Cheney. The impression of a genuine cabinet government is given; meanwhile 'Messianic' Tony Blair in the most extra-ordinary way, dispensed with both his cabinet colleagues and with the traditional forms of British representational democracy. There is no doubt the British people along with the majority of mankind were appalled at the destruction in New York, but the British people and press appeared somewhat mystified as to why Tony Blair who could not move a muscle in recent home domestic crises, suddenly rose to voice in many cases what should have been voiced by President Bush. Tony Blair also appeared alone at the microphone in the *rose garden* of No.10 Downing Street (the Prime Minister's residence) subtly mirroring the traditional presidential press conferences in the White House *rose garden.*

Despite Tony Blair declared a "war on terrorism", appearing in Congress in America, it was not until criticism had been levelled in the press, did Tony Blair finally set up a war cabinet on the 8th Oct 2001 in response to September 11: further, British troops had already been deployed and the bombs had already dropped on Afghanistan. Blair's decision to set up a War Cabinet was the 'machine' responding to input of criticism from the British press. Mo Mowlam (past Secretary of State for Northern Ireland) has commented of the "Presidential" style of Tony Blair, dispensing with cabinet and therefore **accountability**. If Mr Blair took the decision to commit British forces without consulting the full Cabinet, then we might reasonably ask **who** in fact is governing Britain? – There is a background here, which is not being made open. It seems to the author, that whilst the Commons has reached broad agreement on the "war on terrorism", this is traditionally a cause for alarm. Many times in British history has a government proceeded to disaster while supported by all persons of goodwill on both sides of the Chamber. Indeed it is somewhat predictable in the author's view that a further sacrifice of victims will be made by the secret groups, if not an attack on Britain, persuading Britain (if England is left) that an all out war on terrorism is required. The outcome rather depends on which 'script' of the Revelations account that is being dramatized (12 or 13) and which "Jerusalem" has been decided as the religious centre and which as the sacrificial victim. Tony Blair may believe in world peace and the high aspirations that he stated in his speech, which was transmitted around the world, but can he be sure that he will not sacrifice this country in the process and can he be sure that the "knife in the back" of Israel, will not be at a future date be placed swiftly in his own back and that of the British people? Can the Israeli people be sure that they will not once again become sacrificial victims on the world Theatre stage? Indeed the actions of Ariel Sharon against the Palestinians, may in a dangerous way open up Israel for attack – again it rather depends which "Jerusalem" the World Order have decided to maintain – if indeed either in the event that China becomes ally and world communism introduced!

No sooner than the dust had settled on the Twin Towers, than conspiracy theories hit the streets and media and whilst the west without immediate evidence blamed Islamic Fundamentalists, the Arabs turned on the Israelis. This story however as I have been at pains to point out, cannot be laid at the door of ordinary people, who have no inkling of this game. The Israelis cannot collectively be held responsible for the mechanical beings and a World Order policy, any more than any other nation. The fact is however that religion has harboured these beings and religious texts still bear evidence to mind control and magic channelling of Grid Akashic record. The rise in anti-Semitism post 9/11 is merely once again playing into World Order hands, just as is the provocation of the long suffering Palestinian people. Indeed many Jews are very much opposed to the actions of Ariel Sharon against the Palestinians.

Britain is the only European country that has taken such a drastic step in introducing legislation that would nullify Human Rights legislation (compare America). When asked why that is so, the government replied that Britain was and is in special danger, because it is particularly close to America. However here in this book, the nature of the "special relationship" is questioned and whether that depends on secret group alliances – the Rosicrucian's and the whole line back to Stag and Bull-Minos cult, through Druids and Adamites (13th tribe). When this book went to press on August 23rd August 2001, it was too late to prevent the events of 9/11 and indeed there was just time to add the section of 9/11 at the end (1st Edition). The bees were still buzzing however and there were still some nagging questions that I felt I had not answered. Why for instance should the proposed memorial garden (*rose garden*) for the late Princess Diana (which displays co-incidentally or not, many archetypal symbols of Twin Kingship/Minoan Greece) also have a 45' wide rock from China included? (*p.37/38 Vol.II*). There was also the question of why the original statues of Gog and Magog in London destroyed by the blitz in 1940, were simply not replaced by the original design which clearly depicted the Greek connection of the secret groups (Twin Kings as Greek/Roman?) reflecting perhaps the ruling power prior to 1939 and explaining why one Pope was to be found watching an Illuminatus ceremony in New York, where a woman tapped an egg with a wand (Druidic/13th tribe). Why should the new statues erected at the Guidlhall in London after World War II, now represent one Twin King as Celtic (Druid/13th tribe) and the other with the slanted Mongolian-type eyes, reflecting the Masters of the occult groups and which was to turn up in manipulated UFO incidents; where three (Druidic/13th tribe) men in black appeared with slanted Mongolian-type eyes? I did conclude however that this was an attempt to connect alien/extraterrestrial intelligence (the Masters/MRC case or mechanical beings from Sirius?) to an **eastern source** of either Tibet (the traditional source of Masters in occult writing and allegedly a source for Jesus) – **or China?** - The attempt being made to link wisdom and a greater font of knowledge to a source.

Putting the clues together one might tentatively conclude that some deal was arranged with Churchill, whereby America would enter World War II (the bombing of Pearl Harbour was always viewed with some suspicion) and aid the British, if the insistence on a Greek source (extraterrestrial/spiritual intervention) of civilization was dropped, in favour of a Mongolian or Chinese source? This question of source is a pre-occupation of secret groups, when in truth both are wrong, since the knowledge was stolen. Ron Hubbard when he claimed that he had some form of out-of-body experience as the background to *Excalibur,* allegedly accessed all knowledge laid out "like a smorgasbord" and significantly described passing through two very large Chinese-like gates! Hubbard however appeared linked to the Rosicrucians and Illuminati through Jack Parsons (O.T.O) and Aleister Crowley, who was both Illuminatus and a Rose Croix Mason. Hubbard himself wrote a poem about a rose.

Corelli Barnett in *The Collapse of British Power* (*1972*) commented:
> "For, unlike the collapse of French power in 1940 and German power in 1945, the collapse of British power had not been made evident by defeat in the field; its historical moment was not fixed by the entry of conquering troops into the capital, or by well-filmed and photographed ceremonies of surrender. Instead, British power had quietly vanished amid the stupendous events of the Second World War, like a ship-of-the-line going down unperceived in the smoke and confusion of battle".

On 24th March, 2002, *The Observer* reported what was seen as a binding British obligation in that the United Kingdom remained indebted to the United States to the tune of £243,000,000 from the 1939-45 War. This does not seem over-excessive however it has always been a curiosity that the work and genius of Alan Turing was never publicly acknowledged and the Colossus machine he developed as the origin of modern computers was allegedly destroyed after the war. Did the Americans broker a deal on the technology? Hitler as puppet and dupe to the secret groups (more than likely the Bull-Minos cult/Rosicrucians or Scottish Rite Freemasonry - accounting for the inexplicable journey of Rudolf Hess) presumably served his purpose well in setting the stage for a State of Israel to be born along with European Union amongst the dust and ruins of Europe; whilst America now became the world's definitive power. As we have observed in the events of post 9/11 there is no country, which dares to stand against America and the globalisation plan. The "war on terrorism", as with World War II is only a means to an end – and that end will repeat past cycles in a nuclear catastrophe where two "warring civilizations" or two Twin Kings will square up in battle. One might conclude that the battle will involve America and its allies against China; however there appears to have been a deal post World War II, with the possibility that the Illuminati have no intention of introducing a religious kingdom (Rosicrucian) under world communism.

According to the Nostradamus prophesies "Earthshaking fire from the centre of the earth will cause tremors around the New City. Two great rocks will war for a long time, then Arethusa will redden a new river". Those who try to interpret the prophecy fail to identify the symbols (rock- Semitic stone pillar and the Patriarchs from Noah: red – red men, divinity, red men of Knossos and Oak Royal, genetic hereditary line of Twin Kingship – "two great rocks": river (red) – underground stream of wisdom, the Alpheus in Greece, The Holy Grail connected to Twin Kingship – possibly Rosicrucian knowledge sequestered from Minoan Crete). Thus whilst some have extrapolated this prophecy to the attack on New York, the story has a much deeper origin and symbolism.

Further there was the question as to why during a State visit to Britian from Ziam Chang of China, should Tibetan demonstrators have their pro-Tibet flags wrestled from them, whilst a newspaper referred to "policy" – WHAT POLICY! Is there a secret policy here, decided at the end of the Second World War that the new era Twin Kings would become the US and China in some World Order goal of a Communist hive? The true basis of which, would be the common Patriarchal descent of a race of men derived from Noah, or at least Shem or Ham son's of Noah. These sons appear to have given rise to two opposing groups on earth, one supporting The Covenant not to misuse the hidden science again and the other bent on continuation of magical practice and use of Grid energies, perhaps accounting for past atomic wars.

It appears that China by occupying Tibet in the 50's, wished to rid its borders of the influences of hidden Masters of ROSICRUCIAN ORIGIN (and a belief in Re-incarnation?) who have been at the back of virtually all western occult groups through personages such as Alice Bailey, Rudolf Steiner, Blavatsky and allegedly Jesus who increasingly appears as Druid and Rosicrucian. However there are I concluded, **two opposing Rosicrucian groups**, one wishing to release and commercialise the mysteries and the other not wishing to reveal the mysteries (and the message of Re-incarnation) to the "profane". It is difficult to say whether Hubbard belonged to the former group, sold out to it, or was overtaken by the World Order Illuminati in the cull conducted by the Brokers and David Miscavige in the 80's; however from my own experience the communistic (3rd dynamic emphasis to the cost of all other dynamics including indvidual/self/1st – group aberration) thinking I encountered, along with the tedious mechanistic approach to the game, which sucked the life force out of you, did not bode well and certainly was not present (I am told) in the early days of Scientology.

In the cull of the 80's, virtually all senior Scientologists who had known and worked with Hubbard (the man) and privy to events as they happened, were evicted under extremely upsetting circumstances and many were (and still are) deeply spiritually wounded and confused by what had occurred: it was as though the tracks were being dusted and the scene were being set for the myth of Hubbard to be reborn – as opposed to the reality of the man and his life and the true goals of Scientology (spiritual freedom for all not just those who can afford to pay the price tag). When 'new' (or altered?) "tech" (the works of Hubbard) appeared – no-one would be there from the beginning to say - Hey hang on Hubbard did not write this!' and certainly no-one would be there to remember equally embarrassing details such as the comment by Otto Rous that Hubbard had 'rock slammers' and 'witholds' (indicative of wrong actions), that marred the progress of his case. Any one of the above scenarios for the true background to Hubbard would indeed give 'rock slams'. The same scenario appeared in the life of Jesus and whilst James (the brother of Jesus) complained to St Paul that the teachings of Jesus were meant for a Semitic audience, St Paul palmed them off, on the world by enlisting zealots to spread the altered word. Even Hubbard's son (Nibs) would not be there to warn of "magic" and the method I believe Hubbard used to gain access to the OT (Operating Thetan levels) of Inc.1 and Inc.2 –channelling off The Grid Akashic record; which has led to misunderstandings explained in this book as imprints as opposed to "implants". The consequences are of course that the whole religious background to this planet, true source and the exact nature of the catastrophe has been misunderstood as some "implant" - the true nature of the trap has not been revealed. Man believes that his powers and cause will be sufficient to find that miniscule door out, without touching the electro-magnetic web!

It is not immediately clear as to why symbols of Twin Kingship should make an appearance in the proposed Memorial Garden dedicated to the late Princess Diana along with a 45' wide rock from China, unless we remember creationist myths of China in common with Biblical accounts and the majority of world creation myths. In myth a Chinese hero escaped destruction by deluge (Flood) with his wife, *three* sons and *three* daughters and on the mainland of China it is contended that all Chinese are direct descendents of an ancient ancestor called Nu-wah. I have already referred to the Chinese word for 'ship' as an ancient character made up of a picture of a 'boat' and 'eight mouths', with symbolic inference on the figure-of-eight and the number who survived the Flood. 'Nu' also means 'woman' and 'wah' is 'flowery', thus reminding us of the Palaeolithic cave paintings of "The Missionary Woman" and a female spiritual ancestor; indicated in black and white and probably symbolic of Goddess incorporating Twin Kinship (or two lines of Noah?). However we would be wrong to assume that the Chinese consider this a true source, for two small 'mouth' pictures placed beside the name 'Nu-wah', are according to Dr. E. W. Thwing, an indication that the *sound* of the characters and *not the meaning* is intended. Thus the sound may be comparable to Noah or even New World or New Word (of God). Early Chinese history supports the idea of a Noachian involvement in the birth of China and it has been questioned whether Noah and Nu-wah are one and the same.

It appears from archaeological evidence of fused glass (quartz) similar to layers of vitrified sand left after Atomic tests in Nevada in the 1950's that Israel, Southern Iraq (near Babylon), the western Arabian desert (with black rocks showing evidence of being subjected to intense radiation) and the Gobi Desert (of Mongolia) including Lop Nor in Sinkiang near the present Chinese atomic test site (excavated before they became a nuclear power) are sites where atomic activity has occurred. Further, prehistoric towers in Europe (Scotland, South coast of Ireland and Lofoten Islands off Norway) show walls vitrified and stones fused by an unknown energy. This together with the Indian epics (*The Tibetan Stanzas of Dzyan and Mahabharata*) indicate a nuclear pre-Flood battle, which in the majority of myths and legends occurs c. 3,500 – 2,500 B.C, close to the Chinese date set at 2250 B.C as the beginning of their history; whilst The Bible estimates 2448 B.C as the year of the Flood. This is not synonymous with Hubbard's INC 2 (which I equate with a serious magnetic reversal) placed 75 million years ago in the Triassic period and age of dinosaurs (*Fig. 33 p.335 Vol. I*): where vast species extinction along with the dinosaurs occurred and which has been termed "the catastrophe", although hidden from mankind. The reason why it is inaccurate to use channelled information to represent earth track history, is that cutting and splicing of the holograms during a reversal, as the electro-magnetic threads disentangle and reform, similar to the procedure which produces genetic variation in DNA; invariably no longer produces an accurate **sequence** in terms of space time co-ordinates or time track.

The ancient Chinese also recognised that before them there were "giants" or "men twice as tall as us", paralleling the *Genesis* text "there were giants in those days". According to the ancient Chinese they once inhabited "the realm of delight" but lost it by not living by the laws of nature" (misuse of Grid science). The "Dragon Lines" or ley-lines of earth's electro-magnetic energy were known and understood by both the ancient Chinese and the Druids and indeed they may have derived from a common group. Recent archaeological evidence from early man preserved intact in a glacier in the arctic north, has suggested that by way of tattoo, his medical record and acupuncture treatment was recorded on his skin. Acupuncture specialists have noticed the tattoo parallels certain specific acupuncture points or meridians. The magnetic ley-line currents began at certain natural 'energy springs', which perhaps became known as the 'underground stream', so prominently displayed in symbolic art (*The Battle of the Trees*). Such points became marked as religious sites by megalithic monuments e.g. Stone Henge on Salisbury plain in Wiltshire UK and many of the churches including Alfriston and Willmington on the south coast of England are situated on a ley-line system and often prior mounds or hills marked the site. The Nazca Valley lines in Peru illustrate knowledge of this ley-line system. The account of the demi-god Moses on Mount Sinai, whose face was horribly burnt during recording of The Ten Commandments as the alleged word of God, is in all probability an account of the use of such energies. Knowledge of eclipses and the solar lunar calendar was vital in the use of these energies, perhaps in the application of anti-gravity aircraft or 'vinmas' quoted in the Indian epics as used in battle.

Directing magnetic currents was accomplished by the placement of the standing stones along ley-lines and Semitic stone pillar worship which was introduced into Knossos at the time of the Religious Revolution c. 1400 B.C appears to demonstrate the power that was concentrated into such stones by harnessing these earth energy systems. I am reminded of the Cretan shepherd who told me animals in Crete were being born deformed, with the possibility I concluded that manipulation of the Grid is occurring here, altering the morphogenetic bioplasma, which determines species shape and survival mechanisms. Many standing stones also had healing properties and must to a gullible Palaeolithic and Bronze Age public have appeared as magic, which indeed it was as a forerunner of earth energy science. The system of ley-line use did not spring up gradually, but appears to have occurred simultaneously from one source, co-incident with the world survey and presumably a group of men known as "giants" or the survivors of the Flood as Noah and his descendents?

John Mitchell wrote in *The View over Atlantis* "A great scientific instrument lies sprawled over the surface of the globe. At the same period perhaps it was 4,000 years ago – almost every corner of the world was visited by a group of men who came with a particular task to accomplish. With the help of some remarkable power, by which they could cut and raise enormous blocks of stone, these men erected vast astronomical instruments, circles of stone, pillars, pyramids, underground tunnels, cyclopean alignments, from horizon to horizon was marked by stones, mounds and earth-works". The Druids utilized such hills (and caves) for manipulation of this energy. These men were under a single authority and it might be speculated Babel was a significant energy centre in the post Flood epoch. However the fact that they were "giants" all points to a **bodyline that survived a magnetic reversal** and the Flood. In other words the giant bodies evident in the Triassic period prior to the catastrophe 75 million years ago had survived extinction and that catastrophe and the later Flood of creation myths (which appears based on a nuclear incident rather than reversal). The Bible either through editing or deliberate omission, has confused the two events in one creationist story of Genesis, thereby dusting the tracks of what has happened on earth and more importantly hidden data on the trap. The only way such men could have saved the bodyline from a magnetic reversal is to have utilised a craft to escape from Earth, only returning once the event had subsided. The origin of the mechanical beings from Sirius via Mars may mean that these beings survived on Mars during the event, thus giving some credence to the claims in *Alternative 3* of a base on Mars prepared in the 70's (despite NASA's claims that a station is yet to be founded).

The desire for unity and centralization by this group "lest we be scattered abroad on the face of the earth" (*Genesis*) gave rise I would conclude to centres such as Babel, which was the directing power behind the *Genesis* story. The desire to keep the genetic line of the survivors pure in an unbroken line has been continually dramatized not only by groups such as the Jews themselves, but also by the Nazi's and all race hate programmes. Further megalithic sites such as Mystery Hill in North Salem, New Hampshire USA together with the Hermetic white chalk Hill Figure (Druid) previously discussed, all point to this directing power discovering America c. 1225 – 800 B.C long before Columbus. Megalithic monuments have also been found in China, Korea and Japan. One of the oldest Chinese literary works the Shan Hai King, *The Classic of Mountains and Seas*, a treatise on geography (the World Survey?) assigns authorship to "the great Yu" who became Emperor in 2208 B.C and the treatise itself is said to date as far back as 2250 B.C a century after the death of Almodad (Alm-of-Dad? Or branch of the father Noah?) who was a seventh generation of Noah "who measured the earth to its extremities". The question becomes which genetic lines from Noah (and his sons) produced which races, since I have covered a reptilian and ape line which clearly in the faces from La Marche (*fig.50 p.425 Vol.II*) in Palaeolithic times produced very different facial characteristics. Further archaeologists have often been puzzled by lack of human remains in certain strata, as though there was a deliberate attempt to erase racial traces.

The resonance of the particular DNA (as with the rhesus factor) will decide whether the body is tuned to the Grid holographics of the reptilian or ape line and the consequent physiology and behaviour, which perhaps is fully illustrated in the case of the reptilian line in the low harmonics (1.1) of Hubbard's Chart of Human Evaluation (*Science of Survival*). Some record of this reptilian line and the mechanical jaw was previously discussed in UFO witness accounts where past holographics and data had impinged in the 'Onion-Ring Model' (*Alternative 4*). The thorough homogenous mixing of races and DNA will provide various mixes now, unless of course the World Order has preserved a body line, which may account for the obsessional interest in cloning; explaining the myth of "monsters marching over the rainbow bridge" at the end. As I have noted scientists whilst persuaded to genetically alter monkey with jellyfish genes (note Blavatsky's racial origin thesis), are oblivious to the occult background and what appears to be a secret occult directive behind their research.

The Chinese Great Yu was like Noah lame and lameness was a sign of divinity and royalty (the Twin Kings were displayed with heals raised in the Minoan seals). Jesus was also lame and was identified as waxing (New Year babe) and waning Twin King (crucified) in one personage as Hermes, utilising Hermetic mysteries and "a new college of magic". Robert Graves in *The White Goddess* reminds one of the repeated falls of Christ in legend when bearing the cross. A popular Jewish legend relates that Shem son of Noah served as a priest on the landing of Noah's Ark significantly displaying the totem beasts of the descendent Bull-Minos cult in some of its shape-shifting forms, by sacrificing an ox (with sheep, goat, two turtle doves and pigeons). Jacob too limped after wrestling the angel (*Genesis 32:24-32*) and Jacob as father or thirteenth member of a group of twelve sons certainly tied him to 13th tribe and Bull-Minos cult. Thus it is evident that the Spiritual message that arrived on Earth c. 10,000 B.C was from the very beginning silenced and tied to a long system of Twin Kingship and battles for power, with all its dramatizations dating back probably through many cycles of war and precipitated cataclysm, at least to the antediluvian period with its rival kingships and two groups, with misuse of the hidden science.

The mythic image of the lamed king is related to the moon, which is the celestial counterpart of the sacrificed and resurrected bull-king. The moon is lame first on one side, then on the other symbolised as waxing and waning Twin Kings. The full moon rises on the fifteenth day of its cycle and the European flag originally had 15 stars (compare to the original flag of the American Union with 13 stars). On the 15th day the moon in its cycle directly faces the orb of the setting sun and this clue placed alongside the magazine illustration from *Vaincre* (*fig. 48 p.87 Vol.II*) produced by a man close to the cradle of European Union, shows a Hermetic knight with all the symbolism of Knossos and the Bull-Minos cult riding down a road labelled "United States of the West" (European Union) towards/facing a blazing sun; between the labels "Brittany" (the old Merovingian empire derived from a union of the Magdalene and Jesus?) and "Bavaria" (the Illuminati as a secret sun group) with the year "1937" leading up to the Second World War indicated and "1946" as proposals for European Union forged ahead. This implies not only that the war was planned in order to create the goal of European Union, but also implies a union of Illuminati and Rosicrucians (Bull-Minos) portrayed on the obverse side of the One Dollar note of America. In fact in the prior quoted ancient tale from

Greece (Captain 13) the "dollar" was mentioned, despite America had yet to be discovered, let alone a currency name nominated! Thus it would seem that European Union was a joint goal of Illuminati and Rosicrucian Freemasons and furtherance of plan, which really took off with the French Revolution, although conceived at Knossos. Thus prior to World War II it appears that the secret groups were decided on a Greek base as source of civilization and a spiritual impetus conjoined with the political arm of the Illuminati.

Revolving doors and alliances as a method of the Masters means that whilst the Greek base may have been a combined goal before World War 2, following the war that goal of a combined Rosicrucian and Illuminatus Universal political and religious kingdom, illustrated on the One Dollar note of America may have changed, to remove the religious goal altogether, in a secret goal of world communism for the masses run by the elite 'priesthood' and masters: a complete aberration of the 3rd dynamic (group), which in the case of the masters is turned to promote (their) **self**-survival as an obsessional first dynamic (self). For the ordinary man he must make communism and the 3rd dynamic (group) his God, with the soothing knowledge of "we are all in it together" – the trap; whilst the masters make money and power theirs. The notion of a cosmic law is disregarded as irrelevant in communism, but that of a law in human affairs is retained: a law to be known and followed, without the necessity or even possibility of individual choice, conscience or freedom of decision, which removes individuation or free will and the responsibility of each individual not to obey, but to judge and decide freely for himself. In the west 'democracy' is all but communism in name, where media tells man what to think and is owned by the power brokers, who can control public opinion by propaganda and selective coverage of news. There is no idea that men can decide what kind of world (or organisation) they want and then bring that to pass – both east and west have agreed to tragedy, defeat and mortality.

Other than this it is hard to conceive why there should be a "policy" in the UK (and America), which would support China in the light of the Chinese government's crimes against humanity and the people of Tibet. Whilst the west appears to 'strut its stuff' over violations of Human Rights in the former Yugoslavia, the enormity of what has happened in Tibet (as with Iraq) has been ignored by western governments and media alike since the 1950's, indicating that silence is a manifestation of "policy". The World Order development of the idea of a superordinated law to which all human minds must bow (so evident in Bush's "with us or against us" speech) was applied to Tibet horribly from 1950 –1960. *Tibet and the Chinese People's Republic, A Report to the International Commission of Jurists by its Legal Inquiry Committee on Tibet (Geneva: International commission of Jurists, 1960)* is one of the worst documents I have read in terms of crimes against humanity (I particularly draw your attention to Statement No. 45, p.278; Statement No.1, pp. 222-223; Statement 26, p.254; Statement No.11, p.235; Statement No.4, p.225; Statement No.5, p.226; Statement No.7, p. 229-230; Statement No. 2, p.223 – other examples of this treatment appear in Statements No.7 p.230, 10 - p.234, 36 – p.267, 37 – p.269, 38 – p.269, 39 – p.271, 44 – p.277; also Statement No.32 p.260; Statement No.44, p.276 and Statement No.35, p.266. Whilst virtually the whole document makes horrific reading, the above statements are particularly so. Many lamas in Tibet were tortured along with those who supported them; significantly many were crucified. What happened in Tibet was pure vengeance aimed at a peaceful people with a variant religious viewpoint that belonged to the old Orient. The same fate was to befall the Early Minoans and any group or nation that has resisted The World Order dramatization of Unity and the One-ness – globalisation. Tibet however may have housed important documentation on Rosicrucian groups and personages.

The earth-goddess fertilized by the moon-bull who dies and is resurrected appears in the late classical legends of Europa (from which the name Europe is evolved) and the bull of Zeus, Pasiphae and the Bull of Poseidon, Io turned into a cow and the killing of the Minotaur. The earliest Temple compounds in history reinforce the evidence for the bull-god and goddess – cow as fertility symbols. Temple compounds at Obeid (south Mesopotamia) Khafajah and Uquair (north and south of Baghdad in Iraq) are **oval (egg)** in shape surrounded by high walls designed (as with Masonic symbols) to suggest female genitalia and dedication to the goddess as with Indian Temples where the innermost shrine has a form symbolic of the female organs. Masonic groups descended as they are from the all-boys club of Semitic patriarchs have developed severe aberrations on the second dynamic and the subject of sex and woman, which has sub-ordinated half the world's population to a position of domination and non-achievement.

The Biblical quote "ye are all gods" reminds us of Professor Jastrow's remark, that man's separation from the gods did not occur with Sumer but with the later Semitic mind. Whilst Sumerian seals c. 2,300 B.C. illustrate that the new order of the symbolic royal courts was shared by the divinity or "King-god" or "god-king" and woman as priestess, recorded as a ritual marriage during the New Year's Festival; the gold rosette which was to appear at Knossos in the Religious Revolution was evident in important tombs. The dual entombment of a lady named Shub-ad and her lord A-bar-gi contained numerous symbols in common with the Knossos site e.g wagons drawn by *three* oxen. Also evidence of the whole secret group line or ancestry may have been displayed by animals of gold: stags, gazelles, bulls, and goats, with between them the significant cluster of three pomegranates, fruit-bearing branches of a tree (Cabala and Tree of Life) and intervals of gold rosettes.

It was in the Semitic religion that woman as retained in the Jewish prayer today, stood accused of the wrongs of her accusers – the Patriarchs. The tomb also contained a cow in silver, harps each ornamented with the head of a bull: one of copper, the other of gold, with lapis-lazuli horn-tips (sky god and gates of horn – the abode of the dead) – but significantly bearded. The beard was prominent in some heads at La Marche, perhaps meant to signify a certain race derived from one particular son of Noah? Man's separation from the gods or more particularly the message, also belongs to the Greeks in their idea of *hybris* and is the inhabiting principle of tragedy. It underlies the Christian myth of the Fall and Redemption, Tree and Cross. Defeat is the typical outcome of superhuman adventures in the west, whereas in the Orient, as in the legend of Buddha, the hero who sets forth to gain immortality almost invariably wins. Tales of the protagonist's trials are invariably psychological as he confronts the demons of his mind and forces hitherto he believed beyond his ability to confront. This reflects the tragedy of the suppressed Holy Grail message of immortality and continuous existence, where 'past lives' become the demons one has no wish to confront and which consigned man to a belief in his body and not his soul. The age of the hero died as western man resigned himself to guilt and defeat (care of the World Order and the Masters). Communism as a tool and method of the Masters strove to drive everyone down to the same level (the level of the masters themselves with their mechanical minds and lack of create). Communism punished individualism, self-determination and hence ability (including spiritual ability) – genius, cause, self and pan-determinism finds no acknowledgement in Communism. Hubbard having elected himself cause, genius and Saviour, whilst denying his overts/withholds on the subject of source, magical practice and secret groups then consigned his followers into yet another trap of unquestioning obedience. Further what Hubbard maintains are "implants" (of Inc 1 and Inc 2) are I conclude Akashic and Grid memory events on this planet, where symbols such as "spinning dancers" "theatres" "horn" "cherubim" are all records of times when the dominant priesthood utilized high emotion, magical practice/morphic resonance or manipulation of Grid/ley-line energies to access this record and manipulate it for power and profit .

The atomic explosions, which appear to have been designed and used to break up the ley-line master energy points and misuse of natural laws and the hidden science, which caused the downfall of the Atlanteans, also created the sudden demise of the centralized power and priesthood that associated itself with these key points as at Babel. The "giants" or the Masters then organised themselves into a secret Brotherhood (the precursor of today's Masonic and secret groups) that dominated world politics from the earliest times, jealously guarding this secret science, still utilizing aspects of it, such as channelling in order to achieve knowledge, profit and power thus becoming a human Grid or network on earth, spreading out to all four corners of the globe. The sense of tragedy is of such force that the word "catastrophe" (Greek 'Kata', "down" and 'strophein' "to turn") immediately conveys the reason and man's continual Re-incarnation here upon Earth as part of a trap.

If the secret groups are heading towards maat, known as "truth" or "right order", it appears that there are differences in opinion between secret groups, as to what is that right order and truth! Truth, maat, right order, is the principle mythologically personified as the cow-goddess Hathor, which therefore takes us back to the Greek base (source as Hermes) and the philosophy of at least one Rosicrucian group. Hermes however was a downturn of a prior truth as I have covered at length, when the Holy Grail was stolen. The Illuminati however may not today have that particular goal of maat as the revelation of a predestined order. Kingship throughout history was regarded as the vindication of a divinely ordered state of affairs. We may see the push towards a psychocivilised society ('Animal Farm') from this viewpoint of order. Historically war and its cruelty were not violence against nature when prosecuted by the god-king. The same mentality exists today in World Order thinking, where the millions who suffer or die, sacrificed to a cause (globalisation and the plan for order and control) are justified as a means to an end. Further kings (as in the case of Minos) and pharaohs avoided what was once seen as the true maat or order i.e. the celestial stars and heaven, by avoidance of their own ritual sacrifice substituting others to provide the pivotal role of sacrificial victim in the hieratic order governed by heaven: thus saving themselves for the mastery of a religiously rationalized and costumed, yet political order they governed. Hereditary monarchy ensued with the idea that divinity could be inherited through bloodlines, proving to be another manifestation of the masters, themselves obsessed with genetics and bloodlines.

The god-given order was known as *maat* in Egypt, in India as *dharma*, in the Far East, as *tao*, and in Sumer *me*. The emphasis on music in court and temple rituals, with varying instruments e.g. harps that emitted different resonance, coupled with chanting reflects presumably the principle known to the Pythagoreans the "music of the spheres", the cosmic patterning and hum of the cosmos and communication with the heavenly order, not to mention the crystal, UVG120 sphere and Grid holographics of the past! The positioning of the "sea of crystal" at the feet of God in the Apocalyptic Revelations account, merely underlines a conjoining compromise in ancient thought of gods or a God utilising an ordered mathematical pattern to govern man's world: the Grid as vile trap became in this mind a spiritual phenomenon whereby man could communicate with the gods, or a least obtain Akashic record information for power and profit: and Hermes the Master Geomancer as keeper of the Grid had the most truck with profit! This compromise overcame the application of mathematical principles to maat or order in late Sumerian documents, which reshaped man's thinking process towards order in geometry and pattern rather than in the gods: further a mathematical order is antithetic to a doctrine of free will. The concept of order varied from east to west and in Chinese thought and civilization the realization of this order was the chief concern of the Middle Kingdom. Fundamentally the idea became that the individual (microcosm), society (mesocosm), and the universe of heaven and earth (macrocosm), form an indissoluble unit, and that the well being of all, depends upon their mutual harmonization. Such harmonization became a bedrock of communistic doctrine; however harmony was sought in denying any element that would stand to create disharmony e.g. religion, individuation, free will, thought and speech, which denies evolution of mind and spirit.

Religion to the Chinese (communism) lies within the 3rd dynamic or group, which also manifests in various religions, who insist that their particular answer is the only one. It seems that the obsession of secret groups including Adam Weishaupt's Illuminati, with bee hives and ant-heaps reflected a Marxist and communistic goal of harmonization. Secret groups however as in the Indian hierarchal caste system and the Greek Platonic Republic always envisaged rule by a rich hierarchal elite, where women and slaves would have no say: the hive of workers run by a 'queen' bee, enmeshed in the spider's web. The reference to "macrocosm" in the script on the Floor of Cardiff Castle, certainly conveys the idea of maat. The question is, what form of order and truth is envisaged in the Universal political and religious kingdom? The recent suppressive legislation emerging restricting choice and privacy, coupled with secrecy, lies and deterioration in democracy, freedom and liberty in the west, is a strong indicator that order is envisaged as a vast well ordered and grinding machine, with each one as cog. The mechanical beings (MMRC case) due to their inherent psychology will always reduce any system, be it political or religious to that of an efficient machine, which works well for matter, but is catastrophic for spiritual beings.

Peter Mandelson MP (at the time and Minister without portfolio in the U.K) popped up in *The Independent on Sunday (30th Sept 2001)*. Mandelson is not only "an avowed friend of America", but also a member of the Bilderberg secret group. A twelve star global-like circle curiously illustrated the article, with President Bush in the right hand corner (Captain *thirteen*?). Mandelson went on to say: " the terrorist assault on America has revived the West's sense of solidarity (read Unity). It may, I hope, mark the beginning of a fresh understanding and alliance between Europe and America". Well certainly as I have covered in this book, America was deeply worried about a Federal European army and European hostility prior to the terrorist attack, recognised by Mandelson when he stated: "the mood of pessimism that prevailed this summer about European-U.S relations is misplaced. A *twin* (sic) commitment to European and Atlanticism, which is the root of my politics, should encourage us to stress what Europe and America have in common and the combined strength we can devote to tackling the economic inequality and denial of human rights that blights so many parts of the world" (*author's emphasis*) Including England in *my* experience!

I have previously discussed the group 13 consisting of twelve and Captain thirteen or the thirteenth member of a group of twelve. If I were to depict America by way of its national flag it would not be in a global circle, even though some joint implication of the European flag may have been implied – but why *twelve* stars? The history of the American flag is interesting in this respect, since the first national flag of America was raised by George Washington on New Years Day 1776: the 'Grand Union', putting the crosses of English St. George and *Scottish* St. Andrew in the top left hand corner, with *thirteen* stars and stripes. Whilst thirteen has been explained as the number of states at the time, it cannot be dismissed that thirteen is also a significant number as thirteenth tribe. Why indeed should the One Dollar note of America have the Illuminatus symbols on the left of the obverse side of the note and what I concluded was basically *Scottish* Rite and Rosicrucian Freemasonry on the right with its significant symbolism of thirteen? The Union flag offended radicals and federalists and a resolution of the first Continental Congress in Philadelphia, in the summer of 1777, ordered that the union be thirteen stars (one for each state in the revolutionary union), white in a blue field, representing a new constellation. White and blue co-incidentally were also the significant colours relating to the Great Goddess of Crete in her death aspect, reflected in the white gypsum covered site of Knosssos and the white chalk hill figures and also the white barrow of New Grange in Ireland. This might if I cared to extrapolate, bring us back to that curious Millennium icon in the U.K (*Plate 3*) with its similarity to *The Prince* fresco of Knossos. Why on earth Mandelson was coined "Prince of darkness" is anybody's guess, however it is generally acknowledged that he was the architect of New Labour's rise to power, with its emblem of the rose (or is it new rose?). The red men of Knossos (with their rosettes), displayed in the body colour of 'the prince' also depicted royalty, blood lines and Adamites.

To return to the red stars and stripes of America, the story went that Betsy Ross the Quaker seamstress from Philadelphia, was the only woman in the otherwise very male pantheon of the Founding Fathers and it was she who designed the flag's magical circle of 13 stars after meeting with a clandestine congressional committee in a back room of a house. The flag became fifteen stars and fifteen stripes (as was the original flag of European Union with its fifteen circular or *global* stars) when two more states (Vermont and Kentucky) were included in 1795. George

Washington explained the new 15-star flag as: "we take the stars from Heaven, the red from our Mother country, separating it by white stripes, thus showing we have separated from her, and the white stripes shall go down to posterity representing liberty". The "Mother" being Britain presumably (with its red men, Adamites?) Despite the inclusion of more states in 1818 (Tennessee, Ohio, Louisiana, Indiana and Mississippi) a Congressional Act mandated that the number of stripes be fixed at 13 although ostensibly to mark the original states, with one star added on the fourth of July the year following inclusion for each new state. By 1912, there were 48 states and the stars represented in a box or canton to the left hand upper corner – as 6 rows of 8 stars (both patriarchal numbers incidentally). Since 1960 there are 13 horizontal red and white stripes and in the canton 9 rows (female number) alternating 6 (male number) and 5 (female number) making a total of 50 states.

Samuel Huntington, the Harvard political scientist, outlined in a famous article written in the aftermath of the Cold War his vision of the next stage hostilities would take. Rejecting the vision of a New World Order, proposed by President Bush senior, he insisted that mankind had not rid itself of the incubus of violence, but argued that it would take the form of conflict between cultures, in particular between the liberal, secular culture of the West and the religious culture of Islam. Huntingdon's "clash of civilizations" was widely discussed, although it was not taken seriously by some. Since September 11 it has been taken very seriously indeed". *('In this war of civilizations, the West will prevail' – The Daily Telegraph Oct.8 2001 article by Sir John Keegan Defence Editor)* However it is my opinion that this "clash" is being manipulated for a greater goal that turns on political and religious dominance – a "Universal Kingdom" or the "massive project" spoken of in secret Masonic groups, at the time of The French Revolution.

Curiously what Hubbard called Incident 2 ("implants" from the arch controllers) and what I conclude was the downloading of the entire Grid holographics during a magnetic reversal, contained pictures of **skyscrapers and scenes very much like modern day England.** Hubbard did not give each "implant" a space-time co-ordinate or date, thus unless I had worked this entire thesis out from basic first principles of science and inductive logic, one would not have immediately recognised a cycle and specific sequence here, which is a record of **consecutive past events**. In other words during a magnetic reversal the spirit (you) bounces on and off the "umbrella" or Grid, each contact point will leave the soul with an **imprint** (not "implant") of the earth event data. Hence the soul is disorientated for the whole time of a magnetic reversal trying to locate itself within the chaos of data, hence thoughts and memories such as "being oneself", "being animals" etc. Since the Grid contains information for all species this is not surprising. Neither is it surprising that symbols of religion in the past are represented, since priests in the utilization of morphic resonance during ceremonies and in manipulation of earth energy ley-lines (which connect with the Grid) left imprints of thought and ceremonial symbols. The moral of this story is not to go for the "easy wins" as Hitler was warned – utilizing the Grid and ITS MEMORY. The moral is USE YOUR OWN THINKING PROCESS, LOGIC AND MEMORY. The Grid contains data on species (animal and plant) survival and is concerned only with **majority survival** and not the individual as such. It also makes irrational computations when faced with suppression of free will (it will tell you to run or fight in the face of survival threat and if you do neither it will grow you a spare body part!). Communism would find much logic in the Grid as a 'spiritual' phenomenon, with its considerations on majority and group.

John the Evangelist who wrote Revelations was in all probability Rosicrucian and 13th tribe and was a particular patron Saint of Lord Bute (Scottish Rite/Rose Croix Mason?), who had the Floor of Cardiff Castle laid. The 13th tribe however as the Knossos site illustrated removed life force and introduced the Second Plank of Marxism (taxation). The patriarchs always envisaged a system of communism as the political model; and such a system does not lend itself to individual spiritual freedom. The individual is only there to serve the group and be sacrificed for that group. The new religion and era of maat (order and truth) will no doubt dove-tail with tao the Chinese concept of maat, where presumably man as machine, subservient to a machine whose religion becomes the 3rd dynamic group, will best suit the bee-hive or ant-heap vision, philosophical considerations and psychology of a World Order.

Alien Earth-Track History

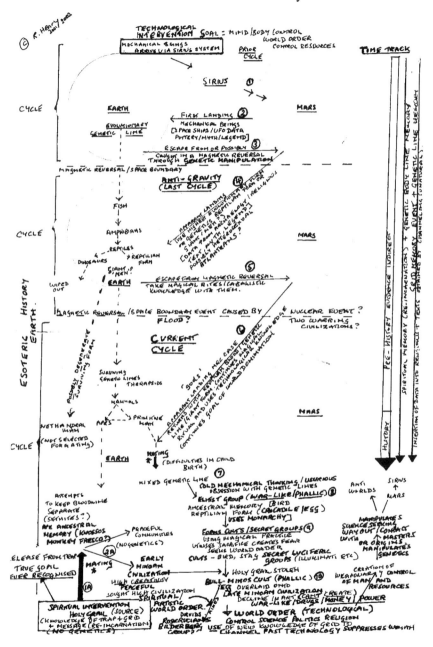

Plate 1:   Dr. Clifford L. Burdick, Arizona geologist, with a set of petrified tracks left in the Paluxy River bed in Texas by a dinosaur and a human being of formidable dimensions. *The human footprints are 15 inches in length, but even though their length is extraordinary, much more significant is the fact that they were found next to the dinosaur tracks. It indicates that man and the dinosaur were contemporaneous, not millions of years apart, cutting the evolutionary timetable to shreds.*

Plate 2: Aura images (*Photo Credit from 'Aura Imaging Photography – Seeing the colours of your Aura by Johanees Fisslinger –sum Press P.O. Box 2431 Fairfield IA, 52556*)

Photo I,1

Photo I,1

Plate 3: The Millennium Experience icon celebrating the millennium in Great Britain. *Note the similarity to the Prince fresco from Knosos –'The Battle of The Trees' and the sun (or mercurial star of Hermes) and crescent moon together with half gold and silver symbology depicting male and female with a male and female appearance or bisexual nature.* Inset the Festival of Britain logo for 1951, *with its hermetic knight quality and four corners of the earth*

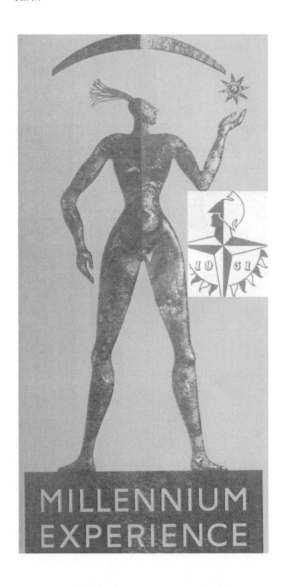

Plate 4: 'Kaluru', the so-called 'Ligtening Man, *(believed responsible for rain, fertility, and thunderstorms indicating Cabalistic ritual) Significantly painted in dark red ochre and white pipeclay.Kalurungari, Calder River, Walcott, N.W.Australia (after A.S. Schu)*

Plate 5:   A Cretan Shrine: Restored by Sir Arthur Evans *(Snake goddesses, or goddess and priestess, "fetish cross", shells, libation jugs, stones hollowed for holding offerings etc.*

Plate 6:   Semitic Stone Pillar at Knossos, incised with the double-axe symbol which signified the labyrinth and Twin Kings.

Plate 7: The Lion Gate at Mycenae. *Note the two lions as Twin Kings, with the upright pillar or herm between them and the feet of the lions resting on the horizontal baetyllic pillar*

Plate 8:   The 'Masked Shaman' (after Breuil). *One shape or form of the World Order – a man masked in deer's fell with the antlers presumably signifying the Cabalistic Tree of Life. The penis obviously relates back to the earlier Bull-Minos phallic cult.*

Plate 9:   Sarcophagus (burial urn) from Gournia, Heraklion Museum Crete. *The fish was the earliest totem beast of the Mother Goddess – note the ellipsoidal shape of the sarcophagus, with the implication of tides 'As I go so shall I return' –The Cycle of Eternal Return and curved space-time. The deceased were often buried in the foetal position with shells- waiting re-birth? Refer to the scalar pattern in the Harvesters vase (Alternative 4 – UFO's Mind and Body Control). This shape of sarcophagus was changed to the square Semitic pillar type after the Religious Revolution.*

Plate 10:   Incised Designs on Neolithic Pottery from Knossos. *From Dr. Mackenzie's "Pottery of Knossos".* Note the zig-zag designs and compare to zig-zag features of UFO phenomena and the windings of the bioplasma filaments (Alternative 4). Note also the insert of a bowl decorated with red lines, discovered in the great "Tholos" of Haghia Triada along with the Phaestos Disc. Compare the pattern to the 'ball of string' of Ariadne in myth and the electro-magnetic windings of the Grid.

Plate 11a: A curious humanlike figure engraved on a bone from Pin Hole Cave, Creswell Crags, Derbyshire, central England.

Plate 11b: Anthropomorphic Figures in Palaeolithic cave art: *From Altamira, N. Spain after Breuil: notice the muzzle-shaped snout and reptilian-type head.*

Plate 12: Head of an Eland. *From Clontarf, near Barkly East, Cape Province, S. Africa. Palaeolithic cave painting that appears to differ from other so-called 'Bushman Art': however this is certainly very different art than was occurring elsewhere in the world at the time, noted for its depiction of reality and actuality, three-dimensional and aesthetic beauty.*

Plate 13:   A Rock Panel: the impressionistic horses, the looming outline of the bison and the mysterious superimposed mauve hands. *Aurignacian to late Magdalenian period after Breuil, from Altimira (Santander), N. Spain. The Bull appears to indicate the Bull-Minos or phallic cult totem beast and past ancestral group or 'shape' of the World Order with the horse cult being one more 'shape': further although not mentioned there is what looks like a Cretan goat with long horns at bottom who was to become Almathea who suckled the infant Zeus on Crete.*

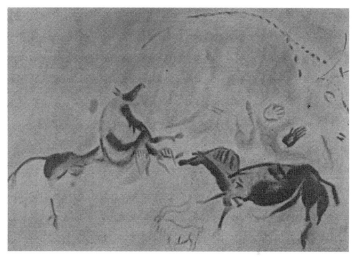

Plate 14a: The Strange Composite Beast: *dark brown outline, late Aurignacian techniqu:. From Lascaux (Dordgne), France. Examples of 'composite' animals may be noted at Nau Gap and also on the seals excavated at the Indus Valley sites (c. 2500 B.C). This may be a depiction of the phallic Bull_minos cult which was to be superimposed on The Holy Grail in Crete during the Religious Revolution.*

Plate 14b: The 'Little Sorcerer': *from Trois-Freres (Ariege), France. The whole scene portrays magicimport and the animals depicted in fear.*

Plate 14c: A Hybrid Man-Beast: *from Trois Freres, France. This however looks remarkably like the Knossos   sealings of man-bull of the Religious Revolution in Crete.*

Plate 15: Examples of Palaeolithic Art: *The objects include: handles of knives and daggers carved in ivory and bone, line drawings of wild animals, faces of men or the demon form which is evidently the muzzle-shaped reptilian form and also shows them with hands raised which compares with the Egyptian "Ka" attitude of adoration that appeared after the Religious Revolution at Knossos. Also the monkey or ape-form makes an appearance, compare to the monkey fresco of knossos.*

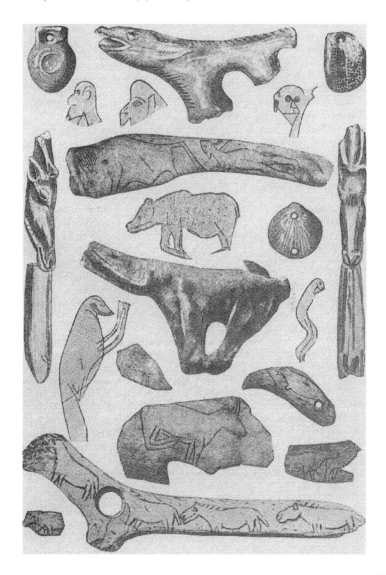

Plate 16a: The so-called 'Missionary Woman' or 'Pink Lady': *Part of a Palaeolithic frieze of Black Figures. The central enigmatic striding figure in pink has not been satisfactorily identified: guesses vary from a 'Greek' or 'Cretan' to a man with penis! From Leopard's Ravine (north of Windhoek) S.W. Africa.*

Plate 16b: Two Animals in bichrome: *stylised but very aesthetic from Leopard's Ravine (north of Windhoek), S.W. Africa. This was found in the same region as the 'Missionary Woman' and bears a quite distinctive Palaeolithic style that for beauty is parallel to the the Eland. This style is quite distinctive also from the shaman-type paintings.*

Plate 17: Human Couples highly stylised, with accompanying figures from Palaeolithic cave art: *From Piedra Escrita, near Fuencaliente, Sierra Morena, S. Spain. (after Breuil): bottom are described two 'dead' women without heads; near is an 'animal' upside down, probably also an emblem of death. This to the author looks like a scale of energy or life comparable to the Tree of Life of Cabalism. Top figures with cone-shaped heads may indicate opening of the crown chakra. The removal of heads was dramatized in the occult driven French Revolution.*

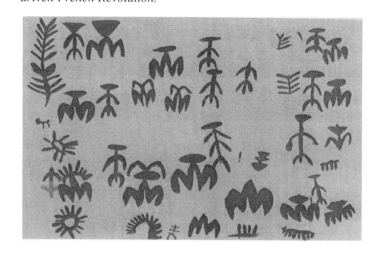

Plate 18: The Aylesford Bucket with its design of stylised horses: *and arched backs reminding one of the arched backs of the so-called 'bull vaulters' of Knossos in Crete (The Battle of The Trees) and presumably harks back to the ancient totem beast (bull); further the heads of the horse resemble a lily and there are scroll designs, which were also present at Knossos.*

Plate 19:   Finglesham Belt Buckle.

Plate 20a: Plan of the Cerne Giant (U.K.) from Flinders Petrie's survey (1926)

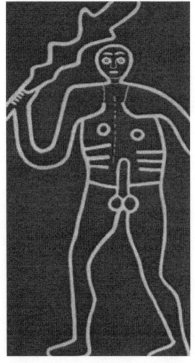

Plate 20b: The Dorset Ooser. Centuries ago it was the custom in Dorset for a wild Bull-masked man to run through the streets and villages demanding food or drink. In Shillingstone it was known as the 'Christmas Bull' with obvious links to Bull-Minos and Divine child as Minotaur from Knossos and the origins of Messiah and idea taken from the truth of Spirtual intervention c. 10,000 B.C

Plate 20c: Stepped crosses on ancient coins

Plate 20d: The Long Man of Wilmington (top) and Evoking Whiteleaf cross.The Cerne Giant (bottom) as reproduced Pleanderleath's The White Horses of the West Of England, 1885. Note two up-right staves or pillars (of Herm) still present (compare to omission in 20a).

Plate 21:   Mummy Heads of notable Pharaohs.

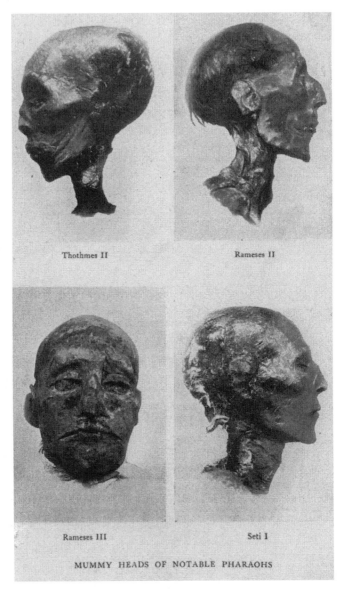

MUMMY HEADS OF NOTABLE PHARAOHS

Plate 22a: Two of the finest surviving mummies of 'commoners' found in Egypt: Yuya (top), master of the king's chariots and Thuya (below), his blond-haired wife: *were found in their intact tomb in 1903. Yuya and Thuya were the parents of Queen Tiye, the wife of Amenhotep III and thus the grandparents of Akhenaton and great-grandparents of Tutankhamun. There are obvious racial origin questions here and 12 tribe and 13 th tribe battles for power.*

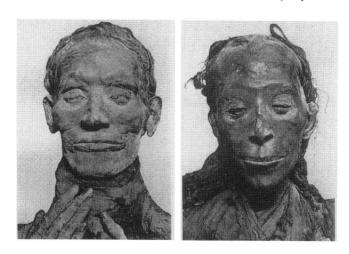

Plate 22b: Amenhotep III: *from the colossal granite bust in the British Museum U.K.*

Plate 23: On Diana's Rock: "The Burial of a King". *Rhodesian so-called 'Bushman Art' from Rusape S. Rhodesia. The King is coloured in red with parallels to the 'red men' of Knossos signifying royalty and monarchy. The king bears the muzzle-shaped snout, which although referred to as an "antelope-mask" does not bear the antlers. The king is covered in dots comparable to the red dots that often appear in Palaeolithic cave art. Note the collection of the 'seed' or king's sperm: from a water-colour by Walter Battiss.*

Plate 24: A Goanna (lizard) with (8) eggs: *Aboriginal bark painting. Ungarinyin tribe from Walcott Inlet, N. W. Australia.*

582

Plate 25: The Central part of the engraved scene at addaura, a cave on Monte Pellegrino, overlooking Palermo in western Sicily. *Note the beaked bir-like appearance Particularly pronounced in the top figure.*

Plate 26: A scene painted in the shaft at the Palaeolithic Lascaux site in France: *note the various 'shapes' or forms of the secret ancestry of the World Order (Bull, bird and man and obvious penis on man ie. phallic cult presumably Bull-Minos)*

Plate 27: Fragment of the sculptured relief at Angles-sur-L'Anglin, Vienne, w. France: *Bull-Minos, or bull-man.*

Plate 28: Some of the innumerable grid-like designs engraved in rock shelters in the Fontaine Bleau Oegion, South of Paris (date unknown). Note the double-axe sign (top upper left) of knossos and the diabolo.

References

1. Khimiyai Zhim: Academy Sciences USSR. 'Is the Earth a Large Crystal?'
2. Keith Critchlo: Time stands still.
3. Willaim Becker and Bethe Hagens: The Planetary Grid – A new Synthesis in Anti-Gravity and The Grid: Ed. David Hatcher Childress – Adventures Unlimited Press; Publisher's Network Stelle, Illinois 60919 (1995).
4. Donald Cyr: Stonehenge Viewpoint.
5. Dick Benson: Research presented in June 1987 to U.S. Psychotronics Association in Atlanta.
6. J. J. Hurtak: Keys of Enoch.
7. Scientific American: April 2 000: 'Quantum Teleportation'.
8. Christopher Bird: New Age Journal May 1975.
9. Rupert Sheldrake: New Science of Life. Granada (1983); Blond and Briggs (1981).
10. Semyon D. Kirlian and Valentina K. Kirlian: Photography and Visual Observations by Means of High Frequency Currents; trans. Foreign Techn. Divn. U.S. Air Force Systems Command (1963).
11. T. E. Bearden, Fer-De-Lance: A Briefing in Soviet Scalar Electro-magnetic Weapons. Tesla Book Co., Millbrae, CA (1986).
12. George Lakhovskky: The Secret of Life. Mac Millan Scientific Publishing, London (1939).
13. Bruce Cathie: The Harmonic Conquest of Space. Nexus Magazine: P.O. Box. 30 Mapleton, Queensland, 4560 Australia (1995). See also The Energy Grid – harmonic 695 - The Pulse of the Universe. Adventures Unlimited Press; One Adventure Place, Kempton, Illinois.
14. Moray B. King: Tapping The Zero – point Energy. Paraclete Publishing. P.O. Box 859, Provo, Ut 84603.
15. J. A. Wheeler: Geometrodynamics. Academic Press, NY, 1962.
16. Rauschning: Hitler Speaks (1939)
17. Charles Berlitz and William Moore: The Philadelphia Experiment. Panther (Granada), St. Albans (1980).
18. Hugh F. Cochrane: gateway to Oblivian. W. H. Allen, London (1980).
19. D. Bohm: Wholeness and the Implicate Order. Routledge and Kegan Paul, London (1980).
20. Richard Lefors Clark, PhD: section in Anti-Gravity and The World Grid (cited in 3 above).

21. Leslie Watkins: Alternative 3. Sphere Books (1978). Also Anglia Television Programme entitled Alternative 3. D. Ambrose and Christopher Miles.
22. John Davidson: New Humanity. Oct-Nov 1988.

23. Robert O. Becker, M.D: Cross Currents. G.P. Putnam and Sons NY (1990).
24. Peter Plichta: God's Secret Formula, Element Books Ltd., (1997) Shaftesbury, Dorset UK.
25. (Op cited in 3 above).
26. G. Dobbs: Correction Needed There Was No Referendum on joining the EEC. Home Publications Bodifyr, Lonpobty, Bangor, Gwynedd, LL57 1HT UK.
27. Sunday Telegraph Magazine 5th Dec. 1999; New Labour New Dome.
28. R. Noorbergen: Secrets of the Lost Races (1978).
29. (Op cited in 3 above).
30. B. Toben, F. Wolk: Space-Time and Beyond. E.P. Dutton NY, 1982.
31. Official History of the Order of Scotland quoted by Bro. Fred. H. Buckmaster in The Royal Order of Scotland publ. at the offices of The Freemason. Also A.E. Waite: Encyclopedia Freemasonry.
32. Gould: History of Freemasonry: III, 92: Mackey's Lexicon of Freemasonry; p. 267.
33. F. Buckmaster (cited).
34. Rev. G. Oliver: the Historical Landmarks of Freemasonry (1865).
35. Vaincre magazine 21st Sept. 1942 (Biblliotheques Nationale Paris).
36. An eithteenth Centgury manuscript of Les Vrais Clavicles du roi Salomon, trans. from Hebrew. Paris
37. Fama and Confessio Societas Rosicruciana in Anglai printed by W.J. Parret (1923).
38. Rev. G. Oliver (cited).
39. Alfred Edersheim: The Life and Times of Jesus the Messiah. II, 6   8   9 (1888).
40. Koran, sura LXXXVII.10.
41. Zohar, section Bereschith, folio 55 and section Lekh-Lekha, folio 76 (De Pauly's trans. Vol. I).
42. Adolphe Franck: La Kabbale p. 68 quoting Talmud treatise Sabbath, folio 34; Dr. Christian Ginsburg.
43. Paul Vulliaud: La Kabbalh Juive - histoire et doctrine 2 vols (1923): vol I, 253; vol I,   p.20.
44. Theodore Reinach: Histoire des Israelites, p. 221; and Salamon Reinach: Opreus, p. 299.
45. M. Vauillaud (cited).

46. Edersheim (cited by M. Vaulliaud) I, p.325.

47. Gaugenot des Mousseaux: Le Juif le Judaime and la Judaisation des Peoples Chretiens, p. 503 (1886).

48. Eliphas Levi: Histoire de la Magie, p. 273.

49. Dr. Mackey: Lexicon of Freemasonry.

50. Zohar, section Toldoth Noah, folio 63b. (de Pauly's trans., I. 373).

51. Drach: De l'harmonie entre l'Eglise et la Synagogue, I. 272.

52. A. E. Waite: The Secret Tradition in Freemasonry, I.8.

53. A.Q.C., XXXII. PartI, p. 40.

54. Le Couteulx de Canteleu: Les Sectes et Societes Secretes, p. 99.

55. Mr. Waite (op cited).

56. A. E. Waite: The Real History of the Rosicrucians.

57. Yarker: The Arcane Schools.

58. Piers Compton: The Broken Cross. Veritas Publsihing Company, Pty Ltd., P.O. Box 42 Cranbrook, western Australia 6321.

59. N. Webster: Secret Societies and Subversive Movements (1924).

60. N. Webster (op cited).

61. Ronald W. Clark: Albert Einstein. Word Publsihing, NY (1971).

62. Diodorus Siculus: Greek History (1923).

63. Martin Short: Inside The Brotherhood. Harper and Collins (1990).

64. J.S.M. Ward: Freemasonry- Its aims and Ideals. Rider (1923).

65. The Journal of Hellenic Studies, Vol. XXI.

66. Robert Graves: The White Goddess. Faber and Faber London.

67. Robert Graves (op cited).

68. M. Short (op cited).

69. Alice Leighton Cleather: H.P. Blavatsky: Her Life and Work for Humanity.

70. R. Guenon: Le Theosophism   (1921).

71. B. Dunford: The Holy Land of Scotland (1996) Brigadoon Books, 1 The Old Bakery, Mill St. Aberfeldy, Perthshire, PHI5 2BT, Scotland, U.K.

72. B. Dunford (op cited).

73. B. Dunford (op cited).

74. George F. Jowett: The Drama of the Lost Disciples (1972).

75. Rev. R. W. Morgan: St. Paul in Britain.

76. W. Rutherford: The Druids – Magicians of the West: The Aquarian Press (1978).

77. Eleanor Murry: The Flaming Door (1962).

78. Douglas Reed: The Controversy of Zion, South Africa (1978).

79. D. Mackenzie: Myths of Pre-Hellenic Europe (1923).

80. D. Mackenzie (op cited).

81. D. Mackenzie (op cited).

82. D. Mackenzie (op cited).

83. Prof. Flinder's Petrie: History of Egypt, Vol. II.

84. D. Mackenzie: Egyptian Myth and Legend (1923).

85. Robert Graves (op cited).

86. D. Ranking A.Q.C., Vol. XXIV.

87. N. Webster (op cited).

88. M.Larson: The Essene Christian Faith (1989).

89-93. Private communication.

94. Owen Morgan: The Light of Britannia.

95. M. Starbird: The woman with the Alabaster Jar (1993).

96. B. Dunford (op cited)

97. B. Dunford (op cited).

98. G. Higgins: Anacalypsis, Vol II (1836).

99. B. Dunford (op cited).

100. P. Beresford Ellis: Celt and Greek, Constable (1997).

102. B. Dunford (op cited).

103. W. Staeglich: Auschwitz – A Judge looks at the evidence Insititute for Historical Review (1990).

104. A.R. Butz: The Hoax of the Twentieth Century (1997) Historical Review Press 199 Maderia Place,
Sussex, BN7 ITN, U.K.

105. Walter N. Sanning: The Dissolution of Eastern European Jewry; Institute for Historical Review
(1990).

106. The Ball Report: ball Resource Ser. Ltd. 160-7231 St., Delta. B.C.V4C 6PJ Canada.

107. N. Webster (op cited).

108. H. Bayley: The Lost Language of Symbolism, London: Williams and Norgate (1968).

109. N. Webster (op cited).

110. The Times Newspaper: 'Pope assures Italians the end is not yet nigh', April 24th (1998).

111. R. Graves (op cited).

112. N. Webster (op cited).

113. C. O'Brien and M. Phillips: Trance Formation of America (1995) P.O. Box 158352 Nashville, Tennessee 37215.

114. B. Dunford (op cited).

115. B.Dunford (op cited).

116. A.E. Waite (op cited).

117. Comyns Beaumont: Britain the key to World History.

118. London Budget 17th Nov. 1912 and 8th Dec. 1912 'The Deeps of the Pacific ocean and their origin'. 'The Great Sea Age – Prehistoric Europe and the Antiquity of Man in Europe'.

119. Prof. Hull: Sub-oceanic Physiography of the Atlantic Ocean (1912) and London Budget Ist Dec. 1912.
120. Dr. Becker: Cross Currents; NY: G.P. Putnam and Sons (1990).
121. E. H. Colbert: The Age of Reptiles, NY: Mc Graw-Hill (1951).
122. Carl Dunbar: Historical Geology; NY: John Wiley (1969).
123. Annual of the British School at Athens, Vol. IX.
124. B. Dunford (op cited).
125. D. Mc Kenzie (op cited).
126. D. Mackenzie (op cited).
127. The Journal of Hellenic Studies, vol. XXI.
128. Proceedings of the Society of Biblical Archaelogy, vol. XXI.
129. Prof. Burrows: The Discoveries of Crete (1923).
130. Private files.
131. J. Vidal: Science et Vie: July 1969.
132. Campbell: the Masks of God, NY: Viking Press.
133. H. Aspden: Aether Science Papers, sabberton Publications P.O. Box 35, Southampton SOI6 7RB
     U.K.
134. R. Noorbergen (op cited).
135. J. Davidson: The Secret of the Creative Vacuum; C.W. Daniel and Co. Saffron Walden, U.K.
136. J. Davidson (op cited).
137. J. Davidson (op cited).
138. F. King: Satan and the Swastika; Mayflower (1976).
139. G. Lakhovsky: The Secret of Life; Mac illan Scientific Publsihing, London (1939).
140. J. Davidson (op cited).
141. J. Davidson (op cited).
142. B. Cathie (op cited).
143. H.Oldfield and R. Coghill: The Dark Side of the Brain; Element books (1988).
144. Ra Bonewitz: Cosmic Crystals, Turnstone Press, Wellingborough (1983).
145. G. Dawson (op cited).
146. V. Woolf: Holodynamics, Harbinger House, NY (1990).
147. H.Oldfield and R. Coghill (op cited).
148. L. Kin: The Pied Pipers of Heaven – who calls the tune? (1994). Science Terra a subdivision of VAP Publishers. VAP Delivery Service: P.O. Box 1180, D-32352 Preussisch Oldendorf, Germany.
149. G. Smoot: Wrinkles in Time – The Imprint of Creation. Little Brown and Co. (1993).
150. S. Hawking: A Brif History of Time. Bantam Books.

151. M. B. King: Tapping the Zero Point Energy. Paraclete Publishing. P.O. Box 859 Provo, UT 84603.

152. W. B. Smith: New Science, Fern-Graphic Publ., Mississauga, Ontario (1964).

153. G. Burridge: The Smith Coil, Psychic Observer, 35 (5), 410-16 (1979).

154. M. B. King (op cited).

155. On Target magazine: vol. 30. Nos 10 and II. Printed and published by Intelligence Publications (U.K.)
26 Meadow Lane, Sudbury, Suffolk, England COIO 2TD.

156. W. A. Tiller: Kirlian Photography – Its Scientific Foundations and Future Potential. Dept. of
Materials Science, Stanford University, unpublished (1975). Also Radionics, Radioesthesia and Physics.
Unpublished MSS presented at Symposium on the Varieties of healing (Amer. Acad. Paraps-Med.).

157. P. Newman: Lost Gods of Albion. Wrens Park Publishing (1997).

158. P. Newman (op cited).

159. A. Yarker (op cited).

160. L. Woolf quoted in P. Newman (op cited).

161. Piers Compton (op cited).

162. E. Mullins: The World Order.Ezra Pound Institute of Civilization. P.O.Box 1105. Staunton, UA. 24401 (1985).

163. N. Chomsky: World Orders Old and New.Redwood Books, Trowbridge (1996).

164. The Spotllight: Special Report on The Bilderberg Group and the World Shadow Government. 300
Independence Avenue Se Washington D.C. 20003.

165. On Target (op cited). Vol 30. Nos 10 and 11; vol. 29 Nos's 12 and 13 (1999).

166. On Target (op cited). Vol.30 Nos 4 and 5 (2000).

167. On Target (op cited). Vol.27 Nos 1 and 2 (1997).

168. The Spotlight (op cited).

169. N. Webster (op cited).

170. N.Webster (op cited).

171. R. Miller: Bare Faced Messiah (p. 454); Sphere Books Ltd. (1987).

172. R. Miller (op cited p.467).

173. Rhodesia Sunday Mail, 22nd May 1966.

174. R. Miller (op cited, p.335).

175. R. Miller (op cited, p. 402).

176. R. Miller (op cited, p.84).

177. R. Miller (op cited, p.479).

178. R.Miller (op cited, p. 176).

179. R. Miller (op cited, p.414).
180. J. Symonds: The Great Beast; Granada Publishing Ltd. (1973) Mayflower Books Ltd.
181. F. King (op cited).
182. R. Miller (op cited, p.174).
183. ECT (Electroconvulsive Therapy) – A Review of the Research, by the Author R. Henry (1990).
184. J.M. Ward (op cited).
185. J. Symonds (op cited).
186. J. Symonds (op cited).
187. B. Dunford (op cited).
188. B. Dunford (op cited).
189. B. Dunford (op cited).
190. J. Symonds (op cited).
191. D. Mc.Kenzie (op cited).
192. Prof. Petrie (op cited).
193. On Target (op cited, vol. 30, 2000).
194. Private papers.
195. C. M. Stoddard: Trail of the Serpent. Black Books (1996).
196. R. Charroux: forgotton Worlds. NY: Walker and Co. (1973).
197. Alan and Sally Landsburg: In Search of Ancient Mysteries: NY Bantam Books (1974).
198. L. Pauwels: The Eternal Man: NY: Avon (1972).
199. A. Thomas: We are Not the First, London: Souvenier Press, 1971.
200. Campbell: The Masks of God. NY: Viking Press.
201. On Target (op cited, Feb. 2001).
202. Ivan T. Sanderson (quoted in ref. Cited at 3).
203. N. R. Melson: Paradox –1980: Durance and Co., Ardmore, Reun.
204. Three Initiates, The Kybalion: A study of the Hermetic Philosophy of Ancient Egypt and Greece: Yogi Publication society, Chicago (1912).
205. Horowitz, Puleo and Barber: Healing Codes of the Biological Apocalypse Tetrahedron Inc. (Oct. 1999).
206. On Target (op cited: vol. 28 Nos 25 and 26 –5th and 19th June 1999).
207. On Target (op cited: vol.28 Nos 21 and 22 1999).

APPENDIX

Sheet 1

Petition from Renee Mary Henry BSc
1st January 1997

To the Honourable the Commons of the United Kingdom of Great Britain and Northern Ireland in Parliament assembled.

The Humble Petition of Renee Mary Henry.

Sheweth

That the Petitioner is extremely concerned to obtain answers to the questions one to six. The Petitioner maintains that the answers to these questions are vital before it is decided whether Britain should remain an independent nation or whether her future will be better served as part of a new country - the Single European Super-State, also known as a Federal Europe. The Petitioner also claims that the questions are not disconnected but are inseparably linked. The Petitioner has been unable to obtain answers to these questions over a number of years and the concern the Petitioner feels is not unfounded but based on her extensive research, which the Petitioner on at least one occasion forwarded to this Government.

The Petitioner's parents fought to keep the door of freedom of choice open for the Petitioner's generation and the Petitioner wishes to do the same for her children and their generation, thus ensuring their democratic legacy. Whereby the Petitioner does below give the questions one to six.

1. The US Government has a new ground-based "Star Wars" weapon which is being tested in the remote bush country of Alaska. This new system manipulates the environment in ways that can; disrupt human mental processes, jam all global communications systems, change weather patterns over large areas, interfere with wildlife migration patterns, negatively affect health of the populous and unnaturally impact the Earth's upper atmosphere. Given these facts and further research forwarded to this Government in Section 5 'The Second Millennium Working Report into Cancer', 'Angels Don't Play this HAARP' and 'Alternative 4 UFOs Mind and Body Control', does it make very good sense to demand the points A-B-C below? - and if not why? and further why has there been no media coverage of this very important issue?

592

Appendix 11 **(continued)**

Sheet II continuation   Object of the Petition - To have the questions answered
                                              by the Right Honourable John Major, Prime Minister.

A.   I demand that an open International Multidisciplinary Symposium be held immediately
      with Independent Scientists free to talk and assess the effects of the Space
      programme, HAARP and GWEN Systems and microwave relay and radio frequency
      technology on biological systems including man and the environment.

B.   I demand that the British Government moves to enlist International pressure to stop
      all further testing of HAARP (High Frequency Active Auroral Research Programme)
      and related advanced secret weaponry and surveillance technology, until the
      recommendations in A are made.

C.   I demand a world ban on Nuclear Tests.

2.   Given this Government's policy of "valuing the individual who takes responsibility", why
      was 'The Second Millennium Working Report into Cancer' ignored? and further why was
      it not disseminated to key Scientific personnel as requested, when as yet no answer has been
      found and millions are suffering?

3.   Given that the UK is a democracy and given that the European Court sits in secret making
      up laws over democratically elected Governments, is it unconstitutional to refuse a FULL
      public debate and referendum on Europe when the fundamental principles on which the State
      is governed and which embody the rights of ALL individual British Citizens are seriously
      challenged?

4.   Are the Secret Groups who formulated European Union ("A Theocratic United States of the
      West" - 'The Battle of the Trees'), still operational in Europe today? and if so are those
      groups still directing executive policy? Particularly in the European Court, and further given
      the facts in 'The Battle of the Trees', why was entry into Europe ever considered in the first
      place?

5.   Given that a definition of History is concerned with events of the past based on or
      constituting FACTUAL material, as distinct from legend or supposition, why does the school
      curriculum persist in teaching our children lies and half truths on the causation of The
      British, French and Russian Revolutions and World War 2? (I quote my son's History book

Appendix 11 **(continued)**

Sheet III continuation Object of the Petition - To have the questions answered
 by the Right Honourable John Major, Prime Minister.

where he states "Documents and books tell us what <u>actually</u> happened in the past" - my emphasis).

6. Is this Government aware that International Finance has been the method of every war and
 Revolution? "Where the debt grip has been firmly established, control of every form of
 publicity and media and political activity follows, together with a grip on industrialists once
 paralysis is achieved by the right hand, the revolutionary left hand strikes and moral
 corruption facilitates the whole process" - 'The Battle of the Trees'. Would it not be
 advisable to look at the lessons of History before signing on the dotted line of monetary
 union and before we suffer a Third World War? - since it is evident control of political
 activity and media is already ongoing.

Note: I refer you to he pyramidal power structure discussed in 'The Battle of the Trees' and
'Alternative 4 - UFOs Mind and Body Control' - It is the most dangerous organisational structure
ever conceived by man.

Wherefore the Petitioner prays that your honourable House do urge the Right Honourable John
Major PM to relieve my concern for the next generation by replying to questions one to six.

And your Petitioner, as in duty bound, will ever pray, &c.

The Petition is written in the Petitioner's own handwriting and she does presently reside at the
Address below:

Signature of Petitioner:

Based on research material obtainable from:

h

CABINET OFFICE
70 Whitehall, London SW1A 2AS
Telephone: **0171-270 0400**

Chancellor of the Duchy of Lancaster
Cabinet Minister for Public Service

RF/97/M/248

Tim Rathbone Esq MP
House of Commons
London   SW1A 0AA

28th   February 1997

Dear Tim,

Thank you for your letter of 12 February 1997 on behalf of your constituent ████████
██
about secrecy surrounding the rejection of her model for cancer.

As you may know, requests for information from the great majority of Government
departments and agencies are governed by the *Code of Practice on Access to Government
Information (2nd Editio*n *1997)* which was published in January and came into effect from
1 February 1997. The first edition had been in force since April 1994.

Under the *Code,* departments must provide information to the general public in response to
specific requests unless the information falls within certain exemptions. The *Code* also has
an appeal procedure that can be invoked if the applicant is dissatisfied with the information
provided. I enclose a copy of the *Code* together with the explanatory leaflet *Open
Government: Explaining the Code of Practice on Access to Government Information.*

You may wish to make Mrs Henry aware of the provisions of the *Code* so that she can take
up the matter of her cancer research with the appropriate body. As it is not clear from Mrs
Henry's letter exactly which department or agency this is and what information has not
been supplied to Mrs Henry, I can unfortunately offer no further advice on her particular
case.

I cannot comment on the substance of Mrs Henry's case but I would imagine that, as it
concerns a model for cancer, that it is a matter for the Department of Health or the Medical
Research Council. I can confirm that the *Code* does apply to both of these bodies.

Yours ever

Roger

ROGER FREEMAN

Tim Rathbone, M.P.

HOUSE OF COMMONS
LONDON SW1A 0AA

28 January 1997

[handwritten] To be Henry

As you know I was only too happy to present your carefully
prepared Petition to Parliament and indeed did so the other
day. Unfortunately I have just heard back from the House of
Commons Clerk of Public Petitions that the matter contained in
your paper is not, *prima facie*, appropriate for a petition.
He explains that a Petition is for use only to obtain redress
of a grievance not to obtain information, as was the general
thrust of the Petition which you have prepared.

I am sorry about this but we have to abide by the rules of the
House of Commons. If, however, you would like to take the
matter further I would only too pleased to take it up with the
Ministers with responsibility for "open Government". If you
would like me to do so please do let me know.

Mrs. Renee Henry Bsc.,

Tim Rathbone, M.P.

HOUSE OF COMMONS
LONDON SW1A 0AA

12th February 1997

Thank you for your further letter of 31st January.

I have now forwarded your petition to the Minister responsible for Open Government in the Office of Public Service asking for his comments and guidance on what you say about secrecy surrounding the rejection of your model for cancer.

As soon as I have any news I will of course be in touch with you again.

Mrs. Renee Henry B.Sc. (Hons) Biochem P.G.C.E
Director
Alpha Education Limited

DECLASSIFIED PER EXECUTIVE ORDER 12356, Section 3.3, *NND 841508*
By *W G Lewis* MARS, Date *Jan 29, 1985* . SECRET

SECRET
Auth CS, USAF

SECRET

DEPARTMENT OF THE AIR FORCE
HEADQUARTERS UNITED STATES AIR FORCE
WASHINGTON 25, D. C.

2 JAN 1952

AFOIN-A

3 JAN 1952

MEMORANDUM FOR GENERAL SAMFORD

SUBJECT: (SECRET) Contemplated Action to Determine the Nature and
Origin of the Phenomena Connected with the Reports of Unusual Flying Objects

1. The continued reports of unusual flying objects requires
positive action to determine the nature and origin of this phenomena.
The action taken thus far has been designed to track down and evaluate
reports from casual observers throughout the country. Thus far, this
action has produced results of doubtful value and the inconsistencies
inherent in the nature of the reports has given neither positive nor
negative proof of the claims.

2. It is logical to relate the reported sightings to the
known development of aircraft, jet propulsion, rockets and range
extension capabilities in Germany and the U.S.S.R. In this connection, it is to be noted that certain developments by the Germans,
particularly the Horton wing, jet propulsion, and refueling, combined with their extensive employment of V-1 and V-2 weapons during
World War II, lend credence to the possibility that the flying objects
may be of German and Russian origin. The developments mentioned
above were completed and operational between 1941 and 1944 and subsequently fell into the hands of the Soviets at the end of the war.
There is evidence that the Germans were working on these projects
as far back as 1931 to 1938. Therefore, it may be assumed that the
Germans had at least a 7 to 10 year lead over the United States in
the development of rockets, jet engines, and aircraft of the Horton-
wing design. The Air Corps developed refueling experimentally as
early as 1928, but did not develop operational capability until 1948.

3. In view of the above facts and the persistent reports of
unusual flying objects over parts of the United States, particularly
the east and west coast and in the vicinity of the atomic energy production and testing facilities, it is apparent that positive action
must be taken to determine the nature of the objects and, if possible,
their origin. Since it is known fact that the Soviets did not detonate
an atomic bomb prior to 1949, it is believed possible that the Soviets
may have developed the German aircraft designs at an accelerated rate
in order to have a suitable carrier for the delivery of weapons of mass
destruction. In other words, the Soviets may have a carrier without the
weapons required while we have relatively superior weapons with relatively

COUPON DESIGNATION MADE _____

X-322.7- ATIC

13 Feb 52

To: File
Edwin Bishop, Jr.
Lt Colonel, USAF

SECRET
SECURITY INFORMATION

598

SECRET

inferior carriers available. If the Soviets should get the carrier
and the weapon, combined with adequate defensive aircraft, they might
surpass us technologically for a sufficient period of time to permit
them to execute a decisive air campaign against the United States and
her allies. The basic philosophy of the Soviets has been to surpass
the western powers technologically and the Germans have given them
the opportunity.

4. In view of the facts outlined above, it is considered
mandatory that the Air Force take positive action at once to definitely
determine the nature and, if possible, the origin of the reported
unusual flying objects. The following action is now contemplated:

a. to require ATIC to provide at least three teams to
be matched up with an equal number of teams from ADC for the purpose
of taking radar scope photographs and visual photographs of the
phenomena;

b. to select sites for these teams, based on the concen-
trations of already reported sightings over the United States; (these
areas are, generally, the Seattle area, the Albuquerque area, and the
New York-Philadelphia area) and

c. to take the initial steps in this project during
early January 1952.

1 Incl
   Tech. Rept #76-45
                  W. M. Garland
                  Brigadier General, USAF
                  Assistant for Production
                  Directorate of Intelligence

U. S. Planes Hunting Discs; Russ Tells of 'Atom Saucers

FBI Probes Story of Soviet Ship Officer

LOS ANGELES, July 6—(Special)—Federal agents today investigated a letter to the Examiner describing Russian supersonic atom-powered planes resembling the "flying saucers."

A top flight atomic scientist to whom the Examiner referred the letter said it was "not all nonsense," and suggested the matter be turned over to the FBI.

The letter writer said he got the information from an officer aboard a Russian tanker recently at Los Angeles harbor.

KILLED EVEN WORMS

The Russian, he said, also described experiments with controlled radioactive clouds in the Arctic, where birds, animals and even worms were killed.

The planes, as described by the Russian to the writer, are only 8 inches thick, with a kidney-shaped outline and no propellors.

The pilot lies on his stomach and is artificially cooled against the heat developed by air friction.

"The outer surface is highly polished," the Russian said. Both upper and lower surfaces are convex, like a giant lens. The lifting force is an entirely different principle found about 10 years ago among unpublished papers of a Russian chemist.

"Energy is required only for climbing, but no energy is needed for support when the airplane goes along the earth's gravitational contour lines."

The writer of the strange letter said he met the Russian officer in Wilmington and, because he wanted to hear about Russia, invited him to dinner.

The Russian first asked where he could sell 18 polar bear pelts which he received "for very dangerous work."

He said he had been assigned to go over the route of the radioactive cloud near Lake Bakal (or Baykal) and pick up dead animals.

ALL LIFE DESTROYED

"They loaded a few small ships with all kinds of animals and directed the cloud over them," the writer said.

"During this experiment, a violent storm blew the cloud far north into the tundra, but before it dissipated it destroyed all life on its way.

"The cloud may be controlled from land, from a plane or from a robot-piloted 'leader.' As I understand it, the control is based on electro-magnetic waves and the cloud has two components: The carrier and the killer."

ENCLOSURE
RECORDED 62-83474
32 JUL 16

Milwaukee Sentinel
Milwaukee, Wis
July 7, 1947

60 OCT 1 1947

NAVAL MEDICAL RESEARCH UNIT 4,
Building. 2909
Great Lakes, Illinois

10 July 1952

U. S. Air Force
Air Technical Intelligence Command,
Washington, D. C.

Gentlemen:

Having recently read an article in "Look" magazine concerning your interest in so-called flying saucers, I have decided to tell you about a peculiar observation made some time ago.

On September 6, 1950 I was at Edison Court, Waukegan, Illinois about 5:40 to 5:50 PM. The day was perfectly clear, no clouds in the sky at that time, and a slight south wind was blowing. I saw an object in the sky over the northern part of Waukegan which I have not been able to identify. It was sausage-shaped, measuring perhaps 80 feet in diameter or greatest length, and perhaps 15 to 20 feet in center thickness. When first seen, it was possibly 5,000 to 7,000 feet north at about 75° angle. It was nearly stationary but had a constant revolution of perhaps 15 to 20 revolutions per minute, with a motion of rotation end over end about a central axis. The object was very clearly visible and I could have made a good picture had a camera been available. It was entirely silent. The outer or convex part was of a silvery color with a peculiar light appearance different from sun reflection and suggestive of luminescence; the concave or under side was of a light gray color.

My first though was that it must be a peculiar large ballon-like object, but I wondered at its large size, constant speed of rotation, and strangely bright appearance. It hovered in nearly one location for about 2 to 3 minutes and then abruptly travelled westward in the direction of the Waukegan airport, which lies NW of Waukegan a few miles. It travelled very rapidly toward this airport, with a speed I would judge to be that of jet planes ocassionally seen here.

As it travelled, it continued to be perfectly silent and also maintained its continual, slow rotation about its central axis. No flashes of light from an exhaust were visible. When it reached a position perhaps 2-3 miles south of the Waukegan airport, it again slowed down and became nearly motionless. At this time a friend of mine arrived and I pointed this object out to him, which was equally puzzling to him.

After remaining rather localized for a few minutes, it again began a fast, westerly movement and in a few seconds rapidly passed beyond sight. When last seen, it has a remarkably fast speed which might have been several hundred miles per hour faster than any aircraft I have seen.

COPY

In summary, the object observed was entirely noiseless, had a
luminescent-silvery appearance, maintained a constant and slow rotation
end-on-end, and was capable of remaining nearly motionless and also very
fast speed.

On the day observed (6 Sept 1950) the University of Chicago had sent
a ballon very high into the air, but it had landed near Lake Forest, Ill.
between 3 and 4 PM. This object was clearly observed for some time and in
no way resembled any ballon or aircraft known to me. Also, it was sighted
several hours after the U. of Chicago ballon had landed.

I reported this observation to the Medical Officer in Charge, CDR
John R. Seal MC USN, of Naval Medical Research Unit 4. I am employed at
that unit as Histopathologist in observation interesting but did not believe
it was a matter requiring a report elsewhere.

Perhaps this observation is of no interest or use to you, but in case
it is, I shall be glad to give you whatever further details I may remember.

Very truly yours,

JOHN J. ROBINSON, M. D.

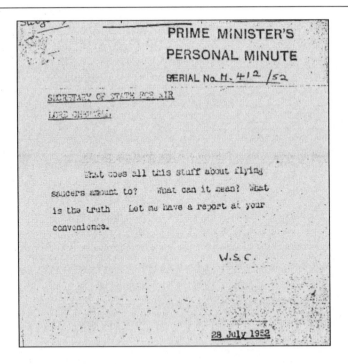

See L.Kin's book: *The Pied Pipers of Heaven –Who calls the tune?*
(*page340*): cited in reference section with address.